MEGARRY'S MANUAL OF
THE LAW OF REAL PROPERTY

AUSTRALIA
The Law Book Co. Ltd.
Sydney : Melbourne : Brisbane

CANADA AND U.S.A.
The Carswell Company Ltd.
Agincourt, Ontario

INDIA
N. M. Tripathi Private Ltd.
Bombay
and
Eastern Law House Private Ltd.
Calcutta and Delhi
M.P.P. House
Bangalore

ISRAEL
Steimatzky's Agency Ltd.
Jerusalem : Tel Aviv : Haifa

MALAYSIA : SINGAPORE : BRUNEI
Malayan Law Journal (Pte.) Ltd.
Singapore

NEW ZEALAND
Sweet & Maxwell (N.Z.) Ltd.
Auckland

PAKISTAN
Pakistan Law House
Karachi

MEGARRY'S MANUAL OF
THE LAW OF
REAL PROPERTY

SIXTH EDITION

BY
DAVID J. HAYTON, LL.D.
of the Inner Temple and Lincoln's Inn, Barrister
Fellow of Jesus College, Cambridge

LONDON
STEVENS & SONS LIMITED
1982

First Edition	1946
Second Impression, revised	1947
Third Impression, revised	1949
Fourth Impression	1951
Second Edition	1955
Second Impression	1960
Third Edition	1962
Second Impression	1967
Fourth Edition	1969
Second Impression	1972
Third Impression	1973
Fifth Edition	1975
Sixth Edition	1982

Published in 1982 by
Stevens & Sons Limited of
11 New Fetter Lane, London
and printed in Great Britain by
Richard Clay (The Chaucer Press) Ltd., Bungay, Suffolk.

British Library Cataloguing in Publication Data

Megarry, *Sir* Robert
  Megarry's manual of the law of real property.—6th ed.
  1. Real property—England
  I. Title   II. Hayton, David J.
344.2064'3   KD829

  ISBN 0–420–46330–5
  ISBN 0–420–46340–2 Pbk

PREFACE

HAVING been given a free hand in preparing this edition there are many changes from the 1975 edition. Naturally, I have had to consider the need to keep the size and the cost down and the special relationship between previous editions of the *Manual* and Megarry & Wade's *The Law of Real Property*.

The *Manual* was first published in 1946 and was founded on a pre-war manuscript. *Megarry & Wade* was first published in 1957 and was similarly founded, though being a work of joint authorship and of greater amplitude. The books were of a common design but different scope.

The *Manual* is now of a different design and a little more ambitious in scope. Little attention is given to the position before the 1925 Property Legislation. Much attention is given to the registration of title system. After all, well over seven million titles are registered (the register setting out the current state of the title except for overriding interests) and over three quarters of conveyancing transactions concern land that is already registered or requires to be registered for the first time. Even under the old unregistered land system, which the registration of title system is replacing, in investigating the title deeds it is only necessary to go back to a good root of title (*e.g.* a conveyance on sale) at least 15 years old. It is thus a rare event when one has to examine pre 1926 documents of title. Resort should then be had to *Megarry & Wade*. The *Manual* is not intended to be an all-embracing work for practitioners but reflects modern land law courses in concentrating on the modern land law in England and Wales.

In such courses there is the perennial problem of how to introduce the subject, how to provide some idea of the picture on the lid of the so-called jig-saw puzzle of land law before commencing with a detailed examination of each interlocking piece of the puzzle. The first four chapters (and, in particular, Chapter 1, Section 2 and Chapter 4) tackle this problem, whilst Chapter 5 attempts to provide some practical perspective by dealing with the transmission of title to land. As reflected in most land law courses today, it is generally considered best to set out in detail the bone-like anatomical structure of unregistered land and of registered land at an early stage, and then to flesh out the skeleton by detailed examination of individual parts. Exceptionally, the topic of rectification and indemnity in registered land has to be left to the end since it cannot properly be appreciated without a sound knowledge of basic land law topics, *e.g.* Settled Land Act Settlements.

The savings accorded by vigorous pruning of pre-1926 material (*e.g.* on future interests, co-ownership and intestacy) and of matters not normally covered in land law courses (*e.g.* construction of wills and much of the old chapter on trusts and powers) afford an opportunity to examine in more detail some problematical aspects of settled land, co-ownership, perpetuities, licences and registered land. Easements are dealt with before restrictive covenants, which now have a chapter to themselves instead of being dealt with after covenants in leases. This enables restrictive covenants to be understood better in their historical context as resembling equitable negative easements, whilst making it possible to appreciate the modern view of restrictive covenants as land obligations similar to easements and thus, perhaps, capable of falling within the ambit of section 62 of the Law of Property Act 1925.

Apart from these changes this edition takes into account the many significant cases and statutes that have emerged since 1975. In this I have been fortunate in the valuable assistance rendered by Simon Taube, B.A., Barrister and by Jonathan Brown, Barrister in the preparation of Chapter 14 and of Chapter 16 respectively. Without such assistance the manuscript would not have been delivered on time. I am most grateful to the publishers for preparing the index and the tables of cases and statutes.

It is hoped that the law is accurately stated as from sources available on October 1, 1981 though some updating has been possible at the proof stage.

By the date of publication the Administration of Justice Bill will have been enacted so as to relax the formal requirements of wills.

DAVID HAYTON

CONTENTS

Chapter 1

INTRODUCTION

Chapter 2

ESTATES

Chapter 3

LAW AND EQUITY

CHAPTER 4

THE STRUCTURE OF LAND LAW AFTER 1925

CHAPTER 5

TRANSMISSION OF TITLE TO LAND

CHAPTER 6

FUTURE INTERESTS

CHAPTER 7

SETTLED LAND AND TRUSTS FOR SALE

CHAPTER 8

CO-OWNERSHIP

CHAPTER 9

LEASES AND TENANCIES

CHAPTER 10

COVENANTS AFFECTING LEASEHOLD LAND

CHAPTER 11

INCORPOREAL HEREDITAMENTS

CHAPTER 12

RESTRICTIVE COVENANTS

CHAPTER 13

MORTGAGES

CHAPTER 14

LIMITATION

CHAPTER 15

RECTIFICATION AND INDEMNITY IN REGISTERED LAND

CHAPTER 16

OWNERSHIP AND ITS LIMITS

TABLE OF CASES

TABLE OF STATUTES

TABLE OF STATUTORY INSTRUMENTS

ABBREVIATIONS

STATUTES

A.E.A.: Administration of Estates Act.
A.H.A.: Agricultural Holdings Act.
C.A.: Conveyancing Act.
I.E.A.: Intestates' Estates Act.
J.A.: Supreme Court of Judicature (Consolidation) Act.
L.C.A.: Land Charges Act.
L.P.A.: Law of Property Act.
L.P.Am.A.: Law of Property Amendment Act.
L.R.A.: Land Registration Act.
R.P.A.: Real Property Act.
S.L.A.: Settled Land Act.
T.A.: Trustee Act.

CASES

I.R.C.: Commissioners of Inland Revenue.
In b.: (In bonis) In the Goods of, In the Estate of.
S.E.: Settled Estate(s).
S.T.: Settlement Trust(s).
W.T.: Will Trust(s).

BOOKS AND PERIODICALS

Bl.Comm.: Blackstone's Commentaries on the Laws of England, 15th ed., 1809.
Camb.L.J.: Cambridge Law Journal.
Challis R.P.: Challis's Law of Real Property (3rd ed. 1911).
Co.Litt.: Coke's Commentary upon Littleton (19th ed., 1832).
Conv.(N.S.): The Conveyancer, New Series, 1936–
Conv.(O.S.): The Conveyancer, Old Series, 1916–36.
Conv.Y.B.: Conveyancers' Year Book.
Col.L.R.: Columbia Law Review.
Cru.Dig.: Cruise's Digest of the Laws of England respecting Real Property (4th ed., 1835).
Digby: Digby's Introduction to the History of the Law of Real Property (5th ed., 1897).
Farrand: Contract and Conveyance (3rd ed., 1980).
Fearne C.R.: Fearne's Essay on the Learning of Contingent Remainders and Executory Devises (10th ed., 1844).
Fry S.P.: Fry's Treatise on the Specific Performance of Contracts (6th ed., 1921).
Gilbert, *Uses*: Gilbert's Law of Uses and Trusts (3rd ed., 1811).
Gray, *Perpetuities*: Gray's Rule against Perpetuities (4th ed., 1942).
Halsbury: Halsbury's Laws of England.
Hanbury & Maudsley: Hanbury & Maudsley's Modern Equity (11th ed., 1981).

Harv.L.R.: Harvard Law Review.
Hayes, *Intrpoduction*: Hayes' Introduction to Conveyancing (5th ed., 1840).
Hayton: Registered Land (3rd ed., 1981).
H.E.L.: Holdsworth's History of English Law, 1922–66 (see (1945) 61 L.Q.R. 346).
Lewis: Lewis's Practical Treatise on the Law of Perpetuity (1843).
Litt.: Littleton's Tenures: see Co.Litt.
L.J.News.: Law Journal Newspaper.
L.Q.R.: Law Quarterly Review.
Maitland, *Equity*: Maitland's Equity (2nd ed., 1936).
     Forms of Action: Maitland's Forms of Action at Common Law, 1936.
Mod.L.R.: Modern Law Review.
M. & W.: Megarry and Wade's Law of Real Property (4th ed., 1975).
N. & M.: Nathan & Marshall's Cases and Commentary on the Law of Trusts (7th ed., 1980).
P. & M.: Pollock & Maitland's History of English Law (2nd ed., 1898) (reprinted with new introduction 1968).
Perk.: Perkins' Profitable Book (15th ed., 1827).
Preston, *Estates*.: Preston's Elementary Treatise on Estates (1820–27).
Prideaux: Prideaux's Forms and Precedents on Conveyancing.
Rob.Gav.: Robinson's Common-Law of Kent, or the Customs of Gavelkind (3rd ed., 1822).
Ruoff & Roper: Ruoff & Roper's Registered Conveyancing (4th ed.)
Sanders, *Uses*: Sanders' Essay on Uses and Trusts (5th ed., 1844).
Scriven: Scriven's Treatise on the Law of Copyholds (7th ed., 1896).
Shep.: Sheppard's Touchstone of Common Assurances (7th ed., 1820).
S.J.: Solicitors' Journal.
Snell: Snell's Principles of Equity (26th ed., 1966).
Theobald, *Land*: Theobald's Law of Land (2nd ed., 1929).
Tudor L.C.R.P.: Tudor's Selection of Leading Cases on Real Property, Conveyancing and the Construction of Wills and Deeds (4th ed., 1898).
Underhill: Underhill's Law Relating to Trusts and Trustees (13th ed., 1979).
Williams R.P.: Williams' Principles of the Law of Real Property (23rd ed. 1920).
V. & P.: Williams' Treatise on the Law of Vendor & Purchaser (4th ed., 1936).

GLOSSARY

The object of this glossary is to provide a ready source of reference to the meanings of some of the more troublesome technical expressions used in the text. For the most part, brief but not necessarily exhaustive definitions have been given, with references by means of numerals in brackets to the pages of the text where further information can be obtained and the terms may be seen in their context; references which are essential to a proper understanding of the terms are in heavy type. Where the text contains a convenient collection and explanation of a number of contrasting terms, a simple reference to the appropriate pages is given instead of setting out the definitions.

Abstract of title: an epitome of documents and facts showing ownership (**148**).

Ademption: the failure of a gift by will, *e.g.* because the property ceases to exist or to belong to the testator.

Ad hoc settlement or trust for sale: one with special overreaching powers (**297**).

Administrators: persons authorised to administer the estate of an intestate (179); compare Executors.

Advowson: a right of presenting a clergyman to a vacant benefice (85).

Alienation: the act of disposing of or transferring.

Ante-nuptial: before marriage.

Appendant: attached to land by operation of law (405); compare Appurtenant.

Approvement: appropriation of portion of manorial waste free from rights of common (428).

Appurtenant: attached to land by act of parties (405); compare Appendant.

Assent: an assurance by personal representatives vesting property in the person entitled (180).

Assignment: a disposition or transfer, usually of a lease.

Assurance: the documentary or other evidence of a disposition or transfer.

Beneficial owner: a person entitled for his own benefit and not, *e.g.* as trustee.

Beneficiaries: those entitled to benefit under a trust or will.

Betterment levy: a charge payable to the State on realising the development value of land (555); see also Development charge.

Bona vacantia: goods without an owner.

Cestui que trust: a beneficiary under a trust.

    ”   ” *use*: a person to whose use property was conveyed (71).

    ”   ” *vie*: a person for whose life an estate *pur autre vie* lasted (51).

Charge: an incumbrance securing the payment of money.

Collaterals: blood relations who are neither ancestors nor descendants.

Consolidation: a requirement that a mortgagor shall not redeem one mortgage without another (487).

Contingent: operative only upon an uncertain event (**190**); compare Vested.

Contractual tenancy: tenancy under a lease or agreement which is still in force; contrast Statutory tenancy.

Conversion: a change in the nature of property either actually or notionally (314).
Conveyance: an instrument (other than a will) transferring property.
Co-parceners: persons together constituting the heir.
Corporeal: accompanied by physical possession (73).
Covenant: a promise contained in a deed.
Coverture: the continuance of a marriage.
Curtesy: a widower's life estate in his wife's realty (177).
Customary heir: the heir according to a local custom.

Deed: a document signed, sealed and delivered.
Deed poll: a deed with only one party (151); compare Indenture.
Defeasance: the determination of an interest on a specified event.
Demise: a transfer, usually by the grant of a lease.
Determine: terminate, come to an end.
Devise: a gift of real property by will.
Distrain, distress: the lawful extra-judicial seizure of chattels to enforce a right, *e.g.* to the payment of rent (337).
Dominant tenement: land to which the benefit of a right is attached; compare Servient tenement.
Dower: a widow's life estate in one-third of her husband's realty (177).
Durante viduitate: during widowhood.

Emblements: growing crops which an outgoing tenant may take (364).
Enceinte: pregnant.
Engross: prepare a fair copy (149).
En ventre sa mère: conceived but not born.
Equities: equitable rights.
Equity of redemption: the sum of a mortgagor's rights in the mortgaged property (**464**).
Escheat: a lord's right to ownerless realty.
Escrow: a document which upon delivery will become a deed.
Estate: 1. the *quantum* of an interest in land (24).
    2. an area of land (24).
    3. the whole of the property owned by a deceased person (24,179).
Estovers: wood which a tenant may take for domestic and other purposes (53).
Execute: 1. to perform or complete, *e.g.* a deed.
    2. to convert, *e.g.* to transform the equitable interest under a use into a legal estate.
Executors: persons appointed by a testator to administer his estate (179); compare Administrators.
Executory: not yet completed (contrasted with "executed") (305).
Executory interest: a valid future interest not complying with the legal remainder rules (**195**).
Executory limitation: a limitation creating an executory interest (**195**).
Executory trust: a trust the details of which remains to be set out in some further document (305).

Fee: base (43), conditional (40), determinable (39), simple (39), tail (29).
Feoffee to uses: a person holding property to the use of another.
Feoffment: a conveyance by livery [delivery] of seisin (32).
Fine: 1. a collusive action partially barring an entail (45); compare Recovery.

2. a premium or a lump sum payment, *e.g.* for the grant of a lease.

Foreclosure: proceedings by a mortgagee which free mortgaged property from the equity of redemption (484).

Freehold: 1. socage tenure (27).
   2. an estate of fixed but uncertain duration (**29**).

Gavelkind: a special custom of descent whereby land descended on intestacy to all children and not to eldest son alone (27).

General equitable charge: an equitable charge of a legal estate not protected by a deposit of title deeds (469).

Good consideration: natural love and affection for near relatives (64).

Hereditaments: inheritable rights in property.

Heritable issue: descendants capable of inheriting.

Hold over: remain in possession after the termination of a tenancy (344).

Hotchpot: the bringing into account of benefits already received before sharing in property (175).

Improved value: the value of land together with improvements to it.

In capite: in chief, immediately holding of the Crown (23).

Incorporeal: not accompanied by physical possession.

Incumbrance: a liability burdening property.

Indenture: a deed between two or more parties (151); compare with Deed poll.

Infant: a person under 18 years of age.

In gross: existing independently of a dominant tenement (396, 406).

Instrument: a legal document.

Interesse termini: the rights of a lessee before entry (**341**).

Intestacy: the failure to dispose of property by will.

Issue: descendants of any generation (168).

Jointure: provision by a husband for his widow, usually under a settlement.

Jus accrescendi: right of survivorship (299).

Lapse: the failure of a gift, especially by the beneficiary predeceasing the testator (167).

Letters of administration: the authorisation to persons to administer the estate of a deceased person (179).

Licence: a permission, *e.g.* to enter on land (370).

Limitation, words of: words delimiting the estate granted to some person previously mentioned (**521**); compare Purchase, words of.

Marriage articles: the preliminary agreement for a marriage settlement (305).

Merger: the fusion of two or more estates or interests (394).

Mesne: intermediate, middle (23).

Minority: the state of being an infant.

Next-of-kin: the nearest blood relations (171).

Nuncupative: oral (of wills).

Overreach: to transfer from land to the purchase money therefor (107).

Override: to render rights void, *e.g.* against a purchaser (107).

Parol: by word of mouth.

Particular estate: an estate less than a fee simple.

Per capita: by heads; one share for each person; compare *Per stirpes*.

Personal representatives: executors or administrators (178).

Per stirpes: by stocks of descent; one share for each line of descendants; compare *Per capita*.

Portions: provisions for children, especially lump sums for the younger children under a settlement (232).

Possibility of reverter: the grantor's right to the land if a determinable fee determines (40).

Post-nuptial: after marriage.

Prescription: the acquisition of easements or profits by long user (404).

Privity of contract: the relation between parties to a contract (79).

Privity of estate: the relation of a landlord and tenant (334).

Probate: the formal confirmation of a will, granted by the court to an executor (179).

Procreation, words of: words confining the persons mentioned to issue of a particular person (36).

Puisne mortgage: a legal mortgage not protected by a deposit of title deeds (92).

Pur autre vie: for the life of another person (51).

Purchase, words of: words conferring an interest on the person they mention (38); compare Limitation, words of.

Purchaser: a person who takes land by act of parties and not by operation of law.

Que estate: dominant tenement.

Recovery: a collusive action completely barring an entail (45); compare Fine, 1.

Remainder: the interest of a grantee subject to a prior particular estate (195).

Rentcharge: (84).

Restraint on anticipation: a restriction on a married woman disposing of capital or future income (185).

Restrictive covenant: a covenant restricting the use of land (73).

Reversion: the interest remaining in a grantor after granting a particular estate (194).

Riparian owner: the owner of land adjoining a watercourse (552).

Root of title: a document from which ownership is traced (10).

Satisfied term: a term of years created for a purpose since fulfilled (357).

Seisin: the feudal possession of land by a freeholder (**31**).

Servient tenement: land burdened by a right such as an easement (396); compare Dominant tenement.

Settlement: provisions for persons in succession (or the instruments making such provisions).

Severance: the conversion of a joint tenancy into a tenancy in common (324).

Severance: words of: words showing that property is to be held in distinct shares.

Spes successionis: a possibility of succeeding to property (34).

Squatter: a person occupying land without any title to it (381).

Statutory owner: persons with the powers of a tenant for life (262).

Statutory tenant: a person holding over under the Rent Restriction Acts (579); compare Contractual tenancy.

Statutory trusts: certain trusts imposed by statute, especially—
   1. the trust for sale under co-ownership (**306**).
   2. the trusts for issue on intestacy (**175**).
Sub-mortgage: a mortgage of a mortgage (503).
Sui juris: "of his own right," *i.e.*, subject to no disability.
Tenement: anything which may be held by a tenant.
Tenure: the set of conditions upon which a tenant holds land (23); compare
   Estate, 1.
Term of years: a period with a defined minimum for which a tenant holds
   land (87).
Terre tenant: a freehold tenant in possession (393).
Title: the evidence of a person's right to property.
Trust: constructive (312), executory (305), resulting (310).
Trust corporation: one of certain companies with a large paid-up capital, or
   one of certain officials (5).

Undivided share: the interest of a tenant in common or co-parcener (301).
Use: benefit (70).
User: use, enjoyment (Note: *not* the person who uses).

Vested: unconditionally owned (**191**); compare Contingent.
Vesting assent (246), deeds (246), instrument (246).
Voluntary conveyance: a conveyance not made for valuable consideration.
Volunteer: a person taking under a disposition without having given valuable
   consideration.

Waste: ameliorating (52), equitable (53), permissive (52), voluntary (52).

CHAPTER 1

INTRODUCTION

Sect. 1. Prefatory

THE English law of real property, traditionally described by Oliver Cromwell as "an ungodly jumble," is justly recognised as being a difficult subject for the beginner, partly because of the intricate interlocking of its component parts and partly because of the complexity of the language, which involves the use of many technical terms. For these reasons, those coming new to the subject must not expect to understand everything at a first reading. In this subject more than any other it is economical of time and effort to read fast and often. Much that is almost incomprehensible at first will become clear on a second reading and perhaps obvious on a third. In order to understand complex ideas expressed in unfamiliar language it is necessary to master the language as soon as possible, and for this purpose a generous use should be made of the glossary which immediately precedes this page.

1. Objects of learning the subject. The objects of learning the law of real property are—
  (a) to acquire a knowledge of the rights and liabilities attached to interests in land; and
  (b) to lay a foundation for the study of conveyancing.

It is not easy to distinguish accurately between real property and conveyancing. In general, it can be said that the former is static, the latter dynamic; real property deals with the rights and liabilities of landowners, conveyancing with the art of creating and transferring rights in land. Yet inevitably the two overlap, and often the exact place at which to draw the line is ultimately a matter of taste. But although this is a book on the law of real property, it is built upon a conveyancing foundation. In deciding what to include and what to exclude, conveyancing has played a large part. The reader's knowledge of land law has to be carried to the point when it will be possible for him to embark with profit on a study of conveyancing; the joints must be true and the overlapping restrained within due limits. It is, indeed, best to regard real property and conveyancing not as two separate though closely related subjects, but as two parts of the one subject of land law; it is convenience of teaching rather than any essential difference of nature that dictates the division.
  Conveyancing necessarily influences any book on real property in

another way, namely, by making it essential to include some historical element. A conveyancer must deal both with ownership and incumbrances; in other words he must see not only that his client gets what he has agreed to buy but also that he gets it free from any burdens such as mortgages or rights of way which would make it less valuable. (In parenthesis, it must be noted that this division between ownership and incumbrances is not rigid; what in one transaction appears as an incumbrance, may appear in another as the subject-matter of ownership. If A owns a mortgage on X's land, the mortgage is regarded as an incumbrance if X sells his land, but as the subject-matter of ownership if A sells his mortgage. Nevertheless, in any particular transaction the distinction is clear). A conveyancer acting for a client who is purchasing property must investigate the title to the land, both as to ownership and as to incumbrances, for a period which is usually at least the last 15 years; those who are engaged in this work must consequently know the law not only as it is but also as it was.

Since modern conveyancing is based on the 1925 Property Legislation enacted over 56 years ago and since conveyancing requires investigation of title only to a good root of title (*e.g.* a conveyance on sale) at least 15 years old it is uncommon for knowledge of the pre-1925 law to be required. Moreover, where the new registration of title system applies—and there are almost eight million registered titles—the register sets out the current state of the title, except for overriding interests as will later be seen. Accordingly, little attention will be paid to the pre-1926 law, which may be discovered from previous editions hereof or from the current edition of *Megarry and Wade, The Law of Real Property*, whilst more attention will be given to the registration of title system.

2. The common law basis of the subject. The law of real property is part of the common law of England. The phrase "common law" or "at law," which will be frequently encountered, is employed in three senses:

    (i) in contrast with local custom;
    (ii) in contrast with statute law; and
    (iii) in contrast with equity.

The third is the most usual sense, the second less usual, the first comparatively rare; the context will normally make it plain which is meant. A word must be said on the third meaning. As will be seen later[1] certain rights could be enforced in the common law courts (*i.e.* the King's ordinary courts), and these were known as legal rights. Other rights were not protected by the common law courts, but came

---

[1] *Post*, pp. 57 *et seq*.

to be protected by the Chancellor if he deemed this equitable. It was the Chancellor who first compelled trustees to carry out their trusts, and remedied wrongs which, because of non-compliance with some formality, the common law courts would not redress. Rights enforced by the Chancellor were known as equitable rights, for the Chancellor's Court, the Court of Chancery, was known as the Court of Equity. Equitable rights were (and still are) inferior to legal rights, in that a legal right would be enforced against everyone, whereas an equitable right would be enforced only against a person who the Chancellor considered was unable in good conscience to deny liability. Thus not only would a trustee be compelled to carry out his trust, but also if he gave or sold the trust property to a third person who knew that the trustee was committing a breach of trust, the equitable rights of the beneficiaries under the trust would be enforced against that third person, who would thus be compelled to carry out the trust. Ultimately, equitable rights became enforceable against the whole world except a bona fide purchaser for value of a legal estate without notice of the equitable right, or someone claiming title under such person, who, in short, may be termed "equity's darling".[2] Legal rights, on the other hand, were enforceable against everyone, without this exception.

The common law affecting real property has in the course of time been profoundly affected by equity, and today most questions on real property law fall for decision in the Chancery Division of the High Court; yet this is merely a procedural arrangement which must not be allowed to obscure the common law basis of the law of real property, though much affected by statute law.

Sect. 2. The Scope of the Subject

1. The complex functions of land. When a person buys a car he does not find that ownership of the car involves obligations (*e.g.* never to drive into Exeter, never to carry groceries in the car, never to fit a sun-roof to the car, always to give a lift to hitch-hikers, always to let A drive the car on Sundays, always to let B siphon off petrol when he wishes, always to carry C in the back seat when she desires to go to Bristol) or carries rights (*e.g.* to have one's children driven to school in D's car and one's goods transported to Reading in E's van when he drives there). A car owner does not find that the boundaries of his car are uncertain or that his car is inextricably linked to another car. He does not find that his car is liable to be compulsorily purchased or to be demolished for want of planning permission or that he is liable for road charges if the road on which his car stands is made up by the

---

[2] See *post*, pp. 62 *et seq.*, where this is more fully discussed.

local authority. He does not find that someone has a life interest in
the car or a 99-year tenancy or a 21-year sub-tenancy in the car.

In contrast, land is virtually indestructible so it may be settled upon
A for life, then his eldest son for life, then his eldest grandson
absolutely, or it may be leased for 99 years to X, who sub-leases for
21 years to Y, who further sub-leases for a year to Z. Laws have to
regulate the relationships between A and the remaindermen, and
between X, Y and Z, and also to regulate the position of a purchaser
of the property in which A or X, Y and Z are interested. Land is
specially apt for satisfying concurrent needs, whether of spouses or of
businessmen, so that land may be owned by H and W as joint tenants
(when by the *ius accrescendi* the survivor will become sole owner) or
by P and Q as tenants in common (when each has a half share which
will pass by his will or under the intestacy rules).

Land is uniquely immovable so that it may be subject to easements
(*e.g.* rights of way, rights of light) or profits (*e.g.* a right to put
animals out to pasture, a right to dig up and take away peat or turf) or
restrictive covenants (*e.g.* a promise in a deed not to build more than
one dwelling-house or not to use a house other than as a private
dwelling-house) which benefit neighbouring land. It is also unique
security for a loan of money where such money is lent by way of
mortgage or charge: if the borrower defaults then the lender can sell
the land and recoup himself.

Land and buildings thereon, which are treated as part of the land
under the maxim "*quicquid plantatur solo, solo cedit*" (whatever is
attached to the soil becomes part of it), are divisible vertically (*e.g.*
semi-detached or terraced houses) or horizontally (*e.g.* maisonettes
and flats) so creating may problems as to mutual rights and
obligations. Further problems arise from the unique inelasticity of
supply of land which has provoked much governmental interference.

2. Legal and equitable interests. To enable land to fulfil as many
functions as possible some interests in land are "legal," having been
originally enforceable in the common law courts, whilst others are
"equitable," having been originally enforceable in the Lord Chancellor's Court of Chancery, otherwise known as the Court of Equity.[3] A
legal interest is enforceable against everyone, whilst an equitable
interest is enforceable against everyone except a bona fide purchaser
of a legal interest without notice of the equitable interest (often
known as "equity's darling") or his successor in title.[4]

Since 1925 there are only two legal estates, giving the estate owner
ownership—the right to use, occupy and enjoy—of a fee simple
absolute in possession or of a term of years absolute.[5] Where a

---

[3] *Post*, pp. 57–62
[4] *Post*, pp. 62–69.
[5] *Post*, pp. 84–88.

layman would say A is the owner of Blackacre a lawyer would say A has a fee simple absolute in possession in Blackacre. Where a layman would say T has a 99-year lease a lawyer would say T has a term of 99 years absolute, and such lawyer, if O had granted the 99 year term, would still say that O had a fee simple absolute in possession because possession covers not just actual occupation but also the right to receive rents. The only significant legal interests—rights over someone else's land—are now mortgages, rent-charges, rights of entry exercisable in respect of legal leases or rent-charges, easements and profits, since it is commercially expedient that such interests can be legal interests.[6] All other interests are equitable interests, *e.g.* restrictive covenants and interests under trusts.

3. The estate owner and overreaching. Nowadays, there is always an estate owner in whom the legal fee simple estate in possession is vested so that such estate is freely alienable, subject to any legal interests that may affect it, so satisfying the economic and commercial needs of a thriving society. The human desire for fragmentation of ownership and for keeping wealth in the family for as long as possible is satisfied by having the estate owner hold the legal estate on trusts giving effect to the fragmented equitable interests. A purchaser concerns himself with obtaining the legal estate from the estate owner and, upon paying the purchase moneys over to two trustees or a trust corporation, will take the legal estate free from the equitable interests which will now be attached to the proceeds of sale (which may be invested in other land or stocks and shares). This process whereby the rights are detached from the land and attached to the proceeds of sale is known as "overreaching."[7]

4. An example of a settlement. Two examples may introduce some further land law concepts and provide a bird's eye view of the land law that the rest of this book is concerned with. Indeed, it will take the rest of the book to understand the examples fully. The examples are intended to operate as does a quick glance at the picture on the lid of a jig-saw puzzle before dealing in detail with the interlocking pieces of the puzzle.

By his will T settles *Great Expectations* on his son H for life, then W for life, remainder in fee tail for such child of H and W as H shall appoint by deed or will, but in default of appointment then in fee tail to their first son to attain 35 years of age.

(a) *The beneficial interests.* Here, H has a life interest vested in possession, W has a life interest vested in remainder, and H has a special power of appointment enabling him to appoint a fee tail to

[6] *Post*, pp. 88–90.
[7] *Post*, pp. 107–108.

one of his children, a fee tail continuing for as long as the original tenant in fee tail or any of his descendants survived. If H has a son aged four and a daughter aged two, then each is an object of the special power with a hope (*spes*) that the power may ultimately be exercised in his or her favour, whilst the son has a contingent entailed interest in remainder, contingent upon attaining 35 years. When he attains 35 he will have a vested entailed interest liable to be divested by an exercise of the power of appointment. Since T has not disposed of his whole fee simple, and it is possible that no child might obtain an entailed interest, or that a child might obtain such an interest but die childless or his descendants die out at some stage, T retains a fee simple in reversion to pass under his will, whether specifically or as part of his residuary estate.

(b) *The Settled Land Act estate owner.* Life would indeed be difficult if a prospective purchaser of the legal estate had to deal with everyone interested in Great Expectations. Instead, the law sensibly provides that he only has to deal with the estate owner holding the legal fee simple and pay over the purchase moneys to two trustees or a trust corporation. The purchaser thereupon obtains the legal estate free from the multifarious equitable interests which become interests in the purchase moneys. In the example the Settled Land Act ensures that H, the current tenant for life, holds the legal fee simple on trust for himself and the other beneficiaries and negotiates the sale price and transers the legal title to the purchaser.[8] The Act arranges for there to be two individuals or a trust corporation to be Settled Land Act trustees to whom the purchase moneys must be paid if the legal estate is to pass to the purchaser.[9]

(c) *The trustees for sale as estate owners.* Since H is the dominant controller of the settled property in the example, it is possible for a settlor to create the same beneficial interests but to vest the legal estate in two trustees (or a trust corporation) on trust to sell the property but with power to postpone sale so that the property may remain unsold for many years. It is then the trustees themselves who are in control and who hold the legal estate and negotiate the sale price and transfer the legal title to the purchaser, themselves receiving the purchase moneys.[10]

(d) *The position of purchasers.* In either case the prospective purchaser is not at all worried by the equitable beneficial interests under the settlement which are overreached. He may, however, be worried if the legal fee simple is subject to burdensome easements or restrictive covenants. Furthermore, if the fee simple be subject to a

[8] *Post,* pp. 243, 267.
[9] *Post,* pp. 262–264.
[10] *Post,* pp. 280–281.

mortgage he will insist that the mortgage be paid off or that the price be appropriately reduced.

It may be that, under his Settled Land Act powers, H had earlier leased the property for 22 years to Mr. and Mrs. L as joint tenants, that Mr. and Mrs. L had assigned the unexpired residue of the lease to Messrs. R, S, V and P as tenants in common, who themselves had sub-let for three years to Mr. and Mrs. Y jointly, who had taken in Z as a lodger. If a prospective purchaser were interested in purchasing as an investment the legal fee simple subject to the various leasehold interests, he would need to clarify the status and responsibilities of the parties, to discover whether the 22 year lease could be forfeited for some breach of covenant and to ascertain what rights might exist under the Leasehold Reform Act and the Rent Acts.

(e) *The position of other interested persons.* Lawyers do not just act for purchasers. A person involved as a tenant, sub-tenant or lodger may seek advice as to his rights. Who is liable to repair the central heating; what happens on the death of R or of Mrs. Y; can the interest be assigned to someone else and, if so, how? A beneficiary under the trust may seek advice. What if H is cutting down valuable growing timber on the property and keeping the proceeds for himself; what if H is proposing to sell the property at what seems too low a figure; if H does exercise the special power conferred on him on what conditions (*e.g.* as to age) may he make the appointment; indeed, is T's gift over in default of appointment valid, when he seems to be trying to govern from the grave for a very long time and there is a special rule, commonly known as the Rule Against Perpetuities or the Rule against Remoteness of Vesting,[11] designed to prevent excesses in this regard?

5. Co-ownership. It may be said that the *Great Expectations* case is an unusual case designed to raise more problems than would normally arise. However, fundamental problems arise in more common situations, especially those involving co-ownership of land.

Before 1926 the major problem with co-owned land was that a purchaser might find that there were 38 (or more) co-owners of the legal estate owning different fractions of the land, some living in Canada, Australia, India and Singapore, some being minors and some mental patients, if there were not already trouble enough in ascertaining the names and addresses of all the co-owners. Obviously, a purchaser had to deal with all co-owners and take a conveyance of the house from all of them if he were to obtain the full legal title. If there were many co-owners it was easier for a purchaser to look for other property to purchase, leaving the co-owned property to stagnate.

[11] See Chap. 6.

Since 1925 the problem has been resolved.[12] There can never be more than four co-owners of the *legal* estate, who must hold the legal estate as *joint tenants*, so that on death the legal estate remains in the survivors (by the *ius accrescendi*) who can appoint others to be joint tenants with themselves of the legal estate so long as their number does not exceed four. The legal estate is held by the joint tenants on *trust for sale* with power to postpone sale (so that the property may remain unsold for a long time) for any number of co-owners, who may be minors or mental patients or live in remote countries, and who have *equitable* interests which may be joint tenancies or tenancies in common. So long as a purchaser pays his purchase moneys to the joint tenants holding the legal estate as trustees—and takes a conveyance of the legal estate from them—he obtains a good legal title free from all the equitable interests of the beneficial co-owners which are now in the proceeds of sale. Thus everyone lives happily ever after.

6. Current co-ownership problems. More recently, problems have arisen where one person holds the legal estate but some other person by some contribution to the purchase or the improvement of the house has obtained an equitable co-ownership interest.

Take H and W who married in 1950 when H purchased the matrimonial home by paying a 10 per cent. deposit and taking on a mortgage for the balance, which he paid off over 25 years. The title deeds show H to be the sole legal estate owner. W stayed at home bringing up their family and in 1977 inherited £30,000. H sold their house for £60,000 and with W's £30,000 purchased in his sole name a £90,000 bungalow called Reality Checkpoint. In 1981 H sold the bungalow for £110,000 to P who paid the money over to H. When P attempted to move into the bungalow he discovered W, who refused to let him in, stating that she owned a third of the bungalow and was staying there, since H had run off with some 30-year-old divorcee.

Technically, since H and W were co-owners, having put up two thirds and one third of the price of the bungalow, H held the legal estate upon trust for sale for H and W as equitable tenants in common as to two thirds and one third respectively. Thus, if W's equitable interest were to be overreached P should have paid the purchase moneys to two trustees for sale (or a trust corporation) instead of to H.

7. Overreachable equitable interests and the doctrine of notice. P will argue that if he had known there was a trust for sale he would not have paid the moneys to H but to two trustees so as to overreach W's equitable interest. However, he was a bona fide purchaser of the legal

---

[12] *Post*, pp. 305–310.

estate without notice of W's equitable interest and so took free of such interest on general equitable principles.[13]

W will argue that even if P had no actual notice of her interest he had constructive notice of it, since a purchaser has constructive notice of all those matters he would have discovered if such inquiries and inspections had been made as ought reasonably to have been made by a purchaser.[14] Nowadays, when so many wives go out to work at some stage, there is a good chance that a wife will have used her money to acquire an interest in the matrimonial home so it is reasonable to inquire of a wife whether she has such an interest.

If P had seen W on the premises he ought to have asked her if she claimed any interest in the bungalow or whether she only lived there because she was the wife of H. If he had done so he would have discovered her equitable interest.

If P had not seen W but had seen signs of a female presence in the bungalow P should have made inquiries. But what if H said the clothes and perfumes belonged to his 15 year old daughter or that he was a transvestite or a drag artist? Surely P cannot rely on anything H says, in any event, since H in his own interest would be doing all he could to appear as sole owner, having contrived P's visit to the bungalow to coincide with W's absence in hospital or at the hairdressers or at her mother's home.

If there had been no obvious signs of a female presence should P have searched in cabinets, trunks and wardrobes to see if H had tried to hide such signs? Should P have examined the public electoral register or have made enquiries of H's neighbours or have employed private detectives to ascertain whether anyone other than H lived in the bungalow?

There is much uncertainty over what inquiries and inspections ought *reasonably* to be made by a purchaser so as to fix a purchaser with constructive notice of an equitable interest so as to be bound by such interest. However, the uncertainty inherent in the doctrine of notice is considered justifiable in the interests of occupiers, who would expect any equitable interest as co-owner to be protected by virtue of their occupation. The law would unfairly favour purchasers too greatly if it required occupiers with such interests to register them in some public register on pain of such interests being void against a purchaser if not registered before the purchase.

8. Equitable interests registrable under the Land Charges Act. However, as will later be seen,[15] there are some other equitable interests involving rights over other persons' property such as

---

[13] *Caunce* v. *Caunce* [1969] 1 W.L.R. 286 though now in the light of *Williams & Glyn's Bank* v. *Boland* [1981] A.C. 487 it seems there would be constructive notice of the wife's equitable interest.

[14] *Post*, pp. 65–69.

[15] *Post*, pp. 90–97.

equitable easements and restrictive covenants which must be registered under the Land Charges Act 1925 or that of 1972 against the name of the owner of the property burdened with the interest, otherwise they will be void against a purchaser. Once a land charge has been registered this gives notice of it to everyone.

Registration of land charges under the Land Charges Act of 1925 or, nowadays of 1972, is distinct from registration of local land charges under what is now the Local Land Charges Act 1975. Land charges registered under the Land Charges Acts are recorded in a national computerised system in Plymouth based on the names of the landowners against whom registration was originally made. Under the Local Land Charges Act 1975 all district councils in England and Wales, the London boroughs and the Common Council of the City of London maintain a register of addresses affected by local land charges. These charges are of a local public nature, for example prohibitions and restrictions on the use of land under planning law, compulsory purchase proceedings, charges for making up a private road.

9. Problems of a purchaser of land. A purchaser obviously has to search the Plymouth Land Charges Register against the name of all the successive estate owners and the local land charges register against the address of the property. He also has to inspect the property and make inquiries of anyone apparently occupying the property[16]: such occupier might be an equitable co-owner or a legal tenant. The purchaser must also check the history of the vendor's title, tracing it back to a good root of title at least 15 years old. A good root of title is a document which deals with the whole legal and equitable interest, describes the property adequately and contains nothing to throw any doubt on the title. If the title consists of a series of conveyances on sale 4, 14 and 30-years old, the root of title will be the 30-year old conveyance. If the purchaser fails to investigate the title at all or else investigates it for only part of the period (*e.g.* because he contracts to accept the 14 year old conveyance as the root of title) he is fixed with constructive notice of everything he would have discovered had he investigated the title for the proper period.

Difficulties arise where a land charge has been registered under the Land Charges Act 1925 against the name of some estate owner whose name is hidden behind the root of title a purchaser can see, for example, if there have been conveyances on sale in 1981, 1976, 1973, 1965, 1960, 1950, 1940 and 1930 when a purchaser can only discover, and so only makes searches against, names in the conveyances of 1981, 1976, 1973 and 1965. Registration of a land charge gives notice of it to the world, so that registration against the name of an estate

---

[16] *Hunt* v. *Luck* [1902] 1 Ch. 428.

owner remains valid even if such name ultimately becomes hidden behind the root of title. All the purchaser can do is to claim compensation from state funds under section 25 of the Law of Property Act 1969 since he is bound by the registered land charge of which he is deemed to have notice.

It is also inconvenient having to trace title back to a good root of title at least 15 years old (such period having been 30 years until 1969), especially when earlier purchasers and their mortgagees will have fully examined the title deeds in checking up on the title.

10. The new registration of title system. How much better it would be if there were kept a register of addresses of titles containing full particulars of the title to each property and setting out the current result of former dealings affecting the property. This obviates the necessity for the repetitive investigations of title deeds on sale and also avoids the problems arising from having land charges registered against the names of estate owners.

Accordingly, under the Land Registration Act 1925 there are over seven million registered titles under a system of registration of title[17] which covers areas inhabited by over 75 per cent. of the population of England and Wales, and which in 1980–81 attracted receipts of £49½ million as against expenditure of £48 million. The system will ultimately cover all England and Wales and replace unregistered land.

Basically, fees simple absolute in possession and terms of over 21 years absolute are registrable estates, the owner of which is known as a registered proprietor, who is issued with a land certificate showing the title recorded in the register of title kept by the nearest of the 14 District Land Registries. The register of title and the land certificate (*a*) describe the land by reference to a filed plan, (*b*) set out the name(s) of the current registered proprietor subject to any "restrictions" on such proprietor's powers of disposition (*e.g.* no disposition to be effective unless purchase moneys are paid to two trustees or a trust corporation) and subject to any "caution" entered by someone claiming an adverse interest who cannot enter a "restriction" or "notice," and (*c*) set out "notices" of leases exceeding 21 years, mortgages, restrictive covenants, easements and other incumbrances adversely affecting the land.

A purchaser of registered land becomes legal estate owner on becoming proprietor and takes the legal estate subject only to entries on the register and to "overriding" interests but free from all other interests whatsoever. "Entries on the register" cover registered charges (*i.e.* mortgages) and "minor interests" protected by entry of a notice or restriction or caution. Overriding interests are interests

---

[17] *Post*, pp. 111–131.

not entered on the register but which fall within a category set out in section 70 of the Land Registration Act 1925, for example, rights being acquired under the Limitation Act 1980 by adverse possession of at least 12 years, rights of persons in actual occupation or in receipt of rents and profits save where inquiry is made of *such* person and such rights are not disclosed, leases for terms of 21 years or fewer granted at a rent without taking a capital sum, and local land charges. The idea is that such overriding interests are easily discoverable, for example, by inspecting the property and making inquiry of occupiers or by search against the property's address in the local land charges register.

The registered land system is clearly superior to the old unregistered land system in the way it deals with the multifarious interests in land that may subsist. It does sometimes, however, have similar weaknesses.

11. Co-ownership problems. Take, in a registered land context, the previously mentioned £110,000 bungalow called Reality Checkpoint vested in H as sole registered proprietor and used by H and W as their matrimonial home, W having an equitable tenancy in common in one third of the bungalow. In unregistered land P would only be bound by W's equitable interest if he had notice of her interest: this would depend upon whether or not he had made those inquiries and inspections that ought reasonably to have been made by a purchaser.

In registered land P is bound by overriding interests which include the rights of a person in actual occupation, save where inquiry is made of such person and such rights are not disclosed.[18] There is no concern with reasonably discoverable rights of reasonably apparent actual occupiers so what is reasonable to expect of P is immaterial. However, so as not to be too hard on P it is possible for the court to take a strict, rather than a liberal, view of "actual occupation," for example, where H hid all traces of W when W was away in hospital or on holiday or on business (*e.g.* as a croupier on an ocean liner or a marketing director) or, perhaps even where H had hidden W in a secret Priest's hole or cellar.

12. Rectification and indemnity. Registered land is inherently different from unregistered land in that it has to be possible to rectify the register of title in certain special cases, for example, fraud, forgery or mistake. If someone suffers loss by reason of rectification or of non-rectification then, subject to certain qualifications, he will obtain an indemnity from state funds. As will later be seen,[19] at face value the jurisdiction to rectify the register is absurdly wide and the

---

[18] L.R.A., s. 70 (1) (*g*); *Williams & Glyn's Bank* v. *Boland* [1981] A.C. 487.
[19] *Post*, pp. 533–537.

court and the Chief Land Register must in due course refine the principles upon which rectification may be ordered. It would seem that just as in unregistered land there is the fundamental "equity's darling" principle, enabling a bona fide purchaser of a legal estate for value without notice to take free of equitable interests, so in registered land there is the fundamental "Registrar's darling" principle enabling a purchaser of a registered estate for value to take free of interests not then protected as overriding interests or by entry on the register, so that rectification should, therefore, never be ordered against the "Registrar's darling."

13. The scope of unregistered and of registered land law. Unregistered and registered land law both deal with the same essential interests in land: fees simple, leases, Settled Land Act settlements, trusts for sale for co-owners or for persons successively, easements, restrictive covenants, mortgages, acquisition by adverse possession of at least 12 years. They differ when it comes to the methods by which such interests in land should be protected in case a conflict ever arises between one interest in land and another. Often the effect of the different methods of protection is the same, but sometimes it is different.

14. The statutory magic of registration of title. The most significant difference between unregistered and registered land results from the statutory "magic" of registration of a title. In unregistered land if F by forgery of a title deed apparently becomes legal estate owner and then purportedly sells and conveys the legal estate to P, P does not become legal estate owner or owner of anything, since the documents on which his alleged title is based are forgeries and nullities. In registered land if F forges a transfer, so as to become registered proprietor and then sells and transfers the registered estate to P, who becomes registered proprietor thereof, P does become the legal estate owner and can validly dispose of it.[20]

In unregistered land if O leases his house to T for 99 years and S ousts T by adverse possession exceeding 12 years then, as between S and T, S is entitled to occupy the house. However, O's rights are unaffected since adverse possession can only commence against O when O has a right to occupy the land, that is, when the 99 year lease has expired. Thus, a valid leasehold relationship remains between O and T, entitling O or his successors in title to possession of the house on expiry of the 99 years or on earlier forfeiture of the lease for breach of covenant or on an earlier surrender of the lease. It follows that if T surrenders the lease to O, O becomes entitled to possession

---

[20] *Haigh's* case reported in Ruoff & Roper, *Registered Conveyancing* (3rd ed.), p. 853 and in Hayton at pp. 185–186.

of the property,[21] just as if the 99 years had expired, and can evict S—and, if he wishes, re-let to T! Thus S's position is precarious.

In registered land if registered proprietor, O, leases his house to T for 99 years and T becomes registered proprietor of the lease and S ousts T by adverse possession, so that the Land Registrar cancels T's registration and registers S as registered proprietor of the lease, then S is entitled to occupy the house. On the same general principles of adverse possession outlined in the unregistered land case S's adverse possession cannot affect O's position. However, since T no longer has any registered title, T has nothing that can be surrendered to O so as to entitle O to immediate possession and to oust S.[22] Thus S's position is not precarious.

15. The need to understand both systems. For many years it will be necessary to understand the structure of both unregistered and registered land law even though ultimately all land will be registered land. The reason is that unregistered land only has to become registered land when (i) that land is within an area of complusory registration of title (designated by Order in Council) and (ii) the fee simple is sold, or a lease for 40 or more years granted (when the leasehold title is registered) or an existing lease sold when it has not less than 40 years unexpired (when the leasehold title is registered). It may take many years before some rural areas, particularly in Wales, become compulsory registration areas and, of course, many properties within existing compulsory registration areas may not be sold for many years yet (*e.g.* if owned by a company) when a purchaser will find himself examining unregistered land and applying unregistered land law principles before he is able to become first registered proprietor of the property.

16. Final comments. That then is a bird's eye view of unregistered and registered land law: some of its strengths, some of its weaknesses, some of its scope for improvement. Obviously, these prefatory pages will only be fully understood when the rest of the book has been studied but it is hoped they give some insight into the nature of land law and stimulate some interest in the law's endeavours to provide a useful framework within which land can satisfy a vast variety of human needs. The complex functions of land in fulfilling such needs must inevitably result in a relatively complex land law. Furthermore, once the law has provided for all sorts of different interests in land it faces the difficult task of trying to balance as harmoniously as possible the interests of purchasers, who want life made as simple as possible for them by having as much as possible

[21] *Fairweather* v. *St. Marylebone Property Co.* [1963] A.C. 510.
[22] *Spectrum Investment Co.* v. *Holmes* [1981] 1 All E.R. 6.

recorded in a register, unregistered matters being void against them, and the interests of occupiers and incumbrancers who would be prejudiced by a requirement that their interests must be recorded in a register to be valid, especially if they themselves could not reasonably be expected to know of the need to record their interests or to have had professional legal advice. How satisfactorily the law operates can only be judged after studying the rest of the book.

Sect. 3. Historical Outline

The history of the law of property in land can be divided into seven periods.

1. Formulation of principles. This was the early period during which the common law courts formulated many of the fundamental rules of land law. A number of important statutes were passed during this period, which extended from the Norman Conquest to the end of the fourteenth century.

2. Growth of Equity. This was the period from about 1400 to 1535, when the jurisdiction of the Chancellor to give relief in cases not covered by the common law rules was firmly established and developed.

3. The Statute of Uses. This was the period from 1535 to the middle of the seventeenth century, when the great changes made by the Statute of Uses 1535 were being worked out.

4. Development of trusts and the rules against remoteness. This encompassed the end of the seventeenth century and the eighteenth century, when trusts, which had been considerably restricted by the Statute of Uses 1535, were once more enforced. The modern form of a strict settlement of land, by which land was "kept in the family," from one generation to another, was fully developed during this period as were rules preventing interests vesting in persons at remote future dates.

5. Statutory reforms. This period consists of the nineteenth and twentieth centuries, when far-reaching reforms were made by Parliament. Many reforms were made during the nineteenth century, particularly between 1832 and 1845 and again between 1881 and 1890; but important though these were, they could not rival the 1925 property legislation in complexity and comprehensiveness. The Law of Property Act 1922 laid the foundation for the Acts of 1925, but most of it, together with extensive amendments of the law made by the Law of Property (Amendment) Act 1924, was repealed and replaced before it came into force. The provisions of these two Acts and of much of the earlier reforms were consolidated and divided up into six Acts; and these Acts and the unrepealed portions of the Act of 1922 all came into force on January 1, 1926. The "1925 property legislation" thus consists of:

The unrepealed portions of the Law of Property Act 1922.
The Settled Land Act 1925.
The Trustee Act 1925.
The Law of Property Act 1925.
The Land Registration Act 1925.
The Land Charges Act 1925.
The Administration of Estates Act 1925.

In addition, some amending statutes were subsequently passed, altering details in the principal Acts.

The genesis of the 1925 property legislation is important when construing it. The Acts of 1925 are all consolidating Acts, and a consolidating Act is presumed to change the law no more than the language necessarily requires. However, the Acts of 1922 and 1924 are professedly amending Acts, so that the presumption is not that the Acts of 1925 have not changed the old law, but that they have not changed the changes in that law made by the Acts of 1922 and 1924. Accordingly, where the Acts of 1922 and 1924 have left the old law unchanged, the Acts of 1925 are presumed not to have changed the law.[23] But where the Acts of 1922 and 1924 have changed the old law, it is those provisions which, though repealed, must first be construed.[24]

Since 1925 several statutes directed to specific reforms have appeared, notably the Perpetuities and Accumulations Act 1964, the Law of Property (Joint Tenants) Act 1964, The Matrimonial Homes Act 1967, the Law of Property Act 1969, the Charging Orders Act 1979 and the Limitation Act 1980. Furthermore, the Land Charges Act 1925 has in turn been replaced by a new consolidating Act, the Land Charges Act 1972.

6. Social control of land. This period overlaps the last; it consists of the last 60 years, during which, in the public interest, Parliament has enacted increasingly drastic provisions curtailing and restricting the rights of landowners.

7. Registered titles superseding unregistered titles. Over the last 30 years ever-increasing numbers of titles to land have been registered

---

[23] See, *e.g. Beswick* v. *Beswick* [1968] A.C. 58.
[24] *Re Turner's W.T.* [1937] Ch. 15; *Grey* v. *Inland Revenue Commissioners* [1960] A.C. 1; *Lloyds Bank Ltd.* v. *Marcan* [1973] 1 W.L.R. 339 at p. 344 (affirmed [1973] 1 W.L.R. 1387).

under the Land Registration Act 1925 which simplifies and facilitates conveyancing and provides state guaranteed titles to land. All land in England and Wales is ultimately intended to be registered under the registration of title system. Almost 80 per cent. of conveyancing transactions currently involve knowledge of such system, either because the title is already registered or because an unregistered title requires to be registered for the first time after completion of the purchase of the unregistered title.

Sect. 4. Meaning of "Real Property"

1. Land. The natural division of physical property is into land (or "immovables" as it is sometimes called) and other objects known as chattels or "movables." This simple distinction is inadequate. In the first place, chattels may become attached to land so as to lose their character of chattels and become part of the land itself.[25] Secondly, a sophisticated legal system of property has to provide not simply for the ownership of physical property, but also for the ownership of a wide variety of *interests* in such physical property, and also for the ownership of interests in non-physical or intangible property such as shares in companies or copyright.[26] Thirdly, for historical reasons English law has developed a distinction between "real property" and "personal property" which only approximately corresponds to that between "land" and other types of property.

2. History. In early law, property was deemed "real" if the courts would restore to a dispossessed owner the thing itself, the "*res*," and not merely give compensation for the loss.[27] Thus if X forcibly evicted Y from his freehold land, Y could bring a "real" action whereby he could obtain an order from the court that X should return the land to him. But if X took Y's sword or glove from him, Y could bring only a personal action which gave X the choice of either returning the article or paying the value thereof. Consequently, a distinction was made between real property (or "realty"), which could be specifically recovered, and personal property (or "personalty"), which was not thus recoverable. In general, all interests in land are real property, with the exception of leaseholds (or "terms of years"), which are classified as personalty.

At first, a dispossessed leaseholder had no right to recover his land from anyone except the lessor who had granted him the lease. Against third parties, he remained without remedy until late in the thirteenth century, when he was enabled to recover damages but not

---

[25] For "fixtures," see *post*, p. 19.
[26] For interests in land, see *post*, p. 24.
[27] 3 H.E.L. 3, 4; and see T.C. Williams (1888) 4 L.Q.R. 394.

possession. Not until 1468 was this rule seriously questioned, and when in 1499 it was finally decided that he might recover the land itself,[28] leaseholds had become too firmly established as personalty for this change to make any difference to their status. Thus, if a testator dies today, leaving a will giving all his realty to R and all his personalty to P, the reason for the leaseholds being included in the property passing to P lies in a rule which ceased to exist over 400 years ago.

3. Reasons for distinction. In early times there were no opportunities for investing in stocks and shares such as there are today. Money was therefore often employed in buying land and letting it out on lease in order to obtain an income from the capital. Further, the relationship between landlord and tenant was regarded as being mainly contractual, the tenant on his part agreeing to pay rent, and the landlord on his side agreeing to allow the tenant to occupy the land.[29] These conceptions were so far removed from the feudal system of landholding that leaseholds remained outside that system[30] and for a long time were hardly regarded as being rights in the land at all.

4. Classification. Although leaseholds are still classified as personalty, they differ from most of the other kinds of personalty in that they fall under the heading of "land" or "immovables" as opposed to "pure personalty," or "movables," such as furniture or stocks and shares. They are accordingly classified as "chattels real," the first word indicating their personal nature (cattle were the most important chattels in early days hence the name), the second showing their connection with land.[31] The three types of interests may therefore be classified thus:

Land / Personalty
(i) Realty.
(ii) Chattels real.
(iii) Pure personalty.

Although strictly a book on real property should exclude leaseholds, it has long been customary and convenient to include them, and that course is adopted here.

5. Modern distinction. The legislation of 1925 has abolished many of the remaining differences between the law governing realty and

[28] See 3 H.E.L. 213–216.
[29] 2 P. & M. 106.
[30] Challis R.P. 63.
[31] See *Ridout* v. *Pain* (1747) 3 Atk. 486 at 492.
[32] For other chattels real, of no importance today, see Co. Litt. 118b and M. & W. 17.

that governing personalty.[33] For example, before 1926, if a person died intestate (*i.e.* without a will), all his realty passed to his heir, while his personality was divided between certain of his relatives; again, realty could be entailed and personalty could not. After 1925, however, realty and personalty both pass on intestacy to certain relatives, and both kinds of property can be entailed. Thus the modern emphasis is on the distinction between land and other property, though the term "real property" still has some significance and is still widely used.

Sect. 5. Fixtures

In law, the word "land" extends to a great deal more than "land" in everyday speech. The general rule is *"quicquid plantatur solo, solo cedit"* (whatever is attached to the soil becomes part of it). Thus if a building is erected on land and objects are attached to the building, the word "land" prima facie includes the soil, the building and the objects affixed to it; and the owner of the land becomes owner of the building, even if it is built with bricks stolen by the builder.[34] The word "fixtures" is the name applied to anything which has become so attached to land as to form in law part of the land. A mortgage or devise of Blackacre or a contract to sell Blackacre thus passes rights to the fixtures to the mortgagee or devisee or purchaser.

A. Definition of Fixtures

In deciding whether or not an object has become a fixture, there are two main elements to be considered, namely—

(1) the degree of annexation, and
(2) the purpose of annexation.

1. Degree of annexation. In general, for an article to be considered a fixture, some substantial connection with the land or a building on it must be shown. An article which merely rests on the ground by its own weight, such as a cistern or a "Dutch barn" which rests upon timber laid on the ground, is prima facie not a fixture.[35] On the other hand, a chattel attached to the land or a building on it will prima facie be a fixture even if it would not be very difficult to remove it.[36]

2. Purpose of annexation. The degree of annexation is useful as showing upon whom the onus of proof lies[37]; thus if the article is

---

[33] See A.E.A. 1925, ss. 45–47, L.P.A. 1925, ss. 60, 130.
[34] *Gough* v. *Wood & Co.* (1894) 10 T.L.R. 318.
[35] See *Wiltshear* v. *Cottrell* (1853) 1 E. & B. 674.
[36] See *Buckland* v. *Butterfield* (1820) 2 Brod. & B. 54; *Jordan* v. *May* [1947] K.B. 427.
[37] *Holland* v. *Hodgson* (1872) L.R. 7 C.P. 328 at p. 335.

securely fixed, the burden of proof lies on the party contending that it is not a fixture. The purpose of the annexation, however, is the main factor; the modern tendency is to regard the degree of annexation as being chiefly of importance as evidence of the purpose of annexation.[38] The more securely an object is affixed and the more damage that would be caused by its removal, the more likely it is that the object was intended to form a permanent part of the land.[39]

In determining the purpose of annexation, the question to be asked is: "Was the intention to effect a permanent improvement of the land or building as such; or was it merely to effect a temporary improvement or to enjoy the chattel as a chattel?"[40] In the first case, the chattel is a fixture, in the second it is not. Thus, a wall composed of blocks of stone, or statues forming part of a general architectural design,[41] or movable dog-grates substituted for fixed grates,[42] or tapestries and portraits in a room designed as an Elizabethan room, have all been held to be fixtures.[43] In each case, the evident intention was to effect a permanent improvement to the land. But tapestry attached by tacks to wooden strips fastened to the wall by two-inch nails,[44] panelling screwed into wooden plugs let into the wall, and a collection of stuffed birds attached to movable wooden trays in glass cases attached to the walls of a bird gallery,[45] and pictures recessed into panelling[46] have been held not to form part of the premises. Although in these cases there was a substantial degree of annexation, the only way in which the chattels could be properly enjoyed was to attach them to the house in some way, and thus it was easy to infer an intent to affix them for the better enjoyment of them as chattels and not for the permanent improvement of the building. So, too, a drainpipe serving a house and laid in adjoining land has been held not to be a fixture; it was put there for the commodious occupation of the *house* and not for the benefit of the land in which it lay.[47] Similar articles may in individual cases remain chattels or become fixtures, depending on the circumstances, *e.g.* tip-up seats fastened to the floor of a cinema or theatre,[48] tapestries,[49] statues.

---

[38] *Leigh* v. *Taylor* [1902] A.C. 157 at p. 162.
[39] *Spyer* v. *Phillipson* [1931] 2 Ch. 183 at pp. 209, 210.
[40] See *Hellawell* v. *Eastwood* (1851) 6 Exch. 295 at p. 312.
[41] *D'Eyncourt* v. *Gregory* (1866) L.R. 3 Eq. 382.
[42] *Monti* v. *Barnes* [1901] 1 Q.B. 205.
[43] *Re Whaley* [1908] 1 Ch. 615.
[44] *Leigh* v. *Taylor* [1902] A.C. 157.
[45] *Viscount Hill* v. *Bullock* [1897] 2 Ch. 482.
[46] *Berkley* v. *Poulett* (1976) 242 E.G. 39.
[47] *Simmons* v. *Midford* [1969] 2 Ch. 415; contrast *Montague* v. *Long* (1972) 24 P. & C.R. 240 (bridge over river).
[48] Contrast *Lyon & Co.* v. *London City & Midland Bank* [1903] 2 K.B. 135 with *Vaudeville Electric Cinema Ltd.* v. *Munset* [1923] 2 Ch. 74.
[49] *cf. Re Whaley* [1908] 1 Ch. 615 with *Leigh* v. *Taylor* [1902] A.C. 157, and *D'Eyncourt* v. *Gregory* (*supra*) with *Berkley* v. *Poulett* (*supra*).

B. Right to Remove Fixtures

If according to the above rules an article is not a fixture, it can be removed by the person bringing it on to the land or by his successors in title; but if it is a fixture, prima facie it cannot be removed from the land and must be left for the fee simple owner, although there are some important exceptions to this. Questions of the right to remove fixtures arise between the following parties.

LIMITED RIGHT OF REMOVAL

1. Landlord and tenant. Prima facie, all fixtures attached by the tenant are "landlord's fixtures," *i.e.* must be left for the landlord. But the exceptions which have arisen nearly swallow up the rule; and fixtures which can be removed under these exceptions are known as "tenant's fixtures." The following are tenant's fixtures, though judgment in some cases blur the issue whether the chattel is removable since it has not become a fixture or whether the chattel has become a fixture but is removable as a tenant's fixture.

(a) *Trade fixtures.* Fixtures attached by the tenant for the purpose of his trade or business have long been removable by the tenant at any time during the term[50] or in such circumstances that he is entitled still to consider himself a tenant,[51] *e.g.* if he surrenders his lease either expressly or by operation of law and retains possession under a new lease or if he holds over as a statutorily protected tenant. An express surrender will not extinguish the tenant's right to remove trade fixtures unless on its true construction it disposes of all his rights in respect of the land.[52] Vats, fixed steam engines and boilers, a shed for making varnish, shrubs planted by a market gardener and the fittings of a public house have all been held to come within the category of trade fixtures.

(b) *Ornamental and domestic fixtures.* This exception appears to be rather more limited than the previous one, and seems to extend only to chattels perfect in themselves which can be removed without substantial injury to the building.[53] An article which can be moved entire is more likely to fall within this exception than one which cannot.[54] Thus while a conservatory on brick foundations has been held not to be removable, looking glasses, ornamental chimney pieces, window blinds, stoves, grates and kitchen ranges have all been held to be removable during the tenancy.

---

[50] *Poole's Case* (1703) 1 Salk. 368.
[51] *Ex p. Brook* (1878) 10 Ch. D. 100.
[52] *New Zealand Property Co. v. H.M. & S. Ltd.* [1982] 1 All E.R. 64.
[53] *See Martin v. Roe* (1857) 7 E. & B. 237 at p. 244.
[54] *Grymes v. Boweren* (1830) 6 Bing. 437.

(c) *Agricultural fixtures.* At common law, agricultural fixtures were not regarded as falling within the exception of trade fixtures,[55] for agriculture was regarded as a normal use of land and not as a trade. But by statute[56] a tenant of an agricultural holding who has attached fixtures to the land may remove them before, or within two months after, the determination of the term, provided the following conditions are observed:

(i) one month's written notice is given to the landlord;

(ii) all rent due is paid and all the tenant's obligations under the tenancy are satisfied by him;

(iii) no avoidable damage is done in the removal, and any damage done is made good; and

(iv) the landlord is allowed to retain the fixtures if he pays a fair price for them.

2. Tenant for life and remainderman. If land is settled on A for life with remainder to B, on the death of A the question arises whether fixtures which A has attached to the land can now be removed and treated as part of A's estate or whether they must be left for B. The position here is similar to that between landlord and tenant. Prima facie, all the fixtures must be left for B, with the common law exceptions of trade, ornamental and domestic fixtures[57]; but the statutory exception of agricultural fixtures does not apply.

NO RIGHT OF REMOVAL

3. Devisee and personal representative. If the land is given by will, the rule is that all fixtures pass under the devise; the testator's personal representatives are not entitled to remove them for the benefit of the testator's estate, whether they are ornamental, trade or any other kind of fixture.[58]

4. Vendor and purchaser. Without exception, all fixtures attached to the land at the time of a contract of sale must be left for the purchaser[59] unless otherwise agreed. The conveyance will be effective to pass the fixtures to the purchaser without express mention[60] but not structures or erections which are not fixtures.

---

[55] *Elwes* v. *Maw* (1802) 3 East. 38.
[56] Agricultural Holdings Act 1948, s. 13, replacing provisions in statutes from the Landlord and Tenant Act 1851, s. 3, onwards.
[57] See *Re Hulse* [1905] 1 Ch. 406 at p. 410.
[58] See *Re Lord Chesterfield's S.E.* [1911] 1 Ch. 237.
[59] *Colegrave* v. *Dias Santos* (1823) 2 B. & C. 76; *Phillips* v. *Lamdin* [1949] 2 K.B. 33.
[60] L.P.A. 1925, s. 62(1); *Dibble Ltd.* v. *Moore* [1970] 2 Q.B. 181.

5. Mortgagor and mortgagee. If land is mortgaged, all fixtures on it are included in the mortgage without special mention; the exceptions as between landlord and tenant do not apply.[61] The mortgagor is not even entitled to remove fixtures which he has attached after the date of the mortgage.[62]

Sect. 6. Tenures and Estates

The basis of English land law is that all land in England is owned by the Crown. A small part is in the Crown's actual occupation; the rest is occupied by tenants holding either directly or indirectly from the Crown.[63] "*Nulle terre sans seigneur*" (no land without a lord): there is no allodial land in England,[64] *i.e.* no land owned by a subject and not held of some lord.

1. Lord and tenant. This position can be traced from the Norman Conquest. William I regarded the whole of England as his by conquest. To reward his followers and those of the English who submitted to him, he granted and confirmed certain lands to be held of him as overlord.[65] These lands were granted not by way of an out-and-out transfer, but to be held from the Crown upon certain conditions. Thus, Blackacre might have been granted to X on the terms that he did homage and swore fealty, that he provided five armed horsemen to fight for the Crown for 40 days in each year, and the like. Whiteacre might have been granted to Y on condition that he supported the King's train in his coronation. X and Y might each in turn grant land to others to hold of them in return for services. Those who held directly of the King (such as X and Y in the examples above) were known as "tenants *in capite*" or "tenants in chief." Those who in fact occupied the land were called tenants in desmesne, and the tenant or tenants (if any) who stood between the King and the tenant in desmesne were called mesne lords, or mesnes. In days when land and its rent and profits constituted nearly the whole tangible wealth of a country,[66] it was more usual to secure the performance of services by the grant of land in return for those services than it was to secure them by payment; the whole social organisation was based on landholding in return for services.[67]

2. Services. These services became to a certain extent standardised. Thus there was one set of services (which included the provision of

---

[61] *Monti* v. *Barnes* [1901] 1 Q.B. 205; L.P.A. 1925, s. 62(1).
[62] *Reynolds* v. *Ashby & Son* [1904] A.C. 466.
[63] 1 P. & M. 232, 233.
[64] Co. Litt. 1b.
[65] Williams R.P. 12.
[66] Challis R.P. 1.
[67] Williams R.P. 10.

armed horsemen for battle) which became known as knight service, and there was another set (which included the performance of some honourable service for the King in person) which was known as grand sergeanty. Each of these sets of services was known as a *tenure*, for it showed how the land was held (*tenere*, to hold).

3. Time. A further essential is the length of time for which the land was held. Land might be granted for life (for as long as the tenant lived), in tail (for as long as the tenant or any of his descendants lived), or in fee simple (for as long as the tenant or any of his heirs, whether descendants or not, were alive). Each of these lengths of tenancy was known as an *estate*, a word derived from *status*.[68] Thus the Crown might grant land to A for an estate in fee simple, and A in turn might grant it to B for life. But the ownership of the land remained in the Crown. A man might own one or more estates in land, yet he never owned any of the land itself. Ownership of the largest estate in land, the fee simple, has come more and more to resemble ownership of the land itself, but even today it is technically true to say that the whole of the land in England is owned by the Crown; a subject can own only an estate. Both in popular speech and in legal parlance, however, the word "estate" is often used in other senses. Thus it may describe an area of land ("the Blank Estate is for sale") or assets generally ("the testator left a net estate of £50,000"). The context will usually leave little doubt about which sense is intended.

4. Basic doctrines. There are thus two basic doctrines in the law of real property. These are known as—

(i) the doctrine of tenures: all land is held of the Crown, either directly or indirectly, on one or other of the various tenures; and

(ii) the doctrine of estates: a subject cannot own land, but can merely own an estate in it, authorising him to hold it for some period of time.

In short, the tenure answers the question "How is it held?" the estate the question "For how long?"

5. Effects of doctrines. It is this doctrine of estates, coupled with the permanence of land as opposed to mere destructible chattels, which makes the law relating to land so much more complex than the law governing chattels. At common law, it can in general be said that only two distinct legal rights can exist at the same time in chattels, namely, possession and ownership. If A lends his watch to B, the ownership of

---

[68] 2 H.E.L. 351, 352.

the watch remains vested in A, while B has possession of it. But in the case of land, a large number of legal rights could and still can exist at the same time. Thus the position of Blackacre in 1920 might have been that A was entitled to the land for life, B to a life estate in remainder (*i.e.* after A's death), and C to the fee simple in remainder. At the same time, D might own a lease for 99 years, subject to a sub-lease in favour of E for 21 years, and the land might be subject to a mortgage in favour of F, a rentcharge in favour of G, easements such as rights of way in favour of H, J and K, and so on, almost *ad infinitum*. Before 1926, all these estates could exist as legal rights, and most, but not all, can exist as legal rights today.

It may thus be said that in the case of pure personalty, the unit of ownership is the chattel or other thing itself; it is either owned by one person (or several persons jointly or in common with each other), or it is not owned at all. In the case of land, however, the unit of ownership is not the land itself (which is necessarily owned by the Crown), but the estates and interests which have been artificially created in the land. In popular speech, one may refer to X's ownership of Blackacre; but technically, one should speak of X owning a lease of Blackacre, or holding Blackacre in fee simple. This conception of the subject-matter of ownership being an abstract estate rather than the corporeal land was a remarkable and distinctive achievement of early English legal thought; it contributed greatly both to the triumphant flexibility of the English system and to its undoubted complexity.

The doctrine of tenures, now greatly attenuated, is briefly described in the following section, while the doctrine of estates, still of great significance, is considered in greater detail in the next chapter.

Sect. 7. Tenures

The disappearance of the social organisation based on landholding in return for services has led over the centuries to extensive changes in the rules of tenure, so that many tenures, formerly important, have now vanished.

1. Extinct tenures. The tenancies which existed at common law were divided into two main classes, free and unfree.

(a) *Free tenures.* There were three classes of free tenures:

    A Tenures in chivalry (or military tenures).
    B Tenures in socage (generally involving agricultural services).
    C Spiritual tenures (involving religious services).

Each of these categories was subdivided, but it is unnecessary to consider in detail the different incidents and services to which each gave rise.[69] The statute *Quia Emptores* 1290, which prohibited the creation of new tenures by anyone except the Crown, the Tenures Abolition Act 1660, which converted tenures in chivalry into common socage, and the Law of Property Act 1922, which abolished almost all[70] the remaining incidents of the free tenures, have contrived to reduce all free tenures to one class, namely socage, now usually called "freehold." The process of attrition of tenures has also brought about the disappearance of all intermediate tenures, so that the courts will now readily act on the presumption that all freehold land is held directly of the Crown.[71]

(b) *Unfree tenures.*[72] The two unfree tenures were villein tenure and, somewhat confusingly, "customary freehold." Their main distinguishing features were the uncertain varying nature of the services to be rendered to the lord, and the absence of protection by the King's Courts. The tenant had to look for his protection to the court of his lord. Both these features disappeared in later centuries, but not before it had been established that land held on an unfree tenure could be transferred only by a surrender and admittance made in the lord's court. The transaction was recorded on the court rolls and the transferee given a copy of the entry to prove his title; he thus held "by copy of the court roll," and the tenure became known as "copyhold."

(c) *Enfranchisement of copyholds.* Before 1926, provision had been made by statute for the enfranchisement of copyholds, *i.e.* the conversion of land of copyhold tenure into socage. The Copyhold Acts of 1841, 1843 and 1844 provided for voluntary enfranchisement, *i.e.* enfranchisement where both lord and tenant agreed. The Copyhold Acts of 1852, 1858 and 1887 (consolidated in the Copyhold Act 1894) enabled either lord or tenant to secure compulsory enfranchisement. But apart from any proceedings taken under these Acts, the various tenures remained substantially unaltered until the legislation of 1925 came into force. Finally, by the Law of Property Act 1922,[73] all remaining copyhold land was converted into land of freehold tenure. However, the incidents of copyhold land, unlike those of freehold land remained important and effective in 1925, and therefore could not be simply abolished without causing injustice to the lord. Some were abolished forthwith subject to the payment of

---

[69] See M. & W., Chap. 2.
[70] A survival is escheat where the trustee in bankruptcy of a landowner disclaims, or a corporation holding land is dissolved: see M. & W. 35, 36.
[71] See, *e.g. Re Lowe's W.T.* [1973] 1 W.L.R. 882.
[72] See M. & W. 23–28.
[73] s. 128 and Sched. 12, para. (1)., Sched 13.

compensation.[74] Others were preserved temporarily, but this class disappeared on or before December 31, 1935.[75] Lastly, there are a few which continue indefinitely unless abolished by written agreement between lord and tenant. These are:

   (i) Any rights of the lord or tenant to mines and minerals;

  (ii) Any rights of the lord in respect of fairs, markets and sporting;

 (iii) Any tenant's rights of common (*e.g.* to pasture beasts on the waste land of the manor); and

 (iv) Any liability of lord or tenant for the upkeep of dykes, ditches, sea walls, bridges and the like.

2. Modern tenures. As a consequence of the developments outlined above, there is only one feudal tenure left today, namely, socage, now called freehold. By contrast, leasehold land has increased in importance[76]; and although leaseholds stood outside the feudal system of tenures, they have long been the most important modern form of tenure. Thus at the present time there are only two forms of tenure, namely, freeholds and leaseholds.

Today little trace remains of the former varieties of tenure and the customs that went with them. Yet some reference must be made to gavelkind and borough English.[77] These were not separate tenures, but customs which applied to certain land of socage tenure and copyhold tenure. The most striking feature of gavelkind, which was mainly found in Kent, was partibility, *i.e.* that on intestacy the land descended to all sons equally and not to the eldest son alone. The main feature of borough English, which was found in Nottingham and places in Sussex and Surrey, was ultimogeniture, *i.e.* that on intestacy the land descended to the youngest son instead of the eldest.

---

[74] L.P.A. 1922, Sched. 12, para. 1; Pt. II, para. 13, as amended.
[75] *Ibid.* Sched. 13, ss. 128, 138, Pt. II.
[76] See *post*, pp. 30, 33 and Chap. 9.
[77] See M. & W. pp. 20–22.

CHAPTER 2

ESTATES

Part 1

CLASSIFICATION

THE nature of an estate has already been discussed[1]; it is essentially an interest in land of defined duration. It is now necessary to consider the different kinds of estate. In doing this, much of the discussion will be in the past tense, for as will be seen[2] some of the estates can no longer exist as such, although corresponding rights can exist as interests (instead of estates) in land.

Estates were divided into two classes:

 1. Estates of freehold;
 2. Estates less than freehold.[3]

It should be noted that "freehold" here has nothing to do with freehold (or socage) tenure; it is merely that the same word is used to express sometimes the quality of the tenure, and sometimes the quantity of the estate. "Freehold" as normally used by the man in the street, unconsciously combines these senses; thus when a house agent advertises "a desirable freehold residence," he refers to a fee simple estate in land of freehold tenure.

Sect. 1. Estates of Freehold

There were three estates of freehold:

 (a) fee simple;
 (b) fee tail; and
 (c) life estate.[4]

The fee simple and the life estate have always existed in English law; the fee tail was introduced by statute in 1285. Before considering the estates in any detail a brief account of each must be given.

1. Fee simple. Originally this was an estate which endured for as long as the original tenant or any of his heirs survived. "Heirs" comprised any blood relations, although originally ancestors were

---

[1] *Ante*, p. 24.
[2] *Post*, pp. 83 *et seq*.
[3] 1 Preston, *Estates*, 22.
[4] Co. Litt. 43b.

excluded; not until the Inheritance Act 1833 could a person be the heir to one of his descendants. Thus at first a fee simple would terminate if the original tenant died without leaving any descendants or collateral blood relations (*e.g.* brothers or cousins), even if before his death the land had been conveyed to another tenant who was still alive. But by 1306 it was settled that where a tenant in fee simple alienated the land, the fee simple would continue as long as there were heirs of the new tenant and so on, irrespective of any failure of the original tenant's heirs.[5] Thenceforward a fee simple was virtually eternal.[6]

2. Fee tail. This was an estate which continued for as long as the original tenant or any of his descendants survived. Thus if the original tenant died leaving no relatives except a brother, a fee simple would continue, but a fee tail would come to an end. The terms "fee tail," "estate tail," "entail" and "entailed interest" are often used interchangeably although "fee tail" is the correct expression for a legal entail[7] and "entailed interest" is usually reserved for an equitable entail.[8]

3. Life estate. As its name indicates, this lasted for life only. The name "life estate" usually denoted that the measuring life was that of the tenant himself, *e.g.* when the grant was to A for life. The form of life estate where the measuring life was that of some other person was known as an estate "*pur autre vie*" (pronounced "per *oh*ter vee," and meaning "for the life of another"), *e.g.* to A so long as B lives.

A common feature of all estates of freehold was that the duration of the estate was fixed but uncertain.[9] Nobody could say when the death would occur of a man and his heirs, or a man and all his descendants, or a man alone. But the duration was not wholly indefinite; the estate was bound to determine if some pre-ordained event occurred. In the case of the fee simple and the fee tail, the word "fee" denoted (a) that the estate was an estate of inheritance, *i.e.* an estate which, on the death of the tenant, was capable of descending to his heir[10]; and (b) that the estate was one which might continue for ever.[11] A life estate, on the other hand, was not a fee. It was an estate of inheritance and it could not continue for ever. On the death of the tenant, an ordinary life estate determined, and an estate *pur autre vie* did not descend to the tenant's heir, but passed under special rules of occupancy which applied till 1926.[12] Life estates were sometimes

---

[5] Y.B. 33–35 Edw. I (R.S.) 362.
[6] 1 Preston, *Estates*, 429; but see T. Cyprian Williams (1930) 69 L.J. News. 369 at p. 385; 70 *ibid.* 4, 20; (1931) 75 S.J. 843 at p. 847.
[7] Litt. 13; 1 Preston, *Estates*, 420; Challis R.P. 60.
[8] See *post*, p. 47.
[9] Williams R.P. 65.
[10] 1 Preston, *Estates*, 262, 419; Challis R.P. 218.
[11] 1 Preston, *Estates*, 419, 480.
[12] See M. & W. 101.

called "mere freeholds" or "freeholds," as opposed to "freeholds of inheritance."

Each estate of freehold could exist in a number of varied forms which will be considered in due course.

Sect. 2. Estates Less than Freehold

At first, the three estates of freehold were the sole estates recognised by law; the only other lawful right to the possession of land was known as a tenancy at will,[13] under which the tenant could be ejected at any time, and which therefore hardly ranked as an estate at all. Terms of years grew up outside this system of estates; the lack of protection given to them by the courts, and early doubts whether terms for longer than 40 years were valid,[14] placed leaseholders in a position of inferiority from which they never recovered. Although by the sixteenth century terms of years had become recognised as legal estates[15] and were fully protected, yet they ranked below the three estates of freehold.[16] Leaseholders were regarded as holding their land in the name of their lords, the possession of the leasehold tenant being regarded as the possession of the lord.[17]

Today, the various forms of leasehold estate are of the first importance. Nevertheless, it is still not easy to find any satisfactory common element in them; perhaps it is not possible to evolve a more precise definition than "an estate not a freehold." The principal categories are as follows; they are dealt with more fully later.[18]

1. Fixed term of certain duration. The tenant may hold the land for a fixed term of certain duration,[19] as under a lease of 99 years. The possibility of the term being extended or curtailed under some provision to this effect in the lease does not affect the basic conception, which is one of certainty of duration in the absence of steps being taken for extension or curtailment. A lease for "99 years if X so long lives" also fell under this head; it was not an estate of freehold,[20] for although X might well die before the 99 years had run, the maximum duration of the lease was fixed. For all practical purposes, there was no chance of X outliving the 99 years, so that the duration of the lease would be the same as an estate granted "to X for life"; yet in law the former was less than freehold and the latter

[13] Challis R.P. 63.
[14] See Co. Litt. 45b at 46a.
[15] Challis R.P. 64.
[16] Co. Litt. 43b; and see *Re Russell Road Purchase Money* (1871) L.R. 12 Eq. 78 at p. 84.
[17] 1 Preston, *Estates*, 205, 206.
[18] *Post*, pp. 340–345.
[19] 1 Preston, *Estates*, 203.
[20] 1 Cru.Dig. 47.

freehold. Partly as a result of the intervention of statute, such leases are comparatively rare today.[21]

2. Fixed term with duration capable of being rendered certain. A lease of land "to A from year to year," with no other provision as to its duration, will continue indefinitely unless either landlord or tenant takes some step to determine it. But either party can give half a year's notice to determine it at the end of a year of the tenancy, and thus ensure its determination on a fixed date. This, coupled with the fact that originally the lease was for an uncertain term of uncertain duration, classifies the estate as less than freehold (of fixed but uncertain duration). The same applies to quarterly, monthly, weekly and other periodical tenancies.[22]

3. Uncertain period of uncertain duration. A tenancy at will is a tenancy which may continue indefinitely or may be determined by either party at any time; it is thus less than freehold. In the same way, a tenancy at sufferance, which is similar in nature, is less than freehold.[23] Indeed, such tenancies are perhaps not estates at all.[24]

Sect. 3. Seisin

1. Meaning. One distinction between freeholders and owners of estates less than freehold was that only a freehold could carry seisin with it. It is difficult to define seisin satisfactorily.[25] It has nothing to do with the word "seizing," with its implication of violence. To medieval lawyers it suggested the very opposite: peace and quiet. A man who was put in seisin of land was "set" there and continued to "sit" there.[26] Seisin thus denotes quiet possession of land, but quiet possession of a particular kind.

2. Freeholder. Although at first the term was applied to the possession of a leaseholder as well as that of a freeholder, during the fifteenth century it became confined to those who held an estate of freehold.[27] A leaseholder merely had possession; only a freeholder could be seised.[28] And since the possession of a leaseholder was regarded as the possession of the freeholder from whom he held, a freeholder remained seised even after he had granted a term of years

---

[21] See *post*, p. 345.
[22] For these tenancies see *post*, p. 341.
[23] For these tenancies see *post*, p. 344.
[24] Consider *Wheeler* v. *Mercer* [1957] A.C. 416 at pp. 427, 428; M. & W. p. 140.
[25] See, generally, Maitland's *Collected Papers*, Vol. 1, pp. 329, 358, 407.
[26] 2 P. & M. 30.
[27] Challis R.P. 99.
[28] Litt. 324; Co. Litt. 17a, 200b.

and gave up physical possession of the land; receipt of the rent was evidence of seisin. Further, only land of freehold tenure carried seisin with it. A copyholder could not be seised, even if he held a fee simple.

From this it will be seen that a person was seised if—

(i) he held an estate of freehold,
(ii) in land of freehold tenure, and
(iii) either he had taken physical possession of the land, or a leaseholder or copyholder held the land from him.

3. Definition. Although it seems impossible to frame a satisfactory definition of seisin, to call it "that feudal possession of land which only the owner of a freehold estate in freehold could have" is to express the most important elements. A man might be seised of many plots of land at the same time, whether or not he had granted any leases of them, for the requirement of physical possession did not mean that the person seised had to be in continuous occupation; seisin was not lost merely because he went away on a visit. Once seisin was acquired, it continued until another person acquired it.

4. Importance. The importance of seisin, which has greatly diminished in modern times, is shown in many ways. For example—

(i) Feudal services could be claimed only from the tenant seised of the land.[29]
(ii) A real action (one in which the land itself could be recovered and not merely damages) could be brought only against the tenant seised.[30]
(iii) Curtesy and dower (the rights of a surviving spouse under the pre 1926 intestacy rules) could be claimed only out of property of which the deceased had been seised.[31]
(iv) Conveyances of freehold land could originally be made only by a feoffment with livery of seisin. This was a solemn ceremony carried out by the parties entering on the land, and the feoffor, in the presence of witnesses, delivering the seisin to the feoffee either by some symbolic act, such as handing him a twig or sod of earth, or by uttering some words such as "Enter into this land and God give you joy" and leaving him in possession of the land.

For these and other reasons, the common law abhorred an abeyance of seisin. Any transactions whereby one person lost seisin without transferring it to another was void.

---

[29] Challis R.P. 100.
[30] *Freeman d. Vernon* v. *West* (1763) 2 Wils. K.B. 165 at p. 166.
[31] See M. & W. pp. 514–518.

Sect. 4. Position of Leaseholds Today

As has been seen, leaseholds were at first regarded as mere contractual rights to occupy land.[32] Despite their subsequent recognition as legal estates, they always remained outside the feudal system of landholding. Today, it is possible to regard leasehold as a tenure. Only in the case of leaseholds does there now arise a relationship of lord and tenant which has any practical importance. The one remaining feudal tenure, socage, has been shorn of all the incidents of any consequence, whereas in the case of leaseholds a valuable rent is nearly always payable, and the lord usually has power to forfeit the lease if the tenant does not fulfil his obligations. Further, the position as regards creating successive interests in leaseholds, is substantially the same as for land held in socage. Thus just as socage land may be given "to A for life, remainder to B in tail, remainder to C in fee simple," so leasehold land may be given "to A for life, remainder to B in tail, remainder to C absolutely." Nevertheless, leaseholds also retain the principal characteristic of an estate, for they mark out the length of time for which the land is held. Consequently, although it may be true that for all practical purposes leaseholds have completed the transition from contract via estate to tenure, it is better to regard them as being in a class by themselves, having features of both estates and tenures.

The details of leaseholds will be considered later.[33]

Part 2

ESTATES OF FREEHOLD

The two main points to be considered concerning estates of freehold are—

(1) the words required to create each of the estates, and
(2) the characteristics of each estate.

Sect. 1. Words of Limitation

1. "Limitation." "Words of limitation" is the phrase used to describe the words which limit (*i.e.* delimit, or mark out) the estate to be taken. Thus in a conveyance today "to A in fee simple," the words "in fee simple" are words of limitation, for they show what estate A is to have.

2. Inter vivos. The rule at common law was that a freehold estate of inheritance could be created in a conveyance *inter vivos* (*i.e.* a

---

[32] *Ante*, p. 17.
[33] *Post*, Chap. 9, p. 332.

transfer of land between living persons) only by a phrase which
included the word "heirs." A life estate could be created without
using this word, but a fee simple or fee tail could not.[34] It is important
to note that no other word would do. "Heirs" was the sacred word of
limitation, and had a magic which no other word possessed.

3. Wills. In the case of gifts by will, the attitude of the courts was
different. Strict words of limitation were not required in wills.
Provided the intention of the testator was clear, it would be
effectuated.[35]

The rules will now be considered, taking the fee simple, fee tail and
life estate in turn and dealing separately under each head with
conveyances *inter vivos* and wills.

A. Words of Limitation for a Fee Simple

I. CONVEYANCES INTER VIVOS

1. At common law. (a) *Natural persons.* At common law, the
proper expression to employ was "and his heirs" following the
grantee's name, *e.g.* "to A and his heirs."[36] "Heir" in the singular
would not suffice, and the word "and" could not be replaced by
"or"[37]: "to A or his heirs" gave A a mere life estate, and so did
expressions not containing the word "heirs," *e.g.* "to A for ever," or
"to A in fee simple."[38]

It is important to note that the words "and his heirs" gave no estate
in the land to the heirs. The words were mere words of limitation,
delimiting or marking out the estate which A was to take; they were
not words of purchase, that is to say, they were not words which
conferred any estates on the heirs themselves. ("Purchase" is here
used in the technical sense as referring to any transaction, whether
for value or not, whereby property is acquired by act of parties, as by
gift, and not merely by operation of law, as on intestacy[39]). Thus if A
had an heir apparent or heir presumptive[40] at the time of the
conveyance, such person acquired no estate by it, but had merely a
spes successionis, *i.e.* a hope of succeeding to the fee simple if A died
without having disposed of it.[41]

(b) *Corporations.* In the case of conveyances to corporations,
different rules applied. A corporation aggregate consists of two or
more persons united together under some name to form a new legal
person having perpetual existence, *e.g.* a Dean and Chapter, or a

[34] Co. Litt. 20a at 20b.
[35] *Throckmerton* v. *Tracy* (1555) 1 Plowd. 145 at pp. 162, 163.
[36] 2 Preston, *Estates*, 1.
[37] Co. Litt. 8b; Challis R.P. 221, 222.
[38] Litt. 1.
[39] See M. & W., p. 509.
[40] A living person has no heir.
[41] *Re Parsons* (1890) 45 Ch.D. 51 at p. 55.

limited company. No words of limitation were needed in such a case; a conveyance to the corporation *simpliciter*, *e.g.* "to the Alpha Co. Ltd.," sufficed to pass the fee simple, for there was no reason to give it any other estate.[42] A corporation sole, on the other hand, comprises only one natural person. Thus the King, the bishop or a parson are all corporations sole in their official capacities. In such cases, a life estate to the individual holder of the office was a conceivable alternative to a fee simple, and so to create a fee simple a formula had to be used which indicated that the corporation rather than the individual should benefit.[43] This formula was "and his successors," *e.g.* "to the Vicar of Bray and his successors."[44] Failure to use this phrase resulted in a mere life estate passing to the individual, though the use of "heirs" perhaps gave a fee simple to the individual.[45]

2. By statute. (a) *After 1881.* It has been seen that at common law a conveyance "to A in fee simple" would create not a fee simple, but only a life estate.[46] This was remedied by the Conveyancing Act 1881[47] enacting that in deeds executed after 1881 the words "in fee simple" would suffice to pass the fee simple. The expressions available at common law still remained effective; the Act merely supplied an alternative, and this alternative had to be employed as strictly as the older expression.

(b) *After 1925.* By the Law of Property Act 1925, the necessity for words of limitation in creating a fee simple was abolished in the case of all deeds executed after 1925, for the grantee takes "the fee simple or other the whole interest which the grantor had power to convey in such land, unless a contrary intention appears in the conveyance."[48] This effect will be produced even if the conveyance is to a corporation sole.[49] In practice, the words "in fee simple" are always inserted to make it clear that there is no contrary intention and to make effective the covenants for title implied in a conveyance.[50]

II. GIFTS BY WILL

1. Before 1838. Before 1838, no formal words of limitation were required in a will, but it was necessary for the will to show an intent to pass the fee simple.[51] Thus "to A for ever," or "to A and his heir," or

---

[42] 2 Preston, *Estates*, 43–47.
[43] See *Ex p. Vicar of Castle Bytham* [1895] 1 Ch. 348 at p. 354.
[44] Co. Litt. 8b, 94b; and see *Bankes* v. *Salisbury Diocesan Council of Education Incorporated* [1960] Ch. 631.
[45] 2 Preston, *Estates*, 48; Co. Litt. 94b, n. (5).
[46] Shep. 106.
[47] s. 51.
[48] s. 60 (1).
[49] s. 60 (2).
[50] p. 153, *post.* A conveyance of whatever the grantor has affords no scope for such covenants: *George Wimpey Ltd.* v. *Sohn* [1967] Ch. 481 at p. 509.
[51] 2 Preston, *Estates*, 68.

"to A to dispose at will and pleasure" all sufficed to pass the fee simple.[52] But it was for the devisee to show that a fee simple was intended to pass; a devise "to A" prima facie carried merely a life estate.[53]

2. After 1837. By the Wills Act 1837[54] the fee simple or other the whole interest of which the testator has power to dispose passes in a gift by any will made or confirmed after 1837[55] unless a contrary intention is shown. This reverses the onus of proof; a devise "to A" now passes the fee simple unless a contrary intention is shown.

B. Words of Limitation for a Fee Tail

I. CONVEYANCES INTER VIVOS

1. At common law. The expression required to create a fee tail was the word "heirs" followed by some words of procreation,[56] *i.e.* words which confined "heirs" to descendants of the original grantee; an example is "to X and the heirs of his body." The word "heirs" was essential, but any words of procreation sufficed. Thus "to A and the heirs of his flesh" or "to A and the heirs from him proceeding" sufficed to create entails. But expressions such as "to A and his issue" or "to A and his seed" would not create a fee tail in a deed, for the vital word "heirs" was missing.

By the addition of suitable words, an entail could be further restricted so that it descended only to a particular class of descendants. There were thus the following types of entail.[57]

(i) a tail general, *e.g.* "to A and the heirs of his body," where any descendants of A, male or female could inherit;

(ii) a tail male, *e.g.* "to A and the heirs male of his body," in which case only male descendants of A who could trace an unbroken descent from him through males could inherit, and not, *e.g.* a son of A's daughter; and

(iii) a tail female, *e.g.* "to A and the heirs female of his body," where corresponding rules applied.

In addition a "special tail" could be created, confining the heirs entitled to those descended from a specified spouse, such as "to A and the heirs of his body begotten upon Mary," when only issue of A and Mary could inherit; Mary of course, took nothing. A special tail could exist in any of the three above forms.

As in the case of a fee simple, the words following A's name were

[52] See, generally, 6 Cru.Dig, Chap XI.
[53] 2 Preston, *Estates*, 78.
[54] s. 28.
[55] s. 34.
[56] 2 Preston, *Estates*, 477, 478.
[57] See Litt. 21–29.

mere words of limitation. "To A and the heirs of his body" gave A a fee tail; it gave his heir apparent or heir presumptive no estate but only a *spes successionis*.

2. By statute. In the case of deeds executed after 1881 the Conveyancing Act 1881[58] made provisions for entails similar to those made for a fee simple. In addition to the expressions which sufficed to create an entail at common law, the words "in tail" (not "in fee tail," it will be noted) following the name of the grantee (*e.g.* "to X in tail") would create a fee tail. If it was desired to restrict the entail to a particular class of descendants, apt words could be added, *e.g.* "to A in tail male."

These rules still apply after 1925, the provisions of the Conveyancing Act 1881 being now replaced by the Law of Property Act 1925.[59] The effect of using informal words such as "to A and his issue" is to pass the fee simple either to A, or to A jointly with such of his issue as are alive at the time of the gift; the former seems the better view.[60]

II. GIFTS BY WILL

1. Before 1926. The rule before 1926 was that any words showing an intent to create an entail sufficed in a will, even if no technical expressions were used. Thus "to A and his seed," "to A and his heirs male,"[61] "to A and his descendants," and "to A and his issue,"[62] all usually sufficed to create entails. A devise "to A and his children" sometimes gave A an entail and sometimes gave the property to A and his children jointly depending on the circumstances under the Rule in *Wild's* case.[63] "Children" prima facie meant descendants of the first generation only, and so was less apt to create an entail than words such as "issue," which prima facie included descendants of any generation and were thus the informal equivalent of "heirs of his body."[64]

2. After 1925. The above rule remained unaffected until the Law of Property Act 1925[65] laid down that informal expressions should no longer suffice to create an entail in a will, but that expressions which would have been effective to create an entail in a deed before 1926 must be employed. Thus in deeds and wills alike either "heirs" followed by words of procreation, or "in tail," must now be used. As in the case of conveyances *inter vivos*, it seems that the effect of using informal expressions such as "to A and his issue" is to pass the fee

---

[58] s. 51.
[59] ss. 60, 130.
[60] See (1936) 6 Camb. L.J. 67; (1945) 9 Camb. L.J. 46; *ibid.* (1946) p. 185.
[61] In a deed this created a fee simple: *Idle* v. *Cook* (1705) 1 P.Wms. 70 at p. 77.
[62] *Slater* v. *Dangerfield* (1846) 15 M. & W. 263 at p. 272.
[63] (1599) 6 Co. Rep. 16b, at 17a, b.
[64] *Re Lord Lawrence* [1915] 1 Ch. 129 at p. 146.
[65] s. 130.

simple either to A, or to A jointly with such of his issue as are alive when the testator dies.[66]

C. The Rule in Shelley's Case

1. The Rule. The Rule in *Shelley's Case*[67] applied before 1926 to both deeds and wills. The Rule may be stated thus:

> It is a rule of law that when an estate of freehold is given to a person, and by the same disposition an estate is limited either mediately or immediately to his heirs or to the heirs of his body, then if both limitations are legal or both equitable, the words "heirs," or "heirs of his body" are words of limitation and not words of purchase.

2. Operation of the Rule. If land was limited before 1926—

"to A for life, remainder to his heirs," or—
"to B for life and to the heirs of his body,"

the natural meaning of the words was that A and B should each take life estates, and that A's heir should take a fee simple and B's heir a fee tail. The Rule in *Shelley's Case*, however, required an unnatural effect to be given to such limitations. Under the rule, the fee simple in remainder did not pass to A's heir, but passed to A in addition to the life estate, with the result that A's life estate in possession and his fee simple in remainder merged together and gave him the fee simple in possession. Similarly B took a fee tail in possession.

3. Abolition of the Rule. The Rule was the product of feudal doctrines which had become obsolete. Hence by the Law of Property Act 1925,[68] the Rule was abolished for all instruments coming into operation after 1925. Accordingly in a limitation "to A for life, remainder to his heirs" the word "heirs" is now a word of purchase and not a word of limitation. Thus A will take a mere life interest, while his heir takes the remainder in fee simple.

D. Words of Limitation for a Life Estate

I. CONVEYANCES INTER VIVOS

A life estate was created before 1926 either by words showing an intention to create a life estate, such as "to A for life," or by the use of expressions insufficient to create a fee simple or fee tail, such as "to A" or "to A for ever."[69]

After 1925, a fee simple (or the whole of the interest the grantor

---

[66] See note 60.
[67] (1581) 1 Co. Rep. 88b; and see Challis R.P. 152–167.
[68] s. 131.
[69] *Re Irwin* [1904] 2 Ch. 752.

has power to convey, if it is less than a fee simple) passes unless a contrary intention is shown.[70] Thus to create a life interest, words showing an intention to do so must normally be used, *e.g.* "to A for life."

Before the Wills Act 1837, a devise passed only a life estate unless an intention to create a fee simple or fee tail was shown. That Act provided that the fee simple passes unless a contrary intention is shown,[71] so that in this case also, words showing an intent to pass only a life interest are now essential.

Sect. 2. Nature of the Estates of Freehold

A. The Fee Simple

The fee simple is the most ample estate which can exist in land. Although in theory it still falls short of absolute ownership, in practice it amounts to this, for nearly all traces of the old feudal burdens have disappeared. Today, a tenant in fee simple may dispose of his estate in whatever way he thinks fit either by will[72] or *inter vivos*, though this has not always been so.

TYPES OF FEE SIMPLE

A fee (or fee simple) may be absolute or modified; a modified fee is any fee except a fee simple absolute. There are four types of fee.

1. Fee simple absolute. This is the type most frequently encountered in practice, and is an estate which continues for ever. "Fee" denotes inheritability,[73] "simple" excludes entails, and "absolute" distinguishes modified fees.

2. Determinable fee. A determinable fee is a fee simple which will automatically determine on the occurrence of some specified event which may never occur. If the event is bound to happen at some time, the estate created is not a determinable fee. Thus before 1926 a grant "to A and his heirs until B dies" gave A an estate *pur autre vie*, and a grant "to C and his heirs" for a fixed term of years gave C a mere tenancy for a term of years. A grant to X and his heirs until a specified lease was made, or to Y and his heirs "as long as such a tree stands," however, created determinable fees.[74] The estates of X and

---

[70] *Ante*, p. 35.
[71] s. 28; see *ante*, p. 36.
[72] Subject to possible claims under the Inheritance (Provision for Family & Dependants) Act 1975.
[73] See *ante*, p. 29.
[74] *Idle* v. *Cook* (1705) 1 P.Wms. 70 at p. 78.

Y might continue for ever, but if the specified state of affairs came about, the fee determined and the land reverted to the original grantor. The grantor thus had a possibility of reverter, *i.e.* a possibility of having an estate at a future time. If the occurrence of the determining event became impossible, the possibility of reverter was destroyed and the fee simple became absolute,[75] as where land was given "to A and his heirs until B marries" and B died a bachelor.

Determinable fees are rarely encountered in practice except under protective trusts[76] where property is initially granted to a person until he becomes bankrupt. A fee simple limited to a corporation does not determine merely because the corporation is dissolved.[77]

3. A fee simple upon condition. In making a grant of a fee simple, a clause may be added providing that the fee simple is not to commence until some event occurs, or that it is to determine on the occurrence of some event. Conditions of the first type are conditions precedent[78]; a gift "to X in fee simple if X attains 21" is a gift of a fee simple with a condition precedent that X must attain 21 before he can take the land. These limitations are dealt with under future interests.[79] A condition subsequent is one which operates to defeat an existing interest, *e.g.* a devise of land to X "on the condition that he never sells it out of the family"[80]; here the land passes to X, but it is liable to be forfeited if the condition is broken: X has a vested interest, liable to be divested.

The difference between a determinable fee and a fee simple defeasible by condition subsequent is not always easy to discern. The essential distinction is that the determining event in a determinable fee is included in the words marking out the limits of the estate, whereas a condition subsequent is a clause added to a limitation of a complete fee simple absolute which seeks to defeat it. Thus a devise to a school in fee simple "until it ceases to publish its accounts" would create a determinable fee, whereas a devise to the school in fee simple "on condition that the accounts are published annually" creates a fee simple defeasible by condition subsequent.[81] Words such as "while," "during," "as long as," "until" and so on are apt for the creation of a determinable fee, whereas words which form a separate clause of defeasance, such as "provided that," "on condition that," "but if," "if it happen that," operate as a condition subsequent.[82]

It will be seen that the difference is primarily one of wording; the

[75] Challis R.P. 83, 254.
[76] See Trustee Act 1925, s. 33.
[77] *Re Strathblaine Estates Ltd.* [1948] Ch. 228.
[78] Pronounced "preeseedent," with the accent on the second syllable.
[79] *Post*, pp. 189, *et seq*.
[80] *Re Macleay* (1875) L.R. 20 Eq. 186.
[81] See *Re Da Costa* [1912] 1 Ch. 337.
[82] See 1 Sanders, *Uses* 156; Shep. 121.

determining event may be worked into the limitation in such a way as to create either a determinable fee or a fee simple defeasible by condition subsequent, whichever the grantor wishes. The question is whether the words limit the utmost time of continuance of the estate, or whether they mark an event which, if it takes place in the course of that time, will defeat the estate; in the first case the words form a limitation, in the second a condition. In short, a limitation marks the bounds or compass of the estate, a condition defeats the estate before it attains its boundary.

There are some practical differences between the two forms of fee:

(a) *Determination:* a determinable fee automatically determines when the specified event occurs, for the natural limits of its existence have been reached.[83] A fee simple upon condition merely gives the grantor (or whoever is entitled to his realty, if the grantor is dead) a right to enter and determine the estate when the event occurs; until entry is made, the fee simple continues.[84]

Since a right of forfeiture arises from a condition subsequent the condition is void (so the grantee takes a fee simple absolute) unless it can be seen from the outset distinctly and precisely what events will cause a forfeiture.[85] The concepts of continuing to reside in Canada[86] and of marrying a person "not of Jewish parentage and of the Jewish Faith"[87] have been held to be uncertain, whilst the concepts of continuing in permanent residence in England[88] and of being or becoming a Roman Catholic have been held to be certain.[89]

In the case of conditions precedent where, upon satisfying the condition, a claimant will qualify as a recipient of the grantor's bounty, then the claimant need only show that, whatever the uncertainty of concept for other persons, he at least clearly satisfies the condition, for example, where a long-standing close friend claims under a devise of "a house to each of my old friends."[90] However, in the case of a class gift (*e.g.* a devise of "all my realty to my trustees on trust to sell it and hold the proceeds on discretionary trust to distribute them as my trustees see fit between my old friends,") the gift will fail unless it is possible to say of any given person that he definitely is or is not a member of the class[91] (so a class gift for old friends will fail[92]).

(b) *Remoteness:* if a condition subsequent may possibly become

---

[83] *Newis* v. *Lark* (1571) 2 Plowd. 403.
[84] *Matthew Manning's Case* (1609) 8 Co.Rep. 94b at 95b.
[85] *Sifton* v. *Sifton* [1938] A.C. 656.
[86] *Ibid.*
[87] *Clayton* v. *Ramsden* [1943] A.C. 320.
[88] *Re Gape* [1952] Ch. 743 "permanent residence" is a concept used in the conflict of laws doctrine of domicile.
[89] *Blathwayt* v. *Lord Cawley* [1976] A.C. 397.
[90] *Re Barlow's W.T.* [1979] 1 All E.R. 296; *Re Allen* [1953] Ch. 810.
[91] *McPhail* v. *Doulton* [1971] A.C. 93; *Re Baden's D.T.* [1973] Ch. 9.
[92] *Brown* v. *Gould* [1972] Ch. 53 at p. 57.

operative at too distant a date, it is void, and the fee simple is absolute, whereas a determinable limitation is probably valid no matter how far in the future the estate may determine.[93] Since July 16, 1964 determinable limitations are subject to the same rules as conditional interests.[94]

(c) *Existence at law:* a determinable fee cannot, it seems, exist as a legal estate after 1925; but a fee simple subject to a condition subsequent apparently can.[95]

(d) *Flexibility:* a determinable fee is more flexible than a fee simple upon condition. There are certain restrictions upon the conditions on which a fee simple may be made liable to be defeated. A condition subsequent is void, and the fee simple is absolute, if the condition infringes any of the following rules:

(i) It must not take away the power of alienation. One of the incidents of ownership is the right to sell or otherwise dispose of the property. A condition against alienation is said to be repugnant to this right, and contrary to public policy, if it substantially takes away the tenant's power of alienation; such conditions are thus void.[96] For example, conditions prohibiting all alienation, or all alienation during the life of some person, or alienation to anyone except X, have all been held void.[97] But certain partial restraints have been held valid; thus where land was devised to A "on the condition that he never sells it out of the family," the condition was held valid on the grounds that it did not prohibit any form of alienation except sale, it did not prohibit sales to members of the family, and it bound only A and not subsequent owners of the land.[98] Moreover, a mere covenant not to alienate is not repugnant to the power of alienation; the covenantee may recover damages (which might be nominal) for breach of the covenant, but the alienation is valid and gives rise to no right of forfeiture.[99]

(ii) It must not be directed against a course of devolution prescribed by law. A condition rendering a fee simple liable to be defeated if the tenant dies intestate, becomes bankrupt, or has the estate seized in execution, is void, for on each of these events the law prescribes that a fee simple shall devolve in a particular way, and this course of devolution cannot be altered by condition.[1]

---

[93] *Post,* p. 214.
[94] See *post,* p. 216.
[95] *Post,* p. 86.
[96] *Bradley* v. *Peixoto* (1797) 3 Ves. 324.
[97] See *Re Cockerill* (1929) 2 Ch. 131.
[98] *Re Macleay* (1875) L.R. 20 Eq. 186; *cf. Re Brown* [1954] Ch. 39; and see (1954) 70 L.Q.R. 15.
[99] *Caldy Manor Estates Ltd.* v. *Farrell* [1974] 1 W.L.R. 1303.
[1] *Re Machu* (1882) 21 Ch.D. 838 (bankruptcy).

(iii) It must not be illegal, immoral or otherwise contrary to public policy. The condition under this head most frequently encountered is a condition in restraint of marriage. Partial restraints, prohibiting marriage with a Papist, or a Scotsman, or a person who had been a domestic servant, have been held good.[2] But total restraints (or restraints which are virtually total, *e.g.* against marrying a person who has not freehold property in 1795 worth £500 per annum) are void unless the intent is not merely to restrain marriage but simply to provide for the tenant until marriage,[3] or unless the tenant has already been married once.[4]

A determinable fee, on the other hand, is not so strictly confined. A devise of freeholds on trust for X "until he shall assign charge or otherwise dispose of the same or some part thereof or become bankrupt . . . or do something whereby the said annual income or some part thereof would become payable to or vested in some other person" has been held to give X a determinable fee.[5] On any of the events occurring X's estate would determine; if he died before any of them occurred, the fee simple would become absolute, for it ceases to be possible for any of them to occur. But although a fee may thus be made determinable on alienation or on bankruptcy or on similar events, a limitation would probably be void if it were contrary to public policy for the fee to be determinable on the stated event, *e.g.* if the event is the return to her husband of a wife who is separated from him.

(e) *Effect of condition or limitation becoming void or impossible.* If a condition subsequent is void or becomes impossible, the donee takes a fee simple absolute, free from any condition[6]; but if a fee is made determinable upon an event contrary to law, the whole gift fails.[7]

4. A base fee. A base fee is a particular kind of determinable fee. The two essentials of a base fee are (a) it continues only so long as the original grantor or any heirs of his body are alive; and (b) there is a remainder or reversion after it.[8] Such estates are more fully dealt with below.[9]

Nature of modified fees. In general, the owner of a modified fee has the same rights over the land as the owner of a fee simple absolute:

[2] *Jenner* v. *Turner* (1880) 16 Ch.D. 188 (domestic servant).
[3] See *Jones* v. *Jones* (1876) 1 Q.B.D. 279.
[4] *Newton* v. *Marsden* (1862) 2 J. & H. 356.
[5] *Re Leach* [1912] 2 Ch. 422.
[6] *Re Greenwood* [1903] 1 Ch. 749.
[7] Consider *Re Moore* (1888) 39 Ch.D. 116 (personalty).
[8] See *post*, p. 45.
[9] *Post*, pp. 45, 49.

thus the common law refused to restrain him from committing acts of waste,[10] such as opening and working mines. Equity, on the other hand, intervened to prevent the commission of equitable waste, *i.e.* acts of wanton destruction,[11] whereas the owner of a fee simple absolute is under no such restraint.

At common law the owner of a modified fee could not convey a fee simple absolute but merely a fee liable to determination, for a man cannot convey more than he has. Statute has qualified this position.[12] Further, such a fee may become enlarged into a fee simple absolute, *e.g.* by the determining event becoming impossible[13]; and there are special rules for the enlargement of base fees.[14]

B. The Fee Tail

I. HISTORY

1. The origins. The fee tail is a creature of statute. Before the Statute *De Donis Conditionalibus* 1285 no such estate existed; the common law recognised only two estates of freehold, the fee simple and the life estate, each existing in varying forms.

The name "fee tail" was given to the estate since the word "tail" showed that the fee was *talliatum* or *taillé*, *i.e.* cut down; unlike the fee simple, which would descend to any class of heirs, a fee tail could descend to only one class, namely, issue of the donee. Notwithstanding any act of the original tenant or his issue the land was bound to descend to the issue in tail in the proper way. The statute did not prevent a tenant in tail from alienating the land, but the estate so created could be defeated by his issue after his death. Nor could the rights of the issue be prejudiced by the tenant levying a fine (a fine being a collusive action which was compromised[15]) or by any act of escheat or forfeiture. For nearly two centuries landowners were thus able to secure the unbroken descent of their land. However, freedom of alienation was ultimately secured by the ingenuity of practitioners and the courts. Two methods of "barring the entail" were evolved: the common recovery and the fine.

2. The barring of entails. (a) *The common recovery. Taltarum's Case*,[16] decided in 1472, shows that there was then in full working order a process whereby a tenant in tail could bar the entail by means of a recently invented collusive action known as a "common recovery." The process employed was that an action claiming the land was brought against the tenant in tail with his consent; the court

---

[10] For waste, see *post*, p. 52.
[11] *Re Hanbury's S.E.* [1913] 2 Ch. 357 at p. 365.
[12] *Post*, p. 266.
[13] *Ante*, p. 40.
[14] *Post*, p. 49.
[15] See *infra*.
[16] Y.B. 12 Edw. 4, Mich., pl. 25, f. 19a.

was prepared to allow this claim, provided judgment was entered against some third party for land of equal value to compensate the disappointed heirs. Consequently some "man of straw" was found against whom the second judgment could be given, and the matter could then proceed. The result of the action was that the tenant in tail was able to dispose of the whole fee simple, thus defeating the claims not only of the heirs of his body, but also those of any person entitled to any subsequent remainder, reversion or other estate. However, the action could be brought only by, or with the concurrence of, the person seised of the land; if land was given "to A for life, remainder to B and the heirs of his body," B could not suffer a recovery without the co-operation of A.

(b) *The fine.* A fine was a solemn form of conveyance whereby an agreement to convey the land was entered in the court records in the form of a compromise to an action. It was of earlier origin than the common recovery, but it did not become available for barring entails until some time later. The judges' dislike of unbarrable entails gave rise to judicial decisions which made it possible for entails to be barred by common recoveries, but as the Statute *De Donis* 1285 expressly prohibited the barring of entails by fines, legislation was necessary to make fines effective. The Statutes of Fines 1489 was thought to have made a fine effective to bar the issue in tail unless they asserted their rights within five years of the fine, and the Statutes of Fines 1540 confirmed this construction and made the fine immediately effective to bar the issue.

A fine could be levied without the concurrence of the person seised, but it was not so effective as a common recovery, for although it barred the rights of the issue in tail, it did not bar the owner of any subsequent remainder, reversion or other estate.[17] The estate produced by a fine was known as a "base fee." In effect a base fee was a fee simple which endured for as long as the entail would have continued if it had not been barred, and determined when the entail would have ended.[18] Thus, if land was limited to A for life, remainder to B in tail, remainder to C in fee simple, and B barred his entail by a fine in favour of X, X took a base fee. X remained entitled to the land for as long as B or any of his issue lived, but when they were all dead, C became entitled to the land.

A fine could be levied by one who had no entail but merely a *spes successionis*, or only a contingent or executory interest in tail, *i.e.* an entail to which he would be entitled only if some specified event occurred.[19]

(c) *Differences between fines and recoveries.* The main difference between fines and recoveries may be summarised as follows:

---

[17] *Margaret Podger's Case* (1613) 9 Co.Rep. 104a.
[18] *Ante*, p. 43.
[19] *The Case of Fines* (1602) 3 Co.Rep. 84a at 90a, b.

FINE	RECOVERY
(i) Action compromised.	(i) Action proceeded to judgment.
(ii) Consent of freehold tenant in possession not required.	(ii) Consent of freehold tenant in possession essential.
(iii) Not confined to owners of vested entails.	(iii) Available only to owners of vested entails.
(iv) Produced a base fee.	(iv) Produced a free simple absolute.

Both these methods of barring entails became purely formal; all that a tenant had to do was to instruct his lawyers to take the necessary steps. However, although there was no legal obstacle to the barring of an entail, fines and recoveries were dilatory, complicated and expensive. By the Fines and Recoveries Act 1833 fines and recoveries were abolished and replaced by a simple method of barring entails.

3. The Fines and Recoveries Act 1833. This substantially preserved the distinction between fines and recoveries, although the actions themselves were abolished. The Act provided that an entail could be barred by any assurance (*i.e.* any conveyance or other transfer) by which a fee simple could be disposed of, except a will. It was essential, however, that the assurance should be either made or evidenced by a deed; and a mere declaration by deed that the entail was barred was not enough, for an assurance was what the Act required.[20] If the tenant barring the entail wished to retain the land himself, he conveyed it to some trustee for him; if he wished to dispose of it, he made the disentailing assurance in favour of the grantee. It was necessary for every disentailing assurance to be enrolled within six calendar months of execution, formerly in the Court of Chancery, and later in the Central Office of the Supreme Court.[21] A conveyance which did not comply with the provisions of the Act did not bar the issue or the reversion or remainderman.

The effect of a disentailing assurance was to transfer a fee simple absolute—

(i) if executed by a tenant in tail in possession or—

(ii) if executed by a tenant in tail in remainder with the consent of the protector of the settlement, who was normally the person with the current estate in possession, for example, the life tenant. If the tenant in tail in remainder did not have the protector's consent then only a base fee was created.

---

[20] Fines and Recoveries Act 1833, ss. 15, 40; see *Carter* v. *Carter* [1896] 1 Ch. 62 declaration of trust sufficient.
[21] Fines and Recoveries Act 1833, s. 41.

This in effect preserved the distinction between fines and recoveries.

II. RIGHTS OF A TENANT IN TAIL

In general, a tenant in tail has the same rights of enjoyment of the land as a tenant in fee simple. He may thus commit all kinds of waste, including equitable waste, even if he is restrained from barring the entail by statute.[22] His position is considered further in the chapter dealing with the Settled Land Act 1925.

III. TYPES OF ENTAIL

The various types of entail, such as special tail and tail male, have already been considered.[23]

IV. PRESENT LAW

The Law of Property Act 1925 has made some important amendments to the law of entails, but the general principles remain as under the Fines and Recoveries Act 1833. The following are the chief points to note.

1. Existence only in equity. It is no longer possible for a legal fee tail to exist.[24] After 1925, all entails must exist behind a trust; this means that the legal estate in fee simple must be vested in some trustees or trustee (who may be the tenant in tail himself) on trust for the person entitled in tail and everyone else interested in the land. This does not impair the benefits accruing from the land; only the bare legal ownership is affected. Since an entail is no longer an estate in the land itself, but only an interest under a trust, the proper title for an entail is no longer "estate tail" or "fee tail," but "entailed interest." Similarly a "base fee" can no longer be a legal estate but exists only as an equitable interest in the nature of a base fee. The Fines and Recoveries Act 1833 applies to these equitable interests in the same way as it applied to the legal estate before 1926.[25]

2. Personalty entailable. Any property, real or personal, may be entailed after 1925.[26] This was not so before 1926, for the Statute *De Donis* 1285 applied only to "tenements."[27] Thus the land itself, and inheritable rights in realty such as perpetual rentcharges (*e.g.* £100 per annum charged on Blackacre), could be entailed, but life estates (which were not inheritable) and leaseholds and other personalty could not be entailed.[28] Before 1926, a gift of personalty "to A and

---

[22] *Lord Glenorchy* v. *Bosville* (1733) Ca.t.Talb. 3 at 16; *Att-Gen* v. *Duke of Marlborough* (1818) 3 Madd. 498.
[23] *Ante*, p. 36.
[24] L.P.A. 1925, s. 1; *post*, pp. 84–85.
[25] L.P.(Am.)A. 1924, Sched. 9.
[26] L.P.A. 1925, s. 130.
[27] Challis R.P. 43, 47, 61.
[28] But see M. & W., p. 102 on quasi-entails of life estates.

the heirs of his body" or "to A in tail" gave A the absolute ownership of the personalty, whether the gift was by deed or will.[29] Informal words such as "to A and his issue" or "to A and his descendants" usually gave the property to A and such of his issue or descendants as were alive at the relevant date.[30]

Since 1925, entails can be created in personalty, and all the rules applying to entails of realty, (*e.g.* as to the words of limitation required, barring the entails, interests equivalent to a base fee, and the like) apply to entails of personalty. However, it is expressly provided that if after 1925 personalty is directed "to be enjoyed or held with, or upon trusts corresponding to trusts affecting," land which is already held in tail, this will be sufficient to entail the personalty.[31]

3. No enrolment. A disentailing assurance made after 1925 need not be enrolled.[32]

4. Barring by will. Under the Law of Property Act 1925, s. 176, a tenant in tail can now bar his entail by will, and thus dispose of the fee simple. However, this power is subject to a number of limitations:

(a) It applies only to entails in possession: there is no power to bar an entail in remainder by will, even if the protector consents.
(b) The tenant in tail must be of full age.
(c) The will must be either executed after 1925 or confirmed by a codicil executed after 1925.
(d) The will must refer specifically either to—
  (i) the property (*e.g.* "Blackacre"),[33]
  (ii) the instrument under which it was acquired (*e.g.* "all the property to which I succeeded under X's will"), or
  (iii) entails generally (*e.g.* "all property to which I am entitled in tail").

This power extends to all entailed property, whether real or personal, whenever the entail was created. Further, it allows the owner of a base fee in possession to enlarge it by a disposition by will, provided he complies with the above conditions, and provided he is capable of enlarging it into a fee simple absolute without the consent of anyone else. But the section does not apply to a tenant in tail after possibility or to a tenant in tail restrained by statute from barring his entail.[34] Except so far as is necessary to give effect to the will, the entail or base fee is unaffected; thus if instead of disposing of the fee

[29] *Dawson* v. *Small* (1874) 9 Ch.App. 651: and see *Portman* v. *Viscount Portman* [1922] A.C. 473.
[30] *Re Hammond* [1924] 2 Ch. 276.
[31] L.P.A. 1925, s. 130 (4).
[32] *Ibid.* s. 133.
[33] See *Acheson* v. *Russell* [1951] Ch. 67.
[34] For these, see *post*, pp. 49, 50.

simple in the entailed land the testator merely devises a life interest, the entail will resume its natural devolution when the life interest ceases.

V. BASE FEES

The nature and mode of creation of base fees have already been considered.[35] The uncertainty of the duration of a base fee makes it an unsatisfactory interest in land, but it can be enlarged into a fee simple absolute in a number of ways. If land is given to A for life, remainder to B in tail, remainder to C in fee simple, a base fee created by B can be enlarged as follows:

(1) *New disentailment:* by the former tenant in tail (*i.e.* B) executing a fresh disentailing assurance with the consent of the protector or after the protectorship has ceased (*e.g.* after A's death). This can be done even after the base fee has been conveyed to a purchaser.[36]

(2) *Acquisition of reversion:* by the owner of the base fee acquiring the whole of the remainder or reversion in fee simple (*i.e.* by B, or any person to whom he has conveyed the base fee, acquiring C's fee simple). This does not merge the base fee in the remainder or reversion and so subject the owner of the base fee to any burdens attached to the remainder or reversion, such as a mortgage, but enlarges the base fee into a fee simple absolute, free from any incumbrances on the remainder or reversion.[37]

(3) *Long possession:* by the owner of the base fee (*i.e.* B or anyone to whom he has conveyed it) remaining in possession of the land for 12 years after the protectorship has ceased.[38]

(4) *Devise:* by a gift by will complying with section 176 of the Law of Property Act 1925.[39] This power is exercisable only by a person who is entitled to a base fee in possession and who could enlarge it without the concurrence of any person. Thus B can enlarge the base fee by will if the protectorship has ceased before he dies; but if B has conveyed the base fee to some third person, neither that person nor B can enlarge it by will in any circumstances.

VI. INTERESTS IN TAIL AFTER POSSIBILITY

On the death of the specified spouse of a tenant in special tail without leaving any issue capable of inheriting the entail, the tenant becomes "a tenant in tail after possibility of issue extinct," the last three words usually being omitted for brevity. For example, if land is given "to A

---

[35] *Ante*, pp. 43, 45.
[36] Fines and Recoveries Act 1833, ss. 19, 35; *Bankes* v. *Small* (1887) 36 Ch.D. 716.
[37] Fines and Recoveries Act 1833, s. 39.
[38] Limitation Act 1939, s. 11.
[39] *Ante*, p. 48.

and the heirs of his body begotten on Mary," on the death of Mary
without leaving issue A is a tenant in tail after possibility. Such a
tenant is in a peculiar position. For—

  (i) He cannot bar the entail.[40]

  (ii) Yet although he is virtually in the position of a tenant for life,
he is still technically a tenant in tail. Thus like all tenants in tail
he is not liable for voluntary waste (damage to the land),
although a tenant for life is. However, he will be restrained
from committing equitable waste (wanton destruction).[41]

An interest in tail after possibility can arise only on the death of the
spouse specified in the limitation; it cannot arise out of a tail general
for even if the tenant in tail is unmarried and of a great age, it is
always deemed possible that he or she will marry and have issue.[42]

VII. UNBARRABLE ENTAILS

1. No unbarrable entails. The common law rule which developed at
the end of the sixteenth century was that it was impossible to create
an unbarrable entail. By means of fines and recoveries, all entails
could be barred, and any attempt to restrain the tenant from doing
this was ineffective. Thus a condition that the tenant should not suffer
a common recovery was repugnant to the entail and so void.[43] This
rule was not affected by the Fines and Recoveries Act 1833.

2. Exceptions. Despite this general rule, there are certain entails
which cannot be barred. These are:

  (i) An interest in tail after possibility.

  (ii) Entails created by the Crown for services rendered to the
Crown, the reversion being in the Crown.[44]

  (iii) Entails made unbarrable by special Acts of Parliament, such
as the entails given to reward the first Duke of Marlborough
and the first Duke of Wellington.[45]

3. Persons. Certain persons are unable to bar an entail, even if the
entail is one which can be barred.

  (i) An infant is generally regarded as being unable effectively to
bar an entail. This disability has been exploited to keep settled
property tied up for as long as possible.[46]

  (ii) A person of unsound mind (under the Mental Health Act 1959

---

[40] Fines and Recoveries Act 1833, s. 18.
[41] *Williams* v. *Williams* (1810) 12 East 209; *Cooke* v. *Whaley* (1701) 1 Eq.Ca.Abr. 400.
[42] Co. Litt. 28a.
[43] *Sir Anthony Mildmay's Case* (1605) 6 Co.Rep. 40a.
[44] Fines and Recoveries Act 1833, s. 18.
[45] 6 Anne, cc. 6, 7 1706; 54 Geo. 3, c. 161, 1814.
[46] See *post*, p. 235.

called a "patient") cannot bar his entails; but his receiver[47] can do so, under an order of the Court of Protection.[48]

(iii) A bankrupt cannot bar his entails; this can be done only by his trustee in bankruptcy.[49]

C. The Life Estate

After 1925 an interest in land for life can no longer exist as a legal estate but only as an equitable interest.[50] In general, the law of life estates set out below applies equally to the corresponding life interests after 1925.

I. TYPES OF LIFE ESTATE

The two types of life estates were the ordinary life estate and the estate *pur autre vie*.

1. Estate for the life of the tenant. The normal type of life estate was one for the life of the tenant. This arose either—

(i) by express limitation, as by a grant "to A for life"[51]; or
(ii) by operation of law, as in the case of a surviving spouse's rights on intestacy under curtesy and dower[52] pre 1925.

2. Estate pur autre vie. An estate *pur autre vie* was an estate for the life of someone other than the tenant,[53] the person whose life measured the duration of the estate being called the "*cestui que vie*" (pronounced "setty ker vee"). An estate *pur autre vie* could arise either—

(i) by the owner of a life estate assigning it to another: *nemo dat quod non habet* (nobody can give what he has not got), so that the assignor could create no interest which would last for longer than his own life; or
(ii) by express grant, *e.g.* "to A for the life of X."

Both types of life estate were estates of freehold, but neither was a freehold of inheritance, for they were not capable of descending to the tenant's heir on his death. A life estate ceased automatically when the tenant died, and although an estate *pur autre vie* continued during the life of the *cestui que vie* despite the tenant's death, pre 1926 it did not descend to the tenant's heir as such but passed according to special rules of occupancy.[54] Since 1926 it passes like other property under a will or intestacy.

---

[47] See *post*, p. 186.
[48] Mental Health Act 1959, s. 103 (1).
[49] Bankruptcy Act 1914, s. 55. The former disability of married women is obsolete.
[50] *Post*, p. 84.
[51] *Ante*, p. 38.
[52] See M. & W., pp. 514–519.
[53] See, generally, *Doe* d. Jeff v. *Robinson* (1828) 2 Man. & Ry. 249.
[54] On this see M. & W. p. 101.

Both types of life estate could be made determinable or subject to conditions subsequent[55] and were in general subject to similar rights and burdens.

II. POSITION OF A TENANT FOR LIFE AT COMMON LAW

In considering the position of a tenant for life at common law, an important part is played by the law of waste (particularly as to timber and minerals), and the rules governing emblements and fixtures.

Waste

Although the law of waste is of importance in other connections, notably in the law of landlord and tenant, it is most suitably considered in relation to life interests, where it is applicable both to ordinary life interests and to interests *pur autre vie*. Technically, waste consists of any act which alters the nature of the land, whether for the better or for the worse, *e.g.* the conversion of arable land into a wood or vice versa. Four types of waste must be considered, namely, ameliorating, permissive, voluntary and equitable.

1. Ameliorating waste. Alterations which improve the land, such as converting dilapidated store buildings into dwellings or a farm into a market garden, constitute ameliorating waste. Since the decision of the House of Lords in *Doherty* v. *Allman*[56] in 1878 the court is unlikely to grant an injunction to restrain such waste or to grant any damages.

2. Permissive waste. This consists of the failure to do that which ought to be done, as by the non-repair of buildings or the failure to clean out a ditch or moat so as to prevent the foundations becoming rotten.[57] But mere non-cultivation of land is not permissive waste.[58] A tenant for life is not liable for permissive waste unless an obligation to repair is imposed upon him by the terms of the limitation under which he holds.[59]

3. Voluntary waste. Voluntary waste is positive conduct: "the committing of any spoil or destruction in houses, lands, etc., by tenants, to the damage of the heir, or of him in reversion or remainder."[60] Literally, this would include equitable waste, but the term voluntary waste is usually reserved for such voluntary waste as does not amount to equitable waste. Such acts as opening and

---

[55] *Brandon* v. *Robinson* (1811) 18 Ves. 429; and see *Re Evans's Contract* [1920] 2 Ch. 469; see also *ante*, pp. 39–40.
[56] 3 App.Cas. 709 (conversion of a dilapidated barracks into dwelling-houses by tenant for years).
[57] See *e.g. Powys* v. *Blagrave* (1854) 4 De G.M. & G. 448.
[58] *Hutton* v. *Warren* (1836) 1 M. & W. 466 at p. 472.
[59] *Re Cartwright* (1889) 41 Ch.D. 532.
[60] Bacon's *Abridgement* (7th ed.), Vol. 8, p. 379, definition of waste.

working a mine in the land (but not merely working a mine already open),[61] or cutting timber,[62] are examples of voluntary waste. Timber consists of oak, ash and elm trees which are at least 20 years old and not too old to have a reasonable quantity of usable wood in them. Other trees may rank as timber by local custom, and custom may also prescribe some qualification other than an age of 20 years for the trees to be considered timber.[63]

A tenant for life is liable for voluntary waste unless his interest was granted to him by an instrument exempting him from liability for voluntary waste, for example, a grant "without impeachment of waste."[64] Where there is such an exception the tenant is said to be "unimpeachable of waste": otherwise he is said to be "impeachable of waste." Thus if nothing is said about waste, the tenant is impeachable; in practice, however, he is usually made unimpeachable.

4. Equitable waste. "Equitable waste is that which a prudent man would not do in the management of his own property."[65] Acts of wanton destruction, such as stripping a house of all its lead, iron, glass, doors, boards, etc., to the value of £3,000,[66] or pulling down houses, or cutting timber planted for ornament or shelter (unless this is necessary for the preservation of part of the timber), fall under the head of equitable waste. A tenant for life is liable for equitable waste unless the document conferring his interest upon him shows an intention to allow him to commit equitable waste. It is not enough that his interest has been given to him without impeachment of waste; he must show that it is intended that he should be allowed to commit equitable as well as voluntary waste.[67]

Timber and Minerals

Although largely governed by the general law of waste, the rights of a tenant for life with regard to timber and minerals are so important as to merit separate treatment.

1. Timber. (a) *Estovers.* Whether impeachable of waste or not, a tenant for life can take reasonable estovers (or botes) from the land. These consist of wood and timber taken as—

(i) house-bote, for repairing the house or burning in it;
(ii) plough-bote, for making and repairing agricultural implements; and

[61] See *Dashwood* v. *Magniac* [1891] 3 Ch. 306 at p. 360.
[62] *Honywood* v. *Honywood* (1874) L.R. 18 Eq. 306.
[63] *Ibid.* at p. 309; *Countess of Cumberland's Case* (1610) Moo.K.B. 812.
[64] *Re Ridge* (1885) 31 Ch.D. 504 at p. 507.
[65] *Turner* v. *Wright* (1860) 2 De G. F. & J. 234 at p. 243.
[66] *Vane* v. *Lord Barnard* (1716) 2 Vern. 738.
[67] L.P.A. 1925, s. 135.

(iii) hay-bote, for repairing fences.

The tenant's right to house-bote does not entitle him to cut down timber in excess of his present needs in order to use it for any repairs which may become necessary in the future, nor does it authorise him to sell the timber, even if he employs the proceeds in repairing, or the timber proves unfit for repairs.[68]

(b) *Timber estate.* On a timber estate (an estate cultivated mainly for the produce of saleable timber which is cut periodically), the tenant can cut and sell timber according to the rules of proper estate management even if he is impeachable of waste. The reason for this rule is that the timber properly cut on such an estate is part of the annual fruits of the land rather than part of the inheritance.[69]

(c) *Timber planted for ornament or shelter.* As has been seen,[70] it is equitable waste to cut timber planted for ornament or shelter, and only a tenant unimpeachable of equitable waste is permitted to do this.

(d) *Trees.* In general, a tenant for life, even if he is impeachable of waste, may cut dotards (dead trees not fit for use as timber) and all trees which are not timber, *e.g.* in most cases willows or larches.[71] But there are a number of exceptions to this. It is voluntary waste to cut trees which would be timber but for their immaturity (unless the cutting is necessary to thin them out and so allow proper development) or to cut fruit trees in a garden or orchard.[72] Further, it is voluntary waste to cut wood which a prudent man would not cut, such as willows which help to hold a river bank together; and it is equitable waste to cut trees planted for ornament or shelter, or to grub up an entire wood. Where by reason of abnormal circumstances, such as extraordinary gales or wartime conditions, trees are severed before they are ripe for cutting, the court will direct that the tenant for life shall receive only part of the proceeds, the balance being held in trust for those entitled after his death.[73]

(e) *Normal rules.* Subject to the above special rules, the position is that a tenant for life who is unimpeachable of waste may cut and sell timber and keep all the proceeds.[74] But if the tenant is impeachable of waste, his only right to cut timber is that given to him by statute.[75] This authorises him to cut and sell timber ripe and fit for cutting, provided—

[68] Co. Litt. 41b, 53b.
[69] *Honywood* v. *Honywood* (1874) L.R. 18 Eq. 306 at pp. 309, 310; *Dashwood* v. *Magniac* [1891] 3 Ch. 306.
[70] *Ante,* p. 53.
[71] *Re Harker's W. T.* [1938] Ch. 323.
[72] *Kaye* v. *Banks* (1770) Dick. 431.
[73] *Re Terry* (1918) 87 L.J.Ch. 577.
[74] *Lewis Bowles's Case* (1615) 11 Co.Rep. 79b.
[75] S.L.A. 1925, s. 66, replacing S.L.A. 1882, s. 35.

(i) the consent of the trustees of the settlement under which he holds his life interest, or an order of the court, is obtained; and

(ii) three-quarters of the proceeds are set aside as capital money: this means that the trustees hold this portion of the price on trust for all persons having any interest in the land, paying only the interest to the tenant for life. The remaining quarter of the proceeds is paid to the tenant for life.

(f) *Ownership of severed timber.* Until timber is severed, a tenant for life has no claim to it, so that if land is sold with the uncut timber on it, the life tenant cannot claim any share of the price even though he could lawfully have cut the timber.[76] Once the timber is severed it belongs to the life tenant if he was entitled to cut it, whether the severance was effected by the tenant, a stranger or an act of God, such as a storm; but if he was not entitled to sever it, it belongs not to him but to the owner of the next vested estate of inheritance.[77]

2. Minerals. The mineral rights of a tenant for life depend on two factors, namely, whether the mine was already open when his tenancy began, and whether he is impeachable of waste.

(a) *Right to work mines.* A tenant for life may work a mine and take all the proceeds unless—

(i) he is impeachable of waste, and

(ii) the mine was not open when his tenancy began.

Where both these conditions are satisfied, he cannot work the mine at all, for to open and work an unopened mine is voluntary waste. But it is not waste to continue working a mine already open[78] even if new pits are made on different parts of the same plot of land to pursue the same or a new vein, for the grantor, by opening or allowing the opening of the mines, has shown an intent that the minerals should be treated as part of the profits of the land.

(b) *Right to lease mines.* The Settled Land Act 1925[79] authorises a tenant for life to grant mining leases for one hundred years or less, whether the mine is open or not, and whether or not the tenant is impeachable of waste. In each case, subject to any contrary intention in the settlement, the tenant for life is entitled to three-quarters of the rent, except that if he is impeachable of waste and the mine is unopened, he is entitled to only one-quarter. The balance of rent is capital money, and is held for the benefit of all those interested under the settlement.[80]

---

[76] *Re Llewellin* (1887) 37 Ch.D. 317.
[77] *Bewick* v. *Whitfield* (1734) 3 P.Wms. 267.
[78] See *Re Hall* [1916] 2 Ch. 488 at p. 493.
[79] ss. 41, 42, 45–47, replacing earlier Acts; see *post*, pp. 268 *et seq.*
[80] S.L.A. 1925, s. 47; *Re Fitzwalter* [1943] Ch. 285.

Emblements and Fixtures

A tenant cannot foresee the date on which an estate *pur autre vie* or for his own life will determine, and so to encourage him to cultivate his land by assuring him of the fruits of his labour, the law gives him a right to emblements (pronounced *em*-blem-ents). This means that the tenant's personal representatives, or in the case of an estate *pur autre vie* the tenant himself, may enter the land after the life estate has determined and reap the crops which the tenant himself has sown.[81] This applies only to annual crops artificially produced, such as corn, hemp and flax, and not to things such as fruit trees and timber; further, it extends only to the crops actually growing at the determination of the tenancy.[82] Where the end of the tenancy is brought about by the tenant's own act (*e.g.* where a life estate is granted to a widow until remarriage and she remarries) there is no right to emblements.[83]

Prima facie any fixtures attached to the land by a tenant for life must be left after his death for the person next entitled to the land; but trade fixtures and ornamental and domestic fixtures are excepted.[84]

---

[81] Co.Litt. 55b; *Grantham* v. *Hawley* (1615) Hob. 132.
[82] *Graves* v. *Weld* (1833) 5 B. & Ad. 105 at p. 119.
[83] *Oland's Case* (1602) 5 Co.Rep. 116a.
[84] See *ante*, p. 22.

CHAPTER 3

LAW AND EQUITY

Part 1

GENERAL PRINCIPLES

THE difference between Law and Equity, which has already been mentioned in brief outline,[1] must now be considered in greater detail.

Sect. 1. The Historical Basis of Equity

1. The common law courts. The existence of Equity can best be explained historically. At the end of the thirteenth century the principal courts were (a) many local courts, held by feudal lords and others; and (b) the Royal courts known as the Courts of Common Law, consisting of the courts of King's Bench, of Common Pleas, and of Exchequer. Each of the Royal courts at first had its own proper sphere, but by the end of the Middle Ages their jurisdiction overlapped so much that a plaintiff often had a choice between the three courts. By this time also they had attracted much of the litigation of the country, and although many of the local courts survived into the eighteenth century, most of them were in decline, or moribund.

2. The writ system. In general, no action could be started in any of the common law courts, until a writ had been issued by the Chancellor. The Chancellor, who was usually an ecclesiastic, was the head of the King's Secretarial Department. As keeper of the Great Seal with which writs were sealed, he was at the head of the English legal system.

The writs issued by the Chancellor differed for each different kind of action. Today, anyone claiming to be entitled to some remedy, such as the recovery of possession of land of which he had been dispossessed, or the payment of money owed to him, can issue a writ claiming the appropriate relief. The writ is in a form which leaves it to the plaintiff to state his claim in his own words. The same form can equally well be filled up with a claim for the possession of land as for payment of a debt, or damages for trespass: there is no special writ of ejectment, or debt, or trespass or any other matter. But in medieval days this was not so. Each different kind of action had its own writ,

[1] *Ante*, p. 3.

57

often with its own special procedure.[2] Often causes of action which seemed very similar in principle had separate writs. Thus if a tenant of land died and before his heir could enter the land a stranger took it, the heir could bring an action against the stranger for possession of the land. If the heir were a son of the tenant the action had to be started by a writ of *mort d'ancestor*; if he was a grandson a writ of *aiel* had to be used, while if he was the great-grandson a writ of *besaiel* was necessary. No action could succeed unless the correct writ was chosen.

The selection of the correct writ was thus of great importance. Not until the Common Law Procedure Act 1852 were the old writs replaced by a single form of writ for all actions, and even then, until the Judicature Acts 1873–75 came into force, it was necessary to observe the form of action based on the old writs which was appropriate to the case. Sometimes there were two or more writs appropriate to the plaintiff's claim. Where this was so one writ usually had procedural advantages over the other or others. A writ which had already been settled was known as a writ *de cursu*, a writ "of course" and could be obtained on paying the prescribed fee. But sometimes there was no known writ to fit the case, and the plaintiff would have to ask for the invention of a new writ.

At first new writs were invented with comparative freedom. But it did not follow that the courts would accept each new writ as being valid. Even if a suitor had surmounted the first obstacle by obtaining a writ, he might still fall at the second fence by failing to obtain the court's recognition of its validity. Nevertheless the Register of Writs rapidly increased during the latter half of the twelfth century and the first half of the thirteenth: many new writs became writs *de cursu*, duly recognised by the courts.

This power to invent new writs was assailed by the barons. Recognising that the power to invent new remedies was a power to create new rights and duties, they procured the making of the Provisions of Oxford 1258, in which the Chancellor swore that he would seal no writ, except a writ *de cursu*, without the command of the King and his Council. Had this remained fully effective, it would have stifled the growth of the common law. But the Statute of Westminster II 1285 provided in the famous Chapter 24, *In Consimili Casu*, that the clerks in Chancery should have a limited power to invent new writs.[3] If there already existed one writ and in a like case (*in consimili casu*), falling under like law and requiring like remedy, there was none, the clerks in Chancery were authorised to agree in making a writ, or else they were to refer the matter to the next

---

[2] Maitland, *Forms of Action*, 5.
[3] It is controversial how far the statute was responsible for this development: see SFC. Milsom, *Historical Foundations of the Common Law* (1981), p. 284, collecting the literature.

Parliament. Consequently a suitor whose grievance was not covered by a writ *de cursu*, or one *in consimili casu*, was still left without a remedy unless he could persuade Parliament to intervene.

3. Petitions to the King referred to the Chancellor. Thus suitors began to petition the King and his Council, for the King, as the Fountain of Justice, was regarded as having a residue of judicial power left in his hands. Such petitions were heard by the King's Council, of which the Chancellor was an important member. The Chancellor, as keeper of the King's Conscience, was particularly well fitted to deal with such petitions, and during the reigns of Edward II and III many were referred to him. After the reign of Edward III petitions were often addressed to the Chancellor alone. But although the Chancery became recognised as a court during the fourteenth and fifteenth centuries, the decisions upon the petitions were made either in the name of the King's Council or else with the advice of the serjeants and judges. Not until 1474, it seems, did the Chancellor make a decree on his own authority, but after that date such decrees became frequent.[4]

4. The Court of Chancery. In this way there gradually came into existence a Court of Chancery in which the Chancellor, acting independently of the King's Council, sat as a judge administering a system of justice called Equity. He could even use a common injunction to prevent a plaintiff from enforcing a judgment obtained in the common law courts. This supremacy of the Court of Chancery was established in the *Earl of Oxfords Case*.[5] After the end of the seventeenth century only lawyers were appointed to the office of Chancellor. Equity, which had varied with each Chancellor, began with Lord Ellesmere (1596–1617) to develop into a code of principles, and the work of Lord Nottingham (1673–82) in systematising the rules earned him the title of the Father of Equity. When Lord Eldon retired in 1827 the rules of equity were almost as fixed as those of the common law, though equity provided a greater range of discretionary remedies than did the common law, for example, in the way of injunctions and decrees for specific performance. However, not until Lord Cairns Act 1858 could the Court of Chancery award damages and then only in addition to or in substitution for an injunction or specific performance.[6]

In the course of time various subsidiary officials were appointed to assist the Chancellor, a system of appeals grew up, and finally in 1875 the Chancery system was merged with the common law courts to form the present Supreme Court of Judicature. In short, what was

[4] 1 H.E.L. 400–404.
[5] (1615) 1 Rep. Ch. 1.
[6] *Lavery* v. *Pursell* (1888) 39 Ch.D. 508.

once a method of petitioning the King for justice in exceptional cases gradually became a way of starting an action before a regular court of justice. But there were important differences between Chancery and the common law courts. The latter decided cases according to strict common law rules, and technicalities often played an important part. Chancery, on the other hand, mitigated the rigour of the common law, deciding cases in the light of what had seemed just and equitable to generations of Chancellors, and technical pleas were usually unsuccessful. Further, the common law courts were mainly concerned with enforcing the strict rights of the plaintiff regardless of his conduct, whereas Chancery was a court of conscience where the court might cleanse the conscience of the defendant, compelling him to disgorge any ill-gotten gains by acting *in personam* (on his person), *e.g.* by imprisoning him and where a remedy might be withheld from a party guilty of unconscionable conduct. Consequently there was a marked difference between legal rights, the name for rights enforced by the courts of law, and equitable rights, enforced only by equity. This will be examined in Section 3 (*post*).

5. Fusion of the Courts of Law and Equity. By the Judicature Act 1873,[7] the superior courts of law and equity were fused into one Supreme Court, divided into a High Court and Court of Appeal. For convenience, the High Court was divided into five divisions, each of which had certain matters assigned to it. In 1880 the Common Pleas Division and Exchequer Division were merged into the Queen's Bench Division, and in 1972 the Probate, Divorce and Admiralty Division was re-named the Family Division, with some adjustments of jurisdiction. There are now three divisions:

> the Chancery Division,
> the Queen's Bench Division, and
> the Family Division.

The Queen's Bench Division hears common law cases, the Chancery Division hears equity cases, and the title of the other Division sufficiently indicates the matters with which it deals. But it is important to notice that these are only divisions of one court, the High Court, and not separate courts; each division of the High Court has jurisdiction to enforce both legal and equitable rights and give both legal and discretionary equitable remedies. This means that it is no longer necessary to go to two separate courts to enforce legal and equitable rights or to obtain legal and equitable remedies. If a point of equity arises in an action in the Queen's Bench Division, for

---

[7] Which, by the Supreme Court of Judicature (Commencement) Act 1874, s. 2, came into force on November 1, 1875. Now see Supreme Court Act 1981.

example, the court can deal with it; and it will not be fatal to an action if it is started in the wrong division, for the case will be transferred to the proper division.

Law and equity nevertheless remain distinct: the systems have not been fused, although they are now both administered by the same court.[8] A legal right is still enforceable against a purchaser without notice, while an equitable right is not. Equitable rights are still enforceable only by equitable remedies, subject to the damages jurisdiction conferred by the Chancery Amendment Act 1858 (otherwise known as Lord Cairns Act). Indeed, the distinction between the two systems is emphasised by the provision that where there is any conflict between the rules of law and those of equity, the rules of equity shall prevail. Conflicts rarely occur, but there have been cases where this provision has been operative and the most important will be considered later.[9] The Court of Chancery is a ghost, but like many other English legal ghosts, its influence can be seen on every side.

Sect. 2. Equity Follows the Law

There could exist a whole range of equitable estates or interests corresponding to the legal estates and interests in land. A fee simple, fee tail, life estate, mortgage, easement and nearly every other interest might be either legal or equitable. Thus if A granted a lease to B to hold on trust for C, B had a legal term of years and C an equitable term. If the fee simple owner of Blackacre granted Y a lease for 99 years, Y's lease would be legal if it was granted by deed, equitable if merely in writing. If a person held an equitable interest it would usually be found either that his interest arose under a trust or else that it was created without employing the formalities necessary at law.

Certain interests could exist only in equity: if Blackacre was bound by a restrictive covenant, this could never cast a legal burden on anyone who subsequently acquired the land, although it might well bind him in equity. But apart from these cases, there was a strict parallel in law and in equity. In most cases the maxim "Equity follows the law" applied: "the Chancery moulded equitable estates and interests after the fashion of the common law estates and interests."[10] The court tended to treat an interest in the land in the same way whether it was legal or equitable.[11] Thus equitable entails had to be

---

[8] *Salt* v. *Cooper* (1880) 16 Ch.D. 544 at p. 549; *Coatsworth* v. *Johnson* (1886) 54 L.T. 520; *United Scientific Holdings Ltd.* v. *Burnley Borough Council* [1978] A.C. 904. See Hanbury and Maudsley (11th ed.), pp. 21–24.

[9] *Post*, pp. 337 *et seq.*

[10] Maitland, *Equity*, p. 108.

[11] See *Re Somerville and Turner's Contract* [1903] 2 Ch. 583 at p. 588.

barred in the same way as legal entails[12]; equitable interests passed
on intestacy to the same persons as legal estates; an equitable tenant
for life was in the same position as regards equitable waste as a legal
tenant for life, and so on. But in certain matters, equity considered
that there was good reason, such as to avoid hardship, for refusing to
follow the law. Thus equitable remainders were not liable to
destruction in the same way as legal remainders; equity allowed a
mortgagor to recover the property mortgaged if he paid all that was
due, even though he no longer had any legal right to redeem the
property.

With regard to words of limitation, equity followed the law in part
only. If the grantor used informal words showing a clear intention to
create a fee simple or fee tail, *e.g.* a limitation on trust for A
"absolutely,"[13] these were as effective as formal words. But if strict
conveyancing language was employed, the limitation was construed
in the same way as a legal limitation and in the absence of proper
words of limitation only a life estate passed. This was so even if a
general intention to pass some other interest could be gathered from
the instrument,[14] although in this case if the court was asked to rectify
the instrument and not merely construe it, words of limitation
necessary to carry out the grantor's intention would be inserted.[15]

It will thus be seen that in some important points equity refused to
follow the law. Nevertheless it has been said with some justice that
"the cases, where the analogy fails, are not numerous; and there is
scarcely a rule of law or equity, of a more ancient origin, or which
admits a fewer exceptions, than the rule, that equity followeth the
law."[16]

Sect. 3. The Nature of Equitable Rights

A. Distinction Between Legal and Equitable Rights

At first sight it might seem that as long as a person had a right which
would be enforced by some court, it mattered little which court it
was. But there is a great difference between legal and equitable
rights. This is sometimes expressed by saying that "legal rights are
rights *in rem*, equitable rights are rights *in personam*." A legal
interest in land is a right in the land itself, so that whoever acquires
the land is bound by that right, whether he knew of it or not. A legal
right is thus like a live electric wire which shocks those who touch it

---

[12] *Kirkham* v. *Smith* (1749) Amb. 518.
[13] *Re Arden* [1935] Ch. 326.
[14] *Re Bostock's Settlement* [1921] 2 Ch. 469.
[15] *Banks* v. *Ripley* [1940] Ch. 719.
[16] Co. Litt. 290b, n. 1, xvi.

whether or not they know of it.[17] Equity, on the other hand, would enforce equitable rights only against certain persons. For example, if land was conveyed to T in fee simple on trust for A in fee simple, there was at first no court which would compel T to carry out his trust. Equity, however, began to intervene on behalf of A if T was guilty of breach of trust, and so A's interest, being enforceable in equity but not at law, was merely equitable. It was a right *in personam* enforceable against T alone, so that if he died or conveyed the land to another, the trust would not be enforced against the new tenant.

Then successive extensions were made. In 1465 it was laid down that a trust would be enforced against anyone who took a conveyance of the land with notice of the trust.[18] In 1483 the Chancellor said that he would enforce a trust against the trustee's heir,[19] and in 1522 it was said that a trust would be enforced against anyone to whom the land had been given.[20] After it had been decided that others such as the executors and creditors of the trustees would be bound by the trust, it finally became established as one of the most important rules of equity that trusts and other equitable rights would be enforced against anyone except a bona fide purchaser of a legal estate for value without notice of these rights, or somebody claiming through such a person. Equitable rights thus gradually came to look less and less like mere rights *in personam* and more and more like rights *in rem*. Although it is possible still to regard them as rights *in personam*, it is perhaps best to treat them as hybrids, being neither entirely one nor entirely the other. They have never reached the status of rights *in rem*, yet the class of persons against whom they will be enforced is too large for mere rights *in personam*.

The difference between legal and equitable rights as regards a purchaser without notice may be illustrated as follows. In 1920 X bought the fee simple in Blackacre. In 1921 he granted a legal easement of way across one corner to L, and an equitable easement of way across the other corner to E.[21] As long as X still owned Blackacre, no substantial difference appeared between the rights of L and E: both were enforceable against X. But as soon as the land was conveyed to a third party, Y, the distinction between the rights of L and E became apparent. Even if Y purchased the land without notice of L's easement, it bound him, for it was a right *in rem*. But if Y could

---

[17] *e.g. Wyld* v. *Silver* [1963] Ch. 243 (unfortunate builder held bound by legal right to hold a fair or wake, last held in 1875, though he could not have discovered the existence of the right).

[18] Y.B. 5 Edw. 4, Mich., pl. 16.

[19] Y.B. 22 Edw. 4, Pasch., pl. 18.

[20] Y.B. 14 Hen. 8, Mich., pl. 5, fo. 7.

[21] Equitable easements created after 1925 are registrable under the Land Charges Act so as to bind everyone if registered but to be void against a purchaser of a legal estate for money or money's worth (irrespective of notice) if unregistered.

prove that he was a bona fide purchaser for value of a legal estate without notice of E's easement, he took free from it.

This doctrine of purchaser without notice must now be considered more fully since it is so fundamental to property law. Indeed, it has been called the "polar star of equity."[22]

B. The Purchaser Without Notice

The plea of purchaser of a legal estate for value without notice is "an absolute, unqualified, unanswerable defence."[23] The onus of proof lies on the person setting it up: it is a single plea, and cannot be regarded as a plea of a purchaser for value, to be met by a reply of notice.[24] The principal points are as follows.

1. Bona fide. The purchaser must act in good faith.

2. Purchaser for value. The words "for value" are included to show that value must have been given, because "purchaser" in its technical sense does not necessarily imply this. "Purchaser" covers persons who receive property otherwise than by the operation of the law (*e.g.* under the intestacy rules) and so includes donees and devisees. "Value" includes money, money's worth (*e.g.* other land, or stocks and shares) and marriage.[25] The value need not be full value,[26] but it must all have been actually paid or given before the purchaser receives notice of the equity.[27] "Money or money's worth" usually consists of some present consideration in the sense used in the law of contract, but it also includes the satisfaction of an existing debt.[28] "Marriage," however, extends only to a future marriage; an ante-nuptial agreement (*i.e.* a promise made in consideration of future marriage) is deemed to have been made for value, but a promise made in respect of a past marriage (a post-nuptial agreement) is not. When an ante-nuptial marriage settlement is made, valuable consideration is deemed to have been given both by the spouse and by the unborn issue of the marriage.[29] "Good consideration" (the natural love and affection which a person has for his near relatives) is of small importance and does not amount to value. "Purchaser" is not confined to a person who acquires a fee simple; it includes, for example, mortgagees and lessees, who are purchasers *pro tanto* (to the extent of their interests).[30]

---

[22] *Stanhope* v. *Verney* (1761) 2 Eden 81 at p. 85, *per* Lord Henley L.C.
[23] *Pilcher* v. *Rawlins* (1872) 7 Ch.App. 259 at p. 269.
[24] *Wilkes* v. *Spooner* [1911] 2 K.B. 473 at p. 486.
[25] *Wormald* v. *Maitland* (1866) 35 L.J.Ch. 69 at p. 73.
[26] *Bassett* v. *Nosworthy* (1673) Rep.t.Finch. 102.
[27] *Tourville* v. *Naish* (1734) 3 P. Wms. 307.
[28] See *Thorndike* v. *Hunt* (1859) 3 De. G. & J. 563.
[29] *Macdonald* v. *Scott* (1893) A.C. 642 at p. 650.
[30] See *Goodright* d. *Humphreys* v. *Moses* (1774) 2 Wm.Bl. 1019.

3. Of a legal estate. The purchaser normally must show that he has acquired some legal estate in the land and not a mere equitable interest.[31] If the purchaser acquires merely an equitable interest, his equity is later in time than the prior equitable interest, and as between competing equities the first in time normally prevails[32]; where part of the equitable interest is already vested in the owner of the prior equity, the subsequent purchaser can take only what remains.[33]

There are three qualifications to this rule.

(a) *Better right to legal estate.* A purchaser without notice who acquires only an equitable interest will nevertheless take free from equities if his purchase gives him the better right to a legal estate. Thus if a legal estate is conveyed not to the purchaser but to a trustee for him and the trustee is also without notice, the purchaser takes free from equities.[34]

(b) *Subsequent acquisition of legal estate.* A purchaser without notice who at the time of his purchase fails to obtain either a legal estate or the better right to one will nevertheless prevail over a prior equity if he subsequently gets in a legal estate, even if he then has notice of the equity. As between himself and the owner of the prior equity, there is equal equity, and the legal estate will prevail.[35] But if the purchaser knowingly acquires the legal estate in breach of trust, he will not take free from the interests of the beneficiaries under that trust.[36]

(c) *Mere equities.* Although a purchaser of an equitable interest without notice of prior equitable interests does not take free from them, he takes free from any "mere equities" of which he has no notice.[37] Mere equities fall short of being actual interests in the land, and in the main are rights to equitable relief in respect of property. They include the right to have a transaction set aside for fraud[38] or to have an instrument rectified for mistake.[39]

4. Without notice. There are three kinds of notice.

(a) *Actual notice.* A person has actual notice of all facts of which he has actual knowledge, however that knowledge was acquired; but he

---

[31] See *Pilcher* v. *Rawlins* (1872) 7 Ch.App. 259 at pp. 268, 269.
[32] *Post*, p. 70.
[33] *Phillips* v. *Phillips* (1862) 4 De G. F. & J. 208 at p. 216; *Cave* v. *Cave* (1880) 15 Ch.D.
[34] See *Assaf* v. *Fuwa* [1955] A.C. 215.
[35] *Bailey* v. *Barnes* [1894] 1 Ch. 25; and see *post*, p. 512.
[36] *Harpham* v. *Shacklock* (1881) 19 Ch.D. 207; *McCarthy & Stone Ltd.* v. *Hodge* [1971] 1 W.L.R. 1547.
[37] *Phillips* v. *Phillips* (1862) 4 De G.F. & J. 208; *Cave* v. *Cave* (1880) 15 Ch.D. 639 at p. 647; *Allied Irish Banks Ltd.* v. *Glynn* [1973] I.R. 188. See p. 69, *post*.
[38] *Ernest* v. *Vivian* (1863) 33 L.J. Ch. 513.
[39] *Re Colebrook's Conveyance* [1972] 1 W.L.R. 1397; *Smith* v. *Jones* [1954] 2 All E.R. 823.

is not regarded as having actual notice of facts which have come to his ears only in the form of vague rumours.[40] By statute, a number of rights have become registrable in the registers of land charges, and it has been provided that registration of such rights constitutes actual notice; this subject is dealt with below.[41]

(b) *Constructive notice.* A person has constructive notice of all facts of which he would have acquired actual notice had he made those inquiries and inspections which he ought reasonably to have made, the standard of prudence being that of men of business under similar circumstances.[42] A purchaser has constructive notice of a fact if he—

(i) had actual notice that there was some incumbrance and a proper inquiry would have revealed what it was, or

(ii) has, whether deliberately or carelessly, abstained from making those inquiries that a prudent purchaser would have made.[43]

It is obviously prudent to inspect the land and to investigate the title.

(I) INSPECTION OF LAND. A purchaser must inspect the land and make inquiry of anything which appears to throw doubt on the title offered by the vendor, for example, the presence of other occupants or a right of way or a doubtful boundary. Thus the occupation of a tenant is notice of all the equitable rights of the tenant in the land,[44] though not of any mere equity,[45] such as his right to have his tenancy agreement rectified on account of a common mistake. However, a purchaser need not ask the tenant to whom he pays his rent, so failure so to inquire does not give the purchaser notice of the rights of the tenant's landlord,[44] who may be a different person from the vendor. Of course, actual knowledge that rent is paid to L, and not to V, will be constructive notice of L's rights.

All persons, other than the vendor, in actual occupation must be asked what rights they claim, for example, as possible co-owners of the land under a trust for sale which arises if a person contributes directly or indirectly to the purchase of the land.[46] Although a wife's presence may be explicable purely by her marital status,[47] there is a fair chance that, as a working wife at some stage, she contributed to the purchase of the property (*e.g.* in paying a deposit or mortgage

---

[40] *Lloyd* v. *Banks* (1868) 3 Ch. App. 488; *Barnhart* v. *Greenshields* (1853) 9 Moo. P.C. 18 at p. 36.
[41] *Post,* p. 90 *et seq.*
[42] L.P.A. 1925, s. 199; *Bailey* v. *Barnes* [1894] 1 Ch. 25 at p. 35.
[43] *Jones* v. *Smith* (1841) 1 Hare 43 at p. 55; *Oliver* v. *Hinton* [1899] 2 Ch. 264.
[44] *Hunt* v. *Luck* [1902] 1 Ch. 428. some equitable interests of tenants now need to be registered under the Land Charges Act, *e.g.* options.
[45] *Smith* v. *Jones* [1954] 1 W.L.R. 1089.
[46] See p. 311, *post.*
[47] In older times where a husband appeared sole legal owner no inquiries had to be made of a wife since only the husband was regarded as being in actual occupation with his wife in his shadow, present merely *qua* chief cook, bottle-washer and bed-warmer! *Cf. Bird* v. *Syme Thomson* [1978] 3 All E.R. 1027.

instalments) so, it seems, even she must be asked if she claims any equitable interest in the property.[48] Even though their presence may be explicable by their relationship to the vendor inquiries must also be made of the equitable rights of his mistress, father, mother, brother, sister, uncle, aunt, etc., if they appear to be living in the property.[49] It seems, indeed, that inquiries should also be made of the vendor's adult children or grandchildren.

Where minor children are concerned, the questions arise whether they should themselves be treated in actual occupation, rather than as appendages present merely because their father-vendor is in occupation, and, in any event, whether it is reasonable to make inquiry of such minors. Obviously, it would be unreasonable to ask a child of six months or six years whether he has an equitable interest under a bare trust or a trust for sale, whether arising from a legacy of his grandfather to his father upon trust for him and used by his father in the purchase of the property in the father's name or arising from a declaration of trust made by his father in better times, but now suppressed in more difficult times. However, if a 38-year-old father and a 17-year-old daughter are the only persons living in the property then inquiries should be made to determine whether the female is the male's wife or mistress for, it seems, constructive notice exists of the equitable rights of wives and mistresses. Once inquiries have begun to be made of the daughter it will be as well to ask her whether she claims any equitable interest and to ask her to execute a document stating that in any event the purchaser is to take free of any equitable interest that she might have.[50]

Where the vendor lives in the property with his wife, and three school-children aged, say, 10, 14 and 17 there is much to be said for the view that the children in their unemancipated state should either be treated as present *qua* children rather than *qua* occupiers or as persons of whom it is unreasonable to make inquiry, especially when they may be open to undue influence by the vendor.[51]

It is noteworthy that inquiry of an emancipated adult child living in the property may protect the interests of unemancipated minor children since notice of the existence of a document which might be expected to be material is notice of its contents,[52] and notice that property is subject to certain trusts is notice of all the trusts to which it is subject in the hands of the vendor-trustee.[53]

So far it has been assumed that it has been obvious whether or not

[48] *Williams & Glyn's Bank* v. *Boland* [1979] Ch. 312; [1981] A.C. 487.
[49] *Hodgson* v. *Marks* [1971] Ch. 992.
[50] Even here problems exist since the purchaser might be deemed to have constructive notice of undue influence exercised by the vendor over his daughter.
[51] Cf. *Re Pauling's S. T.* [1964] Ch. 303.
[52] *Re Valletort Steam Laundry Co.* [1903] 2 Ch. 654, *Bisco* v. *Earl of Banbury* (1676) 1 Ch. 287.
[53] *Perham* v. *Kempster* [1907] 1 Ch. 373 at p. 380.

persons have been living in the property. However, a vendor might so
contrive matters that whenever the purchaser visited the property the
vendor's wife was at the shops or visiting a sick relative or on holiday
or on a business trip or on night-duty work, whilst the vendor's
21-year-old son was at university or playing sport or on holiday, etc.
If the presence of the wife or son was apparent from articles in the
bedrooms, etc., then a purchaser should be put on inquiry which
must be of the wife or son: a purchaser cannot rely on the untrue *ipse
dixit* of the vendor.[54] Thereafter, the question arises of how
reasonable it is to expect the purchaser to examine cupboards,
trunks, cellars, etc., for traces of a wife or adult son, or to make
inquiries of the neighbours as to persons residing in the vendor's
property, or to search the electoral register for adult voters living in
the premises. As a precautionary measure such search of the register
would probably be sensible.

Finally, as might be expected, if an occupier by words or conduct
represents that the purchaser will obtain a title free from any interest
of the occupier then the occupier will be estopped from claiming an
interest adverse to the purchaser.[55]

(2) INVESTIGATION OF TITLE. A purchaser has constructive notice of
all rights which he would have discovered had he investigated the title
to the land for the period allowed by law in the case of an open
contract, *i.e.* one which (*inter alia*) prescribes no special length of
title. This period was originally at least 60 years, but by the Vendor
and Purchaser Act 1874, it was reduced to at least 40 years, and by
the Law of Property Act 1925, to at least 30 years. Under section 23
of the Law of Property Act 1969 it is now at least 15 years. The period
is "at least" 15 years, so the purchaser must call for a good root of
title which is at least 15 years old, and see all documents subsequent
thereto which trace the dealings with the property. A good root of
title is a document which deals with the whole legal and equitable
interest in the land, describes the property adequately, and contains
nothing to throw any doubt on the title. Thus if the title consists of a
series of conveyances respectively 3, 14, 41 and 45 years old, as well
as older deeds, a purchaser under an open contract can require the
production of the conveyance 41 years old and all subsequent
conveyances. If in fact he fails to investigate the title at all, or else
investigates it for only part of this period (*e.g.* because he has agreed
to accept a shorter title), he is fixed with constructive notice of
everything that he would have discovered had he investigated the title
for the full statutory period.[56]

---

[54] *Hodgson* v. *Marks* [1971] Ch. 892 at p. 932 (Russell L.J.).
[55] *Midland Bank Ltd.* v. *Farmpride Hatcheries Ltd.* C.A. (1981) 260 E.G. 493;
Knightley v. *Sun Life Assurance Co. Ltd.*, *The Times* July 23, 1981, *Spiro* v. *Lintern*
[1973] 1 W.L.R. 1002.
[56] See *Re Cox and Neve's Contract* [1891] 2 Ch. 109 at pp. 117, 118.

(c) *Imputed notice.* If a purchaser employs an agent, such as a solicitor, any actual or constructive notice which the agent receives may be imputed to the purchaser.[57] Before the Conveyancing Act 1882, notice received by an agent in a previous transaction was occasionally imputed to a purchaser, but this discouraged the employment of local solicitors with knowledge of local affairs[58] and was modified by the Act. Only actual or constructive notice which the agent acquires as such in the particular transaction in question is now imputed to a purchaser.[59] Where the same solicitor acts for both parties, any notice he acquires may be imputed to both parties, except where he enters into a conspiracy with one to conceal something from the other.[60]

5. Successors in title. The protection given to a purchaser without notice extends also to his successors in title, even if they take with notice[61]; for otherwise, the owner of the equitable interest could, by widely advertising his right, make it difficult for the purchaser without notice to dispose of the land for as much as he had paid for it. To this rule there is one exception, which prevents it being abused. If a person bound by the interest sells to a purchaser without notice and later acquires the property again, he cannot shelter behind the immunity of that purchaser.[62]

C. Mere Equities

Mere equities must be distinguished from equitable interests since equitable interests bind everyone except a bona fide purchaser of a legal estate for value without notice whilst mere equities bind everyone except bona fide purchasers of a legal *or equitable interest* for value without notice.[63] It is unfortunate that many judgments confuse the issue by referring to a purchaser taking subject to equities when they mean subject to equitable interests.

Equitable interests are actually interests in land like estate contracts, unpaid vendor's liens, restrictive covenants, equitable easements and profits, equitable mortgages and beneficial interests under trusts. Mere equities are at a further remove, being rights which are ancillary to or dependent upon some interest in land, for example, rights to have a conveyance or lease set aside for fraud or

---

[57] *Re The Alms Corn Charity* [1901] 2 Ch. 750.
[58] See *Re Cousins* (1886) 31 Ch.D. 671.
[59] L.P.A. 1925, s. 199, replacing C.A. 1882, s. 3.
[60] *Meyer* v. *Chartres* (1918) 34 T.L.R. 589; *Sharpe* v. *Foy* (1868) 4 Ch. App. 35.
[61] *Harrison* v. *Forth* (1695) Prec. Ch. 51; *Wilkes* v. *Spooner* [1911] 2 K.B. 473.
[62] *Gordon* v. *Holland* (1913) 82 L.J.P.C. 81.
[63] *National Provincial Bank* v. *Ainsworth* [1965] A.C. 1175, at pp. 1237–1238 (Lord Upjohn); *Westminster Bank* v. *Lee* [1956] Ch. 7; *Latec Investments Ltd.* v. *Hotel Terrigal Pty. Ltd.* (1965) 113 C.L.R. 265; *Phillips* v. *Phillips* (1862) 4 De G. F. & J. 208 at p. 218.

undue influence or rectified for mistake or a mortgagor's right to re-open a foreclosure.[64]

D. Competing Equitable Interests

An equitable interest as first in time binds subsquent equitable interests even if they were purchased for value without notice, unless its owner's conduct amounts to fraud or negligence or raises an estoppel where such conduct is sufficient to induce the detrimental acquisition of the subsequent interest.[65] If the subsequent acquisition were with notice of the earlier interest then there are, of course, no grounds for displacing the priority accorded by the date of the creation of the interests.[66] The onus is always on the person seeking to displace the priority of time sequence to prove his case.[67]

Part 2

SPECIES OF EQUITABLE RIGHTS

Sect. 1. Trusts

1. Origin. Everyone today is familiar with the nature of trusts, whereby the ownership of property is vested in one or more persons (the trustees) who hold it for the benefit of others (the beneficiaries). The ancestor of the trust is the use, which had substantially the same nature. The word "use" was not derived from the Latin "*usus*" but from the Latin "*opus*" in the phrase "*ad opus*" (on his behalf) *via* the Old French "*al oes*" or "*al ues*" and hence "to the use of": thus land was conveyed "to A and his heirs to the use of B and his heirs."[68]

Although there are records of uses having been created even before the Norman Conquest, the only uses found for some time after the Conquest appear to have been merely temporary uses, for example to ensure that some nobleman in England had seisin and the right to bring a real action, while a knight was on a crusade, otherwise leaving his lands and wife and children defenceless. In about 1225 the Franciscan friars came to England. The rules of their Order prevented their owning property, and so land was conveyed, for

---

[64] M. & W. p. 119. Also see A. R. Everton (1976) 40 Conv. 209, Hanbury & Maudsley, *Modern Equity*, p. 753 *et seq*.
[65] *Abigail* v. *Lapin* [1934] A.C. 491; *Shropshire Union Rly. & Canal Co.* v. *R.* (1875) L.R. 7 H.L. 496; *Taylor* v. *London Banking Co.* [1901] 2 Ch. 231.
[66] *Bailey* v. *Barnes* [1894] 1 Ch. 25 at p. 36; *McCarthy & Stone Ltd.* v. *Hodge* [1971] 1 W.L.R. 1547; *I.A.C. Finance Pty. Ltd.* v. *Courtenay* (1963) 110 C.L.R. 550 at p. 578.
[67] *Strand Securities Ltd.* v. *Caswell* [1965] Ch. 958 at p. 991; *Shropshire Union Rly & Canal Co.* v. *R.* (*supra*).
[68] Maitland, *Equity*, p. 24.

example, to some town to the use of the friars.[69] After this, uses of a permanent nature became more common, and by the middle of the fourteenth century they were frequent.

2. Enforced by equity. After early hesitation, the common law courts refused to recognise uses. If land was conveyed by A "to B and his heirs to the use of C and his heirs" the common law courts refused to compel the feoffee to uses, B, to hold the land for the benefit of C, the *cestui que use* (pronounced "setty ker use"). B was the person seised, and the common law would take notice of his rights alone; C had no interest which the law would recognise, for "uses were but imaginations."[70] Nevertheless, many uses were created in reliance on the honour and good faith of the foeffees to uses, and consequent breaches of trust occurred. Towards the end of the fourteenth century the Chancellor's aid was sought, and although there is no record of a decree in favour of a *cestui que use* until 1446, probably relief was given in the first quarter of the fifteenth century.[71]

3. Duties. The duties of the feoffees to uses towards their *cestui que use* were threefold: they were bound—

   (i) to permit him to take the profits of the land;
   (ii) to dispose of the land in accordance with his instructions; and
   (iii) to take all necessary proceedings to protect or recover the land.[72]

Although at first the *cestui que use* was regarded as merely having a right to compel the feoffees to uses to carry out their duties, the rights of the *cestui que use* were so extensive that it was soon recognised that he had an estate in the land.[73] The legal estate was in the feoffees to uses, the equitable estate in the *cestui que use*: the former had the husk, the latter the kernel. With some qualifications, it could be said in Chancery that "the equity is the land."

4. Legal and equitable interests. Frequently the legal and equitable interests in property go together; a person who has had the legal fee simple in Blackacre conveyed to him normally receives the equitable fee simple as well. But although there is often no need to consider separately the legal and equitable estate in land, in some cases this is the only way to arrive at a proper understanding of the subject.[74] The ability of the beneficial owner of a legal estate (*i.e.* one who has the equitable interest as well as the legal estate for his own benefit) to

---

[69] 2 P. & M. 231–238.
[70] *Chudleigh's Case* (1595) 1 Co.Rep. 113b at p. 140a; and see Maitland, *Equity*, p. 28.
[71] Ames, *Lectures on Legal History*, p. 237.
[72] 4 H.E.L. 431.
[73] *Brent's Case* (1583) 2 Leon. 14 at p. 18.
[74] Consider, *e.g.* joint tenancies and tenancies in common; *post*, pp. 302 *et seq.*

separate the legal from the equitable interest is one of the
fundamentals of English law.

5. The Statute of Uses. It was possible by conveying lands to uses to
evade most feudal liabilities, as they fell only upon the person or
persons who were seised of land. All that was needed was the
selection of suitable and sufficient feofees so that the land was never
vested in a single feoffee whose death would give rise to the feudal
incidents which became due upon the death of the tenant. The
evasion seriously affected the King, who was always lord and never
tenant. After various manoeuvres, in 1535 "the Statute of Uses was
forced upon an extremely unwilling parliament by an extremely
strong-willed King."[75] The effect of this was to "execute" all uses to
which it applied, taking the legal estate out of the feoffees to uses and
converting the equitable interests of the *cestuis que use* into
corresponding legal estates. Thus, if land were conveyed to A, B, C
and D and their heirs to the use of X and his heirs, the effect was to
vest the legal fee simple in X, so that if X attained majority or
married or died the feudal incidents would fall due.

6. The use upon a use. Soon after the staute was passed it was held
that a use upon a use was void,[76] so that a conveyance "to A and his
heirs to the use of B and his heirs to the use of C and his heirs" gave
the whole legal and equitable interests to B and nothing to A or C.
After Cromwell's Republic the feudal incidents were mainly
abolished,[77] and the Chancellor by 1676 was enforcing the use in C's
favour as a trust,[78] so that B held the legal estate on trust for C. For
such a result the conveyancing formula "unto and to the use of B and
his heirs in trust for C and his heirs," came customarily to be used.
The statute survived until its repeal by the Law of Property Act 1925.

7. Post 1925. A trust of land is now created by the landowner
conveying land "to T1 and T2 in fee simple in trust for . . . ." The
legal estate is thus in T1 and T2 while those named as beneficiaries
will have equitable interests. Since 1925 life interests and entailed
interests can only exist as equitable interests under a trust of the legal
estate.

[75] Maitland, *Equity*, p. 34; the King was Henry VIII.
[76] *Tyrrel's Case* (1555) 2 Dy. 155a.
[77] *Ante*, p. 26.
[78] *Grubb* v. *Gwillim* (1676) 73 S.S. 347; *Symson* v. *Turner* (1700) 1 Eq.Ca. Abr. 383.
   For a full treatment of the Statute of Uses and developments therefrom see M. & W.
   pp. 155–170.

Sect. 2. Other Equitable Rights

The Chancellor did not confine his intervention to the enforcement of uses or trusts, though that always remained the most important part of his jurisdiction. There were other important areas of real property in which he intervened.

1. Mortgages. If A conveyed his land to B as security for a loan, equity would allow A at any time after repayment of the loan fell due, and despite any contrary provisions in the mortgage, to recover his land by paying B what was due to him under the loan. The development of this equitable right of redemption, exercisable after expiry of the legal date for redemption is described later.[79]

2. Restrictive covenants. Normally a contract is binding upon and enforceable by the parties alone. But during the nineteenth century it was held that if a landowner covenants not to use his land in a certain way for the benefit of neighbouring land, the covenant could be enforced in equity against successors in title of the covenantor thus imposing an equitable burden on his land.[80] It is crucial that the covenant is not positive but negative in nature.

3. Estate contracts. Where a person contracts to purchase a legal estate in land, he is at once considered to have an equitable interest in that land even before he has paid the price and has had the legal estate of the vendor conveyed to him.[81] This is also the case where he has an option to purchase an interest in land.[82]

4. Informal leases, mortgages and easements. At law, in order to create or transfer a legal estate, certain formalities had to be observed. The rule was that "Corporeal hereditaments lie in livery, incorporeal hereditaments lie in grant." A corporeal hereditament was an inheritable right in realty which was accompanied by physical possession of the land, *e.g.* a fee simple in possession; for such estates, a feoffment with livery of seisin[83] was essential. An incorporeal hereditament was an inheritable right in land not accompanied by physical possession, such as a fee simple in remainder or a rentcharge; for such interests, a feoffment was inappropriate but a deed of grant was essential. Leases for a term of years were not hereditaments and at first could be created orally, but the Statute of Frauds 1677[84] made writing necessary in nearly all

---

[79] *Post*, p. 462.
[80] *Post*, p. 443.
[81] *Lysaght* v. *Edwards* (1876) 2 Ch. D. 499.
[82] *Pritchard* v. *Briggs* [1980] Ch. 338.
[83] *Ante*, p. 32.
[84] s. 1.

cases. The Real Property Act 1845[85] made a deed essential for most leases; it also made a deed an alternative to a feoffment of corporeal hereditaments, and provided that if a feoffment was employed it would be void unless evidenced by a deed. Thus after the Act it became substantially true to say that without a deed no legal estate could be created or transferred.

Equity, on the other hand, was not so strict. In accordance with the maxim. "Equity treats that as done which ought to be done," equity regarded an enforceable contract to create or convey an interest in land as being as effective as if the transaction had been properly carried out. Further, equity would regard an attempt to create or convey an interest in land which failed through lack of a deed as being a contract to carry out the transaction and thus as effective in equity. These rules, however, were subject to the transaction being for value and being sufficiently evidenced in writing or by a sufficient act of part performance[86]; in general, a mere oral transaction relating to land and supported by no act of part performance would not be enforced even in equity. In short, a transaction by deed was normally essential to the creation or transfer of a legal interest; writing or part performance sufficed in equity.

5. Proprietary estoppel. If P, under an expectation created or encouraged by O that P shall have an interest in land, thereafter, on the faith of such expectation and with the knowledge of O and without objection by him, acts to his detriment in connection with such land, O will be estopped from denying P's claim to the expected interest and will be forced to give effect to P's expectation. The estoppel interest will also bind purchasers from O with notice of it.[87] Thus, where a father encouraged his son to build a house on the father's land in the belief that the son was to have the fee simple the court ordered the father's will trustees to convey the fee simple to the son.[88] However, where a son had been encouraged to build a bungalow on his father's land in the expectation that he could live there as long as he wished the court held that he had the right to live in it as his home for as long as he desired.[89] Lord Denning stated,[90] "[Counsel] suggested that the father could sell to a purchaser who

---

[85] ss. 2, 3.

[86] This is intended to summarise very briefly what is dealt with more fully at pp. 336 *et seq., post.*

[87] *Taylor Fashions Ltd.* v. *Liverpool Victoria Trustees Co.* [1981] 1 All E.R. 897 at p. 909; *Ramsden* v. *Dyson* (1866) L.R. 1 H.L. 129 at p. 170.

[88] *Dilwyn* v. *Llewelyn* (1862) 4 De G. F. & J. 517, also see *Pascoe* v. *Turner* [1979] 1 W.L.R. 431.

[89] *Inwards* v. *Baker* [1965] 2 Q.B. 29, also see *Williams* v. *Staite* [1979] Ch. 291. This appears to make the son a Settled Land Act tenant for life according to *Dodsworth* v. *Dodsworth* (1973) 228 E. G. 1115, though see p. 259, *post.*

[90] *Inwards* v. *Baker* [1965] 2 Q.B. 29 at p. 37.

could get the son out. But I think that any purchaser who took with notice would clearly be bound by the equity. So here, too, the present plaintiffs, [the trustees of the father's will], the successors in title of the father are clearly themselves bound by this equity." Similarly, where P built a garage on his own land which was accessible only over O's land and O had led P to believe that there would always be access as of right to the garage, purchasers from O with notice of P's right of access were bound to allow access to the garage.[91]

Proprietary estoppel is distinct from promissory estoppel not only in its older ancestry but in its availability not just by way of defence but as a positive cause of action.[92] The relief granted to the plaintiff is whatever in the circumstances is appropriate to satisfy the plaintiff's equity, for example, the grant of a lease,[93] an easement,[94] an equitable lien for expenditure[95] or for the value of improvements.[96]

Whether a proprietary estoppel interest is a full equitable interest or a mere equity has not yet fallen to be decided by the court and is unlikely to be decided since purchasers will almost invariably have notice (arising from P's occupation or the obviousness of the claimed right, for example, a right of way) and so be bound without the need to categorise the interest. It would seem likely, if the question arose, that it would be categorised as an equitable interest. After all, in some ways it is analogous to a specifically enforceable contract for a legal or equitable interest.

Recently, the Court of Appeal has been extending the scope of proprietary estoppel to its limits. In *Pascoe* v. *Turner*[97] the defendant spent about £230 on repairs and improvements to a house and, perhaps, almost £400 on curtains and carpets in the belief that the plaintiff had orally effectively given the house to her, he having moved out to live with another woman. It was held that the defendant's modest expenditure, whilst the plaintiff stood by knowing it was made in the belief that the house was now the defendant's, entitled the defendant to have the fee simple on the ground of proprietary estoppel. The plaintiff was thus ordered to convey the legal estate to the defendant to perfect his oral gift.

In *Greasley* v. *Cooke*[98] though she had spent no money on the house the defendant was held entitled to occupy the house rent-free for the rest of her life. She lived in the house originally as a maid of the owner, living there with his children. Later she became *de facto*

---

[91] *Ives Investments Ltd.* v. *High* [1967] 2 Q.B. 379, also see *Crabb* v. *Arun District Council* [1976] Ch. 179, *N.P.B.* v. *Hastings Car Mart.* [1964] Ch. 665 at p. 686.

[92] *Central London Property Trust Ltd.* v. *High Trees House* [1947] K.B. 130; *Coombe* v. *Coombe* [1951] 2 K.B. 215.

[93] *Stiles* v. *Cowper* (1748) 3 Atk. 692; *Gregory* v. *Mighell* (1881) 18 Ves. 328.

[94] *Ives Investment Ltd.* v. *High* [1967] 2 Q.B. 380; *Crabb* v. *Arun D.C.* [1976] Ch. 179.

[95] *Unity Joint Stock Mutual Banking Association* v. *King* (1858) 25 Beav. 72.

[96] *Raffaele* v. *Raffaele* [1962] W.A.R. 238, (1963) 79 L.Q.R. 238.

[97] [1979] 1 W.L.R. 431.

[98] [1980] 1 W.L.R. 1306.

wife of a son, K, so that without remuneration for 30 years she looked after the family including K's invalid sister, C till K and C died in 1975, and under K's will his interest (inherited from his father) in the house passed to his brother, H. Because of what K and H had said the defendant believed she would be allowed to live in the house rent-free for as long as she wished. The Court was prepared to presume in these circumstances that she had acted to her detriment[99] on the assurances of K and H which had been intended to influence her. She might otherwise have left C and K and obtained a paid job—and a husband, perhaps.

For a case of proprietary estoppel to be made out against O it was originally thought that O had to be at fault in some way. Thus, if O did not know the true position and so did not know of his right to object when he acquiesced in or encouraged P's activities then O was not to be estopped from subsequently asserting his rights against P.[1]

This may still be the position in cases of acquiescence where all that has happened is that O has stood by without protest whilst his rights have been infringed at a time when he did not realise he had such rights.[2]

Where O has actively encouraged P's activities it no longer seems that fault on O's part is the crucial factor. Instead, attention is focused on P's position to see if it would be unconscionable for him to suffer from O enforcing O's strict rights once O had discovered his rights.[3] Indeed, a broad approach is advocated "directed at ascertaining whether, in particular circumstances, it would be unconscionable for a party to be permitted to deny that which, knowingly *or unknowingly*, he has allowed or encouraged another to assume to his detriment."[4] Knowledge of the true position by O becomes merely one of the relevant factors in the overall inquiry.

Where O did not know the true position at the relevant time an alternative basis for a decision against O may be the doctrine of estoppel by convention, whereby the parties to a transaction may be estopped against each other from questioning a conventional agreed basis accepted by the parties as the true state of affairs.[5] Thus if O

---

[99] Lord Denning remarked that the defendant did not need to prove she acted to her detriment but this must be understood in context as meaning that since in the circumstances it was presumed that she had acted to her detriment it was not necessary for her *to prove* detriment. The other judges required detriment as did the Court of Appeal in *Christian* v. *Christian* [1980] C.A. Transcript 838, [1981] New L.J. 43.

[1] *Willmott* v. *Barber* (1880) 15 Ch.D 96; *Falcke* v. *Scottish Imperial Insurance Co.* (1886) 34 Ch.D 234 at pp. 243, 253, *Re Vandervell's Trusts (No. 2)* [1974] 1 All E.R. 47 at p. 74.

[2] *Taylor Fashions Ltd.* v. *Liverpool Victoria Trustees Co.* [1981] 1 All E.R. 897 at p. 912; *Amalgamated Investment & Property Co.* v. *Texas Commerce International Bank Ltd.* [1981] 1 All E.R. 923 at p. 936.

[3] *Ibid. Pascol Ltd.* v. *Trade Lines Ltd., the Times* February 8, 1982.

[4] *Taylor Fashions Ltd.* (*supra*) at p. 915, *per* Oliver J. approved by Oliver L.J. in *Habib Bank Ltd.* v. *Habib Bank A.G. Zurich* [1981] 2 All E.R. 650 at p. 666.

[5] *Amalgamated Investment & Property Co.* v. *Texas Commerce International Bank Ltd.* [1981] 3 All E.R. 577 at pp. 584, 587, 591.

purchases a freehold subject to T's 14-year lease, which contains an option to renew it for a further 14 years, which unknown to O is void for non-registration under the Land Charges Act, and O and T agree to T paying for improvements to the premises which T would not have agreed to but for their mutual understanding that T had a valid option, then O will be bound to renew the lease.[6]

Sect. 3. The Borderline between Proprietary and Personal Rights

1. Introductory. Proprietary rights in land are interests in land, whether legal interests or equitable interests or mere equities that are ancillary to or dependent upon interests in land. They are rights in reference to land which have the quality of enduring through different ownerships of land according to normal conceptions of title to real property.[7] Before a right can be admitted into the category of proprietary rights it must be definable, identifiable by third parties, capable in its nature of assumption by third parties and have some degree of permanence or stability.[8] Thus the purely personal evanescent and changeable right, exercisable against her husband by the deserted wife—the so-called deserted wife's equity—could not be a proprietary right and affect purchasers.[9]

Through the intervention of equity a contracting party's personal rights to enforce a contract for the sale of land against the vendor and a beneficiary's personal right to have the trustees carry out a trust in the beneficiary's favour have become proprietary rights. Browne-Wilkinson J. has summarised the position as follows[10]:

"Historically the courts of equity acted *in personam*. Whether equity was supplementing the common law by giving additional remedies or correcting the common law by imposing a different legal result, the courts of equity intervened by directing the defendant personally to do, or refrain from doing, a specific act. In deciding whether or not to intervene, the courts of equity required, first, that the plaintiff should have some enforceable right and, secondly, that the conscience of the defendant was affected in some way so as to make the failure of the defendant to give effect to the plaintiff's rights contrary to justice.

The rights which the plaintiff asserted were normally either contractual rights or rights under a trust. In the realm of contracts equity supplemented the common law by ordering the party in default to perform the contract, instead of merely paying damages. In

---

[6] *Taylor Fashions Ltd.* (*supra*).
[7] *National Provincial Bank* v. *Ainsworth* [1965] A.C. 1175 at 1237, *per* Lord Upjohn.
[8] *Ibid.* at p. 1247, *per* Lord Wilberforce.
[9] For her new Class F right see p. 95, *ante*.
[10] *Swiss Bank* v. *Lloyds Bank*. [1979] Ch. 548 at p. 565.

the realm of trusts equity ordered the legal owner of property, the trustee, specifically to carry out the trust which he had accepted. In matters involving property equity intervened by ordering that the defendant must deal with the property in question in a specific manner, whether the plaintiff's rights were founded in contract or trust.

But, although the basis of the equity jurisdiction was, and still is, founded on an order *in personam*, the courts of equity evolved the doctrine that, in the eyes of equity, that which ought to have been done is to be treated as having been done. Thus under a specifically enforceable contract for the sale of land, the purchaser is treated in equity as the owner of the property whether or not an order for the execution of the trust has been made against the trustee. In this way the plaintiff's rights, although founded on the ability of the court to make an order *in personam* against the other contracting party or the trustees, become an interest in the property itself, an equitable interest. Once the position is reached that an order for specific performance could have been made against the legal owner if the matter had been brought before the court, thereafter the legal owner holds the property shorn of those rights in the property which the court of equity would decree belong to another.

Once an equitable interest in property is established, thereafter any third party taking that property from the original contracting party or the original trustee only takes it, in the eyes of equity, shorn of, or subject to, the equitable interest. But as the right and the remedy is equitable only, the court of equity would not enforce the equitable interest against the third party unless it was inequitable for him not to give effect to the prior equitable interest. It is on this ground that a subsequent purchaser for value of a legal interest without notice takes free of prior equitable interests."

2. Options and rights of pre-emption. It is well-established that an option to purchase land creates an equitable interest in the land since the option holder, when he wants, can call for the land irrespective of the landowner's wishes, so long as the conditions for the exercise of the option are fulfilled. It imposes a positive obligation on the prospective vendor to keep the offer open during the agreed period. However, a right of pre-emption confers no immediate right: it merely imposes a negative obligation on the possible vendor, requiring him to refrain from selling to any other person without giving to the holder of the right of first refusal the opportunity of purchasing in preference to any other buyer. The pre-emption holder has a mere *spes*. It is solely within the volition of the landowner whether he will frustrate the right of pre-emption by choosing not to fulfil the necessary conditions or whether he will fulfil the conditions, so effectively converting the right into an option and thus into an equitable interest.

Thus the Court of Appeal[11] has held that a right of pre-emption is purely a personal contractual right, though capable of protection by entry in the Land Charges Register, if unregistered land is involved, or in the Land Register if registered land is involved. However, it does become an equitable interest in land the moment the condition on which it depends is satisfied so that an option to purchase arises.[12] If V grants P a right of pre-emption over Cosyacre, covenanting that if he decides to sell or lease the property in his lifetime he will let P have first opportunity to purchase it at a price determined by a fixed formula, and P registers the right, but V sells and conveys to Q, then Q will take subject to P's equitable interests that arose as soon as V decided to sell the property. If V had only granted Q an option to purchase the property at any time in the three months after V's death, then Q would take free from P's rights since the conditions for the rights to become exercisable and to mature into an option would not have been fulfilled.[13] It is thus crucial that the terms of a right of pre-emption are carefully drafted.

3. Privity of contract. Privity of contract—the notion that only the parties to the contract can sue or be sued in respect of the contract—is fundamental to the law of contract but, as has just been seen, the law of property provides for contracts and options for the purchase of land to create equitable interests enforceable against third parties.

For policy reasons, to enable the proper development of land and the preservation of amenity value, a contractual term embodied in a deed as a restrictive covenant,[14] being negative in nature, in restraining the doing of certain things, and benefiting and burdening nearby properties, can also be an equitable interest, enforceable by whomsoever owns the benefited land against whomsoever owns the burdened land. If, however, the covenant is not entered into between nearby landowners or if it is positive in nature, in forcing money to be spent on the provision of certain things, then the covenant is not proprietary in nature enforceable against third parties who subsequently happen to own the land to which the covenant refers.

4. The possibility of tortious claims. If A and B enter into a contract can A ever sue C or C and D if they prevent the contract from being fully carried out in A's favour? Of course, A can always sue B, with whom he has privity of contract, and, if the contract was for the purchase of land, A can obtain the land from the new landowner if A

---

[11] *Pritchard* v. *Briggs* [1980] Ch. 338 cogently criticised by H.W.R.W. (1980) 96 L.Q.R. 488.

[12] This is the view of Templeman and Stephenson L.JJ but not of Goff L.J.

[13] See *Pritchard* v. *Briggs* [1980] Ch. 338.

[14] See *post*, pp. 443 *et seq*.

had protected his estate contract under the Land Charges Act or the Land Registration Act.

In _Esso Petroleum Co. Ltd._ v. _Kingswood Motors (Addlestone) Ltd._[15] A had B Ltd., the proprietor of a garage, agree for five years to sell A's petroleum products and agree not to sell the garage without obtaining a similar solus tie in A's favour. C Ltd. bought all the shares in B Ltd. and had B. Ltd. sell the garage to D Ltd. (another subsidiary of C Ltd.). D Ltd. claimed to take free of the solus tie which only bound B Ltd. Bridge J. held that C Ltd. and D Ltd. were liable for the tort of knowing interference with contractual relations. By mandatory injunction he ordered the garage to be re-transferred to B Ltd. "to enforce the personal liability incurred by a tortfeasor to undo the consequences of his tort which could have been restrained by injunction before it was committed,"[16] rather than to enforce the contract as such against C and D.

A plaintiff like A has sufficient interest to obtain an injunction by virtue of his rights under the contract even though he has no proprietary interest in the property, but the defendant will only be liable if when he acquired his interest he had actual knowledge of the contract.[17] If he had honest doubts about there being a valid contract in A's favour then the requisite knowledge for the tort is not present.[18]

There will be no tortious liability if the defendant's conduct were justified,[19] for example, where X had contracted to purchase land from V who _subsequently_ contracted to sell the land to Y, who sued X after V had conveyed the land to X[20] (subject to the rights, _if any_, of Y registered under the Land Charges Act or the Land Registration Act) or it would seem, where V had conveyed the land to Y when X's earlier contract had become void for non-registration but X was trying to claim tortious remedies.[21] It would seem that general tortious principles should be limited by special land law principles, especially when there is available in reserve the equitable principle that prevents statutes from being used as an instrument of fraud.[22] If there are two or more defendants a civil conspiracy claim might be contemplated but there is a significant limitation on the scope of such a claim. It is restricted to acts done in the execution of an agreement made for the purpose of injuring the plaintiff's interest

---

[15] [1974] Q.B. 142.
[16] _Ibid._ at p. 156. It might have been better if the case had been decided by lifting the veil of incorporation or on the principle that statute cannot be used as an instrument of fraud: _Jones_ v. _Lipman_ [1962] W.L.R. 832.
[17] _Swiss Bank Corporation_ v. _Lloyds Bank Ltd._ [1979] Ch. 548 at p. 575; _Greig_ v. _Insole_ [1978] 1 W.L.R. 302 at pp. 332–342.
[18] _Smith_ v. _Morrison_ [1974] 1 W.L.R. 659.
[19] R.J. Smith (1977) 41 Conv. 318; _Greig_ v. _Insole_ [1978] 1 W.L.R. 302 at pp. 340–342.
[20] _Pritchard_ v. _Briggs_ [1980] Ch. 338 at p. 415.
[21] _Cf. Miles_ v. _Bull (No. 2)_ [1969] 3 All E.R. 1585 at p. 1590; _Midland Bank Trust Co._ v. _Green_ [1981] A.C. 513.
[22] _Post_, p. 131.

and does not extend to acts predominantly done for furthering the defendants' interests.[23]

5. Contractual licences. A licence is a personal permission given by the landowner which allows the licensee to do some act which otherwise would be a trespass[24] for example, use a hall for delivery of a lecture, view a cinema performance, put posters on a wall, supply refreshments in a theatre, play cricket. A licence may even allow the licensee exclusive possession, for example, an employee's widow may be allowed to live in a cottage without payment for as long as she wishes, so long as she maintains the cottage.

The traditional view is that contractual licences are merely contractual rights, in the protection of which equitable remedies may be available,[25] but that they cannot create interests in land like leases or life interests. However, in the case of irrevocable contractual licences conferring exclusive possession Lord Denning has been striving to elevate them into the status of interests in land. He has argued in a minority judgment[26] that if P contracts with V to purchase land from V, subject to the rights of X in exclusive possession under an irrevocable contractual licence, then P holds the legal estate, on the completion of the purchase, on constructive trust for X; furthermore, that the position would be the same if P had not so expressly agreed with V but merely had notice of X's rights arising from X's occupation. Thus X obtains an equitable interest under a constructive trust.

Goff L.J., in an extempore judgment overlooking his views when Goff J.,[27] has endorsed Lord Denning's views when sitting with Lord Denning in *D.H.N. Food Distributors* v. *Tower Hamlets*,[28] which has alternative grounds for the decision. This led Browne-Wilkinson J. in *Re Sharpe*[29] to consider that he should follow Lord Denning's views, though his decision was also based on the licensee having an equitable proprietary estoppel interest.[30]

---

[23] *Lonrho* v. *Shell Petroleum Co. Ltd.* [1981] 2 All E.R. 456; this supports the approach of Sir Stanley Rees in *Midland Bank Trust Co.* v. *Green* [1980] Ch. 590.

[24] *Post*, pp. 370 *et seq.*

[25] *e.g.* an injunction against the other party; *Chandler* v. *Kerley* [1978] 1 W.L.R. 693; *King* v. *David Allen Billposting Ltd.* [1916] 2 A.C. 54; *Clore* v. *Theatrical Properties Ltd.* [1936] 3 All E.R. 483; *Brynowen Estates Ltd.* v. *Bourne* [1981] New L.J. 1212. See pp. 372 *et seq, post.*

[26] *Binions* v. *Evans* [1972] Ch. 359.

[27] *Re Solomon* [1967] Ch. 573 at pp. 582–586: contractual licences cannot be interests in land. *N.P.B.* v. *Ainsworth* [1964] Ch. 665 at p. 699; [1965] A.C. 1175 at pp. 1240, 1251.

[28] [1976] 1 W.L.R. 852 criticised D.J.H. (1977) Camb L.J. 12.

[29] [1980] 1 W.L.R. 219.

[30] See J. Martin (1980) Conv. 207; A Briggs (1981) Conv. 212. Logically, contractual licences and estoppel interests should be mutually exclusive, a contractual licence arising out of an offer-acceptance agreement that itself confers positive rights while an estoppel interest arises from X's express or implied representation which induces Y to act to his detriment so that X negatively should be prevented from asserting his strict rights. However, to this end Y may positively obtain a property interest.

Neither of these latter cases involved purchasers when, whether they are bound hinges upon whether or not a contractual licence is an equitable interest. If it is, then in unregistered conveyancing it is anomalous that the more weighty "estate contract" will be void for non-registration, whereas the lesser contractual licence will be valid since all purchasers will have notice arising from the licensee's occupation.[31] If a contractual licence is not an equitable interest it is still possible to argue[32] that a purchaser should be liable to be restrained from interfering with the licensee if liable for the tort of interference with contractual relations, an argument, it seems, that is not open where an estate contract is void for non-registration. Such an anomaly could be prevented if "special technical considerations in the law relating to land"[33] led the court to find that a purchaser on obtaining the legal estate had the defence of justification to a tortious claim by the contractual licensee in such circumstances.[34]

---

[31] To use the concept of notice to elevate contractual licenses into interests in land seems a revival of the old heresy that notice of contractual rights (*e.g.* positive or negative covenants) could create proprietary rights: *L.C.C.* v. *Allen* [1914] 3 K.B. 642 at p. 655, *N.P.B.* v. *Ainsworth* [1965] A.C. 1175 at pp. 1237, 1253.

[32] *Binions* v. *Evans*, [1972] Ch. 359 at p. 371, *per* Megaw L.J.

[33] *Ibid.*

[34] After all, a purchaser of land with notice of a restrictive covenant not of a proprietary nature, since not taken for the benefit of nearby land, can disregard such covenant: *Sefton* v. *Tophams Ltd.* [1965] Ch. 1140 at pp. 1157, 1183, 1191, 1199, 1202.

CHAPTER 4

THE STRUCTURE OF LAND LAW AFTER 1925

Part 1

THE POLICY OF THE 1925 LEGISLATION

IT has been seen that a purchaser who buys without notice of some adverse right is bound by that right if it is legal and takes free from it if it is equitable. Many legal estates and interests could subsist (many varieties of fees simple, fees tail, life estates, terms of years, rentcharges, mortgages, easements) so that, obviously, the position of a purchaser would be greatly improved if there were a reduction in the number of such estates and interests that might bind him. Since equity followed the law and also went beyond the law in recognising certain interests as proprietary in nature, there were vast numbers of equitable interests affecting legal estates that were vulnerable if such estates were purchased without notice. The position of purchasers or of equitable owners was not helped by the uncertainties inherent in the doctrine of constructive notice.

Accordingly, the 1925 Legislation drastically altered the old system of legal and equitable interests in order to protect purchasers and to protect equitable owners—and to simplify the law.

First, the number of legal estates was reduced to two, the fee simple absolute in possession and the term of years absolute, and the variety of legal interests was also reduced.

Second, equitable interests of a commercial nature, deriving their value from affecting specific land of another, were made registrable against the landowner under the Land Charges Act 1925 (now replaced by the Land Charges Act 1972). If the interest is registered then this gives notice to everyone so everyone is bound by it. If the interest is not registered then it is void against a purchaser, irrespective of whether or not such purchaser has notice of the interest, since the Act makes registration or non-registration the vital factor. For some few special legal interests which otherwise could be undiscoverable by a purchaser (*e.g.* a legal mortgage not protected by retention of the title deeds by the mortgagee) registration or non-registration under the Land Charges Act is also the vital determining factor.

Third, those equitable interests of a family nature (*e.g.* life or entailed interests) or of co-owners, conferring the right to enjoy the fruits of land ownership, were made overreachable. Thus, on a sale by the legal estate owner, if the purchase moneys are paid to two trustees or a trust corporation, the purchaser will obtain the legal estate free from the rights of the equitable beneficiaries even if he has notice of them. The beneficiaries rights are overreached (*i.e.* detached from the land and attached to the proceeds of sale) but still subsist, though in different assets.

Fourth, the old doctrine of notice was left to apply in what was thought to be a limited number of cases. However, the doctrine of notice is available as a long-stop to cover situations involving equitable interests which are not precisely covered by the Land Charges Act or by the statutory overreaching provisions.

Fifth, the Land Registration Act 1925 was enacted with a view eventually to there being a system of registration of title extending throughout England and Wales, simplifying and facilitating conveyancing and providing state-guaranteed titles to land. The 1925 Act developed a system pioneered in the Land Transfer Act 1875 (concerned with voluntary registration) and the Land Transfer Act 1897 (concerned with compulsory registration on sales of land in London).

Part 2

THE STRUCTURE OF UNREGISTERED LAND LAW

Sect. 1. Reduction in the Number of Legal Estates

Section 1 of the Law of Property Act 1925 reduced the number of legal estates that can exist in land to two, and the number of classes of legal interests to five. The distinction, broadly, is that a legal estate confers full rights to use and enjoy land as one's own while a legal interest is a right over the land of another. The terms of the first three subsections of section 1 are as follows:

"1.—(1) The only estates in land which are capable of subsisting or of being conveyed or created as law are—

(*a*) An estate in fee simple absolute in possession;
(*b*) A term of years absolute.

(2) The only interests or charges in or over land which are capable of subsisting or of being conveyed or created at law are—

(*a*) An easement, right, or privilege in or over land for an interest equivalent to an estate in fee simple absolute in possession or a term of years absolute;
(*b*) A rentcharge in possession issuing out of or charged on land being either perpetual or for a term of years absolute;
(*c*) A charge by way of legal mortgage;

(*d*) Land tax, tithe rentcharge,[1] and any other similar charge on land which is not created by an instrument;

(*e*) Rights of entry exercisable over or in respect of a legal term of years absolute, or annexed, for any purpose, to a legal rentcharge.

(3) All other estates, interests, and charges in or over land take effect as equitable interests."

It should be noted that the section does not provide that the estates and interests mentioned in subsections (1) and (2) are *necessarily* legal, but merely that they alone *can* be legal. If they are to be legal the proper formalities must be employed, *i.e.* a deed must be used except in the creation of leases taking effect in possession for a term not exceeding three years.[2]

Probably the incidents of equitable interests are similar to those attaching to corresponding legal estates before 1926. Thus the position of a tenant for life as regards waste seems to have remained unchanged despite the conversion of his legal life estate into an equitable life interest at the beginning of 1926. There is no express provision on this point but "equity follows the law."[3]

The general scheme of the section is to deal with the legal rights of ownership in the land itself in subsection (1) and with legal rights over the land of another in subsection (2). However, this is complicated by the definition of "land" given by the Act. "Land" is defined as including, unless the context otherwise requires, any corporeal or incorporeal hereditament, and among the latter is mentioned an advowson.[4] An advowson is the right of presenting a clergyman to a living[5] and, oddly enough, is a species of real property. By reading subsection (1) in the light of the definition of "land," it seems clear that a fee simple in possession in an advowson is a legal estate and so is a term of years absolute in an advowson.

It will be noted that the rights mentioned in subsection (1) are called legal estates and those mentioned in subsection (2) are called legal interests or charges. This is a convenient distinction between rights over a person's own land and rights over the land of another, but both types of right are referred to in the Act as "legal estates," and have the same incidents attached to them as attached to legal estates before 1926.[6] The title of "estate owner" is given to the owner of a legal estate.[7] Before 1926, equitable rights in land were frequently and properly called equitable estates, but they should now

---

[1] These four words have been repealed: *post*, p. 89.
[2] L.P.A. ss. 52, 54; p. 335, *post*.
[3] *Ante*, p. 61.
[4] L.P.A. 1925, s. 205 (1) (ix).
[5] It is subject to important restrictions, *e.g.* no advowson may be sold after two vacancies of the benefice have occurred after July 14, 1924: see Benefices Act 1898 and Benefices Act 1898 (Amendment) Measure 1923.
[6] L.P.A. 1925, s. 1(4).
[7] *Ibid.*

be called equitable interests, and the name "estate" reserved for legal rights.

The various legal estates and interests must now be examined more closely.

1 (a). "Fee simple absolute in possession." The meaning of *"fee simple"* has already been considered.[8]

"Absolute" is used to distinguish a fee simple which will continue for ever from a modified fee,[9] such as a determinable fee or a base fee. A fee simple defeasible by condition subsequent[10] would also not be "absolute" but for the Law of Property (Amendment) Act 1926. A fee simple defeasible by condition subsequent used to arise most frequently in connection with rentcharges until the Rentcharges Act 1977 prohibited the creation of rentcharges in most cases. In some parts of the country, particularly Manchester and the north, it was a common practice to sell a fee simple for a comparatively small sum in cash and a perpetual rentcharge (an annual sum charged on the land). The remedies for non-payment of a rentcharge include a right to enter on the land temporarily to collect the rents and profits; further, in a number of cases an express right of re-entry is reserved by the conveyance, entitling the grantor to enter and determine the fee simple and thus regain his old estate if the rent is a specified number of days in arrear. The reservation of a right of re-entry clearly made the fee simple less than absolute, and it was thought by some that even a temporary right of entry might have this effect. This meant that those who had purchased land in this way before 1926 and had obtained legal estates suddenly found that their estates might no longer be legal and that it was doubtful who had the legal estate. Further, the complicated provisions of the Settled Land Act 1925 probably applied.[11]

To remedy this state of affairs the Law of Property (Amendment) Act 1926[12] provided that "a fee simple subject to a legal or equitable right of entry or re-entry is for the purposes of this Act a fee simple absolute." While this undoubtedly meets the difficulty it was meant to deal with, the wide terms in which it was drawn appear to have done more than was intended. The effect of a condition subsequent annexed to a fee simple is to give rise to a right of re-entry exercisable on breach of the condition, and until the right of re-entry is exercised the fee simple continues.[13] Consequently, by virtue of the Amendment Act unless created under a trust, every fee simple defeasible by condition subsequent appears to rank as a legal estate, even though it is far from being "absolute" in the ordinary sense of the word.

[8] *Ante*, p. 28.
[9] See *ante*, p. 39.
[10] *Ante*, p. 40.
[11] *Post*, pp. 258 *et seq.*
[12] Sched., adding a clause to L.P.A. 1925, s. 7 (1).
[13] *Ante*, p. 41.

To deal with the further problem that, by statute, certain land held for special purposes, such as schools or highways, will be divested and revert to the grantor when the special purpose is at an end such a fee simple is expressly declared to be absolute.[14]

"In possession" means that the estate is a present estate and not in remainder or in reversion.[15] It includes not only physical possession of the land but also the receipt of rents and profits or the right to receive them, if any. Thus a fee simple is still "in possession" even though the owner has granted a lease, for he is entitled to the rent reserved by the lease. But if land has been granted "to A for life, remainder to B in fee simple," the interests of both A and B are necessarily equitable, for a life interest cannot now be legal and B's fee simple is not in possession.[16] If a mortgagee takes "possession" of land in exercising his remedies it is expressly provided [17] that this does not convert the mortgagor's interest into an equitable interest.

1 (b). "Term of years absolute." *"Term of years"* is defined as including a term of less than a year, or for a year or years and a fraction of a year, or from year to year.[18] In effect, "terms of years" seems to mean a term for any period having fixed and certain duration as a minimum. Thus, in addition to a tenancy for a specified number of years (*e.g.* "to X for ninety-nine years"), such tenancies as a yearly tenancy or a weekly tenancy are "terms of years" within the definition, for there is a minimum duration of a year or a week respectively. But a lease "for the life of X" cannot exist as a legal estate, and the same, perhaps, applies to tenancies at will or at sufferance (if they are estates at all[19]), for their duration is wholly uncertain.

"Absolute". This has very little effect since a term of years is not prevented from being absolute merely by being liable to determination by notice, re-entry, operation of law or by a provision for cesser on redemption or in any other event (other than the dropping of a life, or the determination of a determinable life interest).[20] This means that a term of years may be absolute even if it contains a clause enabling the parties to determine it at certain specified periods, such as at the end of the first five or ten years, or if it provides (as is almost always the case) that the landlord may determine it if the rent is not paid or a covenant is broken. "Operation of law" is illustrated by the

---

[14] L.P.A. 1925, s. 7 (1): *Tithe Redemption Commission* v. *Runcorn U.D.C.* [1954] Ch. 383; *Re Clayton's Deed Poll* [1979] 2 All E.R. 1133.
[15] See *District Bank Ltd.* v. *Webb* [1958] 1 W.L.R. 148.
[16] See, however, the Welsh Church (Burial Grounds) Act 1945, s. 1, for a curious qualification of L.P.A. 1925, s.1.
[17] L.P.A., s. 95 (4).
[18] L.P.A. 1925, s. 205 (1) (xxvii).
[19] See *ante*, p. 31.
[20] L.P.A. 1925, s. 205 (1) (xxvii).

doctrine of satisfied terms,[21] and a proviso for cesser on redemption by the law of mortgages.[22]

It will be seen from this that by the express provisions of statute, a term of years absolute may consist of a tenancy which is neither a "term of years" nor "absolute" according to the natural meaning of the words, *e.g.* a monthly tenancy liable to be forfeited for non-payment of rent. "Absolute" really has very little meaning here.

It should be noted that, unlike a fee simple absolute, a term of years absolute may be a legal estate even though not "in possession." A lease to commence in five years' time may thus be legal, although there is now a 21 year limit to the length of time which may elapse between the grant of a lease and the commencement of the term.[23] There is no limit to the length of a term of years absolute, *e.g.* it may be 3,000 years.[24] But there is no such thing as a lease in perpetuity.[25]

2 (a). "An easement, right, or privilege in or over land for an interest equivalent to an estate in fee simple absloute in possession or a term of years absolute." This head includes both easements and, it seems, profits *à prendre*.[26] An easement confers the right to use the land of another in some way, or to prevent it from being used for certain purposes. Thus rights of way, rights of water and rights of light may exist as easements. A profit *à prendre* gives the right to take something from the land of another, *e.g.* peat, fish or wood. These rights can be legal only if they are held for interests equivalent to one of the two legal estates: thus a right of way for 21 years may be legal but a right of way for life must be equitable.

2 (b). "A rentcharge in possession issuing out of or charged on land being either perpetual or for a term of years absolute." "*A rentcharge*" is a right which, independently of any lease or mortgage, gives the owner the right to a periodical sum of money, with the payment of which some land is burdened,[27] as where the fee simple owner of Blackacre charges the land with a payment of £50 per annum to X. Under the Rentcharges Act 1977 no new rentcharges can be created except in special circumstances.

"*In possession.*" Under the subsection a rentcharge to start at a date subsequent to that on which it is granted cannot be legal, whether it is perpetual or for a term of years absolute. But the Law of Property (Entailed Interests) Act 1932[28] provides that a rentcharge is

---

[21] *Post*, p. 357.
[22] *Post*, p. 464.
[23] *Post*, p. 340.
[24] See L.P.A., ss. 85 (2), 87 (1).
[25] See *Sevenoaks, Maidstone and Tunbridge Ry.* v. *London, Chatham and Dover Ry.* (1879) 11 Ch.D. 625 at p. 635.
[26] For easements and profits, see *post*, pp. 395. *et seq.*
[27] For rentcharges, see *post*, p. 390.
[28] s. 2.

"in possession" notwithstanding that the payments are limited to commence or accrue at a date subsequent to its creation, unless the rentcharge is limited to take effect in remainder after or expectant on the failure or determination of some other interest.[29] Thus if X conveys land to Y in consideration of a perpetual rentcharge becoming payable one year after the conveyance, the rentcharge may nevertheless be legal; but if a perpetual rentcharge is granted "to A for life, remainder to B absolutely," B's interest cannot be legal until A's death.

"Issuing out of or charged on land." "Land" includes another rentcharge.[30] Thus if P charges his fee simple estate in Blackacre with the payment to Q of £100 per annum in perpetuity, Q can create a legal rentcharge of £50 per annum in favour of R, charged on his rentcharge of £100.

"Being either perpetual or for a term of years absolute." "Perpetual" is used here in place of "fee simple absolute" used in 2(a) above. This verbal difference seems to be of no practical importance.

2 (c). "A charge by way of legal mortgage." This needs no comment here save to point out that this is one of the ways of creating a legal mortgage today, the other being by the grant of a term of years absolute on certain conditions. Both forms are dealt with later.[31]

2 (d). "Land tax, tithe rentcharge, and any other similar charge on land which is not created by an instrument." This group comprises periodical payments with which land is burdened by operation of law (*e.g.* by statute) and not by some conveyance or other voluntary act of parties. The words "land tax, tithe rentcharge" have now been repealed,[32] but they are printed here in order to explain the word "similar."

Land tax was a small annual tax on land first imposed in 1692, but abolished in 1963.[33]

Tithe rentcharge was abolished by the Tithe Act 1936. It was a type of rentcharge imposed by statute in lieu of the former right of parsons and others to one tenth of the produce of land. Under the Act of 1936, tithe owners were compensated with government stock, and there was imposed on the land formerly burdened with tithe rentcharge a "tithe redemption annuity" payable to the Crown.[34] The tithe redemption annuity, however, was extinguished by the Finance Act 1977.[35] Although a tithe redemption annuity was not

[29] See (1932) 73 L.J. News. 321.
[30] L.P.A. 1925, ss. 122, 205 (1) (ix); see *post*, p. 391.
[31] *Post*, pp. 464. *et seq.*
[32] Tithe Act 1936, 9th Sched.; Finance Act 1963, 14th Sched., Pt. VI.
[33] Finance Act 1963, Pt. V, 14th Sched.
[34] Tithe Act 1936, s. 3.
[35] s. 56. See M. & W., pp. 801–805 for further details about tithe, tithe rentcharge and tithe redemption annuity.

expressly stated to be a legal interest, it clearly fell within that category as being a "similar charge on land which is not created by an instrument."

2 (e). "Rights of entry exercisable over or in respect of a legal term of years absolute, or annexed, for any purpose, to a legal rentcharge." As already mentioned,[36] a legal term of years absolute is usually subject to the right of the landlord to re-enter if the tenant fails to pay rent or comply with the covenants. Such a right may be a legal right, and the same applies to any right of re-entry attached to a legal rentcharge, *e.g.* if the rent is not paid. By contrast, a right of entry which is not perpetual or for a term of years and is created on an assignment of a lease in favour of the assignor who retains no other interest in the leasehold land is not a legal interest but merely ranks as an equitable interest.[37] Lord Simon even indicated[38] that such assignor's right of entry could only be equitable even if perpetual or for a term of years though this point was left open by Lord Wilberforce[39] with whom the other Law Lords concurred.

Concurrent legal estates. Any number of legal estates may exist concurrently in the same piece of land.[40] Thus A may have the legal fee simple in Blackacre, subject to a legal mortgage in favour of B, a legal rentcharge in favour of C, a legal lease in favour of D and so on.

Sect. 2 Registration of Land Charges

Before 1926, provision had been made for the registration of certain rights affecting land, such as pending actions. Such rights were unenforceable against a subsequent purchaser of the land if they were not registered before the purchase was made. The rights thus registrable were comparatively few and unimportant. The Land Charges Act 1925 (now replaced by the Land Charges Act 1972) greatly extended this system, and many important rights are void against a purchaser unless duly registered. Wherever a right is void against a person for non-registration, that person is not prejudicially affected even if he has actual notice of the right; but once the right is registered, the registration is deemed to constitute actual notice to all persons and for all purposes connected with the land affected.[41]

Thus, in *Midland Bank Trust Co.* v. *Green*[42] a farmer granted his son an option to purchase his farm at a low price. The son failed to

---

[36] *Ante*, p. 87.
[37] *Shiloh Spinners Ltd.* v. *Harding* [1973] A.C. 691. For assignments of leases, see *post*, p. 348.
[38] *Ibid.* at p. 726.
[39] *Ibid.* at p. 719.
[40] L.P.A. 1925, s. 1 (5).
[41] L.P.A. 1925, ss. 198, 199.
[42] [1981] A.C. 513.

register the option as a Class C(iv) land charge. To defeat the son's option the farmer then sold the farm (worth at least £40,000) for £500 to his wife, who knew all about the option. The House of Lords held that the wife took free from the option since it was void against *"a purchaser of a legal estate for money or money's worth."*[43] It did not matter that the wife had actual notice or had not acted in good faith or had provided only a nominal consideration (if £500 were treated as merely nominal consideration which was very doubtful). The Act was concerned to make notice immaterial and deliberately did *not* state that unregistered Class C(iv) charges would be void against "a purchaser in good faith of a legal estate for money or money's worth other than a nominal consideration."[44]

However, it would seem that where no specific statutory provision applies, *e.g.* to donees or to purchasers for marriage consideration (which is value but not money's worth[45]) claiming to take free from unregistered Class C(iv) or D charges, then it is necessary to fall back upon the equitable doctrine of notice to determine the matter.[46]

It is crucial to register a land charge even though its owner be in actual occupation of the land, as where T occupies premises under an informal lease which ranks as an agreement for a lease, *i.e.* a Class C(iv) estate contract.[47] It is interesting that the land charges legislation was not intended prejudicially to affect such interests of persons *qua* occupiers. However, when section 33 of the Law of Property Act 1922 was consolidated in the 1925 legislation it appeared only as section 14 of the Law of Property Act 1925 and was inadvertently omitted from the Land Charges Act 1925, the Lords and Commons Joint Committee having erroneously certified that the consolidation of the Law of Property Act 1922 and the Law of Property (Amendment) Act 1924 into the various 1925 Acts made no change in the law.

A. Registrable Interests

Five separate registers and an index are kept in the computerised Land Charges Department of the Land Registry at Plymouth.[48] The first of these is much more important than the others.

1. Land Charges.[49] These are divided into six classes, A, B, C, D, E, and F. The most important classes, C and D, are subdivided. Most of the interests are equitable interests which derive their value from affecting another's land.

---

[43] L.C.A. 1925, s. 13 (2).
[44] *Cf.* Lord Denning in *Midland Bank Trust Co.* v. *Green* [1980] Ch. 590 at p. 624.
[45] [1981] .C. 513 at p. 531 *per* Lord Wilberforce.
[46] *McCarthy & Stone Ltd.* v. *Hodge* [1971] 1 W.L.R. 1547.
[47] *Hollington Bros Ltd.* v. *Rhodes* [1951] 2 T.L.R. 691.
[48] L.C.A. 1972, s. 1.
[49] L.C.A. 1972, ss. 2–4.

Class A consists of charges imposed on land by some statute, but which come into existence only when some person makes an application. Thus where a landlord who is not entitled to land for his own benefit has to pay compensation to an agricultural tenant, the landlord may apply to the Minister of Agriculture, Fisheries and Food for a charge on the land for the amount of compensation.[50] A Class A charge is registrable whenever created.

Class B consists of charges which are similar to those in Class A except that they are not created on the application of any person, but are imposed automatically by statute. Most charges thus imposed are local land charges, and as these are registrable in a separate register, few charges are registrable in Class B. An example is a charge on property recovered or preserved for a legally aided litigant in respect of unpaid contributions to the legal aid fund.[51]

Class C land charges are divided into four categories:

C (i): A PUISNE MORTGAGE. This is a legal mortgage not protected by a deposit of documents relating to the legal estate affected. It needs to be a registrable land charge for otherwise it would be a legal right *in rem* unfairly affecting a purchaser who could not possibly have discovered its existence.

C (ii): A LIMITED OWNER'S CHARGE. This is an equitable charge which a tenant for life or statutory owner acquires under any statute by discharging death duties or other liabilities, and to which the statute gives special priority. Thus on the death of a tenant for life of settled land, capital transfer tax is payable; if the next tenant for life finds the money out of his own pocket instead of throwing the burden on the settled property itself, he is entitled to a charge on the land in the same way as if he had lent money to the estate on mortgage. Such a charge is registrable under this head.

C (iii): A GENERAL EQUITABLE CHARGE. This is any equitable charge which—

(a) is not included in any other class of land charge;
(b) is not protected by a deposit of documents relating to the legal estate affected[52]; and
(c) does not arise, or affect an interest arising, under a trust for sale or settlement.[53]

This is a residuary class which catches equitable charges not registrable elsewhere, *e.g.* an unpaid vendor's lien. It includes

---

[50] Agricultural Holdings Act 1948, s. 82.
[51] Legal Aid Act 1974, s. 9 (6).
[52] Retention of title deeds gives the world notice of the retainer's rights so there is no need to make the rights registrable.
[53] Such an interest falls exclusively within the scheme of overreachable rights dealt with at p. 107, *post.*

equitable mortgages of a legal estate but not equitable mortgages of an equitable interest under a settlement or trust for sale or other charges on the proceeds of sale of land.[54] It also includes certain annuities created after 1925.[55]

C (iv): AN ESTATE CONTRACT. This is a contract (whether oral[56] or in writing) to convey or create a legal estate, made by a person who either owns a legal estate or is entitled at the date of the contract to have a legal estate conveyed to him. It suffices if the person who makes the contract owns any legal estate in the land, even if it is less substantial than the estate which he has agreed to convey or create, as where a yearly tenant agrees that if he acquires the reversion he will grant his sub-tenant a lease for ten years.[57]

It is important to realise that registration must be against "the name of the estate owner whose estate is intended to be affected" so that if V contracts to sell to P who contracts to sell to Q then Q must register against V: registration against P will be ineffective even if P subsequently obtains the legal estate.[58]

"Contract" includes a contract, an option of purchase, a right of pre-emption[59] or any other like right such as a right to have a lessee offer to surrender the leased premises before asking for the lessor's consent to an assignment.[60] The option or other right is still registrable notwithstanding that it is set out in a lease for all the world to see[61] and notwithstanding that the option (if it is to renew the lease and not to purchase the reversion[62]) or other right is an obligation running with the land and otherwise automatically binding regardless of notice, so as to fall outside the policy seemingly underlying the Land Charges Act.[63] An informal lease taking effect as an agreement for a lease is still registrable though the lessee be in actual occupation.[64] The "contract" head also includes a notice by a tenant under a long lease exercising his statutory right to purchase the freehold or take another lease.[65] On the other hand, a notice to treat

---

[54] *Georgiades* v. *Edward Wolfe & Co. Ltd.* [1965] Ch. 487 (estate agent's commission charged on proceeds of sale not a C (iii) land charge); and see *Thomas* v. *Rose* [1968] 1 W.L.R. 1797.

[55] *Post*, p. 95.

[56] *Universal Permanent Building Society* v. *Cooke* [1952] Ch. 95 at 104. The contract must be enforceable *e.g.* by some act of part performance.

[57] *Sharp* v. *Coates* [1949] 1 K.B. 285.

[58] *Barrett* v. *Hilton Developments Ltd.* [1975] Ch. 237.

[59] This, initially, is only a personal right but it becomes proprietary and capable of binding third parties when activated by the landowner so as to become exercisable as an option in nature: see *Pritchard* v. *Briggs* [1980] Ch. 338, *ante*, p. 78.

[60] *Greene* v. *Church Commissioners* [1974] Ch. 467.

[61] Contrast restrictive covenants within Class D (ii).

[62] A covenant conferring an option to renew a lease touches and concerns the land and runs with the land as part and parcel thereof: *Weg Motors Ltd.* v. *Hales* [1962] Ch. 49. Cf. *Woodhall* v. *Clifton* [1905] 2 Ch. 257.

[63] *Taylor Fashions Ltd.* v. *Liverpool Victoria Trustees Co.* [1981] 1 All E.R. 897 at pp. 907–909, *Beesly* v. *Hallwood Estates Ltd.* [1960] 1 W.L.R. 549 (on appeal on another point in [1961] Ch. 105).

[64] *Hollington Bros Ltd.* v. *Rhodes* [1951] 2 T.L.R. 691.

[65] Leasehold Reform Act 1967, s. 5 (5); *post*, p. 588.

given in connection with a compulsory purchase is not registrable,[66] nor is a right of entry for securing compliance with covenants in an assignment of a lease[67] nor is a contract authorising an agent to enter into a contract.[68]

Class D land charges are divided into three categories:

D (i): DEATH DUTIES. This class consists of any charge acquired by the Board of Inland Revenue under any enactment for death duties arising on a death after 1925. Since the abolition of legacy duty and succession duty in 1949, and the replacement of estate duty by capital transfer tax with regard to deaths after March 12, 1975, only a charge to capital transfer tax in respect of a transfer on death can give rise to the charge.[69] Personal property, including leaseholds beneficially owned by the deceased immediately before death, is not included in the charge. The tax is, however, chargeable on freeholds, and consequently must be registered if it is to bind purchasers. The charge is rarely registered.

D (ii): RESTRICTIVE COVENANTS. Under this head, any covenant or agreement restrictive of the user of land may be registered, provided it—

  (a) was entered into after 1925, and
  (b) is not between a lessor and a lessee.

Thus restrictive covenants in leases are never registrable even where they relate not to the demised land but to adjoining land owned by the lessor.[70] For leases the normal rules as to privity of contract and privity of estates apply, and when there is neither, the question, as usual, is one of notice. Similarly, restrictive covenants made before 1926 still depend upon notice, being enforceable against everyone except a purchaser for value of a legal estate without notice.

D (iii): EQUITABLE EASEMENTS. Any "easement, right or privilege over or affecting land" is registrable under this head, provided—

  (a) it is merely equitable, and
  (b) it was created after 1925.

Thus a perpetual easement created by a document not under seal, or an easement for life, even if created by deed, is registrable under this head if made after 1925. Each is necessarily equitable, the first for lack of a deed and the second as not falling within section 1 of the

---

[66] *Capital Investments Ltd.* v. *Wednesfield U.D.C.* [1965] Ch. 774.
[67] *Shiloh Spinners Ltd.* v. *Harding* [1973] A.C. 691.
[68] *Thomas* v. *Rose* [1968] 1 W.L.R. 1797. However, a contract to convey a legal estate to such persons as A shall direct is registrable: *Turley* v. *Mackay* [1944] Ch. 37 discussed in *Thomas* v. *Rose* (*supra*).
[69] Finance Act 1975, s. 22, 4th Sched., paras. 20, 21, 12th Sched., para. 1.
[70] *Dartstone Ltd.* v. *Cleveland Petroleum Co. Ltd.* [1969] 1 W.L.R. 1807.

Law of Property Act 1925.[71] Presumably equitable profits *à prendre* are included under this head.[72] But the apparent width of "right or privilege" is restricted by the context, and thus a requisition of land under Defence Regulations,[73] a proprietary estoppel interest,[74] a right to remove fixtures at the end of a lease,[75] and a right of entry to secure compliances with the covenants contained in an assignment of a lease[76] have all been held not to be registrable under this head.

The modern tendency is to construe this head narrowly, with the consequence that a number of informal interests fall within the scope of the old doctrine of notice.

Class E: Annuities created but not registered before 1926.[77] An annuity is a rentcharge or an annuity for a life or lives, or for an estate determinable on a life or lives (*e.g.* "to X for 99 years if he so long lives") not created by a marriage settlement or a will.[78] This class is thus small and diminishing. Annuities as thus defined created after 1925 are registrable in Class C (iii) as general equitable charges.

Class F: A spouse's right to occupy a house owned by the other spouse.

Lord Denning's efforts[79] to create a mere equity in favour of a deserted wife capable of binding purchasers with notice (of the deserted wife's occupation and therefore of her equity) were rejected by the House of Lords[80] in 1965. However, by the Matrimonial Homes Act 1967 as amended by the Matrimonial Homes and Property Act 1981 statutory rights of occupation are automatically given to one spouse in the matrimonial home where the legal estate is held by the other spouse or by trustees for the other spouse under trusts where no-one but the spouses are or could become beneficiaries.

The rights are in favour of the spouse who has no interest at all in the house or who only has an equitable interest.[81] The rights are the right not to be excluded from occupation of the house vested in the other spouse (or trustees) and the right, if not in occupation, with the leave of the court[82] to enter and occupy such house. The rights

---

[71] *Ante*, pp. 85, 88.
[72] *E.R. Ives Investment Ltd.* v. *High* [1967] 2 Q.B. 379 at p. 395.
[73] *Lewisham Borough Council* v. *Maloney* [1948] 1 K.B. 50; and see *E.R. Ives Investment Ltd.* v. *High* [1967] 2 Q.B. 379.
[74] *E.R. Ives Investment Ltd.* v. *High, supra,* where Lord Denning considered that D (iii) only covered interests which before 1926 could have been conveyed or created at law but which after 1925 could only take effect as equitable interests.
[75] *Poster* v. *Slough Estates Ltd.* [1969] 1 Ch. 495 at pp. 506, 507.
[76] *Shiloh Spinners Ltd.* v. *Harding* [1973] A.C. 691; *ante*, p. 90.
[77] See *post,* p. 99 for annuities registered before 1926.
[78] L.C.A. 1972, s. 17 (1).
[79] *Bendall* v. *McWhirter* [1952] 2 Q.B. 466.
[80] *National Provincial Bank* v. *Ainsworth* [1965] A.C. 1175.
[81] M.H.A. 1967 s. 1 (1) (9). A spouse with a legal interest is *ipso facto* sufficiently protected.
[82] M.H.A. 1967 s. 1 (1). The right is registrable before the leave of the court has been obtained: *Watts* v. *Waller* [1973] Q.B. 153.

continue so long as the marriage lasts, though the court can restrict, terminate or suspend them and can even exclude the owning spouse altogether from the house.[83]

The rights operate as an equitable charge on the house with priority from January 1, 1968 or the date of the marriage or the date of the house purchase, whichever is the latest.[84] Thus, once registered as a Class F land charge the rights have retrospective effect, so conferring priority against any later competing equitable interests, *e.g.* estate contracts,[85] equitable mortgages. The rights will not bind a purchaser of any interest (legal or equitable) in the land unless registered against the legal estate owner before completion of the purchase.[86] Though these rights, if unregistered, may be void against a purchaser, the spouse may still rely on any equitable interest in the house to give her a right of occupation against the owning spouse or his successors in title.[87] Exceptionally, even rights registered as a Class F land charge are void against the owning spouse's trustee in bankruptcy or other persons representing creditors in the owning spouse's bankruptcy or insolvency,[88] though the non-owning spouse can, of course, claim in respect of any equitable interest she may have.[89]

The power to register a Class F land charge can be a strong but double-edged weapon in the hands of a non-owning spouse who, for one reason or another, wishes to prevent the sale of the matrimonial home. In *Wroth* v. *Tyler*[90] the wife did not want to move and so, at the last minute, without telling her husband she registered a Class F land charge, so preventing the purchase and making her husband liable for £5,500 damages and costs. The learned judge warned her that the probable consequences would be the bankruptcy of her husband and the sale of the house with vacant possession by his trustees in bankruptcy free from her rights, and so gave her an opportunity to remove her charge, so that specific performance might be ordered, but she failed to take advantage of such opportunity.

The court may set aside the Class F charge if misused as where a husband, who had no intention of entering or occupying the wife's home, had registered a Class F charge in order to enable him to freeze his separated wife's assets to assist him pursue a claim for damages against her.[91]

---

[83] M.H.A. 1967, s. 1 (2) as amended by Domestic Violence and Matrimonial Proceedings Act 1976, s. 3 to reverse *Tarr* v. *Tarr* [1973] A.C. 254. Under s. 4 of the 1976 Act the Court can even exclude one spouse where both spouses are legal co-owners.

[84] M.H.A. 1967, s. 2 (1).

[85] *Watts* v. *Waller* [1973] Q.B. 153, Hayton [1976] Current Legal Problems, 26 at 31–33, 43–50.

[86] L.C.A. 1972, s. 4 (8), M.H.A., s. 2 (9) added by M.H.&P.A. 1981, s. 4 (3).

[87] *Williams & Glyn's Bank* v. *Boland* [1981] A.C. 487.

[88] M.H.A. 1967, s. 2 (5).

[89] *Re Densham* [1975] 1 W.L.R. 1519.

[90] [1974] Ch. 30 where there is a useful detailed discussion of the difficulties concerning Class F rights.

[91] *Barnett* v. *Hassett* [1981] 1 W.L.R. 1385.

The possibility of registration of a Class F charge or of the non-owning spouse claiming an equitable interest[92] means that in conveyancing practice the written concurrence of the non-owning spouse is necessary to any sale by the sole legal owner.[93]

Companies. Most charges on land created by a company for securing money (including a charge created by a deposit of title deeds[94]) require registration within 21 days in the Companies Register maintained under the Companies Act 1948.[95] For floating charges, and charges created before 1970, this suffices[96]; other charges require registration in both registers.[97]

2. Pending actions.[98] This head comprises petitions in bankruptcy and pending land actions. A pending land action (often called a *lis pendens*) is an action or proceeding pending in court relating to any interest in land. There must be a claim to some proprietary right in the land itself, and not merely a claim to the proceeds of sale[99] or a claim to prevent the sale of land until some matter has been dealt with.[1] A claim for the transfer of land under section 24 of the Matrimonial Causes Act 1973 is a *lis pendens* even though it is not a claim to an existing interest in land.[2] Registration ensures that if the present owner tries to sell the land before the case has been decided, the purchaser will be bound by the claim. Registration lasts for five years; if the case has not then been decided, registration may be renewed for successive periods of five years.[3]

3. Writs and orders affecting land.[4] This head does not include writs employed to commence an action relating to land; these come under the head of pending actions. The register of writs and orders is directed towards the writs and orders *enforcing* judgments and orders of the court. The chief writs and orders included in this register are—

(i) writs or orders affecting land made for the purpose of enforcing a judgment or recognisance; this head includes an order of the court charging a judgment debtor's land with payment of the money due.

---

[92] *Williams & Glyn's Bank* v. *Boland* [1981] A.C. 487.
[93] Hayton (1974) 38 Conv. 110, *Williams & Glyn's Bank* v. *Boland* (*supra*).
[94] *Re Wallis & Simmonds (Builders) Ltd.* [1974] 1 W.L.R. 391.
[95] Companies Act 1948, s. 95; see *Re Molton Finance Ltd.* [1968] Ch. 325.
[96] *Property Discount Corp. Ltd.* v. *Lyon Group Ltd.* [1981] 1 All E.R. 379.
[97] L.C.A. 1972, s. 3 (7); L.P.A. 1969, s. 26. See [1982] Conv. 43.
[98] L.C.A. 1972, s. 5.
[99] *Taylor* v. *Taylor* [1968] 1 W.L.R. 378. (co-ownership trust for sale).
[1] *Calgary and Edmonton Land Co. Ltd.* v. *Dobinson* [1974] Ch. 102.
[2] *Whittingham* v. *Whittingham* [1979] Fam. 9. also see *Selim Ltd.* v. *Bickenhall Engineering Ltd.* [1981] 3 All E.R. 210 (pending land action includes landlord's application under the Leasehold Property (Repairs) Act 1938 for leave to commence an action intended to lead to forfeiture of the lease).
[3] L.C.A. 1972, s. 8.
[4] *Ibid.* s. 6.

(ii) an order appointing a receiver or sequestrator of land;

(iii) a receiving order in bankruptcy made after 1925.

Registration remains effective for five years, but may be renewed for successive periods of five years.[5]

Charging orders to enforce judgments or orders for the payment of money[6] could only be imposed on interests in land, *e.g.* D's fee simple or the interest of E and F as legal and equitable joint tenants where they have been held jointly liable on a joint debt.[7] Otherwise, however, the interests of co-owners were treated as interests only in the proceeds of sale of the land so charging orders could not be imposed.[8]

Section 2 of the Charging Orders Act 1979 now allows charging orders to be imposed (a) on any interest held by a debtor beneficially under a trust (*e.g.* the interest of a co-owner under a trust for sale of land[9]) and (b) on any interest held by a person as trustee of a trust if the interest is in land and, in a case where there are two or more debtors all of whom are liable to the creditor for the same debt, they together hold the whole beneficial interest under the trust unencumbered and for their own benefit. Under section 3 the Land Charges Act 1972 applies in relation to charging orders as it applies in relation to other orders or writs issued or made for the purpose of enforcing judgments.

A practical difficulty emerges from the fact that whilst charging orders can now be imposed on a co-owner's interest in the proceeds of sale of land (*e.g.* D's interest where C and D or T1 and T2 hold the legal estate on trust for sale for C and D whether jointly or equally) it does not seem that such orders can be registered in the register of writs and orders since one can only register "any writ or order *affecting land*," the entry being made in the name of the estate owner or other person whose *land* is affected by the writ or order registered.[10] After all, the scheme of the 1925 Property Legislation was to protect purchasers of land held on trust for sale so that they should not be concerned with the application by the vendors of the proceeds of sale of the land, the beneficial interests being over-reached. It thus seems that charging orders can only be registered if to enforce a judgment debt against those who together hold the whole legal and beneficial interest in the land.

In all cases it is open to the judgment creditor to seek the appointment of a receiver by way of equitable execution with liberty

[5] L.C.A. 1972, s. 8.

[6] Administration of Justice Act 1956, s. 35.

[7] *National Westminster Bank* v. *Allen* [1971] 1 Q.B. 718.

[8] *Irani Finance Ltd.* v. *Singh* [1971] Ch. 59; *Stevens* v. *Hutchinson* [1953] Ch. 299.

[9] *National Westminster Bank* v. *Stockman* [1981] 1 All E.R. 800.

[10] L.C.A. 1972, s. 6 (1). s. 18 (1) defines "land" as expressly excluding "an undivided share in land." See also *Irani Finance Ltd.* v. *Singh* [1971] Ch. 59 at pp. 77–79 and *Stevens* v. *Hutchinson* [1953] Ch. 299 at pp. 306–307.

being granted by the court to the receiver in the name of the judgment debtor (with the interest in the proceeds of sale) to take such proceedings as may be necessary under section 30 of the Law of Property Act to enforce a sale of the property.[11]

4. Deeds of arrangement.[12] The Deeds of Arrangement Act 1914 elaborately defines deeds of arrangement. For the present purpose, a deed of arrangement may be taken as any document whereby control over a debtor's property is given for the benefit of his creditors generally, or, if he is insolvent, for the benefit of three or more of his creditors. A common example is an assignment by a debtor of all his property to a trustee for all his creditors.

Registration is effective for five years and may be renewed for successive periods of five years.[13] The registration may be effected by the trustee of the deed or by any creditor assenting to or taking the benefit of the deed.[14]

5. Annuities.[15] This register, opened in 1855, was closed in 1925.[16] There can be few registered annuities left now.

B. Mode of Registration

1. Land charges. All land charges must be registered in the name of the estate owner whose estate is to be affected.[17] The estate owner is the owner of a legal estate.[18] Normally, this does not give rise to any difficulty as the estate owner usually creates the charge. Charges created by beneficiaries of their beneficial interests under trusts are not registrable.[19] However in one common case there is a trap. If V contracts to sell land to P who then contracts to sell it to S, it is against V, the estate owner, and not P, that S must register his estate contract; registration against P will not be effective even if P later acquires the legal estate.[20] Yet S often will be ignorant of the identity and even the existence of V. To be safe S should stipulate for the name of the estate owner to be disclosed as soon as contracts are exchanged.[21]

[11] *Levermore* v. *Levermore* [1980] 1 All E.R. 1. Also see Supreme Court Act 1981 s. 37(4). On s. 30 see p. 316 *post*. A *lis pendens* cannot be registered: *Taylor* v. *Taylor* [1968] 1 W.L.R. 378.
[12] *Ibid*. s. 7.
[13] *Ibid*. s. 8.
[14] *Ibid*. s. 7.
[15] *Ibid*. s. 1, 1st Sched.
[16] For the registration of annuities after 1925, see *ante*, pp. 93–95.
[17] L.C.A. 1972, s. 3 (1).
[18] *Ibid*. s 17 (1), applying the definition of L.P.A. 1925, s. 205 (1) (v).
[19] See *ante*, p. 92.
[20] *Barrett* v. *Hilton Developments Ltd.* [1975] Ch. 237.
[21] See *Patman* v. *Harland* (1881) 17 Ch.D. 353 at p. 359.

2. Other registers. Pending actions and writs and orders affecting land are registrable in the name of the estate owner or other person whose estate or interest is intended to be or is affected.[22] It will be noted that this is not limited to estate owners. Deeds of arrangement are registered in the name of the debtor.[23]

3. The name. The name should be the full correct name of the estate owner or other person so as to ensure that it appears in the correct place in the index and shows up when a search is made in the correct name. The name in the title deeds will be presumed to be the correct name until the contrary is shown.[24] A registration, however, in a name which may fairly be described as a version of the correct name (*e.g.* "Frank" for "Francis") is not a nullity but will bind all except those who make an official search in the correct name and obtain a certificate which does not disclose the entry.[25]

C. *Effects of Registration and Non-Registration*

1. Effect of registration. (a) *Notice.* By section 198 of the Law of Property Act 1925[26] registration under the Land Charges Acts constitutes actual notice of the interest registered to all persons and for all purposes connected with the land affected. This prevents any person claiming to be a purchaser without notice of a registered interest. However, section 198 does not operate to prevent a purchaser otherwise without notice from claiming compensation under the scheme detailed below or from rescinding a contract of sale on discovering a land charge not known of at the date of the contract.[27]

(b) *Names register.* The most serious defect of the system from the point of view of a purchaser is that the registers are registers of the names of persons; an incumbrance is registered against the name of the estate owner at the time and not against the land. Thus on a purchase of 14 Newcastle Street it is not possible to search against 14 Newcastle Street, and a search must be made against the names of all previous owners of the land. The rights most likely to concern a purchaser, namely, Classes C and D, only became registrable after 1925, but in course of time the cost of searches may become

[22] L.C.A. 1972, ss. 5 (4), 6 (2).
[23] *Ibid.* s. 7 (1).
[24] *Diligent Finance Co. Ltd.* v. *Alleyne* (1972) 23 P. & C.R. 346; Class F charge registered against Erskine Alleyne void against mortgagee who searched against Erskine Owen Alleyne (the full name in the title deeds) and obtained clear search certificate.
[25] See *Oak Co-operative B.S.* v. *Blackburn* [1968] Ch. 730, See *post,* p. 105, for searches.
[26] L.P.A. 1969, s. 25 (2).
[27] L.P.A. 1969, s. 24 removing the difficulty arising from *Re Forsey & Hollebone's Contract* [1927] 2 Ch. 379.

considerable. It assists if each purchaser in turn preserves the certificate of the search he made when puchasing the land, and hands the certificates on with the title deeds so that the subsequent owners can rely upon them.

(c) *Compensation scheme.* In 1955, when thirty years had elapsed since 1925, the possibility arose that the names of persons against whom charges were registered might lie behind the root of title. The situation was aggravated in 1969 when the length of title was reduced to fifteen years.[28] A purchaser may be unable to discover the relevant names, but yet will be deemed to have actual notice of the charges registered against them. As it is now impossible to reorganise the registers on a territorial basis, the only long-term solution is to press on with registration of title, and this is taking place.[29] As an interim measure financial compensation at public expense was introduced for purchasers saddled with registered but undisclosed land charges. The two main requirements are that the purchaser should not have any actual knowledge of the charge (the deemed actual notice from registration is disregarded), and that the estate owner against whom the charge is registered should not be a party to any transaction in the relevant title or be concerned with any event in it.[30]

(d) *Lessees.* The doctrine that registration constitutes notice *per se* may work especial hardship in the case of lessees. Where a lease is granted by a tenant in fee simple at a low rent in consideration of a fine, the lessee usually stipulates that he shall be entitled to investigate the lessor's title, whereas if the lease is granted at a rack rent, the lessee usually takes it for granted that the lessor is able to grant it and so does not investigate his title. Further, by statute,[31] under an open contract[32] to grant a lease the lessee is not entitled to investigate the freeholder's title. In *Patman* v. *Harland*[33] it was held that since a lessee under an open contract might have made a special contract entitling him to investigate the lessor's title, he was fixed with notice of all that he would have discovered had he made a proper investigation.

The rule in *Patman* v. *Harland*, which caused some hardship and was much criticised, has been abolished for all leases made after 1925. However, the provisions for the registration of land charges such as restrictive covenants made after 1925 have created a new difficulty due to registration being effected against the name of the person making the covenant and not against the land. A prospective lessee will be able to search against the name of the lessor, but if he

[28] L.P.A. 1969, s. 23.
[29] See Report of Committee on Land Charges 1956 (Cmd. 9825).
[30] L.P.A. 1969, s. 25.
[31] L.P.A. 1925, s. 44, replacing Vendor and Purchaser Act 1874, s. 2.
[32] *Post*, p. 146.
[33] (1881) 17 Ch.D. 353.

does not expressly contract for investigation of the lessor's title he will not know the names of the previous owners of the land and so will not be able to discover restrictive covenants registered against their names. Nevertheless, registration is notice to all persons and for all purposes connected with the land,[34] and so the lessee is deemed to have notice of the covenants. He is, moreover, excluded from the compensation scheme.[35] The position may be summarised thus:

(i) Lease and restrictive covenant both made after 1925: the lessee is caught by the provisions for registration.
(ii) Restrictive covenant made before 1926, lease made after 1925: the lessee is safe unless he has notice in some other way, for *Patman* v. *Harland* does not apply and the restrictive covenant, being made before 1926, is not registrable.[36]

2. Effect of non-registration. The effect of non-registration varies according to the interest and only concerns third parties and not the original contracting parties. There are two main categories:

(a) The incumbrance may be void against a purchaser for value of any interest in the land; or
(b) The incumbrance may be void against a purchaser for money or money's worth of a legal estate in the land.

One difference between (a) and (b) is that a purchaser of an equitable interest is protected by (a) but not by (b). Another is that marriage is "value" but is not "money or money's worth,"[37] and so in the case of land settled on an ante-nuptial marriage settlement the spouses and issue will be protected by (a) but not by (b). In each case "purchaser" has an extended meaning and includes a lessee, mortgageee or other person taking an interest in land for value.

The effect of non-registration may be expressed as follows.[38]

(i) In general, whichever register is concerned, non-registration of any registrable matter in the appropriate register makes it void against a purchaser for value of any interest in the land. It may thus be that the purchase for value of an option might be a means of protection against the subsequent registration of a Class F charge before the purchase of the legal estate.
(ii) If, however, a land charge falls within Class C (iv) (estate contracts) or Class D, and was created after 1925, non-registration makes it void only against a purchaser of a legal estate for money or money's worth. To determine whether a

[34] L.P.A. 1925, s. 198. See *White* v. *Bijou Mansions* [1937] Ch. 610 at p. 619 where Simmonds J. points out that s. 198 prevails over s. 44 (5) L.P.A.
[35] L.P.A. 1969, s. 25 (9) and also (10), for definition of "registered land charge." Assignees have the same problems as lessees: L.P.A. 1925, s. 44 (2), (3).
[36] See, *e.g. Shears* v. *Wells* [1936] 1 All E.R. 832.
[37] *Midland Bank Trust Co.* v. *Green* [1981] A.C. 513 at p. 531.
[38] L.C.A. 1972, ss. 4, 5 (7), (8), 6 (4), (5), (6), 7 (2), 1st Sched., para. 4.

purchaser for marriage consideration is bound resort will have to be made to the equitable doctrine of notice since the Act is silent on the matter.[39]

(iii) Bankruptcy petitions (registrable as pending actions) and receiving orders (registrable as writs and orders) are void only against a bona fide purchaser of a legal estate for money or money's worth without notice of an available act of bankruptcy, *i.e.* an act of bankruptcy not more than three months old.

(iv) Any other pending action is void against a purchaser for value of any interest in the land, provided he had no express notice of it.

It will thus be seen that with the comparatively unimportant exceptions of (iii) and (iv) above, actual knowledge is immaterial. Section 199 of the Law of Property Act 1925 provides that where an interest is void against a purchaser under the Land Charges Act, he shall not be affected by notice thereof. Thus it is immaterial that the purchaser bought with actual knowledge of the unregistered interest[40]; the effect of registration and non-registration is automatic. It should be noted that the crucial time in each case is the completion of the transaction, *i.e.* the purchase of the legal estate or the equitable interest, as the case may be; subsequent registration cannot revive an interest that has been invalidated for non-registration at the time of a purchase.[41]

Where there has not been the purchase of a legal or equitable interest, as the case may be, to make an unregistered land charge void, then priorities of competing equitable interests (such as two estate contracts) must be determined on general equitable principles in the absence of statutory guidance.[42]

The Act does not state that land charges shall rank in order of registration as land charges (except for mortgages registered as Class C (i) or C (iii) charges[43]) but only states that unregistered land charges shall be void against purchasers of a legal or equitable interest as the case may be.[44] An estate contract is only void if not registered before the purchase of the legal estate for money or money's worth,[45] so what happens if X enters into a contract of purchase, then Y enters into a contract of purchase, then Y enters a Class C (iv) land charge, then X enters a C (iv) land charge, so that neither X nor Y has purchased the legal estate?

---

[39] *Cf. McCarthy & Stone Ltd.* v. *Hodge* [1971] 1 W.L.R. 1547, and in a registered land context, *Barclays Bank* v. *Taylor* [1974] Ch. 137.

[40] See *Hollington Bros. Ltd.* v. *Rhodes* [1951] 2 T.L.R. 691, *Midland Bank Trust Co.* v. *Green* [1981] A.C. 513.

[41] *Kitney* v. *M.E.P.C. Ltd.* [1978] 1 All. E.R. 595 at pp. 599, 601, 605, *Hollington Bros. Ltd.* v. *Rhodes* [1951] 2 All E.R. 578 at p. 580.

[42] *McCarthy & Stone Ltd.* v. *Hodge* [1971] 1 W.L.R. 1547, *Barclays Bank* v. *Taylor* (1974) Ch. 137, Hayton [1976] Current Legal Problems 26.

[43] L.P.A. 1925, s. 97.

[44] L.C.A. 1972, s. 4.

[45] *Ibid.* s. 4 (6).

In the absence of statutory guidance X's estate contract as first in time will have priority over Y's later contract unless X's fraud or negligence estops him from claiming priority.[46] If X's contract is an ordinary contract to purchase property it is not conveyancing practice to enter a C (iv) charge: since completion of the contract usually takes place four to five weeks after the date of the contract unnecessary expense and trouble would be caused if a C (iv) charge were entered and then a few weeks later removed. Thus, absence of a C (iv) entry should not lead anyone searching the register to believe that no estate contract subsists. In any event, it is not conveyancing practice to search the register before entering into a contract, so Y could not submit that X's conduct in not entering a C (iv) charge had induced Y to enter into his contract. X is thus entitled to the property free from Y's interest.[47]

3. Companies. If a charge registrable in the Companies Register is not duly registered, it is in addition void as a security as against the liquidator and all creditors of the company, and the money becomes immediately payable: Companies Act 1948, s. 95.

D. Vacation of the Register

A land charge can obviously be a blot on an owner's title and can paralyse any dealings by the owner. Some entries of land charges may be unjustified especially since, if the appropriate form is received, the Land Registry officials automatically make the requisite entry without attempting to ascertain whether there is a valid interest to justify the entry.[48] It is also possible that an estate contract has terminated by expiry of time or by rescision by the vendor.

Accordingly, the court has a wide statutory[49] and inherent[50] jurisdiction to order the vacation of an entry *i.e.* the removal of an entry. This jurisdiction can be exercised speedily on motion and with a certain robustness[51] without awaiting the trial of the action. In an appropriate case, it seems that the court will only allow the entry to remain if the maker of the entry undertakes to pay the landowner any damages suffered if, at the trial of the action, it transpires that the entry was wrongly made, *e.g.* because no estate contract had ever existed or because it had been properly rescinded.[52]

---

[46] *Ante*, p. 70.
[47] Further see Hayton [1976] *Current Legal Problems* 26.
[48] Land Charge Rules 5 & 6.
[49] L.C.A. 1972, s. 1 (6) with additional powers under s. 5 (10) where pending actions have been registered but are not being prosecuted in good faith: *Northern Developments* v. *U.D.T. Securities* [1977] 1 All E.R. 747.
[50] *Calgary & Edmonton Land Co. Ltd.* v. *Dobinson* [1974] Ch. 102.
[51] *Rawplug Co. Ltd.* v. *Kamvale Properties Ltd.* (1968) 20 P. & C.R. 32.
[52] *Cf. Tiverton Estates Ltd.* v. *Wearwell Ltd.* [1975] Ch. 146, *Clearbrook Property Holdings Ltd.* v. *Verrier* [1974] 1 W.L.R. 243.

E. Searches and Priority Notices

1. Searches. The means by which an intending purchaser of land can discover registrable incumbrances is by a search. This may be made in person, but it is advisable to obtain an official certificate of search, for—

(i) it is conclusive in favour of a purchaser or intending purchaser whose application correctly specifies the persons[53] and the land,[54] and so frees him from liability for registered rights which it fails to disclose[55];

(ii) it protects a solicitor or trustee who makes it from liability for any error in the certificate[56]; and

(iii) it provides protection against incumbrances registered in the interval between search and completion. If a purchaser completes his transaction before the expiration of the fifteenth day after the date of the certificate (excluding days on which the registry is not open to the public), he is not affected by any entry made after the date of the certificate and before completion, unless it is made pursuant to a priority notice[57] entered on the register before the certificate was issued.[58]

The official certificate of search is conclusive in favour of purchasers or intending purchasers[59] so if it mistakenly fails to mention a charge properly registered before the search, the owner of the charge will be unjustly deprived of his rights and may suffer loss. It seems that damages for negligence can be obtained against a negligent Registry employee and that the Crown may be vicariously liable[60] except where the loss arises from a discrepancy between the particulars in the search application and the particulars shown in the official search certificate as being the particulars in respect of which the search was made.[61]

A single search is effective for all divisions of all registers.

2. Priority notices. Special provision has been made to provide for a rapid sequence of transactions, such as the creation of a restrictive covenant followed immediately by the creation of a mortgage before there has been time to register the covenant. Thus if V is selling land to P, who is raising the purchase-money by means of a loan on

---

[53] See *Oak Co-operative Building Society* v. *Blackburn* [1968] Ch. 730; *ante*, p. 100.
[54] See *Du Sautoy* v. *Symes* [1967] Ch. 1146.
[55] L.C.A. 1972, s. 10 (4): see *Stock* v. *Wanstead and Woodford B.C.* [1962] 2 Q.B. 479 (local land charge).
[56] L.C.A. 1972, s. 12.
[57] See *infra*.
[58] L.C.A. 1972, s. 11 (5), (6).
[59] L.C.A., s. 10 (4).
[60] *Cf. Ministry of Housing and Local Government* v. *Sharp* [1970] 2 Q.B. 223 (local land charge).
[61] L.C.A., s. 10 (6).

mortgage from M, and is to enter into a restrictive covenant with V, the sequence of events will be—

(i) conveyance from V to P, reserving the restrictive covenant, followed a few minutes later by
(ii) mortgage by P to M.

In such a case, V's restrictive covenant could not be registered in the few minutes between its creation and the making of the mortgage, and so it will be void against M, a purchaser for money or money's worth of a legal estate, unless V has availed himself of the machinery of the priority notice. To do this, he must give a priority notice to the registrar at least fifteen days before the creation of the restrictive covenant, and then, if he registers his charge within thirty days of the entry of the priority notice in the register, the registration dates back to the moment of the creation of the restrictive covenant, *i.e.* to the execution of the conveyance from V to P; once again, days on which the registry is not open to the public are excluded.[62] It will be noted that the notice must be give 15 days before completion; this is to allow the expiry of the 15 days' period of protection given to those who made official searches before the priority notice was lodged.

Priority notices are not, of course, confined to restrictive covenants, but apply to all land charges.

Sect. 3. Local Land Charges Registers

In addition to the registers kept by the Land Charges Department of the Land Registry, registers of local land charges are kept by each district council and also by each London Borough and the Common Council of the City of London[63] These registers differ from those kept at the Land Registry in Plymouth in that the charges are registered against the land itself and not against the owner of it. Thus a series of searches against successive owners is unnecessary. The searches should be made before entry into any contract to purchase land.[64]

The interests registrable are any charges acquired by any local authority by statute. Many widely differing matters are registrable,[65] though in general they may be classified as financial, restrictive or acquisitive; and they have the general nature of being public rights, whereas the land charges registers are essentially registers of private rights. A few examples of local land charges are: charges for making up a road imposed in respect of land fronting the road, and charges for sanitary works; prohibitions or restrictions on the use of land,[66]

---

[62] *Ibid.* s. 11.
[63] Local Land Charges Act 1975.
[64] This avoids the problems created by *Re Forsey & Hollebone's Contract* [1927] 2 Ch. 379.
[65] See, generally, Garner, *Local Land Charges* (8th ed., 1978).
[66] Restrictive covenants are not local land changes.

whether under planning law or otherwise (*e.g.* "building lines," preventing any building nearer a road than the prescribed line); and certain proceedings for compulsory acquisition.

Section 10 of the Local Land Charges Act 1975 reversed the former position[67] so that failure to register a local land charge does not now affect the enforcement of the charge. However, a purchaser is entitled to compensation for any loss suffered by him by reason that the charge was not registered or was not shown as registered by an official search certificate.

Sect. 4. Overreachable Interests

1. Settlements. Where it is desired to give land to persons in succession, *e.g.* to A for life, and then to B for life and then to C in fee simple, two methods are available, namely, the strict settlement and the trust for sale. Under the strict settlement (often called merely a "settlement" and the land "settled land") the legal estate and the control over the land is normally vested in the tenant for life, A: under the trust for sale the trustees have the legal estate and control the land. In each case, if the land is sold, the rights of the beneficiaries are "overreached," *i.e.* they are transferred from the land to the purchase-money, which is paid to trustees. This is independent of any question of notice; provided the purchaser pays the money to the trustees (who must be either not less than two in number or a trust corporation[68]) he takes the land free from the claims of the beneficiaries. Although the beneficiaries lose any prospect of enjoying the land itself, they are not defrauded in any way, for they have corresponding interests in the purchase-money. This distinguishes overreaching from an interest being overridden, *i.e.* being void against a purchaser without notice, or for want of registration: if an interest is overreached it is transferred from the land to money in the hands of trustees; if an interest is overridden, it ceases to be enforceable.

2. Co-ownership and intestacy. Since 1926 trusts for sale have been imposed by statute on an intestate's property,[69] the better to enable it to be sold and the proceeds distributed amongst the next-of-kin, and on co-owned land,[70] the better to enable the legal and beneficial ownership to be transferred to a purchaser. In so many cases is the legal or equitable interest co-owned that there has been a dramatic increase in the number of overreachable interests. So long as the purchaser pays the money to at least two trustees for sale or trust corporation he takes the land free from the interests of the

---

[67] L.C.A. 1925, s. 15.
[68] L.P.A. 1925, s. 27 (2); T.A. 1925, s. 14; S.L.A. 1925, s. 18 (1).
[69] A.E.A. 1925, ss. 46, 47.
[70] L.P.A. 1925, ss. 34, 35, 36.

beneficiaries even if he has actual notice of such interests.[71] If the overreaching machinery of payment to two trustees or a trust corporation is not utilised, as where a vendor purports to sell as sole beneficial owner, having the title deeds in his name alone (despite contribution of a quarter of the purchase price by C who thereby becomes a co-owner in equity) then a beneficiary's interest may be overriden if the purchaser is a bona fide purchaser of the legal estate for value without notice.[72]

3. Other overreaching conveyances. Although settlements and trusts for sale are the most important sources of overreaching conveyances, they are not the only sources. Thus if X has mortgaged his land to M, and then fails to pay the interest, M has a statutory power to sell the estate which X mortgaged to him (even though it is not vested in M), free from X's equitable right to redeem it. X's rights will then be transferred to the purchase-money in M's hands, for M is a trustee for X of any surplus after discharging the mortgage.[73] Again, a conveyance by personal representatives will overreach the claims of the beneficiaries under the will or intestacy.[74] A further example of an overreaching conveyance is one made under an order of the court where any capital money arising from the transaction is paid into, or in accordance with the order of, the court.[75]

In general, only equitable rights can now be overreached; with few exceptions, such as a mortgagee's power to overreach the legal interests of the mortgagor and subsequent mortgagees on exercising his power of sale, there is no power to overreach legal rights.[76]

Sect. 5. The Residuary Role of the Doctrine of Notice

Certain equitable interests, that one might have expected to be registrable under the Land Charges Act or to be overreachable under the Settled Land Act or the Law of Property Act, are neither registrable nor overreachable, so resort has to be had to the equitable doctrine of notice as a long-stop to determine the position. Sometimes this is by design, sometimes by accident.

Such equitable interests may be enumerated as follows.

1. Equitable mortgages protected by deposit of title deeds with the mortgagee. Normally,[77] such interests will be easily discoverable by a purchaser.
2. Restrictive covenants made between a lessor and a lessee.

---

[71] L.P.A. 1925, s. 27.
[72] *Caunce* v. *Caunce* [1969] 1 W.L.R. 286, *Williams & Glyn's Bank* v. *Boland* [1979] Ch. 312.
[73] L.P.A. 1925, s. 105.
[74] A.E.A. 1925, s. 36 (8); S.L.A. ss. 13, 18.
[75] L.P.A. 1925, ss. 2, 50.
[76] See *post*, pp. 476 *et seq.*
[77] Problems may exist if the purchaser of a lease is not entitled to see the superior title due to L.P.A. 1925, s. 44 (2), (3), (4), (5).

Normally,[78] such interests will be easily discoverable by a purchaser, *e.g.* where set out in the lease.

3. Restrictive covenants and equitable easements created before 1926, since it was not feasible to require registration of such interests by having expropriatory legislation making such interests void if not registered within a given period.
4. Equitable rights of entry as in *Shiloh Spinners Ltd.* v. *Harding*[79]
5. The equitable right of the owner of a hired fixture to remove it if the hirer breaks the contract of hire.[80]
6. Equitable proprietary estoppel interests as in *Ives Investment Ltd.* v. *High*.[81]
7. Equitable interests under bare trusts[82] as where A holds the legal estate on trust for B who is *sui juris*.

   Where an equitable interest is registrable under the Land Charges Act or is overreachable there is still scope for the application of the doctrine of notice in those situations not precisely covered by the statutory provisions. Thus there are two further areas covered by the doctrine of notice.

8. Where the Land Charges Act does not specifically provide what is to happen where a land charge has not been registered then the doctrine of notice applies. Thus where an estate contract Class C (iv) land charge is, if unregistered, void against a purchaser of a legal estate for money or money's worth, then if the land were purchased for marriage consideration (which is value but not money or money's worth) the equitable doctrine of notice will, it seems, determine whether or not the purchaser is bound by the unregistered estate contract.[83]
9. Where the statutory overreaching provisions in the Settled Land Act or the Law of Property Act do not specifically provide what is to happen when the statutory overreaching machinery has not been complied with (*e.g.* as to payment to two trustees or a trust corporation) then the doctrine of notice applies. Thus, if H holds the legal estate in his sole name but really holds it on trust for sale for H and W in equal shares, owing to W having contributed half the cost of the house, and P purchases the house from H, paying H alone the purchase price, whether or not P is bound by W's equitable interest will depend upon the doctrine of notice.[84]

---

[78] Problems may exist if the covenants relate not to the land leased but to adjoining land of the lessor: *cf. Dartstone Ltd.* v. *Cleveland Petroleum Co. Ltd.* [1969] 1 W.L.R. 1807.
[79] [1973] A.C. 691.
[80] *Poster* v. *Slough Estates Ltd.* [1969] 1 Ch. 495.
[81] [1967] 2 Q.B. 379.
[82] A has no discretion, he must obey B.
[83] *Cf. McCarthy & Stone Ltd.* v. *Hodge Ltd.* [1971] 1 W.L.R. 1547, [1976] Current Legal Problems 26 (D.J. Hayton).
[84] *Caunce* v. *Caunce* [1969] 1 W.L.R. 286; (1969) 33 Conv. 240 (J.F. Garner); *Williams & Glyn's Bank* v. *Boland* [1981] A.C. 487 though the latter case indicates that there should have been constructive notice of the wife in the former case. Since there are so many working wives who are likely to have acquired an interest in the matrimonial home it is reasonable to inquire whether she has such interest.

Sect. 6. A Summary Classification of Interests in Unregistered Land

It may be useful to classify interests in unregistered land as follows:

1. Legal Estates. These are the basic units of land law conferring full rights of use and enjoyment.
2. Legal Mortgages (otherwise known as legal charges).
   Whilst less than a legal estate, a legal mortgage confers on the mortgagee, if the mortgagor defaults, a right to sell the legal estate over the head of the mortgagor, whose rights are overreached and transferred to such of the proceeds of sale in the mortgagee's hands as are not needed to pay off the mortgage debt. As a legal interest a legal mortgage is a right *in rem* which binds everyone, irrespective of notice. Exceptionally, certain legal mortgages or charges which otherwise could well be undiscoverable by a purchaser have to be registered under the Land Charges Act if they are to bind a purchaser. These comprise legal mortgages not protected by deposit of title deeds with the mortgagee, charges arising under the Finance Act 1975 for payment of capital transfer tax and certain charges arising under the Agricultural Holdings Act or the Legal Aid Act.
3. Legal Interests. This class comprises easements, profits, rent-charges and rights of entry, enduring for a period corresponding to the two legal estates, and which are legal if created by deed and, as such, are rights *in rem* binding everyone irrespective of notice.
4. Equitable Interests Registrable under the Land Charges Act. When registered such interests bind everyone, irrespective of notice; if unregistered such interests do not bind a purchaser, irrespective of notice.
5. Equitable Interests Overreachable under the Settled Land Act or the Law of Property Act. So long as the overreaching machinery is complied with by a purchaser, notice of the equitable interests is immaterial.
6. Equitable Interests that are covered neither by the Land Charges Act nor by the overreaching provisions. These remain fully subject to the equitable doctrine of notice which is available even to cover unintentional lacunae in statutory provisions.

SUMMARY SHOWING EFFECT OF A SALE OF LAND ON LEGAL AND EQUITABLE
RIGHTS OVER IT

1. The purchaser takes subject to all legal rights.

Exceptions: He takes free from—

(a) the very few legal rights which are void against him for want of registration; and
(b) the very few legal rights which are overreached.

2. The purchaser takes subject to all equitable rights.

Exceptions: He takes free from—

(a) equitable rights which are void against him for want of registration: notice is irrelevant;
(b) the many equitable rights which are overreached, *e.g.* under a settlement or trust for sale: again, notice is irrelevant; and
(c) those equitable rights which are neither registrable nor overreachable in respect of which he can show that he is equity's darling or a successor in title thereto;
(d) those equitable rights which are either registrable or overreachable, but where the circumstances are not precisely covered by the statutory registration or overreaching provisions, if he can show that he is equity's darling or a successor in title thereto.

Part 3

THE STRUCTURE OF REGISTERED LAND LAW

Sect. 1. Introductory

1. History. Today, registration of title is of great and increasing importance; but it is by no means new. Acts were passed in 1862 and 1875,[85] providing for voluntary registration of title, but not until the Land Transfer Act 1897 made registration of title compulsory on dealings with land in the County of London were any substantial number of titles registered. The present principal Act is the Land Registration Act 1925, which has been amended by the Land Registration Act 1936, the Land Registration Act 1966, the Land Registration and Land Charges Act 1971, the Administration of Justice Act 1977 and the Housing Act 1980. These Acts are supplemented by the Land Registration Rules 1925, as amended, and a number of other statutory rules. Three quarters of the work of conveyancing is estimated to concern registered land so that this has become an important branch of the law.[86]

2. Basis of the system. The basic idea is to replace the separate investigation of title that takes place on every purchase by a title guaranteed by the State. In the case of unregistered land, a purchaser must satisfy himself from the abstract or epitome of title, the deeds, his requisitions on title, his searches and his inspection of the land

---

[85] Land Registry Act 1862; Land Transfer Act 1875.
[86] Ruoff & Roper, *Registered Conveyancing*, (4th ed.) is the standard practitioners' reference book; otherwise see Hayton, *Registered Land* (3rd ed). The most recent registered land figures are in the Report to the Chancellor on H.M. Land Registry for the year 1980–1981.

that the vendor has power to sell the land and that it is subject to no undisclosed incumbrances. In the case of registered land, on the other hand, the purchaser can discover from the mere inspection of the register whether the vendor has power to sell the land and what the more important incumbrances are; the other incumbrances must be investigated in much the same way as in the case of unregistered land. It can be said that the register acts as a mirror reflecting fully and accurately the current facts material to the title except for what are known as "overriding interests." The complexity of rights in land is such as to render it impossible to make the transfer of registered land as simple as the transfer of shares registered in the books of a company, but the present system of registration of title may be said to go almost as far on that road as is practicable.

3. Classification of rights. The system of registration of title in no way amounts to a separate code of land law. In the main it is concerned with the conveyancing aspects of land law, *i.e.* actual or potential transfers of rights existing under the general law, and, generally, it leaves the main basis of this unaffected. In this connection, the differing classes of interests in land must be distinguished.

(a) *Unregistered land.* The classification of interests in unregistered land that emerged[87] is sixfold: (1) legal estates (2) legal mortgages (3) legal interests (4) equitable interests registrable under the Land Charges Act which, when so protected, bind a purchaser irrespective of notice and which, if unprotected, do not bind a purchaser irrespective of notice (5) equitable interests that are overreachable, irrespective of notice, and (6) equitable interests covered neither by the Land Charges Act nor by the overreaching provisions and which remain fully subject to the doctrine of notice.

(b) *Registered land.* In registered land there is a similar division but the types of interests falling into each class do not correspond exactly and, most remarkably of all, interests in registered land may in some circumstances fall into one class but in other circumstances fall into another class, *e.g.* where someone with a minor interest is in actual occupation of registered land when he may protect his interest by entry on the register or, instead, rely on his actual occupation entitling him to an overriding interest.[88]

The classification of interests in registered land that emerges is: (1) registered estates (fees simple and leases exceeding 21 years); (2) registered charges (legal mortgages); (3) overriding interests, which by definition[89] are interests not protected by entry on the register and which override purchasers like rights *in rem* and include rights under

[87] *Ante*, p. 110.
[88] *Williams & Glyn's Bank* v. *Boland* [1981] A.C. 487.
[89] L.R.A., s. 3 (xvi).

the Limitation Act or the Prescription Act and rights (whether legal or equitable) of persons in actual occupation or in receipt of rents and profits, save where inquiry is made of such person and such rights are not disclosed; (4) minor interests capable of being protected by entry of a notice or caution on the register, which are secure when so protected but which, if unprotected, do not bind a purchaser, irrespective of the doctrine of notice, and which comprise interests that in unregistered land would be registrable under the Land Charges Act; (5) minor interests capable of being overreached even when protected by entry of a restriction on the register and which comprise interests of beneficiaries under trusts for sale or under settlements.

In the registered land system there is no scope for a sixth class of interest dependent upon the new registered proprietor having actual or constructive notice of such interest. He takes the legal estate subject to entries on the register and to overriding interests but otherwise free from all other interests whatsoever[90]: this is the cardinal principle of registered land. As Lord Wilberforce stated in *Williams & Glyn's Bank* v. *Boland*,[91] when speaking of a purchaser of registered land, "In place of the lengthy and often technical investigation of title to which a purchaser [of unregistered land] was committed, all he has to do is consult the register; from any burden not entered on the register, with one exception [overriding interests], he takes free. Above all, the system is designed to free the purchaser from the hazards of notice, real or constructive, which in the case of unregistered land, involved him in inquiries, often quite elaborate. The Law of Property Act 1925 contains provisions limiting the effect of the doctrine of notice, but it still remains a potential source of danger to purchasers. By contrast, the only provisions in the Land Registration Act with regard to notice are provisions which enable a purchaser to take the estate free from equitable interests or equities whether he has notice or not (see, *e.g.* s. 3 (xv)). The only kind of notice recognised is by entry on the register. The exception just mentioned consists of 'overriding interests' listed in s.70. As to these all registered land is stated to be deemed to be subject to such of them as may be subsisting in reference to the land. The land is so subject regardless of notice actual or constructive. In my opinion, therefore, the law as to notice as it may affect purchasers of unregistered land has no application even by analogy to registered land."

(c) *The cardinal principles of registered land.* Whereas in unregistered land a legal fee simple or lease or mortgage or easement is transferred or created as soon as the relevant deed has been signed sealed and delivered, in registered land the legal interest only passes

---

[90] L.R.A., ss. 3 (xv), 5, 9, 20, 23, 59 (6), 74.
[91] [1981] A.C. 487 at p. 503.

when the disposition has been completed by the statutory magic of registration.[92] Thus the purchaser of a fee simple only acquires the legal estate when he becomes registered as proprietor, which occurs when the relevant documents have been delivered to the relevant District Land Registry.[93]

Once a purchaser becomes registered proprietor then he takes a good title subject only to then subsisting entries on the register and overriding interests (which override like legal interests in unregistered land) but free from everything else.[94] The registered land equivalent of "Equity's darling," the bona fide purchaser of an unregistered legal estate for value without notice, is thus a purchaser under a registered disposition for value without there being any entry on the register: he may be termed the "Registrar's darling."

The act of registration itself confers title on the new registered proprietor (subject to any claim for rectification of the register[95]) even though on unregistered land principles he might have no title at all[96] *e.g.* where deriving title under a forgery which, as a nullity, leaves title in the victim of the forgery.

4. Other registrations. If the title to land is registered, there is no question of registration in the Land Charges Department, for entries on the Land Register take the place of this. But entries must still be made on the local land charges registers.[97] Further, most charges created by a company for securing money require registration in the Comapnies Register in addition to protection by an entry on the Land Register.[98]

5. Privacy. Unlike the registers of land charges, the Land Register is not open to inspection by the public. In general, nobody can inspect it without the authority of the registered proprietor.[99] But an Index Map and a Parcels Index are open to public inspection, as also is a list of pending applications, and from these it can be discovered whether or not any particular property has been or is about to be registered.

Sect. 2. Registered Estates

The four types of interest in registered land (namely, registered

---

[92] This requires noting of the interest against the burdened title in the case of leases, mortgages and easements.
[93] Rule 83 (2).
[94] L.R.A. 1925, ss. 5, 9, 20, 23, 59 (6), 74 *Re Boyle's Claim* [1961] 1 W.L.R. 339, *Freer v. Unwins Ltd.* [1976] Ch. 288.
[95] L.R.A., s. 82, *post* p. 532.
[96] *Morelle* v. *Wakeling* [1955] 2 Q.B. 379 at p. 411, *Att-Gen* v. *Parsons* [1956] A.C. 421 at p. 441, *Haigh's Case* (pp. 85–86 of Hayton, *Registered Land*, 3rd ed.); L.R.A. 1925, ss. 20, 23, 33, 69, 75, *Spectrum Investment Co.* v. *Holmes* (1981) 1 All E.R. 6.
[97] See p. 106 *ante*, and L.R.A. 1925, s. 70 (1) (*i*).
[98] Companies Act 1948, s. 95; [1982] Conv. 43 (Hare and Flanagan).
[99] L.R.A. 1925, ss. 112, 112(A).

estates, registered charges, overriding interests and minor interests) will now be considered in turn.

1. Estates which can be registered. After 1925, the only estates in respect of which a proprietor can be registered are estates capable of subsisting as legal estates.[1] Thus a fee simple absolute in possession and (with certain exceptions[2]) a term of years absolute exceeding 21 years (to prevent short leases cluttering up the Land Register) are registrable estates.

2. The register. The register itself is divided into three parts:

(a) *The property register.* This describes the land and the estate for which it is held, refers to a map or plan showing the land, and contains notes of interests held for the *benefit* of the land, such as easements or restrictive covenants of which the registered land is the dominant tenement and other like matters. The boundaries shown on the map are general and are not so exact as to show which side of a hedge or fence they run unless stated by the register to be "fixed."[3]

(b) *The proprietorship register.* This states the nature of the title (*i.e.* whether it is absolute, good leasehold, qualified or possessory[4]), states the name, address and description of the registered proprietor, and sets out any cautions, inhibitions and restrictions[5] affecting his right to deal with the land.

(c) *The charges register.* This contains entries relating to rights *adverse* to the land, such as mortgages or restrictive covenants, and in general all notices[6] protecting rights over the land.

The register is kept at the appropriate District Land Registry. The Land Registry has its headquarters in London but has been decentralised. The three parts of the register in respect of each property are kept together. A copy of these entries is included in the "Land Certificate," and is given to each registered proprietor as his document of title for retention until he sells or charges the land.[7] The title deeds, stamped with a notice of registration, are also usually returned when the title is first registered. But the registered proprietor's proof of title is the register itself and not the Land Certificate, which may well be out of date owing to entries having been made in the register since the certificate was last in the registry.

[1] L.R.A., s.2.
[2] See *post*, pp. 116, 139.
[3] L.R.A. 1925, s. 76; L.R. Rules 1925, r. 278; *Lee* v. *Barrey* [1957] Ch. 251.
[4] See *post*, p. 117.
[5] *Post*, p. 126.
[6] See *post*, p. 125.
[7] See *post*, pp. 121, 156.

3. Compulsory and voluntary registration. (a) *The areas.* The compulsory areas are being continually extended. They are mostly urban, so that although they include over three quarters of the population of the country, they are not much more than half its area.[8] If land is in a compulsory area, that does not mean that the title to it must be registered in any event; registration is compulsory only on a conveyance on sale of the fee simple, or the creation or assignment on sale of certain leases.

(b) *Leases.* The position as to leaseholds, which is a little complicated, may be summarised as follows.[9]

(1) REGISTRATION PROHIBITED. The registration of a lease is prohibited, even if the land is in a compulsory area, if the lease—

(i) was granted for a term of 21 years or less; or
(ii) contains an absolute prohibition against assignment; or
(iii) is a mortgage term still subject to a right of redemption.

(2) REGISTRATION COMPULSORY. The registration of a lease not falling under any of the above heads is compulsory—

(i) if the land is in a compulsory area and the transaction consists of the grant of a lease for 40 years or more, or the assignment on sale of a lease with 40 or more years unexpired; or
(ii) if the title to the freehold or leasehold out of which the lease is granted has been registered, and the transaction consists of the grant of a lease for more than 21 years, whether or not the land is in a compulsory area. This rule springs from the requirement that dispositions by a registered proprietor must themselves be registered; for the grant of a lease is a "disposition."

(3) REGISTRATION OPTIONAL. The registration of any other lease of land in a compulsory area is optional, *e.g.* a lease for 30 years granted by a freeholder whose title is not registered.

(c) *Non-registration.* Where registration is compulsory because the land is in a compulsory area, the purchaser is divested of the legal estate (which will revest in the vendor as a bare trustee) unless application for registration is made within two months, or such extended period as the registrar (or the court) allows.[10] Where registration is compulsory because the lessor's title is registered, no legal estate passes until registration and no time limit applies.[11]

(d) *Voluntary registration.* Since 1966 applications to register titles to land outside the compulsory areas will not be entertained except in

---

[8] The Land Registry issues a free list of the current areas.
[9] L.R.A. 1925, ss. 8, 18, 19, 123.
[10] L.R.A. 1925, s. 123. The Registrar, however, is always willing to allow this whenever some quite ordinary but reasonable excuse for the delay is put forward.
[11] *Ibid.* ss. 19, 22.

very limited classes of cases as the Registrar has specified[12] (*e.g.* building estates consisting of 20 or more plots) and where council houses are sold to tenants under the Housing Act 1980.[13]

4. Titles. There are four classes of title with which an applicant for registration may be registered.

(a) *Absolute.* In the case of freeholds, this vests in the first registered proprietor the fee simple in possession together with all rights and privileges (*e.g.* easements) belonging thereto subject only to—

   (i) entries on the register;
   (ii) overriding interests, except so far as the register states that the land is free from them; and
   (iii) as between himself and those entitled to minor interests, to minor interests of which he has notice, if he is not entitled to the land for his own benefit; thus trustees for sale who are registered as proprietors will still hold subject to the claims of the beneficiaries.[14]

In the case of leaseholds, an absolute title vests the leasehold in the first registered proprietor subject to the rights set out above and in addition to—

   (iv) all the covenants, obligations and liabilities incident to the lease.[15]

An absolute title in the case of leaseholds guarantees not only that the registered proprietor is the owner of the lease but also that the lease was validly granted. Incumbrances affecting the superior title will also appear on the leasehold title so a purchaser of the lease will know of the incumbrances that bind him, unlike the unregistered land position when the purchaser may be bound by incumbrances affecting the superior title which he cannot investigate.[16]

(b) *Qualified.* In the case of freeholds, this has the same effect as an absolute title except that the property is held subject to some defect or right specified in the register. This title is granted when an absolute title has been applied for but the registrar has been unable to grant it owing to some defect in the title. A qualified title to leaseholds has the same effect as an absolute or good leasehold title, as the case may be, except for the specified defect.[17]

(c) *Possessory.* In the case of either freeholds or leaseholds, first

---

[12] L.R.A. 1966, s. 1 (2).
[13] s. 20.
[14] L.R.A. 1925, s. 5.
[15] *Ibid.* s. 9.
[16] *Ante*, p. 101
[17] *Ibid.* ss. 7, 12.

registration with possessory title has the same effect as registration with an absolute title, save that the title is subject to all rights existing or capable of arising at the time of first registration.[18] In short, the title is guaranteed as far as all dealings after the date of registration are concerned, but no guarantee is given as to the title prior to first registration, which must accordingly be investigated by a purchaser in the same way as if the land were not registered.

(d) *Good leasehold.* This is applicable only to leaseholds. It is the same as an absolute title, save that the lessor's right to grant the lease is not guaranteed[19] and it may be that undiscoverable binding incumbrances affect the freehold and thus the leasehold. If it should appear that the lessor was never entitled to grant the lease, the lessee is protected if he has an absolute title, but unprotected if he has a good leasehold title. Since a lessee cannot investigate the freehold title unless he stipulates for this in his contract,[20] he usually cannot give the Registrar evidence of the freehold title where it is or appears to be unregistered, and so he can apply only for a good leasehold title. The Registrar may nevertheless be able to grant an absolute title if the title to the freehold is in fact registered, and, though unknown to the lessee, his landlord is the registered proprietor.

Application may be made in the first instance for any of the above titles except a qualified title, which can only be applied for if an absolute title is refused.

5. Conversion of titles. When registration has taken place with any of the above titles other than absolute, conversion of the title may take place subsequently.[21] There are two classes of case.

(a) *Conversion as of right.* Provided he is satisfied that the proprietor is in possession of the land in question, the Registrar is *bound* to convert the title—

   (i) to absolute, in the case of a freehold registered with possessory title for 15 years;
   (ii) to good leasehold in the case of a leasehold registered with possessory title for 10 years.

(b) *Discretionary conversion.* The Registrar *may* convert the title—

   (i) to absolute or good leasehold, if the land was registered with possessory title before 1926;
   (ii) to absolute or good leasehold, if the land is registered with qualified, possessory or good leasehold title and is transferred for value;

[18] *Ibid.* ss. 6, 11.
[19] *Ibid.* s. 10; *White* v. *Bijou Mansions Ltd.* [1937] Ch. 610.
[20] See *ante*, p. 101.
[21] L.R.A. 1925, s. 77.

(iii) to absolute, if the land has been registered with good leasehold title for 10 years and the registrar is satisfied that the owners of the lease have been in possession for that period.

6. Application for first registration. With the exceptions set out above,[22] an application for registration may be made by an estate owner, including those holding the estate as a trustee. Further, anyone entitled to call for a legal estate to be vested in him (except a mere purchaser under a contract, or a mortgagee) can apply for registration.[23] Thus if A holds land on a bare trust for B, B can apply for registration without first requiring a conveyance to be executed in his favour, though normally A will have to join or concur in the application.

The Registrar examines the title and inquires into any objections that may be made to the proposed registration. He has power to accept a defective title if in his opinion it is "a title the holding under which will not be disturbed."[24] There is no appeal to the court from a refusal to register a title as absolute, though the Registrar's action or inaction could be challenged by an application for judicial review.[25]

7. Cautions. Any person interested in unregistered land who thinks that he may be prejudiced by an application to register any title to it may lodge a caution against first registration with the Registrar.[26] This entitles him to be informed by the Registrar of any application to register the title. Thus a person who claims that the execution by him of a conveyance of his unregistered land was obtained by fraud might lodge a caution against first registration to prevent the grantee registering the title without his knowledge.

Cautions may also be lodged to prevent a conversion of the title, or against dealings by the registered proprietor.[27]

The notice given to the cautioner requires him to make his objections to the registration or conversion within a fixed time, usually 14 days. Abuse of this procedure is discouraged by a provision that any person who causes damage to another by unreasonably lodging a caution is liable to pay him compensation.[28]

8. The effect of first registration. On first registration of P as registered proprietor with title absolute one would expect P to obtain the whole legal and equitable estate. Normally, the conveyance on sale leading to first registration will, indeed, pass the legal and equitable estate to P so that there will be no need for statute to state

---

[22] *Ante*, p. 116.
[23] L.R.A. 1925, ss. 4, 8.
[24] L.R.A. 1925, s. 13.
[25] *Dennis* v. *Malcolm* [1934] Ch. 244; R.S.C., Ord. 53.
[26] L.R.A. 1925, s. 53.
[27] See *post*, p. 127, for cautions against dealings.
[28] L.R.A. 1925, s. 56.

the obvious: namely, that when P is registered proprietor not only does he have the legal estate but also the equitable estate.

However, it might be that the conveyance were void for forgery or that the vendor had no title at all to the land, having overlooked the fact that he had already conveyed the land to someone else before the area had become a compulsory registration area. Section 69 (1) makes it clear that P as registered proprietor has the legal estate, whilst section 5 provides that there is vested in P an estate in fee simple in possession, subject to charges and minor interests protected on the register and subject to overriding interests, but free from all other estates and interests whatsoever. The approach of section 5 in seemingly passing everything subject only to entries on the register and overriding interests, suggests that the legal and equitable fee simple is meant to be vested in P.[29]

However, Templeman J., without giving any reason, has assumed[30] that section 5 only vests the legal estate in the proprietor, leaving the equitable estate in the victim, V, of the forgery or of the double conveyancing. If this be correct then P holds the legal estate as bare trustee for V, so that V has an absolute right to call for the legal estate,[31] despite the fact that P is the Registrar's darling, a purchaser under a registered disposition for value without V being protected by entry on the register—or by an overriding interest. Moreover, if P dutifully complied[32] with V's demand for the transfer of the legal estate to V, P would not be able to claim an indemnity since his loss would arise not from rectification of the register but from his own act in transferring the legal estate to V, quite apart from the further point that, since such transfer merely regularises the fact that P has never had the equitable estate, P, indeed, has suffered no loss.[33] It is thus to be hoped that Templeman J.'s view will not be followed.

Sect. 3. Registered Charges

The formal way of mortgaging registered land is to effect a registered charge by deed. This operates as a charge by way of legal mortgage once it has been registered by entering the charge and the name of the proprietor of the charge in the register of the charged title.[34] The proprietor of the charge is issued with a *charge* certificate with the

---

[29] *Re Suarez (No. 2)* [1924] 2 Ch. 19. *Cf.* L.R.A. s. 70 (1) (*a*) where the reference to profits must include legal and equitable profits. For subsequent transfers of registered land ss. 20 (1) and 23 (1) make it clear that the equitable interest passes since the transfer operates as if the transferor were entitled to the land for his own benefit.

[30] *Epps* v. *Esso Petroleum Ltd.* [1973] 1 W.L.R. 1071 at pp. 1075, 1078.

[31] Under the *Saunders* v. *Vautier* (1841) Cr. & Ph. 240 principle.

[32] If he refused the court might have power directly to order rectification under L.R.A., s. 82 (1) (*a*).

[33] *Cf. Re Chowood's Registered Land* [1933] Ch. 574.

[34] L.R.A., ss. 25, 26, 27; *Grace Rymer Investments Ltd.* v. *Waite* (1958) Ch. 831.

original charge annexed, and so long as the charge subsists the *land* certificate is retained in the Registry.[35] The registered chargee (as the proprietor of the charge is commonly called) has all the powers of a legal mortgagee,[36] *e.g.* the power of sale of the legal estate if the borrower defaults.

A registered charge is *sui generis* in that it is incapable of substantive registration with its own land certificate, it cannot be an overriding interest,[37] nor can it be a minor interest since it is created by and can be disposed of by a registered disposition.[38]

Sect. 4. Overriding Interests

1. Nature. By definition they are interests "not entered on the register."[39] Overriding interests bind the proprietor of registered land, even though he has no knowledge of them and no reference is made to them in the register. In general, they are the kind of rights which a purchaser of unregistered land would not expect to discover from a mere examination of the abstract and title deeds, but for which he would make inquiries and inspect the land. Most are legal rights but many are equitable. It must be emphasised that as far as incumbrances on registered land are concerned, the issue in deciding whether a purchaser is bound where there is no entry on the register is not whether the rights are legal or equitable but whether they are overriding interests or minor interests. It is significant that a purchaser takes subject to overriding interests subsisting at the date of registration of the purchaser's title[40] (not the earlier date when purchase moneys are handed over in return for the appropriate documents).

2. The interests. The most important overriding interests are[41]:

(1) Rights of common, public rights, profits *à prendre*, rights of way, watercourses, rights of water, and other easements not being equitable easements required to be protected by notice on the register. The category thus includes legal easements and legal and equitable profits which came into existence before the land was first registered and legal easements and profits which have subsequently come into existence by virtue of an implied or presumed grant. Once land is registered an expressly granted easement or profit can only be legal if noted on the register, *ipso facto* being incapable of being an overriding interest.

---

[35] *Ibid*. ss. 63, 65.
[36] *Ibid*. s. 34, *post* p. 470.
[37] *Ibid*. s. 3 (xvi).
[38] *Ibid*. ss. 3 (xv) (xxii), 18 (4), 21 (4).
[39] L.R.A. 1925, s. 3 (xvi).
[40] L.R.A. 1925, ss. 5, 9, 20, 23, *Re Boyle's Claim* [1961] 1 W.L.R. 339, *London & Cheshire Insurance Co.* v. *Laplagrene* [1971] Ch. 499.
[41] The full list under 12 headings is given in L.R.A. 1825, s. 70.

(2) Rights acquired or being acquired under the Limitation Acts.

(3) Rights of every person in actual occupation of the land or in receipt of the rents and profits, unless inquiry made of such person fails to disclose the right.[42]

(4) Rights excepted from the effect of registration, such as rights existing at the time of first registration where only a possessory title is granted.

(5) Local land charges, until protected by entry on the register.

(6) Legal[43] leases for not more than 21 years at a rent without a fine; nearly all leases, however, unless entered on the register, will take effect as overriding interests under head (3) above, even if they are for more than 21 years.[44]

3. Entries on register. The registrar *may* make entries on the register stating that the land is free from or subject to certain overriding interests. His only *obligation* is to enter a notice of the existence of any easement, right, privilege or benefit created by an instrument (and not, for example, an easement acquired by prescription) which appears on the title at the time of first registration.[45]

4. Section 70 (1) (g). This sets out the most significant overriding interest: "the rights of every person in actual occupation of the land or in receipt of the rents and profits thereof, save where inquiry is made of such person and the rights are not disclosed."

(a) *"Rights"*. "Rights" means rights of a proprietary and not of a personal nature,[46] so that legal or equitable interests in land and mere equities, which are ancillary to and dependent upon interests in land, may be overriding interests if supported either by actual occupation or by receipt of rents and profits. The following rights have been held to be overriding interests of occupiers: the rights of a beneficiary under a bare trust[47] or under a trust for sale of a house purchased for occupation by the beneficiary,[48] an unpaid vendor's lien,[49] a purchaser's lien for his deposit,[50] an option to purchase the freehold reversion to a lease,[51] a contract for the purchase of land,[52] a

---

[42] See s. 70 (1) (g) heading, *post.*
[43] *City P.B.S.* v. *Miller* [1952] Ch. 840.
[44] See *Strand Securities Ltd.* v. *Caswell* [1965] Ch. 958.
[45] L.R.A. 1925, s. 70 (2), *Re Dances Way* [1962] Ch. 490.
[46] *National Provincial Bank* v. *Ainsworth* [1965] A.C. 1175 at pp. 1237, 1261.
[47] *Hodgson* v. *Marks* [1971] Ch. 892.
[48] *Williams & Glyn's Bank* v. *Boland* [1981] A.C. 487 Query whether rights under trusts for sale as in *Barclay* v. *Barclay* [1970] 2 Q.B. 677 which do not enable the beneficiaries to invoke the protection of L.P.A. 1925, s. 30 can be overriding interests *in land*: see Hayton, pp. 98–100, and *post* pp. 313–315.
[49] *London & Cheshire Insurance Co.* v. *Laplagrene* [1971] Ch. 499.
[50] *Lee-Parker* v. *Izzet* [1971] 1 W.L.R. 1088.
[51] *Webb* v. *Pollmount* [1966] Ch. 584.
[52] *Bridges* v. *Mees* [1957] Ch. 475.

right to rectify a conveyance mistakenly conveying more than the original parties intended.[53] Thus *all* proprietary rights are protected: not just those rights entitling the claimant to occupation or to receipt of rents.

(b) *Occupation or receipt of rents and profits.* Whether or not a purchaser had notice of such rights is immaterial[54] since he is absolutely bound by rights of occupiers or receivers of rents, except only where he made inquiry of such persons and they failed to disclose their rights. Thus it is not enough to ask the vendor about the rights of others[55]: all occupiers must be asked if they claim any proprietary rights and also (unlike the unregistered land position) all persons in receipt of rents and profits. It does not matter that it might be unreasonable to expect a purchaser to discover that O is in actual occupation or that R is in receipt of rents and profits (*e.g.* where T is paying R rent but has not yet gone into occupation) if the court decides that as a matter of fact O was in actual occupation or R in receipt[56] of rents and profits.

To attain a sensible result a court has some leeway in deciding whether or not O was in actual occupation. The problem is most likely to arise where A is sole registered proprietor but O has contributed to the purchase of the property, so as to be tenant in common under a trust for sale entitled, say, to an undivided one-tenth share of the proceeds of sale.[57] It may be that whenever the purchaser visited the house O was in hospital or on holiday or away on business and that A ensured that no obvious visible signs of O's occupation existed. In cases of doubt it seems likely that O's interests will be preferred to those of the purchaser[58] so a purchaser should take as many precautions as possible, *e.g.* search the electoral register or require the sale to be carried out by two trustees for sale, so overreaching all beneficial interests under the trust for sale.[59]

Occupiers over the age of 18 years, even if sons or daughters of the vendor, clearly need to be asked what rights they claim,[60] as, it seems, should persons over the age of 16 years living in emancipated fashion with the vendor as spouse[61] or lover. It may well be that minors living as unemancipated dependants of the vendor should not be treated as being capable of being in actual occupation in their own right.[62]

---

[53] *Blacklocks* v. *J.B. Developments (Godalming) Ltd.* [1981] 3 All E.R. 392.
[54] *Williams & Glyn's Bank* v. *Boland* [1981] A.C. 487 at pp. 503, 511.
[55] *Hodgson* v. *Marks* [1971] Ch. 892. at p. 932.
[56] It should be immaterial that at the time of registration of the new proprietor it so happens that R is not actually in receipt of rent owing to his tenant withholding it: see Hayton, pp. 91–92.
[57] See the situation in *Bull* v. *Bull* [1955] 1 Q.B. 234 and *Williams & Glyn's Bank* v. *Boland* [1981] A.C. 487.
[58] See Hayton, p. 91.
[59] L.P.A. 1925, ss. 2, 27: Martin [1981] Conv. 219.
[60] *Bird* v. *Syme Thomson* [1978] 3 All E.R. 1027 at p. 1030.
[61] *Williams & Glyn's Bank* v. *Boland* [1981] A.C. 487.
[62] See p. 67 *ante.*

(c) *Nevertheless certain rights can only be minor interests.* Certain rights can never be overriding interests but can only be minor interests:

   (i) the rights of a beneficiary under a Settled Land Act settlement[63];

   (ii) the rights of occupation of a spouse under the Matrimonial Homes Act 1967[64];

   (iii) the rights of a tenant arising from a notice under the Leasehold Reform Act 1967 of his request to have the freehold or an extended lease[65];

   (iv) the rights of a mortgagee other than under a registered charge[66]

(d) *The intrinsic nature of the right.* The fact that a right is an overriding interest "does not convert it into something more than it was before registration of the estate or the interest which is alleged to be subject to it."[67] Ordinary land law criteria have to be applied to ascertain the nature of the right. Thus if V contracted to sell his house to P and then declared himelf trustee of the house for O, who happened to be in actual occupation when P became registered proprietor, O's rights are not capable of binding P: by virtue of the contract V held the house as trustee for P and so could not effectively later also hold the house as trustee for O. Similarly, if H and W are registered proprietors and H assigns his equitable half share to A but H and W as trustees for sale subsequently sell to P, then P, even if A is in actual occupation, should take free from A's overreachable rights which are in the proceeds of sale in the hands of H and W, being overreached under sections 2 and 27 of the Law of Property Act 1925.[68]

5. Derivative validity and invalidity. If an interest is created out of a valid overriding interest (*e.g.* a lease created out of an absolute interest under a bare trust) then just as the overriding interest binds a purchaser so will the actual interest derived out of the overriding interest.[69]

However, if an overriding interest is created out of an unprotected minor interest which is void against a purchaser (as where a lease is created out of a Settled Land Act life interest) then just as an underlease created out of a void lease is void so a lease derived from a void minor interest should be void.[70] The tenant's "rights" within section 70 (1) (g) as equitable lessee are void rights.

[63] L.R.A., s. 86 (2).
[64] s. 2 (7).
[65] Leasehold Reform Act 1967, s. 5 (5).
[66] L.R.A., s. 106 (2).
[67] *Schwab* v. *McCarthy* (1976) 31 P. & C.R. 196 at p. 205 *per* Oliver J.
[68] See Hayton pp. 138–140, Martin [1981] Conv. 219.
[69] *Marks* v. *Attallah* (1966) 110 S. J. 209.
[70] See Hayton, pp. 139–140.

Sect. 5. Minor Interests

1. Definition. The Act elaborately defines minor interests,[71] but for present purposes it may suffice to say that minor interests are those which require protection by some entry on the register. The category excludes overriding interests and registered estates and charges. The former require no protection and the latter are necessarily on the register either as a registered title or as a registered charge. All other interests fall into the class of minor interests and so need to be protected by an entry on the register, otherwise they will not bind a purchaser for value under a registered disposition, *i.e.* of the legal estate.[72] Actual notice of the minor interest is immaterial.[73]

2. Protection of minor interests. A minor interest may be protected by a notice, restriction, caution or inhibition. Except in the case of cautions and inhibitions the land certificate normally has to be in the Registry to enable a restriction or notice to be entered.[74]

(a) *Notices.* (1) EFFECT OF NOTICE. In general, the effect of the entry of a notice is to ensure that any subsequent dealing with the land will take effect subject to the right protected by the notice[75]; the mere entry of a notice will not, of course, give validity to an invalid claim. A notice also serves to fix the registered proprietor with notice of the claim as from the moment of entry.

(2) RIGHTS PROTECTED. The rights which can be protected by notice include all land charges under the Land Charges Act 1972 (including a spouse's right to occupy a house owned by the other spouse,[76] and the right conferred on a tenant of a long leasehold to serve a notice of his desire to acquire the freehold or an extended lease[77]), legal rentcharges, legal estates exceeding 21 years, legal charges, legal easements, the rights of creditors when a bankruptcy petition has been presented against the registered proprietor, and charging orders.[78] Where the notice relates to a bankruptcy petition, the notice is called a "creditor's notice."[79] A notice cannot be entered to

---

[71] L.R.A. 1925, s. 3 (xv).
[72] L.R.A. 1925, ss. 5, 9, 20, 23, *Miles* v. *Bull* (*No.* 2) [1969] 3 All E.R. 1585; contrast *Barclays Bank Ltd.* v. *Taylor* [1974] Ch. 137, where the purchaser took an equitable interest only.
[73] L.R.A. 1925, s. 59 (6); and see *De Lusignan* v. *Johnson* (1973) 230 E.G. 499 and *Williams & Glyn's Bank* v. *Boland* [1981] A.C. 487 at p. 503 revealing the error of the contrary approach in *Peffer* v. *Rigg* [1977] 1 W.L.R. 285.
[74] L.R.A. s. 64 (1).
[75] *Ibid.* s. 52. See *Kitney* v. *M.E.P.C. Ltd.* [1977] 1 W.L.R. 981.
[76] Matrimonial Homes Act 1967, s. 2 (7); see *ante*, p. 95.
[77] Leasehold Reform Act 1967, s. 5 (5); *post*, p. 588.
[78] Charging Orders Act 1979, s. 3 (3); L.R.A., s. 49 (1) (g). A notice can only be used where the charging order, if the land had been unregistered, could have been registered as an order affecting land, *i.e.* because the debt is against a sole legal and beneficial owner or against all those who together hold the whole legal and equitable estate: see p. 98 *ante*.
[79] L.R.A. 1925, s. 61.

protect overreachable interests under settlements or trusts for sale (except as a temporary measure pending appointment of two trustees).[80]

(3) MODE OF ENTRY. Normally before the notice can be entered, the land certificate must be produced to the registrar. Thus unless the land is already charged so that the certificate has been deposited at the Land Registry,[81] a notice cannot be entered without the co-operation of the registered proprietor. Exceptionally, a creditor's notice or a spouse's Class F notice or notice of a capital transfer tax charge or notice of a lease can be entered without the production of the land certificate.[82] Notices are entered in the charges register of the burdened title.

(b) *Restrictions.* (1) EFFECT OF RESTRICTION. Entry of a restriction ensures that no subsequent dealing with the land takes effect unless it complies with the terms of the restriction,[83] *e.g.* terms ensuring that capital moneys are paid to two trustees or a trust corporation and, in the case of settled land, that only authorised dispositions under the Settled Land Act take place. This ensures that the proper over-reaching machinery is used so that the beneficial interests protected by the restriction are detached from the land and attached to the capital moneys.

(2) RIGHTS PROTECTED. The equitable interests of beneficiaries under a Settled Land Act settlement or a trust for sale should be pro-tected by a restriction except where the proprietors are beneficially jointly entitled under a trust for sale so that the survivor should be able himself to give a valid receipt for capital money arising on a sale.[84] Restrictions can also be used to record other legal restraints on a proprietor's powers of disposition, *e.g.* no disposition shall take place except with the consent of X or the Charity Commissioners or the Housing Corporation or except in accordance with the New Towns Act 1965 or the Companies Act.

(3) MODE OF ENTRY. The land certificate has to be lodged in the Registry if a restriction is to be entered,[85] and on registering two or more proprietors it is obligatory on the Registrar to enter a restriction (so preventing any disposition by the survivor) unless the survivor will have power to give a valid receipt for capital moneys. Otherwise, entry has to be on the application of or with the consent of the proprietor.

---

[80] L.R.A., s. 49 (2).
[81] L.R.A. 1925, s. 65.
[82] L.R.A. 1925, s. 54, *Strand Securities Ltd.* v. *Caswell* [1965] Ch. 958; Matrimonial Homes & Property Act 1981, s. 4 (1).
[83] L.R.A., s. 58.
[84] *Ibid.* s. 58 (3).
[85] *Ibid.* s. 64 (1) (c).

(c) *Cautions against dealings.* (1) EFFECT OF CAUTION. Where a notice or restriction cannot be entered due to the unavailability of the land certificate, then anyone howsoever interested in the land can enter a caution against dealings.[86] This ensures that no dealing with the land will be registered until notice has been served on the cautioner[87] warning him that if he does not object within 14 days then registration will be effected, the caution having been "warned off." If the cautioner does object then, after hearing both sides and subject to appeal to the Chancery Division, the Registrar has a very broad discretion to do what he thinks appropriate,[88] *e.g.* cancel the caution, refuse to register the projected dealing, allow the dealing to be registered but subject to a notice protecting the interest formerly protected by the caution,[89] or allow the dealing to be registered unless within a fixed period the cautioner institutes some legal proceedings when the caution will remain to protect the pending action. A caution is thus often a temporary "holding" device until some more permanent form of protection is available for the cautioner's interest, *e.g.* entry of a notice or substantive registration of the interest.

Otherwise, a caution has no effect whatever except that a person who lodges a caution without reasonable cause is liable to compensate anyone who thereby sustains damage.[90] It is unclear what is "reasonable cause" so in an interlocutory action to vacate the caution, under the Court's inherent jurisdiction or section 82 (1) (*b*) of the Land Registration Act 1925,[91] the Court may allow the caution to remain only if the cautioner undertakes to pay the proprietor any damages caused by the caution's presence if it is subsequently held that the caution was wrongly entered (*e.g.* because no contract had existed or it had been properly rescinded). If the cautioner is not ready so to undertake then the caution will be vacated.[92] No doubt, the Court could act similarly in respect of a notice entered without the proprietor's consent when the land certificate was in the Registry owing to the land being subject to a registered charge.

(2) RIGHTS PROTECTED. Any person interested under any unregistered instrument, or interested as a judgment creditor, or otherwise howsoever, in any land or charge may lodge a caution,[93] *e.g.* persons

---

[86] *Ibid.* s. 55.
[87] At any time the proprietor can apply for such notice to be served on the cautioner unless Class F rights are concerned.
[88] Land Registration Rule 220. At any stage the Registrar can refer the matter to the Chancery Division.
[89] A caution registered against a proprietor of land will not affect dispositions by the proprietor of a charge on such land. Thus, if the proprietor of land against whom a caution is entered charges the land the cautioner should only consent to registration of the charge subject to a *notice* protecting his interest.
[90] L.R.A., s. 56 (2), (3).
[91] *Lester* v. *Burgess* (1973) 26 P. & C.R. 536; *Price Bros. Ltd.* v. *Kelly Homes Ltd.* [1975] 1 W.L.R. 1512.
[92] *Tiverton Estates Ltd.* v. *Wearwell Ltd.* [1974] 1 Ch. 146.
[93] L.R.A., s. 54 (1).

having the benefit of a contract or option or right of pre-emption or interested under a trust for sale[94] or in a charging order on an interest under a trust for sale. Protection by caution is the residual method of protection where protection by substantive registration or by notice or by restriction is not available for some reason.

(3) MODE OF ENTRY. The land certificate's presence is not needed for entry of a caution, which will be made by the Registrar on receiving a statutory declaration, sworn by the cautioner, referring to the land or charge to which it relates and specifying the interest which warrants the caution.[95] Penalties exist for false declarations and where there are no substantial grounds for a caution the Court may take a robust approach to ordering vacation of the register on interlocutory motion.[96]

(d) *Inhibition.* An inhibition is an order of the Court or an entry of the Registrar which forbids any dealing with the land for a specified period or until further order.[97] It may be made on the application of any person *e.g.* the proprietor who finds that his land certificate has been stolen. Where a receiving order in bankruptcy is made a "bankruptcy inhibition" is automatically entered, preventing any disposition until a trustee in bankruptcy has been registered.[98] Otherwise, inhibitions are very rare.

(e) *Class F Rights Against the Matrimonial Home.* Class F rights should be protected by notice and cannot be overriding interests.[99] This is one of the exceptional cases where the land certificate is not required before entry of a notice[1] and where a caution can no longer be lodged.[2] Without the need for the proprietor's authority a mortgagee can make an official search solely for ascertaining whether Class F rights are protected on the register: this is to enable the mortgagee to comply with his statutory duty of joining as a party to his action against the owning spouse the spouse who has registered Class F rights.[3]

3. Official search certificates. A purchaser can ascertain what minor interests have been protected by entries on the register by making an official search of the register if authorised by the registered

---

[94] *Elias* v. *Mitchell* (1972) Ch. 652.
[95] Land Registration Rule 215 (4).
[96] *Rawplug Co. Ltd.* v. *Kamvale Properties Ltd.* (1968) 20 P. & C.R. 32; *Price Bros. Ltd.* v. *Kelly Homes Ltd.* [1975] 1 W.L.R. 1512.
[97] L.R.A., s. 57.
[98] *Ibid.* s. 61 (3).
[99] Matrimonial Homes Act 1967, s. 2 (7), Matrimonial Homes and Property Act 1981, s. 4(1).
[1] M.H.&.P.A. 1981, s. 4 (1).
[2] *Ibid.* s. 4 (2).
[3] *Ibid.* ss. 2, 4 (4).

proprietor.[4] An official search certificate will afford the purchaser protection against any minor interest protected by entry made in the thirty working days priority period following the date of the certificate.[5] Any entries made in that period will be postponed to the purchaser's interest if the purchaser's application for registration is received at the Registry before expiry of the priority period. If a second application for search is made during the priority period conferred by an earlier search the second search will confer a separate priority period but will not act as an extension of the priority under the first search. A new entry revealed by the second search will thus bind the purchaser if he does not deliver his registration application to the Registry within the priority period afforded by the first clear search certificate.[6]

4. Competing minor interests. Just as date of registration of a land charge affecting unregistered land does not normally govern priority of competing equitable interests in unregistered land,[7] so date of entry of a notice or caution, protecting a minor interest in registered land, does not normally govern priority of competing minor interests.[8] Minor interests take effect only as equitable interests[9] so that the minor interest that was first created has priority over subsequent minor interests (even if they were purchased for value without notice of the earlier interests) unless its owner's conduct amounted to fraud or negligence or raised an estoppel where such conduct was sufficient to induce the detrimental acquisition of the subsequent interest.[10] These general equitable principles apply in the absence of relevant statutory provisions.[11]

Thus, if X enters into an ordinary contract of purchase, then Y enters into such a contract, then Y enters a caution, then X enters a caution, so preventing either from becoming new registered proprietor, X will have priority over Y and be able to obtain the land free from Y's rights.[12] It should make no difference if Y had entered a notice instead of a caution, since the disposition in X's favour would be subject to Y's rights protected by notice "only if and so far as such rights may be valid and are not (independently of this Act)

---

[4] L.R.A., ss. 110 (1), 112.
[5] Land Registration (Official Searches) Rules 1981.
[6] Land Registry Notice (1981) 131 New L.J. 881.
[7] *Ante.* p. 103.
[8] See Hayton, pp. 140 *et seq.*
[9] L.R.A., s. 2 (1).
[10] *Ante*, p. 70.
[11] *Barclays Bank* v. *Taylor* [1974] Ch. 137; *Abigail* v. *Lapin* [1934] A.C. 491 at pp. 500–502; *Strand Securities Ltd.* v. *Caswell* [1965] Ch. 958 at p. 991; L.R.A., ss. 27 (3), 40, 66.
[12] *Ante.* p. 104. If, instead, X had an equitable charge unprotected by entry on the register or by deposit and Y, on obtaining a clear search certificate, had taken an equitable charge by deed, then X would lose his priority since it is standard practice to protect a charge like that of X.

overridden by the disposition." In the eyes of equity Y's rights are not valid as against X.[13]

Sect. 6. Rectification and Indemnity[14]

(a) *Rectification.* Wide powers are given to the court or the registrar to rectify the register when there is any error or omission, as when a person with no title to the land has been registered in place of the true owner. However, if the registered proprietor is in possession, the register cannot be rectified so as to affect his title save in a limited class of cases, *viz.*:

   (i) to give effect to Court orders such as those under section 42 of the Bankruptcy Act 1914;
   (ii) to give effect to an overriding interest;
   (iii) where the proprietor "has caused or substantially contributed to the error or omission by fraud or lack of proper care";
   (iv) where it would be unjust not to rectify.[15]

(b) *Indemnity.* Any person suffering loss by reason of such rectification is entitled to be indemnified out of state funds.[16] The loss, however, must be caused by the rectification. Thus where the registered proprietor bought the land with a squatter in possession of part of it, the subsequent rectification of the register by excluding that part from the title merely gave effect to the squatter's overriding interest, and this formal recognition of the existing position gave no right to compensation.[17] There will similarly be no indemnity if the applicant (or a person through whom he claims otherwise than by a disposition for value which is registered or protected on the register) has caused or substantially contributed to the loss by fraud or lack of proper care.[18] If a claim is made more than six years after the date that the land was registered with an absolute title or with good leasehold title then no indemnity is payable.[19]

(c) *Complexities.* The situations generating claims to rectification and indemnity involve detailed knowledge of land law topics and a consideration of the relationship between registered and unregistered land law principles. Rectification and indemnity will therefore be further examined when a fuller grasp of land law has been obtained.

---

[13] See the approach in *Kitney* v. *M.E.P.C. Ltd.* [1977] 1 W.L.R. 981 and *Barclays Bank* v. *Taylor* [1974] Ch. 137.
[14] See Hayton, Chap. 9 and *post*, pp. 532 *et seq.*
[15] L.R.A. 1925, s. 82 (3) as amended by Administration of Justice Act 1977, s. 24.
[16] L.R.A. 1925, s. 83; Land Registration and Land Charges Act 1971, s.1.
[17] *Re Chowood's Registered Land* [1933] Ch. 574; contrast *Re Boyle's Claim* [1961] 1 W.L.R. 339.
[18] L.R.A. 1925, s. 83 (5), as amended by Land Registration and Land Charges Act 1971, s. 2.
[19] *Ibid.* s. 83 (11), *Epps* v. *Esso Petroleum Ltd.* [1973] 1 W.L.R. 1071.

Sect. 7. The Diagrammatic Structure of Unregistered and Registered Land Law

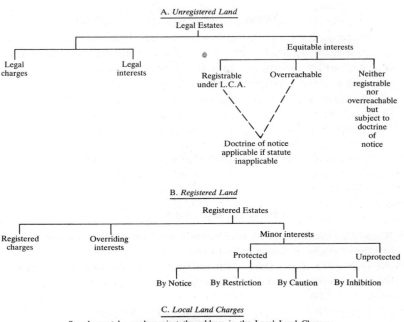

A. *Unregistered Land*

Legal Estates

Legal charges

Legal interests

Equitable interests

Registrable under L.C.A.

Overreachable

Neither registrable nor overreachable but subject to doctrine of notice

Doctrine of notice applicable if statute inapplicable

B. *Registered Land*

Registered Estates

Registered charges

Overriding interests

Minor interests

Protected

Unprotected

By Notice   By Restriction   By Caution   By Inhibition

C. *Local Land Charges*

Search must be made against the address in the Local Land Charges Registers whether the land be unregistered or registered (local land charges ranking as overriding interests).

Part 4

THE EQUITABLE IN PERSONAM JURISDICTION

Sect. 1. Statute cannot be used as an Engine of Fraud

When statutory provisions apply to unregistered or to registered land equity will not allow such provisions to be used as an "engine of fraud."[20] Thus, if a purchaser deliberately misleads the owner of an equitable interest registrable under the Land Charges Act or of a minor interest, capable of protection by entry of a notice, a restriction or a caution, to leave such interest unregistered or unprotected, equity will not allow the purchaser to take advantage of the statutory provisions making such interest void against him.[21] Similarly, if A is contractually bound to sell his land to P but transfers the land for value to the A Co. Ltd., controlled by A, equity will not

---

[20] *Bannister* v. *Bannister* [1948] 2 All E.R. 133. *Hodgson* v. *Marks* [1971] Ch. 892.
[21] *Cf. Montacute* v. *Maxwell* (1720) 1 P.Wms. 618 at p. 620.

allow A or the A Co. Ltd., to take free of P's equitable estate contract unregistered under the Land Charges Act or unprotected as a minor intrest under the Land Registration Act.[22]

It is important to realise that equity is not intervening merely because the defendant has actual notice of the interest of the plaintiff. It is necessary for a plaintiff to show he has been the victim of some fraudulent or dishonest or reprehensible conduct of the defendant so that it would be unconscionable for the defendant to take free of the plaintiff's interest. Normally, if a plaintiff fails to protect his interest when statute specially affords a method of protection, then it is the plaintiff's fault—so he cannot complain if the defendant discovers that the plaintiff's interest is unprotected and so goes on to purchase the property and take advantage of a situation which statute has positively provided for, namely, that the unprotected interest is void against the purchaser.[23]

Sect. 2. Proprietary Estoppel

Regardless of statutory provisions the equitable doctrine of proprietary estoppel may assist a plaintiff. As already seen[24] this may be the case even if the defendant has not been fraudulent or guilty of reprehensible conduct.[25]

Sect. 3. Foreign Land

An English Court has no jurisdiction to adjudicate upon title to, or right to possession of, land abroad.[26] However, if the defendant is personally resident in England and there is some equitable right which the plaintiff could have enforced if the land had been in England then the court will be ready to exercise its *in personam* jurisdiction against the defendant *e.g.* for specific performance of a contract[27] or for rents and profits.[28]

---

[22] *Jones* v. *Lipman* [1962] 1 W.L.R. 832, *Frazer* v. *Walker* [1967] 1 A.C. 569 at p. 585.
[23] *Midland Bank Trust Co. Ltd.* v. *Green* [1981] A.C. 513; *Miles* v. *Bull (No. 2)* [1969] 3 All E.R. 1585.
[24] *Ante*, pp. 74–77.
[25] *Taylor Fashions Ltd.* v. *Liverpool Victoria Trustees Co.* [1981] 1 All E.R. 897.
[26] *British South Africa Co.* v. *Companhia de Mocambique* [1893] A.C. 602.
[27] *Richard West & Partners* v. *Dick* [1969] 2 Ch. 424.
[28] *St. Pierre* v. *South American Stores* [1936] 1 K.B. 382.

CHAPTER 5

THE TRANSMISSION OF TITLE TO LAND

Part 1

RELATIVITY OF TITLE AND ADVERSE POSSESSION

To understand how title to land is transmitted it is necessary to appreciate that the basis of title is possession. As between competing claimants he has title who has the better right to possession. However, though A may have a better right to possession than B, who is in possession, a time must come when A's continuing failure to take steps to recover possession from B will bar any future claim by A.

> "At common law . . . there is no such concept as 'absolute' title. Where questions of title to land arise the court is concerned only with the relative strengths of the titles proved by the rival elements. If party A can prove a better title than party B he is entitled to succeed notwithstanding that C may have a better title than A, if C is neither a party to the action nor a person by whose authority B is in possession of the land."[1]

Possession by itself gives a title to land good against the whole world except a person with a better, *i.e.* earlier, right to possession.[2] Thus if X wrongfully dispossesses A the fee simple owner of Blackacre, X has a right to possession treated as a legal fee simple good against all except A and A's successors in title.[3] A has a better right of possession but after 12 years this right will be barred by the Limitation Acts[4] so that X's fee, freed from the superior claims of A, will then be good against the world except for anyone with an earlier right to possession than A, if the Limitation Act has not barred such right.

Consider the following events:

1926	A is in possession of Cosyacre
1930	A sells and conveys to B
1942	C wrongfully takes possession
1948	C sells and conveys to D
1950	E wrongfully takes possession
1963	E sells and conveys to F
1964	F sells and conveys to G
1978	G sells and conveys to H

[1] *Ocean Estates Ltd.* v. *Pinder* [1969] 2 A.C. 19 at pp. 24–25 *per* Lord Diplock.
[2] *Asher* v. *Whitlock* (1865) L.R. 1 Q.B.
[3] Megarry & Wade, p. 1007.
[4] Now Limitation Act 1980, s. 15, *post* p. 521.

If P is considering purchasing the property he must ascertain who has the legal title, *i.e.* the best right to possession. Ignoring the Limitation Acts, B has the earliest right to possession, having lawfully received it from A. Next D has a right to possession and, last, H has a right to possession. Thus H has a right good against all except D and his successors in title and B and his successors in title, whilst D has a right good against all except B and his successors in title. However, taking the Limitation Acts into account, the rights to possession of D and B have been extinguished so that H can confer a good title on P.

P has to ascertain the person who has the earliest right to possession which has not been extinguished, *e.g.* by adverse possession of another for 12 years. P cannot be expected to trace the title back indefinitely but he can be expected to check that the vendor and those through whom the vendor derived title have possessed the land for a time sufficient to exclude any reasonable probability of a superior adverse claim. Since the limitation period is 12 years[5] it is reasonable to require the purchaser to investigate title to a good root of title at least 15 years old.[6] Thus P will only be entitled to trace H's title back to the 1964 conveyance. This may be sufficient to show that H has a good title which P can be forced to accept.

It may, however, transpire that in 1886 the then fee simple owner, L, had granted a 99 year lease to T, so that L had disposed of his right to possession for 99 years. On expiry of the lease L's successor in title, S, will have an immediate right to possession, derived from L's earlier right to possession, so that S will be able to evict P or P's successors in title[7]—so long as S does so within 12 years of the expiry of the lease. Adverse possession and limitation are fully dealt with in Chapter 14 *post*.

As will be seen the registration of title system is designed to avoid the above problems.

Part 2

CONTRACTS

Having considered the structure of land law it should be obvious that no-one, having selected the house he wishes to purchase, there and then pays over the purchase price in return for a conveyance of the house. Normally a proper formal contract subject to the National Conditions of Sale (20th ed.) or the Law Society Conditions of Sale (1980 edition) is drawn up whether the land is registered or unregistered. This deals fully with the matters that must be dealt with between the date of the contract and the completion of the contract

---

[5] *Ibid.*
[6] L.P.A. 1925, s. 44 (1) as amended by L.P.A. 1969, s. 23.
[7] *Fairweather* v. *St. Marylebone Property Co.* [1963] A.C. 510.

and provides for the resolution of any problems that might arise in this period.

Even before the contract is entered into the purchaser should take some important precautionary steps. He should inspect the property to discover any patent physical or title defects. His solicitor should send a standard form of Inquiries before Contract to the vendor: the Form contains a set of printed inquiries to which may be added any others considered appropriate. A search should also be made of the register of local land charges, and additional inquiries should be made of the relevant local authority on the standard printed form to ascertain other matters within the knowledge of such authority but not registrable in the local land charges register.

A contract to sell or make any other disposition of land is made in the same way as any other contract. As soon as there is an agreement for valuable consideration between the parties on the essential terms, there is a contract between the parties; and this is so whether the agreement was reached orally or in writing.

However, although a valid contract relating to land may be made orally, it will be unenforceable by the most important method of enforcing contracts, namely, by action,[8] unless either the statutory requirements as to written evidence of the contract, or the requirements of equity as to part performance, have been satisfied. Thus, when considering whether an agreement relating to land can be enforced by action, two separate points fall to be considered:

(1) whether there is a contract at all, and
(2) if so, whether that contract is enforceable by action.

In addition, some mention will be made of—
(3) the practice concerning contracts relating to land.

Sect. 1. The Existence of a Contract

There must be a final and complete agreement between the parties on at least the essential terms, namely—

(i) the parties;
(ii) the property;
(iii) the consideration;
(iv) (in the case of the grant of a lease) the commencement and the period of the lease.

If an offer is accepted "subject to contract" or "subject to suitable arrangements being arranged between your solicitors and mine,"[9] or

---

[8] *Tiverton Estates Ltd.* v. *Wearwell Ltd.* [1975] Ch. 146; *post*, p. 136.
[9] *Lockett* v. *Norman-Wright* [1925] Ch. 56.

some similar provision,[10] the effect is that until the necessary contract or arrangements have been made there is no contract and either party can withdraw. An agreement "subject to contract" must be distinguished from an unconditional acceptance of an offer coupled with a statement that the terms should be embodied in some formal document, *e.g.* "I accept your offer and have asked my solicitor to prepare a contract"; in this case, the parties are bound at once, even though no formal contract is ever prepared.[11] An agreement "subject to contract" may subsequently become binding if the parties subsequently execute a document agreeing that they are now to be bound on the terms formerly set out in the subject to contract agreement.[12]

There is no need for a contract to be made by any formal document or phrases. But where a formal agreement is drawn up, usually each party signs one copy, and there is no binding contract until these identical copies have been exchanged.[13] However, a vendor can agree to be bound as soon as he receives the purchaser's copy[14] and a solicitor has ostensible authority by telephone to agree to hold his client's copy to the order of the other party and so effect a notional exchange.[15]

Sect. 2. The Enforceability of the Contract

The contract will be unenforceable by action unless there is either a sufficient memorandum thereof in writing or a sufficient act of part performance.

A. Memorandum in Writing

By the Law of Property Act 1925, s. 40 (1), it is provided that "no action may be brought upon any contract for the sale or other disposition of land or any interest in land, unless the agreement upon which such action is brought, or some memorandum or note thereof, is in writing, and signed by the party to be charged or by some other person thereunto by him lawfully authorised."

1. "No action may be brought." Since 1852 it has been settled that the effect of non-compliance with the statute is not to make the

---

[10] The phrases "subject to the purchaser obtaining a mortgage satisfactory to him" or "subject to survey of the property" have been held not to prevent a binding contract arising: *Janmohamed* v. *Hassam* (1977) 241 E.G. 609, *Ee* v. *Kakar* (1980) 40 P. & C.R. 223.

[11] See *Rossiter* v. *Miller* (1878) 3 App.Cas. 1124 at pp. 1139, 1151.

[12] *Griffiths* v. *Young* [1970] Ch. 675, as explained in *Tiverton Estates Ltd.* v. *Wearwell Ltd.*, *supra*, and see *Daulia* v. *Millbank Nominees* [1978] Ch. 231 at p. 250. An oral waiver of "subject to contract" is insufficient.

[13] *Eccles* v. *Byrant* [1948] Ch. 93; *Harrison* v. *Battye* [1975] 1 W.L.R. 58.

[14] *Storer* v. *Manchester City Council* [1974] 1 W.L.R. 1403.

[15] *Domb* v. *Isoz* [1980] Ch. 548.

contract void but merely to make it unenforceable by action.[16] "The Statute of Frauds does not avoid parol contracts but only bars the legal remedies by which they might otherwise have been enforced."[17] It is true that to deprive a party to a contract of his right to bring an action upon it is to deprive him of one of his most important rights, but it does not render that contract useless; the Act is no bar to the contract being enforced in any way except by action. Thus, if a purchaser pays a cash deposit to the vendor under an oral contract, the vendor may forfeit (*i.e.* keep) that deposit if the purchaser defaults.[18] If there were no contract at all, the deposit would have to be returned.[19] Again, if a cheque is given in part payment under an oral contract for the sale of land, an action will lie if the purchaser refuses to honour it, for the action is not on the contract for the sale of land but it is on the cheque.[20]

2. "The sale or other disposition of land or any interest in land." The section applies to a contract for any disposition of any interest in land, whether by sale, mortgage, lease or otherwise. It applies equally to a contract for the creation of a new interest in land as to the disposition of an existing interest. "Land" is very widely defined.[21] It includes an interest under a trust for sale of land,[22] but not annual crops, such as corn or potatoes, which require the periodical application of labour for their production; these are known as *fructus industriales.*[23] *Fructus naturales*, on the other hand, are sometimes included. This term applies to the natural products of the soil, such as grass and timber, and also the products of those plants and trees which, although needing attention at first, do not require it each year to produce a crop,[24] such as fruit from fruit trees.[25] *Fructus naturales* are treated as land within the statute unless either they are to be severed by the vendor and not by the purchaser[26] or else the contract binds the purchaser to sever them as soon as possible.[27]

The sale by the tenant to his landlord of fixtures which the tenant is entitled to remove is neither a sale of land nor a sale of goods, for the substance of the agreement is merely a waiver by the tenant of his rights to remove the fixtures.[28]

---

[16] *Leroux* v. *Brown* (1852) 12 C.B. 801.
[17] *Maddison* v. *Alderson* (1883) 8 App.Cas. 467 at p. 474, *per* Lord Selbourne L.C.
[18] *Monnickendham* v. *Leanse* (1923) 39 T.L.R. 445.
[19] *Chillingworth* v. *Esche* [1924] 1 Ch. 97.
[20] *Low* v. *Fry* (1935) 152 L.T. 585.
[21] L.P.A. 1925, s. 205 (1) (ix).
[22] *Cooper* v. *Critchley* [1955] Ch. 431; but see *Stevens* v. *Hutchinson* [1953] Ch. 299.
[23] See *Duppa* v. *Mayo* (1669) 1 Wms.Saund. 275.
[24] *Marshall* v. *Green* (1875) 1 C.P.D. 35 at p. 40.
[25] *Rodwell* v. *Phillips* (1842) 9 M. & W. 501.
[26] *Smith* v. *Surman* (1829) 9 B. & C. 561.
[27] *Marshall* v. *Green* (1875) 1 C.P.D. 35 (and see the summary of the decisions at p. 42).
[28] *Lee* v. *Gaskell* (1876) 1 Q.B.D. 700; and see *ante*, pp. 21 *et seq.*

3. "Some memorandum or note thereof, is in writing." (a) *Existence of the document*. The contract itself may be made orally; all that is required is that before the action is begun[29] a written memorandum of the contract should have come into existence. For example, a memorandum made over 14 years after the contract may suffice[30]; and even if it has been lost or destroyed, it may be proved by oral or other secondary evidence, like any other missing document.[31] Even a document made before the contract came into existence may be sufficient, for it is settled that if a written offer is accepted orally, the written offer may be a sufficient memorandum to support an action against the person making it,[32] although the onus of proving such an acceptance is high.[33]

(b) *Form*. The memorandum need not be in any special form, nor is it necessary that it should have been intended to act as a memorandum: "the question is not one of intention of the party who signs the document, but simply one of evidence against him."[34] Nor need the memorandum consist of a single document. If the terms of the contract and the signature cannot be found in any one document, but can be gathered from two or more documents, then these documents can be taken together as the memorandum, provided the signed document refers to the others. Any reference in the signed document, whether express or implied, may be explained by evidence to show that it is another document which is being referred to and to identify that document.[35] Thus a telegram accepting "your offer" may refer sufficiently to a written offer received by the sender.[36] Again, it is not essential that the reference should be in words, for the nature of one document may refer to another; a signed carbon copy of a letter may thus refer sufficiently to the top copy upon which the defendant's signature appeared.[37] And if the signed document merely refers to another transaction, evidence is admissible to identify any document relating to that transaction which will supply the missing terms.[38] But it is essential that there should be some reference in the signed document to the other documents or transaction, for evidence cannot be admitted to connect one document with another when, on being placed side by side, the signed document still does not appear to refer to the other.[39]

Where two documents are both signed, they may be read together

---

[29] *Lucas* v. *Dixon* (1889) 22 Q.B.D. 357.
[30] *Barkworth* v. *Young* (1856) 4 Drew. 1.
[31] *Barber* v. *Rowe* [1948] 2 All E.R. 1050.
[32] *Reuss* v. *Picksley* (1866) L.R. 1 Ex. 342.
[33] *Watson* v. *Davies* [1931] 1 Ch. 455 at p. 468.
[34] *Re Hoyle* [1893] 1 Ch. 84 at p. 99, *per* Bowen L.J.
[35] *Long* v. *Millar* (1879) 4 C.P.D. 450.
[36] *Godwin* v. *Francis* (1870) L.R. 5 C.P. 295.
[37] *Stokes* v. *Whicher* [1920] 1 Ch. 411.
[38] *Timmins* v. *Moreland Street Property Co. Ltd.* [1958] Ch. 110 at p. 130.
[39] See, *e.g. Taylor* v. *Smith* [1893] 2 Q.B. 65.

even if neither refers to the other, provided it can be shown that they each refer to the same subject-matter.[40] Further, two documents which are separable without damage to either may constitute one document where they are in fact treated as one, as with a paper book and a leather cover which are connected only by the former being slipped into latter and habitually used with it.[41]

(c) *Contents*. (1) AGREEMENT. The memorandum must contain an acknowledgment or recognition that a contract has been entered into.[42] Thus, a letter from a solicitor expressed to be "subject to contract" and enclosing a draft contract is not a memorandum of an oral contract, even if all the terms are faithfully recorded.[43]

(2) ALL TERMS. The memorandum must accurately state *all* the terms of the contract.[44] "If the memorandum is not in accordance with the true contract, it is a bad memorandum."[45] Thus a memorandum is defective if it records as a single contract to buy three houses what in fact consisted of three distinct contracts,[46] or if it omits to mention that the purchase price was to be payable by instalments.[47] However, if the memorandum merely omits an unimportant stipulation which is for the benefit of one party alone (and not, *e.g.* an important provision which is for the benefit of both parties, such as one relating to vacant possession[48]), that party can enforce the contract if he waives the stipulation[49]; similarly, if the omitted stipulation is to the detriment of one party alone, he can enforce the contract if he agrees to perform the stipulation.[50]

(d) *Certainty*. The terms of the contract are sufficiently stated if they fall within the rule *id certum est quod certum reddi potest* (that is certain which can be made certain). Thus, while it is essential that the memorandum should disclose each party to the contract, or his agent,[51] it suffices if, without being named, each party is so described that his identity cannot be fairly disputed,[52] *e.g.* if the memorandum refers to the "proprietor"[53] of the property, or states that "the

[40] *Studds* v. *Watson* (1884) 28 Ch.D. 305.
[41] *Jones Brothers* v. *Joyner* (1900) 82 L.T. 768.
[42] *Tiverton Estates Ltd.* v. *Wearwell Ltd.* [1975] Ch. 146, not following *Law* v. *Jones* [1974] Ch. 112.
[43] *Ibid*.
[44] *Beckett* v. *Nurse* [1948] 1 K.B. 535.
[45] *Crane* v. *Naughten* [1912] 2 I.R. 318 at p. 324, *per* Gibson J.
[46] *Smith* v. *MacGowan* [1938] 3 All E.R. 447.
[47] *Tweddell* v. *Henderson* [1975] 1 W.L.R. 1496.
[48] *Hawkins* v. *Price* [1947] Ch. 645, *Heron Garage Properties Ltd.* v. *Moss* [1974] 1 W.L.R. 148.
[49] *North* v. *Loomes* [1919] 1 Ch. 378 at pp. 385, 386.
[50] *Scott* v. *Bradley* [1971] Ch. 850, following *Martin* v. *Pycroft* (1852) 2 De G.M. & G. 785 and not following *Burgess* v. *Cox* [1951] Ch. 383.
[51] *Davies* v. *Sweet* [1962] 2 Q.B. 300.
[52] *Carr* v. *Lynch* [1900] 1 Ch. 613 at p. 615.
[53] *Rossiter* v. *Miller* (1878) 3 App.Cas. 1124.

vendor will convey as legal personal representative."[54] But references to the "vendor"[55] or "landlord"[56] or "my clients"[57] are not sufficient by themselves, for these descriptions may fit many persons; the proprietor of land is not the only person who can be the vendor, for many other persons such as mortgagees or even complete strangers[58] may enter into a contract to sell the land. Similar principles apply to descriptions of the property concerned.

4. "Signed by the party to be charged or by some other person thereunto by him lawfully authorised." (a) *"Party to be charged."* Signature by both parties to the contract or their agents is not required; the statute requires signature by or on behalf of the party to be charged, namely, the party against whom it is sought to enforce the contract. Thus where there is a contract between A and B, and A alone has signed a memorandum, the contract is enforceable by action by B against A but not by A against B.[59]

(b) *"Signed."* The word "signed" has been given an extended meaning by the courts. Provided the name of the party to be charged appears in some part of the document in some form, whether in writing, typewriting, print or otherwise, there will be a sufficient signature if that party has shown in some way that he recognises the document as an expression of the contract.[60] Thus memoranda in the handwriting of A, the defendant, which began "I, A, agree"[61] or "A agrees"[62] or "sold A"[63] without any other signature, have all been held sufficiently signed on the ground that A has shown by his writing that he recognises the existence of the contract mentioned in the document. But the mere occurrence of the defendant's name in a memorandum written by him does not necessarily amount to a signature; thus if A writes out a document beginning "Articles of agreement made between A and B" and ending "As witness our hands," without any signatures, the statute is not satisfied,[64] for A's name must be inserted in such a way as to "have the effect of authenticating the instrument,"[65] or "to govern what follows."[66]

(c) *Agent's authority.* The statute makes no special provision about

[54] *Fay* v. *Miller, Wilkins & Co.* [1941] Ch. 360; but see (1941) 57 L.Q.R. 452.
[55] *Potter* v. *Duffield* (1874) L.R. 18 Eq. 4.
[56] *Coombs* v. *Wilkes* [1891] 3 Ch. 77.
[57] *Lovesy* v. *Palmer* [1916] 2 Ch. 233.
[58] *Donnison* v. *People's Cafe Co.* (1881) 45 L.T. 187.
[59] See *Boys* v. *Ayerst* (1822) 6 Madd. 316.
[60] See *Halley* v. *O'Brien* [1920] 1 I.R. 330 at p. 339; and see *Leeman* v. *Stocks* [1951] Ch. 941.
[61] *Knight* v. *Crockford* (1794) 1 Esp. 190.
[62] *Bleakley* v. *Smith* (1840) 11 Sim. 150.
[63] *Johnson* v. *Dodgson* (1837) 2 M. & W. 653.
[64] *Hubert* v. *Treherne* (1842) 3 Man. & G. 743.
[65] *Ogilvie* v. *Foljambe* (1817) 3 Mer. 53 at p. 62, *per* Grant M.R.
[66] *Lobb* v. *Stanley* (1844) 5 Q.B. 574 at p. 582, *per*, Coleridge J.

the mode in which an agent must receive his authority to sign a memorandum, so that it is not necessary that the authority should be given in writing.[67] However, it must be shown not only that the agent signing the document has authority to act as agent but also that he has authority to sign a memorandum of the same kind of contract as that upon which the plaintiff relies.[68] In the case of auction sales, the auctioneer is an express agent for the vendor, and his authority to sell includes authority to sign a memorandum for him; further, when the purchaser makes the highest bid and the hammer falls, he is deemed to have given the auctioneer authority to sign a memorandum on his behalf.[69] The auctioneer thus has authority to sign for both parties,[70] and although the vendor may revoke his authority before the property is sold, it seems that neither vendor nor purchaser can revoke it after the fall of the hammer.[71] The auctioneer's authority to sign for the purchaser is confined to the time of the sale,[72] but his authority to sign for the vendor, by whom he was expressly constituted agent, is of a more permanent character.[73] A solicitor has no ostensible or apparent authority to sign a contract but where a contract exists it seems he does have authority to sign a memorandum evidencing such contract.[74]

B. A Sufficient Act of Part Performance

Since 1686, equity has addressed itself to what may be described as "the task of decorously disregarding an Act of Parliament"[75] by means of the doctrine of part performance. The fundamental idea behind this doctrine, which was firmly established by a decision of the House of Lords in 1701,[76] is that if the plaintiff has done acts in performance of his part of the contract, it would be fraudulent of the defendant to plead the statute as a defence, and consequently equity will enforce the contract despite the absence of any sufficient memorandum. Equity took the view that it could not allow the statute to be made an instrument of fraud.[77]

Statutory recognition has now been accorded to the doctrine of part performance, for section 40 (2) of the Law of Property Act 1925 provides that subsection (1), which requires writing, "does not affect the law relating to part performance."

---

[67] *Heard* v. *Pilley* (1869) 4 Ch.App. 548; contrast L.P.A. s. 53(1)(c).
[68] *Thirkell* v. *Cambi* [1919] 2 K.B. 590 at p. 598.
[69] *Emmerson* v. *Heelis* (1809) 2 Taunt. 38 at p. 48.
[70] *Chaney* v. *Maclow* [1929] 1 Ch. 461.
[71] See Williams V. & P. 23.
[72] *Bell* v. *Balls* [1897] 1 Ch. 663.
[73] *M'Meekin* v. *Stevenson* [1917] 1 I.R. 348 at p. 354.
[74] *Gavaghan* v. *Edwards* [1961] 2 Q.B. 220, *H. Clark Ltd.* v. *Wilkinson* [1965] Ch. 694 at p. 702.
[75] *Spencer* v. *Hemmerde* [1922] 2 A.C. 507 at p. 519, *per* Lord Sumner (spoken of another statute).
[76] *Lester* v. *Foxcroft* (1701) Colles P.C. 108.
[77] See *Whitbread* v. *Brocklehurst* (1784) 1 Bro. C.C. 404 at p. 413.

For the doctrine of part performance to apply, certain conditions must be satisfied.

1. Evidence of the contract: the court requires clear evidence, whether parol or otherwise, that there was a contract certain and definite in its terms.[78] No amount of what would otherwise be part performance will render certain a contract which is void for uncertainty or make into an agreement that which is not an agreement at all.

2. Contract specifically enforceable: even if the terms of the contract are clear, it is essential that the contract should be one of which, had it been properly evidenced in writing, specific perform-ance would have been granted by equity.[79] Equity would refuse this discretionary remedy on a number of grounds, such as misrepresenta-tion, hardship or unreasonable delay.[80]

3. Act by the plaintiff: the act of part performance must have been done by the plaintiff with the knowledge of the defendant that it was done on the faith of the contract.[81] It will be noticed that whereas in the case of a memorandum in writing it is the signature of the defendant that is necessary, what is required in the case of part performance is an act by the plaintiff who is seeking to enforce the contract[82]; for if the party refusing to perform the contract has done the only act of part performance, there is no fraud but merely a loss to himself.

4. Performance referable to the contract: the act of part perform-ance must be "unequivocally referable to the contract." Yet although the fourth requirement is usually expressed in the above form,[83] this cannot be properly understood without further explanation.

(a) *"Unequivocally referable."* The true meaning of the phrase appears to be that the act or acts of part performance must be such that by themselves they suggest that it is more likely than not that the parties had entered into some contract of the kind alleged.[84] After all "in the nature of things no act of part performance could be so eloquent as to point unequivocally to one particular contract and no other."[85] Thus the part performance must on the balance of

---

[78] *Cooth* v. *Jackson* (1801) 6 Ves. 12 at p. 38.
[79] *Elliot* v. *Roberts* (1912) 28 T.L.R. 436 at pp. 437, 438.
[80] See Fry S.P., Pt. III.
[81] *Dann* v. *Spurrier* (1802) 7 Ves. 231.
[82] See *Caton* v. *Caton* (1865) 1 Ch.App. 137.
[83] See, *e.g. Morphett* v. *Jones* (1818) 1 Swans. 172 at p. 181.
[84] *Steadman* v. *Steadman* [1976] A.C. 536. See H.W.R.W. (1974) 90 L.Q.R. 433.
[85] Williams, *Statute of Frauds,* Sect. IV (1932), p. 253.

probabilities indicate that there is some contract of the kind alleged, leaving the terms of the contract to be established by parol evidence.[86]

(b) *Whether the act must be referable to a contract relating to land.* Until *Steadman* v. *Steadman*[87] it was considered that the acts of part performance must on a balance of probabilities indicate that the parties had entered into some contract concerning land.[88] In the case Lord Reid and Viscount Dilhorne held the acts need only refer to some contract, whilst Lords Salmon and Morris held that the acts need refer to some contract concerning land: Lord Simon thought that it was unnecessary to decide the point. Accordingly, Walton J. in *Re Gonin*[89] felt free to follow the traditional view that the act need refer to some contract concerning land.

(c) *Part performance must be established before the oral contract is considered.* "You must not first look at the oral contract and then see whether the alleged acts of part performance are consistent with it. You must first look at the alleged acts of part performance to see whether they prove there must have been a contract and it is only if they do so prove that you can bring in the oral contract."[90] In *Daulia* v. *Four Millbank Nominees Ltd.*[91] the acts of procuring a banker's draft for the deposit and attending at the vendor's offices with the purchaser's signed copy of the contract were held not to be acts of part performance of an existing contract but acts done in contemplation of making a contract: one had to ignore the evidence of an oral contract whereby the vendor had agreed that if the purchaser attended his offices before 10 o'clock the following day with the banker's draft and a signed copy of the contract then the vendor would enter into a formal written contract for the sale of the property.

(d) *"Part performance."* As just indicated the acts must have been done in performance of the contract and not merely in preparation for its performance. Thus, viewing the land or measuring it, or giving instructions for a lease or a conveyance to be prepared, or applying for planning permission,[92] are insufficient acts of part performance.

Often the act of part performance is concerned with possession of

---

[86] *Frame* v. *Dawson* (1807) 14 Ves. 386 at p. 388; *Kingswood Estate Co. Ltd.* v. *Anderson* [1963] 2 Q.B. 169.
[87] *Steadman* v. *Steadman* [1976] A.C. 536 a controversial decision. See H.W.R.W. (1974) 90 L.Q.R. 433, Megarry & Wade, pp. 566–567.
[88] *Maddison* v. *Alderson* (1883) 8 App.Cas. 467. Query whether the housekeeper might nowadays have a valid proprietary estoppel interest: *Greasley* v. *Cooke* [1980] 3 All E.R. 710.
[89] [1979] Ch. 16.
[90] *Steadman* v. *Steadman* [1976] A.C. 536 at pp. 541–542 *per* Lord Reid.
[91] [1978] Ch. 231.
[92] *New Hart Builders Ltd.* v. *Brindley* [1975] Ch. 34.

the land. If a leasehold tenant agrees to take a new lease[93] or buy[94] the land, and remains in possession after the existing lease has expired, there is no sufficient act of part performance since the tenant's possession might well be due to his holding over as a tenant at sufferance[95] and not because of the alleged contract. But where the owner or tenant (as the case may be) gives possession of the land to a person to whom he has contracted to sell or lease or assign it, there is a sufficient act of part performance on the part of the former party to the contract by his giving possession[96] and on the part of the latter party by his taking possession.[97] The former suffers the detriment of giving up possession of his land: the latter is liable to be treated as a trespasser and evicted unless he is allowed to rely upon the contract under which he claims.[98] It is the change of possession that is the important feature; the duration of the possession is immaterial, a single hour being sufficient. A *fortiori* there is sufficient part performance if the change of possession is followed by the plaintiff, on the faith of the agreement, expending money on improving the premises.[99]

Although the retention of possession by a leasehold tenant whose tenancy has expired is not by itself a sufficient act of part performance, there will be sufficient part performance by such a tenant if he spends money on effecting substantial improvements of the type which a mere yearly tenant could not make[1]; and if an increased rent is paid and accepted under a new contract of tenancy, there will be sufficient part performance both by the tenant[2] and, it seems, by the landlord.[3] It will be noticed that in this case two acts, neither of which would be sufficient by itself, together amount to sufficient part performance.

The mere fact that a landowner builds or repairs a house under an oral contract of sale is not a sufficient act of part performance to enable him to enforce the contract, for his act is equally referable to his ownership of the land.[4] But if a landowner submits to his workmen effecting alterations to a building under the personal supervision of the defendant, who frequently visits the premises and tells the workmen how she wants certain details carried out, this is sufficient part performance by the landowner of a contract to sell or lease the land, for his act in having the work done in the way

---

[93] *Re The National Savings Bank Association* (1867) 15 W.R. 753.
[94] *Lincoln* v. *Wright* (1859) 4 De. G. & J. 16 at p. 20.
[95] See *post*, p. 344.
[96] *Hohler* v. *Aston* [1920] 2 Ch. 420.
[97] *Sharman* v. *Sharman* (1893) 67 L.T. 834.
[98] *Clinan* v. *Cooke* (1802) 1 Sch. & Lef. 22 at p. 41.
[99] *Reddin* v. *Jarman* (1867) 16 L.T. 449.
[1] *Brennan* v. *Bolton* (1842) 2 Dr. & War. 349 at pp. 355, 356.
[2] *Miller & Aldworth Ltd.* v. *Sharp* [1899] 1 Ch. 622.
[3] *Conner* v. *Fitzgerald* (1883) 11 L.R.Ir. 106.
[4] *Rawlinson* v. *Ames* [1925] Ch. 96 at p. 114.

suggested by the defendant clearly indicates that there is some contract between them which relates to the building.[5]

It was considered that payment of money could not be part performance.[6] However, in special circumstances it may now be part performance since in *Steadman* v. *Steadman*[7] it was held that payment of £100 and the sending of a deed for signature by the wife were acts of part performance of an oral compromise that the husband would pay the wife £100 arrears of maintenance and the wife would sell her interest in their house to him for £1,500. It appears from Lord Reid's and Lord Salmon's speeches[8] that it may be that payment of money will only be part performance if the defendant is unable or unwilling to repay the money.

II. EFFECT OF PART PERFORMANCE

1. Evidence of all terms admissible. The effect of a sufficient act of part performance is to enable evidence of all the terms of the contract, including terms to which the acts of part performance have no relation.[9] "The effect of the removal of the barrier set up by the statute . . . is to open the door to parol evidence of the whole agreement."[10] Thus, if a landlord agrees to grant his tenant a lease with an option to purchase the freehold, part performance by the tenant which is unequivocally referable to the agreement to grant a lease entitles him to demand not merely the term of years but also the option.[11]

2. Enforceable only in equity. Nevertheless, a party seeking to enforce a contract merely supported by part performance is not in so good a position as if the contract were evidenced in writing, for part performance makes the contract enforceable only in equity and not in law.[12] A contract properly evidenced in writing is enforceable in law, and the plaintiff, on proving his case, is entitled as of right to an award of damages; equity may in addition grant him the discretionary remedy of specific performance. A contract merely supported by part performance, on the other hand, gives the plaintiff no right to any remedy at all. Equity may award him specific performance if it thinks the case a proper one, but that lies in the discretion of the court; and no damages can be awarded if the case is one where equity has no power to grant specific performance or an injunction.[13]

---

[5] *Rawlinson* v. *Ames* [1925] Ch. 96.
[6] *Maddison* v. *Alderson* (1885) 8 App.Cas. 467 at p. 474, *Broughton* v. *Snook* [1938] Ch. 505 at p. 514.
[7] [1976] A.C. 536.
[8] *Ibid.* at pp. 541 and 571.
[9] *Sutherland* v. *Briggs* (1841) 1 Hare 26 at p. 32.
[10] *Brough* v. *Nettleton* [1921] 2 Ch. 25 at p. 28, *per* P.O. Lawrence J.
[11] *Brough* v. *Nettleton* [1921] 2 Ch. 25.
[12] *O'Herlihy* v. *Hedges* (1803) 1 Sch. & Lef. 123 at p. 130.
[13] See *Lavery* v. *Pursell* (1888) 39 Ch.D. 508.

C. Cases in which neither writing or part performance is required

Neither writing nor part performance is required—

   (i) where the sale is by the court[14];
  (ii) where the defendant does not plead the absence of writing as a defence; the defendant is not bound to take advantage of the section and if he fails to plead it he renounces the benefit of it[15]; or
 (iii) where it was due to the fraud of the defendant that the contract was not put into writing[16]; the court will not allow the section to be used as an engine of fraud.
  (iv) in the case of the statutory contract arising out of a notice to treat served in the compulsory acquisition of land.[17]

Sect. 3. Contracts in Practice

A. Cases where it is Usual to Have a Contract

Whenever a transaction involves a payment of a capital sum, it is usual for it to be governed by a contract. Thus where land is being sold in fee simple, or a lease at a ground rent (a rent representing the value of the land without the buildings on it) being assigned in consideration of a capital payment, a formal contract is normally made. If, on the other hand, no capital payment is involved, there is usually no contract, *e.g.* on the grant or assignment of a lease at a rack rent (a rent representing the full value of the land and buildings). And a mortgage, although involving a capital payment, is rarely preceded by a contract.

B. Types of Contract

There are three main types of contract.

1. Open contracts. In these, only the essential terms[18] have been expressly agreed between the parties, the remaining terms being left to the general law.

2. Contracts by correspondence. In the case of contracts by correspondence, the Law of Property Act 1925[19] provides that the Statutory Form of Conditions of Sale 1925, made by the Lord

---

[14] L.P.A. 1925, s. 40 (2).
[15] *James* v. *Smith* [1891] 1 Ch. 384.
[16] *Maxwell* v. *Montacute* (1719) Prec.Ch. 526.
[17] *Munton* v. *G.L.C.* [1976] 1 W.L.R. 649 at p. 653.
[18] See *ante*, p. 135.
[19] s. 46.

Chancellor, shall govern the contract, subject to any modification or contrary intention expressed in the correspondence.[20]

3. Formal contracts. It is always open to the parties to make a contract in such terms as they think fit, subject to the rule that certain provisions contrary to the policy of the law are void, such as any provision that the conveyance should be prepared by a solicitor appointed by the vendor.[21] In practice, various standard forms of conditions have been settled, and prints of them may be purchased, *e.g.* The Law Society's Conditions of Sale, and the National Conditions of Sale. These conditions, with such emendations as are desirable to fit the particular case, are usually employed, since they avoid the labour of preparing a special set of conditions for each case.

The above division of the types of contracts is not rigid; thus the parties may agree a few special conditions and leave the rest to the ordinary rules of law, thus creating a contract which is in part formal and as to the remainder an open contract.

C. Terms of a Contract

The following are examples of the matters usually dealt with in a formal contract for the sale of land.

1. Provision for the payment of a deposit (usually 10 per cent. of the purchase-money) and for the payment of interest on the purchase-money if completion is delayed.

2. If the title is unregistered the length and nature of the title to be deduced by the vendor, and any special provisions, *e.g.* as to making no objection to some specified defect in title or flaw in evidence of title. If the title is registered the title number of the property, the class of title, authority for the purchaser to inspect the register and copies of documents referred to on the register, *e.g.* as imposing restrictive covenants.[22]

3. The time schedule within which the matters affecting the title must be dealt with.

4. The date and place for completion of the sale.

5. Power for the vendor to rescind the contract or re-sell the property in certain circumstances, such as the purchaser's insistence on objections to the title, or his failure to perform the contract.

6. Power for either party to serve a Completion Notice to make time of the essence if the contract is not completed on the date specified in the contract.

[20] See A.M. Prichard (1974) 90 L.Q.R. 55.
[21] L.P.A. 1925, s. 48 (1).
[22] If the deed imposing restrictive covenants cannot be produced a special condition should be inserted in the contract expressly making the sale subject to whatever those covenants may be: *Faruqi* v. *English Real Estates Ltd.* [1979] 1 W.L.R. 963.

Part 3

CONVEYANCING

Conveyancing may be regarded as the application of the law of real property in practice. It is an immense subject and only a very brief outline of a few of the chief features can be given here.[23] Although conveyancing does not form part of the subject of real property, every student should have some idea of the relationship between the two subjects. The work of a conveyancer is twofold. First, he investigates titles by examining documents and making inquiries and searches. Secondly, he drafts conveyances and other legal documents. The drafting of legal documents demands great skill though books of forms or "precedents" are widely used. The steps taken after a contract has been made will depend on whether the title is registered or unregistered.

Sect. 1. Unregistered Title

A. From Contract to Completion

The usual sequence of events on the sale of a freehold by V to P are as follows; most of the steps are normally taken by the solicitors for the parties rather than by the parties in person.

1. Delivery of abstract or epitome of title. Within the time mentioned in the contract, V must deliver to P the abstract of title. This document provides a consecutive story of the derivation of the title and consists in part of a condensed version of the various documents, and in part of a recital of the relevant events, such as the births, deaths and marriages which affect the title. The abstract starts with a good root of title[24] and traces the devolution of the property down to V. Thus a very simple abstract might consist of—

   (i) a summary of a conveyance by A to B;
  (ii) a recital of B's death;
 (iii) a recital of probate of B's will being granted to X and Y;
 (iv) a summary of the assent by X and Y in favour of V.

In the age of the photocopier it is now customary, as an alternative, to provide an epitome of the title, setting forth the essential facts in the derivation of title and supported by photocopies of the documents mentioned in the epitome.

---

[23] See generally M. & W., pp. 574–612.
[24] *Ante,* p. 68.

2. Consideration of abstract. P then persues the abstract or epitome of title, considers the validity of the title shown, and checks the abstract against V's title deeds.

3. Requisitions on title. P's examination of the abstract or epitome usually discloses a number of points upon which he requires further information. This further explanation is obtained by means of "requisitions on title," a series of written questions which P delivers to V. Requisitions usually consist of a mixture of genuine objections or requests for information (*e.g.* as to the date of some death, or as to the existence of some incumbrance which the abstract does not disclose), and statements of the obvious, *e.g.* that V, having agreed to sell free from incumbrances, must discharge a mortgage or obtain the concurrence of his mortgagee to the sale of the property free from the mortgage. Requisitions also usually seek confirmation of the answers to the inquiries on draft contract sent before conclusion of the contract.[25]

4. Replies to requisitions. V then answers the requisitions within the agreed time; if his answers are unsatisfactory on any point, P may make further requisitions.

5. Draft conveyance. P next prepares a draft conveyance in the form which he thinks it should take. He sends this draft to V for his approval; V makes in red ink any emendations he considers necessary, returns it to P, who makes any further amendments in green ink, and so on until the conveyance is agreed. P then engrosses the conveyance (*i.e.* prepares a fair copy of it) and sends it to V for execution.

6. Searches. A few days before the date fixed for completion, P searches the land charges register.

7. Completion. Completion then takes place, usually at the office of V's solicitor, before expiry of the priority period afforded by the official search certificate. This involves V delivering to P the engrossment of the conveyance duly executed by V; only if P is entering into some obligation towards V, as by binding himself to observe restrictive covenants, will the conveyance be executed by P

---

[25] *Ante*, p. 135.

as well. In addition to receiving the conveyance, P is entitled to receive the title deeds. However, V may retain any deed which—

(i) relates to other land retained by him; or
(ii) creates a trust which is still subsisting; or
(iii) relates to the appointment or discharge of trustees of a subsisting trust.[26]

If V retains any deeds, he must give P an acknowledgment of P's rights to production of the deeds and, unless V is a mortgagee or trustee of the land, an undertaking for their safe custody.[27]

In return, P pays V the purchase money either in cash or by bankers' draft. The exact amount due is settled by the "completion statement" which apportions the rates and other outgoings up to the exact day of completion.

B. The Conveyance

A conveyance of a legal estate must be by deed.[28]

(1) Precedent of a Conveyance

Commencement and date	THIS CONVEYANCE is made the 1st day of June, 1982.
Parties	BETWEEN John Bull of No. 1 Weelkes Street Farnaby in the County of Tye Composer (hereinafter called "the vendor") of the one part and Orlando Gibbons of No. 1 Morley Street Dowland in the County of Tallis Organist (hereinafter called "the purchaser") of the other part
Recitals	WHEREAS— (1) The vendor is the estate owner in respect of the fee simple of the property hereby assured for his own use and benefit absolutely free from incumbrances (2) The vendor has agreed with the purchaser to sell to him the said property free from incumbrances for the price of £29,750.
Testatum Consideration Receipt clause Operative Words	NOW THIS CONVEYANCE WITNESSETH that in consideration of the sum of £29,750 now paid by the purchaser to the vendor (the receipt whereof the vendor hereby acknowledges) the vendor As Beneficial Owner hereby conveys unto the purchaser
Parcels	ALL THAT messuage or dwellinghouse with the yard gardens offices and outbuildings thereto belonging known as No. 1 Byrd Street Purcell in the County of Norcome which premises are more particularly de-

[26] L.P.A. 1925, s. 45 (9).
[27] For the effect, see L.P.A. 1925, s. 64.
[28] L.P.A. 1925, s. 52 (1).

lineated and coloured pink on the plan annexed to these presents

Habendum TO HOLD the same unto the purchaser in fee simple

Certificate of value IT is hereby certified that the transaction hereby effected does not form part of a larger transaction or a series of transactions in respect of which the amount or value or the aggregate amount or value of the consideration exceeds £30,000.

Testimonium IN WITNESS WHEREOF the parties to these presents have hereunto set their hands and seals the day and year first above written

Attestation clause Signed sealed and delivered by the vendor in the presence of Edward Elgar clerk to Messrs. Delius Field and Stanford solicitors JOHN BULL

(2) *Details of the Conveyance*

In considering the very simple form of conveyance set out above, the following points should be noticed.

1. Commencement. The old practice was for the initial words to be "This Indenture." An indenture was a deed with the top of the parchmented indented, *i.e.* having an irregular edge. The deed was written out twice on a single sheet of parchment, which was then severed by cutting it with an irregular edge; the two halves of the parchment thus formed two separate deeds which could be fitted together to show their genuineness. This contrasted with a "deed poll," a deed to which there was only one party, which at the top had been polled, or shaved even. The modern practice is for the commencement to describe the general nature of the document, *e.g.* "This Conveyance," "This Mortgage" and the like.

2. Date. Whatever date is in fact inserted in the conveyance, the document takes effect from the date upon which it was signed, sealed and delivered by the parties to it.[29] A deed which has been signed and sealed but not delivered is ineffective; delivery is effected formally by uttering words such as "I deliver this as my act and deed," or informally by doing some act showing that the deed is intended to be operative. A deed may be delivered in escrow, *i.e.* delivered on the condition that it is not to become operative until some stated event

---

[29] Norton *Deeds* (2nd ed., 1928), p. 189.

occurs.[30] Usually a vendor of land will execute the conveyance some days before completion and deliver it to his solicitor in escrow, the condition being the completion of the purchase by the purchaser.[31] Where a deed is delivered as an escrow it takes effect from the date of delivery of the deed and not from the date on which the conditions of the escrow are satisfied.[32]

3. Parties. If any other person is an essential party to the transaction, such as a mortgagee who is releasing the property from his mortgage, he will be included as a party.

4. Recitals. These are of two types:

(a) *Narrative recitals*, which deal with matters such as how the vendor became entitled to the land; and

(b) *Introductory recitals*, which explain how and why the existing state of affairs is to be altered, *e.g.* that the parties have agreed for the sale of the property.

5. Testatum. This is the beginning of the operative part of the conveyance.

6. Consideration. The consideration is stated to show (*inter alia*) that the transaction is not a voluntary one.[33]

7. Receipt clause. This is inserted to save a receipt being given. Further, a solicitor who produces a conveyance containing such a clause which has been duly executed by the vendor thereby demonstrates that he has authority from the vendor to receive the purchase money.[34]

8. Operative words. These effect the actual conveyance of the property. A most important part of them is the phrase "As Beneficial Owner." It involves some consideration of the subject of covenants for title.

(a) *The covenants.* In order to shorten conveyances and other documents, the Law of Property Act 1925[35] provides that where for

---

[30] See *Beesly* v. *Hallwood Estates Ltd.* [1961] Ch. 105.
[31] *Glessing* v. *Green* [1975] 1 W.L.R. 863.
[32] *Alan Estates Ltd.* v. *W.G. Stores Ltd.*, [1981] 3 All E.R. 481.
[33] This excludes the possibility of a resulting trust.
[34] L.P.A. 1925, s. 69.
[35] s. 76, 2nd Sched., replacing C.A. 1881, s. 7.

valuable consideration a person conveys *and*[36] is expressed to convey land "as beneficial owner" the following covenants for title are implied:

(i) Good right to convey: the vendor has power to convey the land.

(ii) Quiet enjoyment: the purchaser shall have quiet enjoyment of the land (see p. 359 *post*).

(iii) Freedom from incumbrances: the land is free from any incumbrances other than those subject to which the conveyance is expressly made.

(iv) Further assurance: the vendor will execute such assurances and do such things as are necessary to cure any defect in the conveyance.

In the case of a sale of leaseholds, the following additional covenants are implied:

(v) That the lease is valid.

(vi) That the rent has been paid and the covenants in the lease duly performed.[37]

Where a person conveys and is expressed to convey (whether or not for value) "as settlor" the only covenant implied is one for further assurance, binding that person and those claiming under him. Where a person conveys "as trustee," "as mortgagee," "as personal representative," or "under an order of the court" the only covenant implied is that the grantor has not himself incumbered the land.[38]

(b) *Enforceability of the covenants*. The rules for enforcing covenants for title are as follows.

The benefit of the covenants runs with the land, so that each person in whom the land is for the time being vested is entitled to enforce the covenant.[39] Thus if V enters into the covenants with P, and later P sells the land to Q, Q is entitled to enforce the covenants for title against V even though Q was not a party to the conveyance from V to P which created the obligations.

As regards the burden of the covenant, the person liable is the person entering into the covenant. He does not, however, always make himself responsible for the acts of everyone. If land is conveyed

---

[36] If two persons who are trustees for sale purport to convey "as beneficial owner" so that they do not have the actual capacity in which they express to convey, the view has been taken that the covenants are not implied: *Fay* v. *Miller, Wilkins & Co.* [1941] Ch. 360. This seems doubtful: *Re Ray* [1896] 1 Ch. 468; *Parker* v. *Judkin* [1931] 1 Ch. 475; *Butler* v. *Broadhead* [1975] Ch. 97.

[37] L.P.A. 1925, s. 76, 2nd Sched.

[38] *Ibid*. s. 76, 2nd Sched.

[39] L.P.A. 1925, s. 76 (6), s. 78.

"as beneficial owner" the general rule is that the vendor makes himself responsible for the acts and omissions of—

(i) himself, and
(ii) those claiming through, under, or in trust for him, and
(iii) those through whom he claims *otherwise than* by purchase for money or money's worth, and those claiming under them.[40]

Thus if V conveys land to P for value "as beneficial owner," and P subsequently discovers undisclosed incumbrances, he can sue V on the covenants for title if those incumbrances were created by V, or those claiming through, under or in trust for V, or those through whom V claims otherwise than by purchase for money or money's worth, and those claiming under them. This last phrase means that V will *not* be responsible for the acts of someone from whom he *bought* the land, but that he will be responsible for the acts of somebody who made a voluntary conveyance of the land to him, or gave it to him under a marriage settlement.

Where a person creates a mortgage "as beneficial owner," the covenants for title implied are absolute[41]; the mortgagor thus makes himself responsible for the acts of everyone. As stated under (a) above, the liability on the covenants implied by using phrases other than "as beneficial owner" is limited to the grantor's own acts.

9. Parcels. The parcels describe what is conveyed; often the conveyancer employs a plan for this purpose, but this is not essential, *e.g.* if an accurate verbal description can be given, or the property can be described by reference to a plan on an earlier conveyance. The purchaser is entitled on completion to all fixtures attached to the land at the date of the contract,[42] for they are part of it; and the conveyance will transfer them with the land, without special mention.

10. Habendum. This shows that the purchaser is to hold the land for his own benefit and not upon trust for a third party. It also contains the usual words of limitation.[43] It is followed by the acknowledgment and undertaking[44] where these are to be included.

11. Certificate of value. This is so that a reduced rate of stamp duty will be charged where it is certifed that the consideration does not exceed a specified amount: see section 55 of the Finance Act 1963.

---

[40] *Ibid.* 2nd Sched.; *David* v. *Sabin* [1893] 1 Ch. 523 at pp. 532, 533. And see M. & W. 605–610.
[41] L.P.A.s. 76, 2nd Sched.
[42] For fixtures, see *ante*, pp. 19 *et seq.*
[43] *Ante*, pp. 33 *et seq.*
[44] *Ante*, p. 150.

12. Testimonium, and

13. Attestation clause. These need no comment.

Sect. 2. Registered Title

A. From Contract to Completion

On the sale of a freehold by V to P the sequence of steps taken by the parties' solicitors is as follows:

1. Delivery to P of authority to inspect the register and of copies or abstracts of documents noted on the register.[45] Before entry into the contract it is usual for V to have supplied P with office copy entries on the register and, after entry into the contract, V must give P authority to make an up-to-date search of the register. V must also supply copies or abstracts of any documents noted on the register, *e.g.* as imposing restrictive covenants burdening the title.[46] If the registered title is only possessory or qualified then the pre-registration title must be treated as unregistered land,[47] whilst overriding interests, by definition not appearing on the register, require special attention.

2. Examination of title. The entries on the register must be examined to see that the vendor is obtaining what he was expecting. The register provides an instant title (subject to overriding interests) so there is obviously no need to examine the history of the title.

3. Requisitions on title. If P's official search of the register reveals any untoward entries, *e.g.* a recent entry of a caution in favour of X or if a copy of a document noted on the register is not supplied, then P will raise requisitions on these matters, as well as require confirmation of the answers given to his earlier inquiries on draft contract.

4. Replies to requisitions. V then answers the requisitions. If his answers are unsatisfactory on any point then P may make further requisitions till he is satisfied that he is obtaining what he contracted to purchase.

5. Draft transfer. P next fills in a standard form of draft transfer with such special clauses as he considers appropriate to give effect to the contract. He sends this to V for approval. When the draft transfer has been agreed—usually an easy matter—then P sends a fair copy to V to be used as the engrossment for execution by V.

---

[45] L.R.A. 1925, s. 110 (1).
[46] *Cf. Faruqi* v. *English Real Estates Ltd.* [1979] 1 W.L.R. 963.
[47] L.R.A. 1925, s. 110 (2).

6. Searches. A few days before the date fixed for completion P makes an official search of the register to ensure that nothing has been entered against the title since the last search.

7. Completion. Before expiry of the priority period afforded by the official search certificate, P will attend upon V to receive the duly executed transfer and the land certificate in return for P's banker's draft for the moneys due under V's completion statement. Unlike the unregistered land position, the legal title does not pass until P has lodged his application to register the transfer with the appropriate District Land Registry,[48] and P must ensure that this is done before expiry of the priority period afforded by the official search certificate. This period is now 30 working days.[49]

B. The Transfer

1. The Form. Form 19 will be filled in as follows:

H.M. Land Registry   Land Registration Acts 1925–1971

TRANSFER OF WHOLE
(Rule 98 Land Registration Rules 1925)

County and District   Norcome, Purcell
(or name of Greater
London Borough where
applicable)

Title Number   FT 034567
Property   1 Byrd Street Purcell in the County of
                             Norcome

Date   1st of June 1982

In consideration of twenty nine thousand seven hundred and fifty pounds (£29,750) the receipt whereof is hereby acknowledged.
I JOHN BULL of No. 1 Weelkes Street Farnaby in the County of Tye Composer as beneficial owner hereby transfer to ORLANDO GIBBONS of 1 Morley Street Dowland in the County of Tallis Organist the land comprised in the title above referred to

It is hereby certified that the transaction hereby effected does not form part of a larger transaction or a series of transactions in respect of which the amount or value or aggregate amount or value of the consideration exceeds £30,000

SIGNED SEALED AND DELIVERED by
the said JOHN BULL in the
presence of

Edward Elgar
Clerk to Messrs. Delius Field   John Bull
   & Stanford, Solicitors

---

[48] L.R. Rules r. 83 (2).
[49] Land Registration (Official Searches) Rules 1981.

2. Details of the transfer. 1. *The Form.* A registered proprietor's estate is only capable of being disposed of in an authorised manner[50] and the forms set out in the Schedule to the Land Registration Rules must be used in all matters to which they refer or are capable of being applied or adapted. Any amendments or additions can only be made if allowed by the Registrar or the Rules. However, many of the printed forms contain the standard additions, *e.g.* a receipt clause, a certificate of value, the phrase "as beneficial owner" and a blank space for any special clauses, such as a covenant of indemnity by the purchaser in case of breach of any subsisting restrictive covenants. Under Rule 78 the Registrar has an enormous discretion to decline to register an instrument either absolutely or subject to approved modifications.

2. *The date.* The transfer must be dated and takes effect *inter partes* from the date when it was signed sealed and delivered. However, the legal estate only passes when the appropriate application is lodged at the District Land Registry.[51]

3. *The consideration and receipt clause.* These are present for the same reasons as for unregistered land. A disposition made without valuable consideration is subject so far as the transferee is concerned not only to entries on the register and overriding interests but also to all minor interests.[52]

4. *Operative words.* The clause "as beneficial owner hereby transfer" is effective *inter partes* but does not transfer the legal estate, since such occurs only when the appropriate documents have been lodged at the District Land Registry.[53] The clause is intended to import the covenants for title and it is likely that the courts will strive to find that it is effective though some difficult technicalities may need to be overcome.[54]

5. *The land comprised in the title.* The purchaser obtains whatever the vendor owned in the way of a fee simple in the land described in the Register.

6. *Certificates of value.* This is the same as for unregistered land.

---

[50] L.R.A., s. 69 (4), L.R.R., r. 74, *Spectrum Investment Co.* v. *Holmes* [1981] 1 All E.R. 6.
[51] *Lever Finance Ltd.* v. *Needleham's Trustee* [1956] Ch. 375, *Grace Rymer Investments Ltd.* v. *Waite* [1958] Ch. 831 L.R.A., ss. 19 (1), 22 (1), Rule 83 (2).
[52] L.R.A. 1925, ss. 20 (4), 23 (5).
[53] See note 51 *supra.*
[54] P. H. Kenny [1981] Conv. 32, Farrand, pp. 271–272, Hayton, pp. 67–71.

Part 4

WILLS

Sect. 1. Freedom of Testation

From the fourteenth century until 1939 there was in general no restriction upon a testator's power to dispose of property as he thought fit: for good reasons or bad, he might give all his property to a mistress or to charities, and leave his family penniless. The Inheritance (Family Provision) Act 1938 changed this and the position is now governed by the Inheritance (Provision for Family and Dependants) Act 1975.

1. *Ambit of Act.* The Act of 1975 applies to the estate of any person who since April 1, 1976 has died domiciled in England and Wales. If the deceased leaves a spouse, a former spouse who has not remarried, a child of the deceased or of the family where the deceased had married the parent, or any person who immediately before the death of the deceased was being wholly or partly maintained by the deceased[55] and reasonable provision is not made by the will or the rules of intestacy (or both in combination), the court may order reasonable provision to be made out of the estate. Reasonable provision means such financial provision as it would be reasonable in all the circumstances for the applicant to receive *for his or her maintenance* except that this maintenance limitation does not apply to a spouse who was not judicially separated from the deceased.[56] The test is not subjective, but objective: the question is not whether the deceased acted unreasonably in not making any further provision, but whether, in the events which have occurred, reasonable provision has in fact been made.[57] Application must be made to the court not later than six months after the grant of probate or letters of administration, although the court may in its discretion extend the time, *e.g.* if a new will or codicil substantially affecting the situation is discovered.[58] "Child" includes a child *en ventre sa mère*, and an illegitimate child.[59] The provision is to be made out of the "net estate," that is,[60] all property which the deceased had power to dispose of by will, less the amount of funeral and administration expenses, debts and capital transfer tax, and any property treated as part of the net estate under sections 8, 9, 10 or 11, *e.g.* property

---

[55] s. 1 (1). The applicant must not have been maintained because he or she provided the deceased with full valuable consideration (other than marriage or the promise of marriage): ss. 1 (3), 25 (1), *Jelley* v. *Iliffe* [1981] 2 All E.R. 29.
[56] s. 1 (2).
[57] *Re Coventry.* [1980] Ch. 461.
[58] Act of 1975, s. 4, *Re Salmon* [1980] 3 All E.R. 533.
[59] *Ibid.* s. 25 (1).
[60] *Ibid.*

passing on death under a nomination or by *donatis mortis causa* or disposed of in a transaction intended to defeat an application under the Act.

2. *Extent of order.* Where the Act applies, the court may order perodical payments of a specified amount, or payments equal to the whole or any part of the income of the estate, or a lump sum payment or order property to be transferred outright or settled.[61] The court may distribute the burden between those entitled to specific gifts and those entitled to residue, as it thinks fit.[62]

3. *Discretion of court.* The court's power is entirely discretionary and all the relevant factors must be considered,[63] including the conduct of the dependant in question and the financial resources and financial needs of the dependant and of any beneficiaries and any reasons of the deceased for not providing for the dependant. There are limited powers for the court to vary any order[64] and to make an interim order.[65]

Sect. 2. Nature of a Will

1. A will is ambulatory. Until the death of the testator, a will has no effect at all, but operates as a mere declaration of his intention, which may be changed from time to time. For this reason, a will is said to be "ambulatory" and any hopeful beneficiary merely has a *"spes"* and not any interest in property. This distinguishes a will from a conveyance, settlement or other dealing *inter vivos*, which operates at once or at some fixed time and confers an interest in property.

A will is also ambulatory in that it "speaks from death," *i.e.* it is capable of disposing of all property owned by the testator at his death, even if acquired after the date of the will.[66]

2. A will is revocable. Notwithstanding any declaration in the will itself or any other document, a will can be revoked at any time.[67] However, although a binding contract not to revoke a will does not prevent its revocation,[68] and will prima facie be construed as not extending to revocation by marriage,[69] such a contract binds the testator's assets, so that if the will is revoked, the beneficiaries thereunder can compel the person to whom the assets have passed to

[61] *Ibid.* s. 2.
[62] *Ibid.* s. 2 (3).
[63] *Ibid.* s. 3.
[64] *Ibid* s. 6.
[65] *Ibid* s. 5.
[66] Wills Act 1837, s. 24.
[67] *Vynior's Case* (1610) 8 Co.Rep. 81b.
[68] *In b. Heys* [1914] P. 192.
[69] *Re Marshland* [1939] Ch. 820.

hold these on trust for them in accordance with the terms of the contract.[70]

3. Codicils. A codicil is similar to a will and is governed by the same rules. A testamentary document is usually called a codicil if it is supplementary to a will and adds to, varies or revokes provisions in the will: if it is an independent instrument, it is called a will. Although sometimes indorsed on a will, a codicil may be a separate document, and can stand by itself even after the revocation of the will to which it is supplementary.[71] Codicils are construed in such a way as to disturb the provisions of a will no more than is absolutely necessary to give effect to the codicil.[72]

Sect. 3. The Formalities of a Will

A. Formal Wills

I. EXECUTION

The present rules governing the execution of a formal will are as follows.[73]

1. Writing: the will must be in writing. Any form of writing, printing, typewriting and the like may be employed. No special form of words need be used: all that is required is an intelligible document.

2. Signature by testator: the will must be signed by the testator, or by someone else in his presence and by his direction. The testator's signature may be made in any way, provided there is an intention to execute the will. Thus initials,[74] a stamped name, a mark,[75] a signature in a former or assumed name,[76] or "your loving Mother,"[77] all suffice. But a seal is not enough, for the will must be signed and sealing is not signing.[78] Similar principles apply to signature by someone on behalf of the testator. Thus signature of his own name instead of that of the testator is sufficient.[79] But it is essential that the signature should be made in the testator's presence and authorised by him, either expressly or by implication.[80]

---

[70] *Re Cleaver* [1981] 2 All E.R. 1018.
[71] *In b. Savage* (1870) L.R. 2 P. & D. 78.
[72] *Doe* d. *Hearle* v. *Hicks* (1832) 1 Cl. & F. 20.
[73] Wills Act 1837, s. 9.
[74] *In b. Savory* (1815) 15 Jur. 1042.
[75] *In b. Finn* (1936) 53 T.L.R. 153 (thumb-mark).
[76] *In b. Redding* (1850) 2 Rob. Ecc. 339.
[77] *In b. Cook* [1960] 1 W.L.R. 353.
[78] *Wright* v. *Wakeford* (1811) 17 Ves. 454.
[79] *In b. Clark* (1839) 2 Curt. 329.
[80] *In b. Marshall* (1866) 13 L.T. 643.

3. Position of signature: the signature must be at the foot or end of the will. At first this requirement was interpreted liberally, but later the courts insisted upon a strict compliance. Consequently the Wills Act Amendment Act 1852 was passed. As a result if it is apparent from the face of the will that the testator intended to give effect to the will by the signature which the witnesses attested,[81] probate will be granted; but nothing which was inserted after the will was signed, or which follows the signature in space, will be effective. In short, probate will be granted to every part of the will except that which comes after the signature either in time or in space.

For example, where a will ended in the middle of the third page of a sheet of paper and was executed at the bottom of the fourth page, the intervening space being left blank, probate was granted.[82] In another case,[83] the will was written on one sheet of paper, one side of which contained all the bequests and the other the usual opening words "This is the last Will and Testament," the appointment of an executor and, beneath these, the signature of the testatrix. It was held that the proper way to read the will was to start with the bequests and then to turn over; the will was thus admitted to probate. The court may even ignore the numbered order of the pages in order to reduce the signature to the foot or end of the will,[84] or be satisfied with a signature in a space ruled off half-way down the only page of the will,[85] or on the envelope containing the will.[86] But although the court will go to all lengths within the limit of reasonable construction to save a will from defeat by such formal defects it will not resort to physical interference with it, such as folding or bending the paper.[87]

Effect will be given to dispositions contained in a document which has not been executed as a will if the document is incorporated in a will. For this to be the case—

(i) the will must clearly identify the document to be incorporated;
(ii) the will must refer to the document as being already in existence and not as one subsequently to be made; and
(iii) the document must in fact be in existence when the will is executed.[88]

4. Presence of witnesses: the testator must either make or acknowledge the signature in the presence of two witnesses present at the same time. Whether the signature to the will is made by the

[81] *In b. Bercovitz* [1962] 1 W.L.R. 321 (two signatures, only one attested).
[82] *Hunt* v. *Hunt* (1866) L.R. I P. & D. 209.
[83] *In b. Long* [1936] P. 166.
[84] *In b. Smith* [1931] P. 225.
[85] *In b. Hornby* [1946] P. 17 1.
[86] *In b. Mann* [1942] P. 146; contrast *In b. Bean* [1944] P. 83; *Re Beadle* [1974] 1 W.L.R. 417.
[87] See *Re Stalman* (1931) 145 L.T. 339.
[88] See *University College of North Wales* v. *Taylor* [1908] P. 140.

testator or by someone in his presence and by his direction, there is no need for witnesses to be present at the time of the signature if they are present when the testator subsequently makes a proper acknowledgment of the signature. But either the signature or the must be made in the *simultaneous* presence of two witnesses. An express acknowledgment is desirable but not essential; a gesture by the testator may suffice,[89] and an acknowledgment by a third party is effective if it can be shown that it should be taken to be the acknowledgment of the testator.[90]

It is desirable but not essential that the witnesses should be of full age and sound intelligence; yet a blind person cannot be a witness, for the will cannot be signed in his "presence."[91]

5. Signature by witnesses. The witnesses must then sign in the presence of the testator. No form of attestation is necessary although a proper attestation clause showing that the will has been executed in accordance with the statutory requirements will facilitate the grant of probate. All that is necessary is that after the testator's signature has been made or acknowledged in the *joint* presence of two witnesses, they should sign their names in the testator's presence.

There is no provision allowing a witness to acknowledge his signature. Thus if the testator signs in the presence of A, who signs his name, and then B is called in, and both the testator and A acknowledge their signatures to B, who then signs, probate will be refused. The testator did not sign or acknowledge his signature in the presence of two witnesses until B was called in, and A's subsequent acknowledgment of his signature is no substitute for signing after the testator as required by the Act.[92]

There is no need for the witnesses to sign in each other's presence,[93] although this is both usual and desirable.

II. ALTERATIONS

Every obliteration, interlineation or other alteration made after a will has been executed must itself be executed in the same way as a will; in default, it is ineffective unless it revokes any part of the will by rendering it illegible.[94] The signatures of the testator and the witnesses should be written either opposite the alteration (*e.g.* in the margin) or else at the foot or end of, or opposite to, a memorandum referring to the alteration.[95] Signature by means of initial suffices.

---

[89] See *In b. Davies* (1850) 2 Rob.Ecc. 337.
[90] *Inglesant v. Inglesant* (1874) L.R. 3 P. & D. 172.
[91] *In b. Gibson* [1949] P. 434.
[92] *Wyatt v. Berry* [1893] P. 5.
[93] *In b. Webb* (1855) Dea. & Sw. 1.
[94] Wills Act 1837, s. 21.
[95] *Ibid.*

An obliteration or erasure of part of a will, even though unattested, is effective to revoke that part, since it amounts to a destruction of that part,[96] and the same applies to the pasting of paper over part of a will,[97] provided the words are not decipherable by any natural means, such as by the use of magnifying glasses or by holding the will up to the light.[98] The court will not permit physical interference with the will, as by using chemicals or removing paper pasted over the words[99]; and an obliteration is not ineffective merely because the original words can be deciphered by making another document, *e.g.* an infra-red photograph.[1]

III. REVOCATION

A will or codicil may be revoked by another will or codicil, by destruction, or by marriage.

1. By another will or codicil. A revocation clause expressly revoking all former wills is effective provided it is contained in a document executed with the proper formalities.[2] This is so even if the testator had been misled as to the effect of the clause,[3] but not if the testator did not know of the presence of the clause.[4] A will is not revoked merely because a later will is entitled (as is usual) "This is the last will and testament of me" or some similar phrase.[5]

A will is revoked by implication if a later will is executed which merely repeats the former will or is inconsistent with it, although if the repetition or inconsistency is merely partial, those parts of the former will which are neither repeated in the later will nor inconsistent with it remain effective.[6] Any number of testamentary documents may be read together, each being effective except so far as subsequently varied or revoked; the sum total constitutes the testator's will.[7]

2. By destruction. A will is revoked if it is destroyed by the testator, or by some person in his presence and by his direction, with intent to revoke it.[8] There are thus two elements, an act of destruction and an *animus revocandi* (intention to revoke).

---

[96] See *post*, pp. 163, 164.
[97] *In b. Horsford* (1874) L.R. 3 P. & D. 211.
[98] *Ffinch* v. *Combe* [1894] P. 191.
[99] *In b. Horsford, supra*; contrast *In b. Gilbert* [1893] P. 183.
[1] *In b. Itter* [1950] P. 130.
[2] Wills Act 1837, s. 20.
[3] *Collins* v. *Elstone* [1893] P. 1.
[4] *In b. Moore* [1892] P. 378; and see *Re Phelan* [1972] Fam. 33.
[5] *Simpson* v. *Foxon* [1907] P. 54.
[6] *Lennage* v. *Goodban* (1865) L.R. 1 P. & D. 57.
[7] *In b. Fenwick* (1867) L.R. 1 P. & D. 319.
[8] Wills Act 1837, s. 20.

(a) *Destruction.* It is not necessary that the will should be completely destroyed; there must, however, be some burning, tearing or other destruction of the whole will or some essential part of it, as by cutting off the signature of the testator or the witnesses.[9] It is not enough for the testator to draw a line through part of the will, indorse it "all these are revoked" and kick it into the corner.[10] Destruction of part of a will normally revokes that part alone,[11] unless the part destroyed is so important as to lead to the conclusion that the rest cannot be intended to stand alone.[12]

If a will has been destroyed without being revoked (*e.g.* because an *animus revocandi* was lacking), it is proved by means of a draft or copy, or even by oral evidence.[13] A will in the testator's possession which cannot be found at the testator's death is presumed to have been destroyed by him *animo revocandi* and cannot be proved unless the presumption is rebutted by evidence of non-revocation.[14]

(b) *Intent to revoke.* The testator must have an *animus revocandi* at the time of destruction. If a will is intentionally torn up by a testator who is drunk[15] or believes the will to be ineffective, it is not revoked, for an intent to destroy the document is no substitute for the requisite intent to revoke the will. "All the destroying in the world without intention will not revoke a will, nor all the intention in the world without destroying: there must be the two."[16]

Revocation of a will may be conditional, in which case the will remains unrevoked until the condition has been fulfilled. One particular kind of conditional revocation is known as dependent relative revocation. If revocation is relative to another will and intended to be dependent upon the validity of that will, the revocation is ineffective unless that other will takes effect. Thus if a will is destroyed by a testator who is about to make a new will, and the evidence shows that he intended to revoke the old will only if he executed the new one, the old will remains valid if the new will is never executed.[17] Another example arises in the case of revival: if Will No. 1 is revoked by Will No. 2, the revocation of Will No. 2 is not sufficient to revive Will No. 1,[18] so that if the testator revokes Will No. 2 in the mistaken belief that he is thereby reviving Will No. 1, the doctrine of dependent relative revocation applies and the revocation of Will No. 2 is ineffective.[19] Again, if a testator

---

[9] *Williams* v. *Tyley* (1858) Johns. 530.
[10] *Cheese* v. *Lovejoy* (1877) 2 P.D. 251.
[11] *Re Everest* [1975] Fam. 44.
[12] *Leonard* v. *Leonard* [1902] P. 243.
[13] *Sugden* v. *Lord St. Leonards* (1876) 1 P.D. 154.
[14] *Eckersley* v. *Platt* (1866) L.R. 1 P. & D. 281.
[15] *In b. Brassington* [1902] P. 1.
[16] *Cheese* v. *Lovejoy* (1877) 2 P.D. 251 at p. 253, *per* James L.J.
[17] *Dixon* v. *Treasury Solicitor* [1905] P. 42.
[18] *Post,* p. 165.
[19] *Powell* v. *Powell* (1866) L.R. 1 P. & D. 209; *In b. Bridgewater* [1965] 1 W.L.R. 416.

obliterates a legacy and by unattested writing substitutes a new legacy, the old legacy remains effective if the court is satisfied that it was revoked only on the (erroneous) supposition that the new legacy would be effective.[20]

3. By marriage. Marriage automatically revokes all wills made by the parties to the marriage.[21] There are two exceptions to this.

(a) *Certain appointments.* An appointment by will under a power of appointment is not revoked by the marriage of the testator unless, in default of appointment, the property would pass to his heir, customary heir, executor, administrator or the person entitled as his statutory next-of-kin,[22] *i.e.* in effect, to those who would take if he died intestate. The general intention of this provision is that if the testator's new "family" will get the property even if the will is revoked, there is no harm in allowing a marriage ro revoke it. But if the property would pass out of the "family" in default of appointment, the will is allowed to stand so far as it exercises the power of appointment, and no farther.[23]

(b) *Contemplation of marriage.* A will made after 1925 and expressed to be in contemplation of a marriage is not revoked by the solemnisation of the marriage contemplated.[24] The contemplation must be expressed in relation to the making of the whole will, and not merely of some gifts in it,[25] though an inferential contemplation suffices, as in a gift "to my fiancée" X.[26] Moreover, the exception applies only if the will refers to the particular marriage in fact celebrated; it is not enough for the testator to declare in the will that it is "made in contemplation of marriage."[27]

IV. REVIVAL

A will revoked by destruction *animo revocandi* can never be revived.[28] Any other will can be revived, but only re-execution with the proper formalities or by a codicil showing an intention to revive it.[29] If a will has been revoked by a subsequent will, the first will is thus not revived merely by the revocation of the latter will.[30] If a will

---

[20] *In b. Horsford* (1874) L.R. 3 P. & D. 211.
[21] Wills Act 1837, s. 18.
[22] *Ibid.*; for those entitled as statutory next-of-kin, see *post*, pp. 172.
[23] See *In b. Russell* (1890) 15 P. D. 111; *In b. Gilligan* [1950] P.32.
[24] L.P.A. 1925, s. 177.
[25] *Re Coleman* [1976] Ch. 1.
[26] *In b. Langston* [1953] P. 100; *Re Coleman, supra.*
[27] *Sallis* v. *Jones* [1936] P. 43.
[28] *In b. Reade* [1902] P. 75.
[29] Wills Act 1837, s. 22.
[30] *In b. Hodgkinson* [1893] P. 339.

is first partially revoked, then wholly revoked, and then revived, the revival does not extend to the part partially revoked unless an intention to this effect is shown.[31]

B. Informal Wills

Certain persons are excepted from the rules that a testator must be of full age and must comply with the usual formalities.[32]

I. PRIVILEGED TESTATORS

1. A soldier in actual military service. The testator must not merely be in an army; when he makes the will he must be actually serving in connection with military operations which are or have been taking place or are believed to be imminent[33]; in one case service at a camp in England in August 1940 was held sufficient,[34] and, in another, service in Northern Ireland in 1978 at a time of armed and clandestine operations against the government was held sufficient.[35] A soldier is deemed to be in actual military service from the moment he receives mobilisation orders until the full conclusion of the operations. "Soldier" includes both officers and other ranks, a female army nurse,[36] and a member of the Air Force,[37] or Women's Auxillary Air Force.[38]

2. A mariner or seaman at sea. This includes both members of the Royal Navy and merchant seamen, and extends to a female typist employed on a liner.[39] It includes an admiral directing naval operations on a river,[40] a master mariner in his ship lying in the Thames before starting on her voyage,[41] and a seaman whose ship is permanently stationed in harbour.[42] It also extends to a seaman on shore leave from his ship, or under orders to join a new ship.[43]

3. A member of Her Majesty's Naval or Marine Forces so circumstanced that, had he been a soldier, he would have been in actual military service.[44] This enables a member of the navy or marines who has been called up to make an informal will even though he has not joined his ship.[45]

---

[31] Wills Act 1837, s. 22.
[32] *Ibid.* s. 11.
[33] *Re Wingham* [1949] P. 187.
[34] *In b. Spark* [1941] P. 115.
[35] *Re Jones* [1981] 1 All E.R. 1.
[36] *In b. Stanley* [1916] P. 192.
[37] Wills (Soldiers and Sailors) Act 1918, s. 5.
[38] *In b. Rowson* [1944] 2 All E.R. 36.
[39] *In b. Hale* [1915] 2 I.R. 362.
[40] *In b. Austen* (1853) 2 Rob. Ecc. 611.
[41] *In b. Patterson* (1898) 79 L.T. 123.
[42] *In b. M'Murdo* (1867) L.R. 1 P. & D. 540.
[43] *In b. Newland* [1952] P. 71; *In b. Wilson* [1952] P. 92.
[44] Wills (Soldiers and Sailors) Act 1918, s. 2.
[45] *In b. Yates* [1919] P. 93.

A will made by a testator who at the time of making the will comes within one of the above categories has the following privileges:

1. It is immaterial that the testator is a minor. This has always applied to wills of personalty, provided the minor is at least 14 years of age if a male and at least 12 if a female.[46] In the case of realty, this privilege seems to have been accidentally curtailed after 1925 in the case of minors who have never married.[47]

2. The will can be made or revoked informally. The will may be made in writing, with or without witnesses or signature, or it may be nuncupative; thus informal words of farewell spoken at a railway station may suffice.[48] The testator need not know that he is making a will, provided he gives deliberate expression to his wishes as to the destination of his property on his death,[49] *e.g.* "If I stop a bullet everything of mine will be yours."[50] Those entitled to make an informal will (including infants[51]) may also revoke a will, even if it has been made formally, in an informal manner, *e.g.* by an unattested letter to a relative asking that the will should be burned, "for I have already cancelled it."[52]

These privileges have always applied to wills of personalty, and extend to wills of realty if the testator dies after February 6, 1918.[53] A will properly made under the above conditions remains valid indefinitely unless revoked, even after the military or other service is over.[54]

Sect. 4. Operation of Wills

A. Lapse

I. GENERAL RULE

A legacy or bequest (*i.e.* a testamentary gift of personalty) or a devise (*i.e.* a testamentary gift of realty) is said to lapse if the beneficiary dies before the testator. In such a case, unless a contrary intention is shown, the gift fails and the property comprised in it falls into residue, which means that it passes under any general or residuary

---

[46] *Hyde* v. *Hyde* (1711) Prec. Ch. 316.
[47] See A.E.A. 1925, s. 51; *post* p. 184.
[48] *In b. Yates* [1919] P. 93.
[49] *In b. Spicer* [1949] P. 441.
[50] *Re Stable* [1919] P. 7; contrast *In b. Knibbs* [1962] 1 W.L.R. 852.
[51] Family Law Reform Act 1969, s. 3 (3).
[52] *In b. Gossage* [1921] P. 194.
[53] Wills (Soldiers and Sailors) Act 1918, s. 3.
[54] *Re Booth* [1926] P. 118.

gift in the will,[55] such as "all the rest of my property I leave to X." If
there is no residuary gift, or if the gift which lapses is itself a gift of all
or part of the residue, there is a partial intestacy and the property
passes to the person entitled on intestacy.[56]

II. EXCLUSION OF THE GENERAL RULE

1. No lapse. The Wills Act 1837 excludes the general rule in two
important cases:

(a) *Entails:* by section 32, subject to any contrary intention, there
is no lapse if property is given to a person in tail and he
predeceases the testator, leaving issue living at the testator's
death capable of inheriting under the entail.

(b) *Gifts to issue:* by section 33, subject to any contrary intention,
there is no lapse if property is given to a child or other issue of
the testator who leaves issue living (and not merely *en ventre
sa mère*, it seems[57]) at the testator's death. "Issue" includes
legitimated issue[58] and, for testators dying after 1969, illegitimate issue.[59]

In neither case does the Act give anything to the issue whose
survival prevented the lapse; it merely provides that the gift shall take
effect as if the legatee or devisee had died immediately after the
testator. Accordingly if T leaves £2,000 by his will to his daughter D,
who dies some years before him, the legacy lapses unless she left issue
who survived both herself and T, in which case the £2,000 forms part
of D's estate. If D died a bankrupt, it passes to her trustees in
bankruptcy[60]; if she was solvent but bequeathed all her property to
charities or strangers, it passes to them under her will.[61] Only if D's
issue are entitled under her will or intestacy will they benefit.

The fiction that D survived is now applied only so far as is
necessary to prevent a lapse. Thus where it saves from lapse a gift by
a father who died in 1940 to a son who died intestate in 1920, the
property carried to the son's estate passes under the rules of intestacy
in force at the date of the son's real, and not his notional, death.[62]

2. Exceptions. In four cases section 33 does not apply to prevent a
lapse.

[55] Wills Act 1837, s. 25.
[56] *Ackroyd* v. *Smithson* (1780) 1 Bro.C.C. 503.
[57] See *Elliot* v. *Lord Joicey* [1935] A.C. 209, disapproving *Re Griffiths' Settlement*
[1911] 1 Ch. 246.
[58] *Re Brodie* [1967] Ch. 818; Family Law Reform Act 1969, s. 16 (2).
[59] Family Law Reform Act 1969, s. 16.
[60] *Re Pearson* [1920] 1 Ch. 217.
[61] *Re Hayter* [1937] 2 All E.R. 110.
[62] *Re Basioli* [1953] Ch. 367.

(a) *Appointments under special powers:* section 33 does not apply to an appointment by will under a special power,[63] for it is confined to cases where property is "devised or bequeathed." It does, however, apply to appointments under general powers.[64]

(b) *Class gifts:* section 33 does not apply to class gifts,[65] such as a gift to "all my children," even if in fact there is only one member of the class.[66] The reason for this is that membership of a class is normally ascertained at a testator's death, and those dying before the testator fail to become members of the class. Strictly, there is no question of lapse; it is merely that nothing has ever been given to those who predecease the testator. But a gift of property "to be equally divided between my five daughters" is not a class gift, for there is a gift to each individual alive at the date of the will; section 33 will accordingly apply if one of the children predeceases the testator.[67]

(c) *Interests terminable on donee's death:* section 33 does not preserve gifts which would in any case terminate with the donee's death, *e.g.* gifts of a life interest or joint tenancy.[68]

(d) *Certain contingent gifts:* section 33 does not preserve a contingent gift such as a bequest "to X as and when he is 25" if X dies aged 24, even if he would have attained the requisite age had he in fact outlived the testator.[69]

III. COMMORIENTES

Where a devisee or legatee dies at nearly the same time as the testator, it is necessary to determine which survived the other in order to know whether the gift lapsed. Similar questions between *commorientes* (those dying together) arise on intestacy and in respect of joint tenancies. Before 1926, there was no means of settling the question if there was no evidence of the order of deaths. Thus if two people perished in a shipwreck, in the absence of evidence of survivorship, the estate of one could not benefit under the will or intestacy of the other, for it was impossible for the personal representatives to establish the survivorship essential to their case. In the case of deaths after 1925, however, where it is uncertain which survived the other, for all purposes affecting the title to property the younger is deemed to have survived the elder, subject to any order of the court.[70] This rule applies equally to cases of simple uncertainty,

[63] *Holyland v. Lewin* (1883) 26 Ch.D. 266.
[64] *Eccles v. Cheyne* (1856) 2 K. & J. 676.
[65] See *post,* p. 210.
[66] *Re Harvey's Estate* [1893] 1 Ch. 567.
[67] *Re Smith's Trusts* (1878) 9 Ch.D. 117.
[68] See *Re Butler* [1918] 1 I.R. 394.
[69] *Re Wolson* [1939] Ch. 780.
[70] L.P.A. 1925, s. 184. For an exception, see *post,* pp. 174, 175 (intestate spouses).

as where one of the parties is on a ship which founders with all hands on an uncertain date and the other dies at home during that period, and to common disasters, such as virtually simultaneous deaths in an air-raid.[71] But for the purpose of capital transfer tax, the old rule remains, and each is deemed to have died simultaneously, so that there can be no second liability for tax on the death of a notional survivor.[72]

B. Gifts to Witnesses

1. Invalidation of gift. The Wills Act 1837[73] provides that the attestation of a beneficiary or his or her spouse is not to invalidate the will, but the beneficiary can claim no benefit under the will, either as to realty or personalty.

2. Limits of the rule. This rule does not apply in the following cases.

(a) *Informal wills*: where no witnesses at all are necessary for the validity of the will, as where the testator is a soldier in actual military service.[74]

(b) *Sufficient other witnesses*: where the testator dies after May 29, 1968, and the will would be validly executed without regard to the attestation by the beneficiary or his or her spouse.[75]

(c) *Signed not as a witness*: where the person has signed the will not as a witness but merely, for example, to show that he agrees with the testator's leaving him less than his brothers and sisters.[76]

(d) *Subsequent marriage*: where the marriage of the beneficiary to the witness occurred after the date of the will.[77]

(e) *Fiduciary gifts*: where the gift to the witness is to him as a trustee and not beneficially.[78]

(f) *Confirmation*: where the gift is made or confirmed by any will or codicil not attested by the beneficiary. Thus if there is a gift by will confirmed by codicil, a beneficiary who witnesses only one document is entitled to the gift since he can claim under the other document.[79]

(g) *Secret trusts*: where the beneficiary does not take on the face of the will, but under a secret trust, operating outside the will on property given under the will.[80]

---

[71] *Hickman* v. *Peacey* [1945] A.C. 304.
[72] Finance Act 1975, s. 22 (9).
[73] s. 15.
[74] *Re Limond* [1915] 2 Ch. 240.
[75] Wills Act 1968, s. 1, reversing *Re Bravda* [1968] 1 W.L.R. 479.
[76] *Kitkat* v. *King* [1930] P. 266.
[77] *Thorpe* v. *Bestwick* (1881) 6 Q.B.D. 311.
[78] *Cresswell* v. *Cresswell* (1868) L.R. 6 Eq. 69.
[79] *Re Marcus* (1887) 56 L.J.Ch. 830; *Re Trotter* [1899] 1 Ch. 764.
[80] *Re Young* [1951] Ch. 344.

3. Effect. Where the rule applies, the effect is that the will is treated as if it had omitted the offending gift. Where the gift is of a limited interest, the effect is to accelerate the subsequent interests. Hence if property is given to A for life, with remainder to B, the effect of A attesting the will is that B is entitled to the property as soon as the testator dies.[81] Similarly if property is given to X, Y and Z as joint tenants, and X attests the will, Y and Z are entitled to the whole of the property.[82] The notional omission of the offending gift also means that a gift expressed to take effect if the offending gifts fails is itself void.[83]

C. Gifts to Persons Feloniously Causing the Testator's Death

A person guilty of murder or manslaughter can take no benefit under the will or intestacy of his victim,[84] so that a murderer's prospective interest under his victim's intestacy devolves as if the murderer did not exist.[85] This applies where the slayer is convicted of manslaughter through diminished responsibility,[86] but not where the slayer was insane at the time.[87]

Part 5

INTESTACY

The rules relating to intestacy must now be considered. If the deceased died wholly intestate, leaving no effective will, these rules govern the devolution of all his property, while if he died partly testate and partly intestate, they apply to all the property which does not pass under his will.

Before 1926, realty and personalty descended differently. All the realty vested in the heir, whereas the personalty devolved on the next-of-kin. Thus if a widower died intestate leaving three sons and four daughters, the eldest son was the heir and took all the realty, but all seven children shared the personalty equally. In the case of deaths occurring after 1925, both realty and personalty devolve in the same way under the new code of intestacy; and for those dying after 1952, the Intestates' Estates Act 1952 made some important modifications to the new code, though leaving it basically unchanged. Since there is now little occasion to apply the old realty rules or the old personalty rules only the new rules will be considered.[88]

[81] *Jull* v. *Jacobs* (1876) 3 Ch.D. 703.
[82] *Young* v. *Davies* (1863) 2 Dr. & Sm. 167.
[83] *Re Doland's W.T.* [1970] Ch. 267.
[84] *Re Sigsworth* [1935] Ch. 89.
[85] *Re Callaway* [1956] Ch. 559.
[86] *Re Giles* [1972] Ch. 544.
[87] *Re Pitts* [1931] 1 Ch. 546. See *post*, p. 327 for another application of this rule.
[88] For the old rules see M. & W., pp. 509–523 or 5th edition hereof pp. 264–277.

A. The New Rules of Intestacy

Where a person dies intestate after 1925, no distinction is made between realty and personality. By the Administration of Estates Act 1925, all property, whether real or personal, which does not already consist of money is held on trust for sale.[89] The personal representatives of the deceased have power to postpone sale for such periods as they think proper. However, unless required for the purpose of administration for want of other assets, "personal chattels" (see below) are not to be sold without special reason, and reversionary interests (such as an interest in a trust fund which will not fall into the intestate's estate until the life interest of some third person has ceased) are similarly not to be sold without special reason.

Out of the fund thus produced, the personal representatives must pay all funeral, testamentary and administration expenses, debts and other liabilities.[90] The residue must then be distributed to the persons beneficially entitled under rules which are on a much more reasonable basis than those obtaining before 1926, and were in the main laid down by the Administration of Estates Act 1925, though the Intestates' Estates Act 1952 made important modifications for persons dying intestate after 1952: the main changes were directed to improving the position of a surviving spouse. The present rules are set out below.

1. The surviving spouse. The rights of the surviving spouse, whether husband or wife, depend upon whether the intestate left issue, who attain the age of 18 years or marry thereunder,[91] or any "near relations," a convenient term to describe the parents, and the brothers and sisters of the whole blood and their issue, who attain the age of 18 years or marry thereunder, ("issue" as usual meaning any descendant, however remote). There are three categories.[92]

(a) *Issue.* If the intestate leaves any issue, who attain the age of 18 years or marry under that age (whether or not there are any "near relations"), the surviving spouse takes the following interests.

(1) THE PERSONAL CHATTELS ABSOLUTELY. "Personal chattels" are elaborately defined. They include horses, cars, domestic animals, plate, linen, china, books, pictures, prints, furniture, jewellery, "articles of household or personal use or ornament," and wines and consumable stores, but not chattels used for business purposes, money, or securities for money.[93] Roughly speaking, the phrase includes everything that goes to make a home, and rather more

---

[89] s. 33 (1).
[90] A.E.A. 1925, s. 33 (2).
[91] A.E.A. 1925, ss. 46 (1) (i), 47 (1) (i) and (2) (c).
[92] *Ibid.* s. 46.
[93] *Ibid.* s. 55 (1) (x).

besides, but not the house itself; the phrase has a meaning quite distinct from "personalty" or "personal property."

(2) THE FIXED NET SUM OF £40,000[94] ABSOLUTELY, free of death duties and costs, with 7 per cent. interest thereon from the date of death until it is paid or appropriated. Both the £40,000 and the interest thereon are charged on the residuary estate, though the interest is payable primarily out of income and not capital.[95]

(3) A LIFE INTEREST in half the residuary estate (an interest in income).

(b) *No issue but near relations.* If the intestate leaves no issue, who attain 18 years or marry thereunder, but one or more "near relations," the surviving spouse takes the following interests:

(1) THE PERSONAL CHATTELS ABSOLUTELY;

(2) THE FIXED NET SUM OF £85,000[96] ABSOLUTELY; with interest as in (a); and

(3) HALF THE RESIDUARY ESTATE ABSOLUTELY (an interest in capital).

(c) *No issue and no near relations.* If the intestate left no issue who attained 18 or married thereunder and no "near relations," the surviving spouse is entitled to the entire residuary estate absolutely.

These provisions are subject to a number of subsidary rules.

(1) PURCHASE OF LIFE INTEREST. Within 12 months of probate or letters of administration being first taken out (or within such extended period as the court may grant), a surviving spouse who takes a life interest may (even if a minor) by notice in writing to the personal representatives elect that his or her life interest shall be purchased for a capital sum reckoned in accordance with special rules.[97] If the surviving spouse is the sole personal representative, written notice must be given to the principal registrar[98] of the Family Division.

(2) PURCHASE OF MATRIMONIAL HOME. The surviving spouse may by writing require the personal representatives (even if he or she is one of them) to appropriate to him or her any dwelling-house forming part of the residuary estate in which he or she was resident at the death of the intestate; usually this will be the matrimonial home. This

[94] This sum for deaths after 1966 was £8,750, for deaths after June 30, 1972 was £15,000, for deaths after March 14, 1977 until March 1, 1981 was £25,000. Family Provision (Intestate Succession) Order 1981 S. I. 1981 No. 255.
[95] A.E.A. 1925, s. 46 (4), Intestate Succession (Interest & Capitalisation) Order 1977 S. I. 1491.
[96] This sum for deaths after 1966 was £30,000, for deaths after June 30, 1972 was £40,000, for deaths after March 14, 1977 until March 1, 1981 was £55,000.
[97] See Intestate Succession (Interest and Capitalisation) Order 1977 S. I. 1491.
[98] A.E.A. 1925, s. 47 (A).

does not apply where the intestate's interest in the house is a mere tenancy which would determine (or could be determined by the landlord) within two years of his death, nor where the house is part of larger property held by the intestate unless the court is satisfied that the exercise of the surviving spouse's right is not likely to diminish the value of assets in the residuary estate or make them more difficult to dispose of. These provisions of the Act of 1952 in effect give the surviving spouse a power to compel the personal representatives to exercise in respect of the house the general discretionary power of appropriation conferred by the Act of 1925.[99] The property appropriated is taken, at a proper valuation,[1] to have satisfied to that extent the property to which the surviving spouse is absolutely entitled. However, if the house is worth more than the surviving spouse's interest such spouse can still require the house to be transferred to her partly in satisfaction of her interests in the estate and partly for money.[2] The personal representatives must not unnecessarily sell the house within twelve months after probate or letters of administration have first been taken out, and the surviving spouse's right to require an appropriation is exercisable only during that period or any extension granted by the court.[3]

(3) PARTIAL INTESTACY. Under the Act of 1952, the sums of £40,000 or £85,000 mentioned above must be diminished by the value of any beneficial interest acquired by the surviving spouse under the will of the deceased.[4] If, for example, the surviving spouse is given a life interest under the will, and the rest of the property is undisposed of, the spouse may at once claim the £40,000 or £85,000 less the actuarial value of the life interest.[5] Alternatively, the surviving spouse may prefer to disclaim the testamentary life interest and take under the intestacy alone.[6]

(4) SEPARATION. If husband and wife are separated by a decree of judicial separation and the separation is continuing, any property in respect of which either of them dies intestate will devolve as if the other were already dead.[7]

(5) COMMORIENTES. Although the general rule laid down for commorientes[8] applies in general to intestacy, the Act of 1952 has modified its application as between husband and wife. When the intestate and his or her spouse die in circumstances rendering it

---

[99] By s. 41.
[1] At the date of appropriation, not death: *Re Collins* [1975] 1 W.L.R. 309.
[2] *Re Phelps* [1980] Ch. 275.
[3] I.E.A. 1952, 2nd Sched.
[4] A.E.A. 1925, s. 49 (1) (*aa*).
[5] *Re Bowen-Buscarlet's W.T.* [1972] Ch. 463.
[6] See *Re Sullivan* [1930] 1 Ch. 84: *Re Thornber* [1937] Ch. 29.
[7] Matrimonial Causes Act 1973, s. 18 (2), replacing Matrimonial Proceedings and Property Act 1970, s. 40, applying to deaths after July 31, 1970.
[8] See *ante*, p. 169.

uncertain which survived the other, the rules of intestacy apply as if the spouse had not survived the intestate.[9] Thus if the wife, W, is younger than the husband, H, and both perish in a common disaster, then for the purposes of H's intestacy W will be treated as not having survived him. This avoids W taking benefits under H's intestacy which would almost instantly pass under her will or intestacy (probably to her side of the family if she had no issue). H's property accordingly passes as if no spouse had survived him, and so does W's. This exception to the general rule is confined to intestacy as between spouses; it does not affect wills, nor does it apply to other relations, *e.g.* issue.

2. The issue. Subject to the rights of the surviving spouse, if any, the property is held on the statutory trusts for the issue.[10] Under these trusts, the property is held upon trust for all the children of the deceased living at his death in equal shares, subject to three qualifications.

(a) *Subject to representation*, *i.e.* subject to the rule that issue of a deceased child stand in his shoes and take his share; descent is thus *per stirpes*.

(b) *Subject to the rule that no issue attains a vested interest until he is 18 years old*[11] *or married*. This in effect means that if a minor dies without having married, the property must be dealt with from that moment as if the minor had never existed.[12] Thus if X dies leaving a widow and minor son, the widow takes a life interest in half of the residue. If the son dies before either marrying or attaining his majority, the widow forthwith takes absolutely either half the residue, or all, depending on whether any "near relations" survived X.

(c) *Subject to hotchpot.* There are two rules governing this.

(1) INTER VIVOS. If they wish to share in the distribution of the estate, children (but not remoter issue) must bring into account any money or property which the deceased has in his lifetime paid them or settled for their benefit by way of advancement or upon marriage.[13] For example, if the estate is worth £16,000 and there are three children, one of whom has received an advancement of £2,000 in the intestate's lifetime, that child can claim only £4,000 out of the £16,000; the other two children each receive £6,000. Had the first child received an advancement of £10,000, he could not be compelled to refund any part of it for distribution between the others. The

[9] A.E.A. 1925, s. 46 (3), added by I.E.A. 1952, s. 1 (4).
[10] A.E.A. 1925, s. 46 (1).
[11] Family Reform Act 1969, s. 3 (2). For deaths before 1970 the age is 21.
[12] See A.E.A. 1925, s. 47 (2).
[13] A.E.A. 1925, s. 47 (1).

obligation to bring property into hotchpot is subject to any contrary intention appearing from the circumstances of the case. In determining what advances must be brought into hotchpot, a distinction must be drawn between payments made to start a child in life, and casual or periodical sums paid in the ordinary course of events or so as to relieve the child from temporary difficulties; the former alone need be brought into hotchpot.[14]

(2) PARTIAL INTESTACY. In the case of partial intestacy, issue of the deceased, whether children or remoter descendants, must, subject to any contrary intention shown by the deceased, bring into hotchpot any benefit received by him or his issue under his will.[15] Thus if a grandchild of the deceased has received £1,000 from him, neither he nor his parent need bring it into hotchpot if it was an advancement made *inter vivos* (for he is not a child of the deceased), but it must be brought into account if it is given him by will.

If no issue attains a vested interest, then, subject to the claim of the surviving spouse (if any) the relatives of the deceased are entitled in the following order[16]; any member of one class who takes a vested interest excludes all members of subsequent classes.

3. The parents of the deceased are entitled in equal shares absolutely; if one is dead, the survivor is entitled absolutely.

4. The brothers and sisters of the whole blood, on the statutory trusts.

A division must be made here, for at this point the "near relations" end. Those included in the foregoing classes may take an interest even though the intestate left a surviving spouse; those in the subsequent classes cannot.

5. The brothers and sisters of the half blood, on the statutory trusts.

6. The grandparents, if more than one in equal shares.

7. The uncles and aunts of the whole blood, on the statutory trusts.

8. The uncles and aunts of the half blood, on the statutory trusts.

9. The Crown (or the Duchy of Lancaster or Duke of Cornwall) as *bona vacantia* in lieu of any right to escheat.

A number of points arise on the foregoing list.

(1) STATUTORY TRUSTS. The statutory trusts for the brothers, sisters,

---

[14] See *Taylor* v. *Taylor* (1875) L.R. 20 Eq. 155 at p. 157; *Re Hayward* [1957] Ch. 528.
[15] A.E.A. 1925, s. 49; see *Re Grover's W.T.* [1971] Ch. 168.
[16] *Ibid.* s. 46 (1).

uncles and aunts are the same as those for the issue of the deceased, save that the provisions relating to hotchpot do not apply.[17] Thus deceased brothers, sisters, uncles and aunts are represented by their descendants, whose interests in every case are contingent upon their attaining full age or marrying. "Uncles" and "aunts" include only blood relations; an aunt's husband, although bearing the courtesy description of uncle, has no claim.

(2) ILLEGITIMATE CHILDREN. Where the intestate dies after 1969, an illegitimate child (or his issue if he is dead) can take on the intestacy of either parent as if he had been born legitimate; and similarly on his intestacy each of his parents (if surviving) can take.[18] These provisions do not extend to other illegitimate relationships, or to any claim to an entailed interest.[19]

(3) ADOPTED CHILDREN. A formal adoption order (as distinct from a mere *de facto* adoption) puts both child and adoptive parents in the same position for all subsequent intestacies as if the child were their child, born in lawful wedlock, and not the child of any other person.[20]

(4) CROWN DISCRETION. In practice, the Crown modifies its strict rights under head number 9 by making provision for dependants of the deceased, whether related to him or not, and for others for whom he might reasonably have been expected to make provision. This purely discretion power, which the Act of 1925 confirms,[21] is made all the more necessary by the Crown's increased prospects of succeeding to property of an intestate.[22] Before 1926, any relation, however remote, could claim as heir or next-of-kin, and mesne lords could claim land by escheat. After 1925, no relation more remote than a grandparent or the descendant of a grandparent can claim, and there can be no escheat to a mesne lord on intestacy.

B. Survivals of the Old Rules

I. REALTY

In the case of all persons dying after 1925, the foregoing rules supersede the old rules relating to intestacy, and no curtesy or dower can arise in favour of the surviving spouse.[23] However, the old general law of descent of realty still has to be applied in three cases.

1. Lunatic: any realty (including an interest under a trust for sale of realty)[24] which a lunatic of full age at the end of 1925 then owned,

---

[17] *Ibid*. s. 47 (3).
[18] Family Reform Act 1969, s. 14.
[19] *Ibid*.
[20] Adoption Act 1976, ss. 38–46.
[21] A.E.A. 1925, s. 46 (1).
[22] See Ing, *Bona Vacantia* (1971), pp. 104–109.
[23] A.E.A. 1925, s. 45 (1).
[24] And including former copyholds: *Re Sirett* [1969] 1 W.L.R. 60.

and as to which he subsequently dies intestate without having recovered testamentary capacity, descends according to the general law in force before 1926.[25] Curtesy and dower still arise in such cases.

2. Entail: an entail not disposed of by the will of the deceased descends in accordance with the general law in force before 1926.[26] It is curious that while curtesy can still arise out of such an interest,[27] dower cannot.[28]

3. Limitation to heir: if property is limited after 1925, whether *inter vivos* or by will, to the heir of a deceased person, it passes to the heir according to the general law in force before 1926.[29] This is not a case of descent on intestacy, for the heir takes as purchaser.

II. PERSONALTY

In the case of personalty, the old rules[30] never apply to deaths after 1925. These rules still retain some of their importance, however, particularly in showing title to leaseholds, and in the practice of reversion coveyancing. Thus, if in 1920 personalty was settled upon A for life with remainder to B absolutely, and B died intestate in 1925, B's reversion (which is called by this name, although technically a remainder) passed to his next-of-kin. If the person at present entitled to B's reversion (A still being alive) wishes to sell or mortgage it, he will have to prove that he is duly entitled to it, thus invoking the old rules of intestacy.

Part 6

PERSONAL REPRESENTATIVES

Sect. 1. Introductory

1. Vesting of property. The beneficial devolution of property on death has been considered above; it is now necessary to discuss the means by which the property becomes vested in those beneficially entitled. The general rule today is that all property first vests in the personal representatives of the deceased, who in due course (and normally within the "executor's year," *i.e.* one year from the death) are required to transfer to the beneficiaries any of the property not required in the due administration of the estate, *e.g.* for payment of

---

[25] *Ibid.* s. 51 (2); see *Re Bradshaw* [1950] Ch. 582.
[26] L.P.A. 1925, s. 130 (4); A.E.A. 1925, s. 51 (4).
[27] L.P.A. 1925, s. 130 (4).
[28] See A.E.A. 1925, s. 45 (1).
[29] L.P.A. 1925, s. 132; A.E.A. 1925, s. 51 (1).
[30] See M. & W., pp. 519–522 or 5th edition hereof pp. 274–277.

debts. In this context "estate" is used not in the technical sense of an estate in land, but as a collective expression for the sum total of the assets and liabilities of the deceased.

2. Executors. "Personal representatives" is a phrase which includes both executors and administrators. If a person makes a will, he may (but need not) appoint one or more persons to be his executor or executors, with the duty of paying debts, capital transfer tax and funeral expenses, and ultimately of distributing the estate to those entitled. The executor derives his powers from the will,[31] although he must obtain confirmation of his position by "proving the will," *i.e.* obtaining a grant of probate from the court. If a sole or only surviving executor who has obtained probate dies having himself appointed an executor, the latter, on proving the original executor's will, becomes executor of the original testator also. This "chain of representation" may be continued indefinitely until broken by failure to appoint an executor, or failure of an executor to obtain a grant of probate.[32]

3. Administrators. If a person dies without having appointed an executor, or if none of the executors he has appointed is able and willing to act, application must be made to the court by some person or persons interested in the estate for "letters of administration" appointing an administrator or administrators. The duties of an administrator are substantially the same as those of an executor. If the deceased left no will, simple administration is granted; if he left a will, the grant is of administration *cum testamento annexo* ("with the will annexed").[33] Provision is also made for certain limited grants of administration, such as grants confined to settled land,[34] grants "save and except" settled land[35] and grants *durante minore aetate* ("during the minority" of the sole executor).[36] There is no "chain of representation" for administrators. If a sole or last surviving administrator dies without completing the administration of the estate, application must be made for a grant of administration *de bonis non administratis* (more shortly, *de bonis non*), which is a grant "in respect of the goods left unadministered."

Sect. 2. Devolution of Property on Personal Representatives

1. The background.[37] Before the Land Transfer Act 1897 all personalty (including leaseholds) vested in the personal representatives

[31] *Biles* v. *Caesar* [1957] 1 W.L.R. 156.
[32] See A.E.A. 1925, s. 7.
[33] Supreme Court Act 1981, s. 119.
[34] *Ibid.* s. 113.
[35] See A.E.A. 1925, s. 23.
[36] Supreme Court Act 1981, ss. 116, 118.
[37] Further, see M. & W., pp. 534–537.

whilst all realty passed immediately to the heir or devisee as the case might be. The Act made the "personal" representatives also "real" representatives, a testator's realty as well as his personalty passing to his executors. The Administration of Estates Act 1925 now governs the position whereby all realty and personalty vests in the personal representatives, who retain their original name.

2. Vesting. The Administration of Estates Act 1925 substantially repeats the provisions of the Land Transfer Act 1897. In the case of deaths after 1925, all land owned by the deceased, whether freehold or leasehold, vests in the personal representatives,[38] with the following exceptions:

(i) Entails, unless disposed of by the deceased's will.[39]
(ii) Property to which the deceased was entitled as a joint tenant[40];
(iii) Property to which the deceased was entitled as a corporation sole.[41]
(iv) Interests which ceased on the death of the deceased,[42] such as an interest for his life.

As before 1926, property subject to a general power of appointment exercised by the will of the deceased passes to his personal representatives.[43] On an intestacy, both realty and personalty vest in the Probate judge (*i.e.* the President of the Family Division) until administration is granted.[44]

3. Assents. Land, which on a deceased's death devolves on his personal representatives and does not need to be sold by them for payment of debts, etc. (when a deed will be used), could before 1926 pass to a beneficiary by virtue of an assent, which need not be in writing but could be implied from conduct showing that the land was not needed by the personal representatives for paying debts, etc., so that the beneficiary could enjoy the land.[45] The Administration of Estates Act 1925 now provides that no assent made after 1925 (even if the deceased died before 1926) will pass a legal estate in land unless it is in writing and signed by the personal representative.[46] It is even necessary for personal representatives, who have administered the estate and thenceforth are to hold land on trust, to execute a written

---

[38] A.E.A. 1925, ss. 1 (1), 3 (1). For legal estates in settled land see *post* pp. 254–257.
[39] *Ibid.* s. 3 (3).
[40] A.E.A. 1925, s. 3 (4).
[41] A.E.A. 1925, s. 3 (5).
[42] *Ibid.* s. 1 (1).
[43] *Ibid.* s. 3 (2).
[44] *Ibid.* ss. 9, 55 (1) (xv), as amended by Administration of Justice Act 1970, s. 1, 2nd Sched., para. 5. *Wirral B.C.* v. *Smith, The Times,* February 23, 1982.
[45] *Wise* v. *Whitburn* [1924] 1 Ch. 460.
[46] A.E.A. 1925, s. 36 (2), (4).

assent in their own favour as trustees.[47] A bona fide purchaser for value is no longer concerned with the terms of the will; he can rely on the grant of probate or letters of administration, coupled with an assent or conveyance executed by the personal representatives, as constituting his title.[48]

4. Ownership of assets. While the administration is proceeding, the personal representatives are the legal and equitable owners of all assets nor specificially devised and bequeathed. The beneficiaries entitled to residue have no interest, legal or equitable, in any specific assets. They merely have the right to compel the personal representatives to administer the estate properly.[49]

5. Powers. Personal representatives now have all the powers of trustees for sale,[50] and thus all the powers of a tenant for life and trustees under the Settled Land Act 1925.[51] Although they should sell the property only if this is necessary for the purpose of administration, a conveyance to a purchaser for value in good faith is not invalidated merely because he knows that all the debts and other liabilities have been met.[52] Nor is a conveyance to a purchaser for value in good faith invalidated merely because the probate or letters of administration under which the personal representatives acted are subsequently revoked.[53]

Personal representatives have joint and several powers over pure personalty but they have only one joint authority over realty and over leaseholds.[54]

Sect. 3. Number of Personal Representatives

A. Maximum

No grant of probate or letters of administration can be made to more than four personal representatives in respect of the same property.[55] If more than four executors are appointed by a testator, they must decide among themselves who shall apply for probate.

[47] *Re King's W.T.* [1964] Ch. 542. The equitable estate may pass under an assent inferred from conduct: *Re Edwards' W.T.* [1981] 2 All E.R. 941 at p. 949.
[48] *Ibid.* ss. 36 (4), (7), 39 (1).
[49] *Commissioner of Stamp Duties (Queensland)* v. *Livingston* [1965] A.C. 694; *Re Haye's W.T.* [1971] 1 W.L.R. 758 at p. 764.
[50] A.E.A. 1925, s. 39.
[51] *Post*, pp. 266 *et seq. Quaere* whether they have "*ad hoc*" powers (see *post*, pp. 287 *et seq*) as being "approved or appointed by the court."
[52] A.E.A. 1925, ss. 36 (8), 55 (1) (xviii).
[53] *Ibid.* ss. 37, 55 (1) (xviii), retrospectively confirming *Hewson* v. *Shelley* [1914] 2 Ch. 13.
[54] A.E.A. 1925, s. 2 (2), *Fountain Forestry Ltd.* v. *Edwards* [1975] Ch. 1.
[55] Supreme Court Act 1981, s. 114.

B. Minimum

Unlike trustees for sale, there is no provision that a sole personal representative cannot give a valid receipt for purchase money; a sole personal representative, whether original or by survivorship, has full power to give valid receipts for capital money or any other payments.[56] However, if any person interested in the estate is an infant or has a life interest in it, a sole administrator (other than a trust corporation) must not normally be appointed by the court after 1925.[57] A sole executor can act under such circumstances, but the court has power to appoint additional personal representatives.[58]

Part 7

DISABILITIES

Certain persons are subject to disabilities as to the interests in land which they can hold, create or alienate.

Sect. 1. Minors

An infant (or minor[59]) is a person who has not attained full age. For centuries[60] a person attained full age or "majority" at the first moment of the day preceding the twenty-first anniversary of his birth.[61] On January 1, 1970, the age of majority was reduced to 18 years,[62] which is now reached on the first moment of the anniversary of birth.[63] The following are the main points to note concerning a minor's rights in land.

1. Ownership of land. Before 1926, a minor was capable of holding both legal estates and equitable interests in land. After 1925, a minor cannot hold a legal estate in land,[64] although he may still hold an equitable interest.

2. Attempted conveyance to an infant. An attempt after 1925 to convey a legal estate to a minor alone or jointly with other minors operates as a contract for value to make a proper settlement by means of a vesting deed and trust instrument, and in the meantime to

---

[56] L.P.A. 1925, s. 27 (2).
[57] Supreme Court Act 1981, s. 114 (2).
[58] *Ibid*. s. 114 (4).
[59] Family Reform Act 1969, s. 12.
[60] See 3 H.E.L. 510, 511 for the development of the rule in the Middle Ages.
[61] See, *e.g. Re Shurey* [1918] 1 Ch. 263.
[62] Family Reform Act 1969, s. 1; S.I. 1969 No. 1140.
[63] Family Reform Act 1969, s. 9.
[64] L.P.A. 1925, s. 1 (6). There were elaborate transitional provisions which on January 1, 1926, vested in persons of full age legal estates vested in infants before 1926: L.P.A. 1925, 1st Sched., Pt. III; S.L.A. 1925, 2nd Sched., para. 3.

hold the land in trust for the minor or minors.[65] An attempted conveyance of a legal estate to a minor jointly with a person of full age vests the legal estate in the person of full age on the statutory trusts (*i.e.* the trust for sale implied in the case of a tenancy in common[66]) for himself and the minor.[67] These provisions do not apply to a conveyance to a minor as mortgagee or trustee, for which special provisions are made.[68]

3. Mortgages. A minor cannot be a legal mortgagee after 1925. An attempt to grant a legal mortgage to one or more persons who are all minors operates as an agreement for value to execute a proper mortgage when the minor or minors are of full age, and in the meantime to hold the beneficial interest in trust for those intended to benefit.[69] A mortgage to a minor and other persons of full age operates, so far as the legal estate is concerned, as if the minor were not named, although his beneficial interest is not affected.[70]

4. Personal representatives. A minor can be neither an executor[71] nor an administrator[72]; this was so before 1926.[73] If a minor would, but for his infancy, be entitled to be an administrator, or is appointed sole executor, he cannot take a grant until he is of full age; in the meantime a grant may be taken by someone on his behalf, *e.g.* his guardian. In the case of administration, the grant must be made to at least two persons or a trust corporation on the minor's behalf, since an infant is interested in the estate.[74] If a minor is appointed one of several executors, the rest of whom are of full age, he must wait until he attains his majority, when he can join in the grant of probate previously made to the others.

5. Trustees. No minor can be appointed a trustee after 1925.[75] This applies to trusts of any property, real or personal. If there is a purported conveyance of a legal estate in land to a minor as trustee, the effect is as follows:

    (i) If the minor is a sole trustee, the conveyance operates as a declaration of trust by the grantor; the effect is the same if the

---

[65] S.L.A. 1925, s. 27 (1) (a statutory exception to the equitable rule that an imperfect voluntary conveyance will not be treated as a declaration of trust).
[66] *Post*, p. 306.
[67] L.P.A. 1925, s. 19 (2).
[68] See *infra*.
[69] L.P.A. 1925, s. 19 (6).
[70] *Ibid.*
[71] Supreme Court Act 1981, s. 118.
[72] *In b. Manuel* (1849) 13 Jur. 664.
[73] J.A. 1925, s. 165, replaces A.E.A. 1798, s. 6, with amendments.
[74] See *ante*, p. 182.
[75] L.P.A. 1925, s. 20.

conveyance is to two or more trustees, all of whom are minors.[76]

(ii) If the minor is one of two or more trustees, at least one of whom is of full age, the conveyance operates as if the minor were not named, although this does not prejudice any beneficial interest thereby given to him.[77]

These provisions do not prevent an infant from becoming a trustee of property other than a legal estate in land in other ways, *e.g.* under a resulting or constructive trust.[78]

6. Settled land. As was the case before 1926, land to which an infant is entitled in possession is deemed to be settled land.[79] This is so even if the minor is absolutely entitled. In such a case, the statutory powers before 1926 were exercisable by the trustees of the settlement,[80] although the legal estate may still be vested in the infant. After 1925, both the legal estate and the statutory powers are vested in the statutory owner.[81]

7. Voidable dispositions. Any disposition by a minor of any interest in land is voidable at the option of the infant (but not of the grantee[82]) on the minor attaining his majority,[83] or within a reasonable time thereafter[84]; if the infant dies under age, his personal representatives may avoid the disposition within a reasonable time.[85] The same rule applied before 1926. As the disposition is voidable and not void, it is binding if the minor fails to repudiate it within a reasonable time after attaining his majority.[86]

8. Transfer on death. Although normally any equitable interest vested in a minor will pass on his death under his will (exceptionally) or intestacy, there is one exception. By the Administration of Estates Act 1925, s. 51(3), if a minor who dies after 1925 without ever having married was entitled at his death under a settlement to a vested equitable interest in land in fee simple, or an absolute interest in property settled to devolve with such land or as freehold land, he is deemed to have had an entailed intererst.

The objects of this somewhat strange subsection appear to be—

[76] *Ibid.* s. 19 (4).
[77] *Ibid.* s. 19 (5).
[78] *Re Vinogradoff* [1936] W.N. 68.
[79] *Post*, p. 258.
[80] S.L.A. 1882, ss. 59, 60.
[81] *Post*, p. 243.
[82] *Zouch* d. *Abbot* v. *Parsons* (1765) 3 Burr. 1794.
[83] *Ashfield* v. *Ashfield* (1628) W.Jo. 157.
[84] *Carnell* v. *Harrison* [1916] 1 Ch. 328. The Settled Land Act statutory owners can make a binding disposition of the land in which the infant is interested.
[85] 4 Cru.Dig. 69.
[86] *Edwards* v. *Carter* [1893] A.C. 360.

(i) to make it unnecessary always to take out a grant of administration to the minor's estate; and

(ii) to make the land revert to the donor.

For example, if D settled land on A for life with remainder to B (a minor) in fee simple, and B died a minor without having married, he is deemed to have had an entail. Since he can have had no legitimate children, his notional entail comes to an end and D is entitled to the fee simple, subject to A's life interest. This is probably closer to D's intentions than that the land should pass under B's intestacy to, perhaps, his father or uncle. Further, no grant of probate or administration to B's estate is needed in respect of the land. But if B had married, then whether or not he had issue, the subsection would not apply and the land would pass under his will or intestacy.

It is not clear to what extent this provision restricts the power of disposition over realty given by the Wills (Soldiers and Sailors) Act 1918 to minor soldiers and members of the Air Force in actual military service, and mariners at sea[87]; read literally, it deprives them of any testamentary power over realty until they marry, since until then they are deemed to have entails and a minor cannot dispose of an entail by will under section 176 of the Law of Property Act 1925.

9. Leases. Although a legal estate cannot be vested in a minor, a beneficial interest in a lease granted to a minor can only be enjoyed by him subject to the obligation attached to the lease. Further, unless he repudiates the lease within a reasonable time after attaining his majority, he is bound by it.[88] Even if he repudiates the lease, he cannot recover the rent he has paid.[89]

Sect. 2. Married Women

Formerly a married woman was subject to severe disabilities. At common law, the concurrence of her husband was necessary for an effective disposition of her real property. Her leaseholds and personalty were even more completely under his control. Equity intervened on behalf of the wife to a limited extent. It countenanced the setting aside of separate property beyond the control of the husband, and, as regards the separate property, she could be restrained from anticipating it and handing it over to her husband in consequence of his threats or cajolery. The position has been wholly transformed by a series of statutes commencing with the Married Women's Property Act 1882.[90] The effect is that a married woman is

---

[87] *Ante*, p. 166.
[88] *Davies* v. *Beynon-Harris* (1931) 47 T.L.R. 424.
[89] *Valentini* v. *Canali* (1889) 24 Q.B.D. 166.
[90] Also important are the Married Women's Property Act 1907, the Law Reform (Married Women and Tortfeasors) Act 1935, and the Married Women (Restraint upon Anticipation) Act 1949. See M. & W. pp. 993–997 for a full account.

today subject to no disability. She can acquire, hold and dispose of property as if she were a feme sole (pronounced fem soul), *i.e.* an unmarried woman.[91]

Sect. 3. Mental Patients

If a person is of unsound mind, there are two points to consider: first, some control must be exercised over his person, and secondly, someone must be appointed to manage his property. Only the second of these points is relevant here.

1. Control over property. (a) *Jurisdiction.* Ever since the four-teenth-century statute *De Prerogativa Regis* the Crown has exercised a jurisdiction over the property of persons of unsound mind (formerly called lunatics and now patients or mental patients). The current statute is the Mental Health Act 1959.[92] At present the jurisdiction is exercised by a judge of the Chancery Division. In practice the work is done by an office of the Supreme Court called "the Court of Protection" under a Master subject to appeal to the judge.[93] The jurisdiction is exercisable over any person "incapable, by reason of mental disorder, of managing and administering his property and affairs."[94] The normal course of events is for the Court of Protection to appoint a receiver for the patient (usually a near relation), and for the receiver to exercise wide powers under the supervision of the court, including the disposition of property, the management of a business and the conduct of litigation.[95]

(b) *Settlements.* As well as managing the property in the interests of the patient, the court is empowered to make dispositions and other transactions for the benefit of the patient's family or other persons for whom he might have been expected to provide whether in his lifetime or at his death.[96] Thus the court may authorise the making of a settlement[97] or a will[98] by the patient.

2. Capacity. (a) *After proceedings.* If a receiver has been appointed, the patient ceases to have any capacity to deal with his property.[99] He remains the owner but control has been taken from

---

[91] See *ante*, p. 95 for a spouse's rights in the matrimonial home owned by the other.
[92] Replacing Lunacy Act 1890.
[93] Mental Health Act 1959, ss. 100, 111.
[94] *Ibid.* s. 101.
[95] *Ibid.* ss. 103, 105.
[96] *Ibid.* s. 102.
[97] *Ibid.* s. 103 (1) (*d*). See, *e.g. Re D.M.L.* [1965] Ch. 1133; *Re L. (W.J.G.)* [1966] Ch. 135.
[98] *Ibid.* ss. 103 (1) (*dd*), 103A, added by Administration of Justice Act 1969, ss. 17, 18.
[99] *Re Walker* [1905] 1 Ch. 160; *Re Marshall* [1920] 1 Ch. 284.

him. Thus even in a lucid interval, any disposition by him is void,[1] though a will made during a lucid interval is valid.[2]

(b) *Before proceedings.* If there are no proceedings on foot in the Court of Protection, a voluntary disposition of property by the patient is absolutely void, unless made during a lucid interval. A disposition for value is normally not void, but voidable, *i.e.* it remains valid until set aside; however, if the disposition is made during a lucid interval, or takes effect in favour of a person not aware of the insanity, it is valid.[3]

Sect. 4. Traitors and Felons

Since April 18, 1949[4] convicts have been able to deal with their property in the normal way, acting through agents where necessary.[5]

Sect. 5. Aliens

An alien is a person who is not a British subject. At common law, an alien could not hold land, and any conveyance to an alien made the land liable to forfeiture to the Crown. There were certain minor exceptions to this rule, *e.g.* permitting friendly aliens to hold certain short leases. By statute[6] an alien can now in general hold and acquire real and personal property in the same way as a British subject.

Sect. 6. Corporations

1. Mortmain. By the Mortmain and Charitable Uses Act 1888, an assurance to a corporation which had no authority to hold land, either by statute or by licence from the Crown (called a licence in mortmain), made the land, whether freehold or leasehold, liable to forfeiture to the Crown,[7] though any mesne lords were entitled to enter within a limited time, and so secure the forfeiture instead.

2. Origin. This rule had its origin in Magna Carta 1215. Its purpose was to restrict conveyances to monastries, for inasmuch as corporations never died or married and were never minors or convicted of felony, many valuable feudal incidents would have been lost by such a conveyance. With changing conditions, many statutory exceptions were made, but although in modern times few corporations were caught by the rule, it could not be disregarded; in all cases it was

---

[1] *Re Walker, supra.*
[2] *In b. Walker* (1912) 28 T.L.R. 466.
[3] *Imperial Loan Co. Ltd.* v. *Stone* [1892] 1 Q.B. 599; *Re Beaney* [1978] 1 W.L.R. 770.
[4] Criminal Justice Act 1948, s. 70 (1); S.I. 1949 No. 139.
[5] See M. & W., p. 999 for previous position.
[6] Status of Aliens Act 1914, s. 17, replacing Naturalisation Act 1870, s. 2.
[7] *Att-Gen* v. *Parsons* [1956] A.C. 421.

essential to ascertain that the corporation concerned had authority to
hold land.

3. Abolition. The law of mortmain was out of accord with modern
ideas, and on July 29, 1960 it was abolished.[8] Today, no disposition to
a corporation makes the land liable to forfeiture for mortmain.

4. Dispositions. In general, a corporation which has power to hold
land has also the power to dispose of it. This rule is subject to certain
exceptions; thus dispositions by the Universities and colleges of
Oxford, Cambridge and Durham are restricted by provisions
somewhat similar to those which regulate dispositions by tenants for
life.[9]

Sect. 7. Charities

Formerly there were complex and far-reaching restrictions on
dispositions to a charity and by a charity. These have been drastically
curtailed by the Charities Act 1960. The present position is as
follows:

1. Dispositions to a charity. Formerly assurances *inter vivos* to a
charity were subject to one set of conditions and gifts by will to
another. These have all been repealed, and there are now no special
restrictions on such dispositions.[10]

2. Dispositions by a charity. Land held on charitable trusts is settled
land, and the trustees have all the powers given by the Settled Land
Act 1925 to a tenant for life and trustees of the settlement.[11] This
provision does not make the land settled land for all purposes. Thus it
does not require a conveyance to a charity to be made by a vesting
deed and a trust instrument, nor does it disable a sole trustee from
giving a good receipt for capital money if the scheme governing the
charity authorises this.[12] But the powers that it gives are exercisable
only subject to important restrictions. No land which forms part of
the permanent endowment of the charity, or is or has been occupied
by the charity, may be disposed of in any way without an order of the
court or the Charity Commissioners. Other land (*e.g.* land held for
investment purposes) is free from those restrictions; and even where
they apply, leases granted for not more than 22 years without a fine,
and any dispositions of an advowson, are excepted. Further, certain
charities (*e.g.* the Universities of Oxford and Cambridge and their
colleges) are exempt from the restrictions.[13]

---

[8] Charities Act 1960, s. 38.
[9] Universities and College Estates Acts 1925 and 1964.
[10] Charities Act 1960, s. 38 (2), (3), 7th Sched.
[11] S.L.A. 1925, s. 29.
[12] *Re Booth and Southend-on-Sea Estates Company's Contract* [1927] 1 Ch. 579.
[13] Charities Act 1960, s. 29, 2nd Sched.

CHAPTER 6

FUTURE INTERESTS

Part 1

Sect. 1. Introduction

IN feudal times land was especially the basis of wealth and status. It was natural that a landowner, having full powers of disposition over his fee simple, was not so happy to contemplate his heirs having such powers after his death. He wanted his land to remain in the family for generations and this necessitated preventing his heirs from ever having full powers of disposition.

The court, however, felt there had to be limits on a landowner's powers of disposition for, otherwise, a tryannical testator could tie up the future enjoyment of his land and destroy the powers of disposition. There was also the consideration that if land was tied up, then there would be no-one capable of ensuring that the land was used to the fullest advantage, and the country's economy would suffer accordingly. This led Parliament from time to time to increase the powers of limited owners of land.

From earliest times the policy of the law has been to prevent land from being tied up in perpetuity. A condition preventing any disposition of land is void[1]; estate tails can be barred and converted into fees simple[2]; if successive life estates were created then any remainder to the issue of an unborn person was void.[3] Other rules have developed to determine what future interests may be created and these rules will be examined in this chapter, whilst the following chapters will deal with the provisions for selling or otherwise disposing of land in which valid future interests subsist.

This chapter will deal with:

(1) The rule against remoteness of vesting (otherwise known as the rule against perpetuity) which makes void contingent interests which might vest at too remote a future time, *i.e.* outside the perpetuity period.

(2) The rule against inalienability (sometimes known as the rule against perpetual trusts) which makes void current interests under non-charitable trusts if the trust income must be used for specific purposes, so that the income is inalienable, for a period which may exceed the perpetuity period.

---

[1] *Ante*, p. 42.
[2] *Taltarum's Case* (1472) Y.B. 12 Edw. 4 Ed. 19.
[3] The Rule in *Whitby* v. *Mitchell* (1890) 44 Ch.D. 85 abolished by L.P.A. 1925, s. 161.

(3) The statutory rule against accumulations which prevents income from being accumulated and added to capital for longer than an accumulation period.

The modern function of the rule against remoteness. The rule originally ensured that an absolute owner could only create successive limited interests for a period known as the perpetuity period, upon the expiry of which absolute ownership must arise once more and make the land freely alienable again.

Since 1925 there is always an estate owner in whom the legal fee simple estate is vested and who has full powers of disposition of the legal estate. If the land is settled within the Settled Land Act the tenant for life will be the estate owner, whilst if the land is settled under trusts for sale the trustees for sale will be the estate owner. The land or stocks and shares[4] that comprise the capital of the trust fund can always be disposed of and converted into other land or other forms of investment. The subject-matter of the trust fund will change from time to time, though a beneficiary's overreachable interest will remain constant, so that a beneficiary with a life interest will be entitled always to all the income that the trust fund, in whatever form, happens to produce.

The rule against remoteness is now concerned with beneficiaries' interests under trusts: an absolute beneficial owner can create trusts under which limited beneficial interests may subsist for the perpetuity period, whereupon the trust property must belong to an absolute beneficial owner free to dispose of the property as he wishes. Trust capital must thus become risk capital and so the rule against remoteness influences the balance between trust capital and risk capital in the economy. However, nowadays the dichotomy between trust capital (as safe capital) and risk capital is nowhere near as marked as it once was, since many trust instruments confer on the trustees investment powers as broad as those of any sole absolute beneficial owner. The sole justification, nowadays, may therefore be to prevent the dead from ruling the living for too long: to prevent a tyrannical testator's dead hand from tying up the equitable rights to income produced by a trust fund (of land or whatever) in future generations for too long.

In order to appreciate the rule against remoteness it is necessary first to examine the distinction between vested and contingent interests.

Sect. 2. Vested and Contingent Interests

1. Vested interests. A future interest in land is an interest which

---

[4] Trustee Act 1925, s. 1, Trustee Investments Act 1961.

confers a right to the enjoyment of the land at a future time, such as a right to the land after the death of a living person. A future interest may be either vested or contingent. "Vested" when used by itself (as here) means "vested in interest," *i.e.* that there is a present fixed right of future enjoyment; this contrasts with a right "vested in possession," which carries with it a right of present enjoyment. Thus if land is devised on trust for X for life with remainder to his first and other sons successively for life, each son obtains a vested interest at birth, and it is immaterial that the interests of the younger sons may not vest in possession until long after X's death.[5]

2. Conditions for vesting. A future interest is vested if two conditions are satisfied:

(i) that the person or persons entitled to the interest are ascertained; and

(ii) that the interest is ready to take effect forthwith upon the determination of all the preceding estates and interests.[6]

(a) *Conditions satisfied.* Thus if land is given—

"to A for life, remainder to B for life, remainder to C in fee simple,"

the interests of B and C are both vested. Neither is vested in possession, for A has the only interest which is vested both in interest and in possession. But if A's life interest were to terminate forthwith, an ascertained person, B, is ready to take the land, and so B's interest is vested. Even if A is aged 23 and B 97, so that it is most improbable that B's interest will ever vest in possession, B nevertheless has a vested interest; an interest may be vested even if there is no certainty of its taking effect in possession at any time, for otherwise no future life interest or entail would be vested. If land is given to X in tail, remainder to Y in fee simple, Y's remainder is vested, not because X's entail is bound to determine at some time (for this is not the case), but because the whole fee simple has been split up between X and Y, and Y has been *invested* with a portion of it.

(b) *Person not ascertained.* If the person to take is not ascertained, his interest is contingent, even though it is bound to take effect at some time. For example, if property is given—

"to A and B for their joint lives, with remainder to the survivor,"

the death of one before the other is bound to occur at some time, yet since it is uncertain who will be the survivor, the remainder is

---

[5] See *Evans* v. *Walker* (1876) 3 Ch.D. 211; *Pearson* v. *I.R.C.* [1981] A.C. 753.
[6] Fearne C.R. 216; *Re Legh's S.T.* [1938] Ch. 39 at p. 52. For the purposes of the rule against remoteness, there is an additional condition: see *post*, p. 192.

contingent.[7] Similarly, a gift to the heir of a living person is contingent, for until that person dies his heir cannot be ascertained.

(c) *Interest not ready*. Although the gift is in favour of a specified person, it will not be vested if it is made to depend upon some event occurring, *e.g.*—

"to A upon attaining 25 or marrying," or
"to B if he returns to take up permanent residence in England."

In such cases, the interests of A and B are contingent until the event occurs, when they become vested.

3. Size of interest.

(a) *General*. For most purposes[8] an interest will be vested even if the size of the beneficiary's interest has not been finally ascertained. For example, where land is devised in trust for—

"A for life, remainder to all his children who shall attain the age of 18 years,"

each child obtains a vested interest on attaining his majority; but these vested interests are liable to open to let in each child who subsequently attains full age.[9] Thus if X and Y are the only children who have attained their majority, they each have a vested interest in one-half of the property, subject to that interest being partially divested in favour of subsequent children. When Z becomes 18, the shares of X and Y each fall to one-third and Z has the other third; and so on for the other children. X and Y, having vested interests, can dispose of their shares either *inter vivos* or by will, although even in the hands of the transferee the shares will be liable to be diminished by other children attaining full age. But any child of A who dies before he is 18 never has any interest in the property.[10]

(b) *Rule against remoteness*. A long line of cases has established that the size of a beneficiary's interest must be ascertained before the interest is vested for the purposes of the rule.[11] Thus a gift before 1926 to trustees for such of the children of X as attained the age of 25 (X being alive at the date of the gift and having no child aged 25 or more) was totally void because, as will be seen, a child might attain the age of 25 outside the period allowed by the rule.[12] It mattered not that one or more children attained the age within the period, because until it was known how many children would ultimately reach the

---

[7] See *Re Legh's S.T.* [1938] Ch. 39.
[8] For an exception, see below.
[9] See *Re Lechmere and Lloyd* (1881) 18 Ch.D. 524.
[10] See *Rhodes* v. *Whitehead* (1865) 2 Dr. & Sm. 532.
[11] See, *e.g.* *Pearks* v. *Moseley* (1880) 5 App.Cas.714.
[12] *Boreham* v. *Bignall* (1850) 8 Hare 131.

given age, the size of the share to be taken by each beneficiary was uncertain. This aspect of vesting is considered more fully later.[13]

4. Vesting subject to divesting. A remainder may be vested and yet subject to some provision which may operate to defeat the remainder completely. For example, if land is held on trust for A for life, remainder on trust for A's issue as A shall appoint, and in default of appointment on trust for all A's children equally, the remainder to the children is vested, subject to being divested to the extent of any appointment made by A.[14] In cases of doubt, the law favours early vesting, and every interest is construed as being vested forthwith if that is possible; if not, it is treated as becoming vested as soon as possible.

In the case of land held on trust for W for life, remainder for such of her children as attain 25 years, the children have a contingent interest. However, if land is held on trust for W for life, remainder to her children, but if no child attains 25 years then to X, the children will be treated as having vested interests subject to divesting. If the operative event is expressed both as a condition precedent and as a condition subsequent the court favours early vesting and so treats the event as a condition subsequent, the interests being vested subject to divesting,[15] *e.g.* where the trust is for W for life, then to her children if they attain 25 years but if no child attains 25 then to X.

5. Assignability. In the sense that all vested interests give a present right to future enjoyment, the name "future interests" is hardly appropriate. If land is given—

"to X for life, remainder to Y in fee simple,"

Y has a present interest in fee simple which is future only as to the possession of the land. Y can sell, give away, devise or otherwise dispose of his fee simple at any time he wishes. Nevertheless, for convenience, vested interests which are not coupled with a right of present enjoyment are usually dealt with under the head of future interests. Contingent interests are more clearly entitled to be described as future interests, for until the contingency occurs, the person entitled has no estate but merely a possibility of acquiring one. However. contingent interests can be assigned, devised or otherwise disposed of.[16]

Sect. 3. Classification of Future Interests

The two main categories into which future interests fall are

---

[13] *Post*, p. 210.
[14] *Re Master's Settlement* [1911] 1 Ch. 321; *Re Brook's S.T.* [1939] 1 Ch. 993.
[15] *Phipps* v. *Ackers* (1842) 91 C.1 & F. 583; *Re Mallinson* [1974] 1 W.L.R. 1120, *Brotherton* v. *I.R.C.* [1978] 2 All E.R. 267.
[16] L.P.A. 1925, s. 4 (2).

reversions, and future interests other than reversions; these will be considered in turn.

A. *Reversions*

1. Nature of reversions. A "particular estate" in land may be defined as some estate or interest less than a fee simple, *i.e.* either a fee tail, a life interest or a term of years: it is a mere part (*particula*) of the fee simple. If the owner of an estate in land creates one or more particular estates out of his own estate, the residue of his original estate which he retains is known as a reversion. Thus if a tenant in fee simple grants a life interest or a lease for a term of years, the fee simple which he retains is a reversion. If, on the other hand, the tenant creates a particular estate and by the same instrument disposes of some or all of the residue of his estate to one or more other persons, the interests of those other persons are not reversions but remainders. In the case of a reversion, the land reverts to the grantor when the particular estate determines; in the case of a remainder, it remains away from him for the benefit of some third party. It follows that while there may be many remainders created out of one estate, there can be but one reversion. Thus if X, a tenant in fee simple, grants land—

"to A for life, remainder to B for life, remainder to C in tail," he retains the reversion in fee simple, and yet has created two remainders, namely, those of B and C. Further, a reversion arises by operation of law, a remainder by act of parties.

2. All reversions are vested. From its very nature, it follows that a reversion is a vested interest[17]; the grantor, or, if he is dead, his representatives, stand ready to receive the land as soon as the particular estate determines. A freeholder reversioner on a term of years has an estate which is vested both in interest and in possession, for the grant of a lease does not deprive a grantor of seisin, and he therefore has what is properly called a freehold in possession subject to the term. From this point of view, a reversion on a lease is not a reversion or, indeed, a future interest at all; but from a more practical point of view such interests are generally treated as reversions today.

3. Reversions after 1925. Before 1926 a reversion might be legal or equitable, according to whether the estate out of which it was created was legal or equitable. After 1925, a reversion upon an entail or life estate is necessarily equitable; the land will be settled land and the

---

[17] Challis R.P. 67.

legal estate will be vested in the tenant for life or statutory owner.[18] A reversion upon a term of years, however, can still exist as a legal estate, because—

    (a) if the owner of a legal fee simple absolute in possession grants a lease, his estate remains a legal estate, for "possession" includes the right to receive the rents and profits, if any; and

    (b) if the owner of a legal term of years absolute grants a sublease, there is nothing in this to render his estate any the less legal; any number of legal estates can exist concurrently in the same land.[19]

B. Remainders

In addition to reversions, there were three principal types of future interests before 1926, namely legal remainders, future trusts, and, after the Statute of Uses 1535, legal executory interests. Complex rules[20] applied to legal remainders and to legal executory interests but they are no longer significant.

Since 1925:

    (1) the Statute of Uses 1535 has been repealed[21]; and

    (2) no future estates in real property can be legal, for the only legal estate in realty now possible is the fee simple absolute in possession.[22]

The result is therefore that—

    (i) legal remainders can no longer exist, for the second reason above, and

    (ii) legal executory interests can no longer exist, for both reasons; but

    (iii) future trusts can still exist.

After 1925, therefore, all future interests in realty must necessarily be equitable. Legal remainders and legal executory interests existing before 1926 were automatically converted into equitable interests. Thus the comparatively simple law of future trusts, free from feudal rules and statutory modifications, now applies to all future interests. In all cases, the land will either be settled land and subject to the code laid down by the Settled Land Act 1925, or else be subject to a trust for sale. This means that there is full freedom to dispose of the land itself, notwithstanding the rights of the beneficiaries, for their rights

---

[18] *Post*, pp. 258 *et seq.*
[19] *Ante*, p. 90.
[20] See M. & W., pp. 181–199, 5th edition hereof pp. 84–95.
[21] *Ante*, p. 72.
[22] *Ante*, p. 84.

will be transferred from the land to the purchase-money which represents it.[23]

Part 2

THE RULE AGAINST REMOTENESS (OR PERPETUITIES)

Sect. 1. History

1. Need for rule. Under the complex rules applying to legal executory interests and through using trusts estates could be made to spring up or shift at remote future dates, thus leaving the ultimate ownership and right of alienation uncertain for a long time. A rule was finally settled which kept such interests within due limits; this allowed settlors to leave the ultimate ownership uncertain for a maximum period of a lifetime plus a further 21 years. This corresponds to the practice under a strict settlement; if land is settled on H for life with remainder to his son in tail, the maximum period which can elapse before the entail can be barred is H's lifetime plus the son's minority, which before 1970 was 21 years.[24]

2. Development. It was many years before the rule was finally settled. As early as 1662 the limitation of a term of years to several living persons in succession had been held good,[25] and in 1679 an executory devise which might not have vested until the expiration of a lifetime plus 21 years was held valid.[26] But the rule became firmly established only by stages. The *Duke of Norfolk's Case*[27] in 1685 settled beyond doubt that a shifting use bound to take effect, if at all, during a life in being was valid. In 1797 it was settled that a child *en ventre sa mère* (conceived but not born) might be treated as a life in being,[28] thus extending the period by a possible further nine months or so; and by then it had become accepted that the effect of a statute of 1698[29] was that the period of 21 years after the life in being also might be extended to cover a further period of gestation if it existed. In 1805 it was finally settled that the lives in being might be chosen at random and be unconnected with the property,[30] and by 1833 the rule was completed by the decision of the House of Lords in *Cadell* v. *Palmer*[31] that the period of 21 years was an absolute period without

---

[23] *Post*, p. 283.
[24] See *post*, p. 235.
[25] *Goring* v. *Bickerstaffe* (1662) Pollex. 31.
[26] *Taylor* d. *Smith* v. *Biddall*, 2 Mod. 287.
[27] 3 Ch.Ca. 1.
[28] *Long* v. *Blackall*, 7 T.R. 100.
[29] Statute of Posthumous Children 1698.
[30] *Thellusson* v. *Woodford* (1805) 11 Ves. 112.
[31] 1 Cl. & F. 372.

reference to any minority, but that the periods of gestation could be added only if in fact gestation existed.

3. Statutory reform. The rule was invented and developed by the judges without the intervention of Parliament. In the main it achieved a sound solution to the problem of perpetuity, but its undue rigidity produced anomalies requiring reform. Minor amendments were made by the Law of Property Act 1925, followed by revolutionary alterations under the Perpetuties and Accumulations Act 1964. As is customary, these statutes did not sweep away the old law, but built upon it. Thus an understanding of the old law is still essential in order to appreciate the changes. Moreover, the former law still governs future interests taking effect under past dispositions, for the Act of 1964, which came into force on July 16, 1964, applies only to the instruments taking effect after July 15, 1964.[32] Furthermore, there are many cases where pre-Act instruments have created special powers of appointment and the exercise of such powers is governed by the old law.

Sect. 2. The Operation of the Rule

The rule may be stated thus:

(1) A limitation of any interest in any property, real or personal, is void if there is any chance whatever that it might be capable of vesting after the perpetuity period has expired.
(2) The perpetuity period consists of a life or lives in being at the time of the gift, together with a further period of 21 years[33]; and where gestation actually exists, the period of gestation may be added.

The principal points must now be considered in some detail.

1. Meaning of "vest." The meaning of "vest" has already been considered.[34] The rule does not require that an interest should be incapable of vesting *in possession* after the period has run, but only that it should be incapable of becoming vested *in interest* outside the period.[35] Thus if land is devised on trust for X for life with remainder to his first and other sons successively for life, the limitations are valid even if X was a bachelor at the time of the gift. Each of X's sons obtains a vested interest at birth, and these interests are not invalidated by the fact that some of the sons may not be entitled to

---

[32] s. 15 (5).
[33] This is unaffected by the reduction of the age of minority to 18 under the Family Law Reform Act 1969. For further reference see R.H. Maudsley's *The Modern Law of Perpetuities* and Morris & Leach: *The Rule against Perpetuities*.
[34] *Ante,* p. 191.
[35] *Evans* v. *Walker* (1876) 3 Ch.D. 211.

possession of the property until after the period has run[36]; it it is thus immaterial that if X was a bachelor at the time of the gift and his eldest son outlives him by 50 years, the interest of the second son will not vest in possession until 29 years after the perpetuity period has expired.

2. No "wait and see" at common law. In general,[37] the unreformed rule deals with possibilities, not probabilities or actual events. Every limitation must be considered at the time when the instrument creating it takes effect. Thus a deed must be considered at the time when it is executed, while a will must be considered at the moment of the testator's death.[38] If at the relevant moment there is the slightest possibility that the perpetuity period may be exceeded, the limitation is void, even if it is most improbable that this in fact will happen and even if, as events turn out, it does not.[39] For example, if property is given—

> "to A (a bachelor) for life, remainder to his widow for life, remainder to the eldest of his brothers living at the widow's death,"

the remainder to the brother is bad if A's parents are alive. It is just possible that A will marry someone who was not alive at the time of the gift, and if A's wife survived him for more than 21 years, the property might become vested outside the period in a brother born after the date of the gift. This possibility renders the gift to the brother void, even if A is very old and unlikely to marry or in fact marries someone alive at the time of the gift, and even if A's parents are so old that they are most unlikely to have any more children. For the purposes of the perpetuity rule, no person is ever deemed too old to have children,[40] though for other purposes the courts take a more realistic view of preternatural fertility[41]; but statute prevents the lawful marriage (and so lawful issue) of a person under the age of 16 years.[42] Again, a gift of property to certain persons "if the minerals under the said farm should be worked" offends the perpetuity rule and is void because of the possibility that the minerals will be worked after the perpetuity period has expired.[43]

It is immaterial that the gift may never vest at all; the question is whether, if it does vest, it is capable of vesting *outside* the period. A gift to the first son of X, a bachelor, may never vest at all, for X may never have a son. But this possibility does not render the gift

[36] *Re Hargreaves* (1889) 43 Ch.D. 401.
[37] See *post*, pp. 209, 219, for qualifications of this rule.
[38] *Vanderplank* v. *King* (1843) 3 Hare 1 at p. 17.
[39] These words were approved in *Re Watson's S.T.* [1959] 1 W.L.R. 732 at 739.
[40] See *Ward* v. *Van der Leoff* [1924] A.C. 653 (persons aged 66).
[41] See, *e.g. Re White* [1901] 1 Ch. 570.
[42] *Re Gaite's W.T.* [1949] 1 All E.R. 459 (Age of Marriage Act 1929); but see J.H.C. Morris (1949) 13 Conv. (N.S.) 289.
[43] *Thomas* v. *Thomas* (1902) 87 L.T. 58.

void for perpetutity; the gift is incapable of vesting outside the perpetuity period, for if X does have a son, the son must be born or conceived during X's lifetime, and X is the life in being. In short, the gift is bound to vest, *if it vests at all*, within the perpetuity period. Again, a gift by will—

"to the first of my daughters to marry after my death,"

is valid, even though no daughter may marry; for if any daughter does marry, she must do so in her own lifetime, and since the testator is dead when the gift takes effect, no further daughters can be born and all those who are alive or *en ventre sa mère* rank as lives in being. Had the gift been made by deed, it would have been void, for the donor might have had further daughters after the date of the gift (who would not have been lives in being) and one of these might have been the first to qualify for the gift by marrying more than 21 years after the death of the donor and all his other daughters.

A gift which would otherwise be too remote may be validated by the insertion of an express clause confining its vesting to the proper period. Thus a gift by a testator to such of his issue as should be living when some gravel pits should become exhausted is void as it stands, even if it is highly probable that the pits will be worked out in five or six years.[44] The gift would have been valid, however, if worded "to such of my issue living 21 years after my death or when the gravel pits are exhausted, whichever first happens"; and a gift to bodies existing "when the residue of my estate is realised" has been construed as being confined to the "executor's year,"[45] *i.e.* one year from death.[46] But a clause seeking to confine the vesting within the period must do so clearly; a void gift is not validated merely by the addition of words providing that the vesting shall be postponed only "so far as the rules of law and equity will permit."[47]

3. Future parenthood. The Act of 1964 has replaced the rigid rule that no person is too old to have children with a statutory presumption—

(a) that a male can have a child at the age of 14 or over, but not under that age, and

(b) that a female can have a child at the age of 12 or over, but not under that age or over the age of 55.[48]

This presumption may be rebutted by showing that in a particular

---

[44] *Re Wood* [1894] 3 Ch. 381.
[45] See *ante*, p. 178.
[46] *Re Petrie* [1962] Ch. 355; and see *Re Atkins' W.T.* [1974] 1 W.L.R. 761.
[47] *Portman* v. *Viscount Portman* [1922] 2 A.C. 473; contrast *Re Vaux* [1939] Ch. 465; and see *I.R.C.* v. *Williams* [1969] 1 W.L.R. 1197 at p. 1202.
[48] s. 2 (1).

case a living person will or will not be able to have a child at the time in question.[49]

"Having a child" extends to having a child "by adoption, legitimation or other means."[50]

If events falsify the presumptions, the High Court has a general discretion to make such order as it thinks fit for placing the persons interested in the property in the position they would have been if the presumptions had not been applied.[51]

4. "Wait and see" under the Act of 1964. (a) *The new rule.* The common law rule has one great advantage, one can see at the outset whether the gift is good or bad. But it frequently frustrates the intentions of settlors and testators by striking down limitations which almost certainly would vest within the period. To meet these cases the Act of 1964 has introduced the rule of "wait and see" for limitations in instruments taking effect after July 15, 1964,[52] *which would be void at common law*. For such a gift the Act provides that it is to be treated as valid unless and until "it becomes established that the vesting must occur, if at all, after the end of the perpetuity period."[53] It is now permissible to look at actual rather than possible events, so that the disposition does not become void until it is clear that it is going to vest, if it vests at all, outside the period.

(b) *Examples.* The previously given[54] example, "to the first of my daughters to marry," was bad at common law if the gift was made by deed and the donor had at the time no daughter who was married. Even if he had unmarried daughters at that time the gift would be bad, for he might have had further daughters, one of whom might have been the first daughter to marry, and that marriage might have occured more than 21 years after the death of the donor and of all his daughters living at the date of the deed. But under the Act one can wait and see whether one of his daughters, be she a daughter living at the date of the deed or a daughter yet unborn, marries within the period, that is the period which ends 21 years after the death of the donor and those daughters living at the date of the deed. If no daughter marries within that period the gift will fail, even though an after-born daughter marries thereafter.

Similarly, a gift by a testator to such of his issue as should be living when some gravel pits should become exhausted, which is void at common law, will be valid if the pits in fact become exhausted within 21 years of the death of the survivor of those of his issue who are living at his death.

[49] *Ibid.*
[50] s. 2 (4).
[51] Act of 1964, s. 2 (2).
[52] See *ante*, p. 197.
[53] s. 3 (1).
[54] *Ante*, p. 199.

(c) *Consequences*. The practical consequences of the new rule will not be as great as one might suppose from so radical an amendment of the rule. In the first place, the great majority of limitations in fact comply with the old rule, and it is not to be expected that the Act will bring about a relaxation of the standards of drafting. Secondly, the new rule does not extend the period: it does not enable a donor to do anything which he cannot achieve within the framework of the common law rule by the use of an express clause confining the vesting to the proper period, such as a period expiring 21 years after the death of all the descendants of King George VI living at the date of the instrument.

5. The perpetuity period. (a) *At common law.* (1) LIVES IN BEING. For a person to be a life in being for the purposes of the rule, it is unnecessary that he should receive any benefit from the gift or that he should be in any way connected with the beneficiaries.[55] Nor is there any restriction upon the number of lives selected, provided it is reasonably possible to ascertain who they are; "for let the lives be never so many, there must be a survivor, and so it is but the length of that life."[56] "If a term be limited to one for life, with twenty several remainders for lives to other persons successively, who are all alive and in being, so that all the candles are lighted together, this is good enough."[57] For example, gifts by a testator to such of his descendants as are living 21 years after the death of the last survivor of the members of a given school at the testator's death,[58] or 20 years after the death of the last survivor of all the lineal descendants of Queen Victoria living at the testator's death,[59] have been held valid. In the latter case, the testator died in 1926 when there were some 120 lives in being and it was reasonably possible to follow the duration of their lives; a similar limitation today might well be void for uncertainty,[60] though the living descendants of King George VI may safely be selected.[61]

From one point of view, everyone alive at the time of the gift is a life in being in the literal sense, but of course, a perpetuity period expiring 21 years from the death of everyone alive at the date of the gift would be void for uncertainty. Thus the only lives in being which have to be considered in relation to the perpetuity rules are those which may be relevant in restricting the period within which the gift must vest, *i.e.* lives which are mentioned in the gift either expressly or by implication. In the above examples, lives in being have been

---

[55] *Cadell* v. *Palmer* (1833) 1 Cl. & F. 372.
[56] *Scatterwood* v. *Edge* (1697) 1 Salk. 229.
[57] *Howard* v. *Duke of Norfolk* (1681) 2 Swans. 454 at p. 458, *per* Lord Nottingham L.C.
[58] *Pownall* v. *Graham* (1863) 33 Beav. 242 at pp. 245, 247.
[59] *Re Villar* [1929] 1 Ch. 243.
[60] Consider *Re Moore* [1901] 1 Ch. 936.
[61] See *Re Leverhulme* [1943] 2 All E.R. 274.

expressly mentioned, but this is not always the case. If a testator gives property to such of his grandchildren as attain the age of 21, his children can be taken as lives in being. They are all bound to have been born by the time of the testator's death, and a gift to grandchildren presupposes the existence of children. The gift is therefore good, for no grandchild can take longer than 21 years from its parent's death to reach the age of 21. But a gift to the grandchildren of a living person is bad, unless the class is restricted in some way, *e.g.* to those living at the death of a life in being[62]; the living person might have another child after the date of the gift and then, long after all those alive at the date of the gift had died, that child might have a child.

Consequently, it can be said that everyone who is alive at the time of the gift, and whose life the gift contemplates as one which may have some relevance in restricting the period within which the gift must vest, should be considered as a life in being; but other persons, the length or shortness of whose lives have no bearing on the gift, may be ignored.

In the case of limitations made *inter vivos*, the date of the instrument and, in the case of wills, the date of the testator's death, is the time when the period starts running and the facts must be ascertained; to be a life in being, a person must be alive at that moment.

The lives must be human lives, and not the lives of animals.[63]

(2) IF THE LIMTATION IS MADE WITHOUT REFERENCE TO LIVES IN BEING, THE PERIOD IS 21 YEARS. A gift by a testator to all his issue living 50 years after his death, or to all the children of X (who is alive) living 28 years after the testator's death, is void.[64] It is true that in the first case the testator's children and in the second X could be taken as lives in being, but in neither case has the period selected any relation to their lives; it is a period in gross, and neither the immediate death nor the prolonged life of the testator's children or of X will alter the date of vesting. Consequently the gifts must be treated as if there were no lives in being, with the result that the period is 21 years.

(3) A CHILD EN VENTRE SA MÈRE IS TREATED AS HAVING BEEN BORN. For the purposes of the perpetuity period rule, a child *en ventre sa mère* is treated as if it had been born. Two cases can arise:

(i) A child may be *en ventre sa mère* at the beginning of the period, *i.e.* at the time of the gift; in this case, the child is treated as a life in being.[65] Thus if a testator gives property for life to the child with which his wife is enceinte, with a remainder contingent upon certain circumstances existing at

---

[62] *Wetherell* v. *Wetherell* (1863) 1 De G.J. & S. 134 at pp. 39, 140.
[63] See *Re Kelly* [1932] 1 R. 255 at pp. 260, 261.
[64] *Speakman* v. *Speakman* (1850) 8 Hare 180; *Palmer* v. *Holford* (1828) 4 Russ. 403.
[65] *Re Wilmer's Trusts* [1903] 2 Ch. 411 at p. 421.

that child's death, the remainder is good, for the contingency must be resolved at the child's death and the child is treated as the life in being.[66]

(ii) A child may be *en ventre sa mère* during the period; in this case, the period is extended a far as is necessary to include the period of gestation. Thus if property is given to the first of A's sons to be 21 years old, the gift is valid even if A's only son was unborn at A's death; the perpetuity period in such a case is A's lifetime plus the period of gestation and 21 years.

It will be seen from this that two periods of gestation may arise in the same case; both are allowed. If property is given to Jane's eldest child for life, with remainder to the first son of that child to be 21, and Jane is pregnant with her first child at the time of the gift, the remainder does not infringe the perpetuity rule even though Jane's child may be a son who dies leaving his wife enceinte of an only son. Jane's child is treated as a life in being, and the perpetuity period will be extended to cover the period of gestation of the child's son.[67]

These rules do not allow the addition of any period or periods of nine months or so in all cases; they apply only where gestation actually exists.[68]

(b) *Statutory age reduction to bring gift within perpetuity period.* A frequent cause of gifts failing was that they were made contingent upon the beneficiary attaining an age greater than 21. Thus property might be given—

"to the first of A's children to attain the age of 25."

In certain circumstances, the gift would be good; if A was dead at the time of the gift, he could have no further children, and since every possible claimant was a life in being, the gift would be valid.[69] Further, even if A was alive, if one of his children had attained the age of 25 at the date of the gift, the limitation was valid as being an immediate gift to an ascertained person.[70] But if A was alive and no child had attained the age of 25, the gift was bad. This was so even if a child had attained the age of 24, for there was no certainty that he would not die before his twenty-fifth birthday and a child born after the date of the gift be the first child to reach the age of 25.[71]

To deal with cases such as this, section 163 of the Law of Property Act 1925 lays down that in certain circumstances the age of 21 may be substituted for the offending age. This may be done only if—

(i) the limitation is contained in an instrument executed after

---

[66] *Long* v. *Blackall* (1797) 7 T.R. 100.
[67] See *Thellusson* v. *Woodford* (1805) 11 Ves. 112 at pp. 143, 149, 150.
[68] *Cadell* v. *Palmer* (1833) 1 Cl. & F. 372 at pp. 421, 422.
[69] *Southern* v. *Wollaston* (1852) 16 Beav. 276.
[70] *Picken* v. *Matthews* (1878) 10 Ch.D. 264.
[71] See, *e.g. Re Finch* (1881) 17 Ch.D. 211.

1925, or in the will of a testator dying after 1925 but in either
case before July 16, 1964[72]; and
(ii) the limitation would otherwise be void; and
(iii) the excess is in the age of the beneficiary or class of
beneficiaries.

The first point needs no illustration; the second may be illustrated
by considering the limitation mentioned above, namely, "to the first
of A's children to attain the age of 25." Before 1926, if A was alive
and no child had reached the age of 25, the gift failed; if made after
1925, section 163 substitutes "21" for "25" and the gift is good, the
first child to attain the age of 21 taking the property at that age. But if
A had been dead, the gift would have been valid without the aid of
section 163 and so "25" remains undisturbed. In the result, if A's
eldest child is aged 19 at the time of the gift, whether he must wait
two years or six before becoming entitled depends upon whether A is
alive or dead.

The third point may be illustrated by cases where vesting is
postponed for a fixed period of years. A gift to the testator's issue
living 50 years after his death was void before 1926[73] and was not
validated by section 163, for the "50" is not the age of a beneficiary.

(c) *Act of 1964.* (1) LIVES IN BEING. It is controversial whether the
introduction of the "wait and see" principle required any alteration in
the rules for ascertaining the lives in being. It seems likely that no
alteration was necessary on the basis that lives in being at common
law are not confined to those which *necessarily* limit the vesting of the
gift within the perpetuity period, but are those which are so
connected with the gift as to restrict the period of vesting, and they
may or may not restrict it sufficiently to save it at common law.[74]
However, some argue that common law lives in being were only those
lives that *necessarily* limited the vesting of the gift within the
perpetuity period so that the new rule would achieve nothing if it
were tied to the lives in being at common law, as gifts whose vesting is
restricted by those lives are valid anyway without having to wait and
see. Thus where a gift was void at common law so that it was
necessary to wait and see then, unless some definition of the lives in
being for the purposes of the new rule were to be provided, there
would be only a mere 21 year period in which to wait and see.[75]
The framers of the Act of 1964 have avoided such problems by

[72] Except in the case of an instrument made in the exercise of a special power of
appointment created before July 16, 1964: Perpetuities and Accumulations Act
1964, s. 15 (5).
[73] See *ante*, p. 202.
[74] Morris and Wade (1964) 80 L.Q.R. 486 at pp. 495–501; R. Deech (1981) 97 L.Q.R.
593.
[75] Allan (1965) 81 L.Q.R. 106; Maudsley (1970) 86 L.Q.R. 357; Maudsley's *Modern
Law of Perpetuities*, pp. 87 *et seq*.

providing four categories of lives, all of whom must be both in being and ascertainable at the date of the gift. Further, lives in the second and third categories which are defined by description are to be disregarded if they are so numerous as to render it impracticable to ascertain the death of the survivor.[76] If there are no lives in the four categories which satisfy the preceding conditions, the "wait and see" period is 21 years from the date of the gift.[77]

The four categories are as follows.[78]

(a) The donor: "the person by whom the disposition was made."
(b) A donee: "a person to whom or in whose favour the disposition was made, that is to say—
    (i) in the case of a disposition to a class of persons, any member or potential member of the class;
    (ii) in the case of an individual disposition to a person taking only on certain conditions being satisfied, any person as to whom some of the conditions are satisfied and the remainder may in time be satisfied;
    (iii) and (iv) these concern special powers of appointment [discussed below[79]];
    (v) in the case of any power, option or other right, the person on whom the right is conferred."

(c) A donee's parent or grandparent.
(d) The owner of a prior interest.

In many cases these complicated provisions produce the same lives in being as the common law rule, but there are divergences. Often more lives are available under the Act. Thus a gift "to A's first grandson to attain 21" where A is alive and without such a grandson at the date of the gift is void at common law. Under the "wait and see" rule the lives in being are the donor (under (a) above), A and any existing children of A and their spouses (under (c) above), and any existing grandchildren (under (b)(ii) above), so that one waits and sees whether a grandchild reaches 21 within 21 years of the death of the survivor of those lives.

(2) REDUCTION OF FIXED AGES. For instruments taking effect after July 15, 1964,[80] the Act of 1964 has replaced the Law of Property Act 1925, s. 163, with a more flexible provision. It operates where a disposition satisfies the following conditions—

(a) It is limited by reference to the attainment by any person or

---

[76] s. 3 (4) (*a*).
[77] s. 3 (4) (*b*).
[78] s. 3 (5).
[79] *Post*, p. 217.
[80] Except instruments made in the exercise of a special power of appointment created before July 16, 1964: s. 15 (5).

persons of a specified age exceeding 21 years.[81] The corresponding provision of section 163 applied only to the excessive age of a beneficiary; the new provision applies to the excessive ages of others as well, as in a gift to an unborn person "living when A's eldest son attains 25."

(b) It is apparent when the disposition is made or becomes apparent later—

 (i) that it would otherwise be void for remoteness, but

 (ii) that it would not be so void if the specified age had been 21 years.

(c) It is not saved by the "wait and see" rule.

If these conditions are satisfied, the disposition is treated as if it had been limited by reference to the greatest age which would have prevented it from being void.[82] Here again the new provision diverges from section 163 under which the reduction was to 21 years in every case.

Thus if there is a gift by will to A's children at 25, where A is alive at the date of the testator's death, one first "waits and sees" whether the gift is valid without alteration. This will be so if A's children were all alive at the testator's death, or were all over four at A's death. If, however, A's youngest child was not alive at the testator's death but was a year old at A's death, the vesting age will be reduced to 22 years.[83]

The new provision, unlike section 163, also caters for gifts which specify two or more ages. If there is a gift by will to A's sons who attain 30 and his daughters who attain 25, and on A's death after the testator his youngest son is eight and his youngest daughter is three, the vesting ages will be cut down to 29 for sons and 24 for daughters.[84]

(3) SURVIVING SPOUSES. A gift to such of the children of A as should be living at the death of the survivor of A and his widow frequently failed at common law because of the possibility that A might marry a person not born at the date of the gift but who might survive A by more than 21 years. This notorious trap of the "unborn widow" has been eliminated by section 5 of the Act of 1964. If a gift which refers

---

[81] s. 4 (1).

[82] Act of 1964, s. 4 (1).

[83] This seems likely even if A had other children aged four and eight years when attainment of 25 years would be satisfactory for these two if the one year old died within the next 20 years: see M. & W., p. 237. If the gift had been to the first of A's children to attain 25 and on the death of the last statutory life in being there were children aged eight, four, three and 1 it seems one would wait and see whether the eight or four year old qualified, but that if they did not qualify, then reduction should be to the age of 22, rather than to 24, as now being the age which, if specified instead of 25, would certainly have prevented the disposition from being void. Further see M.J. Prichard [1969] Camb. L.J. 286. For class gifts see p. 212 *post*.

[84] See s. 4 (2). This assumes A was the last surviving statutory life in being.

to the death of the survivor of a person in being and his or her spouse is not saved by the "wait and see" rule, it is to be treated as "if it had instead been limited by reference to the time immediately before the end of" the perpetuity period. Thus in the example above, if A is survived by his widow, the gift will vest 21 years after the death of A if the widow is then still living, so that the children then living will take even if one or more of them subsequently die before the widow.

(4) ALTERNATIVE FIXED PERIOD. The Act of 1964 contains one completely new concept. As an alternative to the perpetuity period based on lives in being, it is permissible to specify a fixed period of years not exceeding 80 as the perpetuity period.[85] The period must be expressly specified; it cannot be left to be implied, as in a gift by will to such of the testator's descendants as are living 80 years after his death. There must be some such expression as "which I specify as the perpetuity period for this gift." It will be noted that this period can be used with much the same effect as the "royal lives" clauses at common law. However, nothing in the Act effects the validity of a "royal lives" or similar perpetuity clause where the gift must vest, if at all, within the specified period.

6. Where a deed or will contains several limitations, the rule must be applied to each limitation separately. Thus if there is a gift—

"to A for life, remainder to his eldest son for life, remainder to B's eldest grandson in fee simple,"

the perpetuity rule must be applied to each of the three limitations separately. If all are valid, no difficulty arises; but if one or more are bad, the following rule must be applied.

(a) *No limitation is void merely because it is followed by a void limitation.*[86] A gift "to A for life" standing by itself is clearly good, and it is not invalidated merely because a limitation which infringes the rule is added, *e.g.* "to A for life, remainder to the first of his descendants to marry a Latvian." In such a case, A takes a life interest and after his death the property reverts to the grantor or passes under his will or intestacy, unless the remainder is saved by the Act of 1964.

(b) *A limitation which is subsequent to and dependent upon a void limitation is itself void.*[87] It will be noticed that a limitation is not void merely because it follows a void limitation; it is invalidated by the rule only if an addition to following the void limitation it is also

---

[85] s. 1.
[86] *Garland* v. *Brown* (1864) 10 L.T. 292.
[87] *Re Abbot* [1893] 1 Ch. 54; *Re Hubbard's W.T.* [1963] Ch. 275.

dependent upon it.[88] Thus if a testator devises property in fee simple—

> "to the first of X's sons to become a clergyman, but if X has no such son, to Y in fee simple,"

and when the testator dies X is alive, the first part of the gift is void since the required event might occur more than 21 years after the death of lives in being. The gift to Y is subsequent to and dependent upon this void limitation; not until X and all his sons have died without any son having become a clergyman can it be said that Y is entitled. Thus even though the gift to Y is in favour of a living person, at common law it failed as being dependent upon a void limitation.[89]

On the other hand, if property is given—

> "to A for life, remainder for life to any wife he may marry, remainder for life to any husband whom such wife may marry, remainder to such of A's children as attain the age of 21,"

the gifts to A and his wife are both valid, for A is a life in being and his wife must be ascertained in his lifetime. But at common law the limitation to the wife's husband was void for perpetuity, since A's wife may not be alive at the time of the gift and may marry more than 21 years after A's death. Nevertheless, the gift to A's children is valid, for although it follows a void limitation, it has its own independent date of vesting which cannot exceed the perpetuity period.[90]

The precise meaning of "dependent" in this context is obscure. Sometimes it seems to mean no more than "contingent," so that there is no special rule as to "dependence." But sometimes a remainder which seems plainly vested is struck down as being "dependent" upon a prior void limitation.[91] Such cases can be explained on the principle that if a testator intends the remainder not to take effect until the prior limitation ends, it would be contrary to that intention to allow the remainder to take immediate effect merely because the prior limitation is void for perpetuity. The remainder accordingly falls with the prior limitation. Thus if a testator gives property for life to the first son of A (a bachelor) to marry, and then to B, he may well have intended no immediate gift to B. Further, where a void limitation stands between two or more valid limitations, the limitation following the void limitation will be held dependent on it, and so invalid, unless it will "dovetail in and accord with" the prior limitations.[92]

---

[88] See *Re Coleman* [1936] Ch. 528.
[89] *Proctor* v. *Bishop of Bath and Wells* (1794) 2 Hy. Bl. 358.
[90] See *Re Coleman* [1936] Ch. 528.
[91] *Re Backhouse* [1921] 2 Ch. 51.
[92] *Monypenny* v. *Dering* (1852) 2 De G.M. & G. 145 at p. 182.

(c) *Act of 1964.* The whole doctrine of "dependence" was so unsatisfactory and obscure that the Act of 1964 has abolished it for gifts made after July 15, 1964. Such a gift is not void merely because it is "ulterior to and dependent upon" a void gift. It is only the doctrine of dependence which has been abolished. If the ultimate gift is contingent, the contingency must be satisfied before it can vest. Thus of the gifts mentioned above, that to B is dependent only; but the gift "but if X has no such son, to Y" is contingent as well as dependent. The Act further provides that the existence of the prior void gift will no longer prevent the acceleration of the vesting of the subsequent gift.[93]

7. Alternative contingencies. Where a gift expresses two alternative contingencies upon which the property may vest, and one contingency is too remote and one is not, the gift is good if in fact the valid contingency occurs.[94] Thus in one case,[95] a testator gave property to his grandchildren and issue of his grandchildren living—

> "on the decease of my last surviving child or on the death of the last surviving widow or widower of my children as the case may be whichever shall last happen."

It was held that this gift did not infringe the perpetuity rule as it stood, and that if in fact one of the testator's children outlived all the other children and their spouses, the gift would be valid. There were two alternatives:

> (i) that one of the testator's children (a life in being) would be the last survivor, or
> (ii) that the spouse of one of the testator's children (not necessarily a life in being) would be the last survivor;

if the former actually occurred, the gift did not infringe the rule. To this extent, there is a "wait and see" in the perpetuity rule.

The foregoing applies only if the two alternative contingencies are expressed in the gift.[96] If only one contingency is expressed in the gift and that may be too remote, the gift fails even if there are in fact two contingencies. Thus in *Proctor* v. *Bishop of Bath and Wells*,[97] only one contingency was expressed, namely, that if no son of X became a clergyman, Y should be entitled. In fact, two contingencies were implicit in the gift, namely,

> (i) X might leave no son; this must be known at X's death, which would be within the period;

---

[93] s. 6.
[94] *Hodgson* v. *Halford* (1879) 11 Ch.D. 959.
[95] *Re Curryer's W.T.* [1938] Ch. 952.
[96] *Re Bence* [1891] 3 Ch. 242.
[97] *Ante,* p. 208.

(ii) X might leave one or more sons, who might become clergymen more than 21 years after X's death, which would be outside the period.

Nevertheless, the gift to Y was void *ab initio*, for the only contingency expressed was a void one. Had the gift over been worded—

"but if no son of X shall become a clergyman, or if X shall leave no son, to Y in fee simple,"

the gift to Y would have been valid if X had died leaving no son, *i.e.* if the valid contingency had occurred.[98]

The Act of 1964 has not specifically altered these rules, but its general "wait and see" provisions will apply if the unduly remote contingency occurs, or if there is only one composite contingent gift.

8. Application to class gifts. (a) *At common law.* A class gift is a gift of property to all who come within some description, the property being divisible in shares varying according to the number of persons in the class.[99]

Thus gifts of property—

"to my children who shall live to be 25," or—
"to all the nephews and nieces of my late husband who were living at his death, except A and B"

are class gifts. But gifts of property to be equally divided between—

"the five daughters of X," or—
"my nine children,"

or a gift of £2,000—

"to each of my daughters,"

are not class gifts, for a distinct one-fifth or one-ninth share or the sum of £2,000 is given to each child, exactly as if he or she had been named.

The perpetuity rule applies at common law to class gifts in the following way. If a single member of the class might possibly take a vested interest outside the period, the whole gift fails, even as regards those members of the class who have already satisfied any required contingency.[1] A class gift cannot be good as to part and void as to the rest: "the vice of remoteness affects the class as a whole, if it may affect an unascertained number of its members."[2] Until the total number of members of the class has been ascertained, it cannot be

---

[98] *Miles* v. *Harford* (1879) 12 Ch.D. 691 at p. 703.
[99] *Pearks* v. *Moseley* (1880) 5 App.Cas. 714 at p. 723; *Kingsbury* v. *Walter* [1901] A.C. 187 at p. 192.
[1] *Leake* v. *Robinson* (1817) 2 Mer. 363.
[2] *Pearks* v. *Moseley* (1880) 5 App.Cas. 714 at p. 723.

said what share any member of the class will take, and this state of affairs will continue as long as it is possible for any alteration in the number to be made.

Thus if before 1926 personalty was given—

"to A for life and after his death to be equally divided between all his children who shall attain the age of 25,"

an intent being shown to include every child of A, the remainder was void even as regards children alive at the time of the gift, who were thus lives in being.[3] This was so even if A was in fact many years past the age of child-bearing,[4] for in theory other children might be born, and since one of these might not be 25 until more than 21 years after the death of all lives in being at the time of the gift, the period might be exceeded.

(b) *The impact of the class-closing rules.* To assist in the speedy winding up of a testator's estate and to prevent beneficiaries from having to wait too long to receive their full shares in such estate, the courts have developed some rules to fix the numbers within a class. An incidental effect of the application of such rules may be to save a gift that would otherwise be void for remoteness if, from the outset, it is clear that the rules will apply so as to ensure that the exact size of each beneficiary's share will be ascertained within the perpetuity period.

The basic rule is that a class closes when the first member (or his personal representative) becomes entitled to claim his share, *i.e.* when his interest becomes vested *in possession.*[5] No one subsequently born can enter the class but any potential member of it already born is included. The maximum number of shares is fixed, so that the first taker can receive his share, which may be enlarged if some potential member of the class dies without having become entitled to his prospective share. Exceptionally, where birth is the sole qualification for class membership and no one has been born when the property is available for distribution, the class remains open indefinitely for, otherwise, the first-born would automatically take the whole property himself.[6]

A testator's property will be available for distribution to a class either on his death (*e.g.* a devise to "all my grandchildren who attain 25 years of age") or on the termination of a prior interest (*e.g.* a devise "to my son for life, remainder to his children who attain 25 years of age"). In the former case if one grandchild had attained 25 at the testator's death the class would close to include all the grandchildren alive at the testator's death and to exclude all those

---

[3] *Leake* v. *Robinson, supra.*
[4] Nowadays s. 2 lays down sensible child-bearing age presumptions: *ante* p. 199.
[5] *Andrews* v. *Partington* (1791) 3 Bro. C.C. W.1, *Re Bleckley* [1951] Ch. 740.
[6] *Weld* v. *Bradbury* (1715) 2 Vern. 705.

subsequently born. These grandchildren would be lives in being so that the gift would be valid. In the latter case the class only closes on the son's death if a child has then attained 25 years of age, and such class will include all children alive at the date of the son's death. Since the class could include future-born children who were less than four years old at the son's death it will be possible for such children to attain 25 more than 21 years after the death of the last surviving life in being. The gift to the children was thus void for remoteness before 1926.[7]

The class-closing rules apply to *inter vivos* settlements as well as to wills and are subject to a clearly expressed contrary intention by the testator.[8] Words such as "all and every" or "born or to be born"[9] have been held to be insufficient to oust the class-closing rules, whilst words such as "born or to be born during the lifetime of X" or "whenever born" have been held to be sufficient to oust the rules.

The above rules concern class gifts and not specific gifts[10] to each individual member of a class. If a testator bequeaths £5,000 to each of A's children or £5,000 to such of A's children as attain 25 years of age the class closes when the testator dies, excluding after-born children in each case.[11] If, however, a testator bequeaths his residuary estate to R for life and then directs £5,000 to be paid to each of A's children (or then to each of A's children as attain 25 years of age) the class closes when R dies since there is no additional inconvenience in keeping the class open till then.[12] Of course, any clearly expressed contrary intention will be given effect to.[13]

(c) *Age reduction under the 1964 Act.* If, despite any application of the class-closing rules, a class gift is void at common law then, if it is not saved by the "wait and see" provisions in conjunction with the class-closing rules, it may be saved by the reduction of age provisions in section 4 (1), assuming the courts strive to give effect to what Parliament intended.

The problems may be illustrated by the example of a devise "to my son for life, remainder to his children who attain the age of twenty five years." At common law the gift to the children is void since one cannot be absolutely certain on the testator's death that, at the son's death, the class of children will close to include children who are all over four years of age.

Under the Act it is possible to wait and see what is the position

---

[7] L.P.A. 1925, s. 163 and P.A.A. 1964, s. 4 affect the position after 1925.
[8] *Re Chapman's S.T.* [1978] 1 All E.R. 1122; *Re Clifford's S.T.* [1980] 1 All E.R. 1013.
[9] *Re Wernher's S.T.* [1961] 1 W.L.R. 136 approved by C.A. in *Re Chapman's S.T.* (*supra*).
[10] See p. 210 *ante.*
[11] *Rogers* v. *Mutch* (1878) 10 Ch.D. 25, *Storrs* v. *Benbow* (1853) 3 De G.M. & G. 390. The gift fails if no child of A had then been born.
[12] *Att.-Gen.* v. *Crispin* (1784) 1 Bro. C.C. 386, *Evans* v. *Harris* (1842) 5 Beav. 45.
[13] *Defflis* v. *Goldschmidt* (1816) Mer. 417.

when the son dies. If all his children are then at least four years old the gift to them will be valid since the exact size of share of the children will be ascertained within 21 years of the son's death.

If one child is only two years old at the son's death then the gift to the children will fail in the absence of some saving statutory provision.

Originally, section 163 of the Law of Property Act 1925 was available to save the gift by reducing the age to be attained by the children from 25 years to 21 years.[14] The section has now been repealed by section 4 (6) of the 1964 Act for instruments taking effect after July 15, 1964 (other than instruments made in the exercise of a special power of appointment created before July 16, 1964[15]).

However, the "wait and see" provisions in section 3 of the 1964 Act are only available "where apart from the provisions of this section and sections 4 and 5 of this Act a disposition might be void" for remoteness, and section 4 (1) with its age-reduction provisions, is only available where it is or becomes apparent that a disposition "would, *apart from this section*, be void for remoteness."

If section 4 is ignored then the repeal of section 163 by section 4 (6) has notionally to be ignored when ascertaining whether there is scope for section 3 or section 4 to apply to a disposition. If the repeal is ignored for these notional purposes then the gift to the children would be valid under section 163. Thus no resort can be had to sections 3 and 4 which only apply where, apart from sections 3 and 4, the gift would be void. However, for all other purposes section 163 has been repealed so that after July 15, 1964 no reliance can actually be placed on section 163 to save the gift. The gift to the children therefore fails, though it would have been valid if made after 1925 and before July 16, 1964.

This clearly was not intended so at this stage it may be permissible to seek a second time to apply sections 3 and 4. Having used the above reasoning to conclude that, after all, the gift is going to be void, it can be submitted that the gift is going to be void apart from sections 3 and 4, so that the provisions of sections 3 and 4 can, after all, be used to wait and see and then, if need be, to reduce the age to 23 years to save the gift.[16]

These problems would never have arisen if the draftsman had placed the repeal of section 163 in a separate independent section. Indeed, in the Children Act 1975,[17] in an attempt to remedy his earlier error, the draftsman provided that there should be added to section 4 a new sub-section (7) declaring that a question arising under sections 3 and 4 of whether a disposition would be void apart from

---

[14] See p. 205 *ante*.
[15] s. 15 (5).
[16] See (1965) 81 L.Q.R. 346 (J.D. Davies).
[17] Sched. 3, para. 43.

section 4 should be determined as if sub-section (6) had been in a separate section of the 1964 Act. Since sub-section (7) is itself part of section 4 (so that if section 4 is ignored, so is section 4 (7), so that section 4 (6) remains part of section 4 to be ignored!) it would have been better if the Children Act had added a new section to the 1964 Act. If the court is to strive to assist the draftsman, instead of reading the sections and sub-sections in the order in which they were enacted, it will be necessary to go first to section 4 (7) so that section 4 (6) may then become a separate independent section and then to return to section 3 and section 4 (1).

Somehow or other the court will find a way to validate the gift in the example by allowing a wait and see period and then reducing the age to 23 when it becomes apparent that, on the death of the last statutory life in being, there is a two-year-old child, who in the 21 years remaining can only attain the age of 23.

(d) *Class reduction under the 1964 Act.* The Act has abolished the rule that class gifts cannot be partly good and partly bad. Section 4 (4) eliminates those members of the class who fail to take vested interests within the perpetuity period. Thus if property were devised "to A for life, remainder to his grandchildren whenever born" the gift to the grandchildren is void at common law as the phrase "whenever born" ousts the class-closing rules. Under the Act one first waits to see how many grandchildren are born during the perpetuity period. The property will be divided between them and future-born grandchildren will be excluded.

In an appropriate case the class reduction provisions can be combined with the age reduction provisions.[18] Thus, if property were devised "to such of A's children as attain twenty-five together with such children as attain twenty-five of any children of A who may die under twenty-five" this devise to a composite class is void at common law.[19] Even if the age is reduced to 21 the devise is still void since an as yet unborn grandchild might well attain 21 outside the perpetuity period. The grandchildren are therefore excluded from the class and the qualifying age for A's children may be reduced, assuming that "waiting and seeing" alone does not save the devise.

9. Application to determinable and conditional interests.[20]

(a) *Determinable interests.* "The rule against perpetuities is not dealing with the duration of interests but with their commencement, and so long as the interest vests within lives in being and 21 years it does not matter how long that interest lasts."[21] Thus it can be said

---

[18] s. 4 (3).
[19] *Pearks* v. *Moseley* (1880) 5 App.Cas.714.
[20] See also *ante*, p. 39.
[21] *Re Chardon* [1928] Ch. 464 at p. 468.

that the perpetutity rule does not invalidate a limitation merely because it provides that an interest shall cease at some future date outside the perpetuity period. Accordingly where property is given to an unborn person—

"for life or until she becomes a member of the Roman Catholic Church"

or—

"for life or until marriage,"

the specified event may occur outside the perpetuity period but the limitation is nevertheless valid.[22] The better view is that it is immaterial that the determinable interest is a fee simple and the event on which it will determine may not happen for centuries, *e.g.* where property is conveyed to the X Co. Ltd. in fee simple until the premises are used otherwise than as a biscuit factory. When the event occurs, no new estate arises; the X Co. Ltd.'s fee simple terminates, and the grantor's possibility of reverter (a vested interest which after 1925 can only be an equitable interest) takes effect.[23]

A similar rule applies to resulting trusts.[24] Where land is conveyed to trustees in trust for an orphans' home, and on failure of that trust, in trust for the then owner of other land, the initial gift is good but the gift over is plainly void for perpetuity; instead, there will be a resulting trust for the grantor's estate, and this will not be held void for perpetuity.[25]

(b) *Conditional interests.* A condition may be either precedent or subsequent.[26] A condition precedent is one which must be fulfilled before the beneficiary is entitled to a vested interest, *e.g.*—

"to X and his heirs when he marries."

In such a case the perpetuity rule applies, for a new interest is limited to arise when the event occurs; consequently, if the condition might be fulfilled outside the perpetuity period the whole gift failed at common law.[27] The wait and see principle is now available under the 1964 Act.

A condition subsequent is one which authorises the grantor or his representatives to determine an existing interest. Thus a gift of land to X in fee simple—

"on condition that he never sells it out of the family,"

---

[22] *Wainwright* v. *Miller* [1897] 2 Ch. 255; *Re Gage* [1898] 1 Ch. 498.
[23] But see *Hopper* v. *Corporation of Liverpool* (1944) 88 S.J. 213; contrast 1945 Conv. Y.B. pp. 203–206. And see further M. & W., pp. 244–245.
[24] Any beneficial interest of which the settlor fails to dispose remains in him under a resulting trust.
[25] *Re Cooper's Conveyance Trusts* [1956] 1 W.L.R. 1096.
[26] *Ante*, p. 40.
[27] See, *e.g. Pickford* v. *Brown* (1856) 2 K. & J. 426.

gives the grantor a right of re-entry if the condition is broken. If such a condition infringes the perpetuity rule it is void, but the interest which it was to defeat is not invalidated. Thus if before 1964 there was a valid gift by a testator to his grandchildren followed by a clause providing for the forfeiture of the interest of any grandchild who should forsake the Jewish faith or marry outside that faith, all the beneficiaries took absolute interests; the forfeiture clause was void since it might not take effect until the perpetuity period had expired, but there was nothing to invalidate the gift to the grandchildren.[28] The wait and see principle is now available under the 1964 Act.

It will be noticed that a breach of a condition subsequent gives rise to a right of re-entry, so that some active step must be taken to determine the estate; a determinable limitation, on the other hand, requires no future activity, for the estate automatically determines by force of the original limitation.

(c) *Act of 1964.* Under the Act of 1964 the rules for determinable and conditional interests have been assimilated. The rule against perpetuities applies to possibilities of reverter and resulting trusts created by dispositions made after the Act as if they were in the form of conditions subsequent.[29] If after "waiting and seeing" the determining event has not occurred within the perptuity period then the preceding determinable interest is made absolute.

10. Application to powers. Settlements often authorise trustees, tenants for life and others to do things which they would not otherwise be entitled to do. One class of such powers may authorise acts of administration, such as the sale or leasing of the settled land.[30] Other powers, known as powers of appointment, may authorise an alteration of the beneficial interests. The application of the rule against perpetuities to powers is somewhat complicated.

(a) *Administrative powers.* (1) AT COMMON LAW. In general, an administrative power which was exercisable outside the perpetuity period was void, *e.g.* a power to lease or sell during the lifetime of an unborn person.[31]

(2) ACT OF 1964. It was generally thought that the extension of the rule to administrative powers was unwarranted, and that it ought to be confined to the invalidation of the remote vesting of beneficial interests. Accordingly the Act provides that the rule is not to operate to invalidate a power conferred on trustees and other persons "to sell lease exchange or otherwise dispose of any property for full consideration, or to do any other act in the administration (as

---

[28] *Re Spitzel's W.T.* [1939] 2 All E.R. 266.
[29] s. 12.
[30] See *post*, p. 267.
[31] *Re Allott* [1924] 2 Ch. 498.

opposed to the distribution) of any property."[32] Exceptionally, this provision is retrospective to the extent that it applies to the exercise of a power after July 15, 1964, even if the settlement or will which conferred the power took effect before then.[33]

(b) *Powers of appointment.* A power of appointment is a power for the person to whom it is given ("the donee of the power") to appoint property to such persons ("the objects of the power") as he may select.

(1) GENERAL AND SPECIAL POWERS. A power is a "special power" if the donee's choice is restricted to a limited class of objects, such as X's children, and a "general power" if his choice is unrestricted so that he himself could benefit.

(i) *At common law.* For the purposes of the perpetuity rule, the general test is whether or not the donee of the power is as free to dispose of the property as an absolute owner. Thus for this purpose a joint power of appointment has been held special,[34] and so has a power to appoint with the consent of X,[35] unless, perhaps X's consent is a requisite merely to the exercise of the power and he has no control over the amounts appointed or the persons to benefit, in which case the power may be general. Whether a power to appoint "to anyone except Z" is general or special for this purpose is doubtful. A general power to appoint by will only, though ranking as a general power for the purpose of determining the validity of an appointment, is, exceptionally, treated as a special power for the purpose of determining the initial validity of the power itself.[36]

(ii) *Act of 1964.* The Act of 1964 has codified the distinction between general and special powers. It adopts the formulation worked out in the cases and resolves the doubts which have been mentioned. In dispositions taking effect after July 15, 1964, a power is treated as a special power unless—

(a) it is expressed to be exercisable by one person only, and

(b) it could be exercised by him so as to transfer the property to himself without the consent of any other person or compliance with any condition (apart from a mere formal condition relating only to the mode of exercise of the power).[37]

This provision preserves the exceptional position of general testamentary powers. It will be noted that a power to appoint "to anyone except Z" is general.

---

[32] s. 8 (1).
[33] s. 8 (2). For the general rule, see *ante*, p. 197.
[34] *Re Churston S.E.* [1954] Ch. 334; *Re Earl of Coventry's Indentures* [1974] Ch. 77.
[35] *Re Watts* [1931] 2 Ch. 302.
[36] *Rous* v. *Jackson* (1885) 29 Ch. D. 521, *Morgan* v. *Gronow* (1873) L.R. 16 Eq. 1. The testator cannot, after all, appoint to himself.
[37] s. 7.

(2) VALIDITY OF THE POWER. In connection with the application of the perpetuity rule to powers of appointment, two separate points have to be considered:

(a) Does the power itself infringe the rule?
(b) If it does not, does the appointment made under the power infringe the rule?

(i) *A special power.* A special power of appointment is subject to the ordinary rule relating to powers and is thus void if it could be exercised outside the period; time runs from the date when the instrument creating the power took effect.[38] Thus if the donee of the power will not necessarily be ascertained within the period (if at all) or is capable of exercising the power when the period has expired, it is bad.[39] But a power exercisable only by a person living when it was created can never be void for remoteness.

If a power complies with these conditions, it is not void merely because an appointment which offends the rule might be made under it[40]; thus where a living person is given the power to appoint to his issue, he might make an appointment to his great-great-grandchildren, but this possibility does not invalidate either the power itself or an appointment which in fact complies with the rule.

The Act of 1964 applies the new "wait and see" principle to powers created by instruments taking effect after July 15, 1964. The power is to be treated as void only if and so far as it is not fully exercised within the perpetuity period.[41] If the objects of the power are in existence at the creation of the power and are reasonably ascertainable they are included among the lives in being.[42]

If a power is void for remoteness, a gift in default of appointment (*e.g.* "but if no appointment shall be made, to X and Y equally") is not thereby invalidated; provided it does not itself infringe the rule, it is valid.[43]

(ii) *A general power.* For the purposes of the perpetuity rule, a general power to appoint by deed is so nearly akin to absolute ownership that principles similar to those appropriate to absolute ownership are applied: the perpetuity rule is satisfied if the power must be acquired within the period, if at all, even if the power might be exercised outside the period.[44] But if the power is exercisable by will only, it is treated as a special power and so will be bad if it might be exercised outside the period.[45]

---

[38] *Re De Sommery* [1912] 2 Ch. 662. After all, it is from the bounty of the donor of the power that the limited class of appointees benefits.
[39] *Re Abbot* [1893] 1 Ch. 54.
[40] *Slark* v. *Dakyns* (1874) 10 Ch.App. 35.
[41] s. 3 (3).
[42] s. 3 (5) (*b*) (iii). For lives in being, see *ante*, p. 205.
[43] *Re Abbot, supra.*
[44] See *Re Fane* [1913] 1 Ch. 404.
[45] *Wollaston* v. *King* (1868) L.R. 8 Eq. 165.

Here too, the Act of 1964 applies the new "wait and see" principle. A general power created by an instrument taking effect after July 15, 1964, will not be void on the ground that it might be acquired at too remote a time, but will be valid unless and until it becomes established that it will not be exercisable within the period.[46] Since a general testamentary power is treated as a special power it is to be treated as void only if and so far as it is not fully exercised within the perpetuity period.

(3) VALIDITY OF APPOINTMENTS. If the power itself is void, clearly no valid appointment can be made under it. But even if the power itself is valid, an appointment made under it may nevertheless be too remote.

(i) *A special power.* In the case of a special power of appointment, the property is fettered from the moment the power is created. It can be said at once that either an appointment will be made in favour of one or more of the designated class of persons or else it will pass to those nominated to take in default of appointment, or, if none, to the grantor. The perpetuity period therefore starts to run from the creation of the power.[47] However, as has been seen,[48] the mere fact that the power authorises the making of an appointment which may be too remote does not invalidate it, and until the appointment has been made, it cannot be seen if in fact it is too remote. Consequently, contrary to the general rule in matters of perpetuity, even at common law "the principle seems to be to wait and see."[49] When the appointment is ultimately made, it must be examined to see whether the interests appointed are bound to vest (if at all) within 21 years of the dropping of the lives of persons who were living or *en ventre sa mère*[50] at the time of the creation of the power and not at the time of the appointment. Further, the facts existing at the time of the appointment must be taken into account when deciding this point. In short, in ascertaining the *lives in being* the relevant time is that of the *creation of the power*; in ascertaining the *facts* of the case, the relevant time is that of the *making of the appointment*.

Some examples may make this clearer.

(i) Devise to A for life with power to appoint to his children: A appoints to his son B "when he is 23": B was unborn at the testator's death but aged three at the time of the appointment. A is the only life in being, but since the property is bound to vest (if at all) within 20 years of his death, the appointment is good. Had B been under the age of two at the time of the

[46] s. 3 (2).
[47] *Re Thompson* [1906] 2 Ch. 199.
[48] *Ante*, p. 218.
[49] *Re Witty* [1913] 2 Ch. 666 at p. 673, *per* Cozens-Hardy M.R.
[50] *Re Stern* [1962] Ch. 732.

appointment, then if it had been made before 1926 it would
have been void; if it was made after 1925, B would have taken
when he was 21.[51]

(ii) Marriage settlement upon C for life, remainder as he should
appoint among his issue: C appoints in favour of his daughter
D, postponing the vesting of her interest until her marriage: D
is unmarried at the date of the appointment. The appointment
is void. A few years later, D marries and C then executes a
document confirming the void appointment, D is entitled to
the property, since the confirmation operates as a fresh
appointment, and taking the facts existing at the time of the
appointment the property has vested during the lifetime of a
person alive at the date of the settlement, namely, C.[52]

(iii) Deed giving property to F for life with power to appoint to his
issue: F appoints by will in favour of his grandchildren G and
H (neither of whom was alive at the date of the gift) for their
joint lives as tenants in common, with remainder to the
survivor. The interest for their joint lives is valid but the
remainder is void.[53]

The Act of 1964 has enlarged the scope of the "wait and see" in
relation to the exercise of special powers and the age reduction and
class reduction provisions are also available. If the powers in the
example given above are created after July 15, 1964,[54] the result will
be as follows:

(i) If B is under two years old at the time of the appointment, he
will take when he is 23 if one waits and sees that he attains that
age within the period, *e.g.* if A lives until B is five. But if A
dies before B is two, B will take at whatever age he is when 21
years have elapsed after A's death.[55]

(ii) The first appointment to D will be valid unless and until it
appears that D will not marry within the perpetuity period,
running from the date of the settlement.

(iii) The remainder is valid if it in fact vests within the period, *i.e.*
21 years after the death of the survivor of the donor, F, and
any of F's children living at the date of the deed and any
persons to whom they were married at such date.

(ii) *A general power.* Since the property is unfettered until the
appointment has been made, the donee of the power being able to
deal with it as he wishes, the perpetuity period does not begin to run

---

[51] L.P.A. 1925, s. 163; *ante*, p. 203.
[52] This is based on *Morgan* v. *Gronow* (1873) L.R. 16 Eq. 1.
[53] *Re Legh's S.T.* [1938] Ch. 39.
[54] The Act does not apply to appointments made after July 15, 1964, under a special
power created before that date: s. 15 (5).
[55] See *ante*, p. 205.

until the date of the appointment. Thus for the purposes of the perpetuity rule there is no difference between the exercise of a general power and a conveyance by an absolute owner.

The difference between appointments under general and special powers may be summarised thus. In both cases, the relevant facts are those existing at the time of the appointment; but the time at which the lives in being must be ascertained is the creation of the power in the case of a special power, and the exercise of the power in the case of a general power.

11. Contracts, covenants and options. (a) *At common law.* (1) PERSONAL OBLIGATIONS. The rule against remoteness does not apply to contracts in so far as they create mere personal obligations, *e.g.* to pay mining royalties.[56] The rule is directed against the vesting of interests in some specific property at too remote a date, and personal contracts do not do this. Further, even if a contract confers a right to an interest in some specific property exercisable at too remote a date, the rule did not prevent damages[57] or specific performance[58] being awarded against a party to the contract; for the court is merely enforcing his personal obligations and not any rights of property.

(2) PROPRIETARY INTERESTS. Where, however, the plaintiff's case depends not on a personal obligation but on the existence of an interest in specific property, the rule applies. Thus if a lease for 99 years confers on the lessee and his assigns an option to purchase a freehold at any time during the lease[59] (an option appurtenant to the lease), or a corporation is given an option to purchase or take a lease of land[60] (an option is gross), an action to enforce the option against a successor in title of the person who granted the option cannot be based on any personal obligation, and must depend on the burden of the option running with the land. The rule accordingly makes the option unenforceable against the successor unless its exercise is confined within the period.

(3) COVENANTS TO RENEW LEASE. Exceptionally, a covenant in a lease giving the tenant the right to an extension of the term is not void merely because it can be exercised outside the perpetuity period.[61] The reason for this is that an option to renew a lease (unlike an option to purchase the reversion) "touches and concerns" the land so as to run with the land and be part of the tenant's present interest.

---

[56] *Witham* v. *Vane* (1883) Challis R.P. 440; and see M. & W., pp. 258–263.
[57] *Worthing Corporation* v. *Heather* [1906] 2 Ch. 532.
[58] *Hutton* v. *Watling* [1948] Ch. 26, at p. 398.
[59] *Woodall* v. *Clifton* [1905] 2 Ch. 257.
[60] *London and South Western Ry.* v. *Gomm* (1882) 20 Ch.D. 562.
[61] *Woodall* v. *Clifton, supra*, at pp. 265, 268; *Weg Motors Ltd.* v. *Hales* [1962] Ch. 49; but note that contracts to renew a lease for over 60 years from its termination are void: L.P.A. 1922, 15th Sched., para. 7.

(b) *Statutory modifications.* The Act of 1964 has made three changes in relation to dispositions in instruments taking effect after July 15, 1964.

(1) PERSONAL OBLIGATIONS. The Act reverses the rule that damages or specific performance may be obtained against an original contracting party, despite the proprietary interest conferred by the contract being void for perpetuity. A disposition *inter vivos* which creates an interest in property is void between the original contracting parties wherever it would be void for perpetuity against a third party.[62]

(2) OPTIONS APPURTENANT TO LEASES. The rule against remoteness does not apply to an option for a lessee to purchase the freehold or superior leasehold title which is exercisable only by the lessee or his successors in title and which ceases to be exercisable not later than a year after the end of the lease.[63]

(3) OPTIONS IN GROSS. An option to acquire for value any interest in land is subject to a specially short perpetuity period of 21 years only.[64] The "wait and see" principle applies, so that even if no time limit is specified in the instrument conferring the option, it will remain exercisable for 21 years.

Sect. 3. Exceptions to the Rule against Remoteness

The preceding section has indicated some cases to which the Rule does not apply, namely—

(a) Personal obligations;
(b) Covenants for renewal of a lease; and
(c) Covenants in a lease for the purchase of the landlord's reversion.

There are a few other exceptions.

1. Certain limitations after entails. A limitation which is bound to take effect, if at all, during the continuance, or at the moment of the determination, of an entail is not rendered void by the rule, even though the entail may continue for longer than the perpetuity period.[65] Thus a gift to X in tail, with remainder to such of Y's issue as are alive when the entail determines, is valid, even though the persons entitled to take the remainder may not be ascertained for several hundred years.[66] The justification for this exception is that

[62] s. 10.
[63] s. 9 (1).
[64] s. 9 (2).
[65] *Nicolls* v. *Sheffield* (1787) 2 Bro.C.C. 215.
[66] See *Heaseman* v. *Pearse* (1871) 7 Ch.App. 275 at pp. 282, 283.

since entails are barrable the tenant in tail is potentially an absolute owner so that his power of alienation is not fettered by the remainder.

This exception, however, does not protect limitations which can or must vest when an interval has elapsed after the determination of the entail.[67] If property is given to trustees in trust for A in tail, remainder to the first of the great-grandchildren of B to attain the age of 30, A's entail is valid but the remainder is void, for it might very well vest many years after the period has run and the entail has determined.

2. Certain gifts to charities. The general rule is that a gift to a charity is subject to the rule in the same way as any other gift.[68] However, if there is a gift to one charity followed by a gift over to another charity on a certain event, the gift over is not void merely because the event may occur outside the perpetuity period. Thus if property is given to Charity A with a proviso that it shall go to Charity B if Charity A fails to keep the testator's tomb in repair, the gift over is valid.[69] To this extent alone are charities exempted from the rule against remoteness.[70]

3. Certain rights of entry and re-entry. The right to re-enter and determine a lease if a covenant is broken, which most leases give to the landlord, is excepted from the perpetuity rule.[71] Again, the statutory remedies for enforcing payment of a rentcharge[72] or any like powers or remedies conferred by any instrument were expressly excepted from the rule in 1925[73]; for rentcharges created after July 15, 1964, the Act of 1964[74] extends the exemption to all powers and remedies for enforcing rentcharges.[74] Further, the Law of Property Act 1925[75] sets out a list of certain rights retrospectively excepted from the rule, such as a right of entry created in order to enable minerals to be worked or to enable repairs to be executed.

A right of re-entry in respect of a fee simple is not within this exception and will accordingly be void if exercisable outside the perpetuity period.[76]

4. Mortgages. "The rule has never been applied to mortgages," and thus a clause postponing the mortgagor's right to redeem the

---

[67] See *Bristow* v. *Boothby* (1826) 2 Sim. & St. 465.
[68] *Chamberlyne* v. *Brockett* (1872) 8 Ch.App. 206.
[69] *Re Tyler* [1891] 3 Ch. 252.
[70] See also the exemption from the rule against inalienability, *post*, p. 226.
[71] *Re Tyrell's Estate* [1907] 1 I.R. 292 at p. 298.
[72] *Post*, p. 393.
[73] L.P.A. 1925, s. 121.
[74] s. 11 (1).
[75] s. 162.
[76] *Re Trustees of Hollis' Hospital and Hague's Contract* [1899] 2 Ch. 540; L.P.A. 1925, s. 4; and see *ante*, p. 41.

property is not invalid merely because the right is postponed for longer than the perpetuity period.[77]

Part 3

THE RULE AGAINST INALIENABILITY

1. The rule. It is a fundamental principle of English law that property must not be rendered inalienable. Thus a devise of land to be retained in perpetuity for use as a family burial ground is void.[78]

Nowadays land will always be alienable under the Settled Land Act or under a trust for sale (which may be subject to certain consents) except where there is a bare trust with a direction never to alienate the land, which direction would, of course, be treated as void. Thus, land that forms part of a capital fund will be alienable.

Where the capital fund is directed to be held on certain trusts concerning the income therefrom, the assets from time to time comprising the fund will be alienable under the Settled Land Act or the Law of Property Act or the Trustee Investments Act 1961 but the capital fund (in whatever assets invested) will have to be retained to give effect to the trusts of the income therefrom. This in itself does not infringe the rule against inalienability.[79] It is only where, under the terms of the trust, the income must be used in a specific manner for a period that may exceed the perpetuity period that the rule against inalienability will be infringed.

Thus, if property is given to trustees to be applied for an indefinite period for the upkeep of a monument[80] or grave[81] or the maintenance of specific animals[82] or to provide an annual cup for the best yachtsman in club[83] the gift is void. However, if property is given to trustees on trust to pay the income to the A Charity Co. for such company to dispose of as it wishes for so long as a particular purpose shall be carried out, but as soon as such purpose shall not be carried out, then on trust to pay the income to the B Charity Co. for such company to dispose of ɩs it wishes for so long as the said particular purpose shall be carried out (and so on to the Z Charity Co.) then since the income is alienable the rule against inalienability is not infringed.[84] The rule would have been infringed if the income had been subject to a trust to carry out the particular purpose.

---

[77] *Knighstbridge Estates Trust Ltd.* v. *Byrne* [1939] Ch. 441 at p. 463 *per* Greene M.R.; on appeal, [1940] A.C. 613.
[78] *Yeap Cheah Neo* v. *Ong Cheng Neo* (1875) L.R. 6 P.C. 381.
[79] *Re Gage* [1898] 1 Ch. 506 *Wainwright* v. *Miller* [1897] 2 Ch. 255.
[80] *Musset* v. *Bingle* [1876] W.N. 170.
[81] *Re Hooper* [1932] 1 Ch. 38; *Re Dalziel* [1943] Ch. 277.
[82] *Re Dean* (1889) 41 Ch.D. 552.
[83] *Re Nottage* [1895] 2 Ch. 649.
[84] *Re Chardon* [1928] Ch. 464; *Re Chambers' W.T.* [1950] Ch. 267 For use of charities see p. 223 *ante*.

2. Construction of gift crucial. Problems often arise where a testator leaves property to an unincorporated association which has no legal personality.[85] The heart of such an association is its constitution by which its members are contractually bound. The members are beneficially entitled to the association's property except in so far as the members themselves have, under the constitution, declared trusts of the property and in so far as the donor to the association has expressly subjected the gifted property to trusts.[86]

If a testator's gift is treated as imposing trusts for present and future members of the association then the gift will be void at common law for infringing the rule against remoteness and the rule against inalienability, assuming the gift is not restricted to the perpetuity period.[87] If it is treated as a trust to carry out pure abstract non-charitable purposes (*e.g.* the prevention of animal vivisection) the gift will be void for infringing what is known as the beneficiary principle whereby a non-charitable trust with no beneficiary to enforce it is void, unless it is one of the anomalous cases for the erection or maintenance of graves or monuments or for the maintenance of particular animals.[88]

In view of these problems the courts, originally, were inclined to treat gifts to unincorporated associations not as trusts but as absolute gifts for the benefit of the existing members who could thus call for their aliquot shares.[89] More recently, the courts have become inclined to treat such gifts as an outright accretion to the association's funds subject to the constitution contractually binding the members.[90] No problems then arise so long as under the constitution such funds do not have to be held on trusts which infringe the beneficiary principle or the perpetuity rules.

3. The perpetuity period. The period available for the rule against inalienability seems the same for the rule against remoteness, *i.e.* lives in being, if any, plus 21 years.[91]

4. Section 15 (4) of the 1964 Act. This states "Nothing in this Act shall affect the operation of the rule of law rendering void for remoteness certain dispositions under which property is limited to be applied for purposes other than the benefit of any person or class of persons in cases where the property may be so applied after the end of the perpetuity period." This raises many difficulties.

---

[85] See N. & M., pp. 121–123.
[86] *Re Bucks Constabulary Fund (No. 2)* [1979] 1 All E.R. 623.
[87] *Re Macauley's Estate* [1943] Ch. 435; *Bacon* v. *Pianta* (1966) 114 C.L.R. 634; *Re Grants W.T.* [1979] 3 All E.R. 359.
[88] *Leahy* v. *Att.-Gen. for New South Wales* [1959] A.C. 457; *Re Endacott* [1960] Ch. 232.
[89] *Cocks* v. *Manners* (1871) L.R. 12 Eq. 574; *Re Ogden* [1933] Ch. 678.
[90] *Re Recher's W.T.* [1972] Ch. 526; *Re Lipinski's W.T* [1976] Ch. 235, *Re Bucks Constabulary Fund (No. 2)* [1979] 1 All E.R. 623.
[91] *Re Astor's S.T.* [1952] Ch. 534; *Re Denley's Trust Deed* [1969] 1 Ch. 373.

First, it seems that "the rule rendering void for remoteness certain dispositions" is the rule against inalienability as discussed in these pages, the draftsman elsewhere in the Act using the expression "rule against perpetuities" to cover what is discussed in these pages as the rule against remoteness. This confusion arises since the rule against inalienability has various names (*e.g.* the rule against perpetual trusts or the rule against trusts of excessive duration) as does the rule against remoteness.

Second, it seems that "perpetuity period" means the common law period so that the statutory 80 year period is not available: the statutory period only applies to the "rule against perpetuities" (s. 1 of the 1964 Act) which in the statutory context means the rule against remoteness.

Third, it seems that the clause "for purposes other than the benefit of . . . persons" should be treated not just as covering the anomalous few allowable pure purpose trusts for the erection or maintenance of graves or monuments or for the maintenance of particular animals, but should extend to cover purpose trusts which satisfy the beneficiary principle as indirectly for the benefit of persons, *e.g.* where a recreation ground is given to trustees to retain and to allow to be used within an expressed perpetuity period for the purpose of a recreation or sports ground for the benefit of employees of the donor company.[92]

Thus, it seems, the Act does not affect the rule against inalienability so there can be no wait and see and no use of the 80 year period.[93]

5. Charities. Charities are exempt from the rule against inalienability; no gift for charitable purposes is void merely because it renders property inalienable in perpetuity.[94]

Part 4

THE RULE AGAINST ACCUMULATIONS

This rule resembles the rule against inalienability in that it is directed against remoteness of control over a vested interest rather than against interests which may vest at too distant a date. The rule was first laid down by the ill-drafted Accumulations Act 1800, which was passed as a result of *Thellusson* v. *Woodford*.[95] In that case, Mr.

---

[92] *Re Denley's Trust Deed* [1969] 1 Ch. 373.
[93] M. & W., p. 269, Morris & Leach: *Rule Against Perpetuities* (Supplement), p. 3; though Maudsley's *Modern Law of Perpetuities*, p. 178 suggests that the 80 year period may be available, *sed quaere*.
[94] *Chamberlyne* v. *Brockett* (1872) 8 Ch.App. 206 at p. 211; contrast the rule against remoteness *ante*, p. 223.
[95] (1799) 4 Ves. 227; (1805) 11 Ves. 112; hence the Act is often called "the Thellusson Act."

Thellusson by his will directed that the income of his property should be accumulated during the lives of his sons, grandsons and their issue who were living at his death, and that on the death of the survivor, the accumulated fund should be divided among certain of his descendants. This direction, being confined to lives in being, was held valid, but as it was calculated that the accumulated fund would amount to many millions of pounds, Parliament intervened to prevent further directions of this nature.

At common law, the rule was that a direction to accumulate was valid if it was confined to the perpetuity period,[96] so that Mr. Thellusson might have effectively directed accumulation for a further 21 years; probably he did not do so because the permissibility of the extra period of 21 years after lives in being was not firmly established when he made his will.

A. The Statutory Periods

1. The periods. The present law is contained in the Law of Property Act 1925,[97] and the Perpetuities and Accumulations Act 1964.[98] If the disposition took effect before July 16, 1964, a trust or power[99] to accumulate may be validly given for any one (but not more) of the following periods:

(1) The life of the grantor or settlor.
(2) 21 years from the death of the grantor, settlor or testator.
(3) The minority or respective minorities of any person or persons living or *en ventre sa mère* at the death of the grantor, settlor or testator.
(4) The minority or respective minorities only of any person or persons who under the limitations of the instrument directing accumulation would for the time being, if of full age, be entitled to the income directed to be accumulated.

For dispositions taking effect after July 15, 1964, two further periods have been added.[1]

(5) 21 years from the date of the making of the disposition.
(6) The minority or respective minorities of any person or persons in being at that date.

2. Choice of periods. The question which period has been chosen in each particular case is one of construction.[2] The first two and the fifth

---

[96] *Wilson* v. *Wilson* (1851) 1 Sim. (N.S.) 288 at p. 298.
[97] ss. 164–166.
[98] ss. 13, 14.
[99] *Re Robb* [1953] Ch. 459; Act of 1964, s. 13 (2), *Re Robb* was disapproved in *Re Earl of Berkeley* [1968] Ch. 744, but not so as to affect this point. *Baird* v. *Lord Advocate* [1979] A.C. 666.
[1] Act of 1964, s. 13 (1).
[2] *Jagger* v. *Jagger* (1883) 25 Ch.D. 729.

periods cause little difficulty. Of the first, it should be noted that it is the only period of a life available for accumulation, and that it must be the life of the grantor or settlor himself and not of some third person. The second period is a fixed term of years which starts to run at the beginning of the day after the testator's death and expires at the end of the twenty-first anniversary of his death.[3] Thus if a testator directs accumulations to start at the end of an interval after his death and continue for 21 years, he has exceeded the second period. The second period was of little use save in wills. Now, the fifth period allows the period of 21 years to run from the date of the settlement.

The third, fourth and sixth periods are all minorities. Minority now ends at the age of 18.[4] The periods differ in the following respects:

(i) The third and sixth periods are confined to the minorities of persons alive or *en ventre sa mère* at the death of the grantor, settlor or testator, or at the date of the settlement, as the case may be. The fourth period is not.

(ii) The third and sixth periods are not restricted to the minorities of those who are prospectively entitled to any benefit under the gift, whereas the fourth period is confined to the minorities of those who can say "but for my infancy I should be entitled to the income being accumulated."[5]

(iii) The third and sixth periods can never exceed a single minority; for even if accumulation is directed during a large number of minorities, the period is in effect merely the longest of these minorities. Under the fourth period, on the other hand, accumulation during successive minorities is possible.

An example may make this clear.[6] A testator devises the residue of his property between all the children of his sons, whether born before or after his death, the income of their shares to be accumulated during their respective minorities. At the testator's death, there is only one child of his sons alive, and she is an infant named D. The whole of the income must be accumulated during this minority, the direction to accumulate falling within the fourth period; for if she was of full age she would for the time being be entitled to the whole of the income. After D attains her majority, a child, C, is born to one of the testator's sons. C becomes entitled to one half of the estate, subject to the same liability, *i.e.* that his share may be partially divested by the birth of other children. During the minority of C, the income from his share must be accumu-

[3] *Gorst* v. *Lowndes* (1841) 11 Sim. 434.
[4] Family Law Reform Act 1969, s. 1. The period of 21 years in the second and fifth periods is not affected, nor is the validity of directions for accumulations in dispositions made before 1970 with reference to the previous period of minority ending at the age of 21.
[5] *Jagger* v. *Jagger*, *supra*, at p. 733, as corrected in *Re Cattell*, *infra*, at p. 189.
[6] See *Re Cattell* [1914] 1 Ch. 177.

lated, even though the income from the whole of the residuary estate has already been accumulated once.

If D had not been born until after the testator's death, there could have been no accumulation under the fourth period until her birth, for not until then would her minority have commenced.

3. Purchase of land. Where after June 27, 1892, accumulation is directed for the sole purpose of purchasing land, only the fourth period may be selected. But this restriction does not apply to accumulations to be held as capital money under the Settled Land Act 1925 or any of the Acts which it replaces.[7]

4. Ambit of rules. These rules apply whether the limitations are contained in a deed or a will, whether the accumulation is at compound or, it seems, merely simple interest,[8] and whether the whole or any part of the income of a fund is to be accumulated.[9] Yet there is no accumulation if income is merely retained to meet possible future deficiencies in the income required for paying annuities, and is not added to capital.[10]

B. Excessive Accumulation

1. Exceeding perpetuity period. If the period for which accumulation is directed may exceed the perpetuity period, the direction to accumulate is totally void, *e.g.* where accumulation was directed until a lease with over 60 years to run had "nearly expired."[11] This applies even to accumulations for the benefit of charities.[12] One might have expected that, after 1964, in determining whether an accumulation were void for infringing the perpetuity period one should apply the 1964 wait and see rules and not the old common law rule. However, the 1964 Act does not seem to provide for the wait and see rules to apply in the context of accumulations unless the language of section 3 (3) is strained so that "any power option or other right" is treated as extending to accumulations.[13]

2. Exceeding accumulation period. If the period for which accumulation is directed cannot exceed the perpetuity period but exceeds the relevant accumulation period, the direction to accumulate is good *pro tanto* and only the excess over the appropriate

---

[7] L.P.A. 1925, s. 166; see *post,* p. 285.
[8] See *Re Garside* [1919] 1 Ch. 132.
[9] *Re Travis* [1900] 2 Ch. 541.
[10] *Re Earl of Berkeley* [1968] Ch. 744.
[11] *Curtis* v. *Lutkin* (1842) 5 Beav. 147.
[12] *Martin* v. *Maugham* (1844) 14 Sim. 230.
[13] M. & W., p. 275.

accumulation period is void; the statutory provisions are merely restrictive of the wider powers formerly enjoyed.[14]

Which is the appropriate period depends on the circumstances.[15] Thus where accumulation is directed for the lifetime of any person (other than the settlor in the case of an *inter vivos* settlement), accumulation will take place for 21 years from the date of the settlement or, as the case may be, from the testator's death, if the named person so long lives.[16] This uses the second or fifth period, and these periods are also the most appropriate whenever accumulation is directed for a period of years. The same applies where accumulation is directed until X is 25,[17] or from the time Y remarries until her death,[18] or from the death of either A or B until the death of the survivor. In each of these cases, if accumulation is still continuing 21 years after the date of the settlement or the death of the testator, it must cease forthwith, even if it has been proceeding for only a short period, *e.g.* two years.[19]

Again, if property is given by will to all the children of X (a living person) who attain their majority, and accumulation of the whole fund is directed while any child of X is a minor, the first two periods are clearly not intended and the fourth is not appropriate, for the accumulation is directed to continue for as long as *any* child is a minor even if some of the children are 18; even though the latter children are of full age, they are not entitled to the income to be accumulated within the wording of the fourth period. Consequently the third period is the most appropriate, and so far as it is exceeded the direction is void; accumulation will therefore cease as soon as all children living at the testator's death are 18.[20]

C. Surplus Income

The income for any period during which accumulation is invalidly directed passes to the person who would have been entitled had no excessive accumulation been directed.[21] Thus if there is a gift of a vested interest subject only to an excessive trust for accumulation, the beneficiary with such interest is entitled to any income not validly accumulated. For example, where property is given by will to X, subject to a direction that the income exceeding a certain figure is to be accumulated during X's life for the benefit of Y, the accumulation

---

[14] *Leake* v. *Robinson* (1817) 2 Mer. 363 at p. 389.
[15] See *Re Ransome* [1957] Ch. 348 at p. 361.
[16] *Griffiths* v. *Vere* (1803) 9 Ves. 127. In the case of a settlement *inter vivos* made before July 16, 1964, the first period was the most appropriate, and accumulations continued during the period common to the lives of the settlor and the named person: *Re Lady Rosslyn's Trust* (1848) 16 Sim. 391.
[17] *Crawley* v. *Crawley* (1835) 7 Sim. 427.
[18] *Weatherell* v. *Thornburgh* (1878) 8 Ch.D. 261.
[19] *Shaw* v. *Rhodes* (1836) 1 My. & Cr. 135.
[20] *Re Watt's W.T.* [1936] 2 All E.R. 1555.
[21] L.P.A. 1925, s. 164.

must cease 21 years after the testator's death and the surplus income will go to X.[22] But otherwise, the income reverts to the settlor or his estate, or in the case of a gift by will, passes under any residuary gift, or, in default, to the persons entitled on intestacy.[23]

D. The Rule in Saunders v. Vautier

Under the rule in *Saunders* v. *Vautier*,[24] a beneficiary of full age who has an absolute indefeasible interest in property may at any time, notwithstanding any direction to accumulate, require the transfer of the property to him and terminate any accumulation; a man may do as he likes with his own, and the same applies to a charity.[25] Thus if property is given to A with a direction to accumulate the income for his benefit until he is 24, A can demand payment of both the original property and the accumulations as soon as he is of full age.[26] The rule applies, however, only if the beneficiary or beneficiaries seeking to put an end to the accumulation together comprise every person who has any vested or contingent interest in the property.[27] Thus it will not apply if there is a gift to a class of persons or charities not yet determined, or to beneficiaries whose interests are contingent or liable to be defeated by some event occurring.

E. Exceptions to the Rule against Accumulations

The rule against accumulations does not apply in the following cases.[28]

1. Payment of debts: a provision for accumulation for the payment of the debts of any person.[29] This includes an accumulation directed for the payment of any debts, whether of the settlor or testator, or any other person.[30] Indeed, an accumulation for the payment of the debts of the settlor or testator is valid even if it may exceed the perpetuity period[31]; such a direction can cause little mischief, for the creditors may terminate the accumulation at any time by demanding payment. But an accumulation to pay the debts of any other person must be confined within the perpetuity period.

The exception includes any debts, whether existing or contingent, provided the accumulation is directed bona fide for their payment; thus it extends to accumulations to discharge a mortgage or to

---

[22] *Trickey* v. *Trickey* (1832) 3 My. & Cr. 560. See also *Brotherton* v. *I.R.C.* [1978] 2 All E.R. 267.
[23] *Matthews* v. *Keble* (1867) L.R. 4 Eq. 467 at pp. 473, 474 (affd. 3 Ch.App. 691).
[24] (1841) 4 Beav. 115; affd. Cr. & Ph. 240.
[25] *Wharton* v. *Masterman* [1895] A.C. 186; contrast *Re Levy* [1960] Ch. 346.
[26] *Josselyn* v. *Josselyn* (1837) 9 Sim. 63. A took at 21. Today he would take at 18.
[27] *Berry* v. *Green* [1938] A.C. 575.
[28] See L.P.A. 1925, ss. 164, 165.
[29] L.P.A. 1925, ss. 164, 165.
[30] *Viscount Barrington* v. *Liddell* (1852) 2 De G.M. & G. 480.
[31] *Bateman* v. *Hotchkin* (1847) 10 Beav. 426.

provide for liability under a leasehold covenant not yet broken.[32] It
does not extend to debts not in existence when the instrument
directing accumulation took effect, *e.g.* estate duty payable on the
death of a tenant for life.[33]

2. Portions: a provision for accumulation for raising portions for
any issue of the grantor, settlor or testator or any person to whom an
interest is limited under the settlement.[34] This is an exception from
the rule against accumulations only; such accumulations must be
confined to the perpetuity period. The meaning of "portions" here is
not clear. It is not confined to sums raised out of real estate, nor to
provisions for the benefit of the younger children of a marriage.[35] It
does not, however, apply where there is no existing obligation to use
the fund for portions but a mere future discretionary power,[36] nor
where the direction is to accumulate the income from the whole of a
testator's estate, for "it is nor raising a portion at all, it is giving
everything."[37]

3. Timber or wood: a provision for accumulating the produce of
timber or wood.[38] Although excepted from the accumulation rules,
such a direction will be void it if exceeds the perpetuity period.[39]

4. Maintenance of property: a provision for maintaining property at
its present value. Directions to devote surplus income to maintaining
buildings in a proper state of repair, or to apply a fixed annual sum to
keep up an insurance policy to replace the capital lost by not selling
leaseholds, are outside the rule against accumulations; though they
add income to capital, they merely keep up the property and do not
add to it, so that there is no true accumulation.[40] But they must be
confined to the perpetuity period.[41]

5. Minority: accumulations made during a minority under the
general law or any statutory power. While the person entitled to any
trust property is an infant, a statutory power is given to the trustees to
apply the income for his maintenance; subject thereto, they are
bound to accumulate the residue of the income.[42] It is expressly
provided that the period of such accumulation is to be disregarded

[32] *Re Hurlbatt* [1910] 2 Ch. 553.
[33] *Re Rochford's S.T.* [1965] Ch. 111.
[34] L.P.A. 1925, s. 164, see also *post*, p. 234.
[35] *Re Stephens* [1904] 1 Ch. 322.
[36] *Re Bourne's S.T.* [1946] 1 All E.R. 411.
[37] *Edwards* v. *Tuck* (1853) 3 De G.M. & G. 40 at p. 58, *per* Lord Cranworth L.C.
[38] L.P.A. 1925, s. 164. This exception is said to be due to the need for naval timber in
    1800.
[39] *Ferrand* v. *Wilson* (1845) 4 Hare 344.
[40] *Vine* v. *Raleigh* [1891] 2 Ch. 13; *Re Gardiner* [1901] 1 Ch. 697.
[41] *Curtis* v. *Lukin* (1842) 5 Beav. 147.
[42] T.A. 1925, s. 31.

when determining the period for which accumulations are permitted.[43] Thus if a testator directs accumulation for 21 years after his death and the beneficiary at the end of the period is an infant, the accumulations both for the 21 years and during the minority are valid.[44]

6. Certain commercial contracts: transactions which cannot fairly be described as settlements of dispositions. Many commercial transactions involve a measure of accumulation, such as partnership agreements which provide for the accumulation of certain profits, and investment trusts which capitalise part of their income. Such transactions are outside the Act,[45] which merely provides that no person may "settle or dispose" of property in breach of the Act[46]; and many of them are also outside the perpetuity rule as creating merely personal obligations.

7. Where the settlor is a corporation. A settlement made by a corporation is not subject to the rule against accumulations since the rule only applies to natural persons.[47]

---

[43] L.P.A. 1925, s. 165.
[44] *Re Maber* [1928] Ch. 88.
[45] See *Bassil* v. *Lister* (1851) 9 Hare 177 at p. 184; *Re A.E.G. Unit Trust (Managers) Ltd's. Deed* [1957] Ch. 415.
[46] L.P.A. 1925, s. 164 (1).
[47] *Re Dodwell & Co. Ltd.'s Trust Deed* [1979] Ch. 301.

CHAPTER 7

SETTLED LAND AND TRUSTS FOR SALE

Part 1

BEFORE 1883

IT is now necessary to turn from matters of substance to matters of machinery. The last chapter discussed the rules regulating the various future interests in land which could be created, and this chapter will examine how land which is the subject of future interests is managed and disposed of. The starting point is to consider settlements.

The basic idea of a settlement is to make provision out of property for two or more persons in succession. Settlements were frequently made on marriage, providing for the spouses and issue by giving the property to the husband for life, with remainder to the children in tail, subject to paying the wife an annual sum. But not all settlements are marriage settlements, and for most purposes it can be taken that a settlement exists whenever future interests in property have been created.

By the middle of the nineteenth century two methods of settling land were firmly established; these were the strict settlement and the trust for sale.

Sect. 1. The Strict Settlement

1. Principal provisions. A strict settlement was the type of settlement employed "to keep land in the family." Provided the various rules of law and equity were observed, the settlor might create such limitations as he thought fit, but the type of settlement most frequently encountered has been the marriage settlement giving a life interest to the husband and entails to the children. Provision was also made for the wife by giving her a jointure (an annual income during widowhood), and for the children who did not obtain the land under the entails by giving them portions (lump sums of money to assist them in their careers and in matrimony).[1] This form of settlement was adopted because it made provision for all members of the family and yet preserved the land as a unit. The device of giving the husband a mere life estate with remainder to his son in tail (the son, of course, being unborn at the time of the settlement, which was made shortly before the marriage) was adopted as being the best way

---

[1] For details, see M. & W., pp. 385 *et seq.* and generally see Harvey, *Settlements of Land*.

of keeping the land in the family. If an entail had been given to the husband, he could at once have barred it; and under the rule in *Whitby* v. *Mitchell*,[2] a succession of life estates to the husband, his son, the son's son and so on was invalid after the first gift to an unborn person.

2. Alienation. (a) *Settlement and resettlement*. The effect of such a settlement was to render the land substantially inalienable until the eldest son became able to bar the entail on attaining his majority. Shortly after the son's twenty-first birthday he was usually persuaded (often by some financial inducement) to bar the entail with his father's consent; the land was then resettled on the husband for life, remainder to the son for life, remainder to the son's son in tail. The land was thus tied up for another generation. This process of settlement and resettlement prevented any person of full age from having more than a life estate; and the tenant in possession of the land was always a tenant for life. The tenant for life could alienate his life estate, but that was all; no matter how desirable or necessary it was, he had no power to sell the fee simple in any part of the land, or to grant leases which would be binding after his death. If improvements to the property were required, he could effect them only if he paid for them out of his own pocket. Unless he was unimpeachable of waste, the discovery of valuable minerals beneath the land was of little importance to him, for he could not open mines, and even if he was unimpeachable of waste, he could not grant mining leases with an adequate security of tenure for the lessee. In short, for many purposes the land was sterilised.

(b) *Powers in settlement*. These defects were frequently met by a series of provisions in the settlement. Many powers were given to the tenant for life, such as powers to grant specified leases which would be binding on his successors. He was also empowered to sell the fee simple provided the purchase money was paid to trustees to hold on the trusts of the settlement; his own rights and the rights of his son and the other beneficiaries were thus overreached.[3] Usually the bulk of the land would be retained and not sold, but a power of sale was useful for emergencies.

(c) *Legal estate*. The legal estate in settled land might be either split up between the beneficiaries or vested in trustees, according to the way in which the settlement was made. For example, a conveyance—

> "to T and his heirs to the use of A for life, remainder to B and the heirs of his body, remainder to C and his heirs"

[2] *Ante*, p. 189.
[3] *Ante*, p. 107.

gave A a legal life estate, B a legal fee tail and C a legal fee simple. If the conveyance had been worded—

"unto and to the use of T and his heirs in trust for . . . "

the legal fee simple would have been in T, and A, B and C would have had merely equitable interests. In the first case, the settlement conferred the desired powers upon A by means of legal powers operating under the Statute of Uses 1535; the settlement took effect as if the land had been given to A for life and then, subject to sales, leases and other authorised dealings as A made, to B in tail with remainder to C in fee simple. In the second case, the powers conferred upon A would be merely equitable, but T was bound to give effect to any authorised disposition made by A, and the court would compel him to create or transfer the necessary legal estate.[4]

(d) *Absence of powers.* Although it was thus possible for a settlement to provide the necessary powers, in many cases this was not done, especially where the settlement was made by will. In such cases the land could not be dealt with unless the expense of obtaining a private Act of Parliament was incurred. Further, even if the powers were inserted, difficulties sometimes arose over the construction to be put upon them, and in any case the settlement became of formidable length.

3. Intervention of statute. This position was dealt with by a series of statutes passed in the nineteenth century. Starting with Acts such as the Settled Estates Drainage Acts 1840 and 1845 concerning certain limited improvements, the legislature proceeded to enact the Settled Estates Acts 1856 and 1877, which enabled the court to authorise a number of dealings and even enabled the tenant for life to grant certain leases without application to the court. These comparatively timid measures remained the law until the Settled Land Act 1882, drafted by Mr. Wolstenholme, was piloted through Parliament by Lord Cairns.

Sect. 2. Trusts for Sale

1. Origin. Compared with strict settlements, settlements by way of trust for sale are of comparatively recent origin.[5] (It is true that trusts for sale created by will can be traced back for some 500 years, but most of the earliest of these trusts seem to have been designed to raise sums of money, *e.g.* for the payment of debts, rather than to provide for persons by way of succession.) Trusts for sale created *inter vivos* are more recent in origin; not until nearly 150 years ago do

---

[4] See *Re Brown* (1886) 32 Ch.D. 597 at p. 601.
[5] See generally, J.M. Lightwood (1927) 3 Camb. L.J. 59.

marriage settlements by way of trust for sale appear to have become at all common. The purpose of such trusts for sale usually differed greatly from that of a strict settlement. Where the property to be settled was a family estate on which the beneficiaries would reside and over which the tenant for life would wish to exercise direct control, the settlor usually employed a strict settlement which would keep the land in the family. Where, however, the property was in the nature of an investment (such as a row of shops) there would be no desire to keep it in the family in any particular form, nor would the tenant for life wish to live on it or manage it: in such cases, a trust for sale would be employed, the primary object of such a settlement being to produce a regular income for the beneficiaries.

2. Retention unsold. For these reasons, in a trust for sale the legal estate was vested in the trustees upon trust to sell the land and hold the income until sale and the proceeds thereafter upon specified trusts for the beneficiaries. The trustees were usually given power to postpone sale in their discretion, and to manage the land until sale. Thus as long as the land produced a satisfactory income, it could be retained, and the trustee need not sell until market conditions made an advantageous sale possible. Often the consent of the beneficiaries entitled in possession was made requisite to a sale. The purchase-money arising on a sale was usually directed to be invested in stocks, shares and other securities.

3. Conversion. The effect of creating a trust for sale was that even before sale, the rights of the beneficiaries were deemed to be rights in personalty. Equity treated that as done which ought to be done, and since there was a binding obligation to sell the land sooner or later, the beneficiaries were treated as having forthwith interests in the purchase-money into which the land was to be converted: this is known as the equitable doctrine of conversion. For this reason, trusts for sale are often referred to as "personalty settlements," in common with settlements of stocks and shares and other personal property. They were also sometimes called "traders' settlements," since they are more appropriate to the urban property of business men than the rural estates of the landed gentry.

Part 2

THE SETTLED LAND ACT 1882

The Settled Land Act 1882, which was passed as the result of a period of agricultural depression, had as its paramount object the well-being of settled land. "The leading purpose of the Legislature was to prevent the decay of agricultural and other interests occasioned by the deterioration of lands and buildings in the possession of impecunious life-tenants."[6] The general scheme of the Act was to give the tenant for life under the settlement wide powers of dealing with the land free from the trusts of the settlement without making any application to the court, and to protect the rights of the beneficiaries in the case of a sale by shifting the settlement from the land to the purchase-money, which had to be paid into court or into the hands of the trustees. A purchaser was not concerned with the rights of the beneficiaries, even if he had full knowledge of them; those rights were not destroyed, but, being overreached, were transformed from rights in the land to rights in the money paid for it.

In this legislation, the term "settlement" sometimes means the documents by which the land was settled, but more usually means the state of affairs resulting from them[7]; the context usually indicates which. The Act also applied in a somewhat unsatisfactory way to trusts for sale.[8] The following is a brief statement of the principal provisions of the Act.

Sect. 1. Settled Land

A. Definition of Settled Land

Any land, or any estate or interest therein, which was the subject of any document or documents whereby it stood for the time being limited to, or in trust for, any persons by way of succession, was deemed to be settled land and so subject to the Act, whether the settlement was made before or after the Act.[9] Thus if freehold land was conveyed or given by will—

> "unto and to the use of A and B and their heirs in trust for X for life, remainder in trust for Y and his heirs,"

or freehold land was conveyed—

> "to A for life, remainder to B and his heirs," or
> "to X and his heirs to the use of Y and the heirs of his body,"

in each case the land was settled land whether the legal estate was vested in trustees as in the first example or the person currently beneficially entitled as in the other two examples. Leasehold land might similarly be settled. In the third case the requirement that there should be an element of succession was satisfied by the resulting use to the grantor in fee simple subject to Y's entail.

In one case, land was deemed settled land even if no element of succession was involved: this was where a minor was entitled in possession to land.[10]

---

[6] *Bruce* v. *Marquess of Ailesbury* [1892] A.C. 356 at p. 363 *per* Lord Watson.
[7] See *Re Spencer's S.E.* [1903] 1 Ch. 75 at p. 79; *Re Ogle's S.E.* [1927] 1 Ch. 229 at p. 233.
[8] *Post*, p. 241.
[9] S.L.A. 1882, s. 2.
[10] *Ibid.* s. 59, and see M. & W., p. 289.

B. *Powers of the Tenant for Life*

1. The powers. The object of the Act was to give to one person wide and unfettered powers of sale, exchange, leasing, mortgaging and otherwise dealing with the land.[11] That person was the tenant for life or other limited owner in possession, such as a tenant in tail, tenant in fee simple subject to a gift over, or person entitled to a base fee.[12] For convenience, the phrase "tenant for life" is used to include not only those who had an actual life estate, but any other person who had the powers of a tenant for life. If the tenant for life was a minor, the trustees of the settlement could exercise the statutory powers on the minor's behalf.[13]

2. Tenant for life a trustee. In relation to the exercise of his statutory powers, the tenant for life was deemed to be a trustee for the other beneficiaries, and was bound to consider their interests.[14] This enabled the court to intervene if he sought to sell at a price infinitely below the value of the property[15] or to make an investment which, although not outside his powers, was undesirable. Nevertheless, provided the transaction was a proper one, it would not be invalidated merely because the motive of the tenant for life was not very commendable, *e.g.* that "he is selling out of ill will or caprice, or because he does not like the remainderman, because he desires to be relieved from the trouble of attending to the management of land, or from any other such object, or with any such motive."[16]

3. Powers unfettered. Subject to this restriction, the tenant for life was in general unfettered in the exercise of his powers. They could not be taken away or cut down either directly or indirectly, nor could he curtail or divest himself of them or effectively contract not to exercise them.[17] Additional or larger powers could be conferred by the settlor on the tenant for life or the trustees, and the Act in no way restricted such powers.[18] The tenant for life was thus normally in complete control of the land, even if he was "a spendthrift, who has ruined himself by his own extravagance and folly, who has brought disgrace on the family name, and who has exposed the family estate to destruction for the rest of his life."[19]

---

[11] S.L.A. 1882, ss. 3, 6, 18.
[12] *Ibid.* ss. 2. 58.
[13] *Ibid.* s. 60.
[14] *Ibid.* s. 53; *Re Lord Stamford's S.E.* (1889) 43 Ch.D. 84 at p. 95.
[15] *Wheelwright* v. *Walker (No.* 1) (1883) 23 Ch.D. 752 at p. 762.
[16] *Cardigan* v. *Curzon-Howe* (1885) 30 Ch.D. 531 at p. 540, *per* Chitty J.
[17] S.L.A. 1882, ss. 50–52.
[18] *Ibid.* ss. 56, 57.
[19] *Re Marquis of Ailesbury's S.E.* [1892] 1 Ch. 506 at p. 535, *per* Lindley L.J.

C. The Trustees of the Settlement

The Act contained an elaborate definition of the persons who were
the trustees of the settlement, but in any settlement made after 1882
they normally consisted of those persons expressly appointed as
trustees of the settlement for the purposes of the Act.[20] It is
important to note that whether or not the legal estate was vested in
the trustees, they had no real control over the land. Their most
important function arose from the fact that capital money arising on
any transaction, such as the sale of the land, had to be paid either to
the trustees or into court, and unless the settlement otherwise
provided,[21] the trustees had to be two or more in number to give an
effective receipt.[22]

In short, the full control of the land was in the hands of the tenant
for life, and the trustees merely had certain supervisory functions
designed to protect the interests of the beneficiaries.

D. Effect of a Sale or Other Dealing

The effect of a dealing with the settled land such as a sale was that the
rights of the beneficiaries under the settlement were overreached,
provided that the money was paid to the trustees, being not less than
two in number, or into court.[23] This was so whether the legal estate
was vested in trustees or split up between the beneficiaries. A tenant
for life had a statutory power to convey something not vested in him,
namely, the whole legal estate. The capital money in the hands of the
trustees, which had to be invested in accordance with the Act, was
treated as being land.[24] "The effect of a sale under the Settled Land
Act is merely to substitute money for land, and whatever rights
persons had in the land are preserved to them in the money produced
in its sale."[25] For example, if land was settled on "A for life,
remainder to B for life, remainder to C and his heirs," the effect of a
sale by A was to vest the legal fee simple in the purchaser, free from
the legal rights of A, B and C, who took corresponding rights in the
capital money. Thus C had a fee simple in remainder in the capital
money, which, on his death, would pass with the rest of his realty
under his will or, if he was intestate, to his heir. If the land had been
conveyed "unto and to the use of" trustees on trust for the
beneficiaries, the position was exactly the same: A's statutory power
of sale enabled him to transfer to the purchaser the legal estate vested
in the trustees.

This power of the tenant for life to defeat the expectations of those

---

[20] S.L.A. 1882, s. 2; S.L.A. 1890, s. 16.
[21] Contrast *post*, p. 285.
[22] S.L.A. 1882, ss. 22, 39.
[23] S.L.A. 1882, ss. 20, 22, 39.
[24] *Ibid.* s. 22.
[25] *Hampden* v. *Earl of Buckinghamshire* [1893] 2 Ch. 531 at p. 544, *per* Lindley L.J.

in remainder who wished to enjoy the settled land itself might seem to be unjust, but "what the statute intended to do was to release the land from the fetters of the settlement—to render it a marketable article notwithstanding the settlement."[26] It was more important in the public interest that land should be freely alienable despite any settlement than that "sentimental considerations"[27] should be allowed to sterilise it.

Sect. 2. Trusts for Sale

1. Application of the Act. The original draft of the Act did not apply to land held on trust for sale, but "the unprompted wisdom of Parliament" added a section, section 63, "drafted in a fine style of perplexed verbiage,"[28] which provided that such land was to be deemed settled land, and thus within the Act, if the proceeds of sale or income were to be applied or disposed of for any person or persons for life or any other limited period. The effect of this was to defeat the main purpose of a trust for sale (namely, that the land should be sold as and when the trustees thought best); the hands of the trustees were tied by the prohibition in the Act against their exercising any power to sell given to them by the settlement unless the tenant for life gave his consent.[29] Under a trust for sale, the trustees were normally intended to have control. Yet in consequence of section 63, the wide powers given by the Act were all vested in the tenant for life.

2. Order of court. One solution of the difficulty would have been to repeal the section added by Parliament. Instead, the Settled Land Act 1884, s. 7, provided that in the case of trusts for sale within the Settled Land Act 1882 the tenant for life should be unable to exercise his statutory powers unless he obtained an order of the court. Until such an order was made, the trustees were empowered to sell without the consent of the tenant for life.[30] A purchaser could safely deal with the trustees for sale unless such an order had been registered as a *lis pendens* (pending action).[31]

The result of this was substantially to restore the position as it was before 1883. Land subject to a trust for sale was nominally settled land, but unless the tenant for life had obtained an order from the court, he had none of the statutory powers and the trustees had the sole unfettered power of sale. However, they had no powers of leasing, mortgaging or otherwise dealing with the land except by way

---

[26] *Bruce* v. *Marquess of Ailesbury* [1892] A.C. 356 at p. 361, *per* Lord Halsbury L.C.
[27] *Ibid.* at p. 362, *per* Lord Halsbury L.C.
[28] 27 S.J. 113; 28 S.J. 322.
[29] *Ante*, p. 239.
[30] S.L.A. 1884, s. 6.
[31] See *ante*, p. 97.

of sale unless the trust for sale conferred these powers on them expressly or by implication.[32]

3. Bare trusts. It should be noted that the Settled Land Acts never applied to a trust where one or more persons of full age were entitled in possession absolutely and there was no element of succession, whether there was a trust for sale or a mere trust. Thus a conveyance "unto and to the use of A and his heirs in trust for B and C and their heirs" created a bare trust which was not within the Acts.

Part 3

THE SETTLED LAND ACT 1925

The Settled Land Act 1925 continued the policy of the Act of 1882, but with a number of important alterations to take into account the new simpler principles enshrined in the 1925 legislation as a whole. These alterations will be considered first, before dealing with the other provisions of the Act.

Sect. 1. Basic Alterations Made by the Act of 1925

A. Trusts for Sale are Excluded from the Act

Land subject to "an immediate binding trust for sale" is expressly excluded from the definition of settled land.[33] Trusts for sale are now governed by the Law of Property Act 1925 and are considered later under a separate head.[34]

B. The Legal Estate is Normally in the Tenant for Life

Before 1926, the legal estate in settled land was either vested in trustees or split up between the beneficiaries, depending upon how the settlement was made.[35] After 1925, the settlor has no choice since the only two legal estates are a fee simple absolute in possession and a term of years absolute: with the exceptions stated below, the legal estate is always vested in the tenant for life. Where a settlement is made after 1925, the legal estate must be conveyed to the tenant for life, unless, of course, it is already vested in him,[36] as is the case where the owner of property settles it upon himself as tenant for life, with remainders over ("with remainders over" is a concise way of referring to the remainders following the life interest without setting them out in detail). In the case of a settlement made before 1926, the

---

[32] *Walker* v. *Southall* (1887) 56 L.T. 882; *Re Bellinger* [1898] 2 Ch. 534.
[33] S.L.A. 1925 s. 1 (7), added by L.P. (Am.)A. 1926, Sched.
[34] *Post,* p. 277.
[35] *Ante,* p. 235.
[36] S.L.A. 1925, s. 4.

legal estate was automatically vested in the tenant for life at the first moment of 1926.[37]

Thus today the tenant for life has the legal estate as well as the statutory powers vested in him, and he holds both the estate and the powers on trust for himself and the other beneficiaries under the settlement.[38] This emphasises the dual capacity of a tenant for life: he holds two interests in the land, the legal estate as trustee and his own equitable interest beneficially.[39]

In two cases, however, the legal estate and statutory powers are vested, not in a tenant for life, but in the "statutory owner."[40] These two cases are as follows.

1. Tenant for life a minor. A legal estate cannot be vested in a minor after 1925 and it would be undesirable to give him the statutory powers. Consequently, where the tenant for life is a minor the legal estate and the statutory powers are vested in the statutory owner, consisting of—

    (i) a personal representative if the land is vested in him and no vesting instrument[41] has been executed, *e.g.* where the settlement has been made by the will of a testator who has just died; but otherwise

    (ii) the trustees of the settlement.

2. No tenant for life. Where under a settlement there is no tenant for life, the legal estate and statutory powers are vested in the statutory owner, consisting of—

    (i) any person of full age upon whom the settlement expressly confers the powers; if none,

    (ii) the trustees of the settlement.

The question who is a tenant for life and the cases where there is no tenant for life are dealt with below.[42] For the present, it is sufficient to say that there usually is a tenant for life, but that in those cases where there is not the Act of 1925 has effected a considerable improvement, for in such cases before 1926 the land could not be dealt with at all.

It will be seen from this that whereas before 1926 the legal estate and statutory powers might be vested in different persons (*e.g.* where land was conveyed "unto and to the use of T1 and T2 and their heirs

---

[37] L.P.A. 1925, 1st Sched., Pt. II, para. 6.
[38] S.L.A. 1925, ss. 16, 107.
[39] See generally *Re Liberty's W.T.* [1937] Ch. 176.
[40] S.L.A. 1925, ss. 4, 23, 26, 117; L.P.A. 1925, 1st Sched., Pt. II, paras 3, 5, 6. And on the death of a tenant for life the legal estate normally vests temporarily in personal representatives: see *post*, p. 255.
[41] For vesting instruments, see *post*, p. 245.
[42] *Post*, p. 262.

in trust for A for life, remainder to B and his heirs"), the scheme of
the Act of 1925 is to ensure that they shall not be separated. It should
be noted, however, that the legal estate is never vested in the trustees
of the settlement as such, although they may hold it in some other
capacity, such as statutory owner or special personal
representatives.[43]

C. All Settlements Must be Made by Two Documents

Before 1926, a settlement was usually made by one document. If the
settlement was made by will, the will constituted the settlement,
whereas a settlement *inter vivos* was made by deed. The result was
that if the land was sold, the purchaser had to examine the lengthy
and, for this purpose, mainly irrelevant provisions of the settlement
to discover the principal facts essential to his obtaining a good title;
these were normally—

  (i) that the land he had agreed to buy was included in the
      settlement;
 (ii) that the person who had agreed to sell to him was the duly
      constituted tenant for life; and
(iii) that the persons to whom he was proposing to pay the
      purchase-money were the duly appointed trustees of the
      settlement.

To discover these facts was often a tedious task, for the settlement
was a long document setting out the trusts in full and a purchaser
often had to waste time in reading clauses which were of no interest
to him in order to ascertain the few simple facts he required. In
addition, all the details of the family's arrangements were laid bare to
a stranger's gaze. There was, of course, no question of the purchaser
being prejudiced by the notice he had of the beneficiaries' interests,
for whether they were legal or equitable and whether or not he knew
what they were, statute had laid down that he took free from them
provided he paid his money to the trustees or into court.

The Settled Land Act 1925 avoids these disadvantages by providing
that every settlement made after 1925 must be made by two
documents, a vesting instrument and a trust instrument. The vesting
instrument contains all the information to which a purchaser is
entitled; it gives him, in effect, a short certificate of the few matters
with which he is concerned. The vesting instrument may be regarded
as the tenant for life's warrant card. The trust instrument sets out the
details of the settlement and the purchaser is normally not concerned
with them. The trusts are said to be "behind the curtain" formed by
the vesting instrument, and the curtain is one behind which the
purchaser is not entitled to peep. Settlements made before 1926 are

---

[43] *Post,* p. 255.

brought into line by the provision that the document creating the settlement is to be treated as the trust instrument, and that before the land can be dealt with a vesting instrument must be executed. These provisions must now be examined in greater detail.

1. Settlements made after 1925. (a) *Settlements made inter vivos.* Every settlement of a legal estate in land made *inter vivos* after 1925 must be made by two deeds, a principal vesting deed and a trust instrument.[44] The contents of these deeds are as follows:

TRUST INSTRUMENT

This—
(i) Declares the trusts affecting the settled land.
(ii) Bears any *ad valorem* stamp duty payable in respect of the settlement.
(iii) Appoints trustees of the settlement.
(iv) Contains the power, if any, to appoint new trustees of the settlement.
(v) Sets out, either expressly or by reference, any powers intended to be conferred by the settlement in extension of those conferred by the Act.

PRINCIPAL VESTING DEED

This—
(i) Describes the settled land, either specifically or generally.
(ii) Declares that the settled land is vested in the person or persons to whom it is conveyed, or in whom it is declared to be vested, upon the trusts from time to time affecting the settled land.
(iii) States the names of the trustees of the settlement.
(iv) States the names of any persons empowered to appoint new trustees of the settlement.
(v) States any additional or larger powers conferred by the trust instrument.

It will be noticed that the last three particulars in each document are similar, the only difference being that whereas the trust instrument actually makes the appointment and confers the powers, the vesting deed merely recites what has been done by the trust instrument. The first two particulars in each of the deeds are, of course, completely dissimilar. The second requirement of a vesting deed is worded so as to cover two cases: (i) where the vesting deed acts as a conveyance from the settlor to the tenant for life or statutory owner, as where X settles property on A for life with the remainders over; and (ii) where the same person is both settlor and tenant for

[44] S.L.A. 1925, ss. 4, 5.

life, so that there is no transfer of the legal estate, as where Z on his marriage settles property on himself for life with remainders over.

(b) *Settlements made by will.* Where land is settled by the will of a testator dying after 1925, the will is treated as the trust instrument and the testator's personal representatives, after providing for debts and death duties, hold the land on trust to execute a vesting instrument in favour of the tenant for life or statutory owner on being required to do so.[45] The vesting instrument may be either a vesting deed or a vesting assent. A vesting assent is a document merely in writing containing the same particulars as a vesting deed[46]; it attracts no stamp duty, whereas a vesting deed, being a deed, must carry a stamp. Personal representatives will thus use a vesting assent.

2. Settlements made before 1926. A deed creating a settlement existing at the beginning of 1926 is treated as a trust instrument. The Act provided that as soon as was practicable the trustees of the settlement might, and at the request of the tenant for life or statutory owner must, execute a vesting deed.[47] Normally this conveys no estate but merely declares that the legal estate in the settled land is vested in the tenant for life or statutory owner, for in nearly all cases the Law of Property Act 1925 automatically vested the legal estate in him at the beginning of 1926[48]; but if in fact the legal estate was outstanding, the vesting deed operates to convey it.

This provision is of little asistance to a purchaser, however, for this is one of the two important cases where the trust instrument is not kept behind the curtain.[49] Despite the existence of a vesting deed, a purchaser must verify from the settlement that the vesting deed includes the land in question and that the proper persons are tenant for life and trustees of the settlement.[50]

3. Sections 4 (1) and 13. Some provision had to be made to prevent evasions of the requirement that there should be a vesting instrument. Whilst a vesting deed is not invalidated merely by some error in the statements required to be contained in it,[51] the absence of any vesting instrument at all usually makes it impossible to deal with the land.

First, a settlement *inter vivos* of a legal estate in land made otherwise than by two deeds cannot transfer or create a legal estate; the tenant for life or statutory owner, however, can require the

---

[44] S.L.A. 1925, ss. 4, 5.
[45] S.L.A. 1925, ss. 6, 8.
[46] *Ibid.* s. 8.
[47] *Ibid.* 2nd Sched., para. 1.
[48] L.P.A. 1925, 1st Sched., Pt. II, paras. 3, 5, 6.
[49] For the other case, see *post*, p. 248.
[50] S.L.A. 1925, s. 110.
[51] S.L.A. 1925, s. 5.

trustees of the settlement to execute a vesting deed.[52] Thus if A purports to convey his fee simple to B in fee simple on trust for B for life, remainder to C absolutely then no legal estate passes to B so B cannot dispose of any legal estate.[53]

Secondly, section 13 of the Settled Land Act 1925 (sometimes called the "paralysing section") in effect provides that where a tenant for life or statutory owner has become entitled to have a vesting instrument executed in his favour, no disposition of a legal estate can be made until a vesting instrument has been executed in accordance with the Act; until this has been done, any purported disposition of the land *inter vivos* by any person operates only as a contract for valuable consideration to carry out the transaction after the requisite vesting instrument has been executed. The rule in section 13 is thus available where despite section 4 (1) a tenant for life does have the legal estate, *e.g.* because he was the settlor and so has the legal estate *qua* settlor or because the transitional provisions automatically vested the legal estate in him.

To this rule there are four exceptions.

(a) *Disposition by personal representative.* The section does not apply where the disposition is made by a personal representative.[54] Thus if a settlement was made before 1926 and the tenant for life has just died without a vesting deed having been executed, the legal estate (which was nevertheless automatically vested in the tenant for life at the beginning of 1926) duly passes to his personal representatives, who can dispose of the land without a vesting instrument being executed, *e.g.* if part of the land is sold to raise money for death duties.

(b) *Purchaser without notice.* The section does not apply where the disposition is made to a purchaser of a legal estate without notice of the tenant for life or statutory owner having become entitled to a vesting instrument.[55] For example, if by a deed A settles land on himself for life with remainders over, and then, suppressing the deed, sells the land to a purchaser who is ignorant of the settlement, the purchaser gets a good title even though no vesting deed has been executed.

---

[52] *Ibid.* ss. 4, 9.
[53] If A conveyed her fee simple to B absolutely, who had agreed orally to hold it for A for life, so that by *Bannister v. Bannister* [1948] 2 All E.R. 133 a Settled Land Act settlement arose, and then B purported to sell the whole legal and beneficial interest to C, it would seem that, owing to s. 4, no legal estate would pass, but that A should be estopped from claiming priority over C if C had no notice of her (since she was not living in the property) and that C would have to rely on the Limitation Act to enable him to make title to a purchaser. Alternatively, it may be that s. 4 is inapplicable since it applies only to a settlement and no settlement arises under s. 1 until there is an instrument (e.g. a court order) by virtue of which land stands limited in trust.
[54] *Ibid.* s. 13.
[55] *Ibid.*, as amended by L.P. (Am.)A. 1926, Sched.

(c) *Settlement at an end.* The section does not apply where the settlement has come to an end before a vesting instrument has been executed since there is no "settled land" to enable section 13 to apply. Thus where at the end of 1925 X was a tenant in tail in possession free from any trusts or incumbrances, it has been held that if before any vesting instrument is executed he bars the entail and so terminates the settlement, it is unnecessary for a vesting instrument to be executed before he conveys the land to a purchaser.[56] When the land ceases to be settled, the fetters of section 13 drop off.

(d) *Section 1 of the Amendment Act.* Section 13 does not apply where advantage is taken of section 1 of the Law of Property (Amendment) Act 1926. In a limited class of cases, this allows settled land to be dealt with as if it were not settled; the section is dealt with below.[57]

An illustration of the operation of these provisions is given by the case of a settlor who attempts to make a settlement *inter vivos* after 1925 in favour of his son and family by a single document. In such a case—

(i) If he had purported to convey the legal estate the document is ineffective to transfer or create any legal estate which thus remains vested in him.

(ii) The document is treated as a trust instrument.

(iii) As soon as it is practicable the trustees of the settlement may, and at the request of the tenant for life or statutory owner must, execute a principal vesting deed, which will operate to take the legal estate out of the settlor and vest it in the tenant for life or statutory owner.

(iv) If the settlor had retained his legal estate and declared trusts thereof then until he[58] or the trustees have duly executed the vesting deed, section 13 operates to prevent any disposition of the land being made. If there are no trustees and no persons able and willing to appoint trustees, an application must be made to the court for the appointment of trustees.

(v) Even after a vesting deed has been executed the settlement is not as satisfactory as one made in the proper manner, for the document creating the settlement, although treated as the trust instrument, is not behind the curtain. This is the other of the two important exceptions to the rule that a purchaser is not concerned with the trust instrument.[59] A purchaser must examine the document creating the settlement to see that it

[56] *Re Alefounder's W.T.* [1927] 1 Ch. 360.
[57] *Post*, p. 261.
[58] Properly, the settlor executes the vesting deed contemporaneously with the trust instrument (see Hallett *Conveyancing Precedents*, pp. 898–900) but nothing prevents him from subsequently disposing of his legal estate by vesting deed.
[59] For the first exception, see *ante*, p. 246.

includes the land in question and that the proper persons are tenant for life and trustees of the settlement.

4. Section 18. As has been seen *until* a vesting instrument has been executed section 13 paralyses dealings with the legal estate in settled land. Once a vesting instrument has been executed then section 18 makes void dispositions by a tenant for life (or statutory owner) which do not comply with the requirements of the Act. Section 18 ceases to concern purchasers when a vesting deed or assent has been followed or "cancelled" either, usually, by an ordinary deed or assent, which affords purchasers protection under section 110 (5), or, unusually, by a deed of discharge under section 17.[60]

A problem arises from the fact that section 13 itself contains an exception in favour of a purchaser of a legal estate without notice of a S.L.A. settlement, whilst section 18 contains no such exception. It may be that the draftsman appreciated that until a vesting instrument was executed there was scope for equity's darling to acquire the legal estate but took it for granted that once a vesting instrument had been executed then such instrument would give everyone notice of the settlement, so no-one would be able to claim to be equity's darling.[61] It may also be that the draftsman thought that section 110 (1), in any event, conferred sufficient protection upon a purchaser.

s.110 (1) — what provide?

A. *Weston* v. *Henshaw*

Weston v. *Henshaw*[62] provides a useful starting point. A father sold land to his son but later re-purchased it: he then settled the land by his will on his widow for life, then his son for life, remainder to a grandson. In due course, after the widow's death, the land was vested in the son by a vesting assent. Subsequently, the son pretended to be sole absolute beneficial owner, by showing title up to the sale by his father to himself and suppressing the later title deeds, and obtained money for himself by mortgaging the land as sole absolute beneficial owner. Since the land was actually settled land the mortgages, being for his own personal needs, were not for a purpose authorised under the Act[63] and, even if they had been for such purpose the moneys, as capital moneys, should have been paid to the S.L.A. trustees.[64]

When the son died everything came to light and the grandson claimed that the morgages were void under section 18. The mortgagee claimed protection under section 110 (1): "On a sale, lease, mortgage or other disposition *a purchaser dealing in good faith*

---

[60] *Post,* pp. 254–256.
[61] s. 98 (3) S.L.A. reveals that in cases where a tenant for life might otherwise appear to be sole beneficial owner, it was envisaged that the S.L.A. trustees would have ensured that notice of the vesting instrument was written on the earlier title deed otherwise making the tenant for life appear sole owner.
[62] [1950] Ch. 510.
[63] s.71.
[64] s.18.

with a tenant for life or statutory owner *shall*, as against all parties entitled under the settlement, *be conclusively taken* to have given the best price, consideration or rent, as the case may require, that could reasonably be obtained by the tenant for life or statutory owner, and *to have complied with all the requisitions of this Act.*"

Danckwerts J. summarily dismissed the mortgagee's claim by stating, without giving any reasons, that the section only protected a purchaser dealing with a tenant for life as such, *i.e.* known by the purchaser to be a tenant for life. At first sight this appears ridiculous since, if a purchaser *knows* he is dealing with a tenant for life, he will make a point of complying with the Act, so that there is no need of protection under section 110 (1), which can therefore only be needed where a purchaser does *not* know he is dealing with a tenant for life. However, purchasers knowingly dealing with a tenant for life do need some protection in case remaindermen under the settlement allege that the best price or rent has not been obtained, so that the purchaser has been involved in a breach of trust by the tenant for life, so that the purchaser holds the land on constructive trust for the remaindermen and is accountable as a constructive trustee. Without such protection purchasers would never purchase settled land.

Since the mortgagee, in the opinion of Danckwerts J., had failed to bring himself within the first half of section 110 no consideration was given to the latter half. The startling result was therefore reached that the grandson with his equitable interest took free from the mortgages (made void by section 18) even though the mortagee was a bona fide purchaser for value without notice who could not possibly have discovered the existence of the settlement.

B. Re Morgan's Lease

Later it was held in *Re Morgan's Lease*[65] that section 110 (1) is available *whether or not* a purchaser knows he is dealing with a tenant for life. The plaintiffs took a seven year lease in writing (not by deed as required by section 42 of the settled Land Act) from a person appearing to be sole absolute beneficial owner[66] but who was actually a tenant for life. The lease contained an option to renew it at the same rent for a further seven years. When the option was exercised the tenant for life had died and the new owner refused to renew the lease, especially when the rent was so low.

Ungoed-Thomas J. pointed out that *Weston* v. *Henshaw* had been decided in ignorance of some dicta in *Mogridge* v. *Clapp*[67] of Kay L.J. treating it as self-evident, as it seemed to him also, that the section covered a lessee not knowing he was dealing with a tenant for life. Thus he held that the lessee could rely on section 110 (1) to be

---

[65] [1972] Ch. 1.
[66] There was no constructive notice of his real title: L.P.A. 1925, s. 44 (2), (5).
[67] [1892] 3 Ch. 382 at pp. 400–401.

conclusively taken to have given the best rent and to have complied with all the requisitions of the Act.

C. The modern Weston v. Henshaw position

Re Morgan's Lease only concerned minor irregularities (e.g. the lease should have been by deed) and no capital moneys were payable. What, however, is the position today in a *Weston* v. *Henshaw* situation if a tenant for life holds himself out as sole beneficial owner and mortgages or sells the settled land as if it were unsettled, receiving the capital moneys himself? Will the bona fide purchaser without notice take a good title, even though the most fundamental requirement that capital moneys be paid to two trustees has not been complied with?

There is much to be said for the view that such a purchaser will obtain a good title, being conclusively taken under section 110 (1) to have complied with *all* the requirements of the Act.[68] After all, if land is subject to a trust for sale, because of a statutory co-ownership trust for sale or an express trust for sale, equity's darling may take a good title,[69] as he can if land is settled land and a vesting instrument has not been executed.[70] What rational reason can there be for discriminating against him when a vesting instrument has been executed, especially when it is quite fortuitous that under the title, which *ex hypothesi* he cannot reasonably discover, the land either happens to be held on trust for sale or to be settled land, in respect of which a vesting instrument has been executed, rather than settled land in respect of which no vesting instrument has been executed?

On the other hand, it is possible to argue that the effect of section 112 (2) of the Settled Land Act, requiring (unless the contrary appears[71]) references to sale, mortgaging, leasing or other dispositions to be construed as extending only to sales, mortgages, leases or other dispositions under the Act, is that section 110 (1) should be construed as applying only on a sale, mortgage, lease or other disposition *under the Act*.[72] In such a case a purchaser, dealing in good faith with someone *ex hypothesi* known to be tenant for life, is taken to have given the best price, consideration or rent and to have complied with all the requisitions of the Act. The final clause in section 110 (1) should be construed as an etcetera clause to sweep in all failures to comply with lesser requirements than the requirements

---

[68] *Gilmore* v. *The O'Conor Don* [1947] I.R. 462 at p. 495 *per* Black J.; *Chandler* v. *Bradley* [1897] 1 Ch. 315 at 323.

[69] *Caunce* v. *Caunce* [1969] 1 W.L.R. 286; *Williams & Glyn's Bank* v. *Boland* [1979] Ch. 312 (C.A.) [1981] A.C. 487 (H.L.).

[70] S.L.A., s. 13.

[71] In *Weston* v. *Henshaw* [1950] Ch. 510, s. 112 (2) was held ousted in s. 18 (1) in context, since it would make a nonsense of s. 18 (1) (a) to say that the dispositions it made void were (under s. 112 (2)) dipositions under the Act.

[72] It may be significant that s. 110 (1) and s. 112 (2) S.L.A. 1925 were originally juxtaposed in s. 54 and s. 55 (3) S.L.A. 1882 respectively.

that sales and leases should be at the best price or best rent. It was not intended to cover the most fundamental requirement of all (which otherwise it would have expressly mentioned) that capital moneys be paid to two trustees, since such moneys would always be paid to two trustees since *ex hypothesi* the purchaser would be dealing knowingly with a tenant for life purporting to make a disposition under the Act. Thus, section 110 (1) cannot assist a purchaser without notice of the settlement who pays capital moneys other than to two trustees: it can only assist purchasers knowingly dealing with tenants for life, as held in *Weston* v. *Henshaw* but rejected in *Re Morgan's Lease*.

Section 110 (1) at least leaves open the position of a purchaser who may on general principles take free of an equitable interest if he is equity's darling. Nothing in the Act expressly states that a bona fide purchaser of a legal estate for value without notice of a settlement will be subject to equitable interests under the settlement.

Nevertheless, if a purchaser cannot rely on section 110 (1) to deem him to have complied with the Act and so be treated as if he had acquired a legal estate, is he prevented from acquiring a legal estate by section 18 (1) (*a*): "Any disposition by the tenant for life other than a disposition authorised by this Act . . . shall be void"? On a narrow view it may be argued that the expression "a disposition authorised by this Act" includes a sale for the best consideration in money that can reasonably be required, since sections 38 and 39 authorise such sale, but does not include a lease for residential or office purposes exceeding 50 years (outside section 41) or a mortgage for purposes other than those within section 71. It is true that by section 18 (1) (*b*) "if capital money is payable . . . a conveyance to a purchaser shall only take effect *under this Act* if the capital money is paid to the trustees or into court" and by section 18 (1) (*c*) "capital money shall not, except where the trustee is a trust corporation, be paid to . . . fewer persons than two as trustees of the settlement." However, is there anything to prevent the conveyance of the legal estate taking effect outside the Act on the basic principle that he who holds the legal estate can convey it to another,[73] *assuming* that a sale for full consideration can be a "disposition authorised by this Act," since within sections 38 and 39, though the sale be not expressly made as tenant for life and the capital money be not paid to two trustees as required by the Act?

If this assumption be erroneously facile, as may well be the case, then section 18 prevents any purchaser from obtaining a legal estate and so prevents any purchaser qualifying as equity's darling *if* section 110 (1) is not available to assist a purchaser. Section 110 (1) should thus be available to assist a purchaser.

---

[73] See *Caunce* v. *Caunce* [1969] 1 W.L.R. 286, *Williams & Glyn's Bank* v. *Boland* [1979] Ch. 312 (C.A.) [1981] A.C. 487 (H.L.) despite s. 27 (2) L.P.A. 1925 and s. 14 T.A. 1925.

5. Subsidiary vesting deed. Where a settlement of land is already in existence and other land is brought into the settlement, a subsidiary vesting deed is required to convey the land to the tenant for life or statutory owner. The contents of a subsidiary vesting deed are as follows—

 (i) particulars of the last or only principal vesting deed affecting land subject to the settlement;
 (ii) a statement that the land conveyed is to be held upon and subject to the same trusts and powers as the land comprised in the principal vesting deed;
 (iii) the names of the trustees of the settlement;
 (iv) the name of any person entitled to appoint new trustees of the settlement.[74]

It is unnecessary to refer to the trust instrument or to any additional powers conferred thereby.

6. The "curtain" principle. Since the whole purpose of the vesting instrument is to provide a purchaser with all he needs to know, section 110 (2) lays down that a purchaser of a legal estate in settled land is not entitled to see the trust instrument. He must rely on the vesting instrument which provides a "curtain" behind which he may not peep and which is not to be invalidated by reason only of any errors contained therein.[75] Section 110 (2) further states that a purchaser of a legal estate in settled land is bound and entitled to assume that the particulars required to be set out in the vesting instrument are correct, *e.g.* as to the persons who are the trustees and the tenant for life.

What happens if the particulars are erroneous? A purchaser is safe if he is a "purchaser of a legal estate in settled land." But, suppose that before the purchase an event had occurred that had terminated the interest of the tenant for life and caused the settlement to determine, *e.g.* where land had been settled on W for life or until remarriage, with remainder to S absolutely, and W had remarried before selling the land as tenant for life to P.[76] Since W had the legal estate it seems that the legal estate will have passed under W's conveyance to P.[77] However, since the settlement had terminated on W's remarriage the land is no longer settled land so P cannot be "a purchaser of a legal estate in *settled land*." Thus P takes subject to S's equitable interest of which he will have constructive notice since the vesting instrument makes it clear that some equitable interests subsist. S will obtain the land but P will recover from the trustees the

[74] S.L.A. 1925, s. 10.
[75] s. 5 (3) S.L.A.
[76] See M. & W., pp. 307–308, H. Potter (1946) 10 Conv. 135.
[77] s. 18 S.L.A. is inapplicable since W is no longer tenant for life.

purchase moneys or the investments purchased with such moneys.

It seems effect might be given to the Act's intention to protect purchasers by intepreting "settled land" as including "land which was previously settled land"[78] (as seems necessary in section 36).[79] It seems P must somehow be protected. Otherwise, all purchasers of settled land will, in case the land is no longer settled as in the above example, insist in all cases that they see the trust instrument to ensure that the vesting instrument is really correct in the events which have happened in stating the land is settled land etc. The "curtain" will then have been torn asunder and, indeed, destroyed.

In certain exceptional cases where there is a chance that a vesting instrument may be incorrect then a purchaser can, and therefore must, look at the trust instrument.[80] The main cases are where a settlement was made before 1926, whether by deed or by will, and where after 1925 an imperfect *inter vivos* settlement was made initially using one deed only. The other cases where no proper vesting instrument arises in the constitution of a settlement, so that the subsequently executed vesting instrument should be verified, are where an infant is entitled to land under someone's intestacy[81] or where land is held on trust for charitable, ecclesiastical or public purposes.[82]

D. Transmission of Title to the Legal Estate

The purpose of having settlements created by two documents, a trust instrument and a vesting instrument, is to ensure that the title to the legal estate is independent of the trust instrument. Where under the trust instrument the interest of the tenant for life ceases, whether on his death or on the occurrence of some event in his lifetime, then the fact that someone else has become entitled to have the legal estate must be reflected in some other instrument. If the settlement continues, such instrument must be a vesting deed or vesting assent, so warning prospective purchasers that the land is settled land so that capital moneys must be paid to the Settled Land Act trustees.[83] If the settlement ends, then such instrument in 99 per cent. of cases will be an ordinary deed or ordinary assent, enabling prospective purchasers to rely on the fact that the land is no longer settled land,[84] and, in rare cases, it will be a deed of discharge, revealing that the former tenant for life has now become absolute beneficial owner.[85] It should be

---

[78] After all, under s. 110 (2) (*e*) a purchaser of *settled* land must assume that the statements contained in any deed of discharge are correct and land cannot be settled land if a deed of discharge has been executed—unless, of course, the land has subsequently been freshly settled.

[79] *Re Cugny's W.T.* [1931] 1 Ch. 305 *post* p. 255.

[80] s. 110 (2) S.L.A.

[81] s. 1 (2) S.L.A.

[82] s. 29 S.L.A.

[83] S.L.A. s. 18.

[84] *Ibid.* s. 110 (5).

[85] *Ibid.* s. 17.

noted that only personal representatives can execute assents, whether vesting or ordinary.

1. Death of the tenant for life. (a) *If the settlement continues* then, since the Settled Land Act trustees know the trusts of the trust instrument, the legal estate passes to the trustees as special personal representatives, who take out a grant of probate or letters of administration specially limited to the settled land.[86] They then pass the legal estate to the new tenant for life by a vesting assent.[87]

(b) *If the settlement ends* then, since *ex hypothesi* there can no longer be any Settled Land Act trustees, the legal estate passes in the ordinary way to the tenant for life's ordinary personal representatives who take out a grant of probate or letters of administration to his estate.[88] They then pass the legal estate to the absolutely entitled remainderman or to trustees for sale by an ordinary assent. Exceptionally, where a settlement ends because persons have become entitled as tenants in common so that there is an immediate binding trust for sale for such persons (*e.g.* "to A for life and then to his children, B and C, equally") the ordinary personal repesentatives can be required by the former Settled Land Act trustees to execute an ordinary assent to pass the legal estate to such trustees on trust for sale for the tenants in common,[89] *e.g.* where the tenants in common are minors.[90]

2. Events occurring in lifetime of tenant for life. (a) *If the settlement continues* then the tenant for life must pass his legal estate on to the next remainderman by means of a vesting deed.[91]

(b) *If the settlement ends,* otherwise than by the tenant for life becoming absolutely entitled, then the tenant for life must pass his legal estate on to the absolutely entitled remainderman or to trustees for sale by an ordinary deed of conveyance.[92] Exceptionally, again, where the settlement ends because persons have become entitled as tenants in common, the former Settled Land Act trustees can require the tenant for life to execute an ordinary conveyance to pass the legal estate to them on trust for sale for the tenants in common.[93]

(c) *If the tenant for life becomes absolutely entitled* when the legal estate is already vested in him *qua* tenant for life, then the former

---

[86] *Ibid.* s. 7 (1), A.E.A. 1925, s. 22, Supreme Court Act 1981, s. 113.
[87] S.L.A., s. 8 (4).
[88] *Re Bridgett & Hayes' Contract* [1928] Ch. 163.
[89] S.L.A., s. 36, *Re Cugny's W.T.* [1931] 1 Ch. 305. Despite the dictum at p. 309 the assent should be an ordinary assent: M. & W. p. 425.
[90] If they are absolutely entitled adults they can call for the legal estate to be vested in themselves as joint tenants on trust for sale: L.P.A. s. 3 (1) (*b*) proviso.
[91] S.L.A. ss. 7 (4), 8 (4) (*a*).
[92] *Ibid.* s. 7 (5).
[93] *Ibid.* s. 36.

Settled Land Act trustees must execute a deed of discharge, so neutralising the vesting instrument and enabling a purchaser to assume that the trusts have ceased so as to be able to pay his purchase moneys over to the former tenant for life,[94] *e.g.* where a tenant in tail in possession has barred the entail, or where land was settled on A absolutely subject to a family charge in favour of W for life, and W has died, or where the tenant for life has purchased the interests of the remaindermen.

3. Minors. Where the currently entitled beneficiary is a minor the legal estate will usually be vested in the statutory owners (who will normally be the Settled Land Act trustees).[95] If the minor only has a limited interest then on attaining his majority he can require the statutory owners to vest the legal estate in him by a vesting deed.[96] If he has an absolute interest he can require the statutory owners to vest the legal estate in him by an ordinary deed of conveyance.[97]

4. Reserve powers of the court. If a person refuses to execute an appropriate instrument or is abroad or undiscoverable or any other difficulties arise then any person interested can apply to the Court for an order vesting the legal estate in the appropriate person.[98]

E. Determination of Settlements

1. Duration of settlements. Land once settled remains settled so long as:

    (i) Any limitation, charge or power of charging under the settlement still exists or is capable of being exercised or

    (ii) the person beneficially entitled in possession is a minor,

unless in either case the land is held on trust for sale.[99] Once land is either held on trust for sale or else vested in a person of full age free from all actual or possible rights under the settlement, the settlement is at an end.

2. Need to show settlement has ended. Once a vesting instrument has been executed no dispositions can take effect unless authorised by the Settled Land Act,[1] *e.g.* unless capital moneys are paid to the Settled Land Act trustees. There is thus a need for some subsequent

---

[94] *Ibid.* s. 17.
[95] *Ibid.* ss. 23, 26. It may have been left in personal representatives who will then execute an appropriate assent in due course.
[96] *Ibid.* s. 7 (2).
[97] *Ibid.* s. 7 (5).
[98] *Ibid.* s. 12.
[99] S.L.A. s. 3.
[1] *Ibid.* s. 18. If the settlement ended before a vesting instrument had been executed then title could be made in the ordinary way: *Re Alefounder's W.T.* [1927] 1 Ch. 360.

instrument to show that the land is no longer settled land and so cancel the effect of the vesting instrument.

3. Ordinary conveyance or assent. If a vesting instrument has been executed but there is a subsequent ordinary conveyance or assent which does not contain a statement of the names of the Settled Land Act trustees, a bona fide purchaser for value of a legal estate is both entitled and bound to assume that every statement in the assent or conveyance is correct and that the person in whom the land was thereby vested holds it free from all rights under the settlement.[2] Thus, if a settlement comes to an end on the death of the tenant for life or on the occurrence of some event in his lifetime, so that the legal estate has to pass from the penultimate beneficiary to the ultimate beneficiary, then the ordinary assent or ordinary conveyance, as the case may be, enables the ultimate beneficiary to make good title to a purchaser and to receive the purchase moneys.

4. Deed of discharge. For those few cases where the legal estate does not pass from the penultimate to the ultimate beneficiary, so as to bring an ordinary assent or conveyance into existence, but the settlement has ended then some other instrument is necessary to prove this. Accordingly, the former Settled Land Act trustees must execute a deed of discharge declaring that they are discharged from the trust.[3] A purchaser is then entitled to assume that the land is no longer settled land, *e.g.* where a deed of discharge has been executed after T, the tenant for life, has become absolutely entitled upon barring his entail or upon purchasing the interests of the remaindermen or upon the death of W, subject to whose family charge for life T had been fee simple owner.

Sect. 2. Other Provisions Relating to Settled Land

The other provisions relating to settled land in the main correspond to similar provisions in the Act of 1882, although in a number of cases important extensions and additions have been made.

A. Essentials of Settled Land

The three essential points to consider are—
(1) whether the land is settled land;
(2) who is the tenant for life; and
(3) who are the trustees.

I. DEFINITION OF SETTLED LAND

1. "Settlement." Land is settled land if "it is or is deemed to be the

---

[2] *Ibid.* s. 110 (5).
[3] *Ibid.* s. 17.

subject of a settlement."[4] By section 1 of the Settled Land Act 1925, a settlement is created by any *instrument or instruments* (including an Act of Parliament[5] and, probably, a court order[6]) whereby one of the following conditions is satisfied.

(a) *Succession:* the land stands limited in trust for any persons by way of succession.

In addition to cases such as limitations "to A for life, remainder to B in fee simple," this definition seems to be wide enough to cover the following cases which are somewhat superfluously set out in the section as independent heads, namely, where land is limited in trust for any person in possession—

   (i) for an entailed interest, whether or not capable of being barred or defeated;

   (ii) for an estate in fee simple or for a term of years absolute subject to an executory gift over (*e.g.* a devise to trustees in trust for "A in fee simple but for B in fee simple when B marries");

   (iii) for a base or determinable fee, including a fee determinable by condition, or any corresponding interest in leasehold land;

or where—

   (iv) land is limited in trust for any person for an estate in fee simple or for a term of years absolute contingently on the happening of an event (*e.g.* a devise to trustees in trust for X in fee simple if his brothers die under the age of 21 years).

In all these cases there is an element of succession sufficient to satisfy the definition in (a). Thus if S settles land upon trust for X in tail, the land stands limited in trust for persons by way of succession and the limitations arise under the settlement; for any estate or interest not disposed of under the settlement and remaining in or reverting to the settlor or anyone deriving title under him is deemed to arise under the settlement, with the consequence that S's fee simple reversion upon X's entail is deemed to arise under the settlement.[7]

(b) *Minors:* the land stands limited in trust for an infant in possession for an estate in fee simple or for a term of years absolute.

(c) *Family charges:* the land stands charged, whether voluntarily or in consideration of marriage or by way of family arrangement, with the payment of any sums for the benefit of any persons.

2. "Limited in trust." It will be noted that under heads

---

[4] *Ibid.* s. 2.
[5] See, *e.g. Re Lord Hereford's S.E.* [1932] W.N. 34.
[6] *Griffiths* v. *Williams* (1977) 248 *Estates Gazette* 947; *Bannister* v. *Bannister* [1948] 2 All E.R. 133; if an arrangement between parties is embodied in a court order, such order is the instrument to be considered: *Moss* v. *Moss* [1972] 1 All E.R. 1121 at 1123, but see *Bacon* v. *Bacon* [1947] P. 151.
[7] See *Re Hunter and Hewlett's Contract* [1907] 1 Ch. 46.

(a) (succession) and (b) (minors), but not (c) (family charges), it is necessary for the land to be "limited in trust" if it is to fall within the definition; if there is no trust, the land is not settled land, nor if the trust is an immediate binding trust for sale can the land be settled land: section 1 (7) of the Act. In all cases where property is given by will, there is necessarily a trust for the beneficiaries by reason of the legal estate first vesting in the testator's personal representatives. Where the disposition is made *inter vivos* it will be made either—

(i) by a proper vesting deed and trust instrument, whereupon the legal estate vests in the tenant for life as trustee, or

(ii) by a single instrument, in which case the legal estate will remain in the settlor and only an equitable interest will be transferred; for none of the interests mentioned in (a) is capable of existing at law (except, it seems, a fee determinable by condition[8]), and in (b), by reason of a minor's inability after 1925 to hold a legal estate in land, no legal estate passes. Consequently, on the principle that there is a trust if the legal estate is in one person and the equitable interest in another, the grantor will hold the land in trust even though there may be no express limitation in trust.[9]

Under head (c), no limitation by way of trust is required. Whether the estate which is subject to the family charges is conveyed directly to the beneficiary or whether it is held in trust for the beneficiary, the land is nevertheless settled land.

3. Limited. The expression "limited" is appropriate to indicate that words of limitation have been used to grant limited estates in the land,[10] *e.g.* life estates of an absolute, determinable or conditional nature. If L has a life estate then he can either personally reside in the property or, instead, receive the rents and profits generated by the property. In contrast, if L merely has a licence personally to reside in the property for the rest of his life if he wishes, he has no estate or interest in the land, only a personal non-assignable right which does not entitle him, instead, to rent the property out to some other exclusive occupier.[11]

Where there are successive estates limited in trust it has been held that the tenant for life, for Settled Land Act purposes defined as "The person for the time being beneficially entitled under a settlement to possession of settled land for his life," is the person

---

[8] See *ante,* p. 86. Where the right of entry for breach of condition is only equitable it seems, the legal estate will be held on a contingent trust for a future beneficiary and so be "settled" within head (a) (iv). See M. & W., p. 316.

[9] Lord Denning's minority view in *Binions* v. *Evans* [1972] Ch. 359 that limited means "expressly limited" seems unjustifiable: see *Griffiths* v. *Williams* (1977) 248 E.G. 947.

[10] *Ante* pp. 33–39.

[11] *May* v. *May* (1881) 44 L.T. 412, *Stone* v. *Parker* (1860) 29 L.J. Ch. 874; *Morss* v. *Morss* [1972] 1 All E.R. 1121, *Moore* v. *Royal Trust Co.* [1956] 5 D.L.R. 152.

currently entitled to reside in the property for life irrespective of such entitlement arising under a mere licence or a life estate.[12] Thus, if property is devised "to A for his personal residence (by way of licence) for so long as he wishes in his lifetime, remainder to B for life, remainder to C absolutely" A is tenant for life with all the Settled Land Act powers as such, entitling him to sell (or lease) the property and to live off the income or any proceeds of sale for the rest of his life![13]

It is only a short step to assume, therefore, that if property is devised "to A for his personal residence (by way of licence) for so long as he wishes in his lifetime but otherwise for B absolutely" then A must be tenant for life of settled land,[14] without considering what exactly is the settlement that creates settled land.[15]

However, the land has been limited to B but not to A, since a limitation "is the bounds or compass of an estate or the time how long an estate shall continue,"[16] so it seems that the land is not "limited in trust for any persons by way of succession" and so is not settled land: so A cannot be a tenant for life.[17] This can be inconvenient since, in practice, no purchaser will purchase from B whilst A occupies the property without having A's consent.[18] From a conveyancing point of view it is more convenient for a court to assume that A is a licensee with the powers of a tenant for life or to strive to find that A really has a life estate[19] and so clearly has the powers of a tenant for life. However, if A is tenant for life and so can sell and live off the income from the proceeds of sale the testator's intentions are likely to be frustrated.

(a) *Extension of scope of settled land.* Before 1926 even if settled land had become vested in one person in fee simple, it continued to be settled land if there still existed a jointure or provisions for portions or annuities under a settlement, provided in each case that

---

[12] *Re Llanover's W.T.* [1903] 2 Ch. 16 *Re Boyer's S.E.* [1916] 2 Ch. 404, *Stevenson* v. *Myers* [1929] 47 New South Wales W.N. 95.

[13] S.L.A., s. 106 see *post* p. 274.

[14] *cf.* the *inter vivos* arrangements in *Bannister* v. *Bannister* [1948] 2 All E.R. 133; *Binions* v. *Evans* [1972] Ch. 359, *Dodsworth* v. *Dodsworth* (1973) 228 E.G. 1115.

[15] *Griffiths* v. *Williams* (1977) 248 E.G. 947.

[16] Sheppard's Touchstone p. 117.

[17] J.A. Hornby (1977) 93 L.Q.R. 561 and see *Chandler* v. *Kerley* [1978] 1 W.L.R. 693 at p. 698 and *Ivory* v. *Palmer* [1975] 1. C.R. 340 at p. 347.

[18] In less clearly drafted examples, it may be unclear whether A has a mere personal licence or a life estate, and even if A has a licence there are doubts on the extent to which licences may bind third parties owing to dicta of Lord Denning in *Binions* v. *Evans* [1972] Ch. 359 and *D.H.N. Food Distributors Ltd.* v. *Tower Hamlets* [1976] 1 W.L.R. 852: *post* p. 372.

[19] Prima facie a right to reside will be treated as a licence whilst a right to use and occupy will be treated as a life estate (so the property can be used by allowing someone else to occupy it at a rent): *Re Gibbons* 1920] 1 Ch. 372, *Rabbeth* v. *Squire* (1854) 19 Beav. 70, *May* v. *May* (1881) 44 L.T. 412, *Re Varley* (1893) 68 L.T. 665 (though the decision that the personal licence to reside did not create a S.L.A. tenancy for life is wrong in the light of *Re Llanover's W.T.* [1903] 2 Ch. 16). In *Bannister* v. *Bannister* (*supra*) and *Binions* v. *Evans* (*supra*) surely only personal residential licences were intended.

they were not merely sums presently payable but were limited to arise in the future, thus satisfying the requirement that the land should be limited to persons by way of succession. The provision in the Act of 1925 is wider than this, and contains no requirement of futurity. It is essential that the sum of money should have been charged on the land either voluntarily, or in consideration of marriage, or by way of family arrangement; the Act does not apply if the charge was created for money or money's worth, as where a tenant in fee simple sells his land and takes a charge on it as part of the price. But subject to this requirement, it is immaterial whether the provision is present or future, whether it is for capital or annual sums, or whether it is for a limited period (*e.g.* for life) or in perpetuity. Thus if a testator devises land to trustees on trust to pay a perpetual annuity to X, and subject thereto on trust for A in fee simple the land becomes settled land.[20]

(b) *The detrimental effect of such extended scope.* The effect of this provision was that at the beginning of 1926 much land which had previously not been settled land was forthwith converted into settled land. In a number of cases this caused hardship to those who had purchased such land before 1926. The practice in such cases was that unless the land could be freed from the charges (as by the owners of the charges all releasing them in return for a share of the purchase-money) the vendor conveyed the land to the purchaser subject to the charges but with an indemnity against them, *i.e.* the vendor agreed to pay the charges himself and so ensure that they would not be enforced against the land. In cases where this had been done, the astonished purchaser found (if, indeed, he could understand the matter at all) that at the beginning of 1926 his land had become settled land and that it could be sold only after compliance with the troublesome Settled Land Act procedure, *e.g.* as to the appointing of trustees and the execution of a vesting deed.

(c) *The solution to the problem.* To meet this situation, the Law of Property (Amendment) Act 1926, s. 1, provides that where a person of full age is beneficially entitled in possession to land in fee simple or for a term of years absolute subject to charges of this kind, he can nevertheless create or convey a legal estate subject to the charges in the same way as if the land were not settled land. This applies whether the charges arose before 1926 or after 1925, and whether the person entitled to the land is the tenant under the settlement or a purchaser from him; but it applies only if the sole reason for the land being deemed settled land is that it is subject to the charges and not, for example, when it is also entailed. Where the Amendment Act applies, a vendor may thus sell the land either (i) free from the

---

[20] *Re Austen* [1929] 2 Ch. 155.

charges, by making use of the Settled Land Act procedure, or (ii) subject to the charges, by virtue of the Amendment Act.

II. DEFINITION OF TENANT FOR LIFE

1. Tenant for life. An elaborate definition of "tenant for life" is given by the Settled Land Act 1925.[21] The definition covers any person who is of full age and for the time being beneficially entitled in possession under a settlement and so includes not only a person entitled to a life interest but a tenant in tail, a tenant in fee simple subject to a gift over or to family charges, a tenant for years[22] terminable on life, a tenant *pur autre vie,* and a person entitled to the whole income of land for his own or any other life. It also covers a person beneficially entitled in possession by virtue of a licence for life since possession can be either the right to physical occupation or the right to receive rents and profits.[23] The position where two or more persons are currently entitled to possession jointly or in common is dealt with later,[24] but only joint tenants can be the composite tenant for life.

2. Cases where there is no tenant for life. Although there will normally be a tenant for life under the above provisions, there are some cases where there is no tenant for life, as where land is given to trustees on trust to pay X a fixed annuity[25] or a definite fraction of the income,[26] with a direction to accumulate the balance, or where there is an immediate discretionary trust, such as a direction to trustees to pay the income to such one or more members of a class of persons as they think fit, no member being entitled as of right to any of the income.[27] In these cases the legal estate and statutory powers are in the statutory owner.[28]

The position where the tenant for life is a minor has already been dealt with.[29]

III. DEFINITION OF TRUSTEES OF THE SETTLEMENT

The trustees of the settlement are defined by section 30 of the Settled Land Act 1925. There are five heads, which must be applied in turn; thus if there are any trustees under one head, they exclude any under a subsequent head. The definition is as follows:

---

[21] ss. 19, 20; and see M. & W., pp. 320–323.
[22] If the tenant pays rent under the lease he cannot be tenant for life: *Re Catling* [1931] 2 Ch. 359 (but consider the impact of L.P.A., s. 149 (6) if the widow exercised her option to have a lease for life at £1 p.a.).
[23] *Re Llanover's W.T.* [1903] 2 Ch. 16; S.L.A., s. 117 (1) (*xix*).
[24] *Post,* p. 321.
[25] *Re Jefferys (No.* 2) [1939] Ch. 205.
[26] *Re Frewen* [1926] Ch. 580.
[27] *Re Gallenga W.T.* [1938] 1 All E.R. 106.
[28] *Ante,* p. 243.
[29] *Ante,* p. 243.

(i) The persons who, under the settlement, are trustees with power to sell the land (even if this power is subject to the consent of anyone) or with power of consenting to or approving the exercise of a power of sale.

For example, if in a settlement on A for life, with remainders over, there is a trust giving X and Y a general[30] power to sell the land, this will make them trustees of the settlement, in preference even to any other persons expressly appointed Settled Land Act trustees. X and Y will in fact have no power to sell the land for, as will be seen,[31] this power is taken away from them and given to the tenant for life; nevertheless, the attempt to give them the power suffices to make them trustees of the settlement.

(ii) The persons declared by the settlement to be trustees thereof for any purposes of the Settled Land Acts 1882 to 1890, or 1925, or any of them.

This is the head under which the trustees of the settlement will usually be found, for cases under head (i) are rare. It should be noted that it is not sufficient to appoint X and Y "trustees of the settlement"[32]: the appointment will be ineffective unless words such as "for the purposes of the Settled Land Act 1925" are added.

(iii) Persons who, under the settlement, are trustees with power of sale or of consenting to or approving a sale, or upon trust for sale, of *other* land held under the same settlement and upon the same trusts.

(iv) Persons who, under the settlement, are trustees with a *future* power of sale, or under a *future* trust for sale, or with a power of consenting to or approving the exercise of such a future power of sale, even if the power or trust does not take effect in all events.

Thus if there is a settlement of Blackacre and Whiteacre which gives trustees a power of sale over Blackacre alone, clause (iii) makes those trustees Settled Land Act trustees of both properties.[33] Again, if Greenacre is settled on A for life with remainder to X and Y on trust for sale, clause (iv) makes X and Y Settled Land Act trustees.[34]

(v) The persons appointed by deed by those able to dispose of the whole equitable interest in the settled land.

For example, if land is settled on A for life, remainder to B in tail, remainder to C in fee simple, A and B between them can dispose of

---

[30] See *Re Carne's S.E.* [1899] 1 Ch. 324.
[31] *Post*, p. 274.
[32] Consider *Re Bentley* (1885) 54 L.J. Ch. 782.
[33] *Re Moore* [1906] 1 Ch. 789.
[34] *Re Johnson's S.E.* [1913] W.N. 222.

the whole equitable interest in the land and thus can appoint trustees of the settlement.[35]

Where a settlement arises under a will or intestacy and there are no trustees under any other provisions, the personal representatives of the deceased are trustees of the settlement until other trustees are appointed.[36] This useful provision deals with the most frequent cause of a lack of trustees, namely, a will made without proper legal advice. Where even this provision fails (*e.g.* where there is a home-made settlement created *inter vivos*) the court has power to appoint trustees on the application of any person interested under the settlement.[37]

B. Compound Settlement

1. Definition. Before 1926, difficulties sometimes arose in the case of compound settlements. "Compound settlement" is the term used to describe the state of affairs when the trusts affecting the land in question are created by two or more instruments. The most usual example of a compound settlement arises where land has been settled on A for life with remainder (subject to provisions for others of the family) to his son in tail; on the son attaining his majority, A and the son bar the entail and resettle the property on A for life, remainder to the son for life, with remainders over. Where such a process takes place there are three distinct settlements to consider—

  (1) the original settlement;
  (2) the resettlement; and
  (3) the compound settlement, which is a separate entity.[38]

2. Position of tenant for life. The position of a tenant for life under a compound settlement was as follows.

  (i) He could exercise his powers as tenant for life under the original settlement, and provided there were trustees under that settlement, he could, on disposing of the land, overreach the rights of the beneficiaries under both the settlement and the resettlement[39]; but while acting under the settlement he could not avail himself of any additional powers conferred by the resettlement.

  (ii) He could act as tenant for life under the resettlement, availing himself of any additonal powers conferred by it, but in this case he could not, on disposing of the land, overreach the rights of beneficiaries under the original settlement.[40]

---

[35] *Re Spearman S.E.* [1906] 2 Ch. 502. A and B together can bar the entail.
[36] S.L.A. 1925, s. 30. This rarely applies on intestacies since trusts for sale then normally arise.
[37] *Ibid.* s. 34.
[38] See *Re Coull's S.E.* [1905] 1 Ch. 712 at p. 720.
[39] *Re Lord Wimborne and Browne's Contract* [1904] 1 Ch. 537.
[40] See *Re Mundy and Roper's Contract* [1899] 1 Ch. 275 at p. 295.

(iii) He could act as tenant for life under the compound settlement, exercising any additional powers conferred by either settlement; and provided there where trustees of the compound settlement, he could overreach the rights of the beneficiaries under both the settlement and the resettlement.[41]

3. Tenant for life and trustees of compound settlement. As the third method combined the advantages of the first two methods, it was important to know in any given case whether there were any trustees of the compound settlement and whether the tenant for life could act under the compound settlement. Except where trustees of the compound settlement were appointed by the persons together able to dispose of the whole equitable interest, they could be appointed only by the court; for on making a settlement, the settlor probably had no power to declare who should be the trustees of any resettlement, and on a resettlement being made, an appointment of trustees thereof could not bind beneficiaries under the original settlement.[42] As regards the tenant for life, it was settled law that where one person was tenant for life under both settlements, or under the resettlement alone, he could act as tenant for life under the compound settlement.[43] In the example given above, A could exercise the powers of a tenant for life under either settlement or under the compound settlement.

4. Need for trustees of compound settlement. In most cases the comparative rarity of trustees of the compound settlement caused no difficulty, as, for example, where the tenant for life wished to sell free from the rights of the beneficiaries under both settlements, and he held under the original settlement of which there were properly appointed trustees, or where he held under the resettlement and merely wised to exercise additional powers conferred thereby. But in one case, trustees of the compound settlement were needed in order to achieve the desired object; this was where there was no tenant for life under the original settlement and the tenant for life under the resettlement wished to overreach the rights of beneficiaries under the original settlement. In this case it was impossible to avoid the expense of an application to the court if no such trustee existed.[44]

5. After 1925. After 1925, this difficulty no longer exists. Where before 1926 the court had appointed trustees of the compound settlement, they continue in office. In other cases, it has been provided in effect that even in the case of settlements made before

---

[41] *Re Phillimore's Estate* [1904] 2 Ch. 460.
[42] *Re Spencer's S.E.* [1903] 1 Ch. 75.
[43] *Re Phillimore's Estate* [1904] 2 Ch. 460.
[44] *Re Trafford's S.E.* [1915] 1 Ch. 9.

1926, the trustees of the original settlement, or in default, the trustees of the resettlement, shall be trustees of the compound settlement.[45]

C. Powers of the Tenant for Life

The powers and position of a tenant for life remain substantially the same as under the Act of 1882, although a number of important details have been modified. Such changes as have been made mainly give the tenant for life wider powers. In general, what follows applies to statutory owners as well as to tenants for life. As was the case under the Act of 1882, a tenant for life is normally subject to no control in the exercise of his powers. The chief safeguards against the abuse of his powers are—

(1) his position as a trustee for the beneficiaries;
(2) the provision that in the case of the most important powers, he must give notice to the trustees of his intention to exercise them; and
(3) the provision that in a few exceptional cases he must not exercise his powers without the leave of the trustees or an order of the court.

The position of the tenant for life as trustee has already been mentioned, and will be further considered later.[46] His powers are considered below.

I. POWERS EXERCISABLE UPON GIVING NOTICE[47]

If the tenant for life intends to make a sale, exchange, lease, mortgage or charge, or to grant an option, he must give written notice to the trustees of the settlement, and, if known, to the solicitor for the trustees. The notice must be given by registered letter or recorded delivery posted at least one month before the transaction or contract therefor, and is invalid unless when it is given the trustees consist of two or more persons or a trust corporation; thus if there are no trustees, a tenant for life is not entitled to exercise these powers. The object of this provision for giving notice seems to be to enable the trustees to prevent any fraudulent dealing by applying to the court for an injunction.[48] In fact, however, it affords comparatively little protection, for—

(i) the trustees are apparently under no obligation to interfere with an improper transaction[49];
(ii) except in the case of a mortgage or charge, a general notice suffices, *e.g.* "take notice that I intend from time to time to

[45] S.L.A. 1925, s. 31.
[46] See *ante*, pp. 239, 243, *post*, p. 273.
[47] S.L.A. 1925, ss. 38–48, 51, 71, 101.
[48] *Wheelwright* v. *Walker* (*No.* 1) (1883) 23 Ch.D. 752.
[49] S.L.A. 1925, s. 97.

exercise any or all of my powers under the Settled Land Act 1925." In such cases, however, the tenant for life must, at the request of a trustee of the settlement, give reasonable information as to any sales, exchanges or leases effected, in progress or immediately intended[50];

(iii) any trustee may by writing accept less than one month's notice or waive it altogether[51]; and

(iv) a person dealing in good faith with the tenant for life is not concerned to inquire whether notice has been given.[52] Even if there are no trustees, a bona fide purchaser for value of a legal estate gets a good title if the transaction is one on which no capital money is payable, *e.g.* the grant of a lease for which no premium is payable.[53]

Each of the powers in respect of which notice is normally required must now be examined.

1. Power to sell. A tenant for life may sell the settled land or any part thereof, or any easement, right or privilege of any kind over the land.[54] He may, for example, sell to a railway company the right to tunnel under the land. With certain qualifications, he must obtain the best consideration in money that can reasonably be obtained. In one case[55] a tenant for life was made an offer by another beneficiary, but being unwilling to sell to him, proposed to sell to a third party for a lower price; the court restrained the tenant for life from selling for less than the price offered by the beneficiary, or from selling at all without informing the beneficiary of the proposed price and giving him two days in which to increase his offer. But there is no need for the sale to be by auction. Further, a purchaser is protected by the provision that if he deals in good faith with the tenant for life, he is to be conclusively taken, as against all the beneficiaries, to have given the best consideration reasonably obtainable and to have complied with all the requirements of the Act; this applies both to sales and other dealings such as leases,[56] and applies whether the transaction has been completed or is still the subject of an executory contract.[57] Thus a purchaser who made a good bargain and bought for £2,000 property which he forthwith resold for £3,000 was held to be protected.[58]

---

[50] *Ibid.* s. 101.
[51] *Ibid.*
[52] *Ibid.*
[53] *Mogridge* v. *Clapp* [1892] 3 Ch. 382; *Re Morgan's Lease* [1972] Ch. 1.
[54] S.L.A. 1925, ss. 38, 39. See *post*, p. 321, for joint tenants for life.
[55] *Wheelwright* v. *Walker (No.* 2) (1883) 31 W.R. 912.
[56] S.L.A. 1925, s. 110.
[57] *Re Morgan's Lease* [1972] Ch. 1.
[58] *Hurrell* v. *Littlejohn* [1904] 1 Ch. 689.

2. Power to exchange. Settled land, or any part of it, or any easement, right or privilege over it, may be exchanged for other land or any easement, right or privilege.[59] For "equality of exchange" (*i.e.* to adjust any difference in value) capital money may be paid or received.

3. Power to lease. (a) *The power.* The settled land, or any part of it, or any easement, right or privilege over it, may be leased for any period not exceeding—

(i) 999 years for building or forestry;
(ii) 100 years for mining;
(iii) 50 years for any other purpose.[60]

Before 1926 the periods were 99, 60 and 21 years respectively, and there was no special provision for forestry leases. After 1925, however, the new periods apply even if the settlement was made before 1926. A building lease is one made partly in consideration of erecting, improving, adding to or repairing buildings, or an agreement to do this[61]; the advantage to the settled land is that in return for a reduced rent the lessee must leave on the land at the end of his lease the new or improved buildings. By the Forestry Act 1967, a forestry lease means a lease to the Minister of Agriculture, Fisheries and Food for purposes authorised by the Act.

(b) *Conditions of lease.* Every lease of settled land must comply with the following conditions.[62]

(i) It must be made by deed.
(ii) It must be made to take effect in possession not more than one year after its date, or in reversion after an existing lease with not more than seven years to run at the date of the new lease. Thus if a tenant for life grants a lease to commence in 14 months' time, it is invalid unless it is to commence after the determination of an existing lease.
(iii) It must reserve the best rent reasonably obtainable in the circumstances, regard being had to any fine (*i.e.* a premium or lump sum) taken, and to any money laid out or to be laid out for the benefit of the land. Any fine is capital money. A lease granted by a tenant for life in return for a bribe or the release from a claim for damages against him personally has accordingly been held not to comply with the statutory requirements.[63] A nominal or reduced rent may be reserved

---

[59] S.L.A. 1925, ss. 38, 40.
[60] *Ibid.* s. 41.
[61] *Ibid.* s. 44.
[62] *Ibid.* s. 42. For defective leases, see M. & W. 337, 338; D. W. Elliott (1971) 87 L.Q.R. 338.
[63] *Re Handman and Wilcox's Contract* [1902] 1 Ch. 599.

for not longer than the first five years of a building lease or the first 10 years of a forestry lease, and in the case of mining or forestry leases, there are wide powers to vary the rent, *e.g.* according to the value of the minerals or trees taken.[64]

(iv) It must contain a covenant by the lessee for payment of rent and a conditon of re-entry (*i.e.* a provision for forfeiture of the lease) on rent not being paid within a specified time not exceeding 30 days.

(v) A counterpart (*i.e.* copy) of the lease must be executed by the lessee and delivered to the tenant for life; it is sufficient evidence that this has been done if the tenant for life duly executes the lease.

It will be seen that normally a lease must be by deed and notice must be given to the trustees. In certain cases, however, these requirements are relaxed. A lease at the best rent reasonably obtainable without a fine and not exempting the lessee from liability for waste has two privileges:

(i) if it is for not more than 21 years, it may be made without giving notice to the trustees; and

(ii) if it is for not more than three years, it may also be made merely in writing and not by deed.[65]

As a corollary to his power to grant leases, a tenant for life has wide powers of accepting surrenders of leases and of varying or waiving the terms of any lease.[66] These powers are exercisable without notice to the trustees.

(c) *Rent from leases.* The normal rule is that the tenant for life is entitled to the whole of the rent from leases of the settled land.[67] But as seen above,[68] this does not apply to mining leases, where the capital value of the land is being diminished. The general rule as to rent from mining leases granted under the Act is that, subject to any contrary intention in the settlement, the tenant for life is entitled to three-quarters of the rent unless he is impeachable of waste and the mine is an unopened one, when he is entitled to only one-quarter of the rent; the balance in each case is capital.[69] These provisions, however, apply only to rent from leases granted under the Act, so that if the lease is granted under an express power in the settlement,[70] or if the lease or a contract therefor[71] was made before the land was

---

[64] S.L.A. 1925, ss. 44, 45, 48.
[65] *Ibid.* s. 42.
[66] *Ibid.* ss. 52, 59.
[67] See, *e.g. Re Wix* [1916] 1 Ch. 279.
[68] *Ante,* p. 55.
[69] S.L.A. 1925, s. 47.
[70] *Earl of Lonsdale* v. *Lowther* [1900] 2 Ch. 687.
[71] *Re Kemeys-Tynte* [1892] 2 Ch. 211.

settled or resettled,[72] the tenant for life is entitled to the whole of the income. It must also be remembered that the rules as to the tenant for life working the minerals himself are different from the rules as to leases,[73] and that where the tenant for life has not a life interest but some interest such as a fee simple subject to a gift over, he may be unimpeachable of waste even if the settlement is silent on the subject; the owner of a mere life interest, on the other hand, is impeachable unless the settlement exempts him from liability for waste.[74]

4. Power to mortgage or charge. In the absence of a contrary provision in the settlement, a tenant for life has no power to mortgage or charge the legal estate for his own benefit. If he wishes to raise money for his own use, he can of course do so by mortgaging his beneficial interest, consisting of his life interest, entail or whatever interest he has. The legal estate, on the other hand, can be mortgaged only for certain specified purposes for the benefit of the settled land or those entitled under the settlement, *e.g.* to pay for improvements, discharge incumbrances or provide money which is required to be raised under the provisions of the settlement, such as portions.[75]

5. Power to grant options. A tenant for life may grant an option in writing to purchase or take a lease of all or any part of the settled land or of any easement, right or privilege over it. But—

  (i) the price or rent must be the best reasonably obtainable and must be fixed at the time of granting the option[76]; a tenant for life thus has no power to agree to sell at a price to be fixed by arbitration;

 (ii) the option must be made exercisable within an agreed number of years not exceeding 10; and

(iii) the option may be granted with or without any consideration being paid, but if any is paid, it is capital money.[77]

II. POWERS EXERCISABLE WITH CONSENT OF THE TRUSTEES OR UNDER AN
ORDER OF THE COURT

In the following cases, the tenant for life can exercise his powers only with the consent of the trustees of the settlement or under an order of the court.

---

[72] *Re Arkwright's Settlement* [1945] Ch. 195.
[73] He can keep the whole of the profits unless he is impeachable of waste and the mine is unopened, when he cannot work it at all: *ante*, p. 55.
[74] *Ante*, pp. 44, 47, 53.
[75] S.L.A. 1925, ss. 16, 71; and see M. & W., pp. 339, 340. For portions, see *ante*, pp. 232, 234.
[76] See *Re Morgan's Lease* [1972] Ch. 1, where the option was contained in an existing lease.
[77] S.L.A. 1925, s. 51.

1. Power to dispose of the principal mansion house. If the tenant for life wishes to make a disposition (whether by sale, lease, exchange or otherwise[78]) of the principal mansion house, if any, and the pleasure-grounds and park,[79] and the lands, if any, usually occupied therewith, the consent of the trustees or an order of the court is required—

(i) if the settlement was made before 1926 and does not expressly provide to the contrary; or

(ii) if the settlement was made after 1925 and expressly requires such consent or order to be obtained.[80]

In other cases, no consent is required, but the usual notice must be given.

If a house is usually occupied as a farmhouse, or if the site of a house and the pleasure-grounds and park and lands, if any, usually occupied therewith do not together exceed 25 acres, the house is not deemed a principal mansion house.[81] In other cases, it is a question of fact whether at a given moment a house is a principal mansion house. Where two separate establishments are comprised in the same settlement, there may be two principal mansion houses, or one may be subsidiary to the other, as where one is used as the main residence and the other as a shooting-box.[82] Again, a house may cease to be a principal mansion house, as where it is let as a school; and if the tenant for life then uses a smaller house on the estate as his home, that may become a principal mansion house.[83]

2. Power to cut and sell timber. This has already been dealt with.[84] It is only if the tenant for life is impeachable of waste that he requires the consent of the trustees or an order of the court and three-quarters of the proceeds are capital money; if he is unimpeachable, he needs no consent or order and may keep all the proceeds.

3. Power to compromise claims. Subject to the consent in writing of the trustees, the tenant for life has a wide power to compromise and settle disputes relating to the settled land or any part thereof.[85]

4. Power to sell settled chattels. With the leave of the court the tenant for life may sell any chattels settled to devolve with the land,[86] as furniture, pictures and the like sometimes are.

---

[78] *Ibid.* s. 117.
[79] See *Pease* v. *Courtney* [1904] 2 Ch. 503.
[80] S.L.A. 1925, s. 65.
[81] *Ibid.* s. 65.
[82] *Gilbey* v. *Rush* [1906] 1 Ch. 11 at p. 21.
[83] *Re Feversham S.E.* [1938] 2 All E.R. 210.
[84] *Ante,* pp. 54 *et seq.*
[85] S.L.A. 1925, s. 58.
[86] *Ibid.* s. 67; and see M. & W., pp. 342–344.

5. Power to effect any proper transaction. The court has a statutory jurisdiction to authorise the tenant for life to effect any transaction not otherwise authorised by the Act or the settlement if it is for the benefit of the land or the beneficiaries and is a transaction which an absolute owner could validly effect.[87] This power even permits the court to sanction alterations in the beneficial interests under the settlement.[88]

IIII. OTHER POWERS OF A TENANT FOR LIFE

1. Power to effect improvements.[89] (a) *Making the improvements.* A tenant for life may of course effect improvements to the land at his own expense, but if he wishes the cost to be borne either temporarily or permanently by capital money, or to be raised by a mortgage or charge of the settled land, he must comply with the Act.

The tenant for life must first ascertain that the proposed improvements are within the list of those authorised by the Act. He must then obtain the appointment of a surveyor or engineer, for capital money cannot be applied in paying for improvements unless—

(1) if the money is in the hands of the trustees,
  (a) a certificate is furnished by a competent engineer or able practical surveyor employed independently of the tenant for life, certifying—
    (i) that the work or some specific part thereof has been properly executed; and
    (ii) the amount properly payable in respect therof; or
  (b) an order of the court directs or authorises payment:
(2) if the money is in court,
  (a) a report or certificate of the Minister of Agriculture, Fisheries and Food is given; or
  (b) a report of a competent engineer or able practical surveyor approved by the court is given; or
  (c) such other evidence as the court thinks fit is given.

(b) *Repayment.* When the improvements are paid for out of capital, the question arises whether or not the tenant for life must repay the money.This depends on the nature of the improvements. A long list is set out in the Third Schedule to the Act, which is divided into three parts:

(i) If the improvement falls within Part I (*e.g.* drainage or erection of bridges) or is authorised by the settlement, repayment cannot be ordered. In the case of agricultural land, ordinary repairs reasonably required for proper farming are

[87] S.L.A. 1925, s. 64; Settled Land and Trustee Acts (Court's General Powers) Act 1943, s. 2.
[88] *Re Simmons* [1956] Ch. 125.
[89] S.L.A. 1925, ss. 83–87; and see M. & W., pp. 345–349.

somewhat surprisingly included under this head if effected after April, 1948.[90]

(ii) If the improvement falls within Part II (*eg.* the restoration or reconstruction of buildings damaged or destroyed by dry rot), the trustees or the court have a discretion to order repayment by instalments.

(iii) If the improvement falls within Part III (*e.g.* the installation of artificial light in a building), the trustees or the court must order repayment by instalments.

The number of the instalments is within the discretion of the court or the trustees, except that the trustees may not order more than 50 half-yearly instalments.

2. Power to select investments for capital money. Capital money must be applied in one or more of the 21 methods specified in the Act.[91] These include investment in trustee securities, paying for improvements and the purchase of land held in fee simple or on a lease with 60 or more years unexpired.[92] The tenant for life may select which of these methods of application shall be employed, in default of which the trustees make the choice.

D. Position of the Tenant for Life

1. The tenant for life is trustee both of the land and of his powers. This has been considered above.[93] One further point which must be mentioned concerns the right of the tenant for life to acquire any or all of the settled land for himself. It is a settled rule of equity that any acquisition of trust property by a trustee, either directly or indirectly, is voidable by any beneficiary, no matter how fair the transaction may be, for otherwise the trustee might be in a position where his interest conflicts with his duty.[94] To avoid this difficulty, the Settled Land Act 1925[95] authorises the trustees of the settlement to exercise all the powers of a tenant for life in carrying out any transaction whereby the tenant for life acquires any interest in the settled land.[96]

2. No powers can be given to anyone except the tenant for life. Any power, other than a power of revocation or appointment, which the settlement purports to give to anyone except the tenant for life, is exercisable not by that person but by the tenant for life as if it were an

---

[90] See the cases cited in *Re Lord Brougham and Vaux's S.E.* [1954] Ch. 24; H.W.R. Wade [1954] Camb.L.J. 63.

[91] S.L.A. 1925, s. 73.

[92] See *Re Wellsted's W.T.* [1949] Ch. 296.

[93] *Ante*, p. 239.

[94] N. & M., p. 504.

[95] s. 68.

[96] See *Re Pennant's W.T.* [1970] Ch. 75. If the tenant for life is also one of the trustees, he should join in the conveyance to himself as one of the conveying parties.

additional power conferred by the settlement.[97] Thus if land is devised "to X and Y in fee simple with power to sell, on trust for A for life and then for B absolutely" the power of sale purported to be given to X and Y is divested from them and given to A; this is so even though A already has a statutory power of sale. But the abortive attempt to give a power of sale to X and Y may not be wholly ineffective, for it may make them Settled Land Act trustees.[98]

3. The statutory powers cannot be ousted, curtailed or hampered. The settlor may confer additional powers on the tenant for life, and such powers are exercisable in the same way as if they were conferred by the Act.[99] Further, nothing in the Act in any way restricts powers which the settlement gives to the tenant for life or purports to give to the trustees to be exercised with the approval of the tenant for life; the powers given by the Act and the settlement are cumulative. But in other respects, so far as the settlement and the Act conflict in relation to powers exercisable under the Act, the Act prevails.[1] Thus if the settlement provides that no sale shall be made without the consent of some specified person, this provision is inconsistent with the unfettered power of sale given by the Act, and the latter prevails.[2]

In particular, it is enacted that any provision in any document is void to the extent to which it purports or tends to prevent or discourage the tenant for life from exercising his statutory powers or from requiring the land to be vested in him.[3] This applies even when the attempt to restrain the exercise of the powers is made by way of determinable limitation; a settlement on "Y for life until he ceases permanently to reside in the property" gives Y a life interest which continues despite any change of residence by him. Notwithstanding anything in a settlement, the exercise of a statutory power can never cause a forfeiture.

Section 106 is most frequently invoked by conditions of residence, *e.g.* a proviso in the settlement that the tenant for life shall forfeit his interest on ceasing to reside on the settled land. In such cases, if the tenant for life ceases to reside for some reason other than the exercise of his statutory powers (as where he prefers to move away and allow a relative to live there rent-free) the proviso for forfeiture is operative and he loses his interest.[4] But if the reason for his ceasing to reside is that he has exercised his statutory powers, as by leasing or selling the land, there is no forfeiture and he continues to be entitled as tenant

---

[97] S.L.A. 1925, s. 108.
[98] *Ante*, p. 263.
[99] S.L.A. 1925, s. 109.
[1] *Ibid*. s. 108.
[2] *Re Jefferys (No. 2)* [1939] Ch. 205.
[3] S.L.A. 1925, s. 106.
[4] *Re Trenchard* [1902] 1 Ch. 378.

for life, receiving the rent from the lease or the income from the purchase-money.[5]

The section can also be invoked where the settlor has provided a fund for the payment of outgoings during the tenant for life's personal occupation and the tenant has exercised his statutory powers of leasing.[6] Payment of outgoings may still be claimed. However, if the house is sold the tenant for life cannot invoke the section and claim an amount corresponding to the sums payable if the house had remained in the settlement.[7]

4. The tenant for life cannot assign, release or contract not to exercise his powers.[8] (a) *Exercise of powers.* Once a person has become a tenant for life, he is incapable of divesting himself of his powers, even if he parts with his entire beneficial interest, as he is entitled to do; it is he, and not the assignee of his beneficial interest, who alone can exercise the statutory powers.[9] However, in three cases the statutory powers may become exercisable by someone other than the tenant for life.

(1) EXTINGUISHMENT OF INTEREST. Where the interest of the tenant for life has been assured, with intent to extinguish it, to the person next entitled under the settlement, the statutory powers cease to be exercisable by the tenant for life and become exercisable as if he were dead.[10] Thus if land is settled on A for life, remainder to B for life, remainder to C in fee simple, the effect of A surrendering his life interest to B is to make the statutory powers exercisable by B instead of A, and A must forthwith convey the legal estate to B by a vesting deed. If B then surrenders his life interest to C, he must convey the legal estate to C, but by ordinary conveyance, for the land ceases to be settled land.[11] This exception does not apply if there is an intervening limitation which might take effect, *e.g.* to D for life, remainder to the sons of D, remainder to E for life, and D, aged 80 and childless, surrenders to E.[12]

(2) ORDER OF COURT. If the tenant for life—

(i) has ceased to have a substantial interest in the land, whether by bankruptcy, assignment or otherwise, and

---

[5] *Re Orlebar* [1936] Ch. 147.
[6] *Re Patten* [1929] 2 Ch. 276.
[7] *Re Aberconway's S.T.* [1953] Ch. 647. Exceptionally, if the fund is given to trustees for the upkeep of a settled house with surplus income being payable to T, the tenant for life, but with a gift over if T ceases permanent residence, then section 106 may be invoked after a sale by T so that T will be entitled to the whole income, since something had been given to T of which he was liable to be deprived upon a sale: *Re Ames* [1893] 2 Ch. 479, *Re Herbert* [1946] 1 All E.R. 421.
[8] S.L.A. 1925, s. 104.
[9] *Re Earl of Carnarvon's Chesterfield S.E.* [1927] 1 Ch. 138 at pp. 145, 146.
[10] S.L.A. 1925, s. 105.
[11] See *ante*, p. 255.
[12] *Re Maryon-Wilson's Instruments* [1971] Ch. 789.

(ii) either consents to an order being made or else has unreasonably refused to exercise his statutory powers,

any person interested in the land may apply to the court for an order authorising the trustees to exercise any or all of the statutory powers in the name and on behalf of the tenant for life.[13] Such an order prevents the tenant for life from exercising any of the powers affected by the order, but until it has been registered[14] the order does not affect those dealing with the tenant for life. Such an order vests neither the legal estate nor the statutory powers in the trustees, who do not become the statutory owner; the order merely authorises the trustees to exercise the powers on behalf of the tenant for life and in his name.

(3) MENTAL PATIENT. Where the tenant for life is a mental patient, his receiver may, in his name and on his behalf under an order of the Court of Protection, exercise his statutory powers.[15]

(b) *Position of assignees.* Where the assignment was made after 1925 then even if the assignment was made for money or money's worth, the consent of the assignee is not required for the exercise of the statutory powers by the tenant for life.[16] But for the application of capital money affected by the assignment for any purpose other than for investment in trustee securities, the consent of the assignee is necessary if the assignment so provides or takes effect by operation of the law of bankruptcy, and the trustees have notice of this. Further, unless the assignment otherwise provides, notice of any intended transaction must be given to the assignee.

Of course, if the land is sold the rights of the assignee are transferred to the capital money which represents the land; and provision is made for obtaining consents in any cases of difficulty.

E. Functions of Settled Land Act Trustees

It may be useful to collect together the principal functions of Settled Land Act trustees. They are—

(i) to receive and hold capital money[17];
(ii) to receive notice from the tenant for life of his intention to effect certain transactions[18];
(iii) to give consent to certain transactions[19];
(iv) to act as special personal representatives on the death of a tenant for life[20];

---

[13] S.L.A. 1925, s. 24.
[14] As "an order affecting land": *ante,* p. 97.
[15] Mental Health Act 1959, s. 103 (1). For mental patients, see *ante*, p. 186.
[16] S.L.A. 1925, s. 104.
[17] *Ante,* p. 240, and *post*, p. 285.
[18] *Ante,* p. 266.
[19] *Ante,* p. 270.
[20] *Ante,* p. 255.

(v) to act as statutory owner if the tenant for life is an infant or there is no tenant for life[21];

(vi) to exercise the powers of the tenant for life if he wishes to acquire the settled land for his own benefit[22];

(vii) to exercise the powers of the tenant for life where he has no substantial beneficial interest and either consents to such exercise or unreasonably refuses to exercise his powers[23]; and

(viii) to exercise a general supervision over the well-being of the settled land.[24]

Part 4

TRUSTS FOR SALE AFTER 1925

1. What is a trust for sale. It has been seen[25] that after 1925 land cannot be settled land if it is subject to an "immediate binding trust for sale." Whenever land is limited in trust for persons by way of succession or for some other reason falls within the definition of settled land, it will be governed by the Settled Land Act 1925 unless it can be shown that it is subject to a trust for sale of this nature. The meaning of the phrase is thus of great importance and must be examined carefully.

(a) *There must be a "trust" for sale.* As before 1926, there must be a true trust to sell and not a mere power of sale.[26] Thus a conveyance to trustees on trust for persons in succession, giving the trustees a power of sale, makes the land settled land; the conveyance operates as an imperfect settlement and the trustees cannot sell.[27] Some of the difficulties which arose from trusts "to retain or sell the land" are solved by the provision that in a disposition or settlement coming into operation after 1925, such a trust shall be construed as a trust for sale with power to postpone sale.[28]

(b) *The trust for sale must be "immediate."* Here again, the position is substantially the same as before 1926[29]; a trust to sell at some future date, *e.g.* when X attains the age of 25, does not prevent land from being settled land.[30] But if there is a trust for sale which is immediately operative, this takes the land out of the Settled Land Act 1925, *even* if the trustees have power to postpone the sale and

---

[21] *Ante*, p. 243.
[22] *Ante*, p. 273.
[23] *Ante*, p. 276.
[24] See *ante*, p. 240; *Re Boston's W.T.* [1956] Ch. 395 at p. 405.
[25] *Ante*, p. 242.
[26] See M. & W., p. 294.
[27] *Ante*, pp. 246, 273.
[28] L.P.A. 1925, s. 25.
[29] See M. & W., p. 295.
[30] *Re Hanson* [1928] Ch. 96.

even if a sale cannot be made without the request or consent of some person.[31]

(c) *The trust for sale must be "binding."* The interpretation of the word "binding" has given rise to considerable difficulty, especially in cases where the land is first subject to the Settled Land Act 1925 and then to a trust for sale, as where it is limited to A for life with remainder to trustees for sale. Three views have been put forward.

(i) That it means a trust for sale capable of binding, in the sense of overreaching, as many interests as possible so that if an equitable interest created under the earlier settlement cannot be overreached by the trustees for sale then the trust for sale is not binding.[32]

(ii) That the word "binding" was inserted to emphasise that a revocable trust for sale is excluded, or else that the word is mere surplusage.[33]

(iii) That a "binding" trust for sale is one which is capable of binding the whole legal estate which has been settled.[34] If the legal estate is vested in the trustees for sale as such, the trust for sale is "binding," even if equitable interests such as charges under a former settlement are still outstanding. Normally, however, where such equitable charges still subsist when the tenant for life dies and a trust for sale arises the trustees for sale will not be able to call for the legal estate under section 7 (5) of the Act so there will be no "binding" trust for sale.[35]

It seems safe to say that the first alternative is now generally recognised as being wrong,[35] and that although the second view is innocuous, the third is probably correct. The issue is largely technical: there is clearly a power of sale and the sole question is who is to exercise it?[36]

2. How a trust for sale comes into existence. A trust for sale may arise—

(a) expressly, by land being deliberately limited on trust for sale, or

(b) by operation of statute.

(a) *Express trusts for sale.* With a view to keeping the trusts off the title, the general practice for many years has been to employ two

---

[31] L.P.A. 1925, s. 205 (1) (xxix).
[32] *Re Leigh's S.E. (No. 1)* [1926] Ch. 852.
[33] *Re Parker's S.E.* [1928] Ch. 247 at p. 261.
[34] See *Re Beaumont S.E.* [1937] 2 All E.R. 353; *Re Sharpe's Deed of Release* [1939] Ch. 51.
[35] *Re Norton* [1929] 1 Ch. 84, *Re Parker (supra).*
[36] See further M. & W., pp. 360–362.

documents, namely, a conveyance on trust for sale and a trust instrument; it was this practice which suggested the vesting deed and trust instrument of the Settled Land Act 1925. Although today two documents are almost invariably employed to create a trust for sale *inter vivos*, there is nothing in the 1925 legislation to make this essential. In the case of testamentary trusts for sale, the usual position before 1926 was that the will was the sole document concerned. After 1925, a written assent is required to vest the legal estate in the trustees for sale, so that now there will usually be two documents in such cases. But even if a trust for sale is created by a single document, it is now provided that a purchaser of the legal estate from the trustees for sale is not concerned with the trusts affecting the rents and profits of the land until sale and the proceeds of sale thereafter, whether or not the trusts are declared by the same instrument as that by which the trust for sale is created.[37]

Where a trust for sale was created before 1926, the legal estate remains vested in trustees for sale if it was already vested in them; if not, it automatically vested in them at the beginning of 1926.[38]

(b) *Statutory trusts for sale*. A trust for sale is imposed by statute in a number of cases. For example—

(i) if two or more persons are entitled to land as joint tenants or tenants in common, a trust for sale is normally imposed by the Law of Property Act 1925[39];

(ii) the Administration of Estates Act 1925 imposes a trust for sale on the property of a person dying intestate[40]; and

(iii) if trustees lend money on mortgage and the property becomes vested in them free from the right of repayment (*e.g.* by foreclosure), they hold it upon trust for sale.[41] This preserves the character of the trust property; the money was pure personalty, and under the doctrine of conversion, the rights of the beneficiaries under a trust for sale are treated as interests in pure personalty, even if the subject-matter of the trust is land.

3. Position of trustees for sale. (a) *Power of postponement.* Unless a contrary intention appears, a power to postpone sale is implied after 1925 in every trust for sale of land, even if it was created before 1926.[42] In the absence of an express provision to the contrary, the

[37] L.P.A. 1925, s. 27.
[38] L.P.A. 1925, 1st Sched., Pt. II, paras. 3, 6.
[39] *Post*, p. 306.
[40] *Ante*, p. 172.
[41] L.P.A. 1925, s. 31. Also if trustees of a settlement of personalty invest the trust funds in the purchase of land that land must be held upon trust for sale unless the settlement otherwise provides: L.P.A. 1925, s. 32.
[42] L.P.A. 1925, s. 25.

trustees are not liable in any way if they postpone sale indefinitely in the exercise of their discretion, nor is a purchaser of the legal estate concerned with directions respecting the postponement of sale.[43] If the trustees cannot agree whether or not to postpone sale, the land must be sold, for the *trust* (or duty) to sell must be carried out unless the power to postpone is effectively exercised or unless enforcing the letter of the trust for sale would defeat the spirit or object of the trust or be a breach of contract.[44] If a power is given to trustees, all must concur before it can be exercised, and thus the power of postponement is exercisable only if all trustees concur.[45] Many trusts for sale are created with the intention that the land shall be retained for a long time before being sold, an intention which is effectuated by the trustees duly concurring in exercising their power to postpone the sale. As a means of making a settlement, the trust for sale has become a recognised alternative to settled land.[46]

(b) *Continuance of trust.* Once a trust for sale has been created, the trust is, for the protection of any purchaser thereunder, deemed to be subsisting until the land has been conveyed either to the beneficiaries themselves or to some other person under their direction.[47] This meets the difficulty that if all the possible beneficiaries were of full age and subject to no disability, they could put an end to the trust for sale by electing to have the land retained as land. For this reason, purchasers who knew that all the possible beneficiaries were *sui juris* sometimes raised objections to a sale without the concurrence of the beneficiaries; formerly this difficulty was overcome by requiring one of the beneficiaries to concur in the conveyance, thus showing that there had not been a unanimous election to terminate the trust for sale.[48]

(c) *Powers of trustees.* The powers of trustees for sale have been considerably extended by the Law of Property Act 1925. Before 1926, they had no powers of leasing, mortgaging or otherwise dealing with the land except by way of sale[49]; after 1925 they have all the powers both of a tenant for life of settled land and of Settled Land Act trustees including the powers of management which the Settled Land Act confers during a minority, even if no minority in fact exists.[50] Thus trustees for sale can exercise even those powers which are exercisable by a tenant for life only with the consent of the

[43] *Ibid.*
[44] *Jones* v. *Challenger* [1961] 1 Q.B. 176, *Re Buchanan-Wollaston's Conveyance* [1939] Ch. 738. These problems usually arise in a co-ownership context: see *post* p. 316.
[45] *Re Mayo* [1943] Ch. 302. Contrast joint tenants for life of settled land, *post*, p. 321.
[46] For a comparison of the two methods, see *post,* pp. 290 *et seq.* For the application of income, see M. & W., p. 366.
[47] L.P.A. 1925, s. 23. This can create problems: see *post* p. 292.
[48] See *Re Jenkins and H.E. Randall & Co.'s Contract* [1903] 2 Ch. 362.
[49] *Ante,* p. 241.
[50] L.P.A. 1925, s. 28; see *Re Wellsted's W.T.* [1949] Ch. 296; *Re Gray* [1927] 1 Ch. 242.

trustees of the settlement. Further, where settled land becomes vested in the Settled Land Act trustees in the form of trust for sale known as the "statutory trusts,"[51] the trustees have all the additional powers (if any) conferred by the settlement on the tenant for life, statutory owner or trustees of the settlement.[52] If trustees for sale refuse to exercise their powers a beneficiary can apply to the court for the court to make such order as it thinks fit.[53]

(d) *Curtailment of powers.* The extent to which the powers of trustees for sale can be curtailed by the settlement is uncertain. It is clear that the Law of Property Act 1925 contemplates the exercise of their power of sale or any other of their powers being made subject to the requirement that the consent of specified persons should be first obtained; for if the consent of more than two persons is required, the Act provides that a bona fide purchaser for value is protected if the consent of any two such persons is obtained, and further, that he need not concern himself with the consents of any persons under disability.[54] But this provision applies only to a purchaser: the trustees will be guilty of a breach of trust if they do not obtain the full number of consents stipulated. Any consent required from a minor, however, may be given by his parent or guardian, and that of a mental patient by his receiver; and the court has power to dispense with consents which cannot be obtained.[55] But although it is clear that consents may be made requisite to the trustees exercising their powers, it is by no means clear whether the powers can be taken away or curtailed in any other way. It is arguable that as the trustees have all the powers of a tenant for life and as the powers of a tenant for life cannot be restricted in any way,[56] so the powers of trustees for sale cannot be hampered except so far as is provided by statute: and perhaps this argument[57] will ultimately be accepted by the courts.

4. Rights of the beneficiaries. After 1925, the person for the time being entitled to the income from a trust for sale has none of the powers of a tenant for life of settled land, for all the powers are vested in the trustees for sale. However, this rule is subject to three qualifications.

(a) *Delegation.* The trustees may *revocably* and in writing delegate certain powers to the person of full age (not being merely an annuitant) who for the time being is beneficially entitled in possession

---

[51] See *post*, p. 306.
[52] L.P.A. 1925, s. 28; L.P.(Am.)A. 1926, Sched.
[53] L.P.A. 1925, s. 30.
[54] L.P.A. 1925, s. 26.
[55] *Ibid.* ss. 26, 30; Mental Health Act 1959, ss. 103 (1), 149 (1).
[56] *Ante*, p. 274.
[57] Urged but not decided in *Re Davies' W.T.* [1932] 1 Ch. 530; see at pp. 532, 533.

to the net rents and profits of the land for his life or any less period.[58] The powers which may be so delegated are the powers of, and incidental to, leasing, accepting surrenders of leases and management. The powers thus delegated must be exercised in the names and on behalf of the trustees; but if they are misused, the liability rests not on the trustees but on the person exercising the powers (who is deemed to be in the position of a trustee) except to the extent that the trustees themselves may have erred in not revoking the delegated powers. If the trustees refuse to delegate these powers, an application to the court may be made to compel them to do so.[59]

(b) *Consents.* The duties or powers of the trustees may only be exercisable with the consent of a beneficiary if such consent is made expressly or impliedly requisite by the trust instrument.[60] Such beneficiary may then restrain a projected act of the trustees.

(c) *Consultation.* In some cases the trustees are under an obligation, so far as is practicable, to consult the persons of full age for the time being beneficially interested in possession in the rents and profits of the land until sale, and must, so far as is consistent with the general interests of the trust, give effect to their wishes, or to the wishes of the majority in value. However, there are many express trusts for sale to which this provision does not apply, for it is confined to the trusts for sale which either are created by statute or show an intention that this provison is to apply. Further, the trustees are not bound to follow the wishes of the beneficiaries, nor is a purchaser concerned to see that the trustees have complied with this requirement.[61]

5. The doctrine of conversion. Equity looks upon that as done which ought to be done, and it has long been settled that as soon as land is held upon trust for sale, the rights of the beneficiaries must be regarded as interests in the money into which the trustees are bound sooner or later to convert the land.[62] This doctrine has its roots in the simple principle that it would be wrong that the precise moment at which the trustees carried out their administrative duty of selling should alter the devolution of beneficial interests, especially where a delay in selling might amount to a breach of trust. Important rights may depend on the character of the property. Thus even before the land is sold the beneficiaries are regarded as owning personal

---

[58] L.P.A. 1925, s. 29.
[59] *Ibid.* s. 30.
[60] In *Re Herklot's W.T.* [1964] 1 W.L.R. 583 where a will imposed a trust for sale on a house but gave A a right to reside there for as long as she wished and gave B a right to acquire the house on A's death, it was held implicit that no sale in A's lifetime could occur without the consent of both A and B.
[61] L.P.A. 1925, s. 26; L.P.(Am.)A. 1926, Sched.
[62] *Fletcher* v. *Ashburner* (1779) 1 Bro.C.C. 497.

property. For example, a testator made a will before 1926 leaving all
his realty to R and all his personality to P. He owned a share in
freehold land, and the effect of the 1925 legislation was to impose a
trust for sale on this land.[63] The doctrine of conversion consequently
applied, so that on his death after 1925 his interest in the property
passed under his will to P and not to R.[64]

The imposition of trusts for sale by the 1925 legislation had further
consequences which had scarcely been foreseen. If at the end of 1925
two or more persons were entitled to land as tenants in common in
tail, the land became subject to a trust for sale at the beginning of
1926. The effect of this was to convert the entails into absolute
interests, for the rights of the beneficiaries became personalty and,
although after 1925 personalty can be entailed,[65] there was no
provision by which this could be done by an instrument executed
before 1926.[66] The Law of Property (Entailed Interests) Act 1932[67]
retrospectively amended the law, providing that in such cases an
entail should be deemed to exist in the proceeds of sale.

Part 5

OVERREACHING EFFECT OF DISPOSITIONS

Sect. 1. Under the Settled Land Act 1925

As already explained,[68] an interest in land is said to be overreached if
it is transferred from land to the purchase-money on a sale or other
disposition being made. The Settled Land Act 1925, after first
authorising a tenant for life to effect a sale or other transaction by
deed, goes on to state the overreaching effect of such a deed.

1. Rights under the settlement.[69] The deed is effectual to pass the
land or other interest concerned "discharged from all the limitations,
powers, and provisions of the settlement, and from all estates,
interests, and charges subsisting or to arise thereunder"; it is
immaterial whether or not a purchaser has notice of these rights. In
short, the purchaser takes the land free from all the rights under the
settlement. The Act then makes certain qualifications to this rule: the
land is to pass to the purchaser discharged from the above rights,
"but subject to and with the exception of"[70]—

[63] *Post,* p. 306.
[64] *Re Kempthorne* [1930] 1 Ch. 268.
[65] *Ante,* p. 47.
[66] *Re Price* [1928] Ch. 579.
[67] s. 1.
[68] *Ante,* p. 107.
[69] S.L.A. 1925, s. 72.
[70] See *Re Dickin and Kelsall's Contract* [1908] 1 Ch. 213 at p. 221.

(a) All legal estates and charges by way of legal mortgage having priority to the settlement.

In nearly every case this provision is mere surplusage, for no power is given to overreach rights prior to the settlement and so the qualification is unnecessary. If X makes a legal mortgage of land and later settles the land, the tenant for life has no power to overreach the mortgage, which continues to bind the land.

(b) All legal estates and charges by way of legal mortgage which have been conveyed or created for securing money actually raised at the date of the deed.

This is a true exception, for it excludes something which otherwise would have been included in the overreaching provision. Thus if a tenant for life creates a legal mortgage to pay for improvements or raise portions, and the mortgagee has actually paid the money, the mortgage cannot be overreached even though it is an interest arising under the settlement. "Mortgagees who have actually lent their money on the security of the land are regarded as strangers to the settlement, and are not to have the security which they bargained for on the land itself transferred to the purchase-money at the will of the tenant for life."[71] If the money has not in fact been paid (*e.g.* where a legal term of years has been created to secure portions which have not been raised[72]) the right is overreached.[73]

(c) All leases and grants of other rights (except annuities, limited ower's charges and general equitable charges[74]) which at the date of the deed are—
   (i) binding on the successors in title of the tenant for life, and
   (ii) duly registered if capable of registration.

This is also a true exception, but unlike the previous provisions it is not confined to legal rights. It thus apparently applies to a restrictive covenant creating a mere equitable burden on the land.

2. Rights prior to the settlement. Having dealt with the exceptions to the rule that all rights arising under the settlement can be overreached, the Act proceeds to the converse case, namely, the exceptions to the rule that rights prior to the settlement cannot be overreached. The Act[75] provides that—

(1) an annuity,
(2) a limited owner's charge, and
(3) a general equitable charge

---

[71] *Re Mundy and Roper's Contract* [1899] 1 Ch. 275 at p. 289, *per* Chitty L.J.
[72] For this device, virtually obsolete, see M. & W., pp. 387, 388.
[73] See *Re Du Cane and Nettlefold's Contract* [1898] 2 Ch. 96 at p. 108.
[74] For these rights, see *ante,* p. 92.
[75] S.L.A. 1925, s. 72.

shall be overreached on a disposition under the Act even if they have been duly protected by registration; these rights are treated as if they had been created by the settlement even if in fact they arose before it came into existence. They are all rights which can be represented in terms of money and so will not suffer from being transferred to the purchase-money.

3. Summary. It cannot be said that the overreaching provisions, which in the main reproduce corresponding provisions in the Settled Land Act 1882, are very happily drawn. For those who wish to have a bird's eye view of their effect (necessarily at the expense of some accuracy) the position may be represented as follows:

(i) There is in general no power to overreach legal rights.

(ii) Subject to the three exceptions set out above, there is no power to overreach equitable rights already existing when the settlement was made.

(iii) There is power to overreach all the equitable rights of the beneficiaries under the settlement, including derivative rights, *e.g.* the rights of a mortgagee of the beneficial interest of a tenant for life.

4. Payment of capital money. There is one important condition which must be observed if a deed is to take effect under the Act and so have an overreaching effect. This is the rule that, notwithstanding anything to the contrary in the settlement, any capital money payable in respect of the transaction must be paid either—

(i) to, or by the direction of, all the trustees of the settlement, who must be either two or more in number or a trust corporation (the definition of "trust corporation" includes certain officials such as the Public Trustee and certain companies with a large paid-up capital[76]), or

(ii) into court.[77]

It lies with the tenant for life to decide which of the two methods of payment shall be adopted.[78] If a purchaser fails to pay his money in accordance with these provisions and pays it, for example, to the tenant for life, he will not get a good discharge and will be unable to make a good title to a subsequent purchaser.[79] Where no capital money arises on a transaction (as where a lease is granted without taking a fine), a disposition in favour of a bona fide purchaser for

---

[76] See N. & M., p. 501.
[77] S.L.A. 1925, s. 18.
[78] S.L.A. 1925, s. 75; *Hatten* v. *Russell* (1888) 38 Ch.D. 334 at p. 345.
[79] *Re Norton and Las Casas' Contract* [1909] 2 Ch. 59. See *ante* pp. 249–252 where the purchaser does not know he is purchasing settled land.

value of a legal estate takes effect under the Act and thus has an overreaching effect even though there are no trustees.[80]

5. Capital money as land. The capital money and any investments representing it are for all purposes of disposition, transmission and devolution (but not otherwise, *e.g.* for purposes of death duties[81]) treated as land, and are held for and go to the same persons, in the same manner and for the same estates, interests and trusts, as the land wherefrom they arise would have been held and have gone under the settlement.[82] Thus where settled freeholds were sold and on the life tenant's death X exercised his option under the settlement to purchase the freeholds X became entitled to the proceeds of sale of the freeholds.[83] In short, the state in which the settled property happens to be at any given moment, whether it is land, investments or money, cannot affect the rights of the beneficiaries or those claiming under them.

Sect. 2. Under a Trust for Sale

Strictly speaking, a trust for sale has no overreaching effect; for, by the equitable doctrine of conversion, so long as the land remains unsold the rights of the beneficiaries are already deemed to be rights in the purchase-money into which it will ultimately be converted. Consequently it cannot be said that a sale or other transaction transfers the rights of the beneficiaries from the land to the purchase-money, for strictly they never were attached to the land. Nevertheless, it is convenient to use the term "overreaching" as including the process by which the beneficiaries have their rights in what is money in theory but land in fact, transferred to what is money both in theory and in fact.

A disposition under a trust for sale is effective to overeach the equitable rights of the beneficiaries thereunder; there is no power to overreach legal estates, nor, apparently to overreach rights already existing when the trust for sale was created. As already seen, a purchaser of a legal estate from the trustees for sale is not concerned with the trusts affecting the rents and profits of the land until sale and the proceeds of sale thereafter even if the trusts are declared by the instrument which created the trust for sale.[84] However, to have an overreaching effect, the proceeds of sale or other capital money, notwithstanding anything to the contrary in the trust for sale, must not be paid to or applied by the direction of fewer than two persons as

---

[80] S.L.A. 1925, s. 110 (4).
[81] *Earl of Midleton* v. *Baron Cottesloe* [1949] A.C. 418.
[82] S.L.A. 1925, s. 75.
[83] *Re Armstrong's W.T.* [1943] Ch. 400; *cf. Re Herklot's W.T. (ante,* p. 282).
[84] L.P.A. 1925, s. 27; *ante,* p. 279.

trustees for sale except where the trustee is a trust corporation[85] or a sole personal representative, or where the purchaser is a bona fide purchaser of a legal estate for value without notice that a trust for sale exists.[86] There is no provision for payment into court. Where no capital money arises, it is unnecessary to have more than one trustee.

Proceeds of sale or other capital money arising under a trust for sale may be applied in the same way as capital money arising from settled land.[87] This does not, however, effect a conversion into realty, and the rights of the beneficiaries remain rights in personalty.[88] Any land acquired under this provision must be conveyed to the trustees for sale on trust for sale.[89]

Sect. 3. Under Ad Hoc Settlements and Trusts for Sale

The original intention of the 1925 legislation was that a conveyance under a settlement or trust for sale should overreach not only the interests of the beneficiaries but also prior equities as well. This provision was attacked in Parliament, and ultimately a workable scheme was produced and duly embodied in the 1925 legislation. Clearly some equities cannot be overreached; thus a restrictive covenant (*e.g.* against building) and an equitable easement (*e.g.* an equitable right of way) cannot become corresponding rights in the purchase-money. The present scheme is that dispositions under ordinary settlements and trusts for sale have the overreaching effect considered above, and that those under certain special settlements and trusts for sale have a special wider overreaching effect. To obtain this wider effect the settlement or trust for sale must have "guaranteed" trustees, *i.e.* either trustees appointed or approved by the court, or a trust corporation. The idea is that such trustees are likely to be particularly trustworthy and that this will console those whose rights are overreached but would not have been overreached under an ordinary settlement or trust for sale. That is the theory; in practice, little use is made of such settlements and trusts for sale, for the additional overreaching powers conferred are meagre. The details of such settlements and trusts for sale are as follows.

1. Creation. (a) *Ad hoc settlements.* If a person of full age is beneficially entitled in possession to a legal estate subject to any equitable interests or powers, then for the purpose of overreaching these rights he may by deed declare that the legal estate is vested in him on trust to give effect to all equitable interests and powers

---

[85] L.P.A. 1925, ss. 2, 27; L.P.(Am.)A. 1926, Sched.
[86] *Caunce* v. *Caunce* [1969] 1 W.L.R. 286, *Williams & Glyn's Bank* v. *Boland* [1979] Ch. 312.
[87] L.P.A. 1925, s. 28; *Re Wellsted's W.T.* [1949] Ch. 296; *ante*, p. 273.
[88] *Re Kempthorne* [1930] 1 Ch. 268.
[89] L.P.A. 1925, s. 28.

affecting the legal estate.[90] Such a deed is treated as a vesting deed and must be executed either by two or more individuals approved or appointed by the court, or by a trust corporation, who must be stated to be Settled Land Act trustees. Thereupon the land is deemed to be settled land and the estate owner becomes a tenant for life: the instruments which create his estate and the equitable interests or powers are deemed to be the trust instrument, in default of which a trust instrument must be executed contemporaneously with the vesting deed. It will be noticed that these provisions are inappropriate to land which is already settled, for normally there will be no person *beneficially* entitled in possession to a *legal* estate: the provisions contemplate only settlements set up ad hoc (expressly for the purpose).

(b) *Ad hoc trusts for sale.* If a legal estate is subject to a trust for sale and the trustees thereof are either—

(i) two or more individuals approved or appointed by the court, or their successors in office, or
(ii) a trust corporation,

then the effect of a conveyance is to overreach equities having priority to the trust for sale, with the exceptions set out below.[91] It will be noticed that this provision is not confined to trusts for sale created ad hoc, but extends to any trusts for sale, whether already in existence or set up expressly for the purpose of overreaching equities: provided the conditions as to trustees are satisfied, the wider overreaching powers exist.[92] Nevertheless, "ad hoc trusts for sale" is a convenient name for such trusts even if they have not in fact been set up ad hoc.

2. Overreaching effect of dispositions. As regards the overreaching effect of a conveyance or other disposition, the provisions as to ad hoc settlements and ad hoc trusts for sale are in similar terms.[93] Equitable rights having priority to the settlement or trust for sale are overreached with the exception of—

(a) equitable interests protected by a deposit of documents relating to the legal estate affected;
(b) restrictive covenants;
(c) equitable easements;
(d) estate contracts;
(e) equitable interests protected by registration under the Land

---

[90] S.L.A. 1925, s. 21.
[91] L.P.A. 1925, s. 2.
[92] *Re Leigh's S.E. (No. 2)* [1927] 2 Ch. 13.
[93] S.L.A. 1925, s. 21; L.P.A. 1925, s. 2.

Charges Act 1972,[94] other than—
(i) annuities,
(ii) limited owner's charges and
(iii) general equitable charges.

It will be observed that the last three rights can be overreached under an ad hoc settlement or an ad hoc trust for sale. Such rights can, indeed, be overreached under an ordinary settlement, so that no wider powers are given in this case; but probably they cannot be overreached under an ordinary trust for sale, so that in this respect an ad hoc trust for sale has marked advantages over an ordinary trust for sale. Apart from these three rights, however, the list of exceptions given above covers all the important equitable rights likely to be encountered in practice. The first exception is designed to cover temporary equitable mortgages and charges where the lender has secured himself by obtaining the title deeds. Heads (b), (c) and (d) could not, from their very nature, be overreached. Head (e) adds little to the previous provisions, for apart from the spouse's right to occupy a house owned by the other,[95] the only rights it includes are included under (b), (c) and (d). These rights are, in general, capable of registration only if created after 1925,[96] so that, for example, a restrictive covenant is protected by head (b) if created in 1920 and by heads (b) and (e) if created in 1930.

Although in general ad hoc settlements and trusts for sale may be said to be both complicated and ineffective, there are certain equitable rights which will be overreached by an ad hoc, but not by an ordinary, settlement or trust for sale. A prior equitable right which is not in the catalogue of registrable interests, and is not comprised in heads (a) to (d), will, it seems, be overreached under an ad hoc settlement or trust for sale, but not under an ordinary settlement or trust for sale. Some pre-1926 family interests would qualify, *e.g.* a widow's right of dower or a rentcharge for life created by a marriage settlement.[97] Recently, however, certain commercial interests have been established as being equitable rights which are not registrable; and they do not fall within heads (a) to (d). These rights include proprietary estoppel interests,[98] and certain rights of entry to secure performance of a covenant.[99] From their very nature such rights could not sensibly be "overreached," and despite the statutory language they seem unlikely to be held overreachable under the ad hoc provisions. It is fortunate that these provisions are of so little practical importance.

---

[94] Replacing Land Charges Act 1925.
[95] See *ante*, p. 95.
[96] *Ante*, p. 94.
[97] See Wolstenholme & Cherry, *Conveyancing Statutes*, vol. 3, pp. 30, 82.
[98] *E.R. Ives Investment Ltd.* v. *High* [1967] 2 Q.B.379; *ante*, pp. 74–77.
[99] *Shiloh Spinners Ltd.* v. *Harding* [1973] A.C. 80; *ante*, p. 90.

Sec. 4. Summary of Overreaching Provisions

In broad outline, the position may be said to be as follows:

(a) A conveyance under an ordinary trust for sale overreaches the rights of the beneficiaries thereunder.

(b) A conveyance under an ordinary settlement overreaches—
   (i) the rights of the beneficiaries thereunder, and
   (ii) annuities, limited owner's charges and general equitable charges.

(c) A conveyance under an ad hoc settlement or trust for sale overreaches—
   (i) the rights of the beneficiaries thereunder;
   (ii) annuities, limited owner's charges and general equitable charges; and
   (iii) certain other equities, such as a widow's right of dower.

Part 6

COMPARISON OF SETTLED LAND WITH TRUSTS FOR SALE

A person proposing to settle land today can do so either by making the land settled land or by creating a trust for sale. The changes made by the 1925 legislation have endowed trusts for sale with all the technical advantages of settled land; for example, entails can now be created under trusts for sale, and trustees for sale have all the powers of a tenant for life. A question which sometimes arises is which method to employ in any given case. The following are some of the points which should be considered.

1. Control of the land is in the hands of the trustees under a trust for sale,[1] but in the hands of the tenant for life in the case of settled land. Thus if the land is a family estate on which the tenant for life will reside, the land should be made settled land, but if it consists of a row of shops, a trust for sale should be created to free the beneficiaries from the burden of managing the property. Again, if the proposed tenant for life is not a good business man it may be better to create a trust for sale.

2. Restrictions on dealings. Although it is now impossible to create a settlement which will effectively prevent the land from being sold or otherwise dealt with, some measure of restraint can be imposed

---

[1] A refusal to exercise their powers may be the subject of a beneficiary's application to the court under L.P.A. 1925 s. 30. Joint tenants for life should not be created since the court has no power to resolve disagreements: *Re 90 Thornhill Rd., Tolworth* [1970] Ch. 261.

under a trust for sale, where the trustees may be obliged to obtain the consent of specified persons before dealing with the land so that in the lifetimes of such persons the land will not in fact be sold since no consent will, in practice, be forthcoming. Settlements and trusts for sale have thus changed places since the middle of the last century. In those days, a settlement was a method of keeping a particular piece of land in the family, and a trust for sale was used where the nature of the land was immaterial; today the trust for sale can to some extent achieve what the settlement cannot. Indeed in *Re Inns*[2] it was assumed that land held on trust for sale could be made unsaleable for a considerable period, where sale could only be with the consent of the X Co. Ltd., a contingent remainderman, which was only to benefit under the trust if the land was unsold at the end of a considerable period.

3. Economy. The trust for sale is usually less complicated and expensive than settled land, and so is the more suitable alternative for small estates. The difficulty of discovering in whom the legal estate and statutory powers are vested occurs not infrequently in the case of settled land, but rarely in the case of trusts for sale. A testator who makes his own will leaving his house to his widow during widowhood, then to his daughter until she marries, and then to his children equally, is unwittingly invoking most of the provisions designed by the legislature for large family estates. The whole creaking structure of Settled Land Act trustees, special personal representatives, vesting assents, deeds of discharge and so on may be involved for a house or cottage worth a few thousand pounds. If instead of this the testator had devised his land to trustees on trust for sale, all these difficulties would have been avoided. The trouble is that the words "on trust for sale" or their equivalent are required to take land out of the Settled Land Act, and these words have not reached the consciousness of the average testator who makes his own will.

4. Preservation of a unit. A trust for sale is more convenient than a strict settlement where a settlor wishes to provide for his children equally. A strict settlement, on the other hand, is normally used "to make an eldest son," *i.e.* to give the principal benefit to the eldest son and make provision for the younger children a subsidiary matter. Before 1926, the doctrine of conversion and the impossibility of creating entails in personalty combined to make trusts for sale unsuitable for this purpose. As already seen,[3] this difficulty no longer exists, although the doctrine of conversion must still be considered, *e.g.* when drafting a will for a beneficiary under a trust for sale.

[2] [1947] Ch. 576.
[3] *Ante,* p. 47.

5.. Termination of trusts. With settled land a purchaser does not need to see the trust instrument to check that the settlement has ended. He can safely rely on a deed of discharge or on the ownership of the person in whose name the land is held under an ordinary conveyance or assent.[4] With trusts for sale, where there has been no overreaching sale by the trustees for sale,[5] the purchaser needs to check that "the land has been conveyed to or under the direction of the persons interested in the proceeds of sale"[6] and so will require knowledge of the trusts of such proceeds, *e.g.* where land has been vested in trustees for sale for A for life or until remarriage and then for B absolutely, and B is trying to sell the land after it has been vested in him by the trustees after A's death or remarriage. It may thus be better for B to leave the legal estate in the trustees.

Part 7

REGISTERED LAND

Sect. 1. Settled Land

The Settled Land Act 1925 takes effect subject to the provisions of the Land Registration Act 1925.[7] The legal estate in the settled land will be registered in the name of the tenant for life or statutory owner or personal representatives[8] according to the circumstances.[9] The beneficiaries' interests can only be minor interests[10]—and not overriding interests—and will be protected by entry of a restriction on the register. If the tenant for life is registered proprietor the restriction will state "No disposition by the proprietor of the land under which capital money arises is to be registered unless the money is paid to AB of . . . and CD of . . . (the trustees of the settlement, of which there must be two or a trust corporation) or into court. Except under the order of the Registrar no disposition is to be registered unless authorised[11] by the Settled Land Act."

Where appropriate,[12] vesting transfers and vesting assents will be used on the same occasions as vesting deeds or vesting assents in unregistered land; similarly, where the settlement has ended ordinary transfers or assents will be used, except where a deed of discharge has

---

[4] S.L.A. 1925, ss. 17, 110 (5).
[5] L.P.A. 1925, ss. 27, 2.
[6] *Ibid.* s. 23.
[7] S.L.A. 1925, s. 119 (3).
[8] L.R.A. 1925, ss. 41, 81, 91.
[9] *Ibid.* s. 86 (1), (5).
[10] *Ibid.* s. 86 (2).
[11] This includes powers conferred by the settlement in extension of the statutory powers: rule 58 (2).
[12] Statutory Forms Nos. 21, 23, 56, 57.

been executed, whereupon, on application, the Registrar will remove the restriction from the register.[13]

The Land Registration Act machinery is thus designed to make the Settled Land Act scheme work smoothly. It must always be remembered, however, that whoever happens to be entered as registered proprietor *ipso facto* has the legal estate and enjoys plenary powers of disposition unless there is some contrary entry on the register.[14] However, where the instruments delivered for registration reveal that land is settled land then the Registrar will ensure that the proper form of transfer is used and the appropriate restriction entered on the proprietorship register.

In dealing with informal settlements of registered land it is crucial to remember that the register is everything (but for overriding interests) and that beneficiaries' interests under Settled Land Act settlements are minor interests only. Thus, if registered proprietor R, declares that he holds the land on certain trusts which make the land settled land, but does not send off the appropriate forms to the Registry, so that he seems sole legal beneficial owner, then he can transfer the title to a purchaser who will take free from the beneficiaries' minor interests not protected by entry on the register.[15]

If R had purported to transfer the land to T on certain trusts within the Settled Land Act then the Registrar, on receiving the application to register T as new proprietor, would ensure that the land became vested in the tenant for life and that the appropriate restriction was entered to protect the beneficiaries. If the transfer appeared as a straight-forward transfer to T, then T would become registered proprietor with the legal estate and would be able to transfer it to a purchaser free from the beneficiaries' minor interests not protected by entry on the register.[16]

Under section 82 (1) (g) of the Land Registration Act 1925 there is a discretion to rectify the register "where a legal estate has been registered in the name of a person who, if the land had not been registered, would not have been the estate owner"[17] *e.g.* the register can be rectified to make the tenant for life of a pre-1926 settlement the registered proprietor in place of the trustees since the legal estate in unregistered settled land automatically vested in the tenant for life at the first moment of 1926. However, it is considered that sections 4, 13 and 18 of the Settled Land Act must under section 119 (3) thereof take effect subject to the fundamental principles of the Land Registration Act 1925 whereby registration of a new proprietor for value vests in him the land subject only to overriding interests and

---

[13] L.R.A., s. 87 (4), Form No. 77.
[14] *Ibid.* ss. 18, 20, 21, 23.
[15] *Ibid.* ss. 20 (1), 23 (1).
[16] *Ibid.*
[17] Further see *post* pp. 533–535.

entries on the register.[18] The fact that such a purchaser, if the land had been unregistered, might not have received a good title should be immaterial. Similarly, if a tenant for life forged a deed of discharge, so that the Registrar withdrew the entry of a restriction, a new proprietor for value should receive a good title free from unprotected minor interests and from the possibility of a claim to rectify the register, there being no valid interest on registered land principles to justify such a claim.

Sect. 2. Trusts for Sale

Where registered land is subject to a trust for sale, whether express or statutory, the title must be registered in the names of the trustees for sale, not exceeding four in number.[19] Where he knows of the trust for sale the Registrar will enter a restriction protecting the minor interests of the beneficiaries as follows: "No disposition by one proprietor of the land (being the survivor of joint proprietors and not being a trust corporation) under which capital money arises is to be registered except under an order of the Registrar or of the Court." On compliance with this restriction a purchaser will overreach the interests of the beneficiaries which will be in the proceeds of sale.

If no entry appears on the register to protect a beneficiary then, if he is in actual occupation (or in receipt of rents and profits) he can claim that his interest under the trust for sale is an overriding interest.[20] Such a claim will succeed where the trust for sale was intended to provide a house for occupation by the beneficiary as in *Williams & Glyn's Bank* v. *Boland*.[21]

The position may be otherwise, however, if the object of the trust for sale was not to provide accommodation for a beneficiary but to enable the income or capital to be divided between the beneficiaries.[22] Take the case of H and W who purchase a block of flats comprising 50 units as an investment. The block is vested in their joint names as registered proprietors but no restriction appears on the register since they are entitled for their own benefit as joint tenants, so that the survivor will be entitled to give a valid receipt for capital moneys. Ten years later they execute a trust instrument declaring that they are holding the block of flats on trust for sale to pay half of the income to each of their two sons, A and B, for life and then to distribute half the capital on the death of such a son amongst the children of such son equally. No entry is made on the register to reflect this. Twelve years later H dies and W as sole legal and

---

[18] See *ante*, pp. 113–114.

[19] L.R.A., ss. 94, 95.

[20] *Williams & Glyn's Bank* v. *Boland* [1981] A.C. 487.

[21] *Ibid.* This may be the case if the life tenant's consent is requisite for any sale: *Re Herklot's W.T.* [1964] 1 W.L.R. 159.

[22] *Cf. Barclay* v. *Barclay* [1970] 2 Q.B. 677, *post*, pp. 313–315.

beneficial owner transfers the block for £2 million to P who becomes registered proprietor when A or A's 30 year old son, S, happens to be renting a flat in the block. It may well be that the interest of A or of S will not be treated as an interest in land, so as to be an overriding interest subsisting in reference to the land, but will be treated as an interest in the proceeds of sale, and the income till sale, of the block, as a minor interest.[23] An unprotected minor interest, of course, will not bind the purchaser.

Part 8

VESTING OF TRUST PROPERTY

Sect. 1. Vesting

Some trustees have no property vested in them, as is often the case with trustees of settled land; in such cases, no question of the devolution of trust property arises. But where property is vested in trustees, questions of the transfer of the trust property arise on their death, retirement or removal, or on the appointment of new trustees.

A. On Death

Trustees are always made joint tenants or joint owners of the trust property, whether it is real or personal. The advantage of this is that on the death of one trustee the estate or interest vested in him passes to the surviving trustees by the doctrine of survivorship.[24] If a sole surviving trustee dies the estate or interest held on trust vests in the personal representatives of the deceased trustee notwithstanding any provision in his will.[25] Until new trustees are appointed, the personal representatives may exercise any power or trust exercisable by the former trustee, without being obliged to do so.[26]

B. On Appointment of New Trustees

1. Vesting declaration. On an appointment of new trustees, the trust property has to be vested in the new trustees jointly with any continuing trustees. Formerly, a formal conveyance of the trust property by the persons in whom it was vested was necessary; if A and B were trustees and C was appointed a new trustee on A's death, B had to convey the trust property to himself and C jointly.[27] But by section 40 of the Trustee Act 1925,[28] if an appointment of new

---

[23] Further see Hayton, pp. 98–100.
[24] *Ante,* p. 4, *post,* p. 299.
[25] A.E.A. 1925, s. 1.
[26] T.A. 1925, s. 18 (2). By T.A. s. 36 (1) the personal representatives of the last surviving trustee can appoint new trustees.
[27] See M. & W., 161, 162.
[28] Replacing earlier provisions.

trustees is made by deed, a declaration therein by the appointor that the property shall vest in the trustees (a "vesting declaration") is sufficient to vest the property in them. This applies to all deeds executed after 1881[29]; and if the deed is executed after 1925, a vesting declaration is implied in the absence of an express provision to the contrary.[30]

These provisions apply even if the trust property is not vested in the appointor. He has a statutory power to transfer what he has not got. Thus where A and B are the trustees and X has the power to appoint new trustees, if A dies and X appoints C a trustee in his place, the deed of appointment will vest the property in B and C jointly.

2. Exceptions. In certain cases the trust property cannot be transferred by a vesting declaration, either express or implied. These cases are when the property consists of—

(1) land which the trustees hold by way of mortgage for securing trust money;

(2) land held under a lease with a provision against assigning or disposing of the land without consent, unless—
  (i) the requisite consent has first been obtained, or
  (ii) the vesting declaration would not be a breach of covenant or give rise to a forfeiture;

(3) any share, stock or other property which is transferable only in books kept by a company or other body, or in a way directed by statute[31];

(4) registered land.[32]

In these excepted cases the trust property must be transferred by the method appropriate to the subject-matter, *e.g.* in the case of shares and registered land, by a duly registered transfer. The reason for the inclusion of (1) is to avoid bringing the trusts on to the title, for otherwise when the borrower sought to repay the loan, he would have to investigate the trust documents to see that he was paying the right persons; and (2) is included to avoid accidental breaches of the terms of the lease.

3. Vesting orders. The court has a wide jurisdiction to make vesting orders where this is desirable.[33]

---

[29] T.A. 1925, s. 40 (6).
[30] *Ibid.* s. 40 (1).
[31] T.A. 1925, s. 40 (4), replacing earlier provisions.
[32] The existing registered proprietors should execute a transfer form in favour of the new trustees: Ruoff & Roper, pp. 384–385.
[33] T.A. 1925, ss. 44–56.

C. On Retirement or Removal

Where a trustee retires or is discharged from a trust without a new trustee being appointed, and the transaction is effected by deed, the trust property can be divested from the former trustee and vested solely in the continuing trustees by means of a vesting declaration. This applies only if the deed is executed by the retiring trustee, the continuing trustees and any person with power to appoint new trustees; if the deed is executed after 1925, a vesting declaration is implied.[34] There are the same exceptions as in the case of vesting declarations on the appointment of new trustees. This special provision is necessary since the *jus accrescendi* operates only on death and not on retirement.

Sect. 2. Procedure in the Case of Settled Land and Trusts for Sale

1. One document. Although it is undesirable, a trust for sale may be created by only one instrument. In this case, when a new trustee is appointed, the appointment may be made by a single document. This may be merely in writing, but it should be by deed so that the legal estate may be vested in the new and continuing trustees by virtue of section 40 of the Trustee Act 1925,[35] thus avoiding the necessity of a separate conveyance. In addition, a memorandum must be indorsed on or annexed to the instrument creating the trust for sale, stating the names of those who are the trustees after the appointment is made,[36] and not merely the names of the new trustees.

2. Two documents. Normally, however, a trust for sale is created by two documents. In this case, and in the case of settled land, the procedure is more complicated. There must be[37]—

(i) An instrument to go with the conveyance on trust for sale or the vesting instrument (for purchasers to see).
(ii) An appointment to go with the trust instrument.
(iii) An indorsement on the conveyance on trust for sale or on the vesting instrument stating the names of those who are the trustees after the appointment.

In the case of settled land, the first document must be a deed; it merely states who are now the trustees. In the case of a trust for sale, it may be merely in writing, but, as above, should be by deed in order to take advantage of section 40 of the Trustee Act 1925; in either case it effects the actual appointment of the persons named in it as trustees

---

[34] *Ibid.* s. 40 (2), replacing earlier provisions.
[35] *Ante*, p. 295.
[36] T.A. 1925, s. 35 (3).
[37] *Ibid.* 35; S.L.A. 1925, s. 35 (1).

for sale. A similar procedure applies if a trustee of settled land is discharged without a new trustee being appointed. The second document, both for settled land and trusts for sale, is an appointment which may be either in writing or by deed.[38]

3. Registered land. A duly executed transfer form must vest the legal estate in the new registered proprietors and the names of the new Settled Land Act trustees must appear in the restriction.

---

[38] T.A. 1925, s. 35; S.L.A. 1925, s. 35.

CHAPTER 8

CO-OWNERSHIP

HITHERTO no consideration has been given to cases where two or more persons have been entitled to the simultaneous enjoyment of land. The two modern types of such ownership must be considered:

(1) Joint tenancy.
(2) Tenancy in common.

The terms "co-ownership," "concurrent interests" and "estates and interests in community" may each be used to include these forms of co-ownership. The old forms of co-ownership known as co-parcenary and tenancy by entireties need no longer be considered.

Part 1

JOINT TENANCY AND TENANCY IN COMMON

Sect. 1. Nature of the Tenancies

A. Joint Tenancy

"A gift of lands to two or more persons in joint tenancy is such a gift as imparts to them, with respect to all other persons than themselves, the properties of one single owner."[1] Although as between them-selves joint tenants have separate rights, as against everyone else they are in a position of a single owner. The intimate nature of joint tenancy is shown by the two principal features, the right of survivorship and the "four unities."

1. The right of survivorship. (a) *The right.* This is the distin-guishing feature of a joint tenancy. On the death of one joint tenant, his interest in the land passes to the other joint tenants by the *jus accrescendi* (right of survivorship), and this process continues until there is but one survivor, who then holds the land as sole owner.[2] This *jus accrescendi* takes precedence over any disposition made by a joint tenant's will, and the same principle applies if a joint tenant dies intestate; a joint tenancy cannot pass under a will or intestacy.[3] For this reason it has been said that each joint tenant holds nothing and yet holds the whole.[4] In other words, a joint tenant may become

---

[1] Williams R.P. 143.
[2] Litt. 280.
[3] Litt. 287.
[4] *Murray* v. *Hall* (1849) 7 C.B. 441 at 455n.

entitled to nothing or to all, according to whether or not he survives his fellows. However, if he acts in his lifetime he may convert his interest into a tenancy in common.[5]

(b) *Corporations.* The common law held that although a corporation could be a tenant in common, no joint tenancy could exist between a corporation and a natural person. However, Parliament provided in 1899 that a corporation should be able to acquire and hold any property in joint tenancy in the same manner as if it were an individual.[6] This provision became necessary as banks and other corporations were taking up the work of acting as trustees.

(c) *Trustees.* Trustees are always made joint tenants because of the convenience of the trust property passing automatically by the *jus accrescendi* to the surviving trustees when one trustee dies; if trustees were made tenants in common, a conveyance of the trust property to the surviving trustees by the personal representatives of the deceased trustee would be necessary. Although the *jus accrescendi* of a joint tenacy is often unsuitable for beneficial owners, because it introduces an element of chance, it is ideal for trustees.

2. The four unities must be present. The four unities of a joint tenancy are the unities of possession, interest, title and time.[7]

(a) *Unity of possession.* Each joint tenant is as much entitled to possession of any part of the land as the others.[8] No tenant can point to any part of the land as his own to the exclusion of the others; if he could, there would be separate ownership and not joint tenancy. In this respect, the position is similar to that of partners; no partner can point to any particular asset of the business as being his, for each is entitled to possession of the assets.

Unity of possession is common to all forms of co-ownership.

(b) *Unity of interest.* The interest of each joint tenant is the same in extent, nature and duration, for in theory of law they hold but one estate. This means[9]

    (i) that although in theory of law each tenant has the whole of the property, the rents and profits of the land are divided equally between the tenants;

    (ii) that there can be no joint tenancy between those with interests of a different nature, *e.g.* a freeholder and a tenant for years; and

---

[5] *Post*, p. 324.
[6] Bodies Corporate (Joint Tenancy) Act 1899.
[7] Their initial letters form the convenient mnemonic P.I.T.T.
[8] Litt. 288; *Bull* v. *Bull* [1955] 1 Q.B. 234.
[9] See Co. Litt. 188a; 2 Bl.Com. 181.

(iii) that there can be no joint tenancy between those whose interests are similar but of different duration. Thus before 1926, a tenant in fee simple and a tenant in tail both owned freeholds, but the differing durations of the estates prevented them from being held in joint tenancy.

(c) *Unity of title.* Each joint tenant must claim his title to the land under the same act or document.[10] This requirement is satisfied if all the tenants acquired their rights by the same conveyance or if they simultaneously took possession of land and acquired title to it by adverse possession.[11]

(d) *Unity of time.* The interest of each tenant must vest at the same time. This does not necessarily follow from the existence of unity of title. For example, if land was conveyed before 1926 "to A for life, remainder to the heirs of B and C," and B and C died at different times in A's lifetime, B's heir and C's heir took the fee simple remainder as tenants in common; the heirs could not take as joint tenants, for although there was unity of title, there was no unity of time.[12]

Two exceptions to the necessity for unity of time grew up: neither in a conveyance to uses nor in a gift by will was the rule applied. Thus if a bachelor conveyed land to the use of himself and any wife he might marry, when he married he held as a joint tenant with his wife. Again, if land was devised or conveyed to the use of A for life with remainder to the use of the children of B, each child of B born in A's lifetime acquired a vested interest at birth, yet the disparity of time did not prevent them from taking as joint tenants.[13]

B. Tenancy in Common

A tenancy in common differs greatly from a joint tenancy.

1. The tenants hold in undivided shares. Unlike joint tenants, tenants in common hold in undivided shares: each tenant in common has a distinct fixed share in property which has not yet been divided among the co-tenants.[14] There is no *jus accrescendi*; the share of each tenant is fixed once and for all and is not affected by the death of one of his companions. When a tenant in common dies, his interest passes under his will or intestacy, for his undivided share is his to dispose of as he wishes.[15]

---

[10] Co. Litt. 189a, 299b.
[11] *Post,* Chap. 15, p. 532.
[12] Co. Litt. 188a; 2 Bl.Com. 181. After 1925 the conveyance to uses or on trusts exemption would seem to apply: S.L.A. 1925, ss. 4, 13. Indeed, all future interests in freeholds are equitable, taking effect behind trusts.
[13] *Ruck* v. *Barwise* (1865) 2 Dr. & Sm. 510, *Doe* d. *Hallen* v. *Ironmonger* (1803) 3 East 533.
[14] *Fisher* v. *Wiggs* (1700) 12 Mod. 296 at p. 302.
[15] Challis R.P. 368.

2. Only the unity of possession is essential. Although the four unities of a joint tenancy may be present in a tenancy in common, the only unity which is essential is the unity of possession. In particular, it should be noted that the unity of interest may be absent and the tenants may hold unequal interests, so that one tenant in common may be entitled to a one-fifth share and the other to four-fifths, or one may be entitled for life and the other in fee simple.[16]

Since unity of possession means that each tenant is as much entitled to physical possession of every part of the property as every other tenant, one tenant cannot claim rent from another tenant happening to occupy the whole property on his own,[17] unless excluded by the occupying tenant.[18]

Sect. 2. Estates in which the Tenancies Can Exist

In general, before 1926 joint tenancies and tenancies in common could exist at law or in equity (*i.e.* as legal estates or as equitable interests), and in possession or in remainder, in any of the estates of freehold or in leaseholds.[19] Thus if land was given to A and B as joint tenants for their lives, they enjoyed it jointly for their joint life, and the survivor enjoyed the whole for the rest of his life.[20] If A and B had converted their joint tenancy into a tenancy in common, the survivor would have been entitled only to half for the rest of his life. Again, if X and Y were joint tenants for the life of X, if X survived he became sole tenant of the whole for the rest of his life, whereas if Y were the survivor he took nothing, for the estate which he acquired by survivorship was one which determined at the moment he received it.

After 1925, the position is substantially the same except that a tenancy in common can no longer exist at law; this is dealt with below.[21] Further, since life estates and entails can exist only in equity,[22] even a joint tenancy in these must also be equitable.

Sect. 3. Mode of Creating the Tenancies

The key to a proper understanding of joint tenancies and tenancies in common is always to consider the legal estate separately from the equitable interest.[23] Thus it may be found that at law A and B are joint tenants, while in equity they are tenants in common. The effect

---

[16] Co.Litt. 189a; Williams R.P. 148; 2 Bl.Com. 191.
[17] *Jones* v. *Jones* [1977] 1 W.L.R. 438.
[18] *Dennis* v. *McDonald* [1981] 1 W.L.R. 810. If one tenant leases the premises to a stranger he must account to the other tenants for their shares of the profits.
[19] Williams R.P. 143.
[20] *Moffat* v. *Burnie* (1853) 18 Beav. 211.
[21] *Post*, p. 305.
[22] *Ante*, p. 85.
[23] Despite *Re Selous* [1901] 1 Ch. 921, criticised in Williams V. & P. 501, 502.

of A's death on the legal joint tenancy is that B is solely entitled; in equity, on the other hand, A's share passes under his will or intestacy. In the result, B holds the legal estate on trust for himself as to his share, and for A's personal representatives as to A's share.

The mode of creating joint tenancies and tenancies in common must now be considered.

A. Before 1926.

I. AT LAW

At law, the presumption was in favour of a joint tenancy since this had feudal and conveyancing advantages.[24] The rule was thus that if land was conveyed to two or more persons a joint tenancy of the legal estate was created unless either—

(i) one of the unities was absent; or
(ii) words of severance were employed.

1. Absence of unities. The four unities have already been considered. If there was unity of possession but one or more of the other unities were missing, the parties took as tenants in common; if there was no unity of possession, the parties took as separate owners.

2. Words of severance. Any words in the grant showing that the tenants were each to take a distinct share in the property amounted to words of severance and thus created a tenancy in common. Words which have been held to have this effect include—

"share and share alike"
"to be divided amongst"
"equally"
"between."

Further, words showing that the tenants were to take unequal interests (such as "two-thirds to A and one-third to B") sufficed to create a tenancy in common; and even if there were no clear words of severance, the gift taken as a whole might show that a tenancy in common was intended.[25] Thus there would be a tenancy in common, for example, if there was a settlement on children containing provisions for advancing capital to a child since if an advance was made to one child, it would have to be debited against that child's share and this could not be done unless the child was a tenant in common and so had a distinct share.[26]

---

[24] *Morley* v. *Bird* (1798) 3 Ves. 628.
[25] See, *e.g. Surtees* v. *Surtees* (1871) L.R. 12 Eq. 400.
[26] See *L'Estrange* v. *L'Estrange* [1902] 1 I.R. 467 at pp. 468, 469; *Re Dunn* [1916] 1 Ch. 97.

Despite the feudal and conveyancing advantages of a joint tenancy, equity did not favour it. Equity looked to the beneficial interests of the co-tenants, and preferred the certainty and equality of a tenancy in common to the element of chance which the *jus accrescendi* of a joint tenancy introduced. This preference for a tenancy in common was manifested by equity holding that a tenancy in common would exist in equity not only in those cases where it existed at law, but also in certain other cases where an intention to create a tenancy in common could be discerned. In short, there was a tenancy in common in equity in the following five cases:

1. Tenancy in common at law. There was a tenancy in common in equity whenever there was a tenancy in common at law.[27]

2. Purchase-money provided in unequal shares. If two or more persons together purchased property and provided the money in unequal shares, the purchasers were presumed to take as tenants in common in shares proportionate to the sums advanced[28]; thus if A found one-third and B two-thirds of the price, they were presumed tenants in common as to one-third and two-thirds respectively. If, on the other hand, the purchasers provided the money in equal shares, they were presumed joint tenants. These presumptions could be rebutted by evidence of circumstances showing that those providing the purchase-money equally intended to take as tenants in common or vice versa.

3. Loan on mortgage. Where two or more persons advanced money on mortgage, whether in equal or unequal shares, equity presumed a tenancy in common in the land between the mortgagees. "If two people join in lending money upon a mortgage, equity says, it could not be the intention, that the interest in that should survive. Though they take a joint security, each means to lend his own and take back his own."[29] "It is obvious, however, that this proposition cannot be put higher than a presumption capable of being rebutted."[30] Yet it should be noted that the "joint account clause" which is normally inserted in mortgages to make the mortgagees appear as joint tenants to the outside world and so simplify the mechanism of discharging the mortgage[31] does not affect this presumption of a tenancy in common in the relationship of the mortgagees *inter se*.[32]

---

[27] *Ante*, p. 303.
[28] *Lake* v. *Gibson* (1729) 1 Eq.Ca.Abr. 290 at p. 291. Further see *post* p. 310.
[29] *Morley* v. *Bird* (1798) 3 Ves. 628 at p. 631, *per* Arden M.R.
[30] *Steeds* v. *Steeds* (1889) 22 Q.B.D. 537 at p. 541, *per* Wills J.
[31] *Post*, p. 501.
[32] *Re Jackson* (1887) 34 Ch.D. 732.

4. Partnership assets. Where partners acquired land as part of their partnership assets, they were presumed to hold it as tenants in common.[33] "*Jus accrescendi inter mercatores locum non habet*": the right of survivorship has no place between merchants. The rule extended to any joint undertaking with a view to a profit, even if there was no formal partnership between the parties; the legal estate might be held on a joint tenancy, but in equity the partners were presumed to be entitled in undivided shares, so that the surviving partners (or whoever held the legal estate) would be compelled to hold the legal estate on trust for those entitled to the property of a deceased partner as far as his share was concerned.[34]

5. Executory trusts. These are trusts where the details have not been set out but a further document is to be drawn up to give effect to the settlor's intention; thus "marriage articles," which are the preliminary agreement for a marriage settlement, create executory trusts and the marriage settlement itself creates executed trusts. In such cases there was a tenancy in common where any intention to create such a tenancy could be found or presumed. "Joint tenancy as a provision for the children of a marriage, is an inconvenient mode of settlement,"[35] for no child could rely upon having a distinct share for his family until he had severed his joint tenancy (*i.e.* converted it into a tenancy in common) nor could any advance to a child be set against his share until this had been done.[36] Accordingly the court would readily infer that a provision in marriage articles or other executory trusts for the benefit of a class of children was intended to be a provision for them as tenants in common, despite the absence of words of severance.[37]

B. After 1925

I. AT LAW

In order to benefit purchasers,[38] substantial changes in the law have been made by the Law of Property Act 1925.

1. The legal estate must be held by joint tenants. Even if there are clear words of severance, after 1925 the legal estate cannot be held on a tenancy in common.[39] As a corollary the legal joint tenancy cannot be severed and converted into a legal tenancy in common. As is explained below, a tenancy in common can still exist in equity, but at law the only form of co-ownership possible after 1925 is a joint

---

[33] *Lake* v. *Craddock* (1732) 3 P.Wms. 158.
[34] See *Re Fuller's Contract* [1933] Ch. 652.
[35] *Taggart* v. *Taggart* (1803) 1 Sch. & Lef. 84 at p. 88.
[36] *Ante*, p. 303.
[37] See *Mayn* v. *Mayn* (1867) L.R. 5 Eq. 150.
[38] *Post*, p. 310, *ante*, p. 7.
[39] L.P.A. 1925, ss. 1 (6), 34 (1), 36 (2); S.L.A. 1925, s. 36 (4).

tenancy. Thus a conveyance today "to A, B and C in fee simple as tenants in common" (all being of full age) will vest the legal estate in A, B and C as joint tenants, although in equity they will be tenants in common.[40] If A had been a minor, his rights in equity would not have been affected, but no legal estate would have vested in him.[41] If A, B and C had all been minors, the legal estate would have remained in the grantor, though it is not clear whether the grantor would be deemed to have made an agreement for value to execute a settlement in their favour and in the meantime to hold the land in trust for them, or whether the transaction would be void.[42]

2. The legal estate is held upon trust for sale.[43] (a) *The statutory trusts*. The purpose of the 1925 legislation was to ensure that after 1925, subject to the special provisions relating to settled land,[44] land is held upon the "statutory trusts" whenever it is conveyed to or held by two or more persons beneficially, whether as tenants in common[45] or joint tenants, *i.e.* wherever there is beneficial co-ownership.[46] The "statutory trusts" may be summarised thus:

> upon trust to sell the land, and stand possessed of the net proceeds of sale and of the net rents and profits until sale upon such trusts and subject to such powers and provisions as may be requisite for giving effect to the rights of those interested in the land,[47] whether beneficially or as trustees.[48]

(b) *Beneficial joint tenancy.* "Where a legal estate (not being settled land) is *beneficially* limited to or held in trust for any persons as joint tenants the same shall be held on trust for sale"[49] A trust for sale thus arises where a legal estate is conveyed to B and C jointly or to D and E upon trust for F and G jointly but not where a legal estate is conveyed to M and N upon trust for O.

(c) *Beneficial tenancy in common.* "Where land is expressed to be conveyed to any persons in undivided shares and those persons are of full age, the conveyance shall operate as if the land had been expressed to be conveyed to the grantees, or if there are more than four grantees, to the four first named in the conveyance as joint tenants upon the statutory trusts and so as to give effect to the rights of the persons who would have been entitled to the shares had the conveyance operated to create those shares."[50]

---

[40] *Ibid.* s. 34 (2).
[41] *Ibid.* s. 19 (2).
[42] See M. & W., p. 408.
[43] See M. & W., pp. 410–417.
[44] *Post*, p. 321.
[45] L.P.A. 1925, s. 34 (2), 1st Sched., Pt. IV.
[46] *Ibid.* s. 36 (1).
[47] *Ibid.* s. 35.
[48] *Re Hayward* [1928] Ch. 367.
[49] L.P.A. 1925, s. 36 (1).
[50] *Ibid.* s. 34 (2).

If the land has not been expressly conveyed to persons in undivided shares (*e.g.* because the conveyance has been to A alone, where A and B have contributed to the purchase money in unequal shares, or because a sole owner, X, declares that he holds on trust for Y and himself equally, or because the conveyance on its face has been to P and Q jointly without setting out their beneficial interests,[51] though equity requires P and Q to take as beneficial tenants in common since they are partners or contributed to the purchase moneys in unequal shares[52]) then problems arise. Section 34 (1) of the Law of Property Act states "An undivided share in land shall not be capable of being created except as provided by the Settled Land Act or as hereinafter mentioned" whilst section 36 (4) of the Settled Land Act states, "An undivided share in land shall not be capable of being created except under a trust instrument[53] or under the Law of Property Act and shall *then* only take effect behind a trust for sale." It follows that if the cases exemplified above are not covered by the Settled Land Act or the Law of Property Act then the intended undivided shares will fail and result back to the grantor unless the intended undivided share owner can take advantage of contractual rights or of the equitable principle that statute may not be used as an instrument of fraud.

However Denning L.J., as he then was, in *Bull* v. *Bull*[54] relied on section 36 (4) (*supra*) in stating, "All tenancies in common now are equitable only and they take effect behind a trust for sale," conveniently ignoring the significance of the word "then," when nothing in the Settled Land Act or the Law of Property Act covered the case, that he was concerned with, of a conveyance in the name of the son alone, where the son and his mother had contributed to the purchase price in unequal shares.

Since then no-one has sought to challenge the view that what would have been tenancies in common before 1926 now take effect as undivided shares behind a trust for sale.[55] This is very convenient from a conveyancing point of view but there is obviously some scope for someone not covered by the wording of section 34 (2) of the Law of Property Act to submit that he has an interest under a bare trust and not a trust for sale, so that he has an interest in the land and not in the proceeds of sale,[56] and so that the powers of management and of partitioning of trustees for sale are not available and so that the Court has no powers under section 30 of the Law of Property Act.

---

[51] If an express equitable joint tenancy existed then this would be conclusive as to the position and L.P.A., s. 36 (1) would create a trust for sale.

[52] In *Re Buchanan-Wollaston's Conveyance* [1939] Ch. 738 the Court of Appeal applied L.P.A., s. 36 (1) but this ignores the word "beneficially" in s. 36 (1).

[53] This means a S.L.A. trust instrument: S.L.A. 1925, s. 117 (1) (xxxi).

[54] [1955] 1 Q.B. 234.

[55] *e.g. Cook* v. *Cook* [1962] P. 235; *Williams & Glyn's Bank* v. *Boland* [1981] A.C. 487 where the trust for sale conversion problem could have been avoided by the wife had she had an interest in land under a bare trust.

[56] See *post*, pp. 317–321.

(d) *Devise for persons in undivided shares.* A gift by will to or in trust for persons in undivided shares[57] operates as a gift to the Settled Land Act trustees of the will, if any, but otherwise to the testator's personal representatives upon the statutory trusts. This is really to cope with circumstances where the beneficiaries are minors. If, however, the co-owners are all adults and between them absolutely entitled to the property then they can require the legal estate to be vested in themselves as joint tenants upon trust for sale for themselves as tenants in common.[58]

(e) *Overreaching.* The trusts for sale created by the statutory trusts take effect in the same way as the trusts for sale considered in the preceeding chapter.[59] In particular, the land must be sold unless either all trustees concur in postponing sale (as they often do)[60] or a sale would defeat the object of the trust or be a breach of the contractual obligations of the trustee who seeks to sell.[61] Further, the overreaching provisions apply. Consequently a purchaser is concerned not with the beneficial interests in the land but only with the legal estate vested in the trustees for sale. Provided he pays his purchase-money to trustees for sale who are either two or more in number or a trust corporation or a sole personal representative, he takes free from the rights of the beneficiaries. To a purchaser who does this, it is immaterial whether in equity there are three or thirty people entitled, or whether they are joint tenants or tenants in common. In practice, on a conveyance to joint tenants or tenants in common, it is usual for the conveyance to be made on an express trust for sale.

(f) *Union in sole tenant.* If the whole legal estate and equitable interest become vested in one person, the trust for sale is at an end, as where A and B were joint tenants at law and in equity, and A dies.[62] Further, by the Schedule to the Law of Property (Amendment) Act 1926, it was provided that nothing in the Law of Property Act 1925 was to affect the right of a survivor of joint tenants who is solely and beneficially interested to deal with his legal estate as if it were not held on trust for sale. Thus B can make title by himself despite the fact that a sole trustee for sale is unable to give a proper receipt for purchase-money. There was formerly a practical difficulty of satisfying a purchaser in such circumstances that B was in truth solely entitled in equity. An act of severance might have occurred in A's

[57] L.P.A., s. 34 (3); *Re House* [1929] 2 Ch. 166.
[58] *Saunders* v. *Vautier* (1841) Cr. & Ph. 240; L.P.A., s. 3 (1) (*b*) (ii).
[59] *Ante*, pp. 277 *et seq.*
[60] *Ante*, p. 280.
[61] *Re Buchanan-Wollaston's Conveyancer* [1939] Ch. 738; *Jones* v. *Challenger* [1961] 1 Q.B. 176. See *post*, p. 316.
[62] *Re Cook* [1948] Ch 212. B's interest in personalty is then reconverted into an interest in land.

lifetime[63] causing A and B to become tenants in common so that B held the legal estate on trust for sale so that a purchaser would need to pay the purchase-moneys to two trustees. This situation has been remedied by the Law of Property (Joint Tenants) Act 1964, which is retrospective to January 1, 1926.[64] It provides that in favour of a purchaser of a legal estate, a survivor of one or more joint tenants is "deemed to be solely and beneficially interested if he conveys as beneficial owner[65] or the conveyance includes a statement that he is so interested."[66] Where the survivor has himself died, his personal representatives have similar powers. The Act does not apply if before the conveyance by the survivor, a memorandum recording the severance is indorsed on or annexed to the conveyance which vested the land in the joint tenants.[67] Nor does it apply where a bankruptcy petition or receiving order has been registered,[68] or where the title to the land is registered.[69]

3. The legal estate cannot be vested in more than four persons. The position here is clear in the case of tenancies in common and rather less clear in the case of joint tenancies; each will be dealt with separately.[70]

(a) *Tenancies in common.* If land is conveyed to trustees for sale on trust for tenants in common, the general prohibition against the number of trustees of land exceeding four applies.[71] If the conveyance is expressed to be made to the tenants in common themselves, and they are of full age, statute provides for it to operate as a conveyance "to the grantees, or, if there are more than four grantees, to the first four named in the conveyance, as joint tenants upon the statutory trusts."[72] Further, a gift of land by will to, or in trust for, tenants in common operates as a gift to the Settled Land Act trustees of the will, or, if none, to the testator's personal representatives, upon the statutory trusts[73]; and the number of Settled Land Act trustees or personal representatives cannot exceed four.

---

[63] See *post*, p. 325.
[64] s.2.
[65] See *ante*, p. 152.
[66] s.1.
[67] *Ibid.*
[68] See *ante*, p. 97.
[69] s. 3. It was assumed that interests under trusts for sale could only be minor interests so that a purchaser would take free of any unprotected minor interest. However, interests under trusts for sale can be overriding interests: *Williams & Glyn's Bank* v. *Boland* [1981] A.C. 487.
[70] Elaborate transitional provisions were enacted with the object of ensuring that the legal estate should vest in suitable persons on January 1, 1926. For these, see M. & W., pp. 419–421.
[71] Trustee Act 1925, s. 34.
[72] L.P.A. 1925, s. 34 (2); for infants, see *ante*, p. 182.
[73] L.P.A. 1925, s. 34 (3).

(b) *Joint tenancies.* There are no provisions dealing expressly with the number of persons in whom the legal estate can be vested when two or more persons are beneficially entitled as joint tenants. But the trust for sale arising in such cases involves the general provision that in a trust for sale of land made or coming into operation after 1925, the number of trustees shall not exceed four,[74] and "where more than four persons are named as such trustees, the first four named (who are able and willing to act) shall alone be the trustees."[75] In the case of a devise to joint tenants, the general prohibition against more than four trustees of land coupled with the fact that there is a trust for sale prevents the personal representatives from vesting the legal estate in more than four persons.

4. Benefit to purchaser. It will be noticed that the three main changes introduced by the 1925 legislation all assist the purchaser. The prohibition of a legal tenancy in common and the limitation of the number of tenants of the legal estate to four means that purchasers are no longer exposed to the burden of having to investigate the titles of each of, say, 30 legal tenants in common, some of whom might own a sixty-eighth share, and who might be so scattered about the world that it took six months to get all their signatures to the conveyance.[76] Further, the overreaching effect of a trust for sale enables a purchaser to ignore the equitable rights of the beneficiaries.

II. IN EQUITY

On the position in equity after 1925, there is little to be added to the foregoing. Strictly there can be no "tenancy" in common after 1925 because those interested hold no estate or interest in the land but are entitled merely as beneficiaries under a trust for sale; the 1925 legislation throughout refers not to "tenancies in common" but to "undivided shares." In general, however, the rights of these beneficiaries correspond to the rights of tenants in common before 1926, and the same applies to those entitled in equity as joint tenants.

Sect. 4. The Position of Beneficiaries

A. Qualification as Beneficiary

1. Resulting trusts. A person may qualify as a beneficiary though there is no express trust for sale in his favour. If V conveys land to P where P and A have, as purchasers, provided the purchase-money then P will hold the land for P and A on a resulting trust

---

[74] T.A. 1925, s. 34.
[75] T.A. 1925, s. 34 (2).
[76] See A. H. Cosway (1929) 15 Conv. (o.s.) 83.

proportionate to their contributions to the purchase moneys,[77] and statute treats this as a trust for sale.[78]

If, however, A provided the money only by way of loan[79] or as a gift[80] then P is sole beneficial landowner. If P is the wife or child of A there is a rebuttable "presumption of advancement" which presumes a gift in the absence of any evidence to the contrary.[81]

Where A claims to have provided part of the purchase-money *qua* purchaser such provision may take various direct or indirect forms. If the cost of a house with legal fees and stamp duty is £32,000 and A paid £4,000 of such costs then A will have an eighth share, whether P paid £28,000 out of his own moneys or by borrowing the £28,000 from a Building Society and taking on sole responsibility for the paying of the mortgage. If, however, P and A had an understanding that they would each pay half the mortgage instalments, then A would be treated as having provided £18,000 of the purchase-moneys, *i.e.* a nine-sixteenths share. If, instead, P and A had an understanding that, as co-habitees, A's earnings would be used for food, clothes, holidays etc. whilst P's earnings would be used to pay the mortgage instalments and that A's contributions, whatever their actual amount, should be treated as provision of half the purchase price then A would be treated as having a half share.[82]

Unless at the outset there was an understanding that A's share was to depend upon exactly how much A contributed to paying off the mortgage over the period of the mortgage, a problem arises in respect of contributions made by A subsequent to the purchase, *e.g.* if upon receiving a £12,000 legacy A uses it in paying off part of the mortgage debt or in paying for considerable extensions built on to the house. Is A to be treated as making a gift of £12,000 to P to enable P to pay off P's debt or as voluntarily improving P's share in the house since if "A expends money on the property of B prima facie he has no claim on such property"?[83]

2. Formalities. Where A is claiming an equitable interest or an enlarged equitable interest in land there is the problem that the creation of a trust respecting land must be provable by writing[84] and

---

[77] *Cowcher* v. *Cowcher* [1972] 1 W.L.R. 425, *Re Rogers' Question* [1948] 1 All E.R. 328.
[78] *Bull* v. *Bull* [1955] 1 Q.B. 234 *ante*, p. 307.
[79] "Loan" and "Resulting Trust" are mutually exclusive concepts: *Re Sharpe* [1980] 1 All E.R. 198 at p. 201, *Hussey* v. *Palmer* [1972] 3 All E.R. 744 at p. 749, Underhill, pp. 272–273.
[80] *Standing* v. *Bowring* (1885) 31 Ch.D. 282.
[81] *Pettitt* v. *Pettitt* [1970] A.C. 777 at pp. 793, 811, 813 and 824, Underhill, pp. 276 *et seq.*
[82] *Cowcher* v. *Cowcher* [1972] 1 W.L.R. 425.
[83] *Per* Lord Upjohn in *Pettitt* v. *Pettitt* [1970] A.C. 777 at p. 818. *Hargrave* v. *Newton* [1971] 1 W.L.R. 1611.
[84] L.P.A. 1925, s. 53 (1) (*b*).

that an equitable interest can be disposed of *only* in writing.[85] However, this does not "affect the creation of resulting or constructive trusts."[86]

3. Constructive trusts. A resulting trust is really based on the express or implied intent of the parties that the legal owner's co-purchaser is to obtain a beneficial interest proportionate to the co-purchaser's contribution to the purchase price. A constructive trust arises where there is an express or implied agreement that the legal owner's "partner" is to have a distinct interest in the land and the "partner" has acted to his detriment on the faith of such agreement so that it would be unconscionable for the legal owner to deny the existence of the "partner's" interest.[87]

Thus if H and W agree that a house, which H is purchasing, is to be put in their joint names, with W having a half share, but H deceives W and has the house put in his name alone the Court is ready to assume that W acted to her detriment so that H will become constructive trustee to give effect to W's half share.[88] Similarly, if L and M agree that although a dilapidated house which L is purchasing is to be put in his name alone, M is to have an interest in the house of such fraction as from time to time is reasonable in the light of M's efforts in renovating the house, L will become constructive trustee to give effect to such share of M as is reasonable.[89] The existence of the constructive trust makes it immaterial that the declaration of trust is not evidenced in writing.

If H purchased a house on mortgage for £30,000 and, a few years later, W used a £10,000 legacy to enable H to pay off part of the mortgage debt W may claim that this was not a gift or a loan but that she thereby acquired a one-third share in the house. This is a disposition of H's equitable interest and thus must actually be carried out by some written instrument or be void unless a constructive trust arises. If H had led W to believe that she would acquire a one-third share in the house by utilising her £10,000 in the above fashion then, it seems, H will become constructive trustee of the house to give effect to such one-third share.[90]

If W had, instead, spent the £10,000 on improvements to the house, then, again, unless W could prove some common intention that this was to give her an equitable interest in the house so as to be able to rely on a constructive trust,[91] the Court would treat W as

---

[85] *Ibid.* s. 53 (1) (*c*).
[86] *Ibid.* s. 53 (2).
[87] See Underhill, pp. 276 *et seq.*
[88] *Re Densham* [1975] 1 W.L.R. 1519; *cf. Pascoe* v. *Turner* [1979] 1 W.L.R. 431.
[89] *Eves* v. *Eves* [1975] 1 W.L.R. 1338. This perhaps takes the constructive trust beyond its proper limits: the doctrine of estoppel seems more suitable.
[90] *Re Densham* [1975] 1 W.L.R. 1519 where Goff J. convincingly disagreed with *Cowcher* v. *Cowcher* [1972] 1 W.L.R. 425 on this point.
[91] *Pettitt* v. *Pettitt* [1970] A.C. 777; *Gissing* v. *Gissing* [1971] A.C. 886.

having made a gift or a loan—until the Matrimonial Proceedings and Property Act 1970.

4. Section 37 of the Matrimonial Proceedings and Property Act 1970. This declares that *substantial* contributions in money or money's worth by a husband or wife to the improvement of real or personal property belonging beneficially to either or both of them, are to entitle the contributor to such a share or enlarged share as was agreed or, in default, "as may seem in all the circumstances just."[92]

5. Conclusiveness of declared equitable shares. If the trust instrument declares an equitable joint tenancy or the quantum of the interest which each tenant in common is to have then this is conclusive in the absence of fraud or mistake.[93] If a contradictory expression is used, *e.g.* "to hold as beneficial joint tenants in common in equal shares" then, in the absence of any guidance elsewhere in the instrument, the earlier words will prevail over the later words.[94]

6. Spouses. To do justice between spouses the Courts (especially Lord Denning's Division of the Court of Appeal[95]) have stretched the doctrine of resulting and constructive trusts to their limits (perhaps even beyond) though this is now no longer necessary wherever divorce proceedings are contemplated. Under the Matrimonial Causes Act 1973, sections 24 and 25, it is no longer necessary to ascertain the strict property rights of the parties since the Court's function is to redistribute whatever property either or both owns between the parties, taking various factors into account, *e.g.* the contributions made to the welfare of the family by looking after the home or caring for the family, this being irrelevant where strict property rights are concerned.[96]

B. Occupation by Beneficiary

1. Distribution and occupation trusts. Originally, trusts for sale had to be created expressly when it was intended that the land should be held for the purposes of sale in the near or distant future and that the rents and profits till sale, and then the proceeds of sale, should be distributed between the beneficiaries. The beneficiaries often had successive interests but under a will or a conveyance land (*e.g.* a block of flats and shops) might be held by T and T_2 on trust for sale

---

[92] See *Griffiths* v. *Griffiths* [1974] 1 All E.R. 932; *Re Nicholson* [1974] 1 W.L.R. 476; *Samuels' Trustees* v. *Samuels* (1975) 223 E.G. 149.
[93] *Leake* v. *Bruzzi* [1974] 1 W.L.R. 1528 *Pink* v. *Lawrence* (1977) 36 P. & C.R. 101.
[94] *Joyce* v. *Barker (Bros.) Ltd.* (1980) 40 P. & C.R. 512.
[95] *e.g. Hazell* v. *Hazell* [1972] 1 W.L.R. 301; *Hargrave* v. *Newton* [1971] 1 W.L.R. 1611 ignoring the true impact of *Gissing* v. *Gissing* [1971] A.C. 886. For unmarried couples: *Bernard* v. *Josephs, The Times,* April 1, 1982.
[96] *Kowalczuk* v. *Kowalczuk* [1973] 1 W.L.R. 930; *Button* v. *Button* [1968] 1 W.L.R. 457.

for A, B, C and D as equitable tenants in common with no intent that A, B, C and D should occupy the land. One might term these trusts "distribution trusts" since their purpose is the distribution of the trust capital and income amongst the beneficiaries.

After 1925 with the imposition of a statutory trust for sale—if an express trust for sale has not been created—in all cases of co-ownership there has arisen a vast number of cases where land is held on an express or statutory trust for sale for occupation by the beneficial co-owners. These trusts might be termed "occupation trusts," *e.g.* where A and B purchase, in A's name or both their names, a house for their occupation or where under a will or conveyance a house is given to C and D for their occupation.

2. Distribution trusts. The trust for sale concept has to cope with distribution trusts and occupation trusts. It copes easily with distribution trusts since it developed around such trusts where it is obviously appropriate that the interests of the beneficiaries under the doctrine of conversion[97] are interests in the proceeds of sale and the rents and profits until sale and not interests in land. It is appropriate that the trustees with the legal title manage the land and lease it out. The only right of the beneficiaries who are currently entitled "in possession" (such as A and B where trustees hold on trust for sale for A and B equally for their joint lives, remainder to the survivor for life, remainder to C absolutely) is to the rents and profits. However, as a matter of discretion the trustees may permit[98] those beneficiaries themselves to occupy the land in lieu of receiving rents and profits. Section 29 of the Law of Property Act 1925 now expressly allows the trustees to delegate revocably in writing to the person(s) currently beneficially entitled in possession their powers of management and leasing. If the trustees refuse to delegate these powers then the Court may compel them to do so if it thinks fit,[99] *e.g.* where it considers the trustees are not acting bona fide in the general interest of the trust.

3. Occupation trusts. With occupation trusts problems have arisen where A and B have purchased a house in A's name for their occupation[1] and when A purports in his discretion no longer to

---

[97] See pp. 282, 317.
[98] *Re Bagot's S.T.* [1894] 1 Ch. 177; *Re Earl of Stamford and Warrington* [1925] Ch. 162; (1955) 19 Conv. 146 (F.R. Crane).
[99] It will be significant if the beneficiaries' wishes are to be consulted under the express terms of the trust or because the trust is imposed by statute: see L.P.A., s. 26 (3). If the beneficiaries are co-owners they will need to be unanimous in exercising the delegated powers.
[1] A statutory trust for sale will arise here. Similar problems can arise in the case of express trusts for sale *e.g.* if F and A purchase as express trustees for sale for F and A equally for occupation by A and his wife, B, who is F's daughter and F dies, having left his share to B; or if a house is left by will to M and A as express trustees for sale for M, A and B, a minor, to live there, and B, when adult, wishes to remain living there but M and A do not.

permit B to occupy the land. In *Bull* v. *Bull*[2] the Court of Appeal held that B was concurrently *entitled* with A to occupy the land so that A had no right to evict B. Thus B had a right to occupy the land until sale of the land. However, no sale could take place until a second trustee was appointed by A. Moreover, no sale could, in practice, take place without B's consent since a purchaser would require vacant possession. Under section 30 of the Law of Property Act B's consent was capable of being dispensed with if the Court considered it proper that a sale should take place.[3] This approach ignores the logical implications of the trust for sale[4] but has the sensible effect of treating equitable tenants in common in the same way as legal tenants in common in land were treated before 1926 when legal tenants in common owned property for their own occupation.

Bull v. *Bull* was distinguished by the Court of Appeal in *Barclay* v. *Barclay*[5] a case involving a distribution trust, a testator having left his bungalow on trust for sale for five members of his family so that the proceeds might be distributed between them. A son, who happened to be living in the bungalow on the testator's death, claimed as equitable tenant in common under a trust for sale to be entitled to occupy the bungalow and to prevent any sale. It was held that, whilst in *Bull* v. *Bull* "the prime object of the trust was that the parties should occupy the house together," here "the prime object of the trust was that the bungalow should be sold"[6] and the proceeds distributed, so that the son had no interest in the land but only in the proceeds of sale. There was thus no question of the son having any right to occupy the land nor of his consent being requisite to any sale.

C. Sale and the Law of Property Act, Section 30

1. Need for two trustees or a trust corporation. If there is only one trustee then any beneficiary can obtain an injunction to restrain sale until another trustee has been appointed.[7] However, the sole trustee can easily appoint[8] a crony to act as co-trustee to join in the conveyance and give a good receipt for the purchase-money. The rights of the beneficiaries are then purely in the proceeds of sale so that if they remain in occupation of the sold land the purchaser can evict them as trespassers. A purchaser, however, is not anxious to proceed where such problems with beneficiaries are likely.

---

[2] [1955] 1 Q.B. 234 endorsed by the House of Lords in *Williams & Glyn's Bank* v. *Boland* [1981] A.C. 487.
[3] See *post* p. 316.
[4] See *Re Landi* [1939] Ch. 828 at pp. 835, 836.
[5] [1970] 2 Q.B. 677. In fact, since the trust for sale had not arisen, the legal estate being still vested in the personal representatives, the personal representatives as such had a right to vacant possession of the bungalow: *Williams* v. *Holland* [1965] 1 W.L.R. 739.
[6] *Ibid.* at pp. 684, 685.
[7] *Waller* v. *Waller* [1967] 1 W.L.R. 451.
[8] Trustee Act 1925, s. 36.

2. Duty of consultation. Where a trust for sale is not expressly created but is imposed by statute then the "trustees for sale shall so far as practicable consult the persons of full age for the time being beneficially entitled in possession in the rents and profits of the land until sale, and shall, *so far as consistent with the general interests of the trust*, give effect to the wishes of such persons, or in the case of dispute, of the majority (according to the value of their combined interests) of such persons."[9] A purchaser, however, is under no duty to see that these weak statutory provisions have been complied with.[10]

3. Requisite consents must be obtained. If the trust instrument expressly requires that no sale shall be made except with the consent of certain persons or impliedly so requires[11] (*e.g.* so that effect can be given to a direction that a beneficiary may occupy the property during his life) then such persons can restrain the trustees from selling without their consent. If more than two consents are required a bona fide purchaser is protected if two consents are obtained: moreover, he need not concern himself with the consents of any person under a disability.[12]

In the case of "occupation" trusts[13] an occupying beneficiary has, in effect, an implied right of consent since, in practice, it will not prove possible to find a purchaser if the beneficiary tells prospective purchasers that he will not let them have vacant possession.[14]

4. Dispensing with consents and section 30. "If the trustees for sale refuse to sell or to exercise any of their powers, or any requisite consent cannot be obtained, any person interested[15] may apply to the Court for a vesting or other order for giving effect to the proposed transaction or for an order directing the trustees for sale to give effect thereto and the Court may make such order as it thinks fit."[16]

Where there is a trust for sale there is a duty to sell, which must be discharged, unless the trustees unanimously exercise their power to postpone sale[17] or unless to enforce the letter of the trust for sale would defeat the purpose of the trust.[18] Thus, where persons become co-owners for a particular purpose (*e.g.* joint occupation of a house)

---

[9] L.P.A. 1925, s. 26 (3). Such persons' wishes must also be consulted if expressly required by the trust instrument.
[10] *Ibid.*
[11] *Re Herklot's W.T.* [1964] 1 W.L.R. 583.
[12] L.P.A. 1925, s. 26 (1), (2).
[13] As defined *ante* p. 314.
[14] *Bull* v. *Bull* [1955] 1 Q.B. 234.
[15] A receiver of an undivided half-share by way of equitable execution can take advantage of s. 30 if authorised by the court to bring the proceedings in the debtor's name: *Levermore* v. *Levermore* [1980] 1 All E.R. 1.
[16] L.P.A. 1925, s. 30. A party may be allowed to buy out the other.
[17] *Re Mayo* [1943] Ch. 302.
[18] *Jones* v. *Challenger* [1961] 1 Q.B. 176.

and that purpose still subsists no sale will be ordered.[19] If the purpose
no longer subsists (*e.g.* because of a breakdown of a marriage) then
sale will be ordered[20] with ancillary directions for enabling an
unimpeded sale to go ahead, *e.g.* an order that a disgruntled
beneficiary vacate the premises to enable prospective purchasers to
obtain an unprejudiced view of the premises.

Where a *de iure* or *de facto* matrimonial home remains occupied by
one "spouse" with the children conflicting views have emerged in the
Courts of Appeal. The "Chancery" attitude favours sale and
emphasises the fact that the beneficial co-owners are the spouses, and
not the children as well, so that the interests of the children are only
of minor incidental significance in resolving the dispute between the
spouses.[21] The "Family" attitude favours retention of the property
and emphasises the fact that the house was purchased as a home in
which the family was to be brought up.[22] In the case of *de iure*
spouses it is now clear that disputes as to property should, wherever
possible, be dealt with under the Matrimonial Causes Act 1973 and
not under section 30.[23]

5. Sale at behest of trustees in bankruptcy. A trustee in bankruptcy
steps into the shoes of the insolvent debtor and is bound by statute[24]
to realise the debtor's assets which may include an undivided share in
a house owned by the debtor and his spouse. Where the trustee in
bankruptcy makes a section 30 application the Court has a
discretion[25] whether to order a sale or not but it will usually order
sale, preferring the creditors' interest to the family interest,[26] though
in one case[27] sale was postponed for five years. It seems likely that
sale will less readily be ordered if the application be made by a
mortgagee (or purchaser) of an undivided share who had notice of
the mortgagor's spouse's interest.[28]

D. The Doctrine of Conversion

1. Rationale. If realty is sold it is actually converted into money: if
money is used to purchase realty it is actually converted into realty. If
there is a binding obligation to convert realty into personalty or vice
versa then a notional conversion takes place since "equity looks on
that as done which ought to be done" in order that there may be a

[19] *Bedson* v. *Bedson* [1965] 2 Q.B. 666; *Re Buchanan-Wollaston's Conveyance* [1939] Ch. 738.
[20] *Rawlings* v. *Rawlings* [1964] P. 398; *Bernard* v. *Josephs. The Times*, April 1, 1982.
[21] *Burke* v. *Burke* [1974] 1 W.L.R. 1063; *Re Holliday* [1980] 3 All E.R. 385.
[22] *Williams* v. *Williams* [1976] Ch. 278; *Re Evers' Trust* [1980] 1 W.L.R. 1327.
[23] *Williams* v. *Williams* (*supra*); *Fielding* v. *Fielding* [1978] 1 All E.R. 267.
[24] Bankruptcy Act 1914, ss. 48 *et seq.*
[25] *Re Turner* [1974] 1 W.L.R. 1556; *Re Holliday* [1980] 3 All E.R. 385.
[26] *Ibid. Re Bailey* [1977] 1 W.L.R. 278; *Re Densham* [1975] 1 W.L.R. 1519; *Bird* v. *Syme-Thomson* [1979] 1 W.L.R. 440; *Re Lowrie* [1981] 3 All E.R. 353.
[27] *Re Holliday* [1980] 3 All E.R. 385.
[28] Only a trustee in bankruptcy is under a statutory duty to realise the undivided share.

proper devolution of beneficial interests on death.[29] Before 1926 on intestacy realty passed solely to the heir whilst personalty was divided between the statutory next of kin, and a testator quite commonly provided for realty to devolve differently from personalty. The rights of those respectively entitled to realty and personalty clearly could not be allowed to depend upon the precise moment at which the duty to convert was carried out, especially where a delay in selling might be a breach of trust.[30] Thus realty held on trust for sale is treated as personalty: the land is treated as if it were proceeds of sale of the land.

2. Co-ownership after 1925. The Law of Property Act 1925 ensures that co-owned land is now held by (no more than four) joint tenants on trust for sale for the beneficial co-owners, whether equitable joint tenants or tenants in common. This is to simplify conveyancing, though it has led the Court of Appeal[31] to assert "The whole purpose of the trust for sale is to make sure, by shifting the equitable interests away from the land and into the proceeds of sale, that a purchaser of the land takes free from the equitable interests: to hold these to be equitable interests in the land itself would be to frustrate this purpose." This ignores the real reason why a purchaser takes free from the equitable interests which is because the sale under the trust for sale is a performance of the trust and not a breach of it: the purchaser is thus a bona fide purchaser of a legal estate for value without notice of any breach of trust which would affect him.[32]

3. Beneficial interests under trusts for sale. In general, the shares of beneficiaries in the proceeds of sale under a trust for sale are treated as personalty; indeed, the various 1925 Acts expressly define land as not including an undivided share in land unless the context otherwise requires.[33] Thus, if T by will leaves his realty to R and his personalty to P it will be P who receives T's undivided share in land.[34] The power of the Court to impose a charging order on the land of a judgment debtor to secure payment of the judgment debt did not extend to the debtor's interest as a joint tenant or a tenant in common under a trust for sale of land[35] until expressly extended by the Charging Orders Act 1979[36]: even now a writ or order affecting land cannot be registered in the register of such writs and orders if it only

---

[29] *Fletcher* v. *Ashburner* (1779) 1 Bro. C.C. 497.
[30] *Re Richerson* [1892] 1 Ch. 379 at p. 383.
[31] *Irani Finance Ltd.* v. *Singh* [1971] Ch. 59 at p. 79 endorsed by the Court of Appeal in *Cedar Holdings Ltd.* v. *Green* [1981] Ch. 129.
[32] (1979) 38 Camb.L.J. 23 at p. 25 (M.J. Prichard).
[33] S.L.A. 117 (1) (ix); T.A., s. 68 (6); L.P.A., s. 205 (1) (ix); L.C.A., s. 20 (6).
[34] *Re Kempthorne* [1930] 1 Ch. 268.
[35] *Irani Finance Ltd.* v. *Singh* [1971] Ch. 59.
[36] *Ante,* p. 98.

affects an interest under a trust for sale.[37] A *lis pendens* cannot be registered to protect a claim to an undivided share in land.[38]

For some purposes, however, the statutory context is enough to enable an interest under a trust for sale to be treated as an interest in land. Thus, a contract for sale of land includes a contract for sale of an interest under a trust for sale,[39] *i.e* a contract relating to the proceeds of sale of land. A person interested in the proceeds of sale of land is "howsoever interested in land" to be able to enter a caution against the registered land concerned.[40] Furthermore, a person interested in the proceeds of sale of land under an "occupation trust"[41] for sale, such that he is entitled to occupy the land until removed by the Court under section 30 of the Law of Property Act, has an interest "subsisting in reference to registered land" which can be an overriding interest.[42] It remains doubtful whether an interest under a "distribution trust" can be an overriding interest.[43]

In *Cedar Holdings Ltd.* v. *Green*[44] H and W were legal and equitable joint owners of their matrimonial home. H and X, who impersonated W, executed a legal charge in the plaintiff's favour. Clearly this could not affect the legal estate nor the equitable interest of W. The plaintiff claimed it could act as a charge of H's equitable interest under the trust for sale since "every conveyance [which includes a charge] is effectual to pass all the interest which the conveying parties respectively have in the property conveyed or expressed or intended so to be."[45] The Court of Appeal rejected the claim since under the doctrine of conversion an interest in the proceeds of sale under a trust for sale of land is not "an interest in the property conveyed or expressed or intended so to be." However, this seems no longer good law since Lord Wilberforce in *Williams & Glyn's Bank* v. *Boland*[46] stated that it had "been wrongly decided." It would, after all, be surprising if the wife had an interest in land as against the Bank in *Boland* but the husband had an interest in money where the Bank was concerned in *Cedar Holdings*!

4. Policy considerations. In determining whether an interest in proceeds of sale under a trust for sale of land is an interest in land or merely an interest in money the Courts take into account "current social conditions"[47] and strive for "the achievement of social

[37] *Ante*, p. 98.
[38] *Taylor* v. *Taylor* [1968] 1 W.L.R. 778.
[39] *Cooper* v. *Critchley* [1955] Ch. 431.
[40] *Elias* v. *Mitchell* [1972] Ch. 652.
[41] *Ante*, p. 314.
[42] *Williams & Glyn's Bank* v. *Boland* [1981] A.C. 487.
[43] *Ante*, pp. 294, 315.
[44] [1981] Ch. 129.
[45] L.P.A. 1925, s. 63.
[46] [1981] A.C. 487.
[47] *Williams & Glyn's Bank* v. *Boland* [1981] A.C. 487.

justice"[48] but these matters "can be decisive only if the particular statutory provision under review is reasonably capable of the meaning conducive to the social purpose . . . .If it is not, the remedy is to be found not by judicial distortion of the language used by Parliament but in amending legislation."[49]

In *Williams & Glyn's Bank* v. *Boland*[50] H was sole registered proprietor but held the legal estate on trust for sale for himself and W in undivided shares, owing to contributions made by W to the purchase of the matrimonial home. To help finance H's business H mortgaged the house by registered charge to the Bank. To enforce its rights the Bank claimed possession of the house but W claimed she had an overriding interest[51] being in "actual occupation" and having "rights subsisting in reference to land" as equitable tenant in common entitling her (and thus H) to be in possession to the exclusion of the Bank.

Before the War one could have expected a Court to take the view that the presence of H as sole registered proprietor in occupation excluded the possibility of his wife, W, being in occupation: H alone would have been in actual occupation and W would only have been there in his shadow *qua* wife[52] since social circumstances were such that it was most unlikely that W would have had sufficient money in her own right to have become part owner of the house and so be entitled to be present in her own right, by virtue of her ownership rather than by virtue of her marital status. The changed social and economic condition of women in 1980 led the Court of Appeal and the Lords in *Boland* to treat W as much in actual occupation as H, occupation being a plain factual situation.

Before the War one could have expected a court to have treated it as axiomatic that interests under trusts for sale were exclusively minor interests, requiring protection on the register of title, and could not be overriding interests in land[53]—as was indeed assumed when the Law of Property (Joint Tenants) Act 1964 was passed.[54] The changed social and economic condition of women in 1980 influenced the Court of Appeal and the Lords to treat W's interest under the trust for sale of the matrimonial home as an overriding interest subsisting in reference to land (though *also* capable of protection as a minor interest) since the Land Registration Act did not expressly state that interests under trusts for sale could *only* be

[48] *Ibid.*
[49] *Ibid.*
[50] *Ibid.*
[51] L.R.A. 1925, s. 70 (1) (g).
[52] As held by Templeman J. in *Boland* (1978) 36 P. & C.R. 448.
[53] This was the view of all text-books.
[54] It did not apply to registered land since it was assumed that interests under trusts for sale were minor interests only so that when unprotected they could not affect purchasers.

minor interests and, under *Bull* v. *Bull*,[55] W had a right to occupy the land till evicted under section 30 of the Law of Property Act.

Essentially, in current conditions the Court of Appeal and the Lords felt it unreasonable for purchasers to be able to ignore wives as "unpersons" and reasonable for purchasers to be expected to ascertain a wife's rights. The wife's concurrence is thus necessary for all dealings,[56] Lord Wilberforce's views having changed since 15 years ago when, rejecting the so-called deserted wife's equity, he stated[57] "To hold that the wife acquires a right valid against third parties would create impossible difficulties for those dealing with the property of a married man. It would mean that the concurrence of the wife would be necessary for all dealings."

Mrs. Boland and her husband, no doubt, considered that social justice had been achieved. The Bank might have doubts. The mortgage had been to benefit Mr. Boland's business which would benefit both Mr. and Mrs. Boland if the business prospered (so that if asked at the time Mrs. Boland would have been prepared to join in the mortgage). It can be argued that she who is ready to benefit from the prosperity of a business should also be ready to accept any burden of adversity in the business. The courts overlooked this injustice in concentrating upon creating greater social justice for wives generally. There seems more scope for dealing with the merits of a particular case if the mortgagee claims as assignee of the husband's equitable interest[58] that sale should be ordered under section 30 of the Law of Property Act 1925.

Sect. 5. Position of Settled Land

Before 1926, where land fell within the definition of settled land but two or more persons were together entitled in possession, they together formed a composite tenant for life, whether they held as joint tenants, tenants in common or otherwise.[59] After 1925, their position depends upon whether in equity they are entitled as joint tenants or in undivided shares.

A. Joint Tenants

If two or more persons of full age are entitled as joint tenants of settled land, they together constitute the tenant for life.[60] If any of

---

[55] [1955] 1 Q.B. 234 *ante*, p. 315.
[56] The husband and a crony as two trustees for sale may make title and overreach the wife's rights, but if the wife makes it clear to a prospective purchaser that she will not vacate the premises until he has brought legal proceedings he will usually not be happy to proceed with the purchase.
[57] *N.P.B.* v. *Ainsworth* [1965] A.C. 1175 at p. 1248.
[58] Whether as express or implied assignee, Lord Wilberforce in *Boland* [1981] A.C. 487 having stated that *Cedar Holdings* v. *Green* [1981] Ch. 129 was wrongly decided.
[59] S.L.A. 1882, s. 2 (6).
[60] S.L.A. 1925, s. 19 (2). If they are absolutely entitled the land cannot be settled land.

them are minors, such one or more of them as for the time being is or are of full age constitute the tenant for life[61]; if they are all minors, the legal estate and statutory powers are vested in the statutory owner[62] until one of them is of full age.[63] The land thus remains settled land and there is no trust for sale. All the joint tenants in whom the land is vested must concur in exercising the power of sale and other statutory powers. The court will not compel a dissident tenant to concur unless he is acting in bad faith.[64]

B. Undivided Shares[65]

1. Trust for sale. If after 1925 two or more tenants in common become entitled in possession to settled land, the land forthwith ceases to be settled land and becomes subject to a trust for sale. The Settled Land Act trustees can require the legal estate to be conveyed to them if it is not already vested in them[66]; they will hold it on the statutory trusts, namely, on trust for sale, with power to postpone sale, holding the income until sale and the proceeds thereafter upon such trusts and subject to such provisions are as requisite for giving effect to the rights of the persons interested in the land.[67] Thus if land is settled on A for life, remainder to B and C in equal shares as tenants in common for life, remainder to the children of B and C in fee simple, when A dies the land will be held upon trust for sale and must be vested in the Settled Land Act trustees.

2. Land ceasing to be settled. This provision that the legal estate shall be vested in the Settled Land Act trustees and not in the persons beneficially entitled applies even if the land ceases to be settled at the moment when the tenants in common become entitled in possession. Thus if land is settled on A for life, remainder to his children in fee simple in equal shares as tenants in common, the land ceases to be settled land on the death of A, for it becomes subject to an immediate binding trust for sale. Nevertheless, A's personal representatives must convey the legal estate to the Settled Land Act trustees as joint tenants upon trust for sale, and not to the children[68]; to this extent the land retains traces of its former status as settled land.

3. Overreaching powers. The Settled Land Act trustees hold on a

---

[61] *Ibid.* s. 19 (3).
[62] *Ante,* p. 243.
[63] L.P.A. 1925, s. 26 (4), (5).
[64] *Re 90 Thornhill Road, Tolworth, Surrey* [1970] Ch. 261. Contrast trusts for sale, *ante,* p. 316.
[65] See M. & W., pp. 424–426.
[66] S.L.A. 1925, s. 36 (1); L.P.A. 1925, 1st Sched., Pt. IV, para. 2.
[67] S.L.A. 1925, s. 36 (2), (6).
[68] *Re Thomas* [1939] Ch. 513. If the children are all *sui juris* then they can require the legal estate to be vested in themselves as joint tenants upon trust for sale for themselves in undivided shares: L.P.A. 1925, s. 3 (1) (*b*) (ii).

special form of trust for sale which enables them to overreach not only the rights under the trust for sale but also any other rights existing under a former settlement and not protected by a legal mortgage, even if these rights are prior to the trust for sale.[69] For example, if land is settled on A for life, subject to an equitable rentcharge for B, with remainder to C and D as tenants in common, on the death of A the Settled Land Act trustees hold on trust for sale with power to overreach B's rentcharge even though it has priority to the trust for sale.

Sect. 6. Determination of Joint Tenancies and Tenancies in Common

Joint tenancies and tenancies in common may be determined by partition or by union in a sole tenant; joint tenancies may also be determined by severance, which converts them into tenancies in common.

A. Partition

1. No power at common law. Joint tenants and tenants in common have always been able to make a voluntary partition of the land concerned if all agreed; their co-ownership thus came to an end by each of them becoming sole tenant of the piece of land allotted to him. But at common law there was no right to compel a partition.

2. Partition Acts. By the Partition Acts 1539 and 1540, a statutory right to compel partition was conferred upon joint tenants and tenants in common, one tenant being entitled to insist upon a partition, however inconvenient it might be. It was not until the Partition Act 1868 that the court was empowered to decree a sale instead of partition, an order which might be highly desirable where, for example, the cost of partition proceedings would exceed the value of the property, or where a single house had to be partitioned into thirds, and the owner of two-thirds was given all the chimneys and fireplaces and the only stairs.[70]

3. Sale. The Partition Acts have now been repealed. Instead, subject to certain qualifications, a power is given to the trustees for sale in whom the legal estate is vested to effect a partition with the consent of the beneficiaries.[71] If the trustees or any of the beneficiaries refuse to agree to a partition, any person interested may

---

[69] S.L.A. 1925, s. 36 (2); L.P.A. 1925, 1st Sched. Pt. IV, para. 1 (3), as amended by L.P.(Am.)A. 1926, Sched.
[70] See *Turner* v. *Morgan* (1803) 8 Ves. 143; 11 Ves. 157n.; but if there had been three houses, each share would have consisted of one house and not one-third of each house: *Earl of Clarendon* v. *Hornby* (1718) 1 P.Wms. 446.
[71] L.P.A. 1925, s. 28 (3).

apply to the court, which may make such order as it thinks fit,[72] such as an order for sale.[73]

B. Union in a Sole Tenant

Joint tenancies and tenancies in common may be determined by the entirety of the land becoming vested in a sole tenant. Thus where one of two surviving joint tenants dies, the other becomes sole tenant and the joint tenancy is at an end. Similarly if one joint tenant or tenant in common acquires the interests of all his fellows, as by purchase, the co-ownership is at an end.

Because in theory each joint tenant is seised of the whole of the land, the appropriate way for one joint tenant to transfer his rights to another is by a release operating to extinguish rather than to convey any rights, and so requiring no words of limitation; but any sort of conveyance will be construed as a release,[74] and it has now been retrospectively provided that the transaction can also be effected by grant.[75] A tenant in common, on the other hand, can not release his share to his fellows, but has to convey it by some assurance by which a sole tenant could have conveyed his land, for "a release supposes the party to have the thing in demand."[76]

Co-ownership in land is also extinguished if the land is sold to a purchaser, for the co-ownership is transferred from the land to the proceeds of sale.

C. Severance

The common law mitigated the uncertainty of the *jus accrescendi* by enabling a joint tenant to destroy the joint tenancy by severance which had the effect of turning it into a tenancy in common. "The duration of all lives being uncertain, if either party has an ill opinion of his own life, he may sever the joint tenancy by a deed granting over a moiety [*i.e.* conveying one half] in trust for himself; so that survivorship can be no hardship, where either side may at pleasure prevent it."[77] "Severance" strictly includes partition, but the word is normally used to describe the process whereby a joint tenancy is converted into a tenancy in common, and it is used in this sense here. Although no joint tenant owned any distinct share in the land, yet each had a potential share equal in size to that of his companions, and so depending upon the number of joint tenants at the time in question. Thus if there were five joint tenants, each had the right to sever his joint tenancy and become tenant in common of one

---

[72] L.P.A. 1925, s. 30.
[73] See *Re Solomon* [1967] Ch. 573.
[74] See *Re Schär* [1951] Ch. 280.
[75] L.P.A. 1925, s. 72 (4).
[76] Litt. s. 304, n. 1.
[77] *Cray* v. *Willis* (1729) 2 P.Wms. 529, *per* Verney M.R.

undivided fifth share; if one joint tenant died before the severance, each of the survivors had a potential quarter share, and so on.

I. BEFORE 1926

Before 1926, a joint tenancy could be severed both at law and in equity. Severance was effected by destroying one of the unities. Unity of time could not be severed, and severance of the unity of possession meant partition, but severance of the unity either of title or of interest converted a joint tenancy into a tenancy in common. A joint tenancy could be severed in the following ways.

1. By acquisition of another estate in the land. Although it was not fatal to a joint tenancy that one of the tenants was initially given some further estate in the land than his joint tenancy, the subsequent acquisition of an additional estate in the land destroyed the unity of interest and severed the joint tenancy.[78] Thus if land was limited to A, B and C as joint tenants for life, with remainder to C in fee simple, the mere existence of C's fee simple remainder did not destroy his tenancy for life; however, if A acquired C's fee simple A's life estate merged in the fee simple and severed his joint tenancy for life. It should be noted, however, that this method of severance required that some estate different from the estate held in joint tenancy should be acquired. Thus in the above example if A released his interest to B, B took A's one-third share as tenant in common, but his joint tenancy with C in the remaining two-thirds was not affected.

2. By alienation. If a joint tenant alienated his interest *inter vivos*, his joint tenancy was severed and the person to whom the interest was conveyed took it as a tenant in common with the other joint tenants, for he had no unity of title with them.[79] Such a severance did not affect the other joint tenants, who remained joint tenants *inter se*. Thus if A, B and C were joint tenants, and A sold his interest to X, X became tenant in common of one-third and B and C joint tenants of two-thirds. If B then died, C alone profited by the *jus acrescendi*, X and C being left as tenants in common as to one-third and two-thirds respectively. If one of the tenants mortgaged his interest, this also severed the joint tenancy as to his share, and the same applied if a joint tenant became bankrupt. The better opinion was that if a joint tenant of freehold land granted a lease of his interest, this also effected severance; but this was not clearly settled.

Equity treats that as done which ought to be done, and so far as the equitable interest was concerned, an enforceable contract by a joint

---

[78] *Wiscot's Case* (1599) 2 Co.Rep. 60b.
[79] See *Partriche* v. *Powlet* (1740) 2 Atk. 54.

tenant to alienate his interest was as effective to sever a joint tenancy as an actual alienation.[80]

3. Mutual agreement of all the joint tenants. Whilst a specifically enforceable contract for the alienation of a joint tenant's interest clearly severs such interest (*e.g.* where the contract is with a third party) it will normally be the case that severance occurs at an earlier stage where a contract is being negotiated between one joint tenant and the other tenant. It will not then matter that the contract is unenforceable through lack of writing since the crucial factor is that there is an agreement between the joint tenants which establishes that they have a common intention that the vendor is to be treated as having an undivided share.[81]

4. Mutual course of dealing between all the joint tenants. "There may be a severance by any course of dealing sufficient to intimate that the interests of all were mutually treated as constituting a tenancy in common. . . . It will not suffice to rely on an intention, with respect to the particular share, declared only behind the backs of other persons interested. You must find a course of dealing by which the shares of all the parties to the contract have been affected."[82] No concluded agreement between all the joint tenants is required: negotiations, not otherwise resulting in any agreement, can effect a severance if they sufficiently indicate a common intention of all the joint tenants that a tenant should be regarded as having an undivided share.[83] Thus where one tenant (*e.g.* a husband) negotiates with the other (*e.g.* the wife) for some rearrangement of interest (*e.g.* on divorce) it may be possible to infer from the particular facts a common intention to treat each other as having undivided shares even though the negotiations break down.[84]

A unilateral declaration of an intent to sever was not effective[85] (though now see section 36 (2) of the Law of Property Act 1925).

---

[80] *Brown* v. *Raindle* (1796) 3 Ves. 256; *Burgess* v. *Rawnsley* [1975] Ch. 429.
[81] *Burgess* v. *Rawnsley* [1975] Ch. 429 (oral agreement to purchase the other joint tenant's share for £750).
[82] *Williams* v. *Hensman* (1861) 1 John & H. 546 at pp. 557–558.
[83] *Burgess* v. *Rawnsley* [1975] Ch. 429 where Lord Denning stated that *Nielson-Jones* v. *Fedden* [1975] Ch. 222 was incorrectly decided (as seems implicit in Sir John Pennycuick's judgment, though he expressly refrained from applying his statement of principle to the facts of that case). Also see *Greenfield* v. *Greenfield* (1979) 38 P. & C.R. 570.
[84] As Lord Denning, and, probably, Sir John Pennycuick would have done if deciding *Nielson-Jones* v. *Fedden*: see preceeding footnote and casenote on *Burgess* v. *Rawnsley* in [1976] Camb.L.J. 20 (D.J. Hayton).
[85] *Nielson-Jones* v. *Fedden* [1975] Ch. 222; *Re Wilks* [1891] 3 Ch. 59. Dicta to the contrary in *Re Draper's Conveyance* [1969] 1 Ch. 486, following dicta of Havers J. in *Hawksley* v. *May* [1956] 1 Q.B. 304 based on a fundamental misunderstanding of *Williams* v. *Hensman* (1861) 1 John & H. 546, are wrong. Even where there is a course of dealing a unilateral declaration will not suffice: the other joint tenant(s) must expressly or implicitly agree that he is to be regarded as having an undivided share, though it seems that, in the absence of dissent, agreement may readily be inferred.

5. By homicide. No one may benefit from his own crime.[86] Hence if one joint tenant criminally killed another, the killer could not benefit by survivorship, so that there was necessarily a severance. If there are two joint tenants, the killer would hold the legal estate in the property upon trust as to one-half for himself and one-half for his victim's estate.[87] If there were three, the legal estate would vest in the killer and the other survivor upon trust for the innocent survivor as to one-third and for the killer and the innocent survivor as to the remaining two-thirds jointly.[88]

II. AFTER 1925

After 1925, a legal joint tenancy can never be severed so as to create a legal tenancy in common; but this does not prevent one joint tenant from releasing his interest to the others, nor does it affect the right to sever a joint tenancy in equity.[89]

In equity, a severance can be effected—

1. By the methods available before 1926. These are dealt with above.

2. By unilateral notice in writing. Under section 36(2) of the Law of Property Act "where a legal estate (not being settled land) is vested in joint tenants beneficially, and any tenant desires to sever the joint tenancy in equity, he shall give to the other joint tenants a notice in writing of such desire or do such other acts or things as would, in the case of personal estate, have been effectual to sever the joint tenancy in equity," whereupon the parties concerned are to be treated in equity as if there had been an actual severance. The effect of a severance is, of course, limited to the tenants' interests in equity in the proceeds of sale.

This new method is not available in the case of settled land but is only available where a legal estate is "vested in joint tenants beneficially," *i.e.* where A and B hold the legal estate on trust for sale for A and B jointly.[90] What then if T_1 and T_2 hold the legal estate on trust for sale for A and B jointly or A and B hold for A, B, C and D

---

[86] See *ante*, p. 171 for another application of this rule. See T.G. Youdan (1973) 89 L.Q.R. 235 for a general survey.

[87] *Schobelt* v. *Barber* [1967] 1 O.R. 349; *Rasmanis* v. *Jurewitsch* (1969) 70 S.R. (N.S.W.) 407; *Re Pechar* [1969] N.Z.L.R. 574; *Re Gore* [1972] 1 O.R. 550.

[88] *Rasmanis* v. *Jurewitsch, supra.*

[89] L.P.A. 1925, s. 36 (2). The suggestion of Lord Denning in *Bedson* v. *Bedson* [1965] 2 Q.B. 666 at p. 678 that spouses cannot sever an equitable joint tenancy is heretical: M. & W., p. 410. In *Burgess* v. *Rawnsley* [1975] Ch. 429 at p. 440, when discussing *Nielson-Jones* v. *Fedden* [1975] Ch. 222, Lord Denning assumed that spouses could sever their joint tenancy.

[90] Once sale has occurred so that cash is held for A and B then no notice may be served, but after contract but before completion it seems, despite dicta in *Nielson-Jones* v. *Fedden* [1975] Ch. 222, that it can still be said that the legal estate is vested in A and B beneficially: see M. & W., p. 409.

jointly? There seems to be no logical justification to distinguish between these three examples. Perhaps the clause "vested in joint tenants beneficially" will be benevolently construed as "vested in *persons for* joint tenants beneficially."

Service of a notice of severance is an irrevocable act and the commencement of legal proceedings by writ or originating summons (or an affidavit sworn in such proceedings) can constitute such a notice even though such proceedings may subsequently be discontinued.[91]

It was considered clear that this method of unilateral notice in writing was a new method of severance available only where a legal estate in land was held on trust for joint tenants. Unfortunately, Lord Denning,[92] with whom Browne L.J. concurred, has treated the statutory provision "give . . . a notice in writing . . . or do such *other* acts or things as would in the case of personal estate have been effectual to sever the joint tenancy" as implying[93] that notice in writing would, before 1926, have been effectual to sever a joint tenancy in personalty and continues to be so effectual. However, unilateral notice in writing was not available to sever joint interests in personalty before 1926.[94] If it had been a recognised method then in section 36 (2) the draftsman need not have expressly mentioned giving notice in writing but only need to have provided that "where any tenant desires to sever the joint tenancy in equity he shall do such acts or things as would, in the case of personal estate, have been effectual to sever the joint tenancy."

It is submitted that the proper construction of section 36 (2) is to treat it as if it finished "he shall give to the other joint tenants a notice in writing of such desire or *otherwise* do such acts or things as would in the case of personal estate have been effectual to sever the joint tenancy." Thus a unilateral notice in writing should not be effectual to sever a joint tenancy in pure personalty.

C. Operation of the Present Law

An example illustrating the present position may be useful. In 1960 X purported to convey land to A, B, C, D and E in fee simple; all were of full age. The legal estate vested in A, B, C and D on the statutory

---

[91] *Burgess* v. *Rawnsley* [1975] Ch. 429 at pp. 440, 447 preferring *Re Draper's Conveyance* [1969] 1 Ch. 486 to *Nielson-Jones* v. *Fedden* [1975] Ch. 222.

[92] *Burgess* v. *Rawnsley* [1975] Ch. 429 at pp. 439–440. Sir John Pennycuick was more circumspect: see p. 448.

[93] Even if the draftsman in enacting a new law for severance of joint tenancies in land assumed that notice in writing was already effectual to sever joint tenancies in personalty "the beliefs or assumptions of those who frame Acts of Parliament cannot make the law" *per* Lord Simonds in *Kirkness* v. *John Hudson & Co. Ltd.* [1955] A.C. 696 at p. 714 applied by Goff L.J. in *Pritchard* v. *Briggs* [1980] Ch. 338 at p. 398.

[94] *Re Wilks* [1891] 3 Ch. 59; *Nielson-Jones* v. *Fedden* [1975] Ch. 222; Williams, *Personal Property* (18th ed.), pp. 524–525.

trusts; in equity, A, B, C, D and E were tenants in common if there were words of severance or if it was one of equity's special cases, but otherwise joint tenants. If they were joint tenants and A died, B, C, and D would then hold the legal estate on the statutory trusts for B, C, D and E as joint tenants; E would not automatically fill the vacancy at law, but could, of course, be appointed by the remaining trustees to be a new trustee in place of A. If B afterwards sold his interest to P, then B, C and D would hold the legal estate on the statutory trusts for P as tenant in common of a quarter and C, D and E as joint tenants of three-quarters. If C then severed his joint tenancy (*e.g.* by agreement with D and E), the legal estate would remain in B, C and D as before, on the statutory trusts for P and C as tenants in common of one-quarter each, and D and E as joint tenants of half. On D's death, B and C would hold on the statutory trusts for P, C and E as tenants in common as to one-quarter, one-quarter and one-half respectively.

Part 2

REGISTERED LAND

The position of trusts for sale in registered land has already been considered when dealing with settlements by way of trust for sale.[95] They need to be expressly created and a restriction will appear on the register to protect the beneficiaries' minor interests. More problems are likely where trusts for sale can arise by operation of law in co-ownership cases when the beneficial interest, if protected by actual occupation but not by entry on the register, can rank as an overriding interest.[96]

However, in the case of a "distribution"[97] trust as opposed to an "occupation" trust since the beneficiary has no right to occupy the land and cannot insist that no sale takes place without his consent (unless dispensed with by the court under section 30 of the Law of Property Act 1925) it seems that a case can be made out for such beneficiary's right not to rank as an overriding interest subsisting in reference to the land but only as a minor interest which, if unprotected, will not bind a purchaser.[98]

On a sale under the overreaching machinery of payment to two trustees (or a trust corporation) any "rights" of actual occupiers under trusts for sale will be overreached, becoming rights in the proceeds of sale, so that such rights will not bind the purchaser.

[95] See *ante,* p. 294.
[96] *Williams & Glyn's Bank* v. *Boland* [1981] A.C. 487.
[97] See *ante,* p. 313.
[98] See *ante,* pp. 294, 315, and Hayton, pp. 98–100.

Part 3

PARTY WALLS

Sect. 1. Before 1926

1. Categories. Where a wall separates land owned by A from land owned by B, the wall may be either in the sole ownership of one party, free from any rights of the other, or a party wall. There appears to be no precise legal definition of the term "party wall." Four possible meanings are as follows[99]:

(a) *Tenancy in common*: the two adjoining owners are tenants in common of the wall.

(b) *Divided*: the wall is divided longitudinally into two strips, one belonging to each of the neighbouring owners.

(c) *Divided with easements*: the wall is divided as in (b), but each half is subject to an easement of support in favour of the owner of the other half.

(d) *Ownership subject to easement*: the wall belongs entirely to one of the adjoining owners, but is subject to an easement or right in the other to have it maintained as a dividing wall.

2. Presumption. The presumption was in favour of a party wall falling within the first category, at all events if evidence was given that each owner had exercised dominion over the entire wall.[1] The first category had the disadvantage that either owner could insist upon a partition, but it was less unsatisfactory than the second category, where either owner, acting with reasonable care, could remove his half of the wall and leave a structure which was perhaps incapable of standing alone.[2] Neither owner could pull down a wall of the first kind except for the purpose of rebuilding it with all reasonable dispatch,[3] nor could either prevent the other from enjoying any part of the wall, as by covering the top with broken glass or replacing it with part of a shed.[4] There was no presumption in favour of the third or fourth categories because these could be established only on proof that the appropriate easements existed.

3. Ownership of soil. The presumption in favour of the first category applied only where the exact situation of the boundary could

---

[99] See *Watson* v. *Gray* (1880) 14 Ch.D. 192 at pp. 194, 195.
[1] *Ibid.*
[2] See *Cubitt* v. *Porter* (1828) 8 B. & C. 257 at p. 264.
[3] *Cubitt* v. *Porter* (1828) 8 B. & C. 257.
[4] *Stedman* v. *Smith* (1857) 8 E. & B. 1 at pp. 6, 7.

not be shown, or where the site of the wall could be shown to have been owned in common.[5] Where the wall was built entirely on A's land, the presumption was that the wall was A's; and where the wall was built on the boundary, so that substantially half the soil on which it stood was A's and half B's, the case usually fell into the second or third category, the wall being regarded as divided into two walls each of half the thickness.[6] The principle in these cases was that "as a matter of law, the property in the wall followed the property in the land upon which it stood."[7] Subject to this, the ownership of the wall was a question of fact for the jury. A wall might even be in sole ownership for part of its height and a party wall for the rest.[8]

In some parts of the country, particularly London, these rules have been modified to some extent by statute.[9]

Sect. 2. After 1925

Unless special provision had been made, all party walls in the first category would have become subject to a trust for sale after 1925. It was consequently provided that after 1925 all party walls in this category should be deemed to be severed vertically, and that the owner of each part should have such rights of support and user over the rest of the wall as were requisite for giving the parties rights similar to those which they would have enjoyed had they been tenants in common of the wall.[10] The practical effect of this provision is to translate all party walls in the first category into the third. Apart from this, the law of party walls remains unchanged.

---

[5] See *Wiltshire* v. *Sidford* (1827) 1 Màn. & Ry. 404 at pp. 407, 409.
[6] *Murly* v. *M'Dermott* (1838) 8 A. & E. 138 at p. 142.
[7] *Jones* v. *Read* (1876) 10 Ir.R. C. L. 315 at p. 320, *per* Palles C.B.
[8] *Weston* v. *Arnold* (1873) 8 Ch.App. 1084.
[9] *e.g.* the London Building Acts (Amendment) Act 1939, Pt. VI, replacing earlier statutes.
[10] L.P.A. 1925, s. 38 (2), 1st Sched., Pt. V.

CHAPTER 9

LEASES AND TENANCIES

Part 1

INTRODUCTORY

BEFORE considering leases in detail, some mention will be made of their history and terminology.

Sect. 1. History

1. Leases. A lease, as generally understood today, is a document creating an interest in land for a fixed period of certain duration,[1] usually in consideration of the payment of rent. This has not always been so.

2. Leases for lives. The owner of a life estate in land was able to recover the land itself if he was dispossessed, whereas until the end of the fifteenth century a tenant for a term of years could not do so. One result of this was that in early times it was a common practice for a lessee to take a lease of land for the duration of a specified number of lives, instead of for a specified term of years. Thus, instead of a lease for 99 years, a tenant would take a lease for the life of the survivor of X, Y and Z. The tenant had an estate *pur autre vie*, which, being an estate of freehold and classified as real property,[2] entitled him to recover the land if he was dispossessed. The disadvantage of the uncertainty of the period was outweighed by the advantages it gave to the tenant and sometimes to the lord. The rent payable was usually fairly small, but a fine was paid when the lease was granted; a further fine was payable when, on the termination of the lives, the tenant exercised the right the lease gave him to replace them and so extend the lease. If the lessor was a corporation such as a monastery or college, the fines were treated as income by the then members of the corporation, to the disadvantage of their successors. Leases for life finally lost their popularity when legislation in the first half of the nineteenth century compelled corporations to add such fines to their capital.[3] Nowadays a lease for life is converted into a 90 year determinable term.[4]

---

[1] See *ante*, p. 30.
[2] *Weigall* v. *Brome* (1833) 6 Sim. 99; *ante*, pp. 18, 29.
[3] See Radcliffe, *Real Property* (2nd ed., 1928), p. 28.
[4] *Post*, p. 345.

3. Leases for fixed terms of years. Leases for fixed terms of years are used today for more purposes than one.

(1) The usual type of lease is the occupational lease, where the tenant holds at a rent or in consideration of a fine, or both, and occupies the property himself, or sub-lets it. This type is dealt with in this chapter.

(2) Sometimes leases are granted as a mere conveyancing device. Such leases are granted without a fine and at no rent, in order to provide security for the payment of money. The most important modern example is the lease granted by a mortgagor to the mortgagee as security for the money lent. In this case it is unusual for the lessee to take possession of the land. Such leases are dealt with under mortgages.[5]

Sect. 2. Terminology

It is important to be familiar with the terms used in the law of leases. A lease is sometimes referred to as a "demise" and the premises in question as the "premises demised." The term "tenancy" is normally used for interests lasting for a relatively short period only, while "lease" usually indicates a more enduring interest; there is no hard-and-fast division, and in this chapter "lease" normally includes "tenancy." "Lease" and "term of years" are virtually synonymous terms today; before 1926 a term of years could only be regarded as one kind of lease, since leases for lives were by no means unknown. Today, leases for lives have nearly all disappeared.[6] "Lease" is often used interchangeably for the document and the "term of years" or "leasehold interest" created by it, although strictly it merely means the document.

The grantor of a lease is known as the lessor, the person to whom it is granted as the lessee. On the grant of a lease, the lessor retains a reversion, which he may assign; similarly, the lessee may assign the lease. Instead of assigning the lease (*i.e.* transferring the property for the whole of the period for which it is held), the owner of the lease may grant a sub-lease (or underlease) for some shorter period, the parties to this sub-lease being known as the sub-lessor and sub-lessee respectively. Where the original lessor and original lessee have both assigned their interests, the new owners of the reversion and the lease are sometimes called the lessor and lessee, although it is better to keep these expressions for the original parties to the lease, and refer to the owners for the time being, whether original or by assignment, as the landlord and the tenant.

---

[5] See *post*, p. 464.
[6] *Post*, p. 345.

These expressions may be illustrated as follows:

$$X \longrightarrow Y$$
$$\downarrow \; 99$$
$$A \longrightarrow B$$
$$\downarrow \; 21$$
$$C \longrightarrow D$$

This diagram is the usual way of representing the following events. X grants a 99 years' lease to A and then assigns the reversion to Y. B takes an assignment of A's lease and grants a sub-lease to C for 21 years, C assigning his sub-lease to D. As to the 99 years' lease, X is the "lessor," Y is the "assignee of the reversion" or "landlord," and A the "lessee." B is in a dual position; as to the 99 years' lease, he is the "assignee" or "tenant" and as to the 21 years' lease he is the "sub-lessor" or "landlord." C is the "sub-lessee," and D the "assignee" of the sub-lease, or the "sub-tenant."

For the purpose of enforcing covenants it is important to note that "privity of contract" exists between X and A and between B and C whilst "privity of estate" exists between Y and B (having the same estates as originally vested in X and A) and between B and D.

Part 2

CREATION OF LEASES

Sect 1. Essentials of a Lease

A. The Right to Exclusive Possession must be Given[7]

The tenant must have the right to exclude all other persons from the premises demised. A right to occupy certain premises for a fixed period cannot be a tenancy if the person granting the right remains in general control of the property, as is normally the case with rooms in an inn or boarding-house; a mere lodger has no tenancy.[8] A non-exclusive occupation agreement, if not a sham, is an effective way to oust the Rent Acts which apply only to leases or exclusive licences.[9] There can also be no lease if no defined premises are in question; thus if there is a contractual obligation to store goods but

---

[7] See M. & W., pp. 618–620.
[8] *Appah* v. *Parncliffe Investments Ltd.* [1964] 1 W.L.R. 1064; *Marchant* v. *Charters* [1977] 1 W.L.R. 1181.
[9] *Somma* v. *Hazelhurst* [1978] 1 W.L.R. 1014; *cf. Walsh* v. *Griffiths-Jones* [1978] 2 All E.R. 1002, *post* p. 585.

the rooms in which they are stored may be changed from time to time at the convenience of the owner of the premises, there is no lease.[10] In such a case a mere licence is created, even if the language used clearly indicates that the parties intended to create a lease. But if the premises are clearly defined, the mere imposition of severe restrictions on the use which can be made of them will not prevent a lease from being created.[11]

Although a right to exclusive possession is an important indication that a tenancy and not a licence has been created,[12] even a licence may nowadays confer such a right.[13] The nature of such "possessory licences" is far from clear. In determining whether a document conferring exclusive possession is a lease or a licence the court looks at the substance of what the parties intended rather than to the external form of the document[13] *e.g.* was the occupier to have only a personal non-assignable privilege or was he to have a disposable stake in the property that would bind third parties?

B. The Requirements as to Duration must be Satisfied

The general nature of an estate less than freehold has already been considered,[14] and details of the requisite duration of each particular type of lease or tenancy are set out below.[15] Essentially, a lease cannot be for an uncertain period such as the duration of a partnership or of a Parliament.

C. The Lease must be Created in the Proper Way

I. LEGAL LEASES

To create a legal estate after 1925, a lease must not only grant a term of years absolute within section 1 (1) of the Law of Property Act 1925[16] but also be made with the proper formalities.

A lease cannot create a legal estate unless it is made by deed; the exception is a lease which—

    (i) takes effect in possession (*i.e.* starts forthwith).
    (ii) for a term not exceeding three years, whether or not the lessee is given power to extend the term,
    (iii) at the best rent reasonably obtainable without taking a fine[17]

If all three conditions are complied with, a legal lease can be created orally or in writing.

It should be noted that this concession applies only to the grant of

---

[10] *Interoven Stove Co. Ltd.* v. *Hibbard* [1936] 1 All E.R. 263.
[11] *Joel* v. *International Circus and Christmas Fair* (1920) 124 L.T. 459.
[12] See *Addiscombe Garden Estates Ltd.* v. *Crabbe* [1958] 1 Q.B. 513.
[13] *Barnes* v. *Barratt* [1970] 2 Q.B. 657; *Finbow* v. *Air Ministry* [1963] 1 W.L.R. 697; *Heslop* v. *Burns* [1974] 1 W.L.R. 1241; *Shell Mex* v. *Manchester Garages* [1971] 1 W.L.R. 612; *Addiscombe Garden Estates* v. *Crabbe* (*supra*).
[14] *Ante*, p. 30.
[15] *Post*, pp. 340 *et seq.*
[16] *Ante*, p. 84.
[17] L.P.A. 1925, ss. 52(1), 54.

an actual lease; a *contract* for a lease, for however short a period, will be unenforceable by action unless evidenced by sufficient writing or part performance.[18] Further, once a legal lease has been validly granted, a deed is required to effect a legal assignment of it, no matter how short the term; thus a legal assignment of a yearly tenancy can be effected only by deed, even if the tenancy was created orally.[19]

II. EQUITABLE LEASES

1. Informal lease itself void at law but a legal periodic tenancy can arise. A lease which did not satisfy the above requirements was void at law and passed no legal estate. However, although at law the lease was ineffective to create any tenancy, a tenancy at law might arise independently of the lease; for if the tenant took possession with the landlord's consent, a tenancy at will arose, and as soon as rent was paid and accepted, the tenancy at will was converted into a yearly or other periodic tenancy, depending on the way in which the rent was paid,[20] on such of the terms of the lease as were consistent with the periodic tenancy created. Thus if in 1890 a lease for 99 years was granted orally or merely in writing, the largest estate which the tenancy could claim in a court of law was usually a yearly tenancy; and his claim to this depended not on the lease but upon his possession and the payment and acceptance of rent.

2. Effect as contract. Although such a lease itself failed to create any legal estate, it was not entirely ineffective, for it might be treated as a contract to grant the lease agreed upon. A lease is clearly distinct from a contract to grant a lease: the difference is between "I hereby grant you a lease" and "I hereby agree that I will grant you a lease." Nevertheless, both law and equity concurred in treating an imperfect lease as a contract to grant a lease, provided it was made for value and was sufficiently evidenced in writing, or, so far as equity was concerned, supported by a sufficient act of part performance.[21] The attitude of equity was particularly important, for under the doctrine of *Parker* v. *Taswell*[22] equity would first treat an imperfect lease of this kind as a contract to grant the lease, and then order specific performance of the contract.[23] Once the actual lease had been granted in pursuance of the decree of specific performance, the position of the parties was the same for the future as if the lease had been a legal lease granted by deed in the first place.

---

[18] *Ante*, pp. 136 *et seq.*, pp. 141 *et seq.*
[19] *Post*, p. 348.
[20] *Martin* v. *Smith* (1874) L.R. 9 Ex. 50; *Industrial Properties Ltd.* v. *Associated Electrical Industries* [1977] Q.B. 580 at pp. 611, 612; *post*, pp. 341–343.
[21] See *Tidey* v. *Mollett* (1864) 16 C.B.(N.S.) 298; but see *Harte* v. *Williams* [1934] 1 K.B. 201.
[22] (1858) 2 De G. & J. 559.
[23] *Zimbler* v. *Abrahams* [1903] 1 K.B. 577.

3. Walsh v. Lonsdale.[24] The rights of the parties under an imperfect lease sufficiently evidenced by writing or part performance were thus clear whenever specific performance had been decreed. What was not so clear was the position if, as was far more often the case, no decree of specific performance had been granted but the parties were entitled to obtain one. In equity, the principle is "Equity looks on that as done which ought to be done," so that the parties were treated as if the lease had been granted. But there was no such principle at law, and, indeed, it would have been strange if the positive requirements of statute could have been so easily circumvented. Yet equity might intervene to restrain the parties from exercising their legal rights in opposition to their equitable obligations, and the Judicature Act 1873[25] provided that where the rules of law and equity conflicted, the rules of equity should prevail. Accordingly, in *Walsh v. Lonsdale*[26] it was held that the relationship of the parties was the same as if the lease had actually been granted.

In that case L agreed in writing to grant by deed a lease of a mill to T for seven years, one of the terms being that T should on demand pay a year's rent in advance. No deed was executed, but T was let into possession and for a year and a half paid rent quarterly, although not in advance. L then demanded a year's rent in advance, and on T's refusal to pay, distrained for it. T then brought an action for damages for wrongful distress, and for specific performance of the agreement.

T argued that distress was a legal, and not an equitable, remedy, and that as at law he was only a yearly tenant with no obligation to pay rent in advance, L could not distrain for the rent.[27] It was held, however, that since the distress would have been legal had the lease agreed upon been granted by deed, and since equity treated the parties as if this had been done, the distress was lawful in equity; the equitable rule prevailed over the rule at law and so even at law T could not complain of the distress.

Subsequently, the Court of Appeal[28] has held that if A contracts to sell a freehold to B, who then contracts to grant a lease to C, equity will regard both contracts as performed, with C holding on the same terms as if a lease had actually been granted after conveyance of the freehold.

4. Differences between legal and equitable leases. The effect of *Walsh v. Lonsdale* is to render an enforceable agreement for a lease very nearly as good as a legal lease, and the same applies to an imperfect lease which is enforceable as an agreement for a lease.

---

[24] (1882) 21 Ch.D.9.
[25] s.25(11), then J.A. 1925, s.44 and now Supreme Court Act 1981, s. 49.
[26] *Supra.*
[27] See *Manchester Brewery Co.* v. *Coombs* [1901] 2 Ch. 608 at pp. 617, 618.
[28] *Industrial Properties Ltd.* v. *Associated Electrical Industries Ltd.* [1977] Q.B. 580.

There are still, however, some points of difference.

(a) *Specific performance.* The rule depends upon the willingness of equity to grant the discretionary remedy of specific performance, so that if an agreement for a lease is one of which the court will not[29] grant specific performance, the position under it will be precarious. Further, if the court lacks jurisdiction to order specific performance,[30] a tenant will not be able to enforce the agreement in that court,[31] though he could defend proceedings by the landlord which ignored the agreement, as the court can give effect to an equitable defence.[32]

(b) *Easements.* Certain easements and similar rights may be created under section 62 of the Law of Property Act 1925 on a grant of a legal estate which will not be created by a mere contract.[33]

(c) *No privity of estate.* The doctrine of *Walsh* v. *Lonsdale* does not treat an enforceable agreement for a lease as being as good as a lease as regards third parties, but only as regards the actual parties to the agreement. Thus if a tenant under a lease assigns his interest, there is said to be privity of estate between the landlord and the assignee, so that the assignee becomes entitled to the benefit, and subject to the burden, of the covenants in the lease. But there is no privity of estate between the landlord and the assignee of a tenant under an agreement for a lease merely by virtue of the assignment, even though it is made by deed. The position is governed by the rule that the benefit of a contract is assignable but not the burden. Thus the assignee can sue the landlord[34] but the landlord can only sue the tenant.[35]

(d) *Third parties.* The rights of a tenant under an agreement for a lease, being merely equitable, are subject to the same frailty as all equitable interests, namely, they are void against a bona fide purchaser for value of a legal estate without notice of them. Thus if L makes an agreement for a lease of seven years with T and then grants a legal lease or a legal mortgage to X, or conveys the legal fee simple to him, T's rights will be unenforceable against X if X took his estate

---

[29] *Coatsworth* v. *Johnson* (1886) 55 L.J.Q.B. 220 at p. 222 (the tenant did not come to equity with clean hands since he was in breach of his obligations to the landlord).

[30] *e.g.* County Courts Act 1959, s.52 (1)(*d*).

[31] *Foster* v. *Reeves* [1892] 2 Q.B. 255; contrast *Cornish* v. *Brook Green Laundry Ltd.* [1959] 1 Q.B. 394.

[32] *Kingswood Estate Co. Ltd.* v. *Anderson* [1963] 2 Q.B. 169.

[33] See *post*, p. 414.

[34] Only the original lessor and not subsequent landlord, unless the estate contract has been registered.

[35] Where the assignee has paid rent accepted by the landlord then a common law periodic tenancy will arise and privity of estate will exist enabling enforcement of those obligations that are consistent with the nature of the periodic tenancy: *Doe* d. *Thompson* v. *Amey* (1840) 12 A. & E. 476; *Beale* v. *Sanders* (1837) 3 Bing N.C. 850.

in good faith and for value without notice of T's rights. Before 1926, the usual rules of actual, constructive and imputed notice applied[36]; and if T was in possession of the land, that would normally suffice to give notice of his rights to X.[37] The same rules apply after 1925, save that if T's agreement was made after 1925, it must be registered as a land charge. Registration is deemed to be notice to the whole world; but if the agreement should have been registered and has not, it will be void against a purchaser for money or money's worth of a legal estate in the land.[38] Actual knowledge of the purchaser is immaterial in these cases.[39]

In practice, a written agreement for a lease is virtually as secure as an actual lease, especially if it has been registered, thus ensuring that the whole world has notice of it and so curing the principal defect to which equitable interests are subject. In the case of tenancies for a relatively short period at a rack rent it is usual to accept a mere agreement and not to register it, relying upon the tenant's evident possession of the land to put any prudent purchaser on inquiry, especially since a purchaser will be bound by any common law periodic tenancy arising from rent paid and accepted[40] and which may be protected by the Rent Acts.

III. REGISTERED LAND

If the title out of which a legal lease is granted has been registered then a lease granted for more than 21 years must be registered with its own land certificate.[41] Otherwise, if the land is in a compulsory registration area and there is the grant of a legal lease for 40 years or more or the assignment on sale of a legal lease with 40 or more years unexpired, then the lease must be registered, with its own land certificate.[42] Notice of the lease will be entered against the lessor's title.

Legal leases for a term not exceeding 21 years (which covers periodic tenancies) granted at a rent without taking a fine rank as overriding interests[43] and the Registrar, in practice, will normally refuse to enter a notice on the register which would convert such a lease into a minor interest.[44] He will protect by way of notice leases not exceeding 21 years granted for a fine and also any lease which contains an absolute prohibition against alienation inter vivos (such

---

[36] *Ante,* pp. 65 *et seq.*
[37] See *Hunt* v. *Luck* [1902] 1 Ch. 428 at pp. 432, 433.
[38] L.C.A. 1972, s. 4(6), (7), replacing L.C.A. 1925, s. 13(2); *Hollington Bros Ltd.* v. *Rhodes* [1951] 2 T.L.R. 691; for land charges, see *ante,* pp. 90 *et seq.*
[39] L.P.A. 1925, s. 199(1); *Midland Bank Trust Co.* v. *Green* [1981] A.C. 513.
[40] *Ante,* p. 336.
[41] L.R.A. 1925, ss. 19(2), 22(2).
[42] *Ibid.* s. 123.
[43] *Ibid.* s. 70(1) (*k*); *City P.B.S.* v. *Miller* [1952] Ch. 840.
[44] Ruoff & Roper, p. 452.

leases being incapable of substantive registration with their own land certificate).[45]

Informal equitable leases and agreements for leases can rank as overriding interests within section 70(1)(g) of the Land Registration Act: "the rights of every person in actual occupation of the land or in receipt of the rents and profits thereof." A person in occupation under an informal lease or agreement for lease is thus fully protected,[46] whereas in unregistered land he is only protected if he enters a Class C (iv) Land Charge.[47]

Sect. 2. Types of Leases and Tenancies

A. Classification

Leases and tenancies may be classified under the five following heads.

1. Leases for a fixed period. (a) *Certainty of term.* A lease may be granted for any certain period of certain duration, no matter how long or short. Leases for a week or for 3,000 years are equally valid. Both the commencement and the duration of the term must either be certain or else be rendered certain before the lease takes effect.[48] Thus a lease for 99 years from January 1 next complies with this rule, and so does a lease from the determination of an existing tenancy for as many years as X shall name, once X has named the period; but a tenancy granted during wartime "for the duration of the war" does not.[49] An Act of 1944[50] converted tenancies for the duration of the current war or emergency into valid tenancies for 10 years determinable after the war or emergency by (usually) one month's notice; but there is nothing in the Act to rescue tenancies for other uncertain periods, such as the duration of a partnership, from the common law rule declaring them void.

(b) *Reversionary leases.* Before 1926, there was no restriction upon the length of time that might elapse before the term began; a lease could thus be granted in 1917 to commence in 1946,[51] such a lease being known as a reversionary lease. The perpetuity rule was not infringed by such a grant, for the lessee took a vested interest forthwith; only the vesting in possession was postponed.[52] However, the grant of a term to take effect more than 21 years from the instrument creating it is void if made after 1925 at a rent or in

---

[45] L.R.A. 1925, s. 8(2).
[46] *Bridges* v. *Mees* [1975] Ch. 475; *Grace Rymer Investments* v. *Waite* [1958] Ch. 831.
[47] *Hollington Bros. Ltd.* v. *Rhodes* [1951] 2 T.L.R. 691; *Midland Bank Trust Co. Ltd.* v. *Green* [1981] A.C. 513.
[48] *Harvey* v. *Pratt* [1965] 1 W.L.R. 1025.
[49] *Lace* v. *Chantler* [1944] K.B. 368.
[50] Validation of War-Time Leases Act 1944.
[51] *Mann, Crossman & Paulin Ltd.* v. *Registrar of the Land Registry* [1918] 1 Ch. 202.
[52] *Ibid.*

consideration of a fine, and the same applies to any contract made after 1925 to create such a term, *e.g.* a grant in 1982 of a lease commencing May 1, 2005 or a contract in 1982 to grant in 1983 a lease commencing May 1, 2005, but an option in a 22-year lease to renew the lease on its termination for a further 22 years is valid.[53] It will be noted that this does not affect grants or contracts made before 1926 or leases taking effect in equity under a settlement, *e.g.* portions terms.[54]

(c) *Interesse termini*. Before 1926, there was a common law rule that a lessee acquired no actual estate in the land until he had taken possession during the term of the lease. Until he had exercised his right to take possession, he had a mere *interesse termini* (an interest in the term). This had troublesome effects but the doctrine has been abolished in respect of all leases, whether made before or after 1925.[55]

(d) *Determination*. The general rule is that a lease for a fixed period automatically determines when the fixed period expires; but there are statutory exceptions to this rule.[56]

2. Yearly tenancies. (a) *Creation*. A yearly tenancy is one which continues from year to year indefinitely until determined by proper notice, notwithstanding the death of either party or the assignment of his interest. Such a tenancy may be created either expressly or by implication. Thus an express grant to A "from year to year" or "as a yearly tenant" will create a yearly tenancy. It should be noted, however, that a grant "to X for one year and thereafter from year to year" will give X a tenancy for at least two years; for he has been given a definite term of one year followed by a yearly tenancy which can be determined only at the end of the first year thereof.[57]

A yearly tenancy arises by implication whenever a person occupies land with the owner's consent in circumstances where a tenancy was intended and rent measured with reference to a year is paid and accepted, unless there is sufficient evidence to show that some other kind of tenancy was intended.[58] A yearly tenancy also arises when a tenant under a lease for a fixed term holds over (*i.e.* remains in possession at the end of his term) and, in circumstances where a tenancy was intended,[59] rent is paid and accepted on a yearly basis. In this case, the tenant will hold under such of the terms of the

---

[53] L.P.A. 1925, s. 149(3); see (1947) 63 L.Q.R. 20; *Re Strand and Savoy Properties Ltd.* [1960] Ch. 582; *Weg Motors Ltd.* v. *Hales* [1962] Ch. 49.
[54] M. & W., p. 387.
[55] L.P.A. 1925, s. 149(1), (2).
[56] See *post*, pp. 566 *et seq.*
[57] *Re Searle* [1912] 1 Ch. 610.
[58] *Kemp* v. *Derrett* (1814) 3 Camp. 510.
[59] *Clarke* v. *Grant* [1950] 1 K.B. 104; *Longrigg Burrough & Trounson* v. *Smith* (1979) 251 E.G. 847.

expired lease as are not inconsistent with a yearly holding.[60] Thus
covenants to repair,[61] or to carry on some specified trade on the
premises[62] and provisos for re-entry by the landlord on non-payment
of rent[63] may be implied in a yearly tenancy. But a covenant to paint
every three years[64] and a provision for two years' notice to quit[65] are
inconsistent with a yearly tenancy and cannot be implied in this way.

The payment of rent at more frequent intervals than a year will not
prevent a yearly tenancy from arising by implication. The test is the
period by reference to which the parties calculated the rent. Thus an
agreement for "£1040 per annum payable weekly" prima facie
creates a yearly tenancy; had the agreement been for "£20 per
week," a weekly tenancy would be presumed, despite the fact that in
each case the tenant would in fact have made the same payments,
namely, £20 every week.[66]

(b) *Determination.* A yearly tenancy may be determined by such
notice and at such time as the parties agree.[67] Different periods for
the landlord and tenant may be agreed, and it may be provided that
the landlord should be entitled to give notice only in certain
circumstances,[68] *e.g.* that he requires the premises for his own
occupation.[69] But a term that one party should not be entitled to give
notice at all is void as repugnant to the nature of a periodic tenancy.[70]
In default of such agreement, the tenancy can be determined by at
least half a year's notice expiring at the end of a completed year of the
tenancy. The meaning of "half a year" depends on the day upon
which the tenancy began. If the tenancy began on one of the usual
quarter-days (Lady Day (March 25), Midsummer Day (June 24),
Michaelmas (September 29) or Christmas (December 25)), "half a
year" means "two quarters;" otherwise "half a year" means 182
days.[71] Thus if a yearly tenancy began on March 25, notice to quit
given on or before September 29 is good, although it is less than 182
days[72]; and if a yearly tenancy began on September 29, notice must
be given on or before March 25, even though it is more than 182 days.
In each of these cases, the tenancy began on a quarter-day[73]; had it
started on some other day, *e.g.* March 26, at least 182 days' notice
would have been required.[74] It will be noted that in neither case is the

[60] *Dougal* v. *McCarthy* [1893] 1 Q.B. 736.
[61] *Wyatt* v. *Cole* (1877) 36 L.T. 613.
[62] *Sanders* v. *Karnell* (1858) 1 F. & F. 356.
[63] *Thomas* v. *Packer* (1857) 1 H. & N. 669.
[64] *Pinero* v. *Judson* (1829) 6 Bing. 206.
[65] *Tooker* v. *Smith* (1857) 1 H. & N. 732.
[66] See *Adler* v. *Blackman* [1953] 1 Q.B. 146.
[67] *Re Threlfall* (1880) 16 Ch.D. 274 at pp. 281, 282.
[68] *Re Midland Railway Co.'s Agreement* [1971] Ch. 725.
[69] As in *Breams Property Investment Co.* v. *Stroulger* [1948] 2 K.B. 1.
[70] *Centaploy Ltd.* v. *Matlodge Ltd.* [1974] Ch. 1.
[71] *Anon.* (1575) 3 Dy. 345a.
[72] *Doe* d. *Durant* v. *Doe* (1830) 6 Bing. 574.
[73] *Morgan* v. *Davies* (1878) 3 C.P.D. 260.
[74] Co.Litt. 135b.

period of the notice necessarily six months, although of course the parties may agree that such shall be the notice required.

3. Weekly, monthly and other periodic tenancies. A tenancy from week to week, month to month, quarter to quarter, and the like (including a tenancy for some artificial period, such as for successive periods of 364 days)[75] can be created in a similar way to a yearly tenancy, namely, either by express agreement, or by inference, such as that arising from the payment and acceptance of rent measured with reference to a week, month or quarter, as the case may be, in circumstances where the parties intended there to be a tenancy.[76] In general, the position of the parties under such a tenancy is similar to that under a yearly tenancy, save that notice of termination is not half a period, but a full period, expiring at the end of a completed period, subject to any contrary agreement between the parties.[77] Thus in the absence of any contrary agreement, a weekly tenancy commencing on a Monday can be determined either by notice given on or before one Monday to expire on the following Monday,[78] or, since a week starting on a Monday is complete at midnight on the following Sunday, by notice given on or before one Sunday to expire on the following Sunday.[79] But at least four weeks' notice is now required for premises genuinely let as a dwelling.[80]

4. Tenancies at will. A tenancy at will arises whenever a tenant, with the consent of the landlord, occupies *qua* tenant (and not merely as a servant or agent) on the terms that either party may determine the tenancy at any time. In some cases the tenant holds rent free, as where the vendor of a fee simple, owing to some delay in completion, lets the purchaser into possession of the property before the conveyance has been executed.[81] But unless the parties agree that the tenancy shall be rent free, the landlord is entitled to compensation for the use and occupation of the land[82]; and if a rent is fixed the landlord may distrain for it in the usual way.

A tenancy at will comes to an end when either party does any act incompatible with the continuance of the tenancy, as where the tenant commits voluntary waste,[83] or the landlord enters the land and cuts trees or carries away stone,[84] or either party gives notice to the

[75] *Land Settlement Association Ltd.* v. *Carr* [1944] K.B. 657.
[76] *Cole* v. *Kelly* [1920] 2 K.B. 106 at p. 132; *Clarke* v. *Grant* [1950] 1 K.B. 104; *Longrigg Burrough & Trounson* v. *Smith* (1979) 251 E.G. 847.
[77] *Queen's Club Gardens Estates Ltd.* v. *Bignell* [1924] 1 K.B. 117; *Lemon* v. *Lardeur* [1946] K.B. 613.
[78] *Newman* v. *Slade* [1926] 2 K.B. 328.
[79] *Bathavon R.D.C.* v. *Carlile* [1958] 1 Q.B. 461.
[80] Protection from Eviction Act 1977, s. 5; *Schnabel* v. *Allard* [1967] 1 Q.B. 627.
[81] *Howard* v. *Shaw* (1841) 8 M. & W. 118.
[82] Distress for Rent Act 1737, s. 11; *Howard* v. *Shaw, supra.*
[83] *Countess of Shrewsbury's Case* (1600) 5 Co.Rep. 13b.
[84] *Turner* v. *Doe* d. *Bennett* (1842) 9 M. & W. 643.

other determining the tenancy. The tenancy is also determined if either party dies or assigns his interest in the land.[85] Essentially, the tenancy is only a personal relationship between the landlord and tenant.[86]

If a tenancy at will is created without any agreement as to payment of rent, and rent is subsequently paid and accepted upon some regular periodical basis, a yearly, monthly or other periodical tenancy will be created in accordance with the rules set out under heads 2 and 3 above.

5. Tenancies at sufferance. A tenancy at sufferance arises where a tenant, having entered upon land under a valid tenancy, holds over without the landlord's assent or dissent.[87] Such a tenant differs from a trespasser in that his original entry was lawful, and from a tenant at will in that his tenancy exists without the landlord's assent. No rent, as such, is payable, but the tenant is liable to pay compensation for his use and occupation of the land.[88] The tenancy may be determined at any time, and may be converted into a yearly or other periodic tenancy in the usual way, *e.g.* if rent is paid and accepted with reference to a year in circumstances where the parties intended there to be a tenancy.

There are statutory penalties for tenants who hold over after giving or receiving notice to quit:

(a) *Double annual value.* If the landlord gives the tenant written notice to quit and the tenant is a tenant for life or for years, the tenant is liable to pay the landlord a sum calculated at double the annual value of the land in respect of the period for which he holds over after the notice expired; this can be enforced by action but not otherwise, *e.g.* not by distress.[89] This provision applies to tenancies from year to year as well as to tenancies for fixed terms of years or for a year certain, but not to weekly tenancies.[90]

(b) *Double rent.* If the tenant gives the landlord written or oral notice to quit, then, whatever the type of tenancy, the tenant is liable to pay double rent in respect of the period for which he holds over after the notice expired; payment can be enforced by action or distress.[91]

The curiously differing terms of these aged provisions will be noticed. The rent and the annual value may be the same, but they

[85] See *Pinhorn* v. *Souster* (1853) 8 Exch. 763 at p. 772.
[86] *Wheeler* v. *Mercer* [1957] A.C. 416 at p. 426.
[87] See *Remon* v. *City of London Real Property Co. Ltd.* [1921] 1 K.B. 49 at p. 58.
[88] *Leigh* v. *Dickeson* (1884) 15 Q.B.D. 60.
[89] Landlord and Tenant Act 1730, s. 1.
[90] *Lloyd* v. *Rosbee* (1810) 2 Camp. 453.
[91] Distress for Rent Act 1737, s. 18.

often differ, as where premises have been let at a reduced rent in consideration of a fine.

B. *Statutory Modifications*

Although the parties to a lease can in general create a lease for such periods as they think fit, statute has made some modifications to this position.

1. Leases for lives. By the Law of Property Act 1925,[92] a lease at a rent or a fine for life or lives, or for a term of years determinable with a life or lives or on the marriage of the lessee, is converted into a term of 90 years, whether it was granted before or after 1925; a contract for such a lease is treated in a similar way. The lease continues even after the death or marriage, as the case may be, although either party may determine it thereafter (but not before) by serving on the other one month's written notice to expire on one of the quarter-days applicable to the tenancy, or, if no special quarter-days are applicable, on one of the usual quarter-days. Thus leases at a rent or fine granted—

"to A for life,"
"to B for 10 years if he so long lives," and—
"to C for 99 years if he so long remains a bachelor"

are all converted into terms which will continue for 90 years unless by the proper notice they are determined on any quarter-day (not necessarily the first) after the event has occurred.

Exceptionally, these provisions do not apply where the lease takes effect in equity under a Settled Land Act settlement.[93] This is to distinguish between family leases and commercial leases.

2. Perpetually renewable leases. A perpetually renewable lease was a lease which gave the tenant the right to renew it for another period as often as it expired[94]; usually the tenant had to make some payment on exercising this right. By the Law of Property Act 1922,[95] all such leases existing at the end of 1925 were converted into terms of 2000 years, calculated from the beginning of the existing terms; and perpetually renewable leases granted after 1925 take effect as terms of 2000 years from the date fixed for the commencement of the term. Any perpetually renewable sub-lease created out of a perpetually

---

[92] s. 149(6).
[93] s. 149(6)(*a*); s.205(i) (xxvi).
[94] Contrast, *e.g. Parkus* v. *Greenwood* [1950] Ch. 644 and *Caerphilly Concrete Products Ltd.* v. *Owen* [1972] 1 W.L.R. 372 where the Court of Appeal found sufficient intent that the covenant for renewal was perpetual with *Marjorie Burnett Ltd.* v. *Barclay, The Times,* December 19, 1980, (1981) 131 New L.J. 683 (H.W. Wilkinson) where the contrary was held by Nourse J. A clause for renewal "on the terms and conditions herein contained (including the present covenant for renewal)" is a clause providing for perpetual renewal.
[95] s. 145 and 15th Sched.

renewable lease is converted into a term of 2000 years less one day. The 2000-year lease is subject to the same terms as the original lease, with the following modifications.

(a) *Termination.* The tenant for the time being (but not the landlord) may terminate the lease on any date upon which, but for the conversion by the Act, the lease would have expired if it had not been renewed, provided he gives at least 10 days' written notice to the landlord.

(b) *Assignment.* Every assignment or devolution of the lease must be registered with the landlord or his solicitor or agent within six months, and a fee of one guinea paid.

(c) *Breach of covenant.* A tenant who assigns the lease is not liable for breaches of covenant committed after the assignment. The general rule is that the original lessee is liable for all breaches occurring during the term, even if they occur after he has assigned the lease[96]; perpetually renewable leases are a statutory exception to this rule.

(d) *Fine.* Any fine or other payment for renewal for which the lease provides is converted into additional rent and spread over the period between the renewal dates, except where the lease is granted after 1925, when the obligation for payment is void.

It should be noted that the landlord has no right to determine the lease at the renewal dates. Before 1926, if L granted T a lease for 21 years with a perpetual right of renewal, it was T alone who had the right to decide each 21 years whether or not to renew the lease. This position is preserved, save that now the lease continues unless determined, instead of requiring renewal.

3. Over-lengthy renewals. A contract made after 1925 to renew a lease for over 60 years from its termination is void.[97] This is aimed at single renewals, not perpetual renewals, and does not affect contracts made before 1926.

4. Reversionary leases. A lease at a rent or a fine cannot be granted after 1925 to commence at too distant a future date. This has already been dealt with.[98]

C. Estoppel

1. Estoppel. On the grant of a lease or tenancy, both landlord and tenant and their successors in title are in general mutually estopped from denying the validity of the transaction. Neither landlord nor

---

[96] See *post*, p. 378.
[97] L.P.A. 1922, 15th Sched.
[98] *Ante*, p. 340.

tenant will be permitted to assert that the tenancy which they have purported to create is invalid, and this is so even if the tenancy is merely oral.[99] But this does not prevent a corporation from setting up that it had no power to grant or receive the tenancy; estoppel cannot validate an *ultra vires* act.[1]

2. Tenancy by estoppel. One consequence of this rule is that if the landlord in fact has no estate in the land, then although the lease or tenancy can confer no actual estate on the tenant, and cannot be effective against third parties,[2] it is good between the parties to it and their successors in title.[3] Both landlord and tenant will be estopped from denying the validity of the lease or tenancy; they cannot "blow hot and cold" by claiming that the transaction was valid when entered into, and yet asserting subsequently that it was a nullity.

No tenancy by estoppel arises, however, if the lessor had a legal interest (as distinct from an equitable interest)[4] in the land when he granted the lease. If his interest was greater than the tenancy, the lease takes effect in the ordinary way; if it was equal to or smaller than the tenancy, the grant of the lease operates as an assignment of the lessor's interest.[5] Thus if L grants T a lease for 99 years T will take a lease for 99 years by estoppel if L had no interest in the land when the lease was granted. But if L had a lease for 10 years at that time, the lease for 99 years will operate as an assignment to T of L's lease for 10 years.

3. Feeding the estoppel. If there is a tenancy by estoppel, and subsequently the landlord acquires an interest in the land out of which the tenancy could have been created (*e.g.* the fee simple is devised to him or purchased by him), this is said to "feed the estoppel." From that moment the lease becomes fully effective giving the tenant an actual estate in the land.[6]

4. Problems for mortgagees. If P is allowed possession of a house before completing his purchase, then grants a lease to T, then completes the purchase by executing a mortgage for the purchase-moneys, does the lease bind the mortgagee? It does, since the

---

[99] *E.H. Lewis & Son Ltd.* v. *Morelli* [1948] 2 All E.R. 1021. After going out of possession the tenant is still estopped from denying his landlord's title for the period for which he had possession (*e.g.* if sued on repairing covenants) unless evicted by title paramount: *Industrial Properties Ltd.* v. *Associated Electrical Industries* [1977] Q.B. 580.

[1] *Rhyl U.D.C.* v. *Rhyl Amusements Ltd.* [1959] 1 W.L.R. 465.

[2] *Tadman* v. *Henman* [1893] 2 Q.B. 168.

[3] See *E.H. Lewis & Son Ltd.* v. *Morelli, supra.*

[4] *Universal P.B.S.* v. *Cooke* [1952] Ch. 95 at p. 102 (tenancy by estoppel where lessor had contracted to buy the property let but had not completed the purchase).

[5] *Beardman* v. *Wilson* (1868) L.R. 4 C.P. 57; *Wollaston* v. *Hakewill* (1841) 3 M. & G. 297 at p. 323.

[6] *Macley* v. *Nutting* [1949] 2 K.B. 55.

tenancy by estoppel was "fed" by the conveyance of the legal estate to P a split second before P mortgaged that legal estate.[7]

Part 3

ASSIGNMENT OF LEASES

In order to effect a legal assignment of a lease, a deed must be employed,[8] even if the lease has been created by word of mouth, *e.g.* a yearly tenancy in possession at a rack rent.[9] However, on principles similar to those applicable to the creation of leases, an oral or written assignment which is sufficiently evidenced by writing or part performance[10] will be effective in equity, though only as between assignor and assignee. Thus, unless estopped from so doing, the assignee may deny liability to the landlord on the covenants of the lease since there will be no privity of estate in respect of that lease.[11] On an assignment the assignor can reserve a right of entry to ensure compliance by the assignee and his successors with covenants in the assignment.[12] Other matters concerning assignments are dealt with below.[13]

The grant of sub-leases is governed by the rules relating to the grant of leases.[14]

Part 4

DETERMINATION OF TENANCIES

A lease or tenancy may come to an end in the following ways.

(1) By expiry.
(2) By notice.
(3) By forfeiture.
(4) By surrender.
(5) By merger.
(6) By becoming a satisfied term.
(7) By enlargement.
(8) By disclaimer.
(9) By frustration.

---

[7] *Church of England B.S.* v. *Piskor* [1954] Ch. 553.
[8] L.P.A. 1925, s. 52(1), replacing R.P.A. 1845, s. 3.
[9] *Botting* v. *Martin* (1808) 1 Camp. 317.
[10] *Ante,* pp. 292 *et seq.,* pp. 297 *et seq.,* pp. 314 *et seq.*
[11] *Rodenhurst Estates Ltd.* v. *W.H. Barnes Ltd.* [1936] 2 All E.R. 3. There will be privity of estate in respect of the periodic tenancy arising from payment and acceptance of rent.
[12] *Shiloh Spinners Ltd.* v. *Harding* [1973] A.C. 691.
[13] *Post,* pp. 366, 379, 382, 383, 385.
[14] *Ante,* pp. 335 *et seq.*

Sect. 1. By Expiry

As has been seen,[15] a lease or tenancy for a fixed period automatically determines when the fixed period expires, with certain exceptions. In some cases the tenant may be entitled to be granted a new lease or to remain in possession as a statutory tenant.[16]

Sect. 2. By Notice

A lease or tenancy for a fixed period cannot be determined by notice unless this is expressly agreed upon. Thus a lease for a substantial term such as 21 years often contains provisions enabling the tenant to determine it at the end of the seventh or fourteenth year, in which case the length of the notice required, the time when it is to be given, and other matters of this kind, depend on the terms of the lease. In the absence of any such provision the lease will continue for the full period.

Yearly, weekly, monthly and other periodical tenancies can be determined by notice. These provisions, and the determination of tenancies at will and at sufferance, have already been considered.[17]

Many periodic tenants have statutory protection against eviction.[18]

Sect. 3. By Forfeiture

A. Right to Forfeit

A landlord's right to forfeit a lease (*i.e.* enforce a forfeiture of it) may arise under three heads.

1. Forfeiture clause. Nearly every lease contains a list of things which the tenant shall and shall not do, and these may be framed as conditions or as covenants. If, as is normally the case, they are framed as covenants (*e.g.* "The tenant hereby covenants with the landlord as follows . . . "), the landlord has no right to forfeit the lease if they are broken *unless* the lease contains an express provision for forfeiture on breach of a covenant.[19] There is no necessary connection between the tenant failing to perform a covenant made by him and the determination of the lease; every well-drawn lease consequently contains a forfeiture clause which in a legal lease creates a legal right of re-entry, making the lease voidable at the landlord's option if a covenant is broken.

2. Breach of condition. If the tenant's obligations are worded as

[15] *Ante*, p. 341.
[16] *Post*, pp. 566 *et seq.*
[17] *Ante*, p. 341.
[18] See *post*, pp. 566 *et seq.*
[19] *Doe* d. *Wilson* v. *Phillips* (1824) 2 Bing. 13.

conditions, however (*e.g.* if the lease is granted "upon condition that" or "provided always that" certain things are done or not done), the lease may be forfeited on breach of condition even if there is no forfeiture clause.[20] In such a case, the continuance of the lease has been made conditional upon the tenant performing his obligations, and upon breach of one of them the lease becomes voidable at the landlord's option so the tenant will not be allowed to set up his breach to avoid his liability under the lease if the landlord does not treat it as forfeited.[21]

3. Denial of title. If a tenant denies his landlord's title, as by asserting (even orally) that he or some third party is the true owner, the landlord is forthwith entitled to forfeit the tenancy.[22] But a mere denial of title in a pleading in an action merely puts the other party to proof of his case and so works no forfeiture, especially if it is withdrawn before the landlord elects to take advantage of it.[23]

B. Waiver of Breach

Even if the landlord has shown that he is treating the lease as forfeited, he may subsequently prevent himself from proceeding with the forfeiture if he waives the breach of covenant; and *a fortiori* a waiver of the breach may take place before the landlord has shown that he is treating the lease as forfeited. Waiver may be express or implied. It will be implied if—

(i) the landlord is aware of the acts or omissions of the tenant giving rise to the right of forfeiture, and
(ii) the landlord does some unequivocal act recognising the continued existence of the lease.[24]

Both elements must be present to constitute a waiver. A waiver will be implied where a landlord, with knowledge of the breach, demands or sues for or accepts rent falling due after the breach[25] (even if accepted "without prejudice"[26] or by a clerk of his agents by mistake)[27] or distrains for rent, whether due before or after the breach.[28] The acts, however, will not amount to a waiver if done after

---

[20] See *Doe* d. *Lockwood* v. *Clarke* (1807) 8 East 185.
[21] See *Doe* d. *Bryan* v. *Bancks* (1821) 4 B. & Ald. 401; *Roberts* v. *Davey* (1833) 4 B. & Ad. 664.
[22] *Wisbech St. Mary Parish Council* v. *Lilley* [1956] 1 W.L.R. 121.
[23] *Warner* v. *Sampson* [1959] 1 Q.B. 297; and see *post*, p. 355.
[24] *Matthews* v. *Smallwood* [1910] 1 Ch. 777 at p. 786. Managing agents' knowledge will be imputed to the landlord as will the knowledge of an employee, *e.g.* a porter if under a duty to inform the landlord: *Metropolitan Properties Ltd.* v. *Cordery* (1980) 39 P. & C.R. 10.
[25] *Goodright* d. *Charter* v. *Cordwent* (1795) 6 T.R. 219; *David Blackstone Ltd.* v. *Burnetts* (*West End*) *Ltd.* [1973] 1 W.L.R. 1487 (rent payable in advance).
[26] *Davenport* v. *R.* (1877) 3 App.Cas 115; *Segal Securities Ltd.* v. *Thoseby* [1963] 1 Q.B. 887.
[27] *Central Estates Ltd.* v. *Woolgar* [1972] 1 W.L.R. 1048.
[28] *Ward* v. *Day* (1863) 4 B. & S. 337 at 353; 5 B. & S. 364.

the landlord has shown his final decision to treat the lease as forfeited, as by commencing an action for possession.[29]

As would be expected, the waiver of a covenant or condition extends only to the particular breach in question and does not operate as a general waiver of all future breaches, although the law was once different; the same applies to a licence granted to the tenant to do any act.[30] And waiver of the forfeiture is no bar to an action for damages.[31]

C. Mode of Forfeiture

The normal method of enforcing a forfeiture is by issuing and serving a writ for possession; such a writ usually contains an unequivocal demand for possession, so that the *service* of the writ operates to determine the lease.[32] Alternatively, unless the premises are let as a dwelling-house on a lease and some person is lawfully residing in it or in any part of it,[33] the landlord can enforce his right of forfeiture by making peaceable entry on the land. It is usually inadvisable for a landlord to adopt this method, for if any force is used, he may be criminally (but not civilly)[34] liable under the Forcible Entry Acts 1381, 1391 and 1429.[35]

D. Conditions for Forfeiture

The conditions under which a right of forfeiture can be enforced depend upon whether the right arises from breach of the covenant or condition to pay rent or from breach of any other provision. Moreover, in each case, first, equity, and later, statute, have intervened so as to allow tenants to obtain relief from forfeiture in certain circumstances.[36]

I. FORFEITURE FOR NON-PAYMENT OF RENT

Where a landlord has the right to forfeit a lease for non-payment of rent, two important points to be considered are the landlord's formal demand for the rent and the tenant's right to relief.

1. Landlord's formal demand: the landlord must either have made a formal demand for the rent, or else be exempted from making such a demand.

---

[29] *Grimwood* v. *Moss* (1872) L.R. 7 C.P. 360.
[30] L.P.A. 1925, ss. 143, 148, replacing earlier provisions which altered the law laid down in *Dumpor's Case* (1603) 4 Co.Rep. 119b.
[31] *Stephens* v. *Junior Army and Navy Stores Ltd.* [1914] 2 Ch. 516.
[32] *Elliott* v. *Boynton* [1924] 1 Ch. 236, as explained in *Canas Property Co. Ltd.* v. *K.L. Television Services Ltd.* [1970] 1 Q.B. 433.
[33] Protection from Eviction Act 1977, s. 2.
[34] *Hemmings* v. *Stoke Poges Golf Club* [1920] 1 K.B. 720.
[35] For another disadvantage, see *R.* v. *Hussey* (1924) 18 Cr.App.R. 160.
[36] For the equitable jurisdiction, see *Shiloh Spinners Ltd.* v. *Harding* [1973] A.C. 691.

(a) *Formal demand.* To make a formal demand, the landlord or his authorised agent must demand the exact sum due on the day when it falls due at such covenient hour before sunset as will give time to count out the money, the demand being made upon the demised premises and continuing until sunset.[37]

(b) *Exemption from formal demand.* To avoid the technicalities of a formal demand, every well-drawn lease provides that the lease may be forfeited if the rent is a specified number of days in arrear, "whether formally demanded or not." The words quoted exempt the landlord from making a formal demand. However, even if a lease contains no such clause, the Common Law Procedure Act 1852[38] dispenses with a formal demand in any action for forfeiture if—

    (i) half a year's rent is in arrear, and

    (ii) no sufficient distress (*i.e.* goods available for distraint) can be found[39] upon the premises to satisfy all the arrears due.[40]

2. Tenant's right to relief: the tenant may be able to claim relief against the forfeiture. Equity considered that a right of forfeiture was merely security for payment of the rent, so that if—

    (i) the tenant paid the rent due; and

    (ii) the tenant paid any expenses to which the landlord had been put; and

    (iii) it was just and equitable to grant relief,

equity would restore the tenant to his position despite the forfeiture of the lease.[41] Originally, there was no limit to the time within which application for relief had to be made, apart from the general principle that equity would give no assistance to stale claims.[42] But the Common Law Procedure Act 1852[43] provides that if, before trial, the tenant pays arrears and costs when at least six months rent is in arrear[44] then the proceedings must be stayed. Furthermore, where the landlord has obtained and procured the execution of a judgment for possession, an application for relief must be made within six months of the execution. If the landlord re-enters without an order, the statute does not apply, and the old equitable jurisdiction remains.[45] While the court will tend to adopt the same time limit it

---

[37] See 1. Wms. Saund. (1871) 434 *et seq.*

[38] s. 210, re-enacting the Landlord and Tenant Act 1730, s. 2; County Courts Act 1959, s. 191(2).

[39] See *Hammond* v. *Mather* (1862) 3 F. & F. 151 (no distress can be "found" if the outer doors are locked).

[40] See *Cross* v. *Jordan* (1853) 8 Exch. 149.

[41] See *Howard* v. *Fanshawe* [1895] 2 Ch. 581.

[42] See *Hill* v. *Barclay* (1811) 18 Ves. 56 at pp. 59, 60.

[43] ss. 210–212, replacing L. & T. Act 1730, ss. 2, 4. And see County Courts Act 1959, s. 191(3).

[44] *Standard Pattern Co. Ltd.* v. *Ivey* [1962] Ch. 432 criticised in (1962) 78 L.Q.R. 168 (R.E.M.).

[45] *Thatcher* v. *C.H. Pearce & Sons (Contractors) Ltd.* [1968] 1 W.L.R. 748.

will not "boggle at a matter of days."[46] If relief is granted, the tenant holds under the old lease[47] and the execution of a new document is not required.

Where a lease is forfeited, any underleases created out of it automatically come to an end.[48] However, an underlessee (or mortgagee) has the same right of applying for relief against forfeiture of the head lease as the tenant under the head lease has.[49]

II. FORFEITURE FOR BREACH OF OTHER COVENANTS OR CONDITIONS

The general rule is that forfeiture for breach of a covenant or condition other than for payment of rent is subject to the landlord's obligation to serve a notice in the statutory form and the tenant's right to relief. There are some exceptions to this rule, however, and there are special provisions for sub-tenants. The right to receive a notice and to apply for relief prevail over any stipulation to the contrary.[50] Hence a device such as an undated surrender executed by the tenant as a guarantee against breaches of covenant is void.[51]

1. General rule. (a) *Service of notice.* Before proceeding to enforce forfeiture either by action or re-entry, the landlord must serve on the tenant the statutory notice in writing under the Law of Property Act 1925, s.146.[52] The notice must—

(i) specify the breach complained of; and

(ii) require it to be remedied, if this is possible; and

(iii) require the tenant to make compensation in money for the breach if the landlord requires such compensation.[53]

Thus a notice in respect of immoral use of the premises that has continued for so long as to cast a stigma on the premises, need only specify the breach, for mere discontinuance of this use would not remedy the breach, and the landlord need not soil his hands by claiming compensation out of the tenant's ill-gotten gains.[54] However, exceptionally, where there has been short-lived immoral user by a sub-tenant, owing to prompt steps taken by the tenant stopping such user, so that no stigma has become attached to the premises the

---

[46] *Ibid.* at p. 756, *per* Simon P.
[47] Common Law Procedure Act 1852, s. 212; J.A. 1925, s. 46; and see County Courts Act 1959, s. 191.
[48] *Great Western Ry.* v. *Smith* (1876) 2 Ch.D. 235 at p. 253.
[49] Common Law Procedure Act 1852, s. 210; L.P.A. 1925 s. 146(4); *Belgravia Insurance Co.* v. *Meah* [1964] 1 Q.B. 436; though under L.P.A. relief is only available before re-entry.
[50] L.P.A. 1925, s. 146(12).
[51] *Plymouth Corporation* v. *Harvey* [1971] 1 W.L.R. 549, also see *Richard Clarke & Co. Ltd.* v. *Widnall* [1976] 1 W.L.R. 845.
[52] Replacing C.A. 1981, s. 14, and C.A. 1892, ss. 2, 4.
[53] L.P.A. 1925, s. 146(1); and see *post*, p. 345 (repairs).
[54] *Rugby School (Govenors)* v. *Tannahill* [1935] 1 K.B. 87.

breach will be considered remediable.[55] The safest course is thus for a landlord to require the specified breach to be remedied "if it is capable of remedy."

(b) *Time for compliance*. The landlord must then allow a reasonable time to elapse in which the tenant may comply with the notice. The Act does not define what is a reasonable time, but three months is usually considered to be enough in normal circumstances. Some breaches are incapable of remedy, *e.g.* a breach of a covenant not to assign or sublet,[56] or a forfeiture on bankruptcy of the tenant or a surety who has guaranteed the tenant's obligations. Even then reasonable notice must be given so as to enable the tenant to consider his position; in such cases, two days' notice has been held to be insufficient[57] although fourteen days may be enough.[58]

(c) *Relief*. If within a reasonable time the notice has not been complied with, the landlord may proceed to enforce the forfeiture. This he may do in person or by action, the same considerations applying as before.[59] However, while the landlord "is proceeding" to enforce the forfeiture (*i.e.* at any time before he has actually entered),[60] the tenant may apply to the court for relief, either in any action by the landlord enforcing the forfeiture or by a separate application.[61] The court may grant relief (even in the case of breach of a negative covenant which may technically be irremediable though remediable in fact) on such terms as it thinks fit, and if relief is granted the effect is as if the lease had never been forfeited.[62] If the breach has been remedied, relief is usually granted, but may be refused if the tenant's personal qualifications are important and he has proved unsatisfactory.[63] In cases where the breach involves immoral user relief will not be granted save in very exceptional circumstances.[64] Where there are two parts of the demised property which are physically separated and capable of being distinctly let and enjoyed (*e.g.* a ground-floor and basement) and where the breaches

---

[55] *Glass* v. *Kencakes Ltd.* [1966] 1 Q.B. 611. The technical view that all breaches of negative covenants are irremediable, since what has been done has been done once and for all and cannot be undone, was considered discredited after the *Rugby School* case (*supra*) but now has fresh support in *Scala House Property Co. Ltd.* v. *Forbes* [1974] Q.B. 575 at p. 588, (1974) 33 Camb. L.J. 54 (D.J.H.).

[56] *Scala House & District Property Co. Ltd.* v. *Forbes* [1974] Q.B. 575. Where assignment occurs in breach of covenant the assignment is effective and so the s. 146 notice must be served on the assignee: *Old Grovebury Manor Farm* v. *Seymour Plant Sales Ltd.* [1979] 1 W.L.R. 1397.

[57] *Horsey Estate Ltd.* v. *Steiger* [1899] 2 Q.B. 79.

[58] *Scala House & District Property Co. Ltd.* v. *Forbes, supra.*

[59] *Ante*, p. 351.

[60] *Rogers* v. *Rice* [1892] 2 Ch. 170.

[61] L.P.A. 1925, s. 146(2).

[62] *Dendy* v. *Evans* [1909] 2 K.B. 894; *Scala House* (*supra*).

[63] *Bathurst* (*Earl*) v. *Fine* [1974] 1 W.L.R. 905.

[64] *Central Estates* (*Belgravia*) *Ltd.* v. *Woolgar* (*No.* 2) [1972] 1 W.L.R. 1048 (sick aged tenant carrying on short-lived homosexual brothel and value of premises had not been detrimentally affected).

were committed on one part (*e.g.* immoral user by a sub-tenant) then relief may be granted in respect of the other part only.[65] There is no provision enabling the court to grant relief after forfeiture, even within six months.

2. Exceptional cases. The above provisions concerning the necessity for serving a notice and the tenant's right to apply for relief do not affect forfeiture for denial of title,[66] but they govern all covenants and conditions (other than those for payment of rent) with two exceptions. These two exceptions are as follows:

(a) *Mining lease:* when there has been a breach of a covenant in a mining lease providing for inspection of the books, accounts, weighing machines or other things, or of the mine itself.[67] Since the rent reserved on such a lease usually varies with the quantity of minerals obtained, such a covenant is most important to the landlord; there is consequently no restriction upon the landlord forfeiting the lease without serving a notice, and no provision enabling the tenant to obtain relief.

(b) *Bankruptcy or execution:* when there has been a breach of a condition against the bankruptcy of the tenant or the taking of the lease in execution.[68] This must be divided into two heads.

(1) NO PROTECTION. In five specified cases, on breach of such a condition, section 146 has no application at all; the lease can thus be forfeited at once without service of notice and without possibility of relief. These cases are those where the lease is of—

   (i) agricultural or pastoral land, or
  (ii) mines or minerals, or
 (iii) a public house or beershop, or
 (iv) a furnished house, or
  (v) property with respect to which the personal qualifications of the tenant are of importance for the preservation of the value or character of the property, or on the ground of neighbourhood to the landlord or to any person holding under him.

(2) PROTECTION FOR ONE YEAR. In all other cases, on breach of such a condition, the protection of section 146 applies for one year from the bankruptcy or taking in execution; if during that year the landlord wishes to forfeit the lease, he must serve the notice and the tenant can apply for relief. But once the year has elapsed, the tenant is no longer

[65] *GMS Syndicate Ltd.* v. *Gary Elliott Ltd.* [1981] 2 W.L.R. 478.
[66] *Warner* v. *Sampson* [1958] 1 Q.B. 404; revsd. on other grounds [1959] 1 Q.B. 297; *ante* p. 350.
[67] *Ibid.*
[68] *Ibid.* s. 146(9), (10). This does not apply on the bankruptcy of the tenant's surety: *Halliard Property Co. Ltd.* v. *Jack Segal Ltd.* [1978] 1 W.L.R. 377.

Leases and Tenancies

protected; the landlord can forfeit the lease without serving notice and the court has no power to grant relief.

In one case under this head, however, the provisions as to notice and relief apply without limit of time: if the tenant's lease is sold during the year, the protection of section 146 continues indefinitely. This allows the trustee in bankruptcy or sheriff to dispose of the lease to a purchaser at a reasonable price, for if the lease were liable to be forfeited after the year, without the service of notice or the chance of relief, it would be hard to find a purchaser.

3. Sub-tenants. Under section 146, as amended by the Law of Property (Amendment) Act 1929,[69] a sub-tenant may apply for relief against the forfeiture of his landlord's lease on whatever ground that forfeiture is being enforced; and a mere mortgagee or chargee is a "sub-tenant" for these purposes.[70] A sub-tenant has this right whether the head lease is being forfeited for non-payment of rent, for one of the exceptional cases mentioned above or for any other reason, irrespective of whether the tenant himself can claim relief. If relief is granted, the court will grant the sub-tenant a term not longer than the term he held under his sub-lease,[71] and may impose certain conditions for making good any subsisting breaches.[72] The sub-tenant usually enters into a new lease direct with the reversioner of the forfeited lease on terms similar to (though not necessarily the same as) those of the old sub-lease.

Sect. 4. By Surrender

If a tenant surrenders his lease to his immediate landlord, who accepts the surrender, the lease merges in the landlord's reversion and is extinguished. The surrender must be to the immediate landlord; a transfer of the lease to a superior landlord does not work a surrender but operates merely as an assignment of the lease. Thus if A leases land to B for 99 years and B sub-leases to C for 21 years, C's lease will be extinguished by surrender if he transfers it to B but not if he transfers it to A. If C surrenders his lease to B any sub-lease or mortgage created by C will, however, bind B for as long as it would have bound C had the lease not been surrendered.[73]

Surrender may be either express or by operation of law. For an express surrender, a deed is required,[74] although probably an oral surrender made for value and supported by sufficient evidence in writing or part performance would suffice in equity. There will be

---

[69] s. 1.
[70] *Grand Junction Co. Ltd.* v. *Bates* [1954] 2 Q.B. 160; and see *post*, pp. 465 *et seq.*
[71] L.P.A. 1925, s. 146(4); and see *Ewart* v. *Fryer* [1901] 1 Ch. 499 at p. 515.
[72] *Chatham Empire Theatre Ltd.* v. *Ultrams Ltd.* [1961] 1 W.L.R. 817; *Belgravia Insurance Co. Ltd.* v. *Meah* [1964] 1 Q.B. 436.
[73] *Schwab* v. *McCarthy* (1976) 31 P. & C.R. 196.
[74] L.P.A. 1925, s. 52, replacing R.P.A. 1845, s. 3.

surrender by operation of law if the parties do some act showing an intention to terminate the lease, and the circumstances are such that it would be inequitable for them to rely on the fact that there has been no surrender by deed.[75] Surrender by operation of law will take place if the tenant accepts a fresh lease from his immediate reversioner, even though the new lease is for a shorter term than the old one or starts at a future date[76]; and if a lease is varied by extending the term, this operates by way of surrender and regrant.[77] Other variations, *e.g.* an agreed increase of rent, do not necessarily bring about a surrender and regrant.[78] There will also be a surrender by operation of law if the tenant gives up possession of the premises and the landlord accepts it,[79] but not if there is a mere uncompleted contract by the tenant to purchase the reversion.[80]

Sect. 5. By Merger

Merger is the counterpart of surrender. Under a surrender, the landlord acquires the lease, whereas merger is the consequence of the tenant retaining the lease and acquiring the reversion, or of a third party acquiring both lease and reversion. The principle is the same in both surrender and merger: the lease is absorbed by the reversion and destroyed.

For merger to be effective, the lease and the reversion must be vested in the same person in the same right with no vested estate intervening.[81] Merger may take place even if the immediate reversion consists of a lease shorter than the lease merged.[82] Thus if A, a tenant in fee simple, leases land to B for 1000 years and a few years later leases the same land to C for 400 years, the result is to give C for 400 years the reversion on B's lease. If X then acquires both C's reversion and B's lease, the 1000 years' lease will merge in the 400 years' reversion and leave X with but 400 years.[83] But there is now no merger if the person in whom the two interests vest intends that there shall be none.[84]

Sect. 6. By Becoming a Satisfied Term

If a lease is granted as security for the payment of money, the term becomes satisfied and the lease automatically ceases when all the money has been paid.[85]

---

[75] See *Glynn* v. *Coghlan* [1918] 1 I.R. 482 at p. 485.
[76] *Ive's Case* (1597) 5 Co.Rep. 11a.
[77] *Baker* v. *Merckel* [1960] 1 Q.B. 657.
[78] *Jenkin R. Lewis & Son Ltd.* v. *Kerman* [1971] Ch. 477.
[79] See *Oastler* v. *Henderson* (1877) 2 Q.B.D. 575.
[80] *Nightingale* v. *Courtney* [1954] 1 Q.B. 399.
[81] See *Chambers* v. *Kingham* (1878) 10 Ch.D. 743.
[82] *Hughes* v. *Robotham* (1593) Cro.Eliz. 302.
[83] *Stephens* v. *Bridges* (1821) 6 Madd. 66.
[84] See L.P.A., s. 185, *post*, p. 394.
[85] See *post*, pp. 464, 504.

Sect. 7. By Enlargement

Under certain conditions, not frequently encountered in practice, a lease may be enlarged into a fee simple by the tenant executing a deed of enlargement. Under the Law of Property Act 1926[86] this can be done only if—

   (i) there is not less than 200 years of the lease unexpired; and
  (ii) the lease was originally granted for at least 300 years; and
 (iii) no trust or right of redemption[87] exists in favour of the reversioner; and
 (iv) the lease is not liable to be determined by re-entry for condition broken; and
  (v) no rent of any money value is payable. A rent of "one silver penny if lawfully demanded" is a rent of no money value, but a rent of three shillings is not.[88] A rent under such a lease which does not exceed one pound per annum and which has not been paid for a continuous period of 20 years (five having elapsed since 1925) is deemed to have ceased to be payable and can no longer by recovered.

For a sub-lease to be capable of enlargement under the section, it must be derived out of a lease which is itself capable of enlargement. A fee simple acquired by enlargement is subject to all the provisions which affected the term of years out of which it arose. This seems to be a way of making positive covenants run with freehold land.[89]

Sect. 8. By Disclaimer

A right to disclaim a lease arises only by statute. Thus tenants whose premises were rendered unfit by war damage were given a statutory power to disclaim their tenancies; the effect of a valid disclaimer is the same as if there had been a surrender.[90] Similar rights were given to certain tenants of premises which were requisitioned under emergency powers.[91] But not all statutory provisions for disclaimer take effect as if there had been a surrender; thus a trustee in bankruptcy may disclaim an onerous lease, but by so doing he only terminates any liability of himself and the bankrupt and does not destroy the lease.[92]

---

[86] s. 153, replacing C.A. 1881, s. 65, and C.A. 1882, s. 11.
[87] *e.g.* a right of redemption under a mortgage; see *post*, p. 463. Thus long leases granted as security for money are excluded.
[88] *Re Chapman and Hobbs* (1885) 29 Ch.D. 1007; *Re Smith and Stott* (1883) 29 Ch.D. 1009n.
[89] See generally T.P.D. Taylor (1958) 22 Conv.(N.S.) 101.
[90] Landlord and Tenant (War Damage) Acts 1939 and 1941.
[91] Landlord and Tenant (Requisitioned Land) Acts 1942 and 1944.
[92] Bankruptcy Act 1914, s. 54; *Re Thompson and Cottrell's Contract* [1943] Ch. 97 at p. 99.

Sect. 9. By Frustration

After much uncertainty the House of Lords has recently held that the doctrine of frustration can apply in a rare case to a lease of land so as to bring the lease to an end if a frustrating event (*i.e.* an event such that no substantial use, permitted by the lease and in the contemplation of the parties, remained available to the tenant) occurs during the currency of the term.[93] Closure of the only access to a demised warehouse for 20 months of a 10 year term has been held not to be a frustrating event.[93] Presumably, a three-month lease of a holiday villa would be frustrated if on the first day the villa was burnt down otherwise than through the fault of the tenant.

Part 5

RIGHTS AND DUTIES OF THE PARTIES UNDER A LEASE OR TENANCY

The rights and duties of the landlord and tenant under a lease or tenancy fall under five heads. First, the lease may be silent as to everything except the essential terms as to parties, premises, rent and duration. This is not infrequently the case with weekly and other periodic tenancies. Secondly, the parties may have agreed to be bound by the "usual covenants." Thirdly, the lease may provide in the orthodox way not only for the matters dealt with by the "usual covenants" but also for a number of other matters. Fourthly, there are a number of statutory provisions relating to the rights and duties of the parties to a lease. The subject of fixtures has already been dealt with.[94]

The question how far covenants in a lease can be enforced between persons other than the original lessor and original lessee is considered separately.[95]

Sect. 1. Position of the Parties in the Absence of Express Provision

Except so far as the lease or tenancy agreement otherwise provides, the position of the parties is as set out below.

A. Position of the Landlord

1. Implied covenant for quiet enjoyment. A covenant for quiet enjoyment is deemed to have been given by the lessor.[96] The

---

[93] *National Carriers Ltd.* v. *Panalpina Ltd.* [1981] 2 W.L.R. 45.
[94] *Ante* p. 19.
[95] *Post,* pp. 377 *et seq.*
[96] *Markham* v. *Paget* [1908] 1 Ch. 697; *Kenny* v. *Preen* [1963] 1 Q.B. 499.

covenant extends to *all* acts of the lessor and the *lawful* acts of those claiming under him, but probably not to the acts of someone claiming by title paramount, such as a superior landlord.[97] The covenant gives the tenant the right to recover damages from the landlord if the persons to whom the covenant extends physically and substantially interfere with the tenant's enjoyment of the land demised.[98] The covenant is not one for "quiet" enjoyment in the acoustic sense; the lessor undertakes not that the tenant will be free from the nuisance of noise, but that he will be free from disturbance by adverse claimants to the property.[99] The covenant will be broken if a lessor who has reserved the right to work the minerals under the land demised causes the subsidence of the land by his mining activities.[1]

It should be appreciated that where the lease is not granted by deed, there cannot be any covenant in the technical sense, for the essence of a covenant is that it should be entered into by deed; but there will be corresponding contractual obligations.[2]

A landlord does not use the words "as beneficial owner" when granting a lease, and even if he did, these words would not import the covenants for title applicable to a conveyance.[3]

2. Obligation not to derogate from his grant. It is a principle of general application that a grantor must not derogate from his grant[4]; he must not seek to take away with one hand what he has given with the other. In the case of leases, the covenant for quiet enjoyment will extend to many of the acts which might be construed as a derogation from the lessor's grant; but acts not amounting to a breach of the covenant may nevertheless be restrained as being in derogation of the grant. Thus, if land is leased for the express purpose of storing explosives, the lessor and those claiming under him will be restrained from using adjoining land so as to endanger the statutory licence necessary for storing explosives.[5]

There must, however, be some act making the premises substantially less fit for the purposes for which they were let. No action will lie if the landlord, having let the premises for some particular trade, *e.g.* for use as a wool shop only, lets adjoining premises for purposes which offer trade competition; for the original premises are still fit for use as a wool shop even if the profits will be diminished.[6] Nor will

---

[97] See *Budd-Scott* v. *Daniel* [1902] 2 K.B. 351; *Miller* v. *Emcer Products Ltd.* [1956] Ch. 304; *Baynes & Co.* v. *Lloyd & Sons* [1895] 2 Q.B. 610.
[98] *Owen* v. *Gadd* [1956] 2 Q.B. 99.
[99] *Hudson* v. *Cripps* [1896] 1 Ch. 265 at p. 268.
[1] *Markham* v. *Paget* [1908] 1 Ch. 697.
[2] *Budd-Scott* v. *Daniel* [1902] 2 K.B. 351; *Baynes & Co.* v. *Lloyd & Sons* [1895] 1 Q.B. 820 at p. 826.
[3] See *ante*, p. 152.
[4] *Palmer* v. *Fletcher* (1663) 1 Lev. 122; and see (1964) 80 L.Q.R. 244 (D.W. Elliott).
[5] *Harmer* v. *Jumbil (Nigeria) Tin Areas Ltd.* [1921] 1 Ch. 200.
[6] *Port* v. *Griffith* [1938] 1 All E.R. 295.

mere invasion of privacy, as by erecting an external staircase passing the windows of the flat demised, amount to a breach of the obligation,[7] although interference with the stability of the house by vibrations caused by powerful engines on adjoining land may suffice, and so may excessive noise, such as that caused in altering another flat in the same building.[8]

3. In certain cases, obligations as to fitness and repair. In general, the landlord gives no implied undertaking that the premises are or will be fit for habitation,[9] nor is he liable to repair them. This rule is subject to four qualifications, which to some extent overlap.

(a) *Furnished lettings.* Where a house is let furnished, the landlord impliedly undertakes that it is fit for human habitation when let.[10] If this is not the case, the tenant may repudiate the tenancy and recover damages for any loss he has suffered.[11] But if the premises are fit for human habitation when let, the landlord need do no more; he is under no obligation to keep them in this condition.[12] And the tenant is not deemed to warrant his fitness to occupy the premises, *e.g.* that he is free from contagious diseases.[13]

(b) *Houses let at a low rent.* Under the Housing Act 1957[14] if a house is let for human habitation at a total rent within certain limits, then, notwithstanding any stipulation to the contrary, there is—

(i) an implied condition that it is fit for human habitation at the beginning of the tenancy, and
(ii) an implied undertaking by the landlord that he will keep it in this condition throughout the tenancy.

The limits of rent are £80 a year in London and £52 elsewhere, or half these amounts if the contract of letting was made before July 6, 1957; and these provisions do not apply to leases not determinable for three years or more under which the lessee is to make the premises reasonably fit for human habitation.

The undertaking extends only to defects of which the landlord has notice,[15] and there is now a statutory list of matters to be considered, *e.g.* repair, freedom from damp, natural lighting, ventilation and drainage.[16] A small defect such as a broken sash-cord may constitute a breach of the statute, for the test is not how difficult it is to repair the defect but whether the state of repair of the house "is such that by

---

[7] *Browne* v. *Flower* [1911] 1 Ch. 219.
[8] *Newman* v. *Real Estate Debenture Corporation Ltd.* [1940] 1 All E.R. 131.
[9] *Hart* v. *Windsor* (1844) 12 M. & W. 68.
[10] *Smith* v. *Marrable* (1843) 11 M. & W. 5 (bugs).
[11] *Wilson* v. *Finch-Hatton* (1877) 2 Ex.D. 336; *Charsley* v. *Jones* (1889) 53 J.P. 280.
[12] *Sarson* v. *Roberts* [1895] 2 Q.B. 395.
[13] *Humphreys* v. *Miller* [1917] 2 K.B. 122.
[14] s. 6, extending earlier legislation.
[15] *McCarrick* v. *Liverpool Corporation* [1947] A.C. 219.
[16] Housing Act 1957, s. 4; and see s. 189(1).

ordinary user damage may naturally be caused to the occupier, either in respect of personal injury to life or limb or injury to health."[17]

Local authorities have extensive powers of compelling the person who has control of a house (usually the owner or his agent) to make it fit for human habitation[18]; and many tenants avoid the burdens of directly enforcing their rights by setting the local authority in motion.

(c) *Short leases of houses.* In any lease or agreement for lease[19] of a dwelling-house granted after October 24, 1961, whatever the rent or rateable value, a covenant by the landlord to do certain repairs is implied if the term is less than seven years (unless the tenant can extend it to seven years or more) or if the landlord can determine it within seven years.[20] The covenant cannot be excluded or limited by any agreement to the contrary unless the county court authorises this as being reasonable; and any covenant by the tenant to repair or pay money in lieu thereof is of no effect so far as it is covered by the implied covenant.

The implied covenant is—

(1) to keep the structure and exterior[21] in repair, and
(2) to keep in repair and proper working order the installations in the house[22]—
      (i) for the supply of water, gas and electricity and for sanitation (including basins, sinks, baths and sanitary conveniences,[23] but not other appliances for making use of water, gas and electricity), and
      (ii) for space heating or heating water.

In such cases there is also an implied covenant by the tenant to permit the landlord to enter and view the premises at reasonable times of the day on 24 hours' prior notice in writing to the occupier. The landlord is only liable for defects of which he has notice.[24]

(d) *Duty of care.* In some cases a landlord owes to all persons who might reasonably be expected to be affected by defects in the state of the premises a duty to take reasonable care to see that they and their property are reasonably safe from injury or damage. This duty arises

---

[17] *Summers* v. *Salford Corporation* [1943] A.C. 283 at p. 289, *per* Lord Atkin.
[18] Housing Act 1957, ss. 9–15, 39.
[19] *Brikom Investments Ltd.* v. *Seaford* [1981] 2 All E.R. 783.
[20] Housing Act 1961, ss. 32, 33.
[21] See *Brown* v. *Liverpool Corporation* [1969] 3 All E.R. 1345 (outside steps in Act); contrast *Hopwood* v. *Cannock Chase D.C.* [1975] 1 W.L.R 373 (back yard outside Act). The exterior of a flat comprises the outside walls though excluded from the demise: *Campden Hill Towers Ltd.* v. *Gardner* [1977] Q.B. 823. A service charge cannot validly extend to expenditure on these listed items.
[22] Thus a central heating boiler outside the demised flat is outside the Act: *Campden Hill Towers Ltd.* v. *Gardner* (*supra*).
[23] A defect in the design of lavatory cisterns causing flooding may be a breach of the covenant: *Liverpool C.C.* v. *Irwin* [1977] A.C. 239.
[24] *O'Brien* v. *Robinson* [1973] A.C. 912.

where the landlord is under an obligation to the tenant for the maintenance or repair of the premises, or has a right to enter the premises to maintain and repair them, and he knows or ought to have known of the defect.[25] The landlord cannot contract out of his liability under this provision.[26]

In *Liverpool C.C.* v. *Irwin*[27] the House of Lords held that in the case of a "high-rise block" in multiple occupation the landlord is under an implied obligation to take reasonable care to maintain the common parts (*i.e.* the stairs, the lifts and the lighting on the stairs) in a state of reasonable repair and efficiency.

B. Position of the Tenant

1. Obligation to pay rent. This is discussed below.[28]

2. Obligation to pay rates and taxes. The tenant is under an obligation to pay all rates and taxes except those for which the landlord is liable. The landlord is liable to income tax under Schedule A on the rent.[29] If he fails to pay it, the tenant may be required to pay it up to the amount of his rent, and he may deduct any such payment from any subsequent rent due from him.[30]

3. Obligation not to commit waste. A tenant's liability for waste depends upon the nature of his tenancy. A tenant for a fixed term of years is liable for both voluntary and permissive waste, and must therefore keep the premises in proper repair.[31] A yearly tenant is similarly liable save that his liability for permissive waste is limited to keeping the premises wind- and water-tight.[32] A weekly tenant, on the other hand, is not liable for permissive waste as such, though he must take proper care of the premises, *e.g.* by keeping the chimneys swept and the drain pipes unblocked[33]; it is not clear, though it seems likely, that the same rule applies to monthly and quarterly tenants. A tenant at will is not liable for permissive waste,[34] although if he commits voluntary waste his tenancy is thereby terminated and he is liable to an action for damages.[35] A tenant at sufferance is liable for voluntary waste,[36] though probably not for permissive waste.

---

[25] Defective Premises Act 1972, s. 4.
[26] *Ibid.* s. 6(3).
[27] [1977] A.C. 239.
[28] *Post,* p. 366.
[29] Income and Corporation Taxes Act 1970, s. 67. This Schedule A should not be confused with the former Schedule A tax on the annual value of the land (landlord's property tax) which was discontinued as from 1963–64; see Finance Act 1963, ss. 14, 68.
[30] Income and Corporation Taxes Act 1970, s. 70.
[31] *Yellowly* v. *Gower* (1855) 11 Exch. 274; for waste, see *ante,* p. 52.
[32] *Wedd* v. *Porter* [1916] 2 K.B. 91.
[33] *Warren* v. *Keen* [1954] 1 Q.B. 15.
[34] *Harnett* v. *Maitland* (1847) 16 M. & W. 257.
[35] *Countess of Shrewsbury's Case* (1600) 5 Co.Rep. 13b.
[36] *Burchell* v. *Hornsby* (1808) 1 Camp. 360.

4. Landlord's right to view. A landlord may by statute or by the terms of the tenancy be expressly authorised to enter the premises; and if he is liable to repair the premises has an implied right to enter them for this purpose.[37] Otherwise, he has no right to enter the premises so long as the tenancy endures.[38]

5. Right to take emblements. The nature of emblements has already been considered.[39] A tenant at sufferance has no right to emblements, but at common law a tenant at will, a yearly tenant or a tenant for years determinable with lives was entitled to them, provided the determination of the tenancy was not caused by his own act.[40] A tenant for a fixed term of years could also claim emblements if his lease came to a premature end without his fault, *e.g.* if the landlord had only a life estate and his death brought the lease to an end. However, the importance of these rules has been greatly diminished by statute. By the Landlord and Tenant Act 1851,[41] a tenant at a rack rent whose tenancy determined by the death of the landlord or cesser of his interest was given the right to continue his tenancy on the existing terms until the expiration of the current year of the tenancy, in lieu of any right to emblements. In the case of agricultural holdings, the Agricultural Holdings Act 1948[42] provides that in such a case the tenancy continues until determined at the end of a year of the tenancy by 12 months' notice to quit. These provisions, coupled with the conversion of most leases for lives into terms of 90 years,[43] have made this subject of little consequence.

6. Right to estovers. A tenant for years has the same right to estovers and botes as a tenant for life.[44]

Sect. 2. Position of the Parties under a Lease Containing the Usual Covenants

1. Effect of agreement. If a lease has actually been granted, the obligations of the parties in the absence of any contrary provision in the lease are as set out above. If, on the other hand, the parties have merely agreed that a lease containing the "usual covenants" shall be granted, or if there is an agreement that a lease shall be granted, no reference being made to the covenants it should contain, then, subject to any contrary agreements by the parties, the lease must contain whatever covenants and conditions may be "usual" in the

---

[37] *Saner* v. *Bilton* (1878) 7 Ch.D. 815.
[38] *Stocker* v. *Planet Building Society* (1879) 27 W.R. 877.
[39] *Ante*, p. 56.
[40] See, *e.g. Haines* v. *Welch* (1868) L.R. 4 C.P. 91.
[41] s. 1.
[42] s. 4: for agricultural holdings generally, see *post*, p. 570.
[43] *Ante*, p. 345.
[44] Co.Litt. 41b; and see *ante*, p. 53.

circumstances, and if it does not, it may be rectified to accord with the agreement. Except in so far that they cover the same ground, the obligations imposed by the "usual" covenants and conditions are additional to those set out under Sect. 1 above.

2. The usual covenants. The following covenants and conditions are always "usual."[45]

1. On the part of the landlord—
   a covenant for quiet enjoyment in the usual qualfied form, *i.e.* extending only to the acts of the lessor or the rightful acts of any person claiming from or under him.
2. On the part of the tenant—
   (a) a covenant to pay rent;
   (b) a covenant to pay tenant's rates and taxes, *i.e.* all rates and taxes except those which statute requires the landlord to bear;
   (c) a covenant to keep the premises in repair and deliver them up at the end of the term in this condition;
   (d) a covenant to permit the landlord to enter and view the state of repair, if he is liable to repair; and
   (e) a condition of re-entry for non-payment of rent, but not for breach of any other covenant.

3. Usual by custom or usage. In addition to the above provisions, which are always "usual," other covenants may be "usual" in the circumstances of the case, by virtue, for example, of the custom of the neighbourhood or trade usage; in each case, this is a question of fact for the court, taking into account the nature of the premises, their situation, the purpose for which they are being let, the length of the term, the evidence of conveyancers and the books of precedents.[46] Today, a right of re-entry for breach of *any* covenant will normally be "usual."[47] In the absence of such special circumstances, however, many covenants which in practice are usually inserted in leases and are therefore literally "usual" are nevertheless not deemed to be "usual" in the technical sense of the word. Examples are covenants against assignment, covenants against carrying on specified trades, and provisos for forfeiture if the tenant has a receiving order in bankruptcy made against him or enters into liquidation or suffers any distress or process of execution to be levied upon his goods or makes any assignment or composition for the benefit of his creditors. Such provisions are frequently inserted when (as is usually the case) no contract to take a lease has been made and

---

[45] See *Hampshire* v. *Wickens* (1878) 7 Ch.D. 555.
[46] See *Flexman* v. *Corbett* [1930] 1 Ch. 672.
[47] *Chester* v. *Buckingham Travel Ltd.* [1981] 1 W.L.R. 96.

the terms of the lease are a matter for negotiation between the parties. But if a contract for a lease has been made, no covenant can be inserted in the lease without the concurrence of both parties unless either the contract provides for it or the covenant is technically a "usual" covenant.

Sect. 3. Position under Certain Covenants Usually Found in Leases

A number of covenants have already been considered, but certain other covenants must be mentioned.

1. Covenant to pay rent. Unless the lease provides for payment in advance, rent is normally payable in arrear.[48] It continues to be payable, unless the lease has been frustrated,[49] even if the premises cannot be used, *e.g.* owing to destruction by fire[50] or other calamity, or seizure by military authorites for the occupation of troops.[51] However, this stern common law rule is frequently mitigated by an express provision in the lease, and in the case of war damage and requisitioning (but not other events) the tenant has been given a statutory right to disclaim his tenancy.[52]

The landlord may enforce payment of the rent—

- (a) directly, by—
  - (i) an action for the money, or
  - (ii) distress;
- (b) indirectly, by the threat of forfeiture if the lease contains a forfeiture clause.

Forfeiture has already been dealt with,[53] and there is no need to discuss an action for the money. The subject of distress is extremely intricate,[54] and all that need be said here is that in essence it consists of the right of the landlord, exercisable without application to the court but ordinarily exercised by a court certificated bailiff, to enforce payment by seizing and selling enough of any goods found on the premises.

2. Covenant against assigning, underletting or parting with possession. (a) *The tenant's rights.* If the lease is silent on the matter the tenant is entitled to assign, underlet or part with possession of the premises without the landlord's consent; for during the term the property is the tenant's. However, a covenant against assignment,

[48] *Coomber* v. *Howard* (1845) 1 C.B. 440.
[49] *National Carriers Ltd.* v. *Panalpina Ltd.* [1981] 2 W.L.R. 45.
[50] *Belfour* v. *Weston* (1786) 1 T.R. 310.
[51] *Whitehall Court Ltd.* v. *Ettlinger* [1920] 1 K.B. 680.
[52] *Ante,* p. 358.
[53] *Ante,* pp. 351 *et seq.*
[54] See M. & W., pp. 691–694.

underletting or parting with possession of all or any part of the premises is often inserted in leases; and although an assignment or sub-lease made in breach of covenant is valid,[55] the breach will usually give rise to forfeiture or a claim for damages.

(b) *Unreasonable withholding of consent.* If the covenant is absolute, the landlord is entitled to waive it in any particular instance, although he cannot be compelled to do so even if his attitude is entirely unreasonable. But if the covenant is one against assigning or sub-letting "without licence or consent," the Landlord and Tenant Act 1927[56] lays it down that notwithstanding any contrary provision the covenant shall be deemed to be subject to a proviso that the licence or consent is not to be unreasonably withheld. This does not permit the tenant to assign or sub-let without seeking the landlord's consent; if he does so, he has committed a breach of covenant even if the landlord could not properly refuse his consent.[57] But if he seeks consent and it is unreasonably withheld, he may forthwith assign or sub-let without the consent,[58] or else pursue the safer but slower course of seeking a declaration from the court of his right to do so.[59] The onus is on the tenant to show that the withholding of consent was unreasonable.[60] In most cases no objection will be reasonable unless based on the person of the assignee or sub-tenant or the proposed use of the premises,[61] taking into account the original purpose of the covenant and the effect of subsequent statutes, *e.g.* the Leasehold Reform Act 1967 (allowing certain tenants to purchase the freehold) or the Rent Act 1974 (extending security of tenure to furnished lettings).[62] Moreover, statute provides that it is unreasonable to withhold consent "on the ground of colour race or ethnic or national origins," though this does not apply to a tenancy of part of a dwelling-house in which some of the accommodation is shared with the landlord.[63] Unless the lease provides for it, in most cases the landlord may not require the payment of a fine or other valuable consideration for giving his consent.[64]

(c) *Breach.* To amount to a breach of a covenant against assignment or underletting, there must in general be some voluntary dealing with the property *inter vivos.* Thus a bequest of the lease is no breach,[65] nor is the involuntary vesting of the lease in the trustee in

[55] *Old Grovebury Manor Farm Ltd.* v. *Seymour Plant Ltd. (No.* 2) [1979] 1 W.L.R. 1397.
[56] s. 19(1).
[57] *Eastern Telegraph Co. Ltd.* v. *Dent* [1899] 1 Q.B. 835.
[58] *Treloar* v. *Bigge* (1874) L.R. 9 Ex. 151.
[59] *Young* v. *Ashley Gardens Properties Ltd.* [1903] 2 Ch. 112.
[60] *Shanly* v. *Ward* (1913) 29 T.L.R. 714.
[61] See *Viscount Tredegar* v. *Harwood* [1929] A.C. 72.
[62] *West Layton Ltd.* v. *Ford* [1979] Q.B. 593; *Norfolk Capital Group Ltd.* v. *Kitway Ltd.* [1977] Q.B. 506; *Bickel* v. *Duke of Westminster* [1977] Q.B. 517.
[63] Race Relations Act 1965, s. 5(1).
[64] L.P.A. 1925, s. 144, replacing C.A. 1892, s. 3.
[65] *Fox* v. *Swann* (1655) Sty. 482.

bankruptcy upon the tenant's bankruptcy,[66] or the compulsory sale of the lease under statutory provisions,[67] as distinct from a voluntary sale by the tenant's trustee in bankruptcy.[68] A mortgage made by the grant of a sub-lease is a breach, but one made by a mere deposit of the title deeds is not, nor is a declaration of trust made by the tenant for the benefit of his creditors.[69] A covenant merely against underletting is perhaps not broken by an assignment or by letting lodgings under licence.

(d) *Condition precedent to assignment.* As a condition precedent to an assignment a landlord may validly require that the tenant shall first offer to surrender the lease *gratis* to the landlord.[70] This ranks as a registrable Class (iv) land charge.[71]

3. Covenant to repair. (a) *Construction of covenant.* In long leases, the tenant usually covenants to do all repairs; in short leases, the landlord frequently assumes liability for external and structural repairs, and in some cases is compelled by statute to do so.[72] Subject to this, in every case, the matter is one for negotiation. If no provision is made for repairs, neither party is liable for them, apart from statute and the general law relating to waste.[73]

The extent of the liability of any party under a repairing covenant depends, of course, upon the wording of the covenant, but expressions such as "tenantable repair," "sufficient repair," or "good and substantial repair" seem to add little to the meaning of the word "repair."[74] "Repair" normally includes any necessary replacement of subsidiary parts (*e.g.* the provision of new drainpipes for old). It is, however, a question of degree.[75] The renovations may be so substantial as to be beyond what any reasonable person could contemplate as a repair.[76] However, want of repair due to an inherent defect in the demised premises may fall within the ambit of a covenant to repair where the repairs will not provide the landlord with a building substantially different from the building demised.[77] If the covenant is qualified by words such as "fair wear and tear excepted," they exclude liability for defects due to reasonable use of the premises or the action of the elements, but not for consequential

[66] *Re Riggs* [1901] 2 K.B. 16.
[67] *Slipper* v. *Tottenham & Hampstead Junction Ry.* (1867) L.R. 4 Eq. 112.
[68] *Re Wright* [1949] Ch. 729.
[69] *Gentle* v. *Faulkner* [1900] 2 Q.B. 267.
[70] *Bocardo S.A.* v. *S. & M. Hotels Ltd.* [1980] 1 W.L.R. 17.
[71] *Greene* v. *Church Commissioners* [1974] Ch. 467.
[72] See *ante*, p. 362.
[73] *Ante*, p. 363.
[74] *Anstruther-Gough-Calthorpe* v. *McOscar* [1924] 1 K.B. 716 at pp. 722, 723.
[75] *Lurcott* v. *Wakely* [1911] 1 K.B. 905.
[76] *Brew Brothers Ltd.* v. *Snax (Ross) Ltd.* [1970] 1 Q.B. 612.
[77] *Ravenseft Properties Ltd.* v. *Davstone (Holdings) Ltd.* [1980] Q.B. 12.

damage, *e.g.* caused by rain entering through an unrepaired skylight.[78]

(b) *Measure of damages*. The measure of damages recoverable by a landlord for the breach of a repairing covenant formerly varied according to the time of the breach. If the breach occurred during the term, the damages were calculated on the decrease in the value of the reversion caused by the breach,[79] *i.e.* on the difference between the value of the landlord's interest with the repairs done and its value without. Thus the longer the lease had to run, the less would be the damages. But if the breach occurred at the end of the term, the cost of repairing the premises was recoverable by the landlord[80] even if he did not propose to spend the money in making the repairs but intended to demolish the premises instead. Now, however, by the Landlord and Tenant Act 1927,[81] damages for breach of a repairing covenant are not to exceed the diminution in the value of the reversion, though if the repairs are going to be done, that diminution will usually be measured by the cost of the repairs.[82] Further, no damages are recoverable if the premises are to be demolished, or structurally altered in such a way as to make the repairs valueless, at or soon after the end of the term. There are special provisions enabling the court in certain cases to relieve the tenant from liability for internal decorative repairs.[83]

(c) *Leave to sue*. There are also provisions which protect the tenant of any property (except agricultural holdings) let for a term of years certain of not less than seven years which has at least three years unexpired.[84] The lack of any provision for relief against claims for damages for non-repair often enabled landlords to force tenants to surrender their leases prematurely, and so the Leasehold Property (Repairs) Act 1938[85] provides that no action for damages for breach of a covenant to repair the property can be brought unless the landlord has first served on the tenant a notice in the form required by the Law of Property Act 1925, s. 146[86] and one month has elapsed thereafter. Further, whether the landlord is claiming damages or forfeiture, he cannot proceed without the leave of the court in such cases if within 28 days the tenant serves on the landlord a counter-notice claiming the protection of the Act; and the notice

[78] *Regis Property Co. Ltd.* v. *Dudley* [1959] A.C. 370.
[79] *Ebbetts* v. *Conquest* [1895] 2 Ch. 377 (affd. [1896] A.C. 490).
[80] *Joyner* v. *Weeks* [1891] 2 Q.B. 31.
[81] s. 18(1).
[82] *Smiley* v. *Townshend* [1950] 2 K.B. 311.
[83] L.P.A. 1925, s. 147.
[84] Leasehold Property (Repairs) Act 1938, as extended by Landlord and Tenant Act 1954, s. 51.
[85] s. 1. If L enters and carries out repairs and then claims the cost from T this is a damages claim under the Act: *Swallow Securities* v. *Brand* (1981) 260 E.G. 63.
[86] See *ante*, p. 353.

served by the landlord must inform the tenant of his right to serve a counter-notice. The court can grant leave only on certain specified grounds, *e.g.* that the cost of immediate repair would be small compared with the cost of repair in the future. The application for leave is registrable as a pending land action where leave is sought as a preliminary to forfeiture proceedings.

(d) *Tenant deducting cost of repair from rent.* A tenant may himself do repairs for which the landlord is liable and deduct the cost from the rent. The tenant should ensure that (1) the repair is within the landlord's repairing covenant, (2) the landlord has been notified of the disrepair and has failed to remedy it and it is then sensible (3) to notify the landlord that the rent is going to be withheld to pay for the repairs and (4) to obtain at least two estimates for the landlord to choose the better, but for the cheaper to be chosen if the landlord does not respond.[87]

4. Covenant to insure. A covenant to insure against fire is broken if the premises are uninsured for any period, however short, even if no fire occurs.[88]

Sect. 4. Statutory Protection for Tenants

Three important classes of property are subject to special statutory codes designed to protect the tenant, particularly by giving him security of tenure and restricting the rent. These classes are most agricultural holdings and business premises and many dwelling-houses; and they are dealt with later in the book.[89]

Part 6

LICENCES

1. Nature of licences. A type of transaction which is sometimes used instead of a lease or tenancy, but which is quite distinct from it, is the licence.[90] Traditionally, a licence is a permission given by the occupier of land which, without creating any interest in land, allows the licensee to do some act which would otherwise be a trespass,[91] *e.g.* to go on to the licensor's land to play cricket, or to become a lodger in his house. Unlike a lease or tenancy, a licence need not, and

---

[87] *Lee-Parker* v. *Izzet* [1971] 3 All E.R. 1099; *Asco Developments Ltd.* v. *Gordon* (1978) 248 E.G. 683; A. Waite [1981] Conv. 199.
[88] *Penniall* v. *Harborne* (1848) 11 Q.B. 368.
[89] *Post,* pp. 566 *et seq.*
[90] See *ante,* pp. 81, 335.
[91] See *Thomas* v. *Sorrell* (1673) Vaugh. 330 at p. 351.

usually does not, confer a right to the exclusive possession of the land concerned.[92] Further examples of licences are—

the hire of a concert hall for several days without the hirer being entitled to exclusive possession[93];

permission to erect and use an advertisement hoarding or electric sign[94];

the grant of the "front of the house rights" in a theatre, *i.e.* the exclusive right to supply refreshments coupled with other rights such as the use of refreshment rooms[95];

permission to view a race or cinema performance.[96]

2. Classification. Licences fall into four categories.

(a) *Bare licence.* A bare licence is a licence granted otherwise than for valuable consideration, such as a gratuitous permission to enter a field to see the view. Even if it is granted by deed, the licensor can revoke it at any time, on giving reasonable notice, without being liable in damages[97]; but revocation does not affects acts already done under it.[98] A bare licence binds neither the licensor nor any third party.

(b) *Licence coupled with an interest.* A licence may be coupled with some interest in the land or chattels thereon as a necessary adjunct to the interest which had been granted. Thus the right to enter another man's land to hunt and take away the deer killed, or to enter and cut down a tree and take it away, involves two things, namely, a licence to enter the land and the grant of an interest in the deer or tree.[99] At common law, such a licence was both irrevocable and assignable.[1] But the interest had to be a legal interest such as a legal *profit à prendre* (which could be created only by deed or prescription, *i.e.* long enjoyment[2]), or the ownership of timber lying on the land or to be cut forthwith (which could be transferred by word of mouth).[3] In equity, however, effect will be given to an enforceable agreement to grant an interest, so that an injunction may be granted to protect a licence coupled with a *profit à prendre* granted merely in writing.[4] The licence will bind third parties to the extent that they are bound by the interest coupled with the licence.

---

[92] See *ante*, p. 335.
[93] See *Taylor* v. *Caldwell* (1863) 3 B. & S. 826.
[94] *Walton Harvey Co. Ltd.* v. *Walker & Homfrays Ltd.* [1931] 1 Ch. 274.
[95] *Frank Warr & Co. Ltd.* v. *L.C.C.* [1904] 1 K.B. 713.
[96] *Hurst* v. *Picture Theatres Ltd.* [1915] 1 K.B. 1.
[97] *Wood* v. *Leadbitter* (1845) 13 M. & W. 838 at p. 845.
[98] *Armstrong* v. *Sheppard & Short Ltd.* [1959] 2 Q.B. 384.
[99] See *Thomas* v. *Sorrell* (1673) Vaugh. 330 at p. 351.
[1] *James Jones & Sons Ltd.* v. *Earl of Tankerville* [1909] 2 Ch. 440 at p. 442; *Muskett* v. *Hill* [1839] 5 Bing.N.C. 694 at pp. 707, 708.
[2] See *post*, pp. 415 *et seq.*
[3] See *Marshall* v. *Green* (1875) 1 C.P.D. 35.
[4] *Frogley* v. *Earl of Lovelace* (1859) Johns 333.

(c) *Contractual licence.* If construction of the contract reveals that the parties intended expressly or impliedly[5] that the contractual licence should be irrevocable for a period, then any revocation by the licensor in breach of contract will be restrained by an injunction[6] or specific performance may be ordered,[7] equity supplementing the common law where the remedy of damages is inadequate. If the benefit of the contract is assignable as a matter of construction, then the contract and the licence which is part of the contract[8] may be enforced by the assignee.[9] Whilst the benefit of a contract can pass the burden cannot, so that a contractual licence ought not to be enforceable against third parties.[10] As Lord Wilberforce has stated, "the fact that a contractual right can be specifically performed or its breach prevented by injunction does not mean that the right is any the less of a personal character or that a purchaser with notice is bound by it: what is relevant is the nature of the right, not the remedy which exists for its enforcement."[11]

Lord Denning, however, having dealt with the fact that the common law rule, that contractual licences were always revocable, but remediable in damages only, had been altered by the interposition of equity, has stated,[12] "this infusion of equity means that contractual licences now have a force and validity of their own and cannot be revoked in breach of the contract. Neither the licensor nor anyone who claims through him can disregard the contract except a purchaser for value without notice."

This seems a revival of the "fallacy that because an obligation binds a man's conscience it therefore becomes binding on the consciences of those who take from him with notice of the obligation."[13] After all, a purchaser of a freehold takes free from positive covenants affecting the land and entered into by his predecessor even if he knows of them,[14] just as he will also take free from a known restrictive covenant affecting the land and entered into by his predecessor if the covenantee had no dominant nearby land benefited by the covenant.[15]

---

[5] The courts are now ready to infer that a licence for a period involves an obligation not to revoke the licence for that period.

[6] *Winter Gardens Theatre (London) Ltd.* v. *Millenium Productions Ltd.* [1948] A.C. 173.

[7] *Verrall* v. *Great Yarmouth B.C.* [1980] 1 All E.R. 839.

[8] *London Borough of Hounslow* v. *Twickenham Garden Developments Ltd.* [1971] Ch. 233.

[9] *Clore* v. *Theatrical Properties Ltd.* [1936] 3 All E.R. 483 at pp. 490, 491; *Shayler* v. *Woolf* [1946] Ch. 320.

[10] *Clore* v. *Theatrical Properties Ltd.* [1936] 3 All E.R. 483 at p. 490.

[11] *N.P.B.* v. *Ainsworth* [1965] A.C. 1175 at p. 1251.

[12] *Errington* v. *Errington & Woods* [1952] 1 K.B. 290 at p. 299. The decision can be explained on the basis of proprietary estoppel or on the basis of a volunteer being bound by an estate contract.

[13] *N.P.B.* v. *Ainsworth* [1965] A.C. 1175 at p. 1253 *per* Lord Wilberforce. See also *L.C.C.* v. *Allen* [1914] 3 K.B. 642 at p. 655.

[14] See *post*, p. 441.

[15] *Sefton* v. *Tophams Ltd.* [1965] Ch. 1140 at pp. 1157, 1183, 1191, 1199, 1202.

However, Lord Denning has continued to affirm,[16] "when the licensee is in actual occupation neither the licensor nor anyone who claims through him can disregard the contract except a purchaser for value without notice," so treating the licensee as having an equitable proprietary interest.

He fails to deal adquately with authority for the contrary view in *King* v. *David Allen & Sons Ltd.*[17] and in *Clore* v. *Theatrical Properties Ltd.*[18] In the former case the House of Lords held a licensor liable to a contractual licensee for damages for breach of the contractual licence to post adverts on the wall of a building sold to a purchaser with knowledge of the contract, who refused to honour the licence. As Russell L.J. has stated,[19] the case "necessarily involved a decision that a contractual licence to post advertisements on a wall for a period of years was not binding upon a purchaser from the licensor with actual notice of the licence because it created a mere personal obligation on the licensor and not an interest in land."

In *Clore* the Court of Appeal held that a purchaser with actual knowledge of "front of house" rights under a contractual licence, dressed up in the form of a lease, was not bound by the licence. Lord Wright M.R. stated,[20] "This is not a document which creates an interest in land, but merely one which is a personal contract between the parties named therein and is only enforceable among parties between whom there is privity of contract."

Lord Denning suggests[21] that it is absence of actual occupation under the licence that distinguishes these two weighty cases (though it seems in *Clore* that the licensee was in actual occupation—though not residential occupation—of parts of the theatre such as the bars, cloakrooms and wine cellars).[22] However, actual occupation is merely one form of notice of the right under which the actual occupation arises and in *King* and in *Clore* there was actual notice of the right. Whether notice of a right happens to arise expressly or from actual occupation is surely immaterial.[23] Notice of a right does not

---

[16] *Binions* v. *Evans* [1972] Ch. 359 at p. 369, a minority view, the other Lord Justices deciding the case on the basis of a Settled Land Act tenancy for life. See also Lord Denning in *Tanner* v. *Tanner* [1975] 1 W.L.R. 1346 at p. 1350; *N.P.B.* v. *Hastings Car Mart. Ltd.* [1964] Ch. 665 at p. 686.

[17] [1916] 2 A.C. 54.

[18] [1936] 3 All E.R. 483.

[19] *N.P.B.* v. *Hastings Car Mart. Ltd.* [1964] Ch. 665 at p. 697.

[20] [1936] 3 All E.R. 483 at p. 490. He also accepted that assignees of the benefit of the licence could enforce it against the original licensor.

[21] *N.P.B.* v. *Hastings Car Mart. Ltd.* [1964] Ch. 665 at p. 688; *Binions* v. *Evans* [1972] Ch. 359 at p. 369. There he also indicates that the plaintiff purchaser had expressly agreed with the vendor licensor to take subject to the defendant's contractual licence; this, however, does not seem to bind the purchaser's conscience any more than express actual notice of the licensee's rights as in *King* or *Clore*. Indeed in *Clore* the instrument of sale to the plaintiff stated that the property comprising the theatre excluded the right to manage the bars and the front of house rights: see p. 486.

[22] *N.P.B.* v. *Hastings Car Mart. Ltd.* [1964] Ch. 665 at p. 698 *per* Russell L.J.

[23] *Ibid.*

itself create a proprietary right: the source of a proprietary right must be sought elsewhere. *King* and *Clore* indicate that a contractual licence cannot be a proprietary right, so that notice of such contractual right cannot convert it into a valid proprietary interest, just as notice of an estate contract void as a proprietary interest for non-registration (though a valid contract between the parties) cannot convert it into a valid proprietary interest.[24]

However, Lord Denning reiterated his views in *D.H.N. Food Distributors* v. *Tower Hamlets*[25] where Goff L.J. endorsed them, overlooking his own views when Goff J,[26] so that Browne-Wilkinson J.[27] has felt obliged to hold that the licensor's trustee in bankruptcy is bound by an irrevocable contractual licence, on the basis that the licence is more than a mere contractual interest capable of disclaimer by the trustee in bankruptcy. He was not concerned with the position of a purchaser of the property subject to the contractual licence but expressed[28] "the hope that in the near future the whole question can receive full consideration in the Court of Appeal,[29] so that, in order to do justice to the many thousands of people who never come into court at all but who wish to know with certainty what their proprietary rights are, the extent to which these irrevocable licences bind third parties may be defined with certainty. Doing justice to the litigant who actually appears in the court ought not to involve injustice to other persons who are not litigants before the court but whose rights are fundamentally affected by the new principles." It is submitted that contractual licences, which may come in all sorts of varieties, cannot be elevated into property interests except by legislation,[30] which could then provide for registration of certain types of contractual licence.

(c) *Estoppel licence.* An irrevocable licence to occupy or use land may be acquired not by contract but by estoppel principles. If a landowner encourages, or stands by and allows a person to spend money on the land or otherwise act to his detriment in the belief that he is acquiring an irrevocable licence to occupy or use the land, then the landowner will be estopped from denying the claim to the licence. Since the expectation is the acquisition of a licence (albeit irrevocable) and not the acquisition of an interest in land[31] like a life interest

---

[24] *Hollington Bros. Ltd.* v. *Rhodes* [1951] 2 T.L.R. 496; *Midland Bank Trust Co. Ltd.* v. *Green* [1981] A.C. 513.
[25] [1976] 1 W.L.R. 852. There are other grounds for the decision.
[26] *Re Solomon* [1967] Ch. 573 at pp. 582, 586.
[27] *Re Sharpe* [1980] 1 W.L.R. 219.
[28] *Ibid.* at p. 226.
[29] The House of Lords seems more appropriate, especially whilst Lord Denning presides over the Court of Appeal.
[30] See Dawson & Pearce: *Licences Relating to the Occupation or Use of Land*; H.W.R. Wade (1952) 68 L.Q.R. 337; G.C. Cheshire (1953) 16 M.L.R. 1; R.H. Maudsley (1956) 20 Conv. 281.
[31] This would create a proprietary estoppel interest capable of binding third parties see *ante*, p. 74.

or a leasehold interest, the licence by estoppel should not be capable of binding third parties, assuming that an irrevocable contractual licence is not an interest in land capable of binding third parties. However, Lord Denning's Court of Appeal without due consideration of the issue has assumed that estoppel licences are capable of binding third parties.[32]

3. Contractual licences, estoppel licences and informal arrangements. Often, in a family context an elderly relative comes to live with the family pursuant to an informal arrangement, having contributed money to enable the family to purchase a larger house or to extend the old house. If the relative falls out with the family or if the family tries to sell the house over the head of the relative it will be necessary to resolve the legal status of the relative.[33]

The possibilities are as follows—

(i) The relative may be treated as a bare licensee, there being no intent to create contractual relations[34] and the relative's contributions being treated as a gift to the houseowner or one of the houseowners where a husband and wife are co-owners.

(ii) The relative may still be a bare licensee but be deemed to have loaned the moneys repayable on demand or as otherwise agreed.[35]

(iii) The relative may be treated as a contractual licensee having a contractual right to occupy the house for a period,[36] *e.g.* until repayment of the moneys or until death or until sale of the house whereupon a right to occupy the house purchased with proceeds of sale arises and so on until death. If H and W hold the house on trust for sale, presumably the interest of the relative, even if regarded as a proprietary interest, will be overreached in any event if the purchase-moneys are paid to two trustees for sale.[37] A purchaser, however, may be reluctant to purchase unless the relative is evicted, *e.g.* after an application under section 30 of the Law of Property Act.[38]

(iv) The relative may be treated as having an estoppel licence estopping the owners from denying that the relative has a right to occupy the house for a period[39] on terms similar to those

---

[32] *Inwards* v. *Baker* [1965] 2 Q.B. 29; *Williams* v. *Staite* [1979] Ch. 291.
[33] See J.D. Davies (1979) 8 Sydney L.R. 578; Gray & Symes Real Property and Real People Ch. 14.
[34] *Horrocks* v. *Forray* [1976] 1 W.L.R. 230.
[35] *Hussey* v. *Palmer* [1972] 1 W.L.R. 1286 at p. 1292 *per* Cairns L.J.
[36] *Re Sharpe* [1980] 1 W.L.R. 219; *Tanner* v. *Tanner* [1975] 1 W.L.R. 1346; *Chandler* v. *Kerley* [1978] 1 W.L.R. 693.
[37] L.P.A. 1925, ss. 2, 27. Sale under L.P.A., s. 2(2) should overreach the interest if s. 27(1) alone is not itself sufficient.
[38] See *ante*, p. 316.
[39] *Re Sharpe* (*supra*), *Greasley* v. *Cooke* [1980] 1 W.L.R. 1306.

suggested for contractual licences and, presumably, with the
same consequences.

(v) The relative may be treated as having an equitable proprietary
estoppel interest, such as a life interest creating a Settled Land
Act tenancy for life for the relative,[40] so that the relative
controls the destiny of the house.

(vi) The relative may be treated as having an equitable interest
under a resulting trust proportionate to the moneys used to
purchase or extend the house.[41] Sale under the trust for sale
will overreach the relative's interest, subject to the vacant
possession problem facing a purchaser if the relative is
stubborn.

---

[40] *Binions* v. *Evans* [1972] Ch. 359.
[41] *Hussey* v. *Palmer* [1972] 1 W.L.R. 1286.

CHAPTER 10

COVENANTS AFFECTING LEASEHOLD LAND

Part 1

GENERAL PRINCIPLES

A COVENANT is a promise under seal, *i.e* contained in a deed. The basic principles concerning the enforceability of covenants relating to land are as follows.

1. If there is privity of contract, all covenants are enforceable. There is said to be privity of contract when the parties concerned have made a legally enforceable agreement. Clearly, if two people have agreed to do or not to do certain things, their obligations bind them whether their contract has anything to do with land or not. The covenants can be enforced both at law, by an action for damages, and in equity, by an injunction or specific performance.

2. If there is merely privity of estate, only covenants which touch and concern the land are enforceable. There is said to be privity of estate between the parties when the relationship of landlord and tenant exists between them under the lease which contains the covenant in question, *i.e.* where L granted a legal lease to T but A now has L's legal estate and B now has T's legal estate. In this case, any covenants in the lease which touch and concern the land, such as repairing covenants, are enforceable both in law and in equity. But covenants which do not relate to the land are not enforceable under this head.

3. If there is privity neither of contract nor of estate, then with two exceptions, no covenants are directly enforceable. There is privity neither of contract nor of estate between a lessor and a sub-lessee, or between the vendor of freehold land and a person who buys it from the purchaser. In such cases, the general rule is that covenants concerning the land are not enforceable. To this rule there are two exceptions, the second of which is of great importance.

(a) *Benefit.* First, even the common law allowed the *benefit* of certain covenants (*i.e.* the right to sue on the covenant) to be assigned with land; and equity followed the law. One example already mentioned[1] is that of covenants for title, the benefit of which runs

---

[1] *Ante*, p. 152.

with the land, so that whoever is entitled to the land is entitled to the benefit of the covenants. But the *burden* of a covenant (*i.e.* the liability to be sued on it) cannot be assigned; at law, if there is no privity of estate the covenantor alone can be sued on a covenant.

(b) *Restrictive covenants in equity.* Secondly, equity allows the transmission of the burden (as well as the benefit) of restrictive covenants affecting land, *i.e.* covenants which are negative in nature, restraining the doing of some act, such as building on the land. As usual, however, a purchaser of a legal estate without notice[2] takes free from such burdens.

4. The enforceability of a forfeiture clause may make covenants indirectly enforceable. This is dealt with *infra* at page 389.

These four principles should be borne in mind whenever considering questions of the enforceability of covenants. They should be applied in the given order: if there is privity of contract, there is no need to look further, and if there is privity of estate, there is no need to consider the third or fourth head.

Little more need be said about privity of contract, but the other heads must be considered in some detail.

Part 2

PRIVITY: COVENANTS IN LEASES

Sect. 1. Position of the Original Parties

If a lease is granted by L to T, there is privity of contract between them. The effect of this is not only that L may enforce all the covenants in the lease against T while he retains it, but also that T remains liable on the covenants for the whole term, notwithstanding any assignment of the lease.[3] Thus if T takes a lease for 99 years, he makes himself liable for 99 years, even if he assigns the lease after only one year has run; L may accordingly sue T for unpaid rent or for damages if the covenant to repair is not observed by the assignee. Similarly, L remains liable on his covenants for the whole term, notwithstanding any assignment of the reversion by him.[4] It is, of course, open to the original parties to restrict their contractual obligations for the periods when they respectively retain the lease and the reversion.

---

[2] Subject to the rule that restrictive covenants, other than between a lessor and lessee, require registration under the Land Charges Act if created after 1925, *ante*, p. 94.
[3] *Thursby* v. *Plant* (1670) 1 Wms.Saund. 230; for an exception in the case of perpetually renewable leases, see *ante*, p. 346.
[4] *Stuart* v. *Joy* [1904] 1 K.B. 368; L.P.A. 1925, s. 142 (2); and see *post*, p. 528.

Sect. 2. Position of Assignees of Legal Lease

A. *Covenants Touching and Concerning Land*

The rights and liabilities of assignees, either of the lease or of the reversion, depend on whether or not the covenant in question "touches
and concerns the land" or, to use more modern phraseology,
"has reference to the subject-matter of the lease."[5] Any covenant
which affects the landlord *qua* landlord or the tenant *qua* tenant may
be said to touch and concern the land.[6] If the covenant of its very
nature and not merely through extraneous circumstances affects the
nature, quality or value of the land demised, or the mode of enjoying
it, it falls within the definition.[7] Some examples may be helpful; the
covenants in the left-hand column have been held to touch and
concern the land, while those in the right-hand column have been
held not to do so.

1. Covenants by a lessee

To pay rent.	To pay an annual sum to some
To repair.	third party.[8]
To pay the landlord £40 towards redecoration.[9]	To repair and renew the tools of a smithy standing on the land.[10]
To use as a private dwelling-house only.	Not to employ persons living in other parishes to work in the demised mill.[11]
Not to assign the lease without the landlord's consent.	

2. Covenants by a lessor

To renew the lease[12] (the inclusion of this is somewhat anomalous[14]).	sold.[13]
	To sell the reversion at a stated price.[15]
To supply the demised premises with water.	To pay at the end of the lease for chattels not amounting to fixtures.
Not to build on a certain part of the adjoining land.	
To give the lessee the first refusal if adjoining land is	To pay the tenant £500 at the end of the lease unless a new lease is granted.[16]

---

[5] L.P.A. 1925, ss. 141 (1), 142 (1).
[6] *Breams Property Investments Co. Ltd.* v. *Stroulger* [1948] 2 K.B. 1.
[7] *Horsey Estate Ltd.* v. *Steiger* [1899] 2 Q.B. 79 at p. 89.
[8] *Mayho* v. *Buckhurst* (1617) Cro.Jac. 438. If a lessee by collateral agreement pays
money to the lessor as security for non-payment of rent this confers no right against
the lessor's assignee: *Edenpark Estates Ltd.* v. *Longman* [1980] C.A. Transcripts
417.
[9] *Boyer* v. *Warbey* [1953] 1 Q.B. 234.
[10] *Williams* v. *Earle* (1868) L.R. 3 Q.B. 739.
[11] *Congleton Corporation* v. *Pattison* (1808) 10 East 130.
[12] *Richardson* v. *Sydenham* (1703) 2 Vern. 447.
[13] *Collison* v. *Lettsom* (1815) 6 Taunt. 224.
[14] *Woodall* v. *Clifton* [1905] 2 Ch. 257 at p. 279.
[15] *Re Leeds and Batley Breweries Ltd. and Bradbury's Lease* [1920] 2 Ch. 548.
[16] *Re Hunter's Lease* [1942] Ch. 124.

B. Principles of Transmission

After considering which covenants touch and concern the land, the rights and liabilities of assignees must next be examined. As in every case when the question of enforcing legal liabilties arise, two separate points must be considered:

(i) Is the defendant liable? and

(ii) Is the plaintiff entitled to sue?

In the case of the rights and liabilties of assignees under covenants concerning land, this may be expressed in the form of—

(i) Has the burden of the covenant passed? and

(ii) Has the benefit of the covenant passed?

I. WHERE THE LESSEE ASSIGNS HIS LEASE

If L leases land to T, and T assigns the legal lease by deed to A, the common law rule laid down in *Spencer's Case*[17] is that A is entitled to the benefit, and subject to the burden, of all covenants and conditions touching and concerning the land, for there is a privity of estate. In short, both the benefit and the burden of the covenants run wih the land.

In applying this rule, the following points should be noted.

1. The lease must be in due form. Originally, the benefit and burden of covenants ran only with a lease by deed but it can now run with a lease for three years or less made by unsealed writing.[18] A legal oral tenancy for less than three years has been held not to suffice,[19] but this rule may no longer be law.[20]

2. There must be a legal assignment of the whole term. (a) *Legal assignment.* The benefit and burden of covenants run with the lease only in the case of a legal assignment of the whole of the remainder of the term.[21] Where instead of an assignment there has been a sub-lease, the sub-lessee takes neither the benefit nor the burden of the covenants in the lease, even if his sub-lease is only one day shorter than the head lease. Thus if L leases land to X for 99 years, X assigns the lease to T, and T sub-leases the land to S for the residue of the term of 99 years less one day, S is not an assignee and there is privity neither of contract nor of estate between L and S. T is still the tenant under the lease for 99 years and until he assigns it, he remains liable upon it. Consequently if S does some act which is contrary to a

---

[17] (1583) 5 Co.Rep. 16a.
[18] See *Boyer* v. *Warbey* [1953] 1 Q.B. 234.
[19] *Elliot* v. *Johnson* (1866) L.R. 2 Q.B. 120.
[20] See *Boyer* v. *Warbey, supra,* at p. 246; and see *ante,* p. 335, for the tenancies which can be created orally; see also *post,* p. 385.
[21] *West* v. *Dobb* (1869) L.R. 4 Q.B. 634; *ante,* p. 348.

covenant in the 99 years' lease, L cannot sue S but can sue T. In practice, the covenants inserted in a sub-lease are always at least as stringent as those in the head lease, so that if a sub-tenant does some act forbidden by the head lease, this will constitute a breach of the covenants in the sub-lease and thus make the sub-tenant liable to the tenant.

(b) *Equitable assignment.* No lease—not even a legal lease for three or fewer years created orally or in writing—can be assigned at law except by deed.[22] If the assignment is merely in unsealed writing what is the position of the equitable assignee?

He does not have the legal estate, so there is no privity of estate to make him liable to the landlord on the covenants, and there is no privity of contract or covenant in respect of the covenants to make him liable.[23] He can be liable if estopped from denying that he has a legal assignment[24] or if an implied contract can be found to have arisen directly between him and the landlord[25]; perhaps, if he has accepted the benefit of possession then he should bear the burden of liability on the covenants incurred whilst in possession.[26]

The benefit of covenants (but not the burden) can be assigned so that if thereby the equitable assignee has the benefit of a restrictive covenant or an option then third parties may be bound on ordinary property principles.[27] If the equitable assignee seeks to sue the assignee of the reversion on covenants in the lease it seems he can join as a party the legal lessee, in whom the legal lease is currently "vested," and proceed under section 142 of the Law of Property Act.[28]

(c) *Squatters.* A squatter entitled to the lease of unregistered land by adverse possession under the Limitation Act is not an assignee of the lessee and cannot therefore sue or be sued on the covenants in the lease, there being no privity of legal estate.[29] However, on estoppel

---

[22] *Ante*, p. 348.
[23] *Cox* v. *Bishop* (1857) De G.M. & G. 815; *Friary Holroyd & Healey's Breweries Ltd.* v. *Singleton*, [1899] 1 Ch. 86 at p. 90 (reversed on other grounds [1899] 2 Ch. 261); *London & County Ltd.* v. *Wilfred Sportsman Ltd.* [1971] Ch. 764 at p. 784. The landlord cannot claim specific performance of the informal assignment taking effect as a contract to make a legal assignment between the *tenant* and the *assignee*: *Moore* v. *Greg* (1848) 2 Ch. 717. The landlord thus cannot claim that *he* ought to be treated as having obtained specific performance and so under the *Walsh* v. *Lonsdale* (1882) 21 Ch.D. 9 doctrine have the assignee treated as if a legal assignee.
[24] *Rodenhurst Estates Ltd.* v. *W.H. Barnes Ltd.* [1936] 2 All E.R. 3 where the landlord gave a licence for a legal assignment and the equitable assignee took possession and paid rent, giving the impression that a legal assignment had occurred.
[25] *Ramage* v. *Womack* [1900] 1 Q.B. 116 at pp. 121–122 but see *Cox* v. *Bishop* (1857) 8 De G.M. & G. 815 at p. 822. A claim to a periodic tenancy arising from possession and payment of rent would be inconsistent with the legal term under which the assignee claims.
[26] *Tito* v. *Waddell* (*No. 2*) [1977] Ch. 106 at pp. 299–302.
[27] M. & W., p. 729.
[28] Cf. *Friary Holroyd & Healey's Breweries Ltd.* v. *Singleton* (1899) 81 L.T. 101 at p. 103; R. J. Smith, [1978] Camb. L.J. 98 at p. 120.
[29] *Tichborne* v. *Weir* (1892) 67 L.T. 735.

principles he may estop himself from denying that he is bound by the lease.[30] In the case of registered land where the squatter has become registered as proprietor of the victim's lease[31] it may, perhaps, be that privity of estate will exist[32] so that the squatter may sue or be sued.

3. Covenants relating to things in posse. If a covenant made before 1926 imposed an obligation upon the tenant to do some entirely new thing, such as to erect a building, the burden of the covenant ran with the land only if the lessee expressly covenanted for himself *and for his assigns* that the covenant would be performed.[33] This rule did not apply to covenants relating to things *in esse* (in existence) nor even to covenants relating only conditionally to something *in posse* (not in existence), such as a covenant to repair a new building if it is erected[34]; in such cases it was immaterial whether or not the covenant mentioned assigns. This not very creditable distinction between covenants relating to things *in posse* and those relating to things *in esse* is still in force as regards all leases granted before 1926, but it does not apply to leases made after 1925.[35]

4. Liability of assignees. Although the original lessee is liable for all breaches of covenant throughout the term of the lease, an assignee is liable only for breaches committed while the lease is vested in him. He is under no liability for breaches committed either before the lease was assigned to him[36] or after he has assigned it[37]; but if a covenant is broken while the lease is vested in him, his liability for this breach continues despite any assignment.[38] Thus while the original lessee of an onerous lease cannot divest himself of liability for future breaches, an assignee can do so by assigning the lease, *e.g.* to a pauper.[39]

5. Liability of personal representatives. (a) *Liability.* Personal representatives may incur personal as well as representative liability.

(1) PERSONAL LIABILITY. If a lessee or assignee dies and his personal representatives take possession of the demised premises, the personal representatives occupy the position of assignees of the lease and so become personally liable on the covenants.[40] However, as regards

---

[30] *Ashe* v. *Hogan* [1920] 1 I.R. 159.
[31] *Spectrum Investment Co.* v. *Holmes* [1981] 1 All E.R. 6.
[32] L.R.A. 1925, ss. 75 (1), (2), (3), 11, 9. The point was left open in *Spectrum (supra)*.
[33] *Spencer's Case, supra.*
[34] *Minshull* v. *Oakes* (1858) 2 H. & N. 793.
[35] L.P.A. 1925, s. 79.
[36] *Granada Theatres Ltd.* v. *Freehold Investment (Leytonstone) Ltd.* [1959] Ch. 592.
[37] *Paul* v. *Nurse* (1828) 8 B.& C. 486.
[38] *Harley* v. *King* (1835) 2 Cr.M. & R. 18.
[39] *Hopkinson* v. *Lovering* (1883) 11 Q.B.D. 92.
[40] *Tilney* v. *Norris* (1700) 1 Ld.Raym. 553.

the payment of rent (but not as regards other covenants) a personal representative may by proper pleading limit his liability to the yearly value of the premises.[41] Further, a personal representative who does not take possession of the premises incurs no personal liability upon any covenant.[42]

(2) REPRESENTATIVE LIABILITY. Upon the death of the original lessee, his personal representatives become liable upon the covenants of the lease for the rest of the term, but only to the extent of the assets of the deceased in their hands.[43] Similarly, if the deceased was an assignee, his personal representatives succeed to his liabilities (*e.g.* for breaches of covenant committed while the lease was vested in him), but only to the extent of his assets.[44] It is irrelevant to this head whether or not the personal representatives take possession of the premises.

(b) *Protection.* If the deceased was the original lessee, the personal representatives are in a difficult position since they cannot tell what breaches of covenant may occur in the future. Although it was settled that they need not put aside part of the estate as an indemnity fund for future breaches,[45] their position was precarious in other respects. In order to make it unnecessary for personal representatives to seek the protection of the court in such cases, the Trustee Act 1925[46] provides that if personal representatives in whom a lease is vested—

(i) satisfy any existing liabilities which have been claimed,
(ii) set aside any *fixed* sum agreed to be laid out on the premises, and
(iii) assign the lease to the person entitled under the will or intestacy, or to a purchaser,

they cease to have representative liability in respect of the assets which came to their hands. This does not render the assets immune from liability, for they may be followed into the hands of the beneficiaries; but the personal representatives need not concern themselves with this. These provisions apply equally whether the deceased was a lessee or an assignee. They do not, however, protect the personal representatives, from their personal liability if they had taken possession of the premises.[47]

6. Indemnities by assignees. (a) *Implied indemnity.* If a covenant has been broken, the lessee and the assignee entitled to the lease at

---

[41] *Rendall* v. *Andreae* (1892) 61 L.J.Q.B. 630.
[42] *Wollaston* v. *Hakewill* (1841) 3 Man. & G. 297 at 320.
[43] *Helier* v. *Casebert* (1665) 1 Lev. 127; *Youngmin* v. *Heath* [1974] 1 W.L.R. 135 (weekly tenancy).
[44] See *Re Lewis* [1939] Ch. 232.
[45] *King* v. *Malcott* (1852) 9 Hare 692.
[46] s. 26, replacing L.P. Am.A. 1859, s. 27.
[47] *Re Owers* [1941] Ch. 389.

the time of the breach are each liable to be sued by the lessor. But
although the lessor may sue either or both, he can only have one
satisfaction: he has no right to recover twice.[48] The primary liability is
that of the assignee, and if the lessee is sued, he may claim indemnity
from the assignee in whom the lease was vested at the time of the
breach, whether that assignee obtained the lease from the lessee or
from some other assignee.[49] Usually, the assignee will be insolvent or
have disappeared so that the lessee's rights will be worthless.

(b) *Express indemnity.* In addition to this implied obligation to
indemnify the lessee, it is usual for each assignee to enter into an
express covenant to indemnify his assignor against future breaches of
covenant; and by the Law of Property Act 1925,[50] in any assignment
for value made after 1925 such a covenant is implied.

(c) *Effect.* The effect of these rights of indemnity may be illustrated
thus:

$$A$$
$$| \ 99 \text{ years}$$
$$B— \ C —D—E$$
$$| \ 21 \text{ years.}$$
$$F$$

A has leased land to B for 99 years; by successive assignments E
has become entitled to the lease and has granted a sub-lease to F
for 21 years. If F does some act which is contrary to a covenant in
the head lease, A can sue either B (privity of contract) or E (privity
of estate). If A sues B, B has an implied right to indemnity against
E. Alternatively, if on the assignment to C a covenant of indemnity
was given to B, he may claim indemnity from C. C in turn may
claim indemnity from D, and D from E, provided in each case that
the covenant for indemnity was given on the assignment. The
importance of these various rights is emphasised if one of the
parties is insolvent. Apart from the rules relating to restrictive
covenants,[51] F incurs no liability to anyone except so far as his act
was a breach of a covenant in the sub-lease and so makes him liable
to E.

II. WHERE THE LESSOR ASSIGNS HIS REVERSION

If L, a tenant in fee simple, leased his land to T, and then L conveyed
his fee simple, subject to the lease, to R, the common law rule was
that with the exception of "implied covenants," *i.e.* certain covenants

---

[48] *Brett* v. *Cumberland* (1619) Cro.Jac. 521.
[49] *Wolveridge* v. *Steward* (1833) 1 Cr. & M. 644; *Moule* v. *Garrett* (1872) L.R. 7 Ex. 101.
[50] s. 77 (1) (c); 2nd Sched., Pt. IX.
[51] *Post,* pp. 443 *et seq.*

which the law implied (*e.g.* to pay rent),[52] neither the benefit nor the burden of the covenants in the lease ran with the reversion: R was neither able to sue nor liable to be sued. But by the Grantees of Reversion Act 1540, sections 1 and 2, the benefit and burden of all covenants and provisions contained in a lease which touched and concerned the land (or had reference to the subject-matter of the lease, to use the modern phrase) passed with the reversion. These provisions were subsequently replaced and extended by statute, and are now contained in the Law of Property Act 1925, sections 141 and 142.

The following points should be noted.

1. The lease must be in due form. The Act of 1540 applied only to leases under seal,[53] but under the doctrine of *Walsh* v. *Lonsdale*[54] a specifically enforceable agreement is now treated as a lease by deed for this purpose,[55] and it suffices if the provisions are contained or implied in some document in writing.[56] After 1925, probably even a mere oral tenancy is sufficient, for by section 154 of the Law of Property Act 1925, sections 141 and 142 extend to an underlease "or other tenancy."[57]

2. The reversion may have been assigned by deed in whole or in part. The assignee of the entire reversion takes the benefit and burden of the provisions in the lease. Where the reversion is not assigned in its entirety, the position is not so simple. Two separate cases must be considered:

(a) *Severance as regards the estate.* Where the assignee has part of the reversion, *e.g.* where a fee simple reversioner grants a lease of his reversion to X, the reversion is severed as regards the estate. In this case, the person entitled to the part of the reversion, *e.g.* X falls within the statutory provisions, so that the benefit and burden of both covenants and conditions pass to him as the immediate reversioner.[58]

(b) *Severance as regards the land.* Where the assignee has the reversion of part, *e.g.* where a fee simple reversioner conveys the fee simple of half the land to X, the reversion is severed as regards the land. In this case, under the Act of 1540 the covenants ran with the reversion.[59] But conditions[60] (*e.g.* a condition for forfeiture on non-payment of rent) did not, unless the severance took place by

---

[52] See *Vyvyan* v. *Arthur* (1823) 1 B. & C. 410.
[53] *Smith* v. *Eggington* (1874) L.R. 9 C.P. 145.
[54] *Ante*, p. 337.
[55] *Rickett* v. *Green* [1910] 1 K.B. 253.
[56] *Rye* v. *Purcell* [1926] 1 K.B. 446; *Weg Motors Ltd.* v. *Hales* [1962] Ch. 49.
[57] Contrast *ante*, p. 380.
[58] *Wright* v. *Burroughes* (1846) 3 C.B. 685.
[59] *Twynam* v. *Pickard* (1818) 2 B. & Ald. 105.
[60] See *ante*, p. 349.

operation of law, *e.g.* on a compulsory acquisition.[61] However, this position has been altered by statute; by the Law of Property Act 1925,[62] all conditions and rights of re-entry became severable on the severance of the reversion. The tenancy itself, however, continues as one tenancy.[63]

3. Rights of an assignee of the reversion to sue and forfeit for previous breaches. At common law, a right to sue for damages or to forfeit the lease for breach of covenant could not be assigned, so that if a reversion was assigned after a covenant had been broken, the new reversioner could not sue[64] or forfeit[65] the lease. Now, after an assignment of the reversion, the assignee is alone entitled to sue the tenant for rent or for breaches of covenant, whether such rent accrued or such breaches occurred before or after the assignment.[66] This is brought about by the Law of Property Act 1925,[67] which also provides that rights of re-entry are enforceable by the new reversioner, provided they have not been waived. Waiver may be express or implied.[68] Waiver will not be implied merely because the reversion is assigned "subject to and with the benefit of" the lease[69]; it is "the merest *res inter alios acta*" without any impact on the tenant.[70]

4. Privity of estate not essential. Covenants run with the reversion by statute and not by privity of estate. Hence if an original tenant assigns the lease and subsequently the landlord assigns the reversion, the assignee of the reversion can sue the original tenant even though there has never been privity of estate between them.[71]

Sect. 3. Position of Assignees of Equitable Lease

An equitable lease arises where the necessity for a deed in the case of leases exceeding three years has been overlooked[72] or where there is an enforceable contract for a lease.

The original parties to the equitable lease are obviously bound by

[61] *Piggott* v. *Middlesex County Council* [1909] 1 Ch. 134.
[62] s. 140 (1), replacing L.P. Am.A. 1859, s. 3, as extended by C.A. 1881, s. 12. The old law continues to apply if the lease was made before 1882 and the reversion was severed before 1926.
[63] *Jelley* v. *Buckman* [1974] Q.B. 488.
[64] *Flight* v. *Bentley* (1835) 7 Sim. 149.
[65] *Hunt* v. *Remnant* (1854) 9 Exch. 635.
[66] *Re King* [1963] Ch. 459; *London and County (A. & D.) Ltd.* v. *Wilfred Sportsman Ltd.* [1971] Ch. 764.
[67] s. 141, replacing C.A. 1911, s. 2.
[68] For waiver, see *ante*, p. 350.
[69] *London and County (A. & D.) Ltd.* v. *Wilfred Sportsman Ltd.*, *supra*.
[70] *Ibid.* at pp. 781, 782, *per* Russell L.J.
[71] *Arlesford Trading Co. Ltd.* v. *Servansingh* [1971] 1 W.L.R. 1080.
[72] See *ante*, p. 335.

privity of contract but there is no legal estate between them to which any subsequent occupier may be "privy."

The benefit but not the burden of a contract can be assigned,[73] so that where L and T have entered into a lease in writing exceeding three years and T has assigned his interest to T2 then T2 can specifically enforce the contract against L, but L cannot enforce the contract against T2. Since T2 is entitled to specific performance[74] he will be treated by equity as if a lease had been granted[75] and thus will be able to sue on the covenants. Since L cannot obtain specific performance against T2 L cannot be treated as if a lease had been granted and so will be unable to sue T2 on the covenants.[76]

L can only avoid this unfortunate result if he can rely on T2's possession and payment of rent to prove either the existence of an implied contract, on the terms of the equitable lease, between himself and T2[77] or the existence of a periodic tenancy with such terms of the equitable lease as are consistent with the nature of the periodic tenancy,[78] or if, which is uncertain, he can invoke the principle that whilst T2 claims the benefit of the equitable lease he must take subject to the burdens thereof.[79] Denning L.J.[80] has uttered *obiter dicta*, "There is no valid reason nowadays why the doctrine of covenants running with the land should not apply equally to agreements under hand as to covenants under seal." However, though such approach accords with a policy of commonsense it does fly in the face of authority[81] and of legal principle.[82]

Where L assigns his reversion upon T's equitable lease to L2 then L2 can obtain specific performance against T and so is treated by equity as if a lease had been granted and so can sue T on the covenants.[83] Under section 141 of the Law of Property Act (replacing section 10 of the Conveyancing Act 1881) L2 now has the benefit of

---

[73] *Austerberry* v. *Oldham Corporation* (1885) 29 Ch.D. 750.

[74] It would seem that T2 can obtain specific performance even if he had not complied with the tenant's obligations under the terms of the equitable lease since, not being bound by such obligations, he would "come to equity with clean hands." Once specific performance had been obtained and the legal lease granted then T2 would be subject to liability under such lease.

[75] *Walsh* v. *Lonsdale* (1882) 21 Ch.D. 9.

[76] *Purchase* v. *Lichfield Brewery Co.* [1915] 1 K.B. 184; *Marquis of Camden* v. *Batterbury* (1860) 9 C.B. (N.S.) 864.

[77] *Buckworth* v. *Simpson* (1835) 1 Cr. M. & R. 834; *Cornish* v. *Stubbs* (1870) L.R. 5 C.P. 334.

[78] *Beale* v. *Sanders* (1837) 3 Bing. N.C. 850; *Cole* v. *Kelly* [1920] 2 K.B. 106; *Bradbury* v. *Grimble* [1920] 2 Ch. 548.

[79] *Tito* v. *Waddell (No. 2)* [1977] Ch. 106 at pp. 299–302.

[80] *Boyer* v. *Warbey* [1953] 1 Q.B. 234 at pp. 245–246.

[81] See note 76 (*supra*), *Cox* v. *Bishop* (1857) De G.M. & G. 815; *Friary Holroyd & Healey's Breweries Ltd.* v. *Singleton* [1899] 1 Ch. 86; R. J. Smith [1978] Camb. L.J. 98.

[82] If L cannot obtain specific performance against T2 then L cannot claim under *Walsh* v. *Lonsdale* that he should be treated as if a legal lease had been obtained under a decree of specific performance.

[83] *Manchester Brewery Co.* v. *Coombs* [1901] 2 Ch. 608; *Rickett* v. *Green* [1910] 1 K.B. 253.

covenants having reference to the subject-matter of the "lease" and "lease" (defined as including "an underlease or other tenancy) has been held to include an equitable lease.[84]

It follows that under section 142 L2 also has the burden of covenants having reference to the subject-matter of the "lease" including an equitable lease. Thus T and T2 can enforce such covenants against L2.

Part 3

PRIVITY NEITHER OF CONTRACT NOR OF ESTATE

Privity of estate may be regarded as an extension of privity of contract; the parties are connected by the relationship of landlord and tenant, and the covenants which are enforceable under the doctrine of privity of estate are contained in the contractual document which forms the link between the parties. Where there is privity neither of contract nor of estate, however, the enforceability of covenants no longer depends on any extension of a contractual relationship. Covenants in leases properly fall within this chapter, for they form part of the terms upon which the tenant holds his land, and, indeed, resemble the incidents of feudal tenure.

On the other hand, where no privity exists but covenants are enforceable directly as restrictive covenants or indirectly through rights of re-entry conferred by a forfeiture clause, such covenants properly fall within the general category of rights over the land of another like rentcharges or easements. Restrictive covenants developed as proprietary interests when the list of negative easements (like rights of light preventing someone from doing something on his own land) became closed and are in the nature of equitable negative easements since they have some common requirements with easements *e.g.* the need for nearby benefited and burdened land benefited or burdened *qua* land. They are thus best understood after easements have been fully dealt with, but their operation will briefly be illustrated below in regard to the enforcement of restrictive covenants in a head lease against a sub-tenant. The operation of forfeiture clauses will then be considered.

Sect. 1. Restrictive Covenants[85]

If L leases premises by deed to T, who then sub-leases by deed to S,

---

[84] *Rickett* v. *Green (supra)*; *Rye & Purcell* [1926] 1 K.B. 446; *Boyer* v. *Warbey* [1953] 1 Q.B. 246. There still remains the question of determining whether or not the burden has passed to the defendant, *e.g.* if the defendant is not the original equitable lessee but an assignee thereof.

[85] *Post*, p. 443.

what can L do if the lease contains a covenant that certain things will not be done on the premises but S contravenes such covenant. No privity of contract or of estate subsists between L and S.

L, however, can rely on *Hall* v. *Ewin*[86] to claim an injunction to restrain S—or any other occupier for that matter—from contravening the terms of the restrictive covenant so long as S—or any other defendant with a legal estate—has notice of the covenant. L's reversion is treated as the benefited land and S's interest as the burdened land.[87]

If L's complaint was against someone who had no notice of the restrictive covenant then L would have to rely on a forfeiture clause conferring a right of re-entry for breach of any covenant in the lease. This legal right binds the world irrespective of notice.

Sect. 2. Operation of Forfeiture Clauses

An occupier of leasehold land (*e.g.* a sub-tenant or an equitable assignee of a lease) may not be bound by privity of contract or privity of estate to observe covenants in a lease but may, in fact, have to observe such covenants under penalty of forfeiture under an express forfeiture clause in the lease. Such clause creates a conditional right of re-entry which is a proprietary interest binding third parties[88]: usually, it will be a legal right of re-entry.[89]

Thus if a legal lease contains a repairing covenant by T and T then sub-leases to S or makes an equitable assignment in favour of A, the lessor, L, can re-enter and determine T's lease (and thus the interests of S and A) if the premises are not repaired as required by the repairing covenant.[90] This seems to be the position even if the covenant does not touch and concern the land so that it would be unenforceable on privity of estate principles if the equitable assignee had been a legal assignee.[91]

Usually, forfeiture clauses will be found in leases but they may be made one of the terms of an assignment of a lease[92] or of a grant in fee simple.[93]

---

[86] (1888) 27 Ch.D. 74.
[87] *Regent Oil Co. Ltd.* v. *J.A. Gregory Ltd.* [1966] Ch. 402 at p. 433; *Teape* v. *Douse* (1905) 92 L.T. 319.
[88] L.P.A. 1925, s. 1 (2) (*e*), *ante*, p. 90.
[89] In *Shiloh Spinners* v. *Harding* [1973] A.C. 691 (*ante*, p. 90) the right of re-entry was equitable since exercisable for an uncertain period. A right of re-entry in an equitable lease can only be equitable and its enforcement will depend on the doctrine of notice.
[90] Subject to the statutory provisions for relief against forfeiture: *e.g.* L.P.A., s. 146.
[91] *Shiloh Spinners* v. *Harding* [1973] A.C. 691 so that *Horsey Estate Ltd.* v. *Steiger* [1899] 2 Q.B. 74 at pp. 88–89 is now of unreliable authority.
[92] *Shiloh's Case* (*supra*).
[93] *e.g.* fees simple subject to conditions subsequent: *ante*, p. 40.

CHAPTER 11

INCORPOREAL HEREDITAMENTS

It has already been seen that incorporeal hereditaments are rights in land which do not give the owner present physical possesion of the land.[1] There are two quite distinct classes of incorporeal hereditaments:

1. Those which may ripen into corporeal hereditaments. Thus a grant to A for life with remainder to B in fee simple gave B an incorporeal hereditament which became corporeal after A's death.
2. Those which can never become corporeal hereditaments but are merely rights over the land of another, *e.g.* rentcharges.

The first class has already been dealt with.[2] It is with incorporeal hereditaments in the latter class that this chapter is concerned. Most are either obsolete or of little importance in connection with the modern law of real property, *e.g.* titles of honour, advowsons[3] and tithes.[4] The only incorporeal hereditaments which need to be considered at length are rentcharges, easements and profits. They do not form a homogeneous class. Some, such as easements, can exist only for the benefit of other land, while others, such as rentcharges, lead an independent existence. In one sense, those in the former category are not hereditaments at all, for they cannot be inherited or dealt with except as appendages to the land which they benefit.

Part 1

RENTCHARGES

Sect. 1. Nature of Rentcharges

1. Rentcharges and rent services. Periodical payments in respect of land fall under the two main heads of rentcharges and rent services. Where the relationship of lord and tenant exists between the parties, any rent payable by virtue of that relationship by the tenant to the lord is a rent service. If there is no relationship of lord and tenant, the rent is a rentcharge. Thus if L grants a lease to T at £1,100 per annum and X charges his fee simple estate with the payment of £2,000 per

---

[1] *Ante*, p. 73; and see generally M. & W., pp. 787–792.
[2] *Ante*, Chaps. 6 and 7.
[3] See *ante*, p. 85.
[4] See *ante*, p. 89.

annum to Y, L has a rent service and Y a rentcharge. Since the Statute *Quia Emptores* 1290 it has been impossible for a grantor to reserve any services on a conveyance of freehold land in fee simple for the grantee holds of the grantor's lord, and not of the grantor. Consequently, no rent reserved on a conveyance of freehold land in fee simple after 1290 can be a rent service. Although at law services could be reserved on the grant by a fee simple owner of a life estate[5] or a fee tail, it was most unusual to do so. The only rent service now met with in practice is the rent reserved upon the grant of a lease for a term of years. A rent service is annexed to a reversion, while a rentcharge stands on its own.

2. Legal and equitable rentcharges. A rentcharge is real property, so that both at law and in equity it could be held for any of the usual estates or interests.[6] However, since 1925 an interest in a rentcharge can be legal only if it is—

  (a) in possession, and
  (b) either perpetual or for a term of years absolute.[7]

Further, a rentcharge cannot exist at law unless the proper formalities have been employed for its creation.[8]

3. Rentcharge on a rentcharge. At common law, a rentcharge could be charged only upon a corporeal hereditament. There could be no rentcharge charged upon another rentcharge or other incorporeal hereditament[9]; a right of distress would clearly be inappropriate in such cases. However, since 1925 a rentcharge charged upon another rentcharge is valid, even if created before 1926; and special provisions have been made for enforcing payment.[10]

Sect. 2. Creation and Transfer of Rentcharges

A. Creation

A rentcharge may be created by statute, by an instrument *inter vivos* or by will but the instances where they can now be created have been drastically curtailed by the Rentcharges Act 1977.

1. By statute. A rentcharge may be created either by statute, or by

---

[5] If any rent service is reserved on the grant of a life estate L.P.A. 1925, s. 149 (6) will apply to create a 90 year term.
[6] See, *e.g. Chaplin* v. *Chaplin* (1733) 3 P.Wms. 229 (entail); *Re Fraser* [1904] 1 Ch. 726. (term of years).
[7] *Ante*, p. 88.
[8] *Infra.*
[9] *Re The Alms Corn Charity* [1901] 2 Ch. 750 at p. 759.
[10] L.P.A. 1925, s. 122: *post*, p. 394.

virtue of powers conferred thereby.[11] This is not affected by the 1977 Act.

2. By instrument inter vivos. Apart from statute, a legal rentcharge can be created *inter vivos* only by a deed[12]; but a document merely in writing may create an equitable rentcharge.[13]

3. By will. A will now operates only in equity,[14] so that if a rentcharge is created or devised by will, the beneficiary gets no legal interest until the personal representatives have assented to the gift.[15]

4. The Rentcharges Act 1977. No new rentcharge can be created at law or in equity after August 22, 1977 except for (a) a rentcharge which has the effect of making the land settled land by reason of a family charge[16] or (b) an "estate rentcharge"—this is one created as a means of making covenants enforceable or of ensuring that certain costs are met.[17]

B. Words of Limitation

If an existing rentcharge is being transferred by deed or will, the normal rule for corporeal hereditaments applies and the whole interest in the rentcharge passes without words of limitation unless a contrary intention is shown.[18] But if a rentcharge is being created by will or (perhaps) by deed, only a life interest will be created unless an intention is shown to create some larger interest.[19]

Sect. 3. Means of Enforcing Payment of Rentcharges

A. Rentcharge Charged on Land

There are four remedies available to the owner of a rentcharge if it is not paid. The first remedy, namely, an action for the money, is given by the common law; the other three are created by statute,[20] and replace remedies formerly expressly conferred by most instruments creating rentcharges.

1. Action for the money. A personal action for the rent will lie

---

[11] See, *e.g.* Improvement of Land Act 1864.
[12] See *Hewlins* v. *Shippam* (1826) 5 B. & C. 221 at p. 229.
[13] *Jackson* v. *Lever* (1792) 3 Bro.C.C. 605; L.P.A. 1925, s. 53.
[14] See L.P.A.(Am.)A. 1924, Sched. IX.
[15] For assents, see *ante*, p. 180.
[16] Or would have that effect if the land were not already settled land or held on trust for sale.
[17] Rentcharges Act 1977, s. 2 (4).
[18] *Ante*, p. 35.
[19] See *Nichols* v. *Hawkes* (1853) 10 Hare 342; *Grant* v. *Edmondson* [1930] 2 Ch. 245 at p. 254; [1931] 1 Ch. 1; *ante*, p. 36; M. & W., p. 795.
[20] L.P.A. 1925, s. 121, replacing C.A. 1881, s. 44.

against the "terre tenant" (the freehold tenant in possession of the land upon which the rent is charged) even if the rent was not created by him[21] and exceeds the value of the land.[22] If the land has been divided, the terre tenant of any part is liable for the full amount[23]; but a mere lessee for a term of years is not liable,[24] for the action lies only against the freeholder.

Although the right to sue and the liability to be sued run with the rentcharge and the land respectively, the benefit of an express covenant for payment does not run with the rentcharge without express assignment.[25] Thus if a rentcharge created by A in favour of X is conveyed to Y and the land to B, Y cannot sue A on his covenant for payment if B fails to pay.

2. Distress. If an express power of distress is given by the instrument creating the rentcharge, the extent of the right is a question of construction. If there is no such express power, and the rentcharge was created before 1882, the rentcharge owner can distrain upon the land as soon as the rent or any part of it is in arrear.[26] If the rentcharge was created after 1881, then, subject to any contrary intention, the rentcharge owner can distrain as soon as the rent or any part of it is 21 days in arrear.[27]

3. Entry into possession. If a rentcharge was created after 1881 and shows no contrary intention, the rentcharge owner may, when the rent or any part of it is 40 days in arrear, enter and take possession of the land without impeachment of waste and take the income until he has paid himself all rent due with costs.[28]

4. Demise to a trustee. If the rentcharge was created after 1881 and shows no contrary intention, the rentcharge owner may, if the rent or any part of it is 40 days in arrear, demise the land to a trustee for a term of years, with or without impeachment of waste, on trust to raise the money due, with all costs and expenses, by creating a mortgage, receiving the income or any other reasonable means.[29] If a rentcharge owner has only an equitable interest, he can grant only an equitable lease to the trustees, but the estate owner can be compelled to clothe the equitable lease with the legal estate.[30]

If the rentcharge is created after July 15, 1964, the rule against

[21] *Thomas* v. *Sylvester* (1873) L.R. 8 Q.B. 368.
[22] *Pertwee* v. *Townsend* (1896) 2 Q.B. 129.
[23] *Christie* v. *Barker* (1884) 53 L.J.Q.B. 537.
[24] *Re Herbage* v. *Rents* [1896] 2 Ch. 811.
[25] See *Grant* v. *Edmondson* [1931] 1 Ch. 1, criticised (1931) 47 L.Q.R. 380.
[26] Landlord and Tenant Act 1730, s. 5.
[27] L.P.A. 1925, s. 121 (2).
[28] *Ibid*. s. 121 (3).
[29] *Ibid*. s. 121 (4).
[30] *Ibid*. ss. 3 (1), 8 (2).

perpetuities does not apply to any powers or remedies for enforcing it.[31] If the rentcharge was created before that date the last three statutory remedies were expressly excepted from the rule, together with similar express powers conferred by an instrument.[32] Other, wider, provisions were not considered to be excepted from the rule, *e.g.* a clause which is sometimes inserted entitling the rentcharge owner to effect a permanent forfeiture of the land if the rent is unpaid for a specified period.[33]

B. Rentcharge Charged on Another Rentcharge

Instead of the statutory remedies of distress, entry into possession and demise to a trustee, the owner of a rentcharge charged upon another rentcharge may appoint a receiver if the rent or any part of it is 21 days in arrear.[34] The receiver has all the powers of a receiver appointed by a mortgagee.[35] Thus if Blackacre is charged with a rent of £100 per annum and that rentcharge is charged with a rent of £25 per annum in favour of X, a receiver of the £100 can be appointed by X if the £25 is unpaid for 21 days.

Sect. 4. Extinguishment of Rentcharges

A rentcharge may be extinguished by release, merger, lapse of time, statutory discharge or the expiry of the 60-year period under the Rentcharges Act 1977.

1. Release. The owner of a rentcharge may by deed release the land from the rent, either wholly or in part. A partial release may take the form of releasing all of the land from part of the rent,[36] or releasing part of the land from the whole of the rent.[37] An informal release may be valid in equity.

2. Merger. At common law, if a rentcharge became vested in the same person as the land upon which it was charged, the rentcharge became extinguished by merger, even if this was not the intention.[38] For this to occur, both the rent and the land must have been vested in the same person at the same time and in the same right.[39] This automatic rule of the common law no longer applies for, by the Law

---

[31] Perpetuities and Accumulations Act 1964, s. 11, amending L.P.A. 1925, s. 121 (6); *ante*, p. 223.

[32] L.P.A. 1925, s. 121 (6).

[33] See *Re Trustees of Hollis' Hospital and Hague's Contract* [1899] 2 Ch. 540, criticised in Challis R.P. 190.

[34] L.P.A. 1925, 2. 122 (2), (3).

[35] *Ibid.* s. 122 (2); *post*, p. 483.

[36] Co.Litt. 148a.

[37] L.P.A. 1925, s. 70.

[38] *Capital and Counties Bank Ltd.* v. *Rhodes* [1903] 1 Ch. 631 at p. 652.

[39] *Re Radcliffe* [1892] 1 Ch. 227.

of Property Act 1925,[40] there is to be no merger at law except in cases where there would have been a merger in equity, and the equitable rule is that merger depends upon the intention of the parties.[41] Even if an intention that there should be no merger cannot be shown, there will be a presumption against merger if it is to the interest of the person concerned to prevent it.[42]

3. Lapse of time. If a rentcharge is not paid for 12 years and no sufficient acknowledgment of the owner's title is made, it is extinguished.[43]

4. Statutory discharge. By the Rentcharges Act 1977[44] provision is made for landowners to obtain the discharge of their land from rentcharges on paying to the rentcharge owner the sum representing the capital value certified by the Secretary of State for the Environment (or Wales).

5. Expiry of 60-years period. Every rentcharge (if not already extinguished by then) is to be extinguished 60 years after the Rentcharges Act 1977 was passed[45] or after the date on which the rentcharge first became payable, whichever is the later.[46] This does not apply, of course, to those rare rentcharges that may still be created after the 1977 Act.[47]

Part 2

EASEMENTS AND PROFITS

Sect. 1. Nature of an Easement

An easement may be defined as a right annexed to land to use, or restrict the use of, the land of another person in some way. This definition is neither exact nor particularly helpful, for it includes certain rights which are not easements, such as restrictive covenants, and it fails to illustrate what sort of a right an easement is. Examples of easements are rights of way, rights of light and rights of water. The best way in which to amplify this imperfect definition is to examine—

(a) the essentials of an easement, and

---

[40] s. 185, replacing J.A. 1873, s. 25 (4).
[41] *Ingle* v. *Vaughan Jenkins* [1900] 2 Ch. 368.
[42] *Re Fletcher* [1917] 1 Ch. 339.
[43] See *post*, pp. 524, 531.
[44] ss. 8, 9, 10 replacing L.P.A. 1925, s. 191.
[45] July 22, 1977.
[46] Rentcharges Act 1977, s. 3.
[47] *Ibid.* s. 3(3), *ante*, p. 392.

(b) the distinction between easements and certain analogous rights.

A. Essentials of an Easement

1. There must be a dominant and a servient tenement.[48] If X owns Blackacre and grants a right to use a path across Blackacre to the owner for the time being of the neighbouring plot of Whiteacre, Blackacre is the servient tenement and Whiteacre the dominant tenement. Had X granted the right to A who owned no land at all, A would have acquired a licence to walk over Blackacre, but his right could not exist as an easement, for a dominant tenement is lacking. Put technically, an easement cannot exist in gross[49] (independently of the ownership of land) but only as appurtenant (attached) to a dominant tenement[50]; on any transfer of the dominant tenement, the easement will pass with the land, so that the occupier for the time being can enjoy it,[51] even if he is a mere lessee.[52]

2. The easement must accommodate the dominant tenement. A right cannot exist as an easement unless it confers a benefit on the dominant tenement as a tenement. It is not sufficient that the right should give the owner for the time being some personal advantage unconnected with his land, such as a right to use a wall on the servient tenement for advertising generally and not merely in connection with a business carried on upon the dominant tenement[53]; the test is whether the right makes the dominant tenement a better and more convenient tenement, *e.g.* a right to affix to adjoining premises a signboard for a public house.[54] There thus has to be some nexus between the enjoyment of the right and the use of the dominant tenement so that the grant to a purchaser of the right free of charge to attend a nearby zoo or cricket ground or cinema cannot create an easement.[55]

Obviously if X owns land in Northumberland, he cannot burden it with an easement of way in favour of land in Kent, for although it may be very convenient for the owner of the Kentish land to walk across X's Northumberland estate when he goes north, the right of way does not improve the Kentish land as a tenement.[56] This does not mean that a right cannot exist as an easement unless the dominant

---

[48] *Hawkins* v. *Rutter* [1892] 1 Q.B. 668.
[49] *Rangeley* v. *Midland Ry.* (1868) 3 Ch.App. 306 at p. 310. See M.F. Sturley (1980) 96 L.Q.R. 557.
[50] See *Re Salvin's Indenture* [1938] 2 All E.R. 498 (dominant tenement partly incorporeal).
[51] L.P.A. 1925, s. 187 (1); *Leech* v. *Schweder* (1874) 9 Ch.App. 463 at pp. 474, 475.
[52] *Thorpe* v. *Brumfitt* (1873) 8 Ch.App. 650.
[53] *Clapman* v. *Edwards* [1938] 2 All E.R. 507.
[54] *Moody* v. *Steggles* (1879) 12 Ch.D. 261.
[55] *Re Ellenborough Park* [1956] Ch. 131 at p. 174.
[56] See *Bailey* v. *Stephens* (1862) 12 C.B. (N.S.) 91 at p. 115.

and servient tenements are contiguous; even if they are separated by other land, an easement can still exist, provided it in fact confers some benefit upon the dominant tenement as such,[57] as does a right for the dominant owner to enjoy an adjacent park in the middle of a Square.[58] Nor will a right be any the less an easement merely because it benefits other land as well as the dominant tenement.[59]

In *Ackroyd* v. *Smith*[60] it was held that a right of way granted "for all purposes" to the tenant of Blackacre and his successors in title was not an easement, for the grant permitted the way to be used for purposes not connected with Blackacre. Had the grant been worded "for all purposes connected with Blackacre" it could have created an easement. Probably the words used would be construed in this sense if the case arose today.[61]

In *Hill* v. *Tupper*[62] the owner of a canal leased land on the bank of the canal to Hill and granted him the sole and exclusive right of putting pleasure boats on the canal. Tupper, without any authority, put rival pleasure boats on the canal. The question was whether Hill could successfully sue Tupper. If Hill's right amounted to an easement, he could sue anyone who interfered with it, for it was a right in land. If it was not an easement, then it could only be a licence,[63] *i.e.* a mere personal arrangement between Hill and the canal owner not amounting to an interest in land, so that Hill would have no right to sue those interfering with it. It was held that since the right did not improve Hill's land *qua* land, but gave him a mere personal advantage, it was not an easement and thus he could not sue Tupper. The result would have been different if the right granted had been to cross and recross the canal to get to and from Hill's land. On the facts as they were, the canal owner, of course, could have sued Tupper for trespassing on the canal.[64]

3. The dominant and servient tenements must be owned or occupied by different persons. An easement is essentially a right in *alieno solo* (in the soil of another): a man cannot have an easement over his own land. "When the owner of Whiteacre and Blackacre passes over the former to Blackacre, he is not exercising a right of way in respect of

---

[57] *Todrick* v. *Western National Omnibus Co. Ltd.* [1934] Ch. 561; *Pugh* v. *Savage* [1970] 2 Q.B. 373.
[58] *Re Ellenborough Park* [1956] Ch. 131.
[59] *Simpson* v. *Mayor of Godmanchester* [1897] A.C. 696.
[60] (1850) 10 C.B. 164.
[61] *Thorpe* v. *Brumfitt* [1873] 8 Ch.App. 650 at pp. 655–657; *Todrick* v. *Western National Omnibus Co. Ltd.* [1934] Ch. 561 at p. 583. The nature of the right will be significant: *Clapman* v. *Edwards* [1938] 2 All E.R. 507 ("for advertising purposes" held not restricted to user for dominant tenement's business and so not an easement).
[62] (1863) 2 H. & C. 121. The land facilitated the use of the canal rather than vice versa.
[63] See *ante*, pp. 370, and *post*, p. 403.
[64] See *Lord Chesterfield* v. *Harris* [1908] 2 Ch. 397 at p. 412 (affd.: [1911] A.C. 623).

Blackacre; he is merely making use of his own land to get from one part of it to another."[65]

It should be noted, however, that the same person must not only own both tenements but also occupy both of them before the existence of an easement is rendered impossible. Thus if an easement over Blackacre is appurtenant to Whiteacre, it will not be affected by the fee simple in each plot becoming vested in one person if the plots are occupied by different lessees[66]; unity of ownership without unity of possession is not fatal to an easement. Similarly, if the fee simple in each plot is owned by different persons, the easement will not be destroyed if the plots are leased to the same tenant, creating unity of possession without unity of ownership; during the currency of the lease the easement is suspended but it will revive when the lease ends.[67]

The name "quasi-easements" is often used to describe rights habitually exercised by a man over part of his own land which, if the part in question were owned and occupied by another, would be easements. These are of some importance, for in certain circumstances they may become true easements.[68]

4. The easement must be capable of forming the subject-matter of a grant. No right can exist as an easement unless it could have been granted by deed. This involves the following points.

(a) *There must be a capable grantor.* There can be no claim to an easement if at the relevant times the servient tenement was owned by someone incapable of granting an easement, *e.g.* a statutory corporation with no power to grant easements.[69]

(b) *There must be a capable grantee.* An easement can be claimed only by a legal person capable of receiving a grant. Thus a claim by a company with no power to acquire easements must fail[70]; similarly, a fluctuating body of persons, such as "the inhabitants for the time being of the village of X," cannot claim an easement, for no grant can be made to them. But such bodies may claim similar rights by showing that there is a custom to that effect, such as a customary right of way across land to reach the parish chuch,[71] or a customary right to play games[72] or to dry nets on certain land.[73]

(c) *The right must be sufficiently definite.* The extent of the right

---

[65] *Roe* v. *Siddons* (1888) 22 Q.B.D. 224 at p. 236, *per* Fry L.J.
[66] *Richardson* v. *Graham* [1908] 1 K.B. 39; and see *Buckby* v. *Coles* (1814) 5 Taunt. 311 at p. 315.
[67] *Thomas* v. *Thomas* (1835) 2 Cr.M. & R. 34 (see especially at p. 40).
[68] *Post*, pp. 411 *et seq.*
[69] See *Re Salvin's Indenture* [1938] 2 All E.R. 498.
[70] *National Guaranteed Manure Co.* v. *Donald* (1859) 4 H. & N. 8.
[71] *Brocklebank* v. *Thompson* [1903] 2 Ch. 344.
[72] *New Windsor Corporation* v. *Mellor* [1974] 1 W.L.R. 1504.
[73] *Mercer* v. *Denne* [1905] 2 Ch. 538; *post*, p. 404.

claimed must be capable of reasonable definition. Thus although there can be an easement of light where a defined window receives a defined amount of light, there can be no easement of privacy,[74] nor of prospect (the right to a view), for "the law does not give an action for such things as delight."[75] Again, an easement for the passage of air through a defined channel may exist, but there can be no easement for the general flow of air over land to a windmill or chimney.[76] These limits on the law of easements may be circumvented by restrictive covenants or by the rule against derogation from grant.[77]

(d) *The right must be within the general nature of rights capable of existing as easements.* Although most easements fall under one of the well-known heads of easements, such as way, light, support and so on, the list of easements is not closed. "The category of servitudes and easements must alter and expand with the changes that take place in the circumstances of mankind."[78] But there are limits. "It must not therefore be supposed that incidents of a novel kind can be devised and attached to property, at the fancy or caprice of any owner."[79] It now seems most unlikely that any new negative easements preventing an owner from doing things on his servient land (*e.g.* rights of light or of air) can be created.[80] The right must fall within the general characteristics of an easement, which are almost incapable of definition.

It can be said, however, that it is most unlikely that a right would be admitted as an easement if it involved the servient tenant in the expenditure of money, for no recognised easement does this,[81] except the obligation to fence land in order to keep out cattle,[82] which has been described as "in the nature of a spurious easement."[83] But new rights not involving the servient owner in expenditure have from time to time been recognised as easements. Thus in 1896 the right to go upon the land of another to open sluice gates,[84] in 1915 a right to store casks and trade produce on land,[85] in 1955 the right to use a neighbour's lavatory,[86] in 1956 the right to

---

[74] *Browne* v. *Flower* [1911] 1 Ch. 219.
[75] *William Aldred's Case* (1610) 9 Co.Rep. 57b at p. 58b, *per* Wray C.J.
[76] *Webb* v. *Bird* (1862) 13 C.B. (N.S.) 841; *Bryant* v. *Lefever* (1879) 4 C.P.D. 172.
[77] *Post*, p. 404.
[78] *Dyce* v. *Hay* (1852) 1 Macq. 205 at p. 312, *per* Lord St. Leonards L.C.
[79] *Keppell* v. *Bailey* (1833) 2 My. & K. 517 at p. 535, *per* Lord Brougham L.C.
[80] *Phipps* v. *Pears* [1965] 1 Q.B. 76 at pp. 82–82 (there cannot be an easement to have the wall of a house protected from the weather by an adjoining house).
[81] See *Pomfret* v. *Ricroft* (1669) 1 Wms.Saund. 321; *Regis Property Co. Ltd.* v. *Redman* [1956] 2 Q.B. 612.
[82] *Crow* v. *Wood* [1971] 1 Q.B. 77; *Jones* v. *Price* [1965] 2 Q.B. 618; *Egerton* v. *Harding, supra*; M. & W., p. 879, 880.
[83] *Lawrence* v. *Jenkins* (1873) L.R. 8 Q.B. 274 at p. 279, *per* Archibald J.
[84] *Simpson* v. *Mayor of Godmanchester* [1896] 1 Ch. 214; [1897] A.C. 696.
[85] *Att.-Gen. of Southern Nigeria* v. *Holt* [1915] A.C. 599. The headnote calls the right an irrevocable licence, but it was clearly recognised as an easement: see p. 617 of the report.
[86] *Miller* v. *Emcer Products Ltd.* [1956] Ch. 304.

enjoy a park[87] and in 1973 the right to use an airfield,[88] were recognised as easements.

An easement is a right over another's land so that if the right claimed amounts to exclusive or joint possession of that land as if it were the claimant's land then the right cannot be an easement. Thus a claim by prescriptive long user to have a right to park and repair vehicles on land may be so ill-defined and extensive (amounting to sole or joint possession of the land) as to be outside the class of possible easements.[89] However, it may be that a landowner may expressly or impliedly grant a neighbour the right to park a vehicle on his land and thereby create an easement,[90] the grantor creating a right over his land rather than giving possession of it to another.

B. Distinction between Easements and Certain Analogous Rights

The nature of easements may be further indicated by contrasting them with certain rights.

I. QUASI-EASEMENTS

As already explained,[91] rights exercised by a landowner over his own land which, if he did not own that land, could exist as easements, are sometimes called quasi-easements.

II. NATURAL RIGHTS

In addition to his rights over his own land, every landowner has a natural right to support, *i.e.* a right that the support for his land provided by his neighbour's land should not be removed[92] whether directly or by causing the subsoil to liquefy.[93] A similar right exists in cases where the surface of the land and the soil underneath are owned by different persons; the owner of the surface has a natural right to have it supported by the subjacent soil[94] unless this right is excluded by clear words or necessary implication in some statute or agreement.

This natural right, however, extends only to land in its natural state; there is no natural right to support for buildings or for the additional burden on land which they cause.[95] But if support is withdrawn, and the land would have fallen even it had not been built upon, an action lies in respect of any damage to the buildings.[96]

---

[87] *Re Ellenborough Park* [1956] Ch. 131.
[88] *Dowty Boulton Paul Ltd.* v. *Wolverhampton Corporation (No. 2)* [1976] Ch. 13.
[89] *Copeland* v. *Greenhalf* [1952] Ch. 488; and see *Grigsby* v. *Melville* [1972] 1 W.L.R. 1355 (affirmed [1974] 1 W.L.R. 80); D.J.H. (1973) 37 Conv. 62.
[90] *Sweet & Maxwell Ltd.* v. *Michael-Michael's Advertising Ltd.* [1965] C.L.Y. 2192 (Co. Ct.).
[91] *Ante,* p. 398.
[92] *Backhouse* v. *Bonomi* (1861) 9 H.L.C. 503.
[93] *Lotus Ltd.* v. *British Soda Co. Ltd.* [1972] Ch. 123.
[94] *London & North Western Ry.* v. *Evans* [1893] 1 Ch. 16 at p. 30.
[95] *Wyatt* v. *Harrison* (1823) 3 B. & Ad. 871.
[96] *Stroyan* v. *Knowles* (1861) 6 H. & N. 454; *Lotus Ltd.* v. *British Soda Co. Ltd.,* *supra.*

Similarly, there is no natural right to have buildings supported by neighbouring buildings.[97] If no more damage is done than is necessary, a man may pull down his house without having to provide support for his neighbour's house. The right to have buildings supported by land or by other buildings can, however, be acquired as an easement.[98]

III. PUBLIC RIGHTS

An easement must always be appurtenant to land; it is a right exercisable by the owner for the time being by virtue of his estate in the land. A public right, on the other hand, is a right exercisable by anyone, whether he owns land or not, merely by virtue of being a member of the public.

The public rights which most closely resemble easements are public rights of way. The land over which a public right of way exists is known as a highway, and although most highways have been made up into roads, and most easements of way exist over footpaths, the presence or absence of a made road has nothing to do with the distinction. There may be a highway over a footpath, while a well-made road may be subject only to an easement of way, or may exist only for the landowner's benefit and be subject to no easement at all.

1. Creation. A public right of way may be created in the following ways.

(a) *By statute.* This needs no explanation.

(b) *By dedication and acceptance*

(1) AT COMMON LAW. To establish a highway at common law by dedication and acceptance, it must be shown—

(i) that the owner of the land dedicated the way to the public, and also

(ii) that the public accepted that dedication, the acceptance normally being shown by user of the public.[99]

Dedication may be formal, although this is comparatively infrequent. It is usually inferred from long user by the public, the user thus being effective to prove both dedication and acceptance. But to raise a presumption of dedication, there must have been open use as of right for so long a time that it must have come to the notice of the landowner that the public were using the way as of right, thus justifying the inference that the landowner consented to this user.[1]

---

[97] *Peyton* v. *Mayor of London* (1829) 9 B. & C. 725.
[98] *Post*, p. 411.
[99] See *Cubitt* v. *Lady Caroline Maxse* (1873) L.R. 8 C.P. 704 at p. 715.
[1] *Greenwich District Board of Works* v. *Maudsley* (1870) L.R. 5 Q.B. 397 at p. 404.

User with the landowner's licence is not user as of right,[2] for it acknowledges that the way is being used not because the public has a right to do so but because the landowner has agreed not to treat it as a trespass in the particular case in question. Further, the use must have been without interruption by the owner. A practice frequently adopted to disprove any intention to dedicate is to close the way for one day in each year, for this openly asserts the landowner's right to exclude the public at will.[3]

The length of the enjoyment to be shown depends on the circumstances of the case. Where the circumstances have pointed to an intention to dedicate, eighteen months has been held to be enough,[4] while where the circumstances are against dedication, a substantially greater period may be insufficient.

(2) UNDER THE HIGHWAYS ACT 1959. The Rights of Way Act 1932, now replaced by the provisions of the Highways Act 1959, simplified the position to some extent by laying down a definite period of use which will suffice to show that a right of way exists. The public can still claim a right of way based on use for a shorter period than that laid down by the Act if an intent to dedicate can be inferred.

The Act provides that a way is to be deemed to have been dedicated as a highway if it "had been actually enjoyed by the public as of right and without interruption for a full period of twenty years," unless "there is sufficient evidence that there was no intention during that period to dedicate it."[5] "Interruption" means interruption in fact, and not, *e.g.* the mere closing of the way only at times when nobody used or was likely to use it.[6] The absence of any intention to dedicate can be shown either in one of the usual ways, as by closing the way for one day in each year, or by one of the special ways provided by the Act, namely, by exhibiting a notice visible to those using the way, or by depositing a map with the local council with a statement of what ways the landowner admits to be highways and lodging statutory declarations at intervals of not more than six years stating whether any other ways have been dedicated. A reversioner or remainderman upon an interest for life or *pur autre vie* is entitled to the same remedies against the public as if he were in possession.[7]

The 20-years' period is to be calculated as that next before the time when the right to use the way was brought into question by a notice exhibited to the public negativing the dedication or otherwise.

2. Extinguishment. When a highway has been established, it can only be stopped up or diverted by an order made under certain

---

[2] *R.* v. *Broke* (1859) 1 F. & F. 514.
[3] See *British Museum Trustees* v. *Finnis* (1833) 5 C. & P. 460.
[4] *North London Ry.* v. *The Vestry of St, Mary, Islington* (1872) 27 L.T. 672.
[5] Highways Act 1959, s. 34.
[6] *Lewis* v. *Thomas* [1950] 1 K.B. 438.
[7] Highways Act 1959, s. 36.

statutory provisions[8]; the mere obstruction of the highway or the failure by the public to use it will not destroy the rights of the public, for "once a highway always a highway."[9] And a mere closing order for a highway leaves unaffected any easement over the route of the highway.[10]

IV. LICENCES

Licences resemble easements in that they authorise the use of the land of another in some way. But licences, which cannot exist as legal estates or interests or, on the orthodox view, as equitable interests, are far more flexible and less restricted than easements. Thus they may be created without formality; they require no dominant tenement; and they may authorise the occupation of land.[11]

V. RESTRICTIVE COVENANTS

Easements and restrictive covenants are similar in that an easement, like a restrictive covenant, may entitle a landowner to restrict the use that his neighbour makes of his land; thus the owner of an easement of light may prevent the servient owner from obstructing his light by erecting a building on the adjoining land.[12] There are other resemblances, such as the need for dominant and servient tenements, and in general it is true to say that the law of restrictive covenants may be regarded as an equitable extension of the law of easements. However, certain points of difference should be mentioned.

1. Scope: restrictive covenants are wider in scope and more flexible than easements. As has been seen, an easement to a general flow of air cannot exist.[13] Further, there can be no easement entitling the dominant owner to a view.[14] But by means of suitable restrictive covenants preventing his neighbour from building, a landowner can enjoy both the view and a general flow of air.

2. Visibility: an inspection of the land will suggest the existence of many easements, but it is otherwise with restrictive covenants. Thus footpaths suggest an easement of way and pipes an easement of drainage, but no inspection of the land will reveal the existence of a covenant against trading upon it.

3. Existence at law: an easement may be legal or equitable, whereas the burden of a restrictive covenant runs only in equity.

---

[8] *e.g.* Highways Act 1959, ss. 108–115; Town and Country Planning Act 1971, s. 210.
[9] *Dawes* v. *Hawkins* (1860) 8 C.B. (N.S.) 848 at p. 858, *per* Byles J.
[10] *Walsh* v. *Oates* [1953] 1 Q.B. 578.
[11] For licences, see *ante*, pp. 81, 370.
[12] For restrictive covenants, see *post*, pp. 443 *et seq*.
[13] *Ante*, p. 399.
[14] *Ante*, p. 399.

4. Prescription: an easement may be acquired by prescription; not so a restrictive covenant.

5. Positive nature: a restrictive covenant is entirely negative; it neither entitles the dominant owner nor binds the servient owner to do any positive act. Easements similarly do not bind the servient owner to do any positive act,[15] but as regards the dominant owner certain easements (called "positive easements") entitle the owner to do positive acts, *e.g.* easements of way, while others (called "negative easements") do not, *e.g.* easements of light. Certain easements thus contain a positive element which is lacking in restrictive covenants.

VI. RIGHTS RESULTING FROM THE RULE AGAINST DEROGATION FROM GRANT

A grantor may not derogate from his grant: where he sells or leases land, knowing that the grantee intends to use it for a particular purpose, he may not do anything to impede such purposed use.[16] His successors in title are also bound by the rights of the grantee and successors in title to the grantee. Thus, where a lease was granted to a timber merchant, needing a free general flow of air to his drying timber, a purchaser of the lessor's adjoining land could not build upon it so as to obstruct the ventilation required by the lessee.[17]

VII. CUSTOMARY RIGHTS OF FLUCTUATING BODIES

These have been considered above.[18] They differ from easements in that they are exercisable by all who are included within the custom, independently of ownership of a dominant tenement. Thus the custom may extend to all the inhabitants of a particular locality, whether they own land or not.[19]

Sect. 2. Nature of a Profit à Prendre

A profit *à prendre* has been described as "a right to take something off another person's land."[20] This is too wide; the thing taken must be something taken out of the soil,[21] *i.e.* it must be either the soil, the natural produce thereof, or the wild animals existing on it; and the thing taken must at the time of taking be susceptible of ownership.[22] A right to "hawk, hunt, fish and fowl" may thus exist as a profit,[23] for this gives the right to take creatures living on the soil which, when killed, are capable of being owned. But a right to take water from a

[15] But see the obligations to fence, *ante*, p. 399.
[16] See D.W. Elliott (1964) 80 L.Q. R. 244, M. & W., pp. 820–821.
[17] *Aldin* v. *Latimer Clark & Co.* [1894] 2 Ch. 437.
[18] *Ante*, p. 398; see also *post*, pp. 407–408.
[19] *Race* v. *Ward* (1855) 4 E. & B. 702.
[20] *Duke of Sutherland* v. *Heathcote* [1892] 1 Ch. 475 at p. 484, *per* Lindley L.J.
[21] *Manning* v. *Wasdale* (1836) 5 A. & E. 758 at p. 764.
[22] *Race* v. *Ward, supra*, at p. 709; *Lowe* v. *J. W. Ashmore Ltd.* [1971] Ch. 545 at p. 557.
[23] *Wickham* v. *Hawker* (1840) 7 M. & W. 63.

spring or a pump, or the right to water cattle at a pond, may be an easement but cannot be a profit; for the water, when taken, was not owned by anyone nor was it part of the soil.[24] A right to take water stored in an artificial receptacle, *e.g.* a cistern, is not an easement but may perhaps exist either as a profit or a mere licence, probably the latter.[25]

A. Classifications of Profits à Prendre

I. AS TO OWNERSHIP

A profit *à prendre* may be enjoyed—

(i) by one person to the exclusion of all others; this is known as a serveral profit; or
(ii) by one person in common with others; this is known as a profit in common, or a common.

II. IN RELATION TO LAND

A profit is not necessarily appurtenant to land, as is the case with easements, and may exist in the following forms.

1. A profit appurtenant. This is a profit, whether several or in common, attached to land by act of parties. A profit appurtenant may be acquired either by grant or by prescription. In general, there must be compliance with the four conditions necessary for the existence of an easement, which can exist only as appurtenant to land.[26] Thus a profit of piscary appurtenant cannot be exploited for commercial purposes; the number of fish taken must be limited to the needs of the dominant tenement.[27]

2. A profit appendant. This is a profit annexed to land by operation of law; probably it exists only in the form of a common of pasture.[28] If before the Statute *Quia Emptores* 1290 the lord of a manor sub-infeudated arable land to a freeholder, the freeholder obtained, as appendant to the arable lands, the right to pasture, on the waste land of the manor, animals to plough and manure the land granted to him.[29] This right was known as a common of pasture appendant and was limited both as to the kind and number of animals which could be depastured. It extended only to horses and oxen (to plough the land) and cows and sheep (to manure it),[30] and only to the number of these "levant and couchant" on the land to which the right was appendant,

---

[24] See *Mason* v. *Hill* (1833) 5 B. & Ad. 1 at p. 24; *Manning* v. *Wasdale, supra,* at p. 764.
[25] See J.S. Fiennes (1938) 2 Conv. (N.S.) 203.
[26] *Ante,* pp. 396.
[27] *Harris* v. *Earl of Chesterfield* [1911] A.C. 623.
[28] See 6 Halsbury (4th ed.) 212; but see Tudor L.C.R.P., pp. 713–716.
[29] *Earl of Dunraven* v. *Llewellyn* (1850) 15 Q.B. 791 at p. 810.
[30] *Tyrringham's Case* (1584) 4 Co.Rep. 36b at p. 37a.

i.e. the number which the dominant tenement was capable of maintaining during the winter.[31] It was immaterial that the land was at any particular time used for purposes temporarily rendering the maintenance of cattle impossible, for the test was not the number actually supported but the number which the land could be made to support.

No common appendant could be created after 1290, for a conveyance of freehold land in a manor after that date resulted in the feoffee holding of the feoffor's lord, and the land passed out of the manor altogether.

3. A profit pur cause de vicinage. This exists only in the form of a common of pasture. If two adjoining commons are open to each other, there is a common *pur cause de vicinage* if the cattle put on one common by the commoners have always been allowed to stray to the other common and vice versa.[32] The claim fails if in the past the cattle have been driven off one common by the commoners thereof,[33] or if the commons have been fenced off,[34] or if the two commons are not contiguous to each other, even if they are separated only by a third common.[35]

4. A profit in gross. This is a profit, whether several or in common, exercisable by the owner independantly of his ownership of land; there is no dominant tenement. Thus a right to take fish from a canal without stint (*i.e.* without limit) can exist as a profit in gross,[36] but not, as already seen, as a profit appurtenant.[37] A profit in gross is an interest in land which will pass under a will or intestacy or can be sold or dealt with in any of the usual ways.

B. Distinctions between Profits à Prendre and Certain Analogous Rights

I. QUASI-PROFITS

Similar principles apply here as in the case of easements.[38]

II. OTHER NATURAL RIGHTS

The same applies.[39] An example is the right of a riparian owner to the unimpeded passage of fish from neighbouring portions of the stream.[40]

---

[31] *Robertson* v. *Hartopp* (1889) 43 Ch.D. 484 at p. 516.
[32] *Pritchard* v. *Powell* (1845) 10 Q.B. 589 at p. 603.
[33] *Heath* v. *Elliott* (1838) 4 Bing.N.C. 388.
[34] *Tyrringham's Case* (1584) 4 Co.Rep. 36b.
[35] *Commissioners of Sewers* v. *Glasse* (1874) L.R. 19 Eq. 134.
[36] *Staffordshire & Worcestershire Canal Navigation* v. *Bradley* [1912] 1 Ch. 91.
[37] *Ante*, p. 405.
[38] *Ante*, pp. 398, 400.
[39] *Ante*, p. 400.
[40] See *Barker* v. *Faulkner* (1808) 79 L.T. 24.

III. PUBLIC RIGHTS

The public right which most closely resembles a profit is the right of the public to fish in the sea and all tidal waters. However, since in theory the right is the Crown's, it was formerly possible for the Crown to grant to an individual the exclusive right to fish in a specified part of the sea or tidal waters; such a franchise was known as a free fishery.[41] In short, the public may fish in all tidal waters except a free fishery. But it has been held that the effect of *Magna Carta* 1215 was to prevent the Crown from creating any new free fisheries,[42] although any already existing remain valid and transferable to this day.

The right to fish in non-tidal water is dealt with below.[43]

IV. RIGHTS OF FLUCTUATING BODIES

There can be no custom for a fluctuating body of persons to take a profit.[44] The reason is said to be that otherwise the subject-matter would be destroyed.[45] However, if in fact such a right has been enjoyed for a long time as of right the courts will endeavour to find a legal origin for it. Two methods have been evolved.

1. Presumed incorporation by Crown grant. The reason why a fluctuating body cannot own a profit is that the body is not a legal person to which a grant could be made.[46] However, the Crown is able to incorporate any body of persons (*i.e.* make them into a corporation), and so could, for example, grant a charter to a village making it a city or borough. Consequently there is nothing to prevent the Crown from making a grant of a profit to the inhabitants of a district and providing therein that for the purposes of the grant they should be treated as a corporation, though for other purposes they remain unincorporated. In fact, such grants have been made but rarely.[47] Their chief importance is that the court will presume that a grant of rights of this kind owned by the Crown at the time of the supposed grant has been made, provided—

(a) long enjoyment is proved, and
(b) those claiming the grant, and their predecessors, have always regarded themselves as a corporation and have acted as such as regards the right, as by holding meetings or appointing some officer to supervise the right.[48]

---

[41] 3 Cru.Dig. 261; see, *e.g. Stephens* v. *Snell* [1939] 3 All E.R. 622.
[42] *Malcolmson* v. *O'Dea* (1863) 10 H.L.C. 593 at 618; but see Theobald, *Land*, pp. 58 *et seq.*
[43] *Post*, p. 436.
[44] *Alfred F. Beckett Ltd.* v. *Lyons* [1967] Ch. 449.
[45] *Race* v. *Ward* (1855) 4 E. & B. 702 at pp. 705, 709.
[46] *Fowler* v. *Dale* (1594) Cro.Eliz. 362.
[47] See, *e.g. Willingdale* v. *Maitland* (1866) L.R. 3 Eq. 103.
[48] See *Re Free Fishermen of Faversham* (1887) 36 Ch.D. 329; *Lord Rivers* v. *Adams* (1878) 3 Ex.D. 361.

2. Presumed charitable trust. Even when the court cannot presume
incorporation by Crown grant because the claimants have not acted
as a corporation, if long enjoyment is shown the court may be able to
find a legal origin for the right by presuming a grant of the profit to
some corporation, subject to a trust or condition that the corporation
should allow the claimants to exercise the rights claimed. Thus in
Goodman v. *Mayor of Saltash*[49] the free inhabitants of certain
ancient tenements had for 200 years enjoyed an oyster fishery from
Candelmas (February 2) to Easter Eve each year. This right had been
shared by the local corporation, which had enjoyed the right all the
year round from time immemorial. The House of Lords refused to
presume a grant incorporating the inhabitants for the purpose of the
grant, but held that the corporation was entitled to a profit subject to
a trust or condition in favour of the free inhabitants. Such a trust is
charitable and so not subject to the rule against inalienability.[50]

Sect. 3. Acquisitions of Easements and Profits

An easement or profit can exist as a legal interest in land only if—

(i) it is held for an interest equivalent to a fee simple absolute in
possession or term of years absolute[51]; and
(ii) it is created either by statute, deed or prescription.

A document not under seal cannot create a legal easement or profit,[52]
although if made for value it may create a valid equitable easement or
profit. Similarly, an oral agreement for value may create an equitable
easement or profit if supported by a sufficient act of part performance, such as acting upon the rights granted.[53]

The various methods of acquisition must now be considered.

A. By Statute

Easements created by statute are most frequently found in the case of
local Acts of Parliament, *e.g.* an Act giving a right of support to a
canal constructed under statutory powers.

B. By Express Reservation or Grant

When a landowner sells part of his land and retains the rest, he may
reserve easements or profits over the part *sold*, and *grant* the
purchaser rights over the land *retained*. Today, these transactions can
be achieved quite simply, but this has not always been the case.

---

[49] (1882) 7 App.Cas. 633.
[50] *Ante*, p. 226.
[51] *Ante*, p. 88.
[52] *Duke of Somerset* v. *Fogwell* (1826) 5 B. & A. 875. There is no exception for
easements or profits for a period not exceeding three years unlike the position for
leases.
[53] See, *e.g. Mason* v. *Clarke* [1955] A.C. 778; *ante*, pp. 141 *et seq*.

1. Express reservation. Before 1926, a legal easement or profit could not be created by a simple reservation in favour of the grantor. Being a new right it had to be granted by someone, and a person could not grant to himself. If, however, the conveyance reserved the right to the grantor, *and* the grantee executed the conveyance, it operated as a conveyance to the grantee followed by the re-grant of the easement or profit by the grantee to the grantor.[54] The effect of a simple reservation not executed by the grantee was merely to create an equitable easement or profit.[55]

Since 1925 it has not been necessary for the grantee to execute the conveyance as statute has provided that the reservation of a legal estate or interest shall be effective at law without any execution of the conveyance by the grantee "or any regrant by him."[56] It seems, however, that despite these words, the change merely goes to formalities.[57] The so-called reservation is still deemed to operate as a grant by the purchaser, which may have significant consequences. Where land held on trust was sold, and conveyed to the purchaser by the legal and equitable owners, a reservation by the equitable owners took effect as a grant of an legal easement by the purchaser and not as a reservation of a mere equitable easement by the vendor of the equitable interest.[58] Another consequence is the operation of the rule that where grants are ambiguous they are construed against the grantor.[59]

2. Express grant. The ordinary case of an easement or profit created by the express words of a deed needs little discussion. Normally, the dominant tenement will be expressly specified in the deed but, if it is not, the court is prepared to consider all the relevant circumstances to see whether there is a dominant tenement.[60]

In certain cases, an easement or profit will be created by express grant even though no mention of an easement or profit appears in any deed. The Law of Property Act 1925, s. 62(1),[61] provides that any conveyance made after 1881 shall, subject to any contrary intention expressed in the conveyance,[62] operate to convey with the land all privileges, easements, rights and advantages appertaining or reputed to appertain to the land or part of it. Thus, if a landlord grants his

---

[54] *Durham & Sunderland Ry.* v. *Walker* (1842) 2 Q.B. 940 at p. 967.
[55] *May* v. *Bellville* [1905] 2 Ch. 605.
[56] L.P.A. 1925, s. 65.
[57] *St. Edmundsbury and Ipswich Diocesan Board of Finance* v. *Clark* (*No. 2*) [1975] 1 W.L.R. 468 at pp. 478–480, commenting on *ibid.* [1973] 1 W.L.R. 1572 at pp. 1587–1591 where the view that the change is one of substance was maintained.
[58] *Johnstone* v. *Holdway* [1963] 1 Q.B. 601.
[59] *Bulstrode* v. *Lambert* [1953] 1 W.L.R., p. 1064 at 1068; *St. Edmundsbury and Ipswich Diocesan Board of Finance* v. *Clark* (*No. 2*) [1975] 1 W.L.R. 468 at pp. 477–480; but see *Cordell* v. *Second Clanfield Properties Ltd.* [1969] 2 Ch. 9.
[60] *Johnstone* v. *Holdway* (*supra*); *The Shannon Ltd.* v. *Venner Ltd.* [1965] Ch. 682.
[61] Replacing C.A. 1881, s. 6 (1): see also L.P.A. 1925, s. 62(2).
[62] L.P.A. 1925, s. 62 (4).

tenant a mere licence to use a coal shed for domestic purposes,[63] or to go through the landlord's house to reach the premises demised,[64] a subsequent conveyance to the tenant will operate to grant him the right as an easement. A right to require a neighbour to maintain fences may similarly arise.[65] But the section will not elevate into easements or profits rights which cannot exist as such,[66] or create rights which the grantor had no power to create by express grant. The section is further discussed below.[67]

C. By Implied Reservation or Grant

1. Implied reservation. A grant is normally construed against the grantor and in favour of the grantee. Further, a grantor must not derogate from his grant. Consequently, the general rule is that no easements will be implied in favour of a grantor; if he wishes to reserve any easements he must do so expressly.[68] To this rule there are two exceptions.

(a) *Easements of necessity.* If a grantor grants the whole of a plot of land except a piece in the middle which is completely surrounded by the part granted, there is implied in favour of the part retained a way of necessity over the part granted.[69] This rests not on the basis of public policy but on the implication to be drawn from the fact that unless some way is implied the land will be inaccessible.[70] The implication may thus be excluded by agreement.[71] The former owner of both plots of land may select the particular way to be enjoyed, provided it is a convenient way[72]; once selected, the route cannot subsequently be changed by one party without the consent of the other.[73] A way of necessity will be implied even if some of the surrounding land belongs to third parties; but it is essential that the necessity should exist at the time of the grant and not merely arise subsequently.[74]

(b) *Intended easements.* Easements required to carry out the common intention of the parties will be implied in favour of the grantor even though not expressed in the conveyance. Thus on the

---

[63] *Wright* v. *Macadam* [1949] 2 K.B. 744.
[64] *Goldberg* v. *Edwards* [1950] Ch. 247.
[65] *Crow* v. *Wood* [1971] 1 Q.B. 77; for this "quasi-easement" see *ante*, p. 399.
[66] *International Tea Stores Co.* v. *Hobbs* [1903] 2 Ch. 165 at p. 172. Neither will it make a piece of land which is not the subject-matter of the grant (but which, say, is at the rear of the granted land) the dominant tenement in relation to an easement impliedly granted by the conveyance: *Nickerson* v. *Barraclough* [1981] 2 W.L.R. 773.
[67] *Post*, p. 412.
[68] *Wheeldon* v. *Burrows* (1879) 12 Ch.D. 31 at p. 49.
[69] *Pinnington* v. *Galland* (1853) 9 Exch. 1.
[70] *Nickerson* v. *Barraclough* [1981] 2 W.L.R. 773.
[71] Unless void for contravening public policy.
[72] See *Pearson* v. *Spencer* (1861) 1 B. & S. 571 at p. 585; affd. (1863) 3 B. & S. 761.
[73] *Deacon* v. *South Eastern Ry.* (1889) 61 L.T. 377.
[74] *Midland Ry.* v. *Miles* (1886) 33 Ch.D. 632.

grant of one of two houses supported by each other, the mutual grant and reservation of easements of support will be implied if (as is usual) such an intention can be inferred.[75] A grantor who wishes to show that a reservation was mutually intended has a heavy onus of proof to discharge.[76]

2. Implied grant. If the owner of two plots conveys one of them, certain easements over the land retained are implied in favour of the land conveyed. The express grant of the land is said to be accompanied by the implied grant of the easements. Rights which will arise by implied grant are as follows:

(a) *Easements of necessity* and

(b) *Intended easements.* The rules which apply in these two cases are similar to those in the case of implied reservation save that the court is readier to imply easements in favour of the grantee than in favour of the grantor. Thus, where a landlord let his basement to a tenant to use as a restaurant and, unknown to them, this could not lawfully be done without installing a proper ventilating system, the tenant had an easement to have a duct fixed to the outside of the land-lord's premises since this was necessary to give effect to the common intention of the parties.[77]

(c) *Ancillary easements*, *i.e.* easements necessary for the enjoyment of some right expressly granted. Thus if there is a grant of an easement of the right to draw water from a spring, a right of way to the spring will be implied.[78]

(d) *Easements within the Rule in Wheldon* v. *Burrows.*[79] In *Wheeldon* v. *Burrows* it was laid down that upon the grant of part of a tenement, there would pass to the grantee as easements all quasi-easements over the land retained which—

   (i) were continuous and apparent,
  (ii) were necessary to the reasonable enjoyment of the land granted, and
 (iii) had been, and were at the time of the grant, used by the grantor for the benefit of the part granted.

A "continuous" easement is one giving the right to do some act of a continuous and constant nature. An "apparent" easement is one

---

[75] *Richards* v. *Rose* (1853) 9 Exch. 221.
[76] *Re Webb's Lease* [1951] Ch. 808 (no implied reservation of right to advertise on tenant's walls).
[77] *Wong* v. *Beaumont Property Trust Ltd.* [1965] 1 Q.B. 173.
[78] *Pwlbach Colliery Co. Ltd.* v. *Woodman* [1915] A.C. 634 at p. 646.
[79] (1879) 12 Ch.D. 31; see M. & W., pp. 833–835. The case itself was actually concerned with implied reservation, holding that those rights passing under what is now known as the Rule in *Wheeldon* v. *Burrows* pass only on a grant and not by implied reservation.

which is evidenced by some sign on the servient tenement discoverable on a careful inspection by a person ordinarily conversant with the subject.[80] Thus a drain into which water from the eaves of a house runs,[81] a watercourse through visible pipes,[82] and windows enjoying light,[83] all indicate the existence of continuous and apparent easements. On the other hand, a right to take water from a neighbour's pump from time to time[84] or a right to project the bowsprit of ships when in dock over the land of another[85] have been held to be outside the meaning of "continuous and apparent" easements. Rights of way do not in general fall within the definition, but a way over a made road, or one which betrays its presence by some indication such as a worn track, will pass under the rule in *Wheeldon* v. *Burrows*.[86]

An easement "necessary to the reasonable enjoyment of land" is not an easement of necessity but only an easement without which there cannot be reasonable enjoyment of the land. It is not clear but it seems likely that this requirement and the requirement of "continuous and apparent" user are to be regarded as alternatives,[87] though it can be argued that the requirements should be cumulative, the "continuous and apparent" requirement being a rule of conveyancing convenience to facilitate the discovery of incumbrances and the other requirement being based on non-derogation from grant.[88]

These rules relating to implied grant apply also to cases where the grantor, instead of retaining any land himself, makes simultaneous grants to two or more grantees. Each grantee obtains the same easements over the land of the other as he would have obtained if the grantor had retained it[89]; and similarly for two or more gifts by the same will.[90] The rules relating to implied grant also apply to contracts to make a grant.[91]

IMPLIED GRANT AND SECTION 62 OF THE LAW OF PROPERTY ACT 1925

The importance of the rules relating to implied grant has been considerably lessened by the Law of Property Act 1925, s. 62. If no contrary intention is expressed a conveyance passes "all liberties, privileges, easements, rights and advantages whatsoever, appertain-

---

[80] *Pyer* v. *Carter* (1857) 1 H. & N. 916 at p. 922.
[81] *Pyer* v. *Carter* (1857) 1 H. & N. 816.
[82] *Watts* v. *Kelson* (1870) 6 Ch.App. 166.
[83] *Phillips* v. *Low* [1892] 1 Ch. 47 at p. 53.
[84] *Polden* v. *Bastard* (1865) L.R. 1 Q.B. 156.
[85] *Suffield* v. *Brown* (1864) 4 De. G.J. & S. 185.
[86] See *Hansford* v. *Jago* [1921] 1 Ch. 322.
[87] M. & W., p. 834.
[88] *Sovmots* v. *The Secretary of State* [1979] A.C. 144 at pp. 168–169, C. Harpum (1977) 41 Conv. 415 at p. 422.
[89] *Swansborough* v. *Coventry* (1832) 2 M. & S. 362.
[90] *Schwann* v. *Cotton* [1916] 2 Ch. 459.
[91] *Borman* v. *Griffith* [1930] 1 Ch. 493; *Sovmots* v. *The Secretary of State* [1977] Q.B. 411 at p. 442.

ing or reputed to appertain to the land, or at the time of conveyance, enjoyed with the land." Section 62 is thus broader than the Rule in *Wheeldon* v. *Burrows* since the right does not have to be necessary for the reasonable enjoyment of the land[92] and since it can apply to profits[93] whereas the nature of the Rule in *Wheeldon* v. *Burrows* is such that it can hardly apply to profits.

(a) *Diversity of occupation or continuous and apparent right.* However, for section 62 to apply either there must have been some prior diversity of occupation of the land immediately prior to the conveyance or the right must have been "continuous and apparent."[94] An owner does not "enjoy" or exercise "rights, privileges or easements," over one part of his land for the benefit of another part: he does everything as owner of the whole land. Thus, for a right to be enjoyed with the land at the time of conveyance diversity of occupation is required[95] as where a landlord grants a formal lease to T who, prior thereto, had been enjoying certain privileges over the landlord's adjacent land.[96] Alternatively, a right, privilege or easement may be reputed to appertain to the land if continuous and apparent such as a right of light[97] or a watercourse pipe-way[98] or a made-up road or cinder-track.[99]

(b) *Legal easement or profit.* Section 62 elevates the right in question to the status of a legal easement or legal profit so that the right in its nature must be capable of being an easement or profit[1] and must be for a term of years absolute or a period equivalent to a fee simple absolute in possession. Thus, section 62 cannot apply to a "right" to a constant supply of hot water,[2] or to a "right" of way for such periods as the servient owner may permit owing to the exigencies of his own business,[3] or to a right for a business tenant of rear premises (with adequate rear access) to use the landlord's passageway for goods and customers for so long as the landlord himself personally resides in the front premises.[4]

It is often stated as an independent principle that "the section will not operate if at the time of the conveyance or lease it was, or should have been, apparent to the grantee or lessee that the enjoyment which he claims to have been converted into a right by the section was

---

[92] *Goldberg* v. *Edwards* [1950] Ch. 247, *Watts* v. *Kelson* (1870) L.R. 6 Ch.App. 166 at p. 175.
[93] *White* v. *Williams* [1922] 1 K.B. 727.
[94] *Long* v. *Gowlett* [1923] 2 Ch. 177; C. Harpum [1979] Conv. 113.
[95] *Ibid. Sovmots* v. *The Secretary of State* [1979] A.C. 144 at pp. 169, 176.
[96] *Wright* v.*Macadam* [1949] 2 K.B. 744; *Goldberg* v. *Edwards* [1950] Ch. 247.
[97] *Broomfield* v. *Williams* [1897] 1 Ch. 602.
[98] *Watts* v. *Kelson* (1870) L.R. 6 Ch.App. 166.
[99] *Bayley* v. *G.W.R.* (1884) 26 Ch.D. 434.
[1] *Phipps* v. *Pears* [1965] 1 Q.B. 76.
[2] *Regis Property Co. Ltd.* v. *Redman* [1956] 2 Q.B. 612.
[3] *Green* v. *Ashco Horticulturist Ltd.* [1966] 1 W.L.R. 889.
[4] *Goldberg* v. *Edwards* [1950] Ch. 247.

only temporary."[5] Thus, the purchaser of the first house in the vendor's projected development of houses cannot really expect his enjoyment of light over vacant plots to be other than temporary and so cannot claim a right of light under section 62 so as to prevent the plots being built upon.[6] The underlying rationale for this may be that such a temporary right is for an uncertain period and so cannot become a legal right. This would harmonise with section 62 (4) which states, "this section applies only if and as far as a contrary intention is not *expressed* in the conveyance."

(c) *Conveyances.* The rules relating to implied grant apply both to conveyances and to contracts, as well as to gifts by will[7]: section 62, however, applies only to "conveyances," a word which is defined to include (*inter alia*) mortgages, leases and assents, but which does not include a mere contract, *e.g.* for a lease over three years or for the sale of a fee simple.[8] Thus on the grant of a lease for seven years in writing, the tenant can claim only the easements which fall within the doctrine of implied grant; because the lease is not by deed, and so is not a "conveyance," section 62 does not apply.[9]

(d) *Contracts and rectification.* It will be seen from the preceding paragraph that a conveyance will sometimes convey more than the purchaser is entitled to under his contract. If a contract is silent on the question of easements, the purchaser is entitled to have conveyed to him with the land only those rights which fall within the rules relating to implied grant. If a conveyance which is silent as to easements is then executed, it may operate by virtue of section 62 to convey to the purchaser rights which are not within the comparatively narrow scope of implied grant but which fall within the section. Thus a non-apparent way may be outside the doctrine of implied grant but within section 62 where prior diversity of occupation existed.[10] In such a case, the vendor is entitled to insist upon the conveyance being so worded as to limit the rights conveyed to those to which the purchaser is entitled under the contract.[11] If the conveyance has already been executed, he may seek to have it rectified to produce this result.[12] However, a bona fide purchaser for value of any interest in the land will take free of this equity of rectification if he has no notice of the

---

[5] *Green* v. *Ashco Horticulturist Ltd.* [1966] 1 W.L.R. 889 at p. 897.
[6] *Birmingham Dudley & District Banking Co.* v. *Ross* (1888) 38 Ch.D. 295, *Godwin* v. *Schweppes Ltd.* [1902] 1 Ch. 926. Where s. 62 has applied to privileges enjoyed by a tenant with his landlord's permission before execution of the lease, the privileges have been expected to endure for the duration of the tenant's interest though subject to revocation by the landlord (before the operation of s. 62): *Wright* v. *Macadam* [1949] 2 K.B. 744; *Goldberg* v. *Edwards* [1950] Ch. 247.
[7] *Schwann* v. *Cotton* [1916] 2 Ch. 459.
[8] *Re Peck and the School Board for London* [1893] 2 Ch. 315.
[9] *Borman* v. *Griffith* [1930] 1 Ch. 493.
[10] See *Ward* v. *Kirkland* [1967] Ch. 194.
[11] *Re Walmsley & Shaw's Contract* [1917] 1 Ch. 93.
[12] *Clark* v. *Barnes* [1929] 2 Ch. 368.

discrepancy which generates such equity.[13] Moreover, a vendor seeking rectification must not be guilty of undue delay or of misleading the purchaser.

D. By Presumed Grant, or Prescription

I. GENERAL PRINCIPLES

The basis of prescription is that if long enjoyment of a lawful right is shown, the court will uphold the right by presuming that it had a lawful origin, *i.e.* that there once was an actual grant of the right, even though it is impossible to produce any evidence of such a grant. However, it is not enough to show long user by itself; user of a particular kind is required. There are three types of prescription, namely, prescription at common law, prescription under the doctrine of lost modern grant, and prescription under the Prescription Act 1832.[14] Except so far as the Act otherwise provides, a claim to an easement or profit under any head must be supported by user complying with the following conditions.

1. User as of right: the user must be as of right, which means that it must have been enjoyed *nec vi, nec clam, nec precario* (without force, without secrecy, without permission).[15] The claimant must show that he has used the right as if he were entitled to it. Forcible user (*vi*) occurs not only where the dominant owner breaks down barriers or commits other acts of violence, but also where the user is continued despite the servient owner making continuous and unmistakable protests.[16] Secret user (*clam*) occurred where a dock had been supported by invisible rods sunk under the servient tenement,[17] or where there had been intermittent and secret discharges of injurious chemicals into a sewer.[18] So, too, no easement can be established against an owner who, owing to absence or other reason, is able to prove that he had no knowledge of the user,[19] since acquiescence (with knowledge of the user) is at the root of prescription.[20]

If the servient owner has given the claimant the right to use the easement or profit claimed, so that there has been an actual grant of such a right, the user is not *precario*, and the claimant can rely upon his grant without resorting to prescription. But if the claimant has

---

[13] *Ante*, p. 69.
[14] The co-existence of three methods is anomalous and undesirable: *Tehidy Minerals Ltd.* v. *Norman* [1971] 2 Q.B. 528 at p. 543.
[15] *Solomon* v. *Mystery of Vintners* (1859) 4 H. & N. 585 at p. 602 (common law prescription); *Sturges* v. *Bridgman* (1879) 11 Ch.D. 852 at p. 863 (lost modern grant); Prescription Act 1832, ss. 1, 2 and *Tickle* v. *Brown* (1836) 4 A. & E. 369 at p. 382 (prescription under the Act); and see M. & W., pp. 841–844.
[16] *Dalton* v. *Angus & Co.* (1881) 6 App.Cas. 740 at p. 786.
[17] *Union Lighterage Co.* v. *London Graving Dock Co.* [1902] 2 Ch. 557.
[18] *Liverpool Corporation* v. *H. Coghill & Son Ltd.* [1918] 1 Ch. 307.
[19] *Diment* v. *N.H. Foot Ltd.* [1974] 1 W.L.R. 1427.
[20] *Dalton* v. *Angus & Co.* (1881) 6 App.Cas. 740 at p. 773.

been given permission to use the right claimed "until further notice," or has had to seek permission anew each year, the user is *precario* and no easement or profit can rise therefrom by prescription. Similarly, if applications for permission to use a way have been made by the claimant from time to time,[21] or he has made annual payments for his enjoyment, there is evidence that the user was *precario*, for such acts are inconsistent with the claimant having a right to the easement or profit claimed.

User during unity of possession, *i.e.* while the claimant was in possession of both dominant and servient tenements, is not user as of right,[22] and the same applies to user under the mistaken belief that the claimant was entitled to the servient tenement[23] or that he had the temporary permission of the landlord. But proof that the claimant exercised his right under the mistaken belief that a valid easement or profit had already been granted to him will not prevent the user from being as of right.[24] The principle involved is that the right must have been exercised *qua* easement or profit and not, for example, under any actual or supposed right of an occupant of both tenements.

2. User in fee simple: the user must be by or on behalf of a fee simple owner against a fee simple owner who both knows of the user and is able to resist it. In general, only easements or profits in fee simple can be acquired by prescription.[25] An easement or profit for life or for years, for example, may be expressly granted but cannot be acquired by prescription, for the basis of prescription is a presumed grant by the owner of the servient tenement, and only a grant in fee simple will be presumed. Consequently the claimant must show either that he is the fee simple owner himself or that he claims on behalf of the fee simple owner. A tenant under a lease must thus prescribe on behalf of the fee simple owner and not merely on his own behalf.[26]

As prescription rests on acquiescence,[27] a claim will fail if user can be proved only when the servient land was occupied by a tenant for life[28] or for years,[29] for the fee simple owner may not be able to contest the user. But if the user began against the fee simple owner it will not become ineffective because the land is later settled or let.[30] Further, if A leases two plots of his land to two tenants, one tenant cannot prescribe for an easement against the other, for otherwise the

---

[21] *Monmouth Canal Co.* v. *Harford* (1834) 1 Cr.M. & R. 614.
[22] *Bright* v. *Walker* (1834) 1 Cr.M. & R. 211 at p. 219.
[23] *Lyell* v. *Lord Hothfield* [1914] 3 K.B. 911.
[24] *Earl de la Warr* v. *Miles* (1881) 17 Ch.D. 535.
[25] See, *e.g. Kilgour* v. *Gaddes* [1904] 1 K.B. 457 at p. 460.
[26] *Gateward's Case* (1607) 6 Co.Rep. 59b; *Dawnay* v. *Cashford* (1697) Carth. 432.
[27] *Dalton* v. *Angus & Co.* (1881) 6 App.Cas. 740 at pp. 773, 774.
[28] *Roberts* v. *James* (1903) 89 L.T. 282.
[29] *Daniel* v. *North* (1809) 11 East 372.
[30] *Pugh* v. *Savage* [1970] 2 Q.B. 373.

result would be that A would acquire an easement over his own land.[31]

There are certain modifications of this rule. First, profits in gross may be acquired by prescription at common law,[32] or under the doctrine of lost modern grant. In this case, the right is not claimed in respect of any estate but on behalf of the claimant personally. Such prescription is known as prescription in gross. The claimant must show that he and his predecessors in title to the profit (often his ancestors) have enjoyed the right,[33] instead of showing that he and his predecessors in title to the dominant tenement have enjoyed it. There can be no prescription in gross for easements (which cannot exist in gross), nor can a profit in gross be claimed under the Prescription Act 1832.[34] Secondly, certain modifications are made in claims under the Prescription Act 1832. Thus under the Act easements of light can be acquired by one tenant against another tenant of the same landlord.[35] This is anomalous; it applies only to light and only to claims under the Act. Other modifications under the Act will be noted later.

3. Continuous user: the claimants must show a continuity of enjoyment. This is interpreted reasonably; in the case of easements of way it is clearly not necessary to show ceaseless user by day and night. User whenever circumstances require it is normally sufficient,[36] provided the intervals are not excessive. Moreover, continuity is not broken if the user is varied by agreement, as where the parties vary the line of a way for convenience.[37]

The three types of prescription must now be considered in turn.

II. PRESCRIPTION AT COMMON LAW

1. Length of user. User of the nature discussed above must be shown to have continued since time immemorial, namely, since 1189. If this is shown, the court presumes that a grant was made prior to that date. The reason for 1189 being adopted is that from time to time limits were fixed within which actions for the recovery of land were to be brought. Instead of adopting a specified period of years, events such as the beginning of the reign of Henry I or the last voyage of Henry II to Normandy were periodically selected. The last choice to be made was the beginning of the reign of Richard I, namely, 1189. These periods originally had nothing to do with prescription, but the courts adopted the last date as the period of time immemorial upon

---

[31] *Kilgour* v. *Gaddes* [1904] 1 K.B. 457.
[32] *Johnson* v. *Barnes* (1873) L.R. 8 C.P. 527.
[33] *Welcome* v. *Upton* (1840) 6 M. & W. 536.
[34] *Shuttleworth* v. *Le Fleming* (1865) 19 C.B. (N.S.) 687.
[35] See *post*, p. 427.
[36] *Dare* v. *Heathcote* (1856) 25 L.J.Ex. 245.
[37] *Davis* v. *Whitby* [1974] Ch. 186.

which all claims based on custom or prescription depended. Modern legislation has altered the rule for claims to land, but 1189 remained the essential date for custom and prescription.[38]

2. Presumption. It is clearly impossible in most cases to show continuous user since 1189. and so the courts adopted the rule that if unexplained user for 20 years or more is shown, the court will presume that that user has continued since 1189; user for less than 20 years requires supporting circumstances to raise the presumption.[39] However, this presumption may be met by showing that at some time since 1189 the right could not or did not exist.[40] Thus an easement of light cannot be claimed by prescription at common law for a building which is shown to have been erected since 1189.[41] Consequently it was virtually impossible to establish a claim to light at common law, and many claims based on enjoyment lasting for centuries were liable to be defeated by evidence that there could have been no enjoyment of the right in 1189. Again, if it could be shown that any time since 1189 the dominant and servient tenements had been in the same ownership and occupation, any easement or profit would have been extinguished and so any claim at common law would fail.[42] To meet this state of affairs, the courts invented what has been called the "revolting fiction"[43] of the lost modern grant.

III. LOST MODERN GRANT

1. The presumption. The weakness of common law prescription was the liability to failure if it was shown that user had begun at some date after 1189. The doctrine of lost modern grant avoided this by presuming from long user that an actual grant of the easement or profit was made at some time subsequent to 1189 but prior to the user supporting the claim, and that unfortunately this grant had been lost.[44] "Juries were first told that from user, during living memory, or even during 20 years, they might presume a lost grant or deed; next they were recommended to make such presumption; and lastly, as the final consummation of judicial legislation, it was held that a jury should be told, not only that they might, but also that they were bound to presume the existence of such a lost grant, although neither judge nor jury, nor anyone else, had the shadow of a belief that any such instrument had ever really existed."[45] In their anxiety to find a legal origin for a right of which there had been open and

---

[38] See generally *Byrant* v. *Foot* (1867) L.R. 2 Q.B. 161 at pp. 180, 181.
[39] *Bealey* v. *Shaw* (1805) 6 East 208 at p. 215.
[40] *Hulbert* v. *Dale* [1909] 2 Ch. 570 at p. 577.
[41] *Duke of Norfolk* v. *Arbuthnot* (1880) 5 C.P.D. 390.
[42] See *post*, p. 430.
[43] *Angus & Co.* v. *Dalton* (1877) 3 Q.B.D. 85 at p. 94, *per* Lush J.
[44] See, *e.g. Dalton* v. *Angus & Co.* (1881) 6 App.Cas. 740 at p. 813.
[45] *Byrant* v. *Foot* (1867) L.R. 2 Q.B. 161 at p. 181, *per* Cockburn C.J.

uninterrupted enjoyment for a long period, unexplained in any other way, the courts presumed that a grant had been made, and so made it immaterial that enjoyment had not continued since 1189. User for 20 years normally sufficed to raise the presumption.[46]

2. Evidence. Rather stronger evidence of user is required to induce the court to presume a lost modern grant than is required for prescription at common law.[47] Further, the doctrine can be invoked only if something prevents the application of common law prescription.[48] Since the doctrine is admittedly a fiction, the claimant will not be ordered to furnish particulars of the fictitious grant (*e.g.* as to the parties), but he must plead whether the grant is alleged to have been made before or after a particular date.[49] The presumption cannot be rebutted by evidence that no grant was in fact made.[50] But the claim is defeated by proof that during the entire period when the grant could have been made there was nobody who could lawfully have made it.[51] Thus the court has refused to presume a lost grant of a way where the land had been in strict settlement (under which there was no power to make a grant) from the time when the user began down to the time of action.[52]

IV. PRESCRIPTION ACT 1832

1. The Act. The Prescription Act 1832 was passed to meet the difficulties and uncertainties mentioned above, and in particular the difficulty of persuading juries to presume grants to have been made when they knew this was not the case. It is ill-drafted, but in many cases it has substituted certainty for uncertainty. The Act makes special provision for easements of light, so that the other rights under the Act will be dealt with first, and then easements of light.

2. Easements (other than light) and profits. The Act is perhaps best dealt with by giving a summary of the effect of each section and annotating the sections in groups.

Section 1: No claim to a *profit* shall be defeasible by showing that user commenced after 1189 if 30 years' uninterrupted enjoyment as of right is shown. If 60 years' uninterrupted enjoyment as of right is shown, the right is deemed to be absolute unless it has been enjoyed by written consent or agreement.

---

[46] *Penwarden* v. *Ching* (1829) Moo. & M. 400.
[47] *Tilbury* v. *Silva* (1890) 45 Ch.D. 98 at p. 123.
[48] *Byrant* v. *Lefever* (1879) 4 C.P.D. 172 at p. 177.
[49] *Tremayne* v. *English Clays Lovering Pochin & Co. Ltd.* [1972] 1 W.L.R. 657, not following *Gabriel Wade & English Ltd.* v. *Dixon & Cardus Ltd.* [1937] 3 All E.R. 900.
[50] *Tehidy Minerals Ltd.* v. *Norman* [1971] 2 Q.B. 528.
[51] *Neaverson* v. *Peterborough R.D.C.* [1902] 1 Ch. 557.
[52] *Roberts* v. *James* (1903) 89 L.T. 282.

Section 2 makes exactly similar provisions for all *easements* except the easement of light, the periods, however, being 20 and 40 years respectively instead of 30 and 60.

Section 3 concerns the easement of light and is dealt with below.[53]

Section 4: All periods of enjoyment under the Act are those periods next before some action in which the claim is brought into question. Further, no act is to be deemed an interruption until it has been submitted to or acquiesced in for one year after the party interrupted had notice both of the interruption and of the person making it.

The chief points to note on this group of sections are as follows.

(a) *"Next before some action."* The Act does not say that an easement or profit comes into existence after 20, 30, 40, or 60 years' user in the abstract; all periods under the Act are those next before some action in which the right is questioned. Thus until some action is brought, there is a mere inchoate right to an easement or profit, however long the user.[54] Further, even if there has been user for longer than the statutory periods, the vital period is always that period (*e.g.* of 20 years) next before some action. Thus if user commenced 50 years ago but ceased 5 years ago, a claim will fail if the action is commenced today, for during the 20 or 40 years next before the action, there has not been continuous user.[55] Similarly a claim under the Act will fail if there had been unity of possession for a substantial period immediately before the action, for there has not been user *as an easement* during the whole of the vital period.[56]

(b) *"Without interruption."* The user must be "without interruption"; but a special meaning is given to "interruption." If D has used a way over S's land for over 20 years, and then a barrier is erected barring his way, D can still succeed in establishing an easement, provided that at the time an action is brought he has not acquiesced in the obstruction for one year after he has known both of the obstruction and of the person responsible for it.[57] "Interruption" means some hostile obstruction and not mere non-user.[58] A protest against an interruption normally endures for some time after it has been made, so that there is no acquiescence in an interruption for a year merely because a year has elapsed since the last protest was made.[59]

---

[53] *Post,* pp. 425 *et seq.*
[54] *Hyman* v. *Van den Bergh* [1908] 1 Ch. 167.
[55] *Parker* v. *Mitchell* (1840) 11 A. & E. 788.
[56] *Aynsley* v. *Glover* (1875) 10 Ch.App. 283.
[57] *Seddon* v. *Bank of Bolton* (1882) 19 Ch.D. 462.
[58] *Smith* v. *Baxter* [1900] 2 Ch. 138 at p. 143. For interrupted user of a common see *post,* p. 424.
[59] *Davies* v. *Du Paver* [1953] 1 Q.B. 184.

User for 19 years and a day followed by 364 days' interruption is thus, for the purposes of the Act, 20 years' user upon which a claim will succeed. But this does not mean that 364 days is in fact deducted from the periods in the Act. To say that user for 19 years and a day is as good as user for 20 years is not accurate for—

(i) no action can be brought to establish an easement if only 19 years and a fraction has elapsed since the user began,[60] whereas after 20 years' user, an action can be started forthwith; and

(ii) if an interruption commences after user for 19 years and a day, not until it has lasted for 364 days can the dominant owner commence an action to establish his easement, for not until then is there a period of 20 years.[61] If he waits another day, the interruption will have lasted for a year and his claim must fail. Thus he has only one day on which to issue his writ, whereas if he has enjoyed user for 20 years when an interruption commences, he may issue his writ on any of the next 364 days; and

(iii) if the servient owner issues a writ before the 20 years have elapsed this does not rank as an "interruption" but determines the calculating period so that the dominant owner cannot show a full 20 years reckoned down to the date of the action brought.[62]

(c) *User "as of right."* Sections 1 and 2 provide that the enjoyment must be by a "person claiming right thereto," and section 5 provides that it is sufficient to plead enjoyment "as of right." The effect is that claims under the Act must be based on user which would have sufficed at common law, *i.e. nec vi, nec clam, nec precario.*[63]

At common law, any consent or agreement by the servient owner, whether oral or written, rendered the user *precario*. Under the Act, this rule applies to the shorter periods (20 years for easements, 30 years for profits), but a special meaning is given to *precario* in the case of longer periods (40 years for easements, 60 years for profits) by the provision that the right shall be absolute unless enjoyed by written consent or agreement. A mere oral consent given at the beginning of the period and not renewed will thus not defeat a claim based on one of the longer periods, although it would be fatal at common law. However, oral consents repeatedly given during a period will defeat a claim based even on the longer periods.[64]

---

[60] *Lord Battersea* v. *Commissioners of Sewers for the City of London* [1895] 2 Ch. 708.
[61] *Reilly* v. *Orange* [1955] 1 W.L.R. 616.
[62] *Ibid.*
[63] *Gardner* v. *Hodgson's Brewery Co. Ltd.* [1903] A.C. 229 at pp. 238, 239.
[64] *Gardner* v. *Hodgson's Kingston Brewery Co. Ltd.* [1903] A.C. 229.

(d) *Effect of consents.* The effect of consents may be summarised thus[65]:

(i) Any consents, whether oral or written, which have been given intermittently during the period make the user *precario* and defeat a claim based on either the shorter or longer periods.

(ii) A written consent given at the beginning of the user (and extending throughout) defeats a claim based on either the shorter or longer periods.

(iii) An oral consent given at the beginning of the user (and extending throughout) defeats a claim based on the shorter periods but not a claim based on the longer periods.

If user commences by consent, the question whether it continues by consent is one of fact.[66] In the case of a written consent or agreement, signature by the servient owner is not essential; a document signed by the dominant owner or his leasehold tenant may suffice.[67]

The remaining sections of the Act must now be dealt with.

Section 5 deals with pleadings.

Section 6 provides that enjoyment for less than the statutory periods shall give rise to no claim. This does not prevent a lost grant being presumed from user for less than a statutory period if there is some evidence to support it in addition to the enjoyment.[68]

Section 7 provides that any period during which the servient tenant has been a minor, lunatic or tenant for life shall automatically be deducted from the shorter periods; further, the period during which an action is pending and actively prosecuted is also to be deducted.

Section 8 provides that if the servient tenement has been held under a "term of life, or any term of years exceeding three years from the granting thereof," the term shall be excluded in computing the period of 40 years in the case of a "way or other convenient [*sic*] watercourse or use of water," provided the claim is resisted by a reversioner upon the term within three years of its determination.

No more need be said about sections 5 and 6. Sections 7 and 8 are complicated and can conveniently be dealt with together. The following points should be noted.

(a) *Deduction.* Where either section applies, the period deducted is excluded altogether when calculating the period next before action.

---

[65] See *Tickle* v. *Brown* (1836) 4 A. & E. 369; *Healey* v. *Hawkins* [1968] 1 W.L.R. 1967.
[66] *Gaved* v. *Martyn* (1865) 19 C.B.(N.S.) 732; *Healey* v. *Hawkins, supra.*
[67] *Hyman* v. *Van den Bergh* [1908] 1 Ch. 167.
[68] *Hammer* v. *Chance* (1865) 4 De G.J. & Sm. 626 at p. 631.

Thus if there has been enjoyment of a profit for 45 years in all, consisting of 25 years' user against the fee simple owner, then 19 years against the life tenant, and then a further year against the fee simple owner, the claim fails, for by section 7 the period of the life tenancy is deducted when calculating the period next before action brought, and thus less than 30 years' user is left. But if the user continues for another four years, the claim would succeed, for there is 30 years' user consisting of 25 years before and five years after the life tenancy; since the period of the life tenancy is disregarded, the 30 years' period is, for the purposes of the Act, next before action within section 4.[69] The sections in effect connect the periods immediately before and after the period deducted, but they will not connect two periods separated in any other way, *e.g.* by a period of unity of possession.[70]

(b) *Application.* Section 7 applies to the shorter periods both for easements and profits; but section 8 does not apply to profits at all, and applies to the longer period only in the case of easements of way "or other convenient watercourse or use of water." Probably "convenient" is a misprint for "easement," and the phrase should read "or other easement, watercourse or use of water" as in section 2. If so, section 8 applies to all easements (except light): but the point is unsettled.[71]

(c) *Ambit.* Section 7 applies to the servient owner being a minor, lunatic or tenant for life: section 8 applies where the servient tenement has been held under a term for over three years, or for life. Thus a life tenancy can be deducted under both sections, but infancy or lunacy affect only the shorter periods. If D has enjoyed a way against S's land for 25 years, but S has been insane for the last 15 of those years, section 7 defeats D's claim. If D continues his user for another 15 years, however, his claim succeeds even though S continues insane throughout.

Further, it should be noted that the only provision for deduction of leasehold terms is in section 8. Thus, where there had been user of a way for 20 years, the servient land being under lease for 15 of the 20 years, but free from any lease at the beginning and end of the period, an easement was established[72]: for section 7 makes no mention of leaseholds, and section 8 does not apply to the 20 years' period. It will be noted that here the user commenced against the fee simple owner who, by leasing the land, voluntarily put it out of his power to resist the user: had the lease been granted before the user commenced and continued throughout, the position would have been different, for no

---

[69] *Clayton v. Corby* (1842) 2 Q.B. 813.
[70] *Onley v. Gardiner* (1838) 4 M. & W. 496.
[71] See *Laird v. Briggs* (1881) 19 Ch.D. 22 at p. 33.
[72] *Palk v. Shinner* (1852) 18 Q.B. 568; *Pugh v. Savage* [1970] 2 Q.B. 373; *ante*, p. 416.

user as against a fee simple owner able to resist it could be shown.[73] In short, a lease may affect a claim in two ways:

(i) by showing that there has been no user against a fee simple owner who knows of it and can resist it; and
(ii) by falling within the provisions of section 8 allowing deduction.

The first of these is a common law rule not affected by the Act; the second is a creature of the statute and can apply only to claims under the Act based on the 40 years' period.

(d) *Right to deduct.* In section 7, the provision for deduction is absolute: in section 8, it is conditional, the condition being that the reversioner shall resist the claim within three years of the determination of the term of years or life. Thus if the reversioner fails to resist the claim within three years, he has no right of deduction. Further section 8 extends only to a reversioner and not to a remainderman,[74] so that it will rarely apply to the usual kind of settlement.

It will be seen from this that section 7 is wide in its scope, giving an absolute right of deduction from the shorter periods for both easements and profits; section 8, on the other hand, is very narrow, giving only a reversioner a conditional right of deduction from the 40 years' period in the case of (possibly) only two classes of easements.

(e) *Commons.* An additional right to deduct from both longer and shorter periods is available in the case of commons. Where during the period a right to graze animals could not be exercised for reasons of animal health or because the common was requisitioned by a government department, the time of non-user is to be left out of account.[75] Moreover, non-user for such reasons does not rank as an interruption.[76]

(f) *Difference between longer and shorter periods.* In the case of the shorter periods, the only benefits which the Act confers upon a claimant are that the period for which he must show user is clearly laid down, and that he cannot be defeated by proof that his enjoyment began after 1189. The nature of the user required is still substantially the same, so that the claimant must show continuous, uninterrupted user as of right by or on behalf of a fee simple owner against a fee simple owner who both knew of the user and could resist it.

In the case of the longer periods, however, although uninterrupted user as of right is expressly required, and easements can be acquired only on behalf of a fee simple owner, the Act provides that the right

[73] *Bright* v. *Walker* (1834) 1 Cr.M. & R. 211.
[74] *Symons* v. *Leaker* (1885) 15 Q.B.D. 629. But see *Holman* v. *Exton* (1692) Carth 246 (remainderman held to be within a statute applicable to reversioners).
[75] Commons Registration Act 1965, s. 16.
[76] *Ibid.*

becomes absolute after the required period next before action has elapsed. User against a fee simple owner who both knew of it and is able to resist it is therefore not required[77]; the only exceptions to this are those provided by section 8. Thus user of a way for 20 years against land held under a life tenancy will give no claim under the Act,[78] but user for 40 years will suffice, subject to section 8.[79] It seems, therefore, that although all prescription is, in general, founded upon the presumption of a grant, there is no need to presume a grant in the case of claims based on the longer periods under the Act, *e.g.* where the servient company has no power of grant. This is clearly so in the case of claims to light under the Act,[80] and in the case of other easements "forty years' user has the same effect which (under the third section) twenty years' user has as to light."[81] But the point cannot be regarded as settled,[82] and the fact that *actual* enjoyment confers an easement of light, whereas user *as of right* is required for other easements, is some indication that it is light alone which requires no presumption of a grant.

The difference between the longer and the shorter periods may be summarised thus:

(i) A presumption of a grant is required in the case of the shorter periods, though possibly not in the case of the longer periods.

(ii) An oral consent given at the beginning of the period defeats a claim based on one of the shorter periods, but not one based on one of the longer periods.

(iii) The shorter periods are subject to the provisions of section 7 but not section 8: the 40 years' period is subject to section 8 though, perhaps, in the case of easements of way and water alone, and is not subject to section 7.

3. Easements of light. Easements of light are in some respects on a footing different from that of other rights under the Act. Section 3 provides in effect that after the actual enjoyment of the access of light to a dwelling-house, workshop, greenhouse[83] or other building has continued for 20 years without interruption, the right is deemed absolute unless enjoyed by written consent or agreement. On the effect of this, the main points to note are the following.

(a) *Resemblances.* Light resembles other rights claimed under the Act in that—

---

[77] *Wright* v. *Williams* (1836) 1 M. & W. 77.
[78] *Bright* v. *Walker* (1834) 1 Cr.M. & R. 211.
[79] *Wright* v. *Williams, supra,* not cited in *Davies* v. *Du Paver* [1953] 1 Q.B. 184.
[80] *Tapling* v. *Jones* (1865) 11 H.L.C. 290 at p. 304.
[81] *Dalton* v. *Angus & Co.* (1881) 6 App.Cas. 740 at p. 800, *per* Lord Selbourne L.C.
[82] See M. & W., p. 860.
[83] *Allen* v. *Greenwood* [1980] Ch. 119. The ordinary amount of light for normal use of the building in question will be the plaintiff's entitlement though it may be possible to acquire an exceptional amount of light by prescription for a use which reasonably requires such light and which was known to the servient owner.

(1) SECTION 4 APPLIES, so that the period in question is that next before action,[84] and with the modification noted below "interruption" has the same meaning as in other cases[85]; and

(2) WRITTEN CONSENT: the rules relating to written consent are the same as for other claims under the Act.

(b) *Differences.* Light differs from other rights claimed under the Act in the following respects.

(1) ONLY ONE PERIOD. There is only one period for light, namely, 20 years.

(2) DISABILITIES. Sections 7 and 8 do not apply.

(3) OBSTRUCTION. Wartime restrictions and later planning control made it difficult to interrupt the enjoyment of inchoate rights of light with screens or other erections. Instead, a servient owner may now provide a notional obstruction. He must first obtain from the Lands Tribunal a certificate either of exceptional urgency or that due notice has been given to those likely to be affected. He may then register as a land charge a notice identifying the dominant and servient tenements and specifying the size and position of the notional obstruction; and for a year this notice takes effect as an obstruction known to and acquiesced in by all concerned. While the notice is in force, the dominant owner may sue for a declaration as if his light actually had been obstructed, and for the cancellation or variation of the registration. Futher, for this purpose he may treat his enjoyment as having begun a year earlier than it did; this avoids the "19 years and a day" type of problem.[86]

(4) ACTUAL USER SUFFICES. User as of right is not required[87]: actual enjoyment suffices, provided there has been no written consent. Thus the provision that written consent defeats the claim is the only fragment of *nec vi, nec clam, nec precario* which is left in claims to light under the Act; oral consent is no bar, even though evidenced by annual payments.[88] But there must be enjoyment of the light *qua* easement: enjoyment during unity of possession is not enough.[89]

(5) NO GRANT. There is no need to presume a grant, because the Act provides that 20 years' actual enjoyment confers an absolute right[90]; in other words, it is not necessary to show user by or on behalf of one tenant in fee simple against another. Thus the mere fact that the

[84] *Hyman* v. *Van den Burgh* [1908] 1 Ch. 167.
[85] *Smith* v. *Baxter* [1900] 2 Ch. 138.
[86] Rights of Light Act 1959; ss. 2, 3; and see *ante*, p. 421.
[87] *Colls* v. *Home & Colonial Stores Ltd.* [1904] A.C. 179 at p. 205.
[88] *Plasterers' Co.* v. *Parish Clerk's Co.* (1851) 6 Exch. 630.
[89] *Ladyman* v. *Grave* (1871) 6 Ch.App. 763.
[90] *Tapling* v. *Jones* (1865) 11 H.L.C. 290 at pp. 304, 318.

servient tenement has been under lease for the whole period does not prevent the acquisition under the Act of an easement of light valid against the reversioner.[91] This has been taken to its logical conclusion, so that under the Act one tenant can acquire an easement of light over land occupied by another tenant of the same landlord,[92] or by the landlord himself.[93] In the former case, on the expiration of the lease of the servient tenement, the easement is effective against the landlord and all subsequent owners of the land.[94]

(6) CROWN NOT BOUND. Sections 1 and 2 mention the Crown: section 3 does not. A statute does not bind the Crown unless it so provides either expressly or by necessary implication,[95] and so an easement of light cannot be acquired under the Act against the Crown,[96] although other easements and profits can.

4. Limits to the Act. The Prescription Act 1832 does not enable claimants to establish as easements or profits rights which could not be established as such at common law. Thus a claim by the freemen and citizens of a town to enter land and hold races thereon on Ascension Day cannot be established under the Act.[97] Nor has the Act abolished the other methods of prescription. Consequently, it is usual to plead all three methods of prescription, although the claimant does this at his own risk as to costs, *e.g.* if this form of pleading needlessly increases the other party's expenses.[98] If a claim is made solely under the Act, it is liable to be defeated by showing unity of possession at any time during the period[99]; this is not so under the doctrine of lost modern grant[1] or at common law.[2] Again, if the claim is made solely at common law, it will be defeated if it is shown that the enjoyment started after 1189. But as seen already, this would not defeat a claim by lost modern grant or under the Act. Nor should a claim be based on lost modern grant alone, for the court will not presume a modern grant if the right can be established in any other way.[3] However, a method of prescription under which it is legally impossible for a claim to succeed should never be pleaded. Thus a profit in gross should not be claimed under the Act,[4] although it may be claimed by prescription at common law.[5]

---

[91] *Simper* v. *Foley* (1862) 2 J. & H. 564.
[92] *Morgan* v. *Fear* [1907] A.C. 429.
[93] *Foster* v. *Lyons & Co. Ltd.* [1927] 1 Ch. 219 at p. 227.
[94] *Morgan* v. *Fear, supra.*
[95] *Perry* v. *Eames* [1891] 1 Ch. 658 at p. 665.
[96] *Wheaton* v. *Maple & Co.* [1893] 3 Ch. 48.
[97] *Mounsey* v. *Ismay* (1865) 3 H. & C. 486.
[98] *Harris* v. *Jenkins* (1882) 22 Ch.D. 481 at p. 482.
[99] *Damper* v. *Bassett* [1901] 2 Ch. 350.
[1] *Hulbert* v. *Dale* [1909] 2 Ch. 570.
[2] *Dalton* v. *Angus & Co.* (1881) 6 App.Cas. 740 at p. 814.
[3] *Gardner* v. *Hodgson's Kingston Brewery Co. Ltd.* [1903] A.C. 229 at p. 240.
[4] *Shuttleworth* v. *Le Fleming* (1865) 19 C.B.(N.S.) 687.
[5] *Johnson* v. *Barnes* (1873) L.R. 8 C.P. 527.

Sect. 4. Extinguishment of Easements and Profits

A. By Statute

An Act of Parliament may extinguish an easement or profit expressly or by implication. Under this head must be considered the extinguishment of commons by approvement, by inclosure, and by failure to register.

1. Approvement. The lord of a manor had a common law right to "approve" the manorial waste over which the tenants exercised rights of pasture. Approvement was effected by the lord taking part of the waste for his separate enjoyment. The Statutes of Merton 1235[6] and Westminster II 1285[7] confirmed this practice, but obliged the lord to leave sufficient land for the commoners. The onus of proving sufficiency was on the lord, and there had to be enough pasture for all the animals which the commoners were entitled to turn out, and not merely for those in fact turned out in recent years.[8] Since the Commons Act 1876, a person seeking to approve a common otherwise than in accordance with the strict procedure for inclosures under that Act must advertise his intention in the local Press on three successive occasions[9]; and the consent of the Secretary of State for the Environment,[10] given after holding a local inquiry, is required to validate the approvement.[11]

2. Inclosure. Inclosure involves the discharge of the whole manorial waste from all rights of common, whereas approvement applies only to commons of pasture appendant or appurtenant, and discharges only part of the land. From the middle of the eighteenth century, a large number of private inclosure Acts were passed. The policy of Parliament was to encourage the efficient production of food, which was hardly possible under the relics of the feudal system. The Inclosure (Consolidation) Act 1801 and the Inclosure Act 1845 facilitated inclosures, but public opinion was aroused by the disappearance of open spaces, and the Inclosure Act 1852 prevented inclosures being made without the consent of Parliament. The procedure is now governed by the Commons Act 1876. An application must first be made to the Secretary of State for the Environment (or Wales), and if a prima facie case is made out, regard being had to the benefit of the neighbourhood, a local inquiry is held. A provisional order is then submitted to Parliament for confirmation.[12]

---

[6] c. 4.
[7] c. 46.
[8] *Robertson* v. *Hartopp* (1889) 43 Ch.D. 484.
[9] s. 31.
[10] Or the Secretary of State for Wales.
[11] Law of Commons Amendment Act 1893, ss. 2, 3; S.I. 1970 No. 1681.
[12] Commons Act 1876, ss. 10–12.

3. Registration. Rights of common may be lost through failure to register under the Commons Registration Act 1965. The Act came into force on January 2, 1967, and required the registration with the appropriate local authority of all rights of common (other than rights held for a term of years or from year to year) within a period which was fixed to expire on July 31, 1970.[13] From the end of that period, no unregistered rights of common are exercisable.[14] The registration is provisional only pending the determination of any objections, which had to be lodged before August 1972. The objections are in process of being investigated by Commons Commissioners appointed under the Act.[15] Their jurisdiction is subject to a right of appeal to the High Court on a point of law, but otherwise the courts have no jurisdiction to investigate rights of common save in cases of bad faith.[16] New rights of common may be created and registered in respect of land over which no rights had been previously registered.[17]

B. By Release

1. Express release. At law, a deed is required for an express release.[18] In equity, however, an informal release will be effective provided it would be inequitable for the dominant tenant to claim that the right still exists, as where he has orally consented to his light being obstructed and the servient tenant has spent money on erecting the obstruction.[19]

2. Implied release. If the dominant owner shows any intention to release an easement or profit, it will be extinguished by implied release. Mere non-user is never enough by itself: an intention to abandon the right must be shown.[20] Nevertheless, non-user for a long period may raise a presumption of abandonment, and 20 years will usually suffice.[21]

It is a question of fact whether an act was intended as an abandonment. Alterations to the dominant tenement which make the enjoyment of an easement or profit impossible or unnecessary may show an intent to abandon the right. Thus if a mill to which an easement of water is appurtenant is demolished without any intent to replace it, the easement is released.[22] Similarly the demolition of a house to which an easement of light is appurtenant may amount to an implied release, unless it is intended to replace the house by another

---

[13] Commons Registration Act 1965, ss. 1 (1), 2 (1), 22 (1); S.I. 1970 No. 383.
[14] Commons Registration Act 1965, s. 1(2).
[15] For procedure, see S.I. 1971 No. 1727.
[16] *Wilkes* v. *Gee* [1973] 1 W.L.R. 742.
[17] S.I. 1969 No. 1843.
[18] Co.Litt. 264b.
[19] *Waterlow* v. *Bacon* (1866) L.R. 2 Eq. 514.
[20] *Swan* v. *Sinclair* [1924] 1 Ch. 254; affd. [1925] A.C. 227; and see *Tehidy Minerals Ltd.* v. *Norman* [1971] 2 Q.B. 528.
[21] *Moore* v. *Rawson* (1824) 3 B. & C. 332 at p. 339.
[22] *Liggins* v. *Inge* (1831) 7 Bing. 682 at p. 693.

building.[23] It is not essential that the new windows should occupy exactly the same positions as the old, provided they receive substantially the same light[24]; the test is identity of light, not identity of aperture. Further, if the dominant tenement is so altered that the burden of the easement is substantially increased, the right may be extinguished altogether.[25] Acquiesence in obstructions in the servient land may show an intent to abandon, but not if it can be explained, *e.g.* by the use of an alternative, precarious way.[26]

C. By Unity of Ownership and Possession

If the dominant and servient tenements come into the ownership and possession of the same person, any easement[27] or profit[28] is extinguished. Unity of possession without unity of ownership is not enough[29]: the right is merely suspended until the unity of possession ceases. Similarly, unity of ownership without unity of possession effects no extinguishment[30]: the right continues until there is also unity of possession. Thus if both dominant and servient tenements are under lease, the easement or profit will not be extinguished merely by both leases being assigned to X, nor will it be extinguished merely by Y purchasing both reversions; but if both leases and both reversions become vested in Z, the right is gone.

Sect. 5. Species of Easements

A. Rights of Way

1. Extent of easements of way. An easement of way may be either general or limited. A general right of way is one which may be used by the owner of the dominant tenement at any time and in any manner. A limited right of way is one which is subject to some restriction. The restriction may be as to time, *e.g* a way which can be used only in the daytime,[31] or it may be as to the mode in which the way can be used, *e.g.* a way limited to foot passengers, or to cattle and other animals in the charge of a drover, or to wheeled traffic,[32] and the like.

A right of way can normally be used only as a means of access to

---

[23] *Ecclesiastical Commissioners for England* v. *Kino* (1880) 14 Ch.D. 213.
[24] *Scott* v. *Pape* (1886) 31 Ch.D. 554.
[25] *Ankerson* v. *Connelly* [1906] 2 Ch. 544; affd. [1907] 1 Ch. 678; and see *Ray* v. *Fairway Motors (Barnstaple) Ltd.* (1968) 20 P. & C.R. 261 (extra burden insufficient).
[26] *Treweeke* v. *36 Wolseley Road Pty. Ltd.* (1973) 128 C.L.R. 274; and see *Ward* v. *Ward* (1852) 7 Exch. 838.
[27] *Buckby* v. *Coles* (1814) 5 Taunt. 311.
[28] *Tyrringham's Case* (1584) 4 Co.Rep. 36b at p. 38a; *White* v. *Taylor* [1969] 1 Ch. 150.
[29] *Canham* v. *Fisk* (1831) 2 Cr. & J. 126.
[30] *Richardson* v. *Graham* [1908] 1 K.B. 39.
[31] *Collins* v. *Slade* (1874) 23 W.R. 199.
[32] *Ballard* v. *Dyson* (1808) 1 Taunt. 279.

the dominant tenement. A right to pass over Plot A to reach Plot B cannot be used as a means of access to Plot C lying beyond Plot B.[33]

In the absence of a contrary agreement or special circumstances,[34] it is for the grantee of a way, not the grantor, to construct the way and to repair it when constructed[35]; the grantee may enter the servient tenement for these purposes.[36] If the way becomes impassable, there is no right to deviate from it unless the servient owner has obstructed it.[37]

2. Effect of mode of acquisition. The extent of an easement of way depends upon how it was acquired.

(a) *Express grant or reservation.* Here the question is primarily one of construction. If the intention is not made clear, a grant is construed most strongly against the person making it, in accordance with the general rule, while a reservation is construed in his favour, for it takes effect as a regrant by the other party.[38] Thus an easement granted in general terms is not confined to the purpose for which the land is used at the time of the grant.[39] A right of way for general purposes granted as appurtenant to a house can accordingly be used for the business of an hotel if that house is subsequently converted into an hotel.[40]

If a way is granted "as at present enjoyed," prima facie these words refer to the quality of the user (*e.g.* on foot or with vehicles) and do not limit the quantity of the user to that existing at the time of the grant.[41] In case of difficulty, the surrounding circumstances must be considered: thus both the condition of the way (*e.g.* whether it is a footpath or a metalled road) and the nature of the dominant tenement (*e.g.* whether it is a dwelling-house or a factory) may be of assistance.[42]

(b) *Implied grant or reservation.* A way of necessity is limited to the necessity existing at the time the right arose; thus if an encircled plot is used for agricultural purposes at the time of the grant, the way of necessity over the surrounding land is limited to agricultural purposes and cannot be used for the carting of building materials.[43]

---

[33] *Harris* v. *Flower* (1904) 74 L.J. Ch. 127; *Bracewell* v. *Appleby* [1975] Ch. 408, *Nickerson* v. *Barraclough* [1981] 2 W.L.R. 773.
[34] See *Saint* v. *Jenner* [1973] Ch. 275 (failure to repair results in obstruction).
[35] See *Miller* v. *Hancock* [1893] 2 Q.B. 177 (not affected by *Fairman* v. *Perpetual Investment Building Society* [1923] A.C. 74 on the duty to the dominant owner).
[36] *Newcomen* v. *Coulson* (1877) 5 Ch.D. 133.
[37] *Selby* v. *Nettlefold* (1873) 9 Ch.App. 111.
[38] For this rule, see *ante*, p. 409.
[39] *South Eastern Ry.* v. *Cooper* [1924] 1 Ch. 211.
[40] *White* v. *Grand Hotel, Eastbourne Ltd.* [1913] 1 Ch. 113 (affd. on another point, 84 L.J. Ch. 938).
[41] *Hurt* v. *Bowmer* [1937] 1 All E.R. 797.
[42] *Cannon* v. *Villars* (1878) 8 Ch.D. 415 at pp. 420, 421; *St. Edmundsbury & Ipswich Diocesan Board of Finance* v. *Clark (No. 2)* [1973] 1 W.L.R. 1672 at pp. 1591–1596 affd. [1975] 1 W.L.R. 468.
[43] *Corporation of London* v. *Riggs* (1880) 13 Ch.D. 798.

In other cases of implied grant, the circumstances of the case must be considered. Thus where a testator devised adjoining plots of land to different persons and one plot was bought by a railway company for conversion into a railway station, it was held that a way which had been used in the testator's lifetime for domestic purposes and for the purposes of warehouses on the land could not be used as a public approach to the station.[44]

(c) *Prescription.* Where an easement of way is acquired by long user, the extent of the way is limited by the nature of the user. Thus a way acquired by long user for farming purposes cannot be used for mineral purposes or for the cartage of building materials.[45] It has been held that user during the prescriptive period as a carriageway does not authorise user for cattle,[46] although it covers use as a footway[47] (since prima facie the greater includes the less) and it extends to use for motor traffic even if the user proved was for horse-drawn vehicles alone.[48] Moreover, unless there is a radical change in the nature of the dominant tenement, the user is not limited to the number or frequency of vehicles or pedestrians using the way during the prescriptive period.[49]

B. Rights of Light

1. No natural right. There is no natural right of light; a landowner may so build on his land as to prevent any light from reaching his neighbour's windows,[50] unless his neighbour has an easement of light or some other right such as a restrictive covenant against building. The access of light to windows is sometimes deliberately obstructed in order to prevent an easement of light being acquired by prescription.[51]

2. Quantum of light. The amount of light to which the dominant owner is entitled was finally settled in *Colls* v. *Home and Colonial Stores Ltd.*[52]; this amount is enough light according to the ordinary notions of mankind for the comfortable use of the premises as a dwelling, or, in the case of business premises, for the beneficial use of the premises for ordinary shop or other business purposes, or in the case of a greenhouse for ordinary use as a greenhouse, requiring not just illumination but the receipt of the suns's rays.[53] The test is thus

---

[44] *Milner's Safe Co. Ltd.* v. *Great Northumberland and City Ry.* [1907] 1 Ch. 208.
[45] *Wimbledon Conservators* v. *Dixon* (1875) 1 Ch.D. 362.
[46] *Ballard* v. *Dyson* (1808) 1 Taunt. 279.
[47] *Davies* v. *Stephens* (1836) 7 C. & P. 570.
[48] *Lock* v. *Abercester Ltd.* [1939] Ch. 861.
[49] *British Railways Board* v. *Glass* [1965] Ch. 538; *Woodhouse & Co. Ltd.* v. *Kirkland (Derby) Ltd.* [1970] 1 W.L.R. 1185.
[50] *Tapling* v. *Jones* (1865) 11 H.L.C. 290.
[51] See *ante*, p. 426.
[52] [1904] A.C. 179.
[53] *Allen* v. *Greenwood* [1980] Ch. 119.

"ordinary user": the dominant owner is not entitled to object even to a substantial diminution in his light, provided enough is left for the ordinary purposes. The test is not "How much light has been taken away?" but "How much light is left?"[54] Exceptionally, an easement of a greater amount of light than that required for ordinary purposes can be acquired, *e.g.* if for 20 years or more the dominant owner has, to the knowledge of the servient owner, enjoyed that quantity of light and has used the premises for purposes reasonably requiring an extraordinary amount of light.[55] Otherwise, the quantum of light to which the dominant owner is entitled is not affected by the fact that he has used the room in question for purposes requiring but little light,[56] for a right of light is a right to have the access of light for all ordinary purposes to which the room may be put.[57]

3. Alteration of apertures. An easement of light can exist only in respect of a window or other aperture in a building, such as a skylight.[58] If the dominant owner alters the size or position of the window, the burden on the servient owner cannot be increased; an obstruction which would not have been actionable before the alteration will not be actionable even if it deprives the altered window of most of its light.[59] But if it is established that an obstruction is an infringement of an easement of light for one set of windows, and another set of windows (for which no easement exists) is also obstructed by it, the dominant owner can recover damages in respect of both sets of windows, for the obstruction is illegal and the damages to both sets of windows the direct and foreseeable consequence of it.[60]

4. Standards of light. The standard of light varies to some extent from neighbourhood to neighbourhood,[61] the test in each case being that laid down in *Coll's* case. There is no "45 degrees" rule, *i.e.* no rule that an interference with light is actionable only if the obstruction rises above a line drawn upwards and outwards from the centre of the window at an angle of 45 degrees; at the most the test provides a very slight presumption.[62]

5. Other sources. In considering whether an easement of light has

---

[54] *Higgins* v. *Betts* [1905] 2 Ch. 210 at p. 215.
[55] *Allen* v. *Greenwood* (*supra*).
[56] *Price* v. *Hilditch* [1930] 1 Ch. 500.
[57] *Yates* v. *Jack* (1866) 1 Ch.App. 295.
[58] *Easton* v. *Isted* [1903] 1 Ch. 405.
[59] *Ankerson* v. *Connelly* [1907] 1 Ch. 678.
[60] *Re London, Tilbury & Southend Ry., etc.* (1889) 24 Q.B.D. 326.
[61] *Fishenden* v. *Higgs & Hill Ltd.* (1935) 153 L.T. 128.
[62] *Ibid*; *Ough* v. *King* [1967] 1 W.L.R. 1547. For scientific tests as to "sill ratio" and "grumble points," see *Charles Semon & Co. Ltd.* v. *Bradford Corporation* [1922] 2 Ch. 737 and *Fishenden* v. *Higgs & Hill Ltd.*, *supra*.

been obstructed, other sources of light of which the dominant owner cannot be deprived must be taken into account, such as vertical light through a skylight.[63] In one case[64] a room was lit though two sets of windows, one set facing A's land and the other facing B's land. It was held that the light received by both sets of windows had to be considered, but that A could not obscure the greater part of the light passing over his land in reliance upon B supplying a large quantity of light. Neither servient owner could build to a greater extent than, assuming a building of like height on the other servient tenement, would still leave the dominant tenement with sufficient light according to the test in *Coll's* case.

C. Rights of Water

A variety of easements may exist in connection with water, such as rights—

to take water from a river[65] or spring or a pump;
to water cattle at a pond;
to pollute the waters of a stream or river;
to discharge water on the land of another;
to enter the land of another to open sluice gates;
to permit rain water to drop from a roof on to a neighbour's land ("easement of eavesdrop").

D. Rights of Support

These have already been considered.[66]

E. Rights of Air

These have already been considered.[67]

F. Miscellaneous Easements

There are a variety of miscellaneous easements, such as rights—

to create a nuisance by the discharge of gases, fluids or smoke, or by making noises or vibrations;
to hang clothes on a line passing over another's land[68];
to mix manure on the servient tenement for the benefit of the adjoining farm;
to use a wall for nailing trees thereto or for supporting a creeper;
to extend the bowsprits of ships over a wharf[69];

---

[63] *Smith* v. *Evangelisation Society (Incorporated) Trust* [1933] Ch. 515.
[64] *Sheffield Masonic Hall Co. Ltd.* v. *Sheffield Corporation* [1932] 2 Ch. 17.
[65] The requirement of a licence from the water authority must always be considered: Water Resources Act 1963; *Cargill* v. *Gotts* [1981] 1 All E.R. 682.
[66] *Ante*, pp. 401, 411.
[67] *Ante*, p. 399.
[68] *Drewell* v. *Towler* (1832) 3 B. & Ad. 735.
[69] *Suffield* v. *Brown* (1864) 4 De G.J. & Sm. 185.

to use a coal shed for domestic purposes[70];

to store casks and trade produce on the servient tenement;

to let down the surface of land by mining operations under it;

to use an airfield[71];

to enter the servient tenement to repair buildings on the dominant tenement[72];

to enjoy a garden or park (a "*jus spatiandi*").[73]

Certain rights are not easements but resemble them. A right to use a pew in a church has been described as not being an interest in land but an interest of a peculiar nature in the nature of an easement created by Act of Parliament[74]; and the right to require a neighbouring landowner to repair his fences exists as a spurious easement.[75]

Sect. 6. Species of Profits à Prendre

The following are the main types of profit *à prendre*. Some are usually met with as commons, and some as several profits.

A. Profit of Pasture

A profit of pasture may exist in the following forms.[76]

1. Appendant. A profit of pasture appendant is limited to horses, oxen, cows and sheep, the numerical test being levancy and couchancy.[77]

2. Appurtenant. A profit of pasture appurtenant is not confined to any particular animals, but depends on the terms of the grant or, in the case of prescription, the animals habitually turned out to pasture. The number of animals may either be tested by levancy and couchancy, or be fixed; it cannot be unlimited.[78]

3. Pur cause de vicinage. Under a common of pasture *pur cause de vicinage*, the commoners of one common may not put more cattle upon it than it will maintain; thus if Common A is 50 acres in extent and Common B 100 acres, the commoners of A must not put more

---

[70] *Wright* v. *Macadam* [1949] 2 K.B. 744.
[71] *Dowty Boulton Paul Ltd.* v. *Wolverhampton Corporation* (*No. 2*) [1973] 2 W.L.R. 618.
[72] *Ward* v. *Kirkland* [1967] Ch. 194.
[73] *Re Ellenborough Park* [1956] Ch. 131.
[74] *Brumfitt* v. *Roberts* (1870) L.R. 5 C.P. 224 at p. 233.
[75] *Ante*, p. 399.
[76] There may be a correlative duty on frontagers to a common to fence against animals grazing on the common: *Egerton* v. *Harding* [1975] Q.B. 262.
[77] *Ante*, p. 405.
[78] *Benson* v. *Chester* (1799) 8 T.R. 396 at p. 401.

cattle on A than the 50 acres will support, in reliance on their cattle straying to B.[79]

4. In gross. A profit of pasture in gross may exist for a fixed number of animals or *sans nombre*. The last phrase means literally "without number" (an alternative form is "without stint"), but such a right is limited to not more cattle than the servient tenement will maintain in addition to any existing burdens.

5. Limitation of numbers. Rights of common registrable under the Commons Registration Act 1965[80] must be registered for a definite number of animals. After registration has become final, the right is only exercisable in relation to the number so registered.[81]

B. Profit of Turbary

A profit of turbary is the right to dig and take from the servient tenement peat or turf for use as fuel in a house on the dominant tenement. It may exist as appurtenant, or, where it is limited to some specified quantity, in gross.[82] Where it is appurtenant, the turves can be used only for the benefit of the dominant tenement and not, *e.g.* for sale, even if the dominant owner is entitled to a fixed quantity.[83]

C. Profit of Estovers

A profit of estovers is the right to take wood from the land of another as hay-bote, house-bote or plough-bote.[84] It may exist as appurtenant, or, if limited to a specified quantity, in gross.

D. Profit of Piscary and Other Sporting Rights

A profit of piscary is a right to catch and take away fish. It can exist in gross (when it may be unlimited) or as appurtenant (when it must be limited to the needs of the dominant tenement). Other sporting rights, such as a right of hunting, shooting, fowling and the like, may also exist as profits *à prendre*.[85] It is no infringement of such a right for the servient owner merely to cut timber in the ordinary way, even if he thereby drives away game,[86] but it is otherwise if fundamental changes in the land are made, as where the whole or a substantial part of the land is built upon or converted into racing stables.[87]

---

[79] *Corbet's Case* (1585) 7 Co.Rep. 5a.
[80] See *ante*, p. 429 for registration.
[81] Commons Registration Act 1965, s. 15.
[82] *Mellor* v. *Spateman* (1669) 1 Wms.Saund. 339 at p. 346.
[83] *Hayward* v. *Cunnington* (1668) 1 Lev. 231.
[84] *Ante*, p. 53.
[85] *Ewart* v. *Graham* (1859) 7 H.L.C. 331 at p. 345.
[86] *Gearns* v. *Baker* (1875) 10 Ch.App. 355.
[87] *Peech* v. *Best* [1931] 1 K.B. 1.

E. Profit in the Soil

A profit in the soil is the right to enter the servient tenement and take sand, stone, gravel and the like.[88] It may exist as appurtenant or in gross.

Sect. 7. Registered Land

A. Easements or Profits existing at First Registration

1. First registration of servient land. Any easement or profit *created by an instrument* and appearing adversely to affect the title must be noted on the register.[89] Other easements or profits may be noted against the title if admitted or proved to the Registrar's satisfaction[90] but their omission from the register will not affect the dominant owner where they exist as legal easements under the general law,[91] since they then rank as overriding interests binding the servient owner.[92]

2. First registration of dominant land. On first registration the proprietor has vested in him all easements and profits appertaining or reputed to appertain to the land without these being expressly mentioned on the register.[93] However, the benefit of a legal easement or profit may be entered in the property register as appurtenant to the registered estate.[94]

B. Easements or Profits created after First Registration

1. Express grant or reservation. If a legal easement or profit is to be expressly created not only must it satisfy the general law requirements for the creation of such legal interest but it must also be completed by registration,[95] *i.e.* notice must be entered against the servient title (in the charges register) and, if the dominant title is registered, the easement or profit should be registered as appurtenant thereto (in the property register). If no notice of the easement appears on the servient title then it will rank only as an equitable easement (which cannot rank as an overriding interest[96]) so that a subsequent transferee for value of the servient title will take free from the easement. Oddly enough, it seems that an equitable profit can rank as an overriding interest[97] so as to bind a subsequent transferee.

---

[88] Co.Litt. 122a.
[89] L.R.A., s. 70(2); *Re Dances Way* [1962] Ch. 490.
[90] *Ibid*. s. 70(3).
[91] *e.g.* L.P.A. s. 62, prescription.
[92] L.R.A., ss. 5, 70(1) (a).
[93] *Ibid*. ss. 5, 72.
[94] L.R.R. 257, *Re Evans Contract* [1970] 1 W.L.R. 583.
[95] L.R.A., ss 19(2), 22 (2).
[96] *Ibid*. s. 70 (1)(a), *ante*. p. 121.
[97] *Ibid*.

2. Implied grant or reservation. Easements and profits can be acquired on registration of a title by virtue of section 62 of the Law of Property Act and (probably) of the Rule in *Wheeldon* v. *Burrows* in the same way as if the land were unregistered.[98] They take effect as overriding interests.[99] If admitted or sufficiently proved they may be noted against the servient title and registered as appurtenant to the dominant title.[1]

Where implied reservation is concerned (*i.e.* ways of necessity or mutually intended easements) no special provision is made by the Land Registration Act or the rules made thereunder. It seems the reservation will be treated as a disposition by the purchaser[2] and so require to be completed by registration[3] if a legal easement is to be reserved. Otherwise, it will only be an equitable easement incapable of ranking as an overriding interest so that a subsequent transferee for value will take free from it.[4]

3. Prescription. Easements or profits acquired by prescription take effect as legal interests[5] and as overriding interests[6] unless noted on the charges register of the servient title[7] after the Registrar has satisfied himself that the right has been acquired by prescription. In such a case he will register the right as appurtenant to the dominant title so conferring an absolute, good leasehold qualified or possessory title to the right according to the nature of the registered title.[8]

---

[98] L.R.A., ss. 20(1) 23(1); L.R.R. 251; Ruoff & Roper, p. 98.
[99] L.R.R. 258.
[1] L.R.R. 252, 253, 254. They then cease to be overriding interests.
[2] Reservation operates as a re-grant by the purchaser: *Ante.* p. 409.
[3] L.R.A. ss. 18 (5), 19(2), *ante*, p. 113. Thus *legal* implied reservation *sub silentio* cannot exist, unlike the unregistered conveyancing position.
[4] L.R.A., ss. 70(1) (*a*), 20(1), 23(1).
[5] L.R.R. 250.
[6] L.R.A., s. 70(1) (*a*).
[7] *Ibid.* s. 70(3).
[8] L.R.R. 250(2), 254(1).

CHAPTER 12

RESTRICTIVE COVENANTS

Sect. 1. Divergence of Law and Equity

Law and equity have taken different views of the rights and liabilities of parties affected by covenants where there is privity neither of contract nor of estate between the parties. At law, the rule is that, provided certain conditions are satisfied, the benefit of a covenant may be assigned, but not the burden. Thus if P, on buying land from V, enters into certain covenants with V, the benefit of those covenants may at law be assigned by V to X, thus enabling X to enforce the covenants against P. But this does not apply to the burden of the covenants; if Y buys P's land, he will not be bound by the covenants.

As regards the benefit of covenants, equity followed the rule at law, with some relaxation of the conditions to be satisfied. The important contribution of equity in this sphere, however, was the rule that subject to certain conditions, the *burden* of covenants could be transferred. This transformed the law of covenants in cases where there was privity neither of contract nor of estate. The effectiveness of a covenant concerning land was no longer confined to the period for which the original covenantor retained the land, but might continue indefinitely. Once it could be shown that the necessary conditions had been satisfied, a covenant might continue to burden one plot of land for the benefit of another, irrespective of the number of times each plot changed hands. This intervention of equity came soon after the outburst of building and increase of population associated with the Industrial Revolution. It became plain that the law lacked any other effective means of securing privacy and maintaining the general character of a district since the courts were not prepared to extend the category of negative easements which prevent the servient owner from doing things on the servient land, *e.g.* a right of light or right to a defined flow of air. Restrictive covenants are thus in the nature of *equitable* negative easements.[1]

This position must now be examined in some detail; for completeness, the position of the original parties to the covenant will be considered here, although privity of contract is involved.

---

[1] *Re Nisbet and Potts' Contract* [1906] 1 Ch. 386 at p. 409; *Reid* v. *Bickerstaff* [1909] 2 Ch. 305 at p. 320; *L.C.C.* v. *Allen* [1914] 3 K.B. 642 at p. 660; *Kelly* v. *Barrett* [1924] 2 Ch. 379 at p. 405; *Newton Abbot Co-operative Society* v. *Williamson* [1952] Ch. 286 at p. 293.

Sect. 2. At Law

A. The Benefit of the Covenant

I. THE ORIGINAL COVENANTEE

An original covenantee who has not assigned the benefit of the covenant can always enforce it against the original covenantor, even if the covenantee has parted with the dominant tenement,[2] unless as a matter of construction the covenant is to benefit the covenantee only whilst he owns the benefited land. Normally the original covenantee will be a party to the deed creating the covenant, but by statute this is not now essential.

Under section 56 of the Law of Property Act 1925[3] a person may now take a benefit under a deed even if he is not named as a party to it, provided that the deed purports to confer that benefit upon him.[4] Thus if V sells land to P, and P binds his land by a covenant expressed to be for the benefit of V and the owners for the time being of certain adjoining plots of land, these adjoining owners can sue on the covenant as original covenantees, even though they were not parties to the conveyance creating the covenant.[5] In such a case, the adjoining owners are clearly identifiable persons in existence at the time of the conveyance; but those who subsequently acquire the adjoining plots cannot claim to be original covenantees under the statutory provisions even though the covenant was expressed to be for the benefit of V and adjoining owners of certain plots and their successors in title.[6] Similarly, if a covenant is made expressly for the benefit of the present owner of a plot of land and his successors in title, the owner at the time of the conveyance is an original covenantee but future owners are not; they can enforce the covenant only under the rules relating to assignees.

II. ASSIGNEES

If V sells part of his land to P in fee simple and P enters into covenants binding the land he buys, the benefit of P's covenant may run at law with V's fee simple estate in the land he retains, so that a subsequent purchaser of V's land can enforce the covenant against P. It is immaterial whether the covenant is negative (not to do something) or positive (to do something). Thus the common law doctrine applies equally to a covenant not to build on the land purchased by P or a covenant to supply pure water to the land

---

[2] See *L.C.C.* v. *Allen* [1914] 3 K.B. 642 at p. 664, Damages will only be nominal.
[3] Replacing R.P.A. 1845, s. 5; see *Beswick* v. *Beswick* [1968] A.C. 58 at pp. 102–107.
[4] See *White* v. *Bijou Mansions Ltd.* [1937] Ch. 610 at p. 625; [1938] Ch. 351 at p. 365.
[5] See *Re Ecclesiastical Commissioners for England's Conveyance* [1936] Ch. 430 (where the liability was equitable and so fell under Sect. 3, *post*, p. 443).
[6] *Westhoughton U.D.C.* v. *Wigan Coal and Iron Co. Ltd.* [1919] 1 Ch. 159 at pp. 169, 170.

retained by V.[7] In fact it is also immaterial that the covenant has nothing to do with P's land or indeed that the covenantor has no land.[8] For a covenant to be enforceable in this way, the following conditions must be satisfied.

1. The covenant must touch and concern land of the covenantee.[9] It is essential that the covenant should be made for the benefit of land owned by the covenantee (*i.e.* V in the above examples) at the time of the covenant. In general, the test for determining whether a covenant touches and concerns the land is similar to that applicable to covenants in a lease.[10]

2. The covenant must be intended to run with the legal estate. Where there was an intent to benefit the land of the covenantee and his successors in title the land being identified in, or identifiable from, the deed then the benefit of the covenant is annexed to the legal estate vested in the covenantee.[11] At law, it is not enough to show that the covenantee has an equitable interest in the land retained. It must be shown that the covenant was made for the benefit of some legal estate into whomsoever's hands it might come, and not for the mere personal advantage of the covenantee.[12]

3. Ownership of the land: an assignee who seeks to enforce a covenant made before 1926 must show that he has the legal estate to which the benefit of the covenant was attached.[13] But a covenant made after 1925 is enforceable by those claiming under the covenantee,[14] so that whether a mere tenant under a lease can enforce a covenant annexed to the legal fee simple depends on the date of the covenant. It is immaterial whether the person enforcing the covenant knew of its existence when he obtained the land,[15] since an annexed covenant passes with the land like hidden treasure.

B. The Burden of the Covenant

As stated above, the rule at law is that the burden of a covenant will

---

[7] See *Shayler* v. *Woolf* [1946] 1 All E.R. 464 at p. 467 (affd. [1946] 2 All E.R. 320).
[8] *Smith* v. *R. Douglas Catchment Board* [1949] 2 K.B. 500.
[9] *Rogers* v. *Hosegood* [1900] 2 Ch. 388.
[10] *Ante*, p. 379.
[11] After Judicature Act 1873, s. 25 (6) replaced by law of Property Act 1925, s. 136 it became possible at law to assign the benefit of a covenant but this was unnecessary where the covenant had been annexed to the land so as automatically to pass therewith.
[12] *Rogers* v. *Hosegood, supra.*
[13] *Westhoughton U.D.C.* v. *Wigan Coal and Iron Co. ltd.* [1919] 1 Ch. 159 at pp. 170–171 though in *The Prior's Case* (1368) Y.B. 42 Edw. III pl. 14 fol. 3A the covenantee was tenant in fee simple but the successful plaintiff, his successor was tenant in tail. See also *Lougher* v. *Williams* (1673) 2 Lev. 92.
[14] L.P.A. 1925, s. 78 which deems the covenant "to be made with the covenantee and his successors in title and the persons deriving title under him or them."; *Smith* v. *R. Douglas Catchment Board* [1949] 2 K.B. 500.
[15] *Rogers* v. *Hosegood, supra.*

not pass with freehold land.[16] Yet what cannot be accomplished directly may be secured indirectly. There are four heads.

1. Chain of covenants. If V sells land to P, and P covenants, for example, to erect and maintain a fence, P will remain liable to V on the covenant by virtue of privity of contract even if P sells the land to Q. P will accordingly protect himself by extracting from Q a covenant of indemnity against future breaches of the covenant to fence. If Q then fails to maintain the fence, V cannot sue Q, but he can sue P, and P can then sue Q on the covenant for indemnity. However, although in theory liability can be maintained indefinitely in this way, with each sale of the land the chain of covenants for indemnity becomes longer, and more liable to be broken by the insolvency or disappearance of one of the parties to it. This indirect enforcement of covenants by means of indemnities is thus an imperfect substitute for the direct enforceability which the common law refuses to allow.

2. Enlarged long lease. A more effective but more artificial method is to insert the covenant in a lease which can be enlarged into a fee simple, and then to enlarge the lease.[17]

3. Conditional benefit. A man who claims the benefit of a conveyance or other deed must submit to its burden. Thus if a conveyance of land on a housing estate gives the purchaser the right to use the estate roads but imposes on him the liability to contribute to the costs of upkeep, a successor in title cannot use the roads without paying the contributions.[18] The liability is thus not absolute but conditional: he who does not enjoy need not submit. Yet often there will be little real choice.

4. Right of entry. On a conveyance or assignment a right of re-entry may be reserved to the grantor, allowing him to re-enter and retake the property if covenants in his favour are not observed.[19]

C. Summary of the Position at Law

It will be observed that only within narrow limits does the common law enforce covenants outside the confines of privity of contract or privity of estate. As will be seen shortly, equity became far more flexible and would enforce covenants in many cases where the common law would not. This does not, however, render the rules at law obsolete, for if a covenant is enforceable at law, the plaintiff, on

---

[16] *Austerberry* v. *Corporation of Oldham* (1885) 29 Ch.D. 750 at pp. 781–785; *E. & G.C. Ltd.* v. *Bate* (1935) 79 L.J.News. 203; *Cator* v. *Newton* [1940] 1 K.B. 415.
[17] See *ante*, p. 358; *Re M'Naul's Estate* [1902] 1 I.R. 114.
[18] *Halsall* v. *Brizell* [1957] Ch. 169; *Ives Investments Ltd.* v. *High* [1967] 2 Q.B. 379; *Tito* v. *Waddell (No. 2)* [1977] Ch. 106 at p. 289 *et seq.*
[19] *Shiloh Spinners Ltd.* v. *Harding* [1973] A.C. 691; *ante* pp. 90, 389.

proving his case, is entitled as of right to a judgment for damages (even though they may be nominal), whereas if a covenant is enforceable only in equity the court has a discretion in deciding whether to give any remedy. However, since the equitable remedy of an injunction is the one usually desired, this point is not of great practical importance. Yet it should be remembered that at law it is quite immaterial whether the covenantor has any land and whether the covenant is negative or positive, and that in the case of a positive covenant, damages will usually be the most suitable remedy.

Sect. 3. In Equity: Restrictive Covenants

A. The Burden of the Covenant

It will later be seen[20] that the rules in equity as to the benefit of a covenant are in the main merely a more relaxed and detailed version of the rules at law. As to the burden of the covenant, however, the rules in equity are now completely different in that if the covenant is negative in nature and, like an easement, benefits dominant land and burdens nearby servient land, then the burden of the covenant can run with the land burdening the occupier thereof, whether freeholder or tenant or squatter.

Until *Tulk* v. *Moxhay*[21] was decided in 1848 (a time when the full effects of the vast expansion in industrial and building activities were being felt), equity had gone no further than the common law.[22] In that case it was decided that a covenant to maintain Leicester Square uncovered with any buildings would be enforced by injunction against a purchaser of the land who bought with notice of the covenant. For some while the question was thought to be one of notice; a person who took land with notice that it had been bound by some restriction could not disregard that restriction. On this footing, it was immaterial whether the restriction has been imposed to benefit other land or merely the covenantee personally; it sufficed that there was some contractual restriction on the use of the land and that the land had been acquired with notice of it.[23] But since 1882[24] it has been accepted that equity will enforce a restrictive covenant against a purchaser only if it was made for the protection of other land. Restrictive covenants came to resemble easements as being rights over one plot of land ("the servient tenement") existing for the benefit of another plot of land ("the dominant tenement"). In short, at a leap, the law of restrictive covenants passed from the sphere of contract to the sphere of property.

---

[20] *Post*, p. 446.
[21] (1848) 2 Ph. 774.
[22] Despite *Whatman* v. *Gibson* (1838) 9 Sim. 196, the question was regarded as still being open in *Bristow* v. *Wood* (1844) 1 Coll.C.C. 480.
[23] See *Luker* v. *Dennis* (1877) 7 Ch.D. 227.
[24] See *London & South Western Ry.* v. *Gomm* (1882) 20 Ch.D. 562 at p. 583.

The original covenantor usually remains liable on the covenant, even if he has parted with the servient tenement, for the common form of covenant extends to the acts of persons claiming under him[25]; but today, words limiting its ambit are often inserted.

An assignee of land of the original covenantor is bound by the covenant only if three conditions are fulfilled.

1. The covenant must be negative in nature. After a few cases in which the court was prepared to enforce positive covenants, the rule was settled in 1881 that none except negative covenants would be enforced by equity.[26] The question is whether the covenant is negative in nature: it is immaterial whether the wording is positive or negative. Thus the covenant in *Tulk* v. *Moxhay*[27] itself was positive in wording, but part of it was negative in nature (to keep land in Leicester Square "in an open state, uncovered with any buildings"), so that this part merely bound the covenantor to refrain from building, without requiring him to do any positive act.

The test is whether the covenant requires expenditure of money for its proper performance; if the covenant requires the covenantee to put his hand in his pocket, it is not negative in nature.[28] A covenant to give the first refusal of a plot of land is negative in nature, for in effect it is a covenant not to sell to anyone else until the covenantee has had an opportunity of buying; but a covenant "not to let the premises get into disrepair," despite its apparently negative form, is in substance positive, for it can be performed only by the expenditure of money on repairs. Among the restrictive covenants most frequently met with in practice are covenants against building on land, and against carrying on any trade or business (or certain specified trades or businesses[29]) on the premises concerned.

2. The covenantee must, at the date of the covenant, own land which will benefit therefrom. Here again, as mentioned above,[30] the rule was not settled at first. It is now accepted, however, that with statutory exceptions in favour of local authorities,[31] a restrictive

---

[25] *L.C.C.* v. *Allen* [1914] 3 K.B. 642 at pp. 660, 673; and see L.P.A. 1925, s. 79(1).

[26] *Haywood* v. *Brunswick Permanent Benefit Building Society* (1881) 8 Q.B.D. 403.

[27] *Ante*, p. 443.

[28] *Haywood* v. *Brunswick Permanent Benefit Building Society, supra*, at pp. 409, 410.

[29] Such covenants are not apparently subject to the doctrine of restraint of trade when given on the acquisition of new property: *Esso Petroleum Co. Ltd.* v. *Harper's Garage (Stourport) Ltd.* [1968] A.C. 269 at pp. 298, 309, 316, 325, 334; and see *Cleveland Petroleum Co. Ltd.* v. *Dartstone Ltd.* [1969] 1 W.L.R. 116 (covenant in lease).

[30] *Ante*, p. 443.

[31] See, *e.g.* Town and Country Planning Act 1971, s. 52(2); Housing Act 1957, s. 151.

covenant is similar to an equitable easement, and that the burden of the covenant will run with land only if the covenant was made for the protection of land belonging to the covenantee; as with easements,[32] there must be a dominant tenement benefited or accommodated by the restrictive covenant.[33] Thus covenants binding land in Hampstead will be too remote to benefit land in Clapham,[34] and if the covenantee retains no other land, a purchaser of the Hampstead land will take free from the covenant. Yet a landlord's reversion on a lease is a sufficient interest to entitle him to enforce the covenant against a sub-tenant, even though he has no other adjoining land.[35]

3. The burden of the covenant must have been intended to run with the covenantor's land. A covenant may be confined, either expressly or by implication, so as to bind the covenantor alone.[36] In this case, assignees of the covenantor's land are not bound by the covenant. But if the covenant was made by the covenantor for himself, his heirs and assigns, the burden will normally be attached to his land. Covenants relating to the covenantor's land which are made after 1925 are deemed to have been made by the covenantor on behalf of himself, his successors in title, and the persons deriving title under him or them, unless a contrary intention appears.[37]

Burden of covenant runs in equity. If these conditions are satisfied, the burden of the covenant runs *in equity*. There are two main consequences.

(a) *Equitable remedies.* Only equitable remedies are available, and these are discretionary remedies. However, since the Chancery Amendment Act 1858,[38] equity has been entitled to award damages in any case where an injunction or specific performance would have been awarded, although the plaintiff is not, as in an action at law, entitled to insist upon some damages being awarded if he makes out his case.[39]

(b) *Purchaser without notice.* The covenant suffers from the infirmity of all equitable interests, namely, that it will not be enforced against a bona fide purchaser for value of a legal estate without notice

---

[32] *Ante*, p. 396.
[33] See *Formby* v. *Barker* [1903] 2 Ch. 539; *L.C.C.* v. *Allen* [1914] 3 K.B. 642; D.J.H. (1971) 87 L.Q.R. 539 at p. 545.
[34] *Kelly* v. *Barrett* [1924] 2 Ch. 379 at p. 404.
[35] *Regent Oil Co. Ltd.* v. *J. A. Gregory (Hatch End) Ltd.* [1966] Ch. 402 at p. 433.
[36] See *Re Fawcett and Holmes' Contract* (1889) 42 Ch.D. 150; *Re Royal Victoria Pavilion, Ramsgate* [1961] Ch. 581.
[37] L.P.A. 1925, s. 79 (1).
[38] s. 2. Though the Act has been repealed the jurisdiction still exists: *Leeds Industrial Co-operative Society* v. *Slack* [1924] A.C. 851. See now Supreme Court Act 1981, s. 50.
[39] See *ante*, p. 61.

of the covenant, or someone claiming through such a person.[40] It is enforceable against others such as squatters.[41]

The doctrine of notice has been significantly affected by the Land Charges Act 1925.[42] Covenants made before 1926, and covenants in leases, whenever made, are still subject to the old rules as to notice and are not registrable; but a restrictive covenant made after 1925 otherwise than between a lessor and a lessee must be registered as a land charge.[43] If not registered, it will be void against a subsequent purchaser for money or money's worth of a legal estate in the land. A registered restrictive covenant will bind everyone.[44] However, a lessee or sub-lessee or assignee who cannot investigate the superior title[45] is not to be deemed to have constructive notice of an *unregistrable* restrictive covenant[46] and so will be bound only if the covenant is referred to in the documents available for inspection or actual notice arises *aliunde*.

B. *The Benefit of the Covenant*

The rules in equity are similar to those at law, since they are a refined development of the common law rules.[47] These refinements, however, have led to problems in ascertaining whether a plaintiff has the benefit of the covenant.

I. THE ORIGINAL COVENANTEE

The position in equity is similar to that at law. In particular, section 56 of the Law of Property Act 1925 applies.[48] It should be noted, however, that if the original covenantee parts with the land for the benefit of which the covenant was taken, he ceases to be able to enforce it in equity[49] since the covenant is presumed to be for the benefit of the covenantee *qua* landowner only.

II. ASSIGNEES

For anyone except the original covenantee to be entitled to enforce a covenant in equity, he must show that the following conditions have been satisfied.

1. The covenant must touch and concern land of the covenantee. Equity follows the law here, and the legal rules apply,[50] though it

---

[40] *Wilkes* v. *Spooner* [1911] 2 K.B. 473; *ante*, p. 69.
[41] *Re Nisbet and Potts' Contract* [1906] 1 Ch. 386.
[42] Now Land Charges Act 1972.
[43] *Ante*, p. 94.
[44] *White* v. *Bijou Mansions Ltd.* [1937] Ch. 610.
[45] L.P.A. 1925, s. 44, *ante*, pp. 101–102.
[46] L.P.A. 1925, s. 44 (5).
[47] For a general survey, see S.J. Bailey (1938) 6 Camb.L.J. 339. See also H.W.R. Wade [1972B] C.L.J. 157; D.J.Hayton (1971) 87 L.Q.R. 539.
[48] *Ante* p. 440.
[49] *Chambers* v. *Randall* [1923] 1 Ch. 149 at pp. 157, 158.
[50] *Re Union of London and Smith's Bank Ltd.'s Conveyance* [1933] Ch. 611.

may be better to draw an analogy with easements and to require the covenant to accommodate the dominant tenement.[51]

2. The covenant must be intended to run with the land and the plaintiff must show he is entitled to the benefit of the covenant. He can satisfy this condition by showing either—

(a) that the benefit of the covenant has been annexed to land and that he owns some interest in that land; or

(b) that the benefit of the covenant has been assigned to him and that he owns some interest in land for the benefit of which the covenant was made; or

(c) that there is a building scheme or other scheme of development.

These provisions will be considered in turn.

(a) *Covenant annexed to land*: the benefit of the covenant has been annexed to land, and the plaintiff now owns some interest in that land. Equity follows the law, and these provisions correspond closely to the rules at law,[52] the main difference being that the equitable rules are rather less strict. There are two separate elements to consider.

(1) THE ANNEXING OF THE COVENANT. A landowner who extracts a covenant from another landowner may do so merely for his direct personal advantage. Alternatively, he may take the covenant for the benefit of his identified land so that the covenant will pass automatically therewith, he deriving an advantage for as long as the land is his. Covenants of the first kind will not automatically run with the covenantee's land, but those of the second type will. The benefit of a covenant will be effectively annexed to the land so as to run with it if in the instrument the covenant is stated either to be for the benefit of the land, or else to be made with the covenantee in his capacity of owner of the land.[53] In both cases the dominant land must be identified in the deed or be ascertainable from the terms of the deed as elucidated by extrinsic evidence (*e.g.* "the adjoining lands of the vendor").[54]

(2) ANNEXURE FOR LAND AS A WHOLE ONLY OR FOR THE WHOLE AND EACH AND EVERY PART. It is a question of construction whether the covenant is intended to benefit the land whilst enjoyed as a whole only (or so long as a substantial part of the whole remains) or whether

---

[51] *Newton Abbot Co-operative Society* v. *Williamson* [1952] Ch. 286 (covenant against competing with a business on the convenantee's land held enforceable); D.J.H. (1971) 87 L.Q.R. 539 at p. 545.

[52] *Ante*, p. 441.

[53] See *Drake* v. *Gray* [1936] Ch. 451 at p. 466; *Rogers* v. *Hosegood* [1900] 2 Ch. 388. *Cf. Renals* v. *Cowlishaw* (1878) 9 Ch.D. 125.

[54] *Newton Abbot Co-operative Society* v. *Williamson* [1952] Ch. 286 at p. 289.

it is intended also to benefit each and every part of the land.[55] In the former case the covenant is only enforceable by the owner of the whole or of substantially the whole.[56] The old presumption of annexation to the whole only has now been displaced by a presumption of annexation to each and every part.[57]

Even if a clear intention is shown to annex the benefit of a covenant to land whilst enjoyed as a whole only, there will be no effective annexation if the area of the land is greater than can reasonably be benefited. Thus, where on a sale of land restrictive covenants were stated to be made for the benefit of the "owners for the time being of the Childwickbury estate" (which was about 1,700 acres in extent), it was held that the benefit of a covenant could not run with the estate even in favour of someone acquiring the whole of the estate; the covenant could not benefit the whole of the estate, and the court could not sever the covenant.[58] Had the covenant been expressed to be for the benefit of the whole *or any part* of the estate, it could have been enforced by the successor in title to any part of the land which the covenant in fact benefits.[59]

(2) OWNERSHIP OF THE LAND. The rule at law (relaxed by statute for covenants made after 1925[60]) is that the plaintiff must show that he is entitled to the same estate in the land as that to which the covenantee was entitled. But in equity, the plaintiff need only show that he has *some* interest in the land to which the benefit of the covenant has been attached; if the covenant was made before 1926 with a fee simple owner of land for the benefit of the land, a tenant for years can enforce the covenant in equity,[61] though not at law.

If the plaintiff has only part of the land to which the benefit of the covenant was attached he can nevertheless enforce it, provided he can show from the wording of the covenant that it was made for the benefit of the whole or any part of the land.[62] Alternatively, it has been held that he will succeed if the benefit of a covenant annexed only to the whole has been expressly assigned to him,[63] but there is surely a logical contradiction in saying that one can assign to a purchaser of *part* of the dominant land the benefit of a covenant which *ex hypothesi* is so expressed as to confine that benefit to the

---

[55] *Drake* v. *Gray (supra).*
[56] *Wrotham Park Estate Co.* v. *Parkside Homes* [1974] 1 W.L.R. 798.
[57] *Federated Homes Ltd.* v. *Mill Lodge Properties Ltd.* [1980] 1 W.L.R. 594.
[58] *Re Ballard's Conveyance* [1937] Ch. 473. The courts are now prepared to presume a covenant capable of benefiting land as a whole unless such view cannot reasonably be held: *Wrotham Park Estate Co.* v. *Parkside Homes* [1974] 1 W.L.R. 798 at p. 808.
[59] *Marquess of Zetland* v. *Driver* [1939] Ch. 1.
[60] See *ante*, p. 441.
[61] *Taite* v. *Gosling* (1879) 11 Ch.D. 273.
[62] See *Drake* v. *Gray* [1936] Ch. 451; *Russell* v. *Archdale* [1964] Ch. 38.
[63] *Stilwell* v. *Blackman* [1968] Ch. 508.

land while it is enjoyed by one owner and as a *whole* and not otherwise.[64]

If the above conditions are satisfied, the benefit of the covenant attaches to the land and passes to each successive owner for the time being, even if he was ignorant of it when he took the land.[65] As soon as the covenantee or other owner has parted with all of the land to which the benefit of the covenant was attached, he loses his equitable right to take advantage of subsequent breaches of the covenant.[66]

(b) *Assignment of benefit of covenant*: the benefit of the covenant has been assigned to the plaintiff and he owns some interest in the land for the benefit of which the covenant was made.[67]

There are the following points to consider.

(1) ASSIGNMENT OF THE BENEFIT. The plaintiff must show that he has had the benefit of the covenant assigned to him. Where the benefit of a covenant has not been annexed to land, it will not pass automatically to the subsequent owners of the land,[68] *e.g.* where the covenant is with "V and his assigns" as opposed to "V and his assigns, the owners from time to time of Mayacre" so that the intent is to benefit the current landowner and, if the covenant is assigned, future landowners, rather than an intent to benefit current and future landowners in any event. The covenantee may, if he wishes, expressly assign the benefit of the covenant to someone who takes all or some of the land intended to be protected by it.[69] There seems to be a presumption that the covenant is taken the better to enable the covenantee to dispose of the whole and each and every part of the land.[70]

The assignment must, it seems be made at the time of the conveyance of the land which is to be protected.[71] Once the land has been sold, the benefit of the covenant cannot be assigned: one purpose of the covenant is to make the covenantee's land more readily saleable, and if he has succeeded in disposing of the whole of his land without assigning the benefit of the covenant, it ceases to be assignable.[72] If only part of his land has been disposed of, he can assign the benefit of the covenant when he sells any of the parts still retained, but he cannot assign it to those who have already purchased parts of the land.[73] Although there must have been no separation

---

[64] D.J.H. (1971) 87 L.Q.R. 539 at pp. 553, 562–563. Now that annexed covenants are, like assignable covenants, to be presumed to be for the benefit of each and every part there is no need for the court to temper one illogicality with another.
[65] *Rogers* v. *Hosegood* [1900] 2 Ch. 388.
[66] *Chambers* v. *Randall* [1923] 1 Ch. 149 at pp. 157, 158.
[67] *Re Union of London and Smith's Bank Ltd.'s Conveyance* [1933] Ch. 611.
[68] *Renals* v. *Cowlishaw* (1878) 9 Ch.D. 125.
[69] *Re Union of London and Smith's Bank Ltd.'s Conveyance, supra.*
[70] D.J.H. (1971) 87 L.Q.R. 539 at pp. 555–557.
[71] *Chambers* v. *Randall* (1923) 1 Ch. 149.
[72] *Re Rutherford's Conveyance* [1938] Ch. 396.
[73] *Re Union of London and Smith's Bank Ltd.'s Conveyance, supra* at p. 632.

between the title to the land and the covenant, equitable entitlement to the covenant under a settlement or contract or will or intestacy will suffice.[74]

The assignment need not necessarily be made by the original covenantee. If, for example, the original covenantee dies, both the covenant and the land that it benefits will devolve on his personal representatives, who may hold it as bare trustees for a devisee under the covenantee's will or for some other successor to the land. As owner in equity, the successor can sue on the covenant without joining the personal representatives,[75] and can assign it to a purchaser.[76]

(2) ASCERTAINABILITY OF DOMINANT LAND. A restrictive covenant prevents the covenantor from doing something on his own land and so in itself does not indicate whether any other land is intended to be benefited. For annexation it seems the intent to benefit land must appear from the deed itself, the land being identified in, or capable of ascertainment from the terms of the deed.[77] For assignment Bennett J. held[78] it necessary "that the deed containing the covenant defines or contains something to define the property for the benefit of which the covenant was entered into." On appeal, Romer L.J., without criticising Bennett J., stated[79] "the court will readily infer an intention to benefit the other land of the vendor where the existence and situation of such land are indicated in the conveyance or otherwise shown with reasonable certainty." In uttering these last six words Romer L.J. was probably contemplating a case where the dominant land was referred to as "the adjoining lands of the vendor" rather than by specific description. However, Upjohn J. relied on the dicta of Romer L.J. to hold that the intent to benefit dominant land need not appear from the wording of the deed so long as the surrounding circumstances clearly establish it.[80]

This broad and reasonable view has commended itself to Wilberforce J.[81] and is in line with the liberal approach to the ascertainment

---

[74] *Ives* v. *Brown* [1919] 2 Ch. 314; *Northbourne* v. *Johnson* [1922] 2 Ch. 209; *Newton Abbot Co-operative Society* v. *Williamson* [1952] Ch. 586.

[75] *Earl of Leicester* v. *Wells-next-the-Sea U.D.C.* [1973] Ch. 110.

[76] *Newton Abbot Co-operative Society Ltd.* v. *Williamson & Treadgold Ltd.* [1952] Ch. 286.

[77] *Drake* v. *Gray* [1936] Ch. 451; *Marquess of Zetland* v. *Driver* [1939] Ch. 1 at p. 8; *Newton Abbot Co-operative Society Ltd.* v. *Williamson* [1952] Ch. 286 at p. 289. There are some dicta of dubious authority in older cases suggesting that annexation might be implied from strong surrounding circumstances: M. & W., p. 764.

[78] *Re Union of London and Smith's Bank Ltd.'s Conveyance* [1933] Ch. 611 at p. 625.

[79] *Ibid.* at p. 631

[80] *Newton Abbot Co-operative Society Ltd.* v. *Williamson* [1952] Ch. 286 (covenant not to carry on ironmonger's business, the vendor-covenantee's address as party to the conveyance was 'Devonia' in Fore St., the street where the sold premises were situate: it so happened the vendor carried on an ironmongery business in 'Devonia').

[81] *Marten* v. *Flight Refuelling Ltd.* [1962] Ch. 115.

of dominant land in the case of easements,[82] though easements should be obvious enough from inspection of the premises, unlike restrictive covenants. If, 50 years ago, P covenanted with V and his successors in title not to carry on the trade of a chemist or publican at the purchased premises when the conveyance did not refer to V's nearby chemist's shop in any way and V's address in the conveyance was his home address in a village 10 miles away, should a purchaser of the servient land today not be entitled to assume that the covenant was a personal one, taken for the personal benefit of someone against drink and drugs, rather than be put to the expense of hiring detectives to inquire into the situs of shops and their ownership 50 years ago, just in case V might then have owned a nearby pub or chemist's shop?

(3) NEED FOR A CHAIN OF ASSIGNMENTS. In *Re Pinewood*[83] it was assumed that a plaintiff seeking to enforce an assignable covenant had to show a continuous chain of assignments of the benefit of the covenant contemporaneously with each transfer of land to successive transferees. Dicta in other cases[84] indicated that on the first assignment of the covenant together with the dominant land annexation occurred, the doctrine of assignment thus being a doctrine of delayed annexation.[85] After all, the very assignment of the covenant in the conveyance of the dominant land sufficiently indicates the dominant land so as to annex the covenant to the land.

However, John Mills Q.C. as deputy judge of the High Court[86] rejected the view that the first express assignment of an assignable covenant annexes the covenant to the land. This did not matter since he accepted the novel submission that section 62 of the Law of Property Act automatically passes the benefit of restrictive covenants unless a contrary intention is manifested. Previously, it had been assumed that section 62 only covered interests like easements and profits that lay in grant rather than depended on covenant, so that section 62 had not been taken at its face value.[87]

(4) THE IMPACT OF L.P.A. 1925, SECTION 78. Section 78 (1) states, "A covenant relating to any land of the covenantee shall be deemed to be made with the covenantee and his successors in title and the persons deriving title under him or them, and shall have effect as if such successors and other persons were expressed. For the purposes of this sub-section in connexion with covenants restrictive of the user of land 'successors in title' shall be deemed to include the owners and

---

[82] *Johnstone* v. *Holdway* [1963] 1 Q.B. 601 though the deed there, perhaps, did contain sufficient to identify the dominant land: J.F. Garner, (1962) 26 Conv. 248.
[83] [1958] Ch. 280.
[84] *Stilwell* v. *Blackman* [1968] Ch. 508; *Renals* v. *Cowlishaw* (1878) 9 Ch.D. 125 at pp. 130–131; *Rogers* v. *Hosegood* [1900] 2 Ch. 388 at p. 408; *Reid* v. *Bickerstaff* [1909] 2 Ch. 305 at p. 326.
[85] D.J.H., (1971) 87 L.Q.R. 539 at pp. 565–567.
[86] *Federated Homes Ltd.* v. *Mill Lodge Properties Ltd.* [1980] 1 All E.R. 371 at p. 378.
[87] D.J.H., (1971) 87 L.Q.R. 539 at pp. 570–571.

occupiers for the time being of the land of the covenantee intended to be benefited."

Section 79 states, "(1) A covenant relating to any land of a covenantor or capable of being bound by him, shall, unless a contrary intention is expressed, be deemed to be made by the covenantor on behalf of himself his successors in title and the persons deriving title under him or them, and, subject as aforesaid, shall have effect as if such successors and other persons were expressed. (2) For the purposes of this section in connexion with covenants restrictive of the user of land 'successors in title' shall be deeemed to include the owners and occupiers for the time being of such land."

Section 79 has been held to be a "word-saving" provision which does not change the law.[88] Thus, the fact that a covenantor is treated as covenanting for himself and his successors in title and occupiers for the time being of the land does not mean that the burden passes to his successors in title and occupiers of the land unless, under the general law, the burden of the covenant passes to them.

Section 78, too, was assumed to be a "word-saving" provision.[89] Thus, the fact that a covenant is treated as being with the covenantee and his successors in title and the occupiers for the time being of the land does not mean that the benefit passes to the successors in title and occupiers for the time being of the land unless, under the general law, the benefit can pass to them, *e.g.* by annexation or assignment. The section cannot annex since its covenanting terms are general or neutral and so cannot reveal an intention to benefit identified dominant land such as Blackacre or the vendor's adjoining lands. If the section intended annexation it would need to be drafted after the fashion of sections 76 (6) and 77 (5) with a further sentence like "The benefit of such covenants shall be annexed and incident to and shall go with each and every part of the land of the covenantee intended to be benefited unless a contrary intention is expressed." Indeed, section 78 does not allow of any contrary intention, which is a reason for taking it only as a word-saving provision, for otherwise it would bring about automatic annexation in the case of all restrictive covenants relating to land and thus abolish the doctrine of assignment.

Nevertheless, without appreciating this, the Court of Appeal in *Federated Homes Ltd.* v. *Mill Lodge Properties Ltd.*[90] took the view that section 78 annexes restrictive covenants to the land intended to be benefited, simply stating, without giving reasons that "section 79

---

[88] *Tophams Ltd.* v. *Earl of Sefton* [1967] 1 A.C. 50 at pp. 73 and 81 *per* Lords Upjohn and Wilberforce.

[89] Though in *Smith* v. *R. Douglas Catchment Board* [1949] 2 K.B. 500 the Court of Appeal seemed prepared to make a covenantor liable at law not just to the fee simple owner but also to a tenant on the basis of s. 78: *ante*, p. 441, D.W. Elliott (1956) 20 Conv. 43; G.H. Newsom, (1981) 97 L.Q.R. 32 at pp. 44–46.

[90] [1980] 1 W.L.R. 594, D. J. Hurst (1982) 2 *Legal Studies* 53.

involves quite different considerations."[91] In the case, the vendor sold off his blue land to the defendant but took an assignable restrictive covenant for the benefit of his adjacent red and green land which he then sold to B, expressly assigning the benefit of the defendant's covenant. B then conveyed the green land to the plaintiff, expressly assigning the benefit of the covenant. As a result of this unbroken chain of assignments the Court held[92] "that that is sufficient to entitle the plaintiff to relief and that the plaintiff's right to relief would be no greater if it were held it also had the benefit of the covenant in its capacity as owner of the red land." However, since the judge had dealt with both areas of land the Court went on to do the same.

The red land had been conveyed with an express assignment of the covenant to U.D.T. who had later transferred it to the plaintiff, but without expressly assigning the covenant. The judge had granted an injunction to the plaintiff on the basis that the covenant was vested in the plaintiff as owner of the green land by virtue of a chain of assignments, and as owner of the red land by virtue of implied assignment under section 62 of the Law of Property Act.

The Court of Appeal, without expressing any view upon section 62, boldly seized upon section 78 as operating from the outset to annex the covenant to each and every part of the red and green land so as automatically thereafter to pass therewith, so the plaintiff was entitled to an injunction. The court made the assumption that since section 78 mentions successors in title and occupiers for the time being it necessarily follows that such persons must be able to enforce the covenant, and for this to be possible it follows the covenant must be treated as annexed to the land. However, this reasoning in respect of section 79 has been rejected[93] and, similarly, under section 56 a person named as successor in title cannot enforce the benefit of a covenant unless under the general law entitled so to do.[94]

The Court of Appeal's views are thus highly controversial,[95] and may even be obiter alone,[96] so that the law is in an unsatisfactory state requiring consideration by the House of Lords. One must accept that there is Court of Appeal authority for section 78 automatically annexing all restrictive covenants relating to land to each and every part of the land. One might have had more confidence in such view if the court had appreciated that this abolishes the doctrine of assignment for all post 1925 restrictive covenants.[97]

---

[91] *Ibid.* at p. 606.
[92] *Ibid.* at p. 603.
[93] *Tophams Ltd.* v. *Earl of Sefton* [1967] 1 A.C. at pp. 73, 81.
[94] *Ante*, p. 440.
[95] D.J. Hayton, (1980) 43 M.L.R. 445; G.H. Newsom, (1981) 97 L.Q.R. 32.
[96] The green land covenant entitled the plaintiff to relief against the defendant who was the original covenantor and so liable at law.
[97] Many cases since 1925 have thus been decided *per incuriam* if this be correct.

(c) *Scheme of development.* (1) MUTUAL ENFORCEABILITY. Where land has been laid out in lots which are to be sold to purchasers and built upon, restrictions are often imposed on the purchasers of each lot for the benefit of the estate generally, such as covenants restraining trading on the estate, prohibiting the erection of cheap buildings and the like. In the ordinary way, these covenants would be enforceable only by the vendor. But much of the purpose of the covenants given by a purchaser of one lot would be lost if they could not be enforced—

(i) by those who have previously bought lots, and
(ii) by those who subsequently buy the unsold lots.

Each of these results could be achieved without any special rules for schemes of development. The first would be achieved if the purchaser's covenants were expressly made with those who had previously bought lots as well as with the vendor. The second could be achieved by the covenant being expressed to be for the benefit of the whole or any part of the land retained by the vendor, and so attaching the benefit of them to each lot sold in the future, or by the vendor expressly assigning the benefit of the covenants with each lot sold.[98]

(2) GENERAL PRINCIPLE OF DEVELOPMENT SCHEMES. It is, however, unnecessary for these arrangements to be made. There is a wide principle that where an owner of a defined[99] area of land deals with it on the footing of imposing restrictive obligations on the use of various parts of it as and when he sells them off, for the common benefit of himself (insofar as he retains any land) and of the various purchasers *inter se*, and the purchasers purchase on this footing then the common intention gives rise to an independent equity which binds each owner (including the vendor) as soon as the first part is sold.[1] This common intention may appear either expressly from the terms of a deed of mutual covenant[2] or the construction of a series of conveyances[3] or impliedly from extrinsic evidence of the conditions for a building scheme.[3]

(3) BUILDING SCHEME IN PARTICULAR. The conditions of a building scheme were for the most part laid down in *Elliston* v. *Reacher.*[4] These are as follows:

[98] See *ante*, pp. 447–453.
[99] *Lund* v. *Taylor* (1975) 31 P. & C.R. 167.
[1] *Baxter* v. *Four Oaks Properties Ltd.* [1965] Ch. 816 at p. 825; *Re Dolphin's Conveyance* [1970] Ch. 654; *Brunner* v. *Greenslade* [1971] Ch. 993 at pp. 1003–1005 stating the principles.
[2] *Baxter* v. *Four Oaks Properties Ltd.* (*supra*).
[3] See *Re Dolphin's Conveyance, supra*, at pp. 662, 663; D.J.H., (1971) 87 L.Q.R. 539 at pp. 546–551.
[4] [1908] 2 Ch. 374 at p. 384; affd. [1908] 2 Ch. 665. The first real hint of the doctrine was in *Western* v. *MacDermott* (1866) L.R. 1 Eq. 499; but see *Re Pinewood Estate, Farnborough* [1958] Ch. 280 at pp. 286, 287.

(i) The plaintiff and defendant must both have derived title from a common vendor or a successor in title thereto who is bound in equity by the obligations of the common vendor.[5]

(ii) Previously to the sale of the plaintiff's and defendant's plot, the common vendor must have laid out or intended to lay out the estate in lots subject to restrictions which were intended to be imposed on all of them and were consistent only with some general scheme of development.

(iii) The common vendor must have intended the restrictions to be for the benefit not merely of himself but of all lots sold.[6]

(iv) The plaintiff's and defendant's plots must both have been bought from the common vendor on the footing that the restrictions were to be for the benefit of the other lots.

(v) The area to which the scheme extends must be clearly defined.[7]

The whole essence of a building scheme is that each purchaser should know when he buys his plot from the common vendor that the covenants given by him are to be enforceable by the owners of all the other lots. It is not necessary to prove an express undertaking by him that this should be so, provided the circumstances show that he must have realised it. If before his purchase he saw some plan of the estate with the restrictions endorsed thereon, as in *Elliston* v. *Reacher*, this suffices; but the absence of a proper plan may be fatal.[8] The reservation by the common vendor of a power to release all or part of the land from the restrictions does not negative a building scheme, nor is it essential that the restrictions imposed on each plot should be identical; it suffices that there is some general scheme of development.[9]

(4) SUB-SCHEMES. Where a lot has been divided into sub-lots, the scheme may be enforceable by and between the purchasers of the sub-lots.[10] Correspondingly, where two or more lots come into the same hands, the covenants are not *pro tanto* extinguished but become enforceable between the owners of the lots if and when they are again separated.[11]

---

[5] *Re Dolphin's Conveyance* [1970] Ch. 654. The scheme crystallises when the first plot is sold so that if the owner then dies his devisee is bound to continue with the scheme: *Brunner* v. *Greenslade (supra)*.

[6] Which may be hard to prove: see, *e.g. Tucker* v. *Vowles* [1893] 1 Ch. 195.

[7] This last condition was added by *Reid* v. *Bickerstaff* [1909] 2 Ch. 305: see *Kelly* v. *Barrett* [1924] 2 Ch. 379 at p. 401.

[8] *e.g. Osborne* v. *Bradley* [1903] 2 Ch. 446; *Harlow* v. *Hartog* (1977) 245 E.G. 140.

[9] *Pearce* v. *Maryon-Wilson* [1935] Ch. 188; *Reid* v. *Bickerstaff* [1909] 2 Ch. 305 at p. 319.

[10] *Brunner* v. *Greenslade* [1971] Ch. 993.

[11] *Texaco Antilles Ltd.* v. *Kernochan* [1973] A.C. 609. Contrast restrictive covenants where no scheme exists: they become extinguished if the dominant and servient land are owned and occupied by the same person: *Re Tiltwood* [1978] Ch. 269.

(5) BUILDINGS ALREADY ERECTED. If a fully-built upon estate is disposed of in sections, and conditions analogous to those laid down for schemes are satisfied, the covenants will be enforceable as in schemes.[12] Again, the principle of a scheme has been applied to a block of residential flats, preventing the landlord from letting or using any of them otherwise than for residential purposes,[13] but the court will be slow to infer a letting scheme from the mere similarity of the covenants when each floor of a large house is sub-let separately.[14]

Sect. 4. Enforceability of Restrictive Covenants

The enforceability of a restrictive covenant may come into question in any of three ways.

1. In an action to enforce the covenant.
2. On application to the court for a declaration.
3. On application to the Lands Tribunal for the discharge or modification of the covenant.

1. Action to enforce the covenant. Prima facie, a restrictive covenant remains enforceable indefinitely.[15] In certain cases, however, the court may refuse to enforce an action brought by the person entitled to the benefit of a covenant. Thus if the person entitled to enforce the covenant has remained inactive in the face of open breaches for so long and in such circumstances that a reasonable person would believe that the covenant no longer applies, the court will not enforce it[16]; and the same applies if the neighbourhood is so completely changed (as from a residential to a shopping area) that an action to enforce the covenant would be unmeritorious, not bona fide and brought with some ulterior motive.[17]

2. Declaration by the court. Sometimes a landowner will be content to break a covenant and rely upon being able to establish one of the above defences if an action is brought. This, however, will not always be satisfactory, as where it is desired to sell or lease the land and the purchaser or lessee wishes to be assured that he is in no danger from the covenant. Consequently, provision has now been made permitting an application to the court for a declaration whether any freehold land is affected by any restriction, and if so, the nature, extent and enforceability of it.[18] This provision is often used in respect of the

---

[12] *Torbay Hotel Ltd.* v. *Jenkins* [1927] 2 Ch. 255 at p. 241.
[13] See *Hudson* v. *Cripps* [1896] 1 Ch. 265.
[14] *Kelly* v. *Battershell* [1949] 2 All E.R. 830.
[15] See *Mackenzie* v. *Childers* (1889) 43 Ch.D. 265 at p. 279.
[16] *Chatsworth Estates Co.* v. *Fewell* [1931] 1 Ch. 224.
[17] *Ibid.*; *Westripp* v. *Baldock* [1939] 1 All E.R. 279.
[18] L.P.A. 1925, s. 84 (2).

many nineteenth-century covenants which are today unenforceable through non-compliance with the rules governing the transfer of the benefit of the covenants. There is no power under this head to modify or discharge a valid covenant.

3. Discharge or modification by the Lands Tribunal. In some cases a covenant may still be enforceable, but it may be undesirable for this state of affairs to continue. Consequently, a discretionary[19] power has been given to the Lands Tribunal[20] to modify or discharge the restrictive covenant with or without the payment of compensation.[21] The applicant must bring his case within one of four heads.

(a) *Obsolete.* By reason of changes in the character of the property or neighbourhood or other material circumstances the restriction is obsolete.

(b) *Obstructive.* Its continued existence would impede some reasonable use of the land for public or private purposes, and either it confers no practical benefit of substantial value or is contrary to the public interest and (in either case) any loss can be adequately compensated in money.[22]

(c) *Agreement.* The persons of full age and capacity entitled to the benefit of the restrictions have agreed, either expressly or by implication by their acts and omissions, to the discharge or modification sought.

(d) *No injury.* The discharge or modification would not injure the persons entitled to the benefit of the covenant.

The provisions under paragraphs 2 and 3 above apply to restrictions whenever made, but do not apply to restrictions imposed on a disposition made either gratuitously or for a nominal consideration for public purposes. They apply to restrictions on freehold land, and to restrictions on leasehold land if the lease was made for more than 40 years and at least 25 have expired[23]; but they do not apply to mining leases.[24]

There is also provision for the county court to authorise the conversion of a house into two or more tenements in contravention of a restrictive covenant or a provision in a lease if owing to changes in

---

[19] *Driscoll* v. *Church Commissioners for England* [1957] 1 Q.B. 330.
[20] Lands Tribunal Act 1949, s. 1 (4).
[21] L.P.A. 1925, s. 84 (1), as extended by L.P.A. 1969, s. 28. An applicant may be required to accept reasonable alternative restrictions.
[22] See *Re Bass Ltd.'s Application* (1973) 26 P. & C.R. 156; H.W. Wilkinson (1979) 129 N.L.J. 523.
[23] *Ridley* v. *Taylor* [1965] 1 W.L.R. 611.
[24] L.P.A. 1925, s. 84 (12), as amended by Landlord and Tenant Act 1954, s. 52.

the neighbourhood the house cannot be readily let as a whole, or if planning permission for the conversion has been granted.[25]

Sect. 5. Restrictive Covenants and Town Planning

In recent years, the extension of town and country planning control[26] has to some extent reduced the importance of restrictive covenants. If planning control imposes restrictions which will preserve the amenities of a neighbourhood, landowners have little incentive to impose restrictive covenants with the same object. Nevertheless, restrictive covenants have not been superseded by planning control. A landowner must see that what he proposes to do will contravene neither the private system of restrictive covenants nor the public system of planning control; and restrictive covenants sometimes extend to matters not usually dealt with by planning law. Further a covenantee has the enforcement of the covenant under his control, whereas a landowner may be disappointed in the way in which the local planning authority imposes or enforces planning control against his neighbours. Nevertheless, the practical advice to give a landowner whose neighbour's activities are objectionable is often not to launch proceedings to enforce any apposite restrictive covenant, with consequent delay, expense and uncertainty, but to encourage the local planning authority to exercise its powers of enforcing planning control.[27]

Sect. 6. Registered Land

Just as the burden of a restrictive covenant affecting unregistered land only binds such land if the covenant (created after 1925 and not made between a lessor and lessee) has been protected by entry of a Class D (ii) land charge,[28] so in the case of registered land such land is only bound if the covenant (not being made between a lessor and lessee[29]) is protected by entry on the register of a notice.[30] A person taking under a registered disposition for value will take free from an unprotected restrictive covenant[31]: it ranks as a minor interest.[32]

The fact that a notice protects a restrictive covenant does not mean that such covenant is necessarily enforceable since a notice only

---

[25] Housing Act 1957, s. 165. See *Josephine Trust Ltd.* v. *Champagne* [1963] 2 Q.B. 160.
[26] *Post*, pp. 553 *et seq.*
[27] For these powers, see *post*, p. 559.
[28] See *ante*, p. 94.
[29] The lease containing restrictive covenants will be available for inspection.
[30] L.R.A., s. 50. In case of difficulty with the alleged covenantor a caution could, of course, be entered.
[31] L.R.A., ss. 20 (1), 23 (1).
[32] *Hodges* v. *Jones* [1935] Ch. 657 at p. 671.

protects rights to the extent that they are valid.[33] In the past[34] it was often the case that the benefit of the covenant could not be shown to have passed to the plaintiff.

Except in the case of building schemes it has usually been difficult for an applicant to establish clearly that he has the benefit of a restrictive covenant. It has thus not been normal practice for the benefit of restrictive covenants to appear on the register.[35] In some cases, though, the Registrar has entered a note on the register that a transfer or conveyance contains covenants which were expressed to be imposed for the benefit of the land in this title.[36]

Any release, discharge or modification of a restrictive covenant should be noted on the register.[37]

[33] L.R.A., s. 52; *Cator* v. *Newton* [1940] 1 K.B. 415.
[34] Before *Federated Homes Ltd.* v. *Mill Lodge Properties Ltd.* [1980] 1 W.L.R. 594.
[35] Ruoff & Roper, pp. 347, 718.
[36] *Ibid.* This leaves open the question of enforceability.
[37] L.R.R. 212.

CHAPTER 13

MORTGAGES

Part 1

NATURE OF A MORTGAGE

1. Security. When one person lends money to another he may be content to make the loan without security, or he may demand some security for the payment of the money. In the former case, the lender has a right to sue for the money if it is not duly paid, but that is all; if the borrower becomes insolvent, the lender may lose part or all of his money. But if some security of adequate value is given for the loan, the lender is protected even if the borrower becomes insolvent, for the lender has a claim to the security which takes precedence over the claims of other creditors.

The most important kind of security is the mortgage. The essential nature of a mortgage is that it is a conveyance of a legal or equitable interest in property, with a provision for redemption, *i.e.* that upon repayment of a loan or the performance of some other obligation the conveyance shall become void or the interest shall be reconveyed.[1] The borrower is known as the "mortgagor," the lender as the "mortgagee."

2. Other transactions. A mortgage must be distinguished from a lien, a pledge and a charge.

(a) *Lien.* A lien may arise at common law, in equity or under certain statutes. A common law lien is the right to retain possession of the property of another until a debt is paid; thus a garage proprietor has a common law lien upon a motor-car repaired by him. This lien is a mere passive right of retention, giving no right to sell or otherwise deal with the property,[2] and is extinguished if the creditor parts with possession to the debtor or his agent.[3]

An equitable lien is not dependent upon a continued possession of the property[4] and in this respect resembles a mortgage. But it differs from a mortgage (*inter alia*) in that a mortgage is a right founded on contract whereas an equitable lien arises from general principles of equity which do not permit a man who has acquired property under a

---

[1] See *Santley* v. *Wilde* [1899] 2 Ch. 474.
[2] But see Disposal of Uncollected Goods Act 1952.
[3] *Pennington* v. *Reliance Motor Works Ltd.* [1923] 1 K.B. 127.
[4] *Wrout* v. *Dawes* (1858) 25 Beav. 369.

contract to keep it without payment.[5] Thus a vendor of land who has conveyed it without receiving the full purchase price has an equitable lien upon it for the balance unpaid.[6]

A statutory lien is the creature of the statute under which it arises, and the rights which it confers depend on the terms of that statute. Railways, shipowners and solicitors have been given such rights.

(b) *Pledge.* A pledge or pawn consists of the loan of money in return for the delivery of possession of chattels to the lender. Although the lender has certain powers of sale, the general property in the goods remains in the borrower and the lender has possession; in a mortgage, on the other hand, the lender acquires ownership and the borrower usually retains possession.

(c) *Charge.* For most practical purposes, a charge is regarded as a species of mortgage, and is dealt with accordingly in this chapter. Nevertheless, there is an essential difference between a mortgage and a charge. A mortgage is a conveyance of property subject to a right of redemption, whereas a charge conveys nothing and merely gives the chargee certain rights over the property concerned as security for the loan.[7]

Part 2

CREATION OF MORTGAGES

Sect. 1. Methods of Creating Legal Mortgages and Charges of Unregistered Land

The methods of creating a legal mortgage differ for freeholds and leaseholds. In each case, some mention must be made of the history of the subject before considering the position before 1926 and after 1925.

A. Freeholds

I. HISTORY

1. Twelfth and thirteenth centuries. In the twelfth and thirteenth centuries, the mortgagor leased the land to the mortgagee, who went into possession. This, as seen above, resembled a pledge. If the income from the land was used to discharge the mortgage debt, the transaction was known as *vivum vadium* (a live pledge), since it was self-redeeming. If the mortgagee kept the income, it was known as *mortuum vadium* (a dead pledge). This latter form was not unlawful,

---

[5] See *Mackreth* v. *Symmons* (1808) 15 Ves. 329 at p. 340.
[6] *Chapman* v. *Tanner* (1684) 1 Vern. 267.
[7] See *London County and Westminster Bank Ltd.* v. *Tompkins* [1918] 1 K.B. 515.

but the Church regarded it as sinful for a Christian to take the income. In either case, if the money was not repaid by the time the lease expired, the mortgagee could enlarge his lease into a fee simple.

2. Fifteenth century. By the middle of the fifteenth century, the usual form of mortgage had changed. Even in the thirteenth century, a form of mortgage by conveyance of the fee simple had been known and this form gradually ousted the others, for it gave seisin to the mortgagee. The mortgagor conveyed the land to the mortgagee in fee simple, subject to a condition that the mortgagor might re-enter and determine the mortgagee's estate if the money lent was repaid on a named date. The mortgagee still took possession forthwith. The condition was construed strictly; if the mortgagor was a single day late in offering to repay the money, he lost his land for ever and yet remained liable for the debt.

3. Seventeenth century. By the beginning of the seventeenth century two changes had taken place. First, the form of a mortgage was usually a conveyance in fee simple with a covenant to reconvey the property if the money was paid on the fixed date. This is the modern form, and it simplified proof of title; whether the fee simple was vested in the mortgagor or not no longer depended merely upon whether the money had been paid within the fixed time, but depended upon whether a reconveyance had been executed.[8]

Secondly, a far more important change had been made by the intervention of equity. Equity took the view that the property mortgaged was merely a security for the money lent, and that it was unjust that the mortgagor should lose his property merely because he was late in repaying the loan. At first, equity intervened in the cases of accident, mistake, special hardship and the like, but soon relief was given in all cases. Even if the date fixed for repayment had long passed, equity compelled the mortgagee to reconvey the property to the mortgagor on payment of the principal with interest and costs. The mortgagor was thus given an equitable right to redeem at a time when the agreement between the parties provided that the mortgagee was to be the absolute owner.[9] In short, for 300 years a mortgagor has had two separate rights of redemption:

(a) *Legal right to redeem on the fixed day.* At law, a mortgagor has no right to redeem either before or after the date fixed by the mortgage for redemption, but on that one day alone.

---

[8] See *Durham Brothers* v. *Robertson* [1898] 1 Q.B. 765 at p. 772.
[9] See *Salt* v. *Marquess of Northampton* [1892] A.C. 1 at pp. 18, 19; and see M. & W., pp. 888–892.

(b) *Equitable right to redeem thereafter.* Equity allowed the mortgagor an equitable right to redeem on any day after the date fixed for redemption by the mortgage. This is a right which can be exercised only on equitable terms.

This equitable right to redeem revolutionised mortgages, and probably lies at the root of Lord Macnaughten's statement that "No one . . . by the light of nature ever understood an English mortgage of real estate."[10] The sum total of the mortgagor's rights in equity is known as his equity of redemption. This must be distinguished from his equitable right to redeem; the latter does not exist until the legal date for redemption is past, whereas the equity of redemption exist as soon as the mortgage is made.[11] The equity of redemption is the mortgagor's right of ownership of the property subject to the mortgage,[12] and is an interesst in land which can be granted, devised, entailed and, in short, dealt with like any other interest in land.[13] The equitable right to redeem, on the other hand, is but one of the adjuncts of the equity of redemption; it is not the equity of redemption itself.

II. BEFORE 1926

As seen above, the usual method of creating a mortgage of freeholds before 1926 was by a conveyance of the fee simple subject to a proviso for redemption, namely, a covenant by the mortagee that he would reconvey the property if the money was repaid on a fixed date. That date was usually six months after the date of the mortgage, even though there was no real expectation by either party that the money would be repaid then.

Although a mortgage in this form left the mortgagor with a mere equity of redemption, this might be of considerable value (*e.g.* if the loan was £1,000 and the property worth £15,000) and could itself be mortgaged. But since it was merely equitable, any mortgage of it would also be equitable, for there could be no legal mortgage of something which existed only in equity. Thus before 1926 there could be only one legal mortgage of this kind on any property; all other mortgages were necessarily equitable.

III. AFTER 1925

By the Law of Property Act 1925,[14] freeholds can no longer be

---

[10] *Samuel* v. *Jarrah, etc., Corporation Ltd.* [1904] A.C. 323 at p. 326; and Maitland remarked that a mortgage is "one long *suppressio veri* and *suggesto falsi*" (*Equity,* p. 182).
[11] *Brown* v. *Cole* (1845) 14 Sim. 427; *Kreglinger* v. *New Patagonia Meat and Cold Storage Co. Ltd.* [1914] A.C. 25 at p. 48.
[12] *Re Wells* [1933] Ch. 29 at p. 52.
[13] See *Casborne* v. *Scarfe* (1738) 1 Atk. 603 at p. 605.
[14] s. 85 (1).

mortgaged by conveyance of the fee simple. Two methods only are possible:

(i) by a demise for a term of years absolute, subject to a provision for cesser on redemption; or

(ii) by a charge by deed expressed to be by way of legal mortgage.

1. Demise for a term of years absolute. (a) *Mortgages made after 1925.* The term of years granted to the mortgagee is usually a long term, *e.g.* 3,000 years. The provision for cesser on redemption is a clause providing that the term of years shall cease when the loan is repaid; it is really unnecessary, for on repayment the term becomes a satisfied term and automatically ceases.[15] In other respects, the position is much as it was before 1926. A fixed redemption date is still named, and it is still usually six months after the date of the mortgage; thereafter the mortgagor has an equitable right to redeem in lieu of his legal right. The difficulty that a mortgagee by demise has no right to the title deeds is obviated by an express provision giving a first mortgagee the same right to the deeds as if he had the fee simple.[16]

The principal change brought about by the new legislation is that the mortgagor now retains the legal fee simple. This does not mean that the equity of redemption has lost its importance; a fee simple giving the right to possession of land only when a lease for 3,000 years has expired is of little value compared with the right to insist that the fee simple shall forthwith be freed from the term of 3,000 years on payment of the money due. Indeed, the term "equity of redemption" is sometimes used as including the mortgagor's legal estate. But the change means that the mortgagor has, in addition to his equity of redemption, a legal fee simple out of which a further term of years may be granted. Consequently, second, third and subsequent mortgages may all be legal after 1925. Thus A, the fee simple owner of Blackacre, may create successive legal mortgages in favour of X, Y and Z. The term he grants to each mortgagee is usually at least one day longer than the term under the previous mortgage. Thus X may be given 2,000 years, Y 2,000 years and a day, and Z 2,000 years and two days, so that each mortgagee has a reversion upon the prior mortgage term.

The rights of Y and Z, though seemingly rather nebulous, are in fact quite substantial. Thus if A defaults and the property is sold by X under his power of sale,[17] the money is paid first to X to discharge his mortgage, the balance to Y to discharge his, the balance to discharge Z's mortgage and any surplus to A; in short, the parties rank in the

---

[15] See *ante*, p. 357.
[16] L.P.A. 1925, s. 85 (1).
[17] *Post*, pp. 475 *et seq.*

order X, Y, Z, A. Further, any mortgagee always has the right, upon giving proper notice, to insist upon redeeming any prior mortgage[18]; thus Y might insist upon buying up X's mortgage and so succeeding to X's position.

An attempt to create a first mortgage by conveyance of the fee simple now operates as the grant of a term of 3,000 years without impeachment of waste but subject to cesser on redemption.[19] An attempt to create a second or subsequent mortgage in the same way takes effect as the grant of a term one day longer than the preceeding term.[20] The system is thus foolproof.

(b) *Transitional provisions.* Mortgages made before 1926 were automatically brought into line with the new scheme by being converted into mortgages by subdemise, subject to cesser on redemption.[21]

2. Charge by deed expressed to be by way of legal mortgage. This is a new creation of the Law of Property Act 1925,[22] which is sometimes for brevity called a "legal charge." To be effective, it must be—

(i) made by deed: a charge merely in writing will have no effect at law; and

(ii) expressed to be by way of legal mortgage: the deed must contain a statement that the charge is made by way of legal mortgage, though such a statement is not required where the title to the land is registered.[23]

The effect of such a charge of freeholds is that the chargee (whether first or subsequent) gets the same protection, powers and remedies as if he had a term of 3,000 years without impeachment of waste.[24] Although he gets no actual legal term of years, he is as fully protected as if he had one.[25] The name "charge" is thus a little misleading because although a legal charge is by nature a charge and not a mortgage,[26] for all practical purposes it is indistinguishable from a mortgage.

The advantages of a legal charge are considered below.[27]

---

[18] *Post*, pp. 497–499.
[19] L.P.A. 1925, s. 85 (2).
[20] *Ibid.*
[21] *Ibid.* 1st Sched., Pt. VII.
[22] s. 87.
[23] *Cityland and Property (Holdings) Ltd.* v. *Dabrah* [1968] Ch. 166, Ruoff & Roper, p. 492.
[24] L.P.A. 1925, s. 87 (1).
[25] See *Regent Oil Co. Ltd.* v. *J.A. Gregory (Hatch End) Ltd.* [1966] Ch. 402.
[26] *Ante*, p. 461.
[27] *Post*, pp. 467–468.

B. Leaseholds

I. HISTORY

The intervention of equity in the case of mortgages of leaseholds closely resembles that in the case of freeholds.[28]

II. BEFORE 1926

A legal mortgage of leaseholds could be made before 1926 in either of two ways:

(i) By assignment of the lease to the mortgagee with a covenant for reassignment on redemption; or
(ii) By the grant to the mortgagee of a sub-lease at least one day shorter than the lease, with a proviso for cesser on redemption.

The first method was rarely employed, for it meant that the mortgagee became liable on such of the covenants in the lease as touched and concerned the land. This was not so if the second method was employed, for then the mortgagee was only an underlessee and there was privity neither of contract nor of estate between him and the lessor.[29] Whichever form was employed, the mortgage normally contained the usual provision for redemption on a fixed date six months ahead, and thereafter the mortgagor had an equitable right to redeem.

Where a mortgage had been made by assignment, second and subsequent mortgages were made by a mortgage of the mortgagor's equity of redemption. Where the prior mortgage had been made by sub-lease, subsequent mortgages were made by the grant of other sub-leases, each normally being longer than the previous one.

III. AFTER 1925

By the Law of Property Act 1925,[30] leaseholds can no longer be mortgaged by assignment. Two methods only are possible:

(i) By a subdemise for a term of years absolute, subject to a provision for cesser on redemption, the term being at least one day shorter than the term vested in the mortgagor; or
(ii) By a charge by deed expressed to be by way of legal mortgage.

1. Subdemise for a term of years absolute. (a) *Mortgages made after 1925*. The term of the sub-lease must be at least one day shorter than the term of the lease which is being mortgaged, otherwise it would operate as an assignment.[31] If the lease requires the tenant to obtain

---

[28] *Ante*, pp. 461–465.
[29] *Ante*, p. 377.
[30] s. 86 (1).
[31] *Beardman* v. *Wilson* (1868) L.R. 4 C.P. 57; *ante*, p. 347.

the landlord's licence before a subdemise by way of mortgage is made, the licence cannot be unreasonably refused.[32] The first mortgagee has the same rights to the deeds as if his mortgage had been made by assignment.[33] It is usual to make the sub-term 10 days shorter than the lease, so as to allow room for second and subsequent mortgages. Thus if T's 50 years' lease is mortgaged, the first mortgage will be secured by a lease for 50 years less 10 days, the second by 50 years less 9 days, and so on. But this is not essential, for the old rule[34] that a lease may take effect in reversion upon another lease of he same or greater length has been confirmed by the Law of Property Act 1925.[35] Thus if the first mortgage was made by a sub-term of 50 years less one day, the second mortgage would be secured by a sub-term of the same length and so on; each mortgage would take effect in its proper order.

An attempted mortgage by way of assignment after 1925 operates as a subdemise for a term of years absolute subject to cesser on redemption. A first or only mortgagee takes a term 10 days shorter than the lease mortgaged. Second and subsequent mortgages take terms one day longer than under the previous mortgage, if this is possible; in every case, however, the sub-term must be at least one day shorter than term mortgaged.[36]

(b) *Transitional provisions.* On January 1, 1926, mortgages made by assignment before 1926 were automatically converted into mortgages by subdemise, subject to cesser on redemption.[37]

2. Charge by way of legal mortgage. (a) *Rights and remedies.* A charge by deed expressed to be by way of legal mortgage gives the mortgagee (whether first or subsequent) the same rights and remedies as if he had a sub-term one day shorter than the term vested in the mortgagor.[38] As in the case of freeholds, he gets no actual term of years but is as fully protected as if he had one. He thus ranks as if he were a sub-lessee for the purposes of seeking relief from forfeiture of the lease under section 146 (4) of the Law of Property Act 1925.[39]

(b) *Advantages of a legal charge.* There is nothing in the Law of Property Act 1925 which suggests any reason why a legal charge, either of freeholds or leaseholds, should be preferred to an ordinary mortgage. But there seem to be three practical advantages in using a legal charge.

---

[32] L.P.A. 1925, s. 86 (1).
[33] *Ibid.*
[34] *Re Moore & Hulme's Contract* [1912] 2 Ch. 105.
[35] s. 149 (5).
[36] L.P.A. 1925, s. 86 (2); *Grangeside Properties Ltd.* v. *Collingwood Securities Ltd.* [1964] 1 W.L.R. 139.
[37] *Ibid.* 1st Sched., Pt. VIII.
[38] L.P.A. 1925, s. 87 (1).
[39] *Grand Junction Co. Ltd.* v. *Bates* [1954] 2 Q.B. 160.

(i) It is a convenient way of mortgaging freeholds and leaseholds together; the deed is shortened by stating that all the properties specified in the schedule are charged by way of legal mortgage, instead of setting out the length of the mortgage terms in each case.

(ii) Probably the granting of a legal charge on a lease does not amount to a breach of any covenant in that lease against sub-letting, for the charge creates no actual sub-lease in favour of the mortgagee but merely gives him the same rights as if he had a sub-lease.

(iii) The form of a legal charge is short and simple.

Nowadays, mortgages are usually effected by way of legal charge so that Professor Fairest has commented,[40] "It may be doubted whether the preservation of the mortgage by demise continues to serve any useful purpose."

(c) *Protection of legal mortgages and legal charges.* As will later be seen,[41] a legal mortgage or charge, if not protected by deposit of title deeds should be registered as a Class C (i) land charge.

Sect. 2 Methods of Creating Equitable Mortgages and Charges of Unregistered Land

A. Equitable Mortgages

1. Mortgage of an equitable interest. If the mortgagor has no legal estate but only an equitable interest, any mortgage he effects must necessarily be equitable. Beneficiaries under a trust have mere equitable interests and so can create only equitable mortgages.

The 1925 legislation has not affected the form of equitable mortgages of equitable interests. Such mortgages are still made by a conveyance of the equitable interest with a proviso for reconveyance. The actual form of words employed is immaterial provided the meaning is plain.[42] Nor need the mortgage be made by deed, as is essential for a legal mortgage; but it must either be in writing signed by the mortgagor or his agent authorised in writing, or else be made by will.[43] The mortgagee should give notice to the trustees to secure priority under the Rule in *Dearle* v. *Hall*.[44]

2. Informal mortgages. Under the same principles as apply to leaseholds,[45] equity treats an enforceable contract to create a legal

---

[40] *Mortgages* (2nd ed.), p. 15.
[41] *Post,* p. 505.
[42] See *William Brandt's Sons & Co.* v. *Dunlop Rubber Co. Ltd.* [1905] A.C. 454 at p. 462.
[43] L.P.A. 1925, s. 53 (1).
[44] (1828) 3 Russ. 1, *post,* p. 510.
[45] *Ante,* p. 337.

mortgage as an actual mortgage,[46] provided it is supported by sufficient evidence in writing or a sufficient act of part performance. Similarly, an imperfect legal mortgage satisfying these requirements is treated as an agreement for a mortgage and thus as an equitable mortgage.[47]

Evidence in writing and part performance have been discussed above.[48] All that need be said here is that since 1783[49] the rule has been that a mere deposit of the title deeds which cannot be accounted for in any other way is taken as part performance of a contract to create a mortgage, even if not a word about such a contract has been said[50]; such a deposit thus creates an equitable mortgage. The deposit must be made for the purpose of giving a security, however; delivery of the deeds by mistake or to enable a mortgage to be drawn up does not suffice.[51] But it is not essential that all the title deeds should be deposited, provided those which are delivered are material evidence of title.[52] The mortgagee has no lien on the deeds apart from his right to retain them under the mortgage, and so if the mortgage contract is void the deeds must be given up.[53]

In practice, mortgages by deposit of title deeds are nearly always accompanied by a deed setting out the terms of the mortgage, or requiring the mortgagor to execute a legal mortgage when so requested. This prevents disputes, and the execution of the deed gives the mortgagee additional powers.[54] It is a matter of construction whether the mortgage was created by the deposit of the deeds, to which the accompanying deed is ancillary, or by the execution of the deed, to which the deposit is ancillary.[55]

B. Equitable Charges

An equitable charge is created where certain property is appropriated to the discharge of some debt or other obligation without there being any change in ownership either at law or in equity.[56] Thus if a man signs a written contract agreeing that he thereby charges his real estate with the payment of £500 to A, an equitable charge is created[57]; the same applies where a will or voluntary settlement

---

[46] See *Ex p. Wright* (1812) 19 Ves. 255 at p. 258.
[47] *Parker* v. *Housefield* (1834) 2 My. & K. 419 at p. 420.
[48] *Ante*, pp. 136 *et seq.*, 141 *et seq.* Advancement of the money will not normally be sufficient part performance: *Rogers* v. *Challis* (1859) 27 Beav. 175 but *cf. Steadman* v. *Steadman* [1976] A.C. 536.
[49] *Russel* v. *Russel* (1783) 1 Bro.C.C. 269.
[50] *Bozon* v. *Williams* (1829) 3 Y. & J. 150 at p. 161.
[51] *Norris* v. *Wilkinson* (1806) 12 Ves. 192.
[52] *Lacon* v. *Allen* (1856) 3 Drew. 579.
[53] *Re Molton Finance Ltd.* [1968] Ch. 325.
[54] *Post*, pp. 476, 485.
[55] *Paul* v. *Nath Saha* [1939] 2 All E.R. 737.
[56] *London County and Westminster Bank Ltd.* v. *Tompkins* [1918] 1 K.B. 515 at p. 528.
[57] *Matthews* v. *Goodday* (1861) 31 L.J.Ch. 282 at pp. 282, 283.

charges money on land.[58] An enforceable contract to create a legal charge presumably creates an equitable charge.[59]

C. Protection of Equitable Mortgages and Charges

Equitable mortgages and charges should be protected by entry of a Class C (iii) land charge[60] if protection has not been obtained by having the title deeds to the land deposited with the mortgagee.

Sect. 3. Methods of Mortgaging Registered Land

A mortgage or charge of registered land will either be a registered charge or it will be a minor interest.

A. Registered Charges

Legal mortgages or charges are created in the same way as for unregistered land[61] but need to be perfected by entry of a notice of the registered charge against the charged title and by issue of a charge certificate to the chargee, the land certificate remaining deposited in the Land Registry.[62]

The deed creating the charge may operate by way of demise or subdemise but, in the absence of any provision causing the deed to operate in this way, it will take effect as a charge by way of legal mortgage[63] as in the vast majority of cases: it is thus not strictly necessary to include the words "by way of legal charge."[64]

The registered charge is only fully effective when a notice is entered against the charged title in favour of the chargee or registered proprietor of the charge. Until then the deed is only effective between the parties.[65] On delivery of the relevant documents to the Land Registry the registered chargee obtains full legal title and thenceforth[66] can exercise the statutory powers of a mortgagee. As of such date, the registered chargee is subject to then-existing overriding interests and entries on the register.[67] This can create problems[68] where overriding interests may arise between the date of handing over the mortgage moneys and the date of registration of the charge.

---

[58] *Re Owen* [1894] 3 Ch. 220.
[59] *Swiss Bank* v. *Lloyds Bank* [1979] Ch. 548.
[60] *Ante*, p. 92.
[61] L.P.A., ss. 85, 86; L.R.A. s. 25.
[62] L.R.A., s. 65. If the land certificate is not deposited at the Registry (*e.g.* because already deposited with an equitable mortgagee) then no registered charge can be created, so no legal mortgage can be created, unlike the unregistered land position; Hayton, p. 120. The mortgagor will usually be pressurised by the prospective second mortgagee seeking a registered legal charge to persuade the first mortgagee to become a registered chargee.
[63] L.R.A., s. 27 (1).
[64] *Cityland & Property (Holdings) Ltd.* v. *Dabrah* [1968] Ch. 166.
[65] *Grace Rymer Ltd.* v. *Waite* [1958] Ch. 831.
[66] *Lever Finance Ltd.* v. *Needleman's Trustees* [1956] Ch. 375, L.R.A., ss. 19, 20, 26.
[67] L.R.A., ss. 5, 9, 20, 23; *Re Boyle's Claim* [1961] 1 W.L.R. 339.
[68] *Post*, pp. 517–518.

Nothing in the Act or the Rules expressly states that only legal mortgages or charges can be registered but, from the framework of the Act, it seems that this is intended to be the case.[69] It is, however, possible to argue that the Registrar ought to be prepared to allow equitable mortgages to be entered as registered charges since sections 27 and 34 of the Act allow, subject to any contrary entry in the register, for registered charges to take effect as legal mortgages and for registered chargees to have the powers of a legal mortgagee.[70] The "contrary entry" could relate to the charge being equitable. However, equitable mortgages or charges can be adequately protected as minor interests in any event where a deed contains a conveyancing device,[71] like a power of attorney, to enable the sale of the legal estate of the mortgagor in case of default by the mortgagor.

B. Minor Interests

Instead of using the registered charge a proprietor may mortgage his land in any of the ways permissible for unregistered land.[72] Until such mortgage becomes a registered charge it takes effect only in equity and is capable of being overridden as a minor interest unless protected[73] in one of the following ways.

1. Notice. If the land certificate is produced to the Land Registry then a notice of the mortgage may be entered against the mortgaged title so as to affect all subsequent dispositions of the title.[74]

2. Notice of deposit operating as a caution. Where a land certificate has been deposited with a mortgagee by way of security then a notice of deposit may be entered on the mortgaged title.[75] However, it only operates as if it were a mere caution against dealings.[76]

3. Caution against dealings. As someone interested in the land the mortgagee can take advantage of the residual method of protection, namely a caution against dealings,[77] where he does not have the land certificate[78] to enable him to enter a notice.

4. Possession of the land certificate. Possession of the land certificate on its own affords a measure of de facto protection, in that

---

[69] L.R.A., ss. 2, 3 (xi), 18 (4), 25–36; 106 (2); *Re White Rose Cottage* [1965] Ch. 940 at p. 949 *per* Lord Denning M.R. disagreeing with Wilberforce J. in the court below.
[70] Professor E.C. Ryder (1966) 19 Current L.P. 26 at p. 37.
[71] *Post*, p. 485.
[72] L.R.A., s. 106 (1).
[73] *Ibid.* s. 106 (2).
[74] *Ibid.* ss. 106 (3) (*a*), 49, 52, *ante*, p. 125.
[75] *Ibid.* s. 106 (3) (*b*), L.R.R. 239. Notice of intended deposit can first be entered: L.R.R. 240–242.
[76] I.R.R. 239 (4), *ante*, p. 127.
[77] L.R.A., ss. 54, 106 (3) (*c*).
[78] *Ibid.* s. 65.

it prevents the proprietor of the land from entering into any disposition that can only be effected by production of the land certificate.[79] However, this affords no protection against a lease for 21 or fewer years taking effect as a registered disposition under section 19 (2), so enabling the lessee to take free from minor interests not entered on the register.[80] Furthermore, leases exceeding 21 years can be substantively registered without production of the freehold land certificate,[81] the lessee taking subject to entries on the register and overriding interests but free from all other interests whatsoever.[82] A mortgagee should thus never rely merely on protection by possession of the land certificate.

It is important to ascertain whether a mortgage was created by deposit and supported by an ancillary deed or was created by a deed to which the deposit of the land certificate was ancillary.[83] Section 66 applies to the former but not the latter[84] and may affect questions of priority.[85] Where a land certificate has been deposited with a mortgagee to secure a loan it is customarily known as a lien by deposit rather than a mortgage by deposit, though in nature it is the same as a mortgage by deposit.[86]

C. Interests under Trusts

If someone with a life interest or interest in remainder in land held on trust for sale or under the Settled Land Act 1925 mortgages his interest by way of assignment, then the mortgagee should protect himself by priority caution entered in a minor interests index kept by the Land Registrar.[87] Date of entry of the priority caution governs priorities.[88]

Part 3

RIGHTS OF THE PARTIES UNDER A MORTGAGE OR CHARGE

The rights of the parties under a mortgage or charge will be considered under three heads:

  (i) The rights of the mortgagee or chargee;
  (ii) Rights common to both parties; and
  (iii) The rights of the mortgagor or chargor.

[79] *Barclays Bank Ltd.* v. *Taylor* [1974] Ch. 137.
[80] L.R.A., ss. 18 (3), 20 (1), 21 (3), 23 (1), 59 (6).
[81] *Strand Securities Ltd.* v. *Caswell* [1965] Ch. 958.
[82] Further see Hayton, pp. 122–123.
[83] *Ante,* p. 469.
[84] *Re White Rose Cottage* [1964] Ch. 483 at pp. 490–491 (Wilberforce J.)
[85] *Post,* p. 516, Hayton, p. 123.
[86] L.R.A., ss. 66, Ruoff & Roper, Chap. 27.
[87] L.R.A., s. 102, L.R.R. 229, Ruoff & Roper, Chap. 8. The Minor Interests Index has no other function. It is ripe for abolition.
[88] L.R.A., s. 102 (2).

Sect. 1. Rights of the Mortgagee or Chargee

A. Remedies for Enforcing Payment

Unless the parties have otherwise agreed, a mortgagee or chargee has five remedies available for enforcing payment. Three of the remedies are primarily directed to recovering the capital due and putting an end to the security: these are an action for the money, foreclosure, and sale. The other two remedies are taking possession and appointing a receiver. The latter primarily seeks merely to recover the interest due as originally did the former though, nowadays, it is in practice invariably sought so as to facilitate sale with vacant possession. Sale and appointing a receiver are rights which used to be conferred by the mortgage deed but are now given by statute; the other remedies are inherent in the nature of the transaction. A mortgagee will not be restrained from enforcing payment merely because the mortgagor has some large cross-claim against him.[89] The remedies available differ according to whether the mortgage or charge is legal or equitable.

I. LEGAL MORTGAGEE OR LEGAL CHARGEE

A legal mortgagee or legal chargee has the following remedies for enforcing his security.

1. To sue for the money due. At any time after the date fixed for payment the mortgagee may sue for the money lent.[90] This remedy is, of course, in no way peculiar to mortgages.

2. To foreclose. (a) *The right of foreclosure.* By giving the mortgagor an equitable right to redeem after he had lost his legal right of redemption, equity interfered with the bargain made between the parties. But equity prescribed limits to the equity of redemption which it created. Thus before 1926, a legal first mortgagee of freeholds had the fee simple vested in him, and once the legal date for redemption had passed, the mortgagor's right to redeem was merely equitable.[91] "Foreclosure" was the name given to the process whereby the mortgagor's equitable right to redeem was extinguished and the mortgagee left owner of the property, both at law and in equity. Equity had interfered to prevent the conveyance of the legal fee simple from having its full effect, and on foreclosure "the court simply removes the stop it has itself put on."[92] From the first the mortgagee was absolute owner at law, and foreclosure, for which *an*

---

[89] *Samuel Keller (Holdings) Ltd.* v. *Martins Bank Ltd.* [1971] 1 W.L.R. 43; *Inglis* v. *Commonwealth Trading Bank of Australia* (1972) 126 C.L.R. 161.
[90] See *Bolton* v. *Buckenham* [1891] 1 Q.B. 278.
[91] See *ante*, p. 463.
[92] *Carter* v. *Wake* (1877) 4 Ch.D. 605 at p. 606, *per* Jessel M.R.

order of the court is essential, made him an absolute owner in equity as well.

After 1925, a mortgagee does not have the whole legal estate of the mortgagor vested in him, but has, or is treated as if he has, only a long term of years in the case of freeholds and an underlease in the case of leaseholds. Consequently it is no longer sufficient for a decree of foreclosure merely to destroy the mortgagor's equity of redemption, and so the Law of Property Act 1925[93] provides that a foreclosure decree absolute shall vest the mortgagor's fee simple or term of years in the mortgagee.

The right to foreclose does not arise until the legal right to redeem has ceased to exist, *i.e.* until the legal date for redemption has passed[94] or until breach of a condition which had to be complied with to keep alive the legal right of redemption.[95] Once this has happened, the mortgagee may commence foreclosure proceedings unless he has agreed not to do so,[96] for sometimes the mortgagee contracts not to enforce the security by foreclosure or other means until he has given some specified notice or until the mortgagor has broken one of his covenants in the mortgage. If no redemption date is fixed or if the loan is repayable on demand, the right to foreclose arises when a demand for repayment has been made and a reasonable time thereafter has elapsed.[97]

(b) *Parties to a foreclosure action.* An action for foreclosure can be brought by any mortgagee of property, whether he is the original mortgagee or an assignee, and whether he is a first or subsequent mortgagee. The effect of a foreclosure order absolute in an action brought by the first mortgagee is to make him the sole owner both at law and in equity, free from any subsequent mortgages; if the action is brought by a second or subsequent mortgagee, he will hold the property subject to prior incumbrances, but free from all subsequent incumbrances.

As will be seen shortly,[98] a foreclosure action gives the mortgagor and all others interested in the equity of redemption an opportunity of redeeming the mortgage. Consequently, all persons interested in the equity of redemption must be made parties to the action. Thus if X has made successive mortgages of his property to A, B and C, and B starts foreclosure proceedings, A will not be affected by them and so need not be made a party to the action. But if the action is successful, C will lose his mortgage and X his equity of redemption, and so both must be made parties to the action.

---

[93] ss. 88 (2), 89 (2).
[94] *Williams* v. *Morgan* [1906] 1 Ch. 804.
[95] *Twentieth Century Banking Ltd.* v. *Wilkinson* [1977] Ch. 89.
[96] *Ramsbottom* v. *Wallis* (1835) 5 L.J.Ch. 92.
[97] *Toms* v. *Wilson* (1862) 4 B. & S. 442.
[98] *Post*, p. 497.

(c) *Procedure.* The first step in a foreclosure is to obtain from the court a foreclosure order *nisi.* This provides that if the mortgagor repays the money lent on a fixed day (usually six months from the accounts being settled by the master), the mortgage shall be discharged, but that if this is not done, the mortgagor shall be foreclosed. If there are several mortgagees and the first mortgagee is foreclosing, each mortgagee is given the alternative of either losing his security or else redeeming (paying off) the first mortgage. Sometimes the court will give the mortgagees successive periods to effect this redemption, but usually there will be only one period between them.[99] At the request of the mortgagee or of any person interested (*e.g.* the mortgagor) the court may order a sale of the property instead of foreclosure.[1]

(d) *Opening a foreclosure absolute.* If no order for sale is made and the property is not redeemed on the date fixed, a foreclosure order absolute is made. This destroys the mortgagor's equity of redemption and transfers his fee simple or term of years to the mortgagee,[2] who thus becomes sole owner at law and in equity, subject only to prior incumbrances. For registered land the order for foreclosure is completed by the registration of the proprietor of the charge as the proprietor of the land and by the cancellation of the charge.

However, although the order of foreclosure absolute appears to be final, it is not necessarily so, for the court will sometimes open a foreclosure absolute. Circumstances which may influence the court to do this are an accident at the last moment preventing the mortgagor from raising the money, any special value which the property had to the mortgagor (*e.g.* if it was an old family estate), a marked disparity between the value of the property and the amount lent, and the promptness of the application. Even if the mortgagee has sold the property after foreclosure absolute, the court may still open the foreclosure; this is unlikely, however, if the purchaser bought the property some time after foreclosure and without notice of circumstances which might induce the court to interfere.[3] The risk of this may reduce the purchase-price so that with this in mind a mortgagee might ask the court to order a sale instead of a foreclosure if he has no power of sale himself.[4]

3. To sell. (a) *History.* There is no right, either at common law or in

---

[99] *Platt* v. *Mendel* (1884) 27 Ch.D. 246. Under Administration of Justice Act 1973, s. 8 (3) the court may adjourn the proceedings if it appears that the mortgagor may be able within a reasonable period to pay the sums due: see *post*, p. 481.
[1] L.P.A. 1925, s. 91 (2) *Twentieth Century Banking Co. Ltd.* v. *Wilkinson* [1977] Ch. 99. See below, p. 481, for the discretionary powers of the court in the case of instalment mortgages of dwelling-houses.
[2] *Ibid.* s. 88 (2) L.R.A., 1925; s. 34 (3).
[3] *Campbell* v. *Holyland* (1877) 7 Ch.D. 166 at pp. 172, 173.
[4] See note 1 (*supra*).

equity, for a mortgagee to sell the mortgaged property free from the equity of redemption, although of course he can freely transfer the estate which is vested in him subject to the equity of redemption. Consequently, an express power was usually inserted in mortgage deeds enabling the mortgagee to sell the property free from the equity of redemption if certain specified events occurred. Lord Cranworth's Act 1860 gave a limited power of sale in the case of mortgages made after 1860, but this was usually thought too narrow to be relied upon. The Conveyancing Act 1881, however, gave a satisfactory power of sale which is now contained in the Law of Property Act 1925.[5]

(b) *The power.* Every mortgagee whose mortgage shows no contrary intention has a power of sale, provided—

(a) the mortgage was made by deed (and all legal mortgages must be made thus); and

(b) the mortgage money is due, *i.e.* the legal date for redemption has passed[6]; if the mortgage money is payable by instalments, the power of sale arises as soon as any instalment is in arrear.[7]

When these conditions have been fulfilled, the statutory power of sale *arises*; nevertheless, the power does not become *exercisable* unless one of the three following conditions has been satisfied[8]—

(i) notice requiring payment of the mortgage money has been served on the mortgagor and default has been made in payment of part or all of it for three months thereafter; or

(ii) some interest under the mortgage is two months or more in arrear; or

(iii) there has been a breach of some provision contained in the Act or in the mortgage deed (other than the covenant for payment of the mortgage money or interest) which should have been observed or performed by the mortgagor or by someone who concurred in making the mortgage.

(c) *Protection of purchaser.* The difference between the power of sale arising and becoming exercisable is as follows. If the power has not arisen, the mortgagee has no statutory power of sale at all; the most he can do is to transfer his mortgage. But if the power of sale has arisen, he can make a good title to a purchaser free from the equity of redemption even if the power has not become exercisable; the title of a purchaser in good faith is not impeachable merely

---

[5] ss. 101–107, applicable to mortgages made after 1881.
[6] L.P.A. 1925, s. 101. If this is not the case then if foreclosure is possible a sale may be ordered in lien thereof under L.P.A. 1925, s. 91 (2); *Twentieth Century Banking Co. Ltd.* v. *Wilkinson* [1977] Ch. 99.
[7] *Payne* v. *Cardiff R.D.C.* [1932] 1 K.B. 241.
[8] L.P.A. 1925, s. 103.

because none of the three specified events has occurred or the power of sale has in some way been irregularly or improperly exercised. Any person injured by an unauthorised, improper or irregular exercise of the power has a remedy in damages against the person exercising it.[9] Thus while a purchaser from a mortgagee must satisfy himself that the power of sale has arisen, he need not inquire whether it has become exercisable. However, if he has actual or Nelsonian[10] knowledge that the power is not exercisable or that there is some impropriety in the sale he will not obtain a good title free from the mortgagor's interest.[11]

(d) *Mode of sale.* In general, the statutory power of sale is exercisable without any order of the court being required. The mortgagee may sell by public auction or private contract and has a wide discretion as to the terms and conditions upon which the sale is made.[12] The power is unaffected by any disposition by the mortgagor so that a contract of sale entered into by the mortgagee will prevail over an earlier contract of sale concluded by the mortgagor.[13] The power becomes exercised as soon as a contract, albeit conditional, is made, so that thereupon the equity of redemption is suspended unless and until the contract goes off.[14] To prevent the mortgagee entering into a contract the mortgagor must tender the redemption moneys in full.[15]

The mortgagee is not a trustee for the mortgagor of his power of sale,[16] for the power is given to the mortgagee for his own benefit to enable him the better to realise his security. Thus he need not delay the sale to obtain a better price, nor does he have to attempt to sell by auction before selling by private contract.[17] Moreover, his motive for selling, such as spite against the mortgagor, is immaterial.[18] But the sale must be a true sale; a "sale" by the mortgagee to himself, either directly or through an agent, is no true sale and may be set aside.[19]

---

[9] *Ibid.* s. 104 (2).
[10] *i.e.* turns a Nelsonian blind eye to suspicious circumstances: *cf. Belmont Finance Ltd.* v. *Williams* [1979] Ch. 250 at pp. 267, 275.
[11] *Bailey* v. *Barnes* [1894] 1 Ch. 25 at p. 30; *Lord Waring* v. *London & Manchester Assurance Co. Ltd.* [1935] Ch. 310 at p. 318; *Northern Developments* v. *UDT Securities* (1976) 32 P. & C.R. 376 at p. 380. Constructive notice cannot affect a purchaser.
[12] L.P.A. 1925, s. 101 (1), (2).
[13] *Duke* v. *Robson* [1973] 1 W.L.R. 267.
[14] *Property & Bloodstock Ltd.* v. *Emerton* [1968] Ch. 94.
[15] *Payne* v. *Cardiff R.D.C.* [1932] 1 K.B. 241.
[16] *Kennedy* v. *De Trafford* [1897] A.C. 180.
[17] *Davey* v. *Durrant* (1857) 1 De G. & J. 535 at pp. 553, 560. It seems unlikely that he will be held to be under a duty to gazump like a trustee as in *Buttle* v. *Saunders* [1950] W.N. 255.
[18] *Nash* v. *Eads* (1880) 25 S.J. 95.
[19] *Downes* v. *Grazebrook* (1871) 3 Mer. 200; *Williams* v. *Wellingborough* [1975] 1 W.L.R. 1327. Except in this case, if a mortgagor submits that a proposed sale is at such an under-value that the court should restrain it, he will be met by the argument that if the property is that valuable then he should have had no trouble in finding a new mortgagee ready to lend enough to redeem the existing mortgagee which *ex hypothesi* is not the case.

Further, a mortgagee is under a duty to take reasonable care to obtain a proper price,[20] so that he will be liable to the mortgagor if he advertised the property for sale by auction without mentioning a valuable planning permission, so that the sort of purchaser likely to pay a high price for land with such permission failed to attend the auction.[21]

(e) *Proceeds of sale.* Although the mortgagee is not a trustee of his power of sale, he is a trustee of the proceeds of sale. After discharging any payments properly due, any balance must be paid to the next subsequent incumbrancer,[22] or if none, to the mortgagor.[23] A mortgagee who has a surplus should therefore search in the registers of land charges[24] or the register of title,[25] as the case may be, to discover the existence of any subsequent mortgages, since if he pays the money to the mortgagor he will be liable to any mortgagee (of whom he has actual or constructive notice) who is thereby prejudiced.[26] But a sale by a mortgagee does not affect any prior mortgagee; the purchaser takes the property subject to any such mortgage, though free from the rights of the vendor, subsequent mortgagees, and the mortgagor.[27] This is achieved for registered land by section 34 (4)[28] which provides that the statutory power of sale operates as a transfer for value by the proprietor of the land at the time of the registration of the charge would have operated.[29]

4. To take possession. (a) *The right.* Since a legal mortgage gives the mortgagee a term of years, he is entitled to take possession of the mortgaged property as soon as the mortgage is made, even if the mortgagor is guilty of no default[30]; a legal chargee has a corresponding statutory right.[31] If the property is already lawfully let to a tenant, the mortgagee cannot take physical possession, but instead takes possession by directing the tenants to pay their rents to him instead of to the mortgagor.[32]

[20] For building societies the duty is statutory: Building Societies Act 1962, s. 36, requiring "the best price reasonably obtainable."
[21] *Cuckmere Brick Co. Ltd.* v. *Mutual Finance Ltd.* [1971] Ch. 949; *Bank of Cyprus* v. *Gill* [1979] 2 Ll. Rep 508.
[22] See *Samuel Keller (Holdings) Ltd.* v. *Martins Bank Ltd.* [1971] 1 W.L.R. 43.
[23] L.P.A. 1925, s. 105; see *Thorne* v. *Heard* [1895] A.C. 495. And see *post,* pp. 524 for the effect of the Limitation Act 1980.
[24] See *ante,* p. 92.
[25] L.R.R. 289; Ruoff & Roper, pp. 499, 536.
[26] *West London Commercial Bank* v. *Reliance Permanent Building Society* (1885) 29 Ch.D. 954.
[27] L.P.A. 1925, ss. 88(1), 89(1), 104(1).
[28] L.R.A. 1925.
[29] A purchaser should ensure that the mortgagee sells under the statutory powers *qua* mortgagee rather than purchase from the mortgagor with the mortgagee's concurrence if he wishes to take free from intervening incumbrances, *e.g.* a judgment creditor's charging order: *Re White Rose Cottage* [1965] Ch. 940.
[30] *Birch* v. *Wright* (1786) 1 T.R. 378 at p. 383.
[31] L.P.A. 1925, s. 87 (1).
[32] *Horlock* v. *Smith* (1842) 6 Jur. 478.

However, the mortgagee's right to possession may be excluded for a period if the terms of the mortgage expressly or impliedly[33] confer a right of possession on the mortgagor, *e.g.* for so long as he keeps up his instalment payments.[34] The onus is on the mortgagor to establish this since the mortgagee's right is not to be lightly abrogated or restricted.[35] A mortgagee will not normally exercise his right until some default has occurred which will enable him to exercise his power of sale.

(b) *Strict account.* In practice unless he plans to sell the property, or it is already fully let, a mortgagee is slow to take possession, because if he does he is liable to account strictly on the footing of wilful default; this means that he must account not only for all that he receives but also for all that he ought to have received.[36] Thus where the mortgagee was a brewer and the mortgaged property a "free" house, a mortgagee who took possession and let the property as a "tied" house was held liable for the additional rent he would have obtained if he had let the property as a "free" house.[37] Again, if the mortgagee occupies the property himself instead of letting it he is liable for a fair occupation rent,[38] though he need pay no rent if through decay or otherwise the land is incapable of being beneficially occupied[39] or if his occupation is essential to preserve the value of the premises *e.g.* to carry on the mortgagor's business.[40] Of course where the property is already let, there is little risk in his taking possession.

(c) *Powers while in possession.* While in possession, a mortgagee whose mortgage was made by deed may cut and sell timber and other trees ripe for cutting which were not planted or left standing for shelter or ornament, or contract for this to be done within 12 months of the contract.[41] Although he is not liable for waste, he will be liable if he improperly cuts timber; and despite his right to work mines already opened, he may not open new mines. However, if the property becomes insufficient security for the money due, the court will not interfere if he cuts timber and opens mines, provided he is not guilty of wanton destruction.[42]

A mortgagee in possession must effect reasonable repairs,[43] and may without the mortgagor's consent effect reasonable but not

---

[33] *Birmingham Citizens P.B.S.* v. *Caunt* [1962] Ch. 883 at p. 890.
[34] *Esso Petroleum Co. Ltd.* v. *Alstonbridge Properties Ltd.* [1975] 1 W.L.R. 1474 at p. 1484.
[35] *Western Bank Ltd.* v. *Schindler* [1977] Ch. 1; R.J. Smith [1979] Conv. 266.
[36] *Chaplin* v. *Young (No. 1)* (1863) 33 Beav. 330 at pp. 337, 338.
[37] *White* v. *City of London Brewery Co.* (1889) 42 Ch.D. 237.
[38] *Marriott* v. *Anchor Reversionary Co.* (1861) 3 De G.F. & J. 177 at p. 193.
[39] *Marshall* v. *Cave* (1824) 3 L.J. (o.s.) Ch. 57.
[40] *Fyfe* v. *Smith* [1975] 2 New South Wales L.R. 408.
[41] L.P.A. 1925, s. 101 (1).
[42] *Millett* v. *Davey* (1863) 31 Beav. 470 at pp. 475, 476.
[43] *Richards* v. *Morgan* (1853) 4 Y. & C.Ex. 570.

excessive improvements; the cost will be charged to the mortgagor in the accounts.[44]

(d) *Relief of mortgagor.* (i) COURT'S INHERENT DISCRETION. In general, since the mortgagee is entitled to an order for possession, the court will not adjourn an application or suspend an order for possession save for a short period to allow the mortgagor a chance of paying off the mortgage in full or otherwise remedying his default, assuming that there is a reasonable prospect of the chance being utilised.[45] This discretion is so limited that statute has conferred much wider discretionary powers in the case of dwelling-houses as will shortly be seen.[46]

Recently Lord Denning M.R., however, has suggested[47] that "in modern times equity can step in so as to prevent a mortgagee, or a transferee from him, from getting possession of a house contrary to the justice of the case. A mortgagee will be restrained from getting possession except when it is sought bona fide and reasonably for the purpose of enforcing the security, and then only subject to such conditions as the court thinks fit to impose. When the bank itself or a building society lends the money, then it may well be right to allow the mortgagee to obtain possession when the borrower is in default. But so long as the interest is paid and there is nothing outstanding, equity has ample power to restrain any unjust use of the right to possession."

In *Quennell* v. *Maltby*[48] Q, who owned a house worth over £30,000, mortgaged it to the bank to secure an overdraft of £2,500. The mortgage deed prohibited the creation of tenancies without the bank's consent. However, Q let the house to M without the bank's consent. Later Q sought to sell the house with vacant possession and so asked the bank to claim possession, as mortgagee, from M, whose Rent Act protected tenancy did not bind the mortgagee.[49] The bank refused, so that Mrs. Q then paid off the overdraft and took a transfer of the mortgage. She then sought possession as mortgagee of the house.

The judge gave effect to her absolute right to possession as mortgagee. As Lord Denning pointed out,[50] this "opens the way to widespread evasion of the Rent Act. If the owner of a house wishes to obtain vacant possession all he has to do is charge it to the bank for a small sum; then grant a tenancy without telling the bank; then get his wife to pay off the bank and take a transfer; then get the wife to sue

---

[44] *Shepard* v. *Jones* (1882) 21 Ch.D. 469.
[45] *Birmingham Citizens P.B.S.* v. *Caunt* [1962] Ch. 883.
[46] *Post*, p. 481.
[47] *Quennell* v. *Maltby* [1979] 1 W.L.R. 318 at p. 322.
[48] *Ibid.*
[49] *Dudley & District Benefit B.S.* v. *Emerson* [1949] Ch. 707.
[50] [1979] 1 W.L.R. 318 at p. 322.

for possession." Thus, acting on his earlier cited dicta and taking the view that she and Q had the ulterior motive of obtaining possession to re-sell the house at a profit free from the tenancy, he dismissed the possession action.

The dicta of Lord Denning conflict with authority[51] and, indeed, render completely unnecessary the protection accorded the mortgagor under the Administration of Justice Acts 1970 and 1973.

As appears from the judgments of Bridge and Templeman L.JJ.[52] the decision is better based on the ground that the action, though in form brought by Mrs. Q herself as mortgagee, was in substance brought by Mrs. Q as agent on behalf of Q, and an action by Q for possession would clearly have failed.

(ii) COURT'S STATUTORY DISCRETION. Since tenants were already well protected it was felt that mortgagors should receive some protection. Thus, in the case of dwelling-houses the court has been given powers to adjourn possession proceedings or to suspend its order or to postpone the giving up of possession for such periods as the court thinks reasonable.[53] For this it must appear to the court that "the mortgagor is likely to be able within a reasonable period to pay any sums due under the mortgage" or to remedy some other default.

The "sums due" are not the whole outstanding capital where, as is usual, the whole capital sum is expressed to be payable on default in payment of interest or of instalments of capital and interest: they are just the outstanding sums due in respect of interest or instalments.[54] In deciding whether the mortgagor is likely to be able to pay the "sums due" in a reasonable time,[55] the court must take into account not only the arrears but also the accruing sums.[56] The court's discretion is available whether the mortgage is an instalment mortgage where each payment is part capital and part interest or a mortgage where after a short fixed period, such as six months, all the money is repayable so that the legal date for redemption arises, but the principal is intended to be repaid much later (*e.g.* when an endowment policy matures or when demanded by the mortgagee) so that interest alone is payable meanwhile.[57]

---

[51] *Robertson* v. *Cilia* [1956] 1 W.L.R. 1502; *Birmingham Citizens P.B.S.* v. *Caunt* [1962] Ch. 883 at p. 896; *Alliance Perpetual B.S.* v. *Belrun Investments Ltd.* [1957] 1 W.L.R. 720 at p. 722; *Four-Maids Ltd.* v. *Dudley Marshall (Properties) Ltd.* [1957] Ch. 317 at pp. 320, 322.

[52] [1979] 1 W.L.R. 318, at pp. 323–234.

[53] Administration of Justice Act 1970, s. 36.

[54] A.J.A. 1973, s. 8 (1) nullifying *Halifax B.S.* v. *Clark* [1973] Ch. 307 which had been circumvented by *First Middlesbrough Trading Co.* v. *Cunningham* (1974) 28 P. & C.R. 69 where the Court of Appeal surprisingly held "reasonable period" in s. 36 could be the whole 25 years mortgage term. The reasonable period of s. 8 for payment of arrears certainly seems much shorter.

[55] The court may take into account the fact that the mortgagor has a good chance of speedily selling the property for a sensible price enabling him to pay off the mortgage: *Royal Trust Co. Ltd.* v. *Markham* [1975] 1 W.L.R. 1416.

[56] A.J.A. 1973, s. 8 (2).

[57] *Centrax Trustees Ltd.* v. *Ross* [1979] 2 All E.R. 952.

The court's powers will normally be exercised subject to conditions, *e.g.* as to payment of arrears and current sums[58] but any adjournment must be for a fixed period and not be indefinite.[59]

(e) *Parties*. Under section 1 (5) of the Matrimonial Homes Act 1967 a mortgagor's spouse has a statutory right to tender mortgage payments on the mortgagor's behalf so as to prevent the mortgagee from exercising his right to take possession and so as to invoke the relief afforded by the Administration of Justice Acts.

To enable the spouse to learn of the mortgagor's default and to become a party to the possession proceedings, the Matrimonial Homes and Property Act 1981 improves the spouse's position.[60] Where the spouse has protected her rights of occupation as a Class F land charge or by entry of a caution or notice then the mortgagee must notify her of the proceedings.[61] To this end the mortgagee has a right to search the land register so far as necessary for the right of occupation to be revealed.[62] The spouse can then apply to the court to be made a party to the possession proceedings. The court should accede to this if it does not see special reason against it and it seems that she might be expected to be likely to be able to pay the sums due within a reasonable period under the Administration of Justice Act.[63]

(f) *Attornment clause*. Many legal mortgages still contain an attornment clause, which is a clause whereby the mortgagor attorns, or acknowledges himself to be, a tenant at will or from year to year of the mortgagee, usually at a nominal rent such as a peppercorn or five pence. Formerly this was inserted because a speedy procedure in the High Court was available to enable landlords to recover possession of the demised property from their tenants, and no such procedure was available for mere mortgagees; the attornment clause enabled mortgagees to sue for possession *qua* landlords. But changes in the rules of court in 1933, 1936 and 1937 made the speedy procedure available to mortgagees as such, so that this reason for its use has gone. A surviving advantage of the clause is that covenants by the mortgagor in the mortgage relating to the premises will be enforceable against an assignee of the mortgagor under the doctrine that covenants in a lease which touch and concern the land will run with the lease and the reversion.[64] Notice to quit must be given as a necessary preliminary to any possession action[65] and the Rent Acts

[58] A.J.A. 1970, s. 36 (3); R.J. Smith [1974] Conv. 266.
[59] *Royal Trust Co. Ltd.* v. *Markham* [1975] 1 W.L.R. 1416.
[60] Previously it was unsatisfactory: *Hastings & Thanet B.S.* v. *Goddard* [1970] 1 W.L.R. 1544; Nevitt & Levin (1973) 36 M.L.R. 345 at p. 349.
[61] M.H.A. 1967, s. 7A (3) (*a*) added by Matrimonial Homes and Property Act 1981, s. 2.
[62] M.H. & P.A. 1981, s. 4 (4).
[63] *Ibid.* s. 2 adding M.H.A. 1967 s. 7A (2).
[64] *Regent Oil Co. Ltd.* v. *J. A. Gregory* (*Hatch End*) *Ltd.* [1966] Ch. 402. For the doctrine, see *ante*, pp. 379 *et seq.*
[65] *Hinckley & Country B.S.* v. *Henny* [1953] 1 W.L.R. 352.

and the Agricultural Holdings Act 1948 confer no protection upon the tenant mortgagor.[66]

5. To appoint a receiver. (a) *History.* In order to avoid the dangers of taking possession mortgages used to provide for the appointment of a receiver with extensive powers of management of the mortgaged property. At first, the appointment was made by the mortgagor at the request of the mortgagee, but later, mortgagees began to reserve a power for themselves, acting in theory as agents for the mortgagor, to appoint a receiver. In such circumstances the receiver was deemed the agent of the mortgagor and the mortgagee was not liable to account strictly[67] in the same way as would have been the case if he had taken possession or the receiver had been his agent.

Lord Cranworth's Act 1860 gave a somewhat unsatisfactory statutory power to appoint a receiver, but the Conveyancing Act 1881, and now the Law of Property Act 1925,[68] confers a power which satisfies most mortgagees. In the case of registered land the power can only be exercised by the mortgagee after he has become registered as proprietor of the charge.[69]

(b) *The power.* The statutory power to appoint a receiver arises and becomes exercisable in the same circumstances as the power of sale.[70] The mortgagor makes the appointment by writing, and may remove or replace the receiver in the same way. The receiver is deemed the agent of the mortgagor, who is solely responsible for his acts unless the mortgage otherwise provides,[71] or unless the mortgagee represents him as being the mortgagee's agent.[72] The receiver has power to recover the income of the property by action, distress or otherwise, and to give valid receipts for it. The money received by the receiver, after discharging outgoings, interest on prior incumbrances and payment of the receiver's commission and other expenses, is used to pay the interest due under the mortgage. If the mortgagee so directs in writing, any surplus may be applied towards discharge of the principal money lent on mortgage; otherwise, it is payable to the person who would have been entitled to it had the receiver not been appointed, normally the mortgagor.[73]

(c) *Limitation Act.* Appointment of a receiver has one minor disadvantage when compared with taking possession. Possession for

---

[66] *Portman B.S.* v. *Young* [1951] 1 All E.R. 191, *Alliance Building Society* v. *Pinwill* [1958] Ch. 788 at p. 792.
[67] *Ante,* p. 479.
[68] s. 101.
[69] *Lever Finance Ltd.* v. *Needleman's Trustees* [1956] Ch. 375.
[70] L.P.A. 1925, ss. 101 (1), 109 (1).
[71] L.P.A. 1925, s. 109 (2); *White* v. *Metcalf* [1903] 2 Ch. 567.
[72] *Chatsworth Properties Ltd.* v. *Effiom* [1971] 1 W.L.R. 144. Care must be taken in the terms of the letter to the mortgagor's tenant.
[73] *Ibid.* s. 109.

12 years without acknowledging the mortgagor's title or receiving any payment of principal or interest from him will extinguish the mortgagor's title in favour of the mortgagee.[74] The appointment of a receiver cannot help the mortgagee in this way since the receiver is treated as the mortgagor's agent.[75]

The mortgagee's remedies are cumulative. A mortgagee is not bound to select one of the above remedies and pursue that and no other: subject to his not recovering more than is due to him, he may employ any or all of the remedies to enforce payment.[76] Thus if he sells the property for less than the mortgage debt, he may then sue the mortgagor upon the personal covenant for payment[77]; and this is so even if the sale was by the court and the mortgagee, bidding by leave of the court, has purchased the property.[78]

However, if he wishes to sue after foreclosure, he can do so only on condition that he opens the foreclosure[79]; for despite the foreclosure he is treating the mortgage as being still alive. Consequently, if by disposing of the property after foreclosure the mortgagee has put it out of his power to open the foreclosure, he cannot sue upon the personal covenant.[80]

It may be noted that two of the mortgagee's remedies are derived from the common law (an action on the covenant, and the right to take possession), one is equitable (foreclosure) and two were formerly contractual and are now statutory (sale, and the appointment of a receiver).

II. EQUITABLE MORTGAGEE OR CHARGEE

The extent to which the foregoing remedies are exercisable by an equitable mortgagee or chargee is as follows.

1. To sue for the money due. The position is the same as for a legal mortgage.

2. To foreclose. An equitable mortgagee may foreclose in the same way as a legal mortgagee save that the court order will direct the mortgagor to convey the legal title to the mortgagee.[81] An equitable chargee, however, has no right of foreclosure,[82] for a charge effects no conveyance of a legal or equitable interest.

---

[74] *Young* v. *Clarey* [1948] Ch. 191.
[75] L.P.A. 1925, s. 109 (2).
[76] *Palmer* v. *Hendrie* (1859) 27 Beav. 349 at p. 351.
[77] *Rudge* v. *Richens* (1873) L.R. 8 C.P. 358.
[78] *Gordon Grant & Co. Ltd.* v. *Boos* [1926] A.C. 781.
[79] *Perry* v. *Barker* (1806) 13 Ves. 198; and see *ante*, p. 475.
[80] *Palmer* v. *Hendrie* (1859) 27 Beav. 349.
[81] *James* v. *James* (1873) L.R. 16 Eq. 153.
[82] *Re Lloyd* [1903] 1 Ch. 385.

3. To sell. The statutory power of sale[83] applies in unregistered land wherever the mortgage or charge was made by deed; other mortgagees or chargees have no power of sale though they may apply to the court for sale under section 91 (2) of the Law of Property Act 1925. Although an equitable mortgagee or chargee by deed has the statutory power of sale, this probably does not enable him to convey the legal estate to the purchaser.[84] To overcome this defect, either or both of two conveyancing devices are employed.

    (a) *Power of attorney*: an irrevocable power of attorney is inserted in the deed empowering the mortgagee or his assigns to convey the legal estate.[85]

    (b) *Declaration of trust*: a clause is inserted in the deed whereby the mortgagor declares that he holds the legal estate on trust for the mortgagee and empowers the mortgagee to appoint himself or his nominee as trustee in place of the mortgagor. The mortgagee can thus vest the legal estate in himself or the purchaser.

    In the case of registered land only a registered chargee has the statutory power of sale[86] but equitable mortgagees may use the above conveyancing devices to sell the legal estate.[87]

4. Possible right to take possession. Although it is usually said that an equitable mortgagee, having no legal estate, has no right to possession, on principle there seems no reason why, like a tenant under an equitable lease, he should not be entitled to it.[88] In any event, he can obtain possession if a clause in the mortgage empowers this upon default by the mortgagor. If the land is let, he cannot collect the rent from the tenant, for that is payable to the legal reversioner[89] with whom there is privity of estate. An equitable chargee, who has not even the benefit of a contract to create a legal mortgage, cannot even claim possession.

5. To appoint a receiver. As in the case of the power of sale, the statutory power to appoint a receiver[90] exists only if the mortgage or charge was made by deed and in the case of registered land, if a registered charge.[91] In other cases, a receiver can be obtained only by application to the court.

---

[83] *Ante*, pp. 475 *et seq.*
[84] See *Re Hodson and Howes' Contract* (1887) 35 Ch.D. 668; contrast *Re White Rose Cottage* [1965] Ch. 940 at p. 951.
[85] These powers are now regulated by the Powers of Attorney Act 1971, ss. 4 (1), 5 (3).
[86] L.R.A., s. 34 (1); *Lever Finance Ltd.* v. *Needleman's Trustees* [1956] Ch. 375.
[87] See, *e.g. Re White Rose Cottage* [1964] Ch. 483 at pp. 495–496 (endorsed in this respect on appeal [1965] Ch. 940.
[88] See M. & W., pp. 923, 924; *ante*, p. 337.
[89] *Finck* v. *Tranter* [1905] 1 K.B. 427.
[90] *Ante*, pp. 483 *et seq.*
[91] *Lever Finance Ltd.* v. *Needleman's Trustees* [1956] Ch. 375.

B. Other Rights of a Mortgagee

Certain other rights of a mortgagee must now be considered. The position of these and other matters is in general the same for both mortgages and charges, whether legal or equitable, and "mortgage" will accordingly be used hereafter to include all such incumbrances unless the contrary is indicated.

1. Right to fixtures. It is a question of construction to determine what property is included in a mortgage. However, subject to any contrary intention, a mortgage includes all fixtures attached to the land either at the date of the mortgage or thereafter; the exceptions as between landlord and tenant do not apply.[92]

2. Right to possession of the title deeds. A first mortgagee has the same right to the title deeds as if he had the fee simple or an assignment of the lease which has been mortgaged, as the case may be[93]; but under all mortgages made since 1881, the mortgagor is entitled to inspect and make copies of the deeds, despite any contrary agreement.[94] If the mortgage is redeemed by the mortgagor, the mortgagee must deliver the deeds to him, unless he has notice of some subsequent incumbrance, in which case the deeds should be delivered to the incumbrancer next in order of priority of whom the mortgagee has notice. Contrary to the general rule that registration is notice, registration under the Land Charges Act 1972 is not notice for this pupose,[95] although as has been seen a mortgagee is bound to search before he distributes any surplus after a sale.[96] If a mortgage becomes statute-barred by lapse of time,[97] the mortgagee must return the deeds even if no part of the mortgage debt has been or will be paid.[98] In the case of registered land the land certificate has to be deposited at the Land Registry for the duration of any registered charge.[99]

3. Right to insure against fire at the mortgagor's expense. Under the Law of Property Act 1925[1] a mortgagee or registered chargee may insure the mortgaged property against fire and charge the premiums on the property in the same way as the money lent; this power, which is given only where the mortgage was made by deed, is exercisable as soon as the mortgage is made. The amount of the insurance must not exceed the amount specified in the deed, or, if none, two-thirds of the

---

[92] *Ante*, p. 21.
[93] L.P.A. 1925, ss. 85 (1), 86 (1).
[94] *Ibid.* s. 96 (1).
[95] *Ibid.* s. 96 (2), added by L.P.(Am.)A. 1926, Sched.
[96] *Ante*, p. 478.
[97] *Post*, p. 524.
[98] *Lewis* v. *Plunket* [1937] Ch. 306; and see *ante*, p. 469.
[99] L.R.A. 1925, s. 65.
[1] ss. 101 (1), 108, replacing C.A. 1881, ss. 19 (1), 23.

amount required to restore the property in case of total destruction. But the mortgagee cannot exercise his power if—

(i) the mortgage deed declares that no insurance is required; or
(ii) the mortgagor keeps up an insurance in accordance with the mortgage deed; or
(iii) the mortgage deed is silent as to insurance and the mortgagor keeps up an insurance to the amount authorised by the Act with the mortgagee's consent.

4. Right to consolidate. (a) *The right.* Consolidation may be described as the right of a person in whom two or more mortgages are vested to refuse to allow one mortgage to be redeemed unless the other or others are also redeemed. In its basic form, the principle is simple. If A has mortgaged both Blackacre and Whiteacre to X, each property being worth £25,000 and each loan being £20,000, it would be unfair, if the value of Blackacre subsequently sinks to £15,000 and the value of Whiteacre doubles, to allow A to redeem Whiteacre and leave Blackacre unredeemed. In such a case, equity permits X to consolidate, and so to oblige A to redeem both mortgages or neither; in seeking redemption, A is asking for the assistance of equity and equity puts its own price upon its interference, saying that he who seeks equity must do equity.

This simple concept has been elaborated to some extent; different considerations may arise where third parties are concerned, *e.g.* by transfer of a mortgage. The rules on the subject may be stated as follows.

(b) *Conditions.* There can be no consolidation unless the following four conditions are satisifed:

(1) RESERVATION OF RIGHT: either both the mortgages were made before 1882, or at least one of the mortgages shows an intent to allow consolidation. Before 1882, the right existed automatically, provided the other conditions were satisfed; but after 1881, the Conveyancing Act 1881 made it necessary to reserve the right. The Law of Property Act 1925, s. 93, now provides that with the two exceptions stated above there is no right to consolidate. It is common practice for a mortgage to contain a clause excluding the operation of section 93, so permitting consolidation.

(2) REDEMPTION DATES PASSED: in the case of both mortgages, the legal dates for redemption have passed.[2] Consolidation is an equitable doctrine and does not come into play unless only the equitable rights to redeem are concerned.

(3) SAME MORTGAGOR: both mortgages were made by the same

---

[2] *Cummins* v. *Fletcher* (1880) 14 Ch.D. 699.

mortgagor.[3] Mortgages made by different mortgagors can never be consolidated, even if both properties later come into the same hands. This is so even if X makes one mortgage and Y, as trustee for X, makes the other, or if A makes one mortgage and A and B jointly make the other.[4] But it is immaterial whether or not the mortgages were made to the same mortgagees.

(4) SIMULTANEOUS UNIONS OF MORTGAGES AND EQUITIES: there has been a time when both the mortgages have been vested in one person and simultaneously both the equities of redemption have been vested in another.[5] If this state of affairs exists at the time when redemption is sought, the mortgagee can consolidate, subject to the other conditions being fulfilled. Even if this state of affairs has ceased to exist when redemption is sought, and the equities of redemption are then owned by different persons, a mortgagee who holds both mortgages can consolidate.

(c) *Illustrations.* There is no need to illustrate (1) and (2), but the following examples may be given of the operation of (3) and (4).

(i)

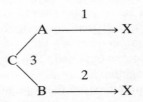

This represents the following steps:

    (1) A mortgages one estate to X.
    (2) B mortgages another estate to X.
    (3) C purchases the equities of redemption of both properties.

There can be no consolidation here, even though Condition (4) is satisfied, for the mortgages were made by different mortgagors.

(ii)

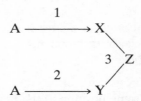

    (1) A mortgages one estate to X.
    (2) A mortgages another estate to Y.
    (3) Z purchases both mortgages.

---

[3] *Sharp* v. *Rickards* [1909] 1 Ch. 109.
[4] *Thorneycroft* v. *Crockett* (1848) 2 H.L.C. 239.
[5] See *Pledge* v. *White* [1896] A.C. 187 at p. 198.

Here Z can consolidate, provided Conditions (1) and (2) are satisfied. Condition (3) is satisfied and so is Condition (4).

(iii)

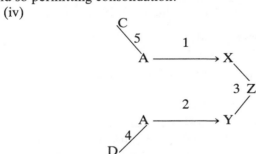

(1) A mortgages one estate to X.
(2) A mortgages another estate to Y.
(3) C purchases the equity on the first estate.
(4) D purchases the equity on the second estate.
(5) Z purchases both mortgages.

There can be no consolidation here, for Condition (4) is not satisfied. It is true that at one stage (after Step (2)) both equities were in one person's hands, and that an another stage (Step (5)) both mortgages were in another person's hands; but at no one moment have both these conditions obtained. The equities separated before the mortgages came together.

If C instead of D had purchased the equity on the second estate, Z could have consolidated, even though at the time of C's purchase no right to consolidate had arisen; the purchaser of two or more equities takes subject to the risk of the mortgages coming into the same hand and so permitting consolidation.

(iv)

This represents the same position as the previous example, except that Steps (3) and (5) have changed places. As Z has now purchased both mortgages *before* A parted with either equity, Z may consolidate the mortgages provided Conditions (1) and (2) are satisfied. In this event, if C seeks to redeem his mortgage, Z can refuse redemption unless C purchases the mortgage on D's property as well as redeeming his own mortgage.

(d) *More than two mortgages.* These rules of consolidation apply equally when it is sought to consolidate more than two mortgages. Sometimes it will be found that while Mortgage I can be consolidated with Mortgages II and III, there is no right to consolidate Mortgages II and III with each other, *e.g.* if only Mortgage I contains a consolidation clause. Examples containing more than two mortgages are best worked out by taking the mortgages in pairs and applying the rules to each pair in turn.

(e) *Extent of doctrine.* The nature of the mortgages or the property mortgaged is immaterial. There can be consolidation even if one mort-gage is legal and one equitable, or if both are equitable, or if one mortgage is of personalty and the other of realty,[6] or if both are mortgages of personalty. The doctrine has even been applied to two mortgages on the same property.[7] Further, it is immaterial whether the equity of redemption has been conveyed *in toto* or whether it has merely been mortgaged; a mortggagee of an equity of redemption is a purchaser *pro tanto, i.e.* to the extent of his interest. Thus if a mortgagee has a right of consolidation, it is effective against subsequent mortgagees of the property as well as the mortgagor.

(f) *Purchasers.* The doctrine of consolidation makes it dangerous to buy property subject to a mortgage without careful inquiry. If a right to consolidate has once arisen, a person who subsequently acquires one or both of the equities of redemption is liable to have the mortgages consolidated against him; and even if no right to consolidate has arisen, a person who acquires two equities of redemption is liable to have the mortgages consolidated if one person acquires both of them. But a person who acquires only one equity of redemption at a time when no right to consolidate has arisen normally suffers no risk of consolidation.[8]

5. Right to tack. This is considered below.[9]

Sect. 2. Rights Common to Both Parties

A. Power of Leasing

1. Leases not binding. The most important right common to both parties is the right of leasing the mortgaged property. Apart from any statutory or contractual provisions, the position of a mortgagor as soon as he has made a mortgage is that he has granted a long term of years to the mortgagee and retains merely the reversion on that lease together with an equity of redemption. The mortgagor consequently has no right to possession of land and so cannot grant a lease giving

---

[6] *Tassell* v. *Smith* (1858) 2 De G. & J. 713.
[7] *Re Salmon* [1903] 1 K.B. 147; *sed quaere.*
[8] *Harter* v. *Coleman* (1882) 19 Ch.D. 630.
[9] *Post,* pp. 512 *et seq.*

anyone else the right to possession. In practice, however, the mortgagor is usually left in possession of the land, and it was held before 1926, when mortgages were created by conveying the whole of the mortgagor's estate, that if the mortgagor granted a lease, he was unable subsequently to deny the validity of that lease and eject the tenant, for the lease bound both the mortgagor and the tenant under the doctrine of estoppel.[10] But the mortgagee is not bound, and in the same way that he can take possession from the mortgagor, he can take possession from a tenant of the mortgagor.[11] As to the mortgagee, although he is entitled to possession of the land at law, leases granted by him will cease to be binding on the mortgagor if he redeems the mortgage,[12] for in equity the mortgagor is entitled to redeem his property as free from incumbrances as it was when mortgaged.

It will be seen from this that once property has been mortgaged, a satisfactory lease could be made only if both mortgagor and mortgagee concurred in granting it, or if the mortgage gave either or both of the parties power to grant binding leases. However, statute has materially altered this position, and the following provisions apply to all mortgages made after 1881 if the parties have not expressed a contrary intention, either in the mortgage or otherwise in writing.[13] It is common for mortgages to preclude the mortgagor from exercising any power to grant leases or tenancies. Any lease granted by the mortgagor in breach of the mortgage deed will not bind the mortgagee.[14]

2. Power to lease. A power to grant leases which will be binding on both mortgagor and mortgagee is exercisable—

(1) by the mortgagee, if he is in possession or has appointed a receiver who is still acting; otherwise,
(2) by the mortgagor, if he is in possession.

3. Term of lease. A lease may be granted for the following terms—

(1) if the mortgage was made before 1926, for not more than—
    (i) 21 years for agricultural or occupation purposes;
    (ii) 99 years for building:
(2) if the mortgage was made after 1925, for not more than—
    (i) 50 years for agricultural or occupation purposes;
    (ii) 999 years for building.

---

[10] *Cuthbertson* v. *Irving* (1859) 4 H. & N. 742 at p. 754; *ante* p. 347.
[11] *Rogers* v. *Humphreys* (1835) 4 A. & E. 299 at p. 313.
[12] See *Chapman* v. *Smith* [1907] 2 Ch. 97 at p. 102.
[13] L.P.A. 1925, s. 99, replacing C.A. 1881, s. 18.
[14] *Dudley & District Benefit B.S.* v. *Emerson* [1949] Ch. 707.

4. Conditions of lease. To fall within the statutory powers, any lease granted must comply with the following conditions:

(1) It must be limited to take effect in possession not later than 12 months after its date.
(2) It must reserve the best rent reasonably obtainable, and with certain qualifications no fine may be taken.
(3) It must contain a covenant by the lessee for payment of rent and a condition of re-entry on the rent not being paid for a specified period not exceeding 30 days.
(4) A counterpart of the lease must be executed by the lessee and delivered to the lessor. A counterpart of any lease granted by the mortgagor must be delivered within one month to the mortgagee.[15]

These conditions do not preclude the grant of oral leases in exercise of the statutory power[16]; such leases need not comply with the last two conditions.[17] Neither the statutory power of leasing nor any provision in the mortgage excluding these powers (as is common in the case of the mortgagor) deprives either party of his common law right to grant a lease which will not bind the other unless adopted by him.[18] Further, the parties may extend the statutory powers by an agreement in writing, whether in the mortgage or not.[19]

B. Power of Accepting Surrenders of Leases

In the case of a mortgage made after 1911, if the parties have not expressed a contrary intention, either in the mortgage or otherwise in writing, statute[20] enables a surrender of any lease or tenancy to be effected, binding the parties to the mortgage, on the following terms.

(a) *Power to accept.* The surrender may be accepted—

(1) by the mortgagee, if he is in possession or has appointed a receiver who is still acting; otherwise,
(2) by the mortgagor, if he is in possession.

(b) *Conditions of surrender.* For the surrender to be valid—

(1) an authorised lease of the property must be granted to take effect in possession within one month of the surrender;
(2) the term of the new lease must not be shorter than the unexpired residue of the surrendered lease; and

---

[15] See *Public Trustee* v. *Lawrence* [1912] 1 Ch. 789.
[16] L.P.A. 1925, s. 99 (17). For oral leases, see *ante*, p. 335.
[17] *Rhodes* v. *Dalby* [1971] 1 W.L.R. 1325 at pp. 1331, 1332.
[18] *Rust* v. *Goodale* [1957] Ch. 33; contrast *Taylor* v. *Ellis* [1960] Ch. 368.
[19] L.P.A. 1925, s. 99 (14).
[20] *Ibid.* s. 100, replacing C.A. 1911, s. 3.

(3) the rent reserved by the new lease must not be less than the rent reserved by the surrendered lease.

The statutory power of accepting a surrender is thus exercisable only for the purpose of replacing one lease by another[21]; but the power may be extended by an agreement in writing, whether in the mortgage or not.

Sect. 3. Rights of the Mortgagor

A. Right of Redemption

I. PROTECTION OF THE MORTGAGOR

One aspect of equity's protection of the mortgagor's equity of redemption is to be found in the maxim "once a mortgage, always a mortgage." This is applied in two ways.

1. The test of a mortgage is substance, not form: if a transaction is in substance a mortgage, equity will treat it as such, even if it is dressed up in some other guise, as by the documents being cast in the form of an absolute conveyance.[22] Thus if a mortgage is expressed in the form of a conveyance with an option for the mortgagor to repurchase the property in a year's time, the mortgagor is entitled to redeem it even after the year has expired.[23]

2. No clogs on the equity: there must be no clog or fetter on the equity of redemption. This means not only that the mortgagor cannot be prevented from eventually redeeming his property, but also that he cannot be prevented from redeeming it free from any conditions in the mortgage.

(a) *No irredeemability*: it is impossible to provide that a mortgage shall be totally irredeemable[24] or that the right of redemption shall be confined to certain persons or to a limited period.[25] A provision in a mortgage that the property shall become the mortgagee's absolutely when some specified event occurs is void.[26] In all such cases, the owner of the equity of redemption may redeem as if there had been no such restriction. But once the mortgage has been made, equity will not intervene if the mortgagor, by a separate and independent transaction, gives the mortgagee an option of purchasing the property and thus of depriving the mortgagor of his equity of redemption.[27] While

---

[21] See *Barclays Bank Ltd.* v. *Stasek* [1957] Ch. 28.
[22] *Barnhart* v. *Greenshields* (1853) 9 Moo.P.C. 18.
[23] *Waters* v. *Mynn* (1850) 15 L.T.(o.s.) 157. Also see *Grangeside Properties Ltd.* v. *Collingwood Securities Ltd.* [1964] 1 W.L.R. 139.
[24] *Re Wells* [1933] Ch. 29 at p. 52.
[25] *Salt* v. *Marquess of Northampton* [1892] A.C. 1.
[26] *Toomes* v. *Conset* (1745) 3 Atk. 26.
[27] *Reeve* v. *Lisle* [1902] A.C. 461 (option ten days after mortgage unlike *Samuel* v. *Jarrah Timber Ltd.* [1904] A.C. 323 where the mortgage deed contained the option).

the mortgagor is in the defenceless position of seeking a loan, or arranging for a transfer of the mortgage,[28] equity will protect him; but once he has obtained the loan or secured the transfer, this protection is not needed.

A provision postponing the date of redemption until some future period longer than the customary six months, *e.g.* for 40 years, is valid, provided the mortgage as a whole is not so oppressive and unconscionable that equity would not enforce it, and provided it does not make the equitable right to redeem illusory.[29] In one case, a lease for 20 years was mortgaged on conditions which prevented its redemption until six weeks before the end of the term; such a provision rendered the equitable right to redeem illusory and so was held void.[30] Generally, however, the court will not interfere with a bargain made between two parties on an equal footing, even if this does postpone redemption for a considerable period.

Limited companies are not protected by this rule, for by statute a debenture may be made wholly or partly irredeemable, and even an ordinary mortgage by a company is a debenture.[31]

(b) *Redemption free from conditions in the mortgage*: the mortgagor cannot be prevented from redeeming exactly what he mortgaged, *i.e.* the property free from all conditions in the mortgage. The essence of a mortgage is a loan of money in return for security. Sometimes terms are inserted in a mortgage which give the mortgagee some other advantage in addition to his security. If this advantage is obtained by fraud or oppression, it will be set aside, but otherwise there is no objection to an advantage which ceases whenever the mortgage is redeemed, such as a provision making the mortgaged property, a public-house, a "tied" house until redemption.[32] The general enforceability of advantages which end on redemption represents an advance on the attitude which the courts had at one time adopted, rendering all collateral advantages for the mortgagee void on the basis that they were a disguised form of interest contravening usury laws.[33] After the last of the statutes dealing with usury was repealed in 1854, the courts gradually became

---

[28] *Lewis* v. *Frank Love Ltd.* [1961] 1 W.L.R. 261.
[29] *Knightsbridge Estates Trust Ltd.* v. *Byrne* [1939] Ch. 441 (affirmed on other grounds: *infra*, note 31). Both parties were bound to allow the full 40 year period.
[30] *Fairclough* v. *Swan Brewery Co. Ltd.* [1912] A.C. 565; *Santley* v. *Wilde* [1899] 2 Ch. 474, unless justified in terms of partnership law, seems of doubtful authority since a 10 year lease was irredeemable until its expiry, since it was security for the mortgagor's obligation to pay one-third of the theatre's profits to the mortgagee throughout the duration of the lease. It has been criticised in *Noakes* v. *Rice* [1902] A.C. 24 at pp. 31, 34.
[31] Companies Act 1948, s. 89; *Knightsbridge Estates Trust Ltd.* v. *Byrne* [1940] A.C. 613.
[32] *Biggs* v. *Hoddinott* [1898] 2 Ch. 307; *Noakes* v. *Rice* [1902] A.C. 24.
[33] See *Jennings* v. *Ward* (1705) 2 Vern. 520 at p. 521.

more liberal and it is now settled that in certain cases a collateral advantage may remain effective even after redemption.

A collateral advantage that is part and parcel of a mortgage transaction must cease on redemption so that the mortgagor can redeem exactly what he mortgaged.[34] Thus a "free" public house which is mortgaged in a deed tying it to products of a brewery mortgagee can no longer be a "tied" house once the mortgagor has redeemed the mortgage.[35] However, if the free house had become tied to the brewery a month *before* it had been mortgaged to the brewery, then, since a "tied" house had been mortgaged, it would not be objectionable that on redemption the mortgagor obtained a "tied" house.[36] If the tie had been entered into a month *after* the mortgage then this would be a distinct independent bargain capable of continuing in independent existence after redemption of the mortgage.[37] Indeed, it seems that a collateral advantage stipulated for by a mortgage on the same day as the mortgage and actually contained in the mortgage deed can still be regarded as a distinct independent bargain: equity looks at the substance of the parties' intentions and not merely at the form in which such intentions are expressed.

This emerges from *Kreglinger* v. *New Patagonia Meat and Cold Storage Co. Ltd.*[38] where a meat company raised a loan from a firm of woolbrokers on a mortgage by way of floating charge and agreed in the mortgage to let the woolbrokers have an option for five years to purchase any sheepskins the company had for sale. The woolbrokers agreed not to call in the loan for five years but the company could redeem the mortgage earlier if it wished. The company repaid the loan after two years and claimed to take free from the option. The House of Lords held the company bound by the option since the parties did not intend the option to be part and parcel of the mortgage and stand or fall with the mortgage but to be a distinct independent bargain. This marks the commencement of the increasing unwillingness of the courts to interfere on technical grounds with freely negotiated agreements made between equal parties at arms' length. Collateral advantages are now likely to be allowed to persist beyond redemption if so intended by the parties, so long as not oppressive and unconscionable and not in restraint of trade. In practice, the collateral advantage should be conferred in a document separate from the mortgage and signed on a different date.

---

[34] *Bradley* v. *Carritt* [1903] A.C. 253 (freely alienable shares mortgaged which, in fact, on redemption would be inalienable if the former mortgagor was to ensure, via that shareholding, that the former mortgagee should be tea broker to the company whose shares the mortgagor held).
[35] *Noakes* v. *Rice* [1902] A.C. 24.
[36] *De Beers Consolidated Mines Ltd.* v. *British South Africa Co.* [1912] A.C. 52.
[37] *Kreglinger* v. *New Patagonia Meat and Cold Storage Co. Ltd.* [1914] A.C. 25.
[38] [1914] A.C. 25.

3. "Oppressive and unconscionable" terms. The courts have a general equitable jurisdiction to strike down terms in a mortgage which are oppressive and unconscionable.[39] Thus where a company sold a house to one of its tenants, advancing £2,900 under a mortgage which required repayment of £4,553, it was held[40] that this £1,653 premium in lieu of interest was unconscionable since it represented far more than a fair rate of interest[41] and the charge exceeded the value of the house. The mortgagor could therefore redeem by paying £2,900 with interest at a reasonable rate, fixed by the court at 7 per cent.[42]

In *Multiservice Bookbinding Ltd.* v. *Marden*[43] a £36,000 loan on mortgage was index-linked to the Swiss franc, the loan not being repayable for 10 years and not being capable of being called in for 10 years. On expiry of the 10 years the dramatic depreciation of the pound sterling meant that £87,588 capital was due and £45,380 interest had been payable. It was held that though the mortgage terms might be unreasonable they were not oppressive and unconscionable "The parties made a bargain which the plaintiffs, who were businessmen, went into with their eyes open with the benefit of independent advice, without any compelling necessity to accept a loan on these terms and without any sharp practice by the defendant."[44] The plaintiffs had to be consoled with the fact that the value of the mortgaged premises had trebled during the mortgage.

4. Extortionate credit bargains. The Consumer Credit Act 1974[45] gives the courts power to re-open[46] extortionate credit bargains entered into by individuals but not companies. "A credit bargain is extortionate if it (a) requires the debtor or a relative of his to make payments (whether unconditionally or on certain contingencies) which are grossly exorbitant or (b) otherwise grossly contravenes ordinary principles of fair dealing."[47] The court must have regard to interest rates prevailing at the time. In relation to the debtor it must have regard to his age, experience, business capacity and state of health and the degree to which, at the time of the bargain, he was under financial pressure, and the nature of that pressure. In relation to the creditor it must have regard to the degree of risk accepted by him

---

[39] *e.g. Knightsbridge Estates Trust Ltd.* v. *Bryne* [1939] Ch. 441 at p. 457.
[40] *Cityland and Property (Holdings) Ltd.* v. *Dabrah* [1968] Ch. 166.
[41] It represented 19 per cent. over the mortgage period or 57 per cent. if, on default, the capital became payable forthwith.
[42] Goff J. treated "unreasonable" and "unconscionable" as being interchangeable terms which he would not have done had *Knightsbridge (supra)* been cited to him: see *Multiservice Bookbinding Ltd.* v. *Marden* [1979] Ch. 84 at p. 110 where Browne-Wilkinson J. also points out that the premium was unconscionable.
[43] [1979] Ch. 84.
[44] *Ibid.* at p. 110.
[45] ss. 137–139. It does not matter that the agreement is not regulated or that the credit exceeds £5,000: ss. 16 (7), 140, 137 (2) (*e*).
[46] It can set aside obligations and alter the terms of the agreement: s. 139.
[47] s. 138 (1).

(taking account of the value of any security provided) and his relationship to the debtor. An annual rate of interest of 48 per cent. has been held[48] not to be extortionate where a loan had been obtained at very short notice to enable a contract to purchase a flat be completed and a high risk had been accepted by the lender.

5. Restraint of trade. A provision which is neither oppressive nor a clog may be void on other grounds. Thus it may be invalid under the ordinary law of contract as being in unreasonable restraint of trade, *e.g.* if a mortgage is to last for 20 years, the mortgagee not to be able to call in the money before expiry of the period and the mortgagor not to be able to redeem the mortgage before expiry of the period, and for the period the mortgagor is obliged to purchase fuels for his mortgaged petrol filling station only from the mortgagee.[49]

II. WHO CAN REDEEM

Redemption is usually sought by the mortgagor; but the right to redeem is not confined to him and may be exercised by any person interested in the equity of redemption.[50] Thus the right to redeem extends to assignees of the equity of redemption, subsequent mortgagees, and even a lessee under a lease granted by the mortgagor but not binding on the mortgagee.[51]

III. EFFECT OF REDEMPTION

Where redemption is effected by the only person interested in the equity of redemption, and the mortgage redeemed is the only incumbrance on the property, the effect of redemption is to discharge the mortgage and leave the property free from incumbrances. But if there are several mortgages on the property, the effect of redemption will normally be that the person paying the money takes a transfer of the mortgage, as where a second mortgagee redeems the first mortgage. If several incumbrancers seek to redeem a mortgage, the first in order of priority has the best claim.[52] However, if the mortgagor redeems a mortgage which has priority over one or more subsequent mortgages, the redemption discharges the mortgage and the mortgagor cannot claim to have it kept alive to the prejudice of the subsequent mortgagees,[53] for his mortgage to them included all

---

[48] *Ketley Ltd.* v. *Scott* [1981] I.C.R. 241 (the borrowers were already protected tenants of the flat and they had failed to disclose the existence of a prior charge to secure a bank overdraft). See also H.W. Wilkinson (1980) 130 N.L.J. 749.
[49] *Esso Petroleum Co. Ltd.* v. *Harper's Garage (Stourport) Ltd.* [1968] A.C. 269.
[50] *Pearce* v. *Morris* (1869) 5 Ch.App. 227 at p. 229.
[51] *Tarn* v. *Turner* (1888) 39 Ch.D. 456.
[52] *Teevan* v. *Smith* (1882) 20 Ch.D. 724 at p. 730.
[53] *Otter* v. *Lord Vaux* (1856) 6 De G.M. & G. 638, recognised by L.P.A. 1925, s. 115 (3); *Parkash* v. *Irani Finance Ltd.* [1970] Ch. 101.

the rights he had, including those against the prior mortgagee. But no such rule binds his successors in title.[54]

IV. TERMS OF REDEMPTION

A mortgage may be redeemed either in court or out of court; the latter is the more usual. If a mortgagee unreasonably refuses to accept a proper tender of the money due and so makes an action for redemption necessary, he may be penalised in costs.[55]

The mortgagor may redeem on the legal date for redemption without giving notice of his intention to do so. After that date, when he is forced to rely upon his equitable right to redeem, it is a rule of practice that he must either give the mortgagee reasonable notice of his intention to redeem (six months usually sufficing), or else pay him six months' interest in lieu thereof,[56] it is only fair that the mortgagee should have a reasonable opportunity of finding another investment for his money. But the mortgagee is not entitled to any notice or interest in lieu thereof—

   (i) if he has taken steps to enforce his security, as by taking possession, or commencing foreclosure proceedings, or giving the mortgagor notice to repay the loan so as to entitle the mortgagee to sell on default being made[57]; or
   (ii) if the loan is merely of a temporary nature, as is usually the case in an equitable mortgage by deposit of title deeds.[58]

If the mortgagor gives six months' notice and fails to pay on the proper day, he must usually give a further six months' notice or pay six months' interest in lieu thereof,[59] unless he can give a reasonable explanation of his failure to pay, in which case it suffices to give reasonable notice, *e.g.* three months.[60] Even if the mortgage makes no provision for interest, the mortgagor must pay it at a rate which the court will, if necessary, fix.[61]

V. "REDEEM UP, FORECLOSE DOWN"

The maxim "Redeem up, foreclose down" applies where there are several incumbrancers and one of them seeks by action to redeem a superior mortgage. The effect is best shown by an example. X has mortgaged his property successively to A, B, C, D, and E, the mortgages ranking in that order; X thus ranks last, *e.g.* in claiming any surplus if the property is sold. Suppose that D wishes to redeem

---

[54] *Whiteley* v. *Delaney* [1914] A.C. 132.
[55] *Graham* v. *Seal* (1918) 88 L.J.Ch. 31.
[56] *Johnson* v. *Evans* (1889) 61 L.T. 18. The mortgage deed may contain provision to the contrary.
[57] See *Bovill* v. *Endle* [1896] 1 Ch. 648.
[58] *Fitzgerald's Trustee* v. *Mellersh* [1892] 1 Ch. 385.
[59] *Re Moss* (1885) 31 Ch.D. 90 at p. 94.
[60] *Cromwell Property Investment Co. Ltd.* v. *Western,* [1934] Ch. 322.
[61] See *Cityland and Property (Holdings) Ltd.* v. *Dabrah* [1968] Ch. 166.

B and owing to the complexity of the accounts or some other circumstance an action for redemption is commenced. Before B can be redeemed, the exact amount due to him must be settled by the court. This amount, however, does not affect only B and D, for C, E and X are all concerned with the amount which has priority to their interests; thus if the property were to be sold, C, E and X would all wish to know whether what B was entitled to was, say £6,000 or £7,000, for upon that figure might depend their chances of receiving anything from the proceeds of sale. Consequently, the court will insist upon their being made parties to D's action for redemption so that they can be represented in the taking of the accounts between B and D and thus be bound by the final result.

However, it would be unfair to give C, E and X the trouble and expense of taking part in the action merely to watch accounts being taken,[62] with the risk of a similar event taking place in the future, and so the court insists that the rights of all parties concerned in the action shall be settled once and for all. A is not concerned: it is immaterial to him what is due to B, for A's mortgage has priority to B's.[63] But all the other parties are concerned, and the order of the court will be that D shall redeem not only B, but also C, for both their mortgages have priority to D's. Further, E and X must be foreclosed: that is, each of them will have the opportunity of saving his rights by paying off the prior mortgages concerned in the action, but if he fails to do so, he will be foreclosed. Thus if E and X fail to redeem and are foreclosed, the final result wil be that D, at the price of redeeming B and C, now holds the equity of redemption subject only to the first mortgage in favour of A.

The principle may be stated thus:—a mortgagee who seeks to redeem a prior mortgage by action must not only redeem any mortgages standing between him and that prior mortgage,[64] but must also foreclose all subsequent mortgagees and the mortgagor[65]; in short, "redeem up, foreclose down."

It should be noted that this rule does not apply to redemptions out of court,[66] and that there is no rule "foreclose down, redeem up"; a mortgagee who forecloses is under no obligation to redeem any prior mortgages,[67] although he must foreclose all subsequent mortgagees as well as the mortgagor.[68] In other words, for foreclosure the rule is simply "foreclose down": a mortgagee cannot foreclose a subsequent mortgagee or the mortgagor unless he forecloses everyone beneath him.

---

[62] *Ramsbottom* v. *Wallis* (1835) 5 L.J.Ch. 92.
[63] *Brisco* v. *Kenrick* (1832) 1 L.J.Ch. 11.
[64] *Teevan* v. *Smith* (1882) 20 Ch.D. 724 at p. 729.
[65] *Farmer* v. *Curtis* (1829) 2 Sim. 466.
[66] See *Smith* v. *Green* (1844) 1 Coll.C.C. 555.
[67] *Richards* v. *Cooper* (1842) 5 Beav. 304.
[68] *Anderson* v. *Stather* (1845) 2 Coll.C.C. 209.

VI. TERMINATION OF EQUITY OF REDEMPTION

An equity of redemption may be extinguished against the mortgagor's will:

    (i) by foreclosure[69];

    (ii) by sale[70]; or

    (iii) by lapse of time.[71]

In addition, the mortgagor may himself extinguish it by releasing it to the mortgagee, or by redeeming.

B. Other Rights

The mortgagor has various other rights, including the right to have the property sold by the court, the right to inspect the title deeds, the right to compel a transfer of the mortgage[72] and the right to bring actions. As to the right to bring actions, before 1926 the mortgagor normally had no legal estate in the land and so could bring no actions which depended on having such an estate, *e.g.* on the covenants of a lease or tenancy which had been granted before the mortgage was made, so that the legal reversion on it had passed to the mortgagee[73]; and after 1925 the mortgagor's only interest is normally a reversion upon a long lease. But by statute,[74] provided the mortgagee has not given notice of his intention to take possession or enter into receipt of the rents and profits, the mortgagor in possession may sue in his own name for possession or for the rents and profits; he may bring an action to prevent, or recover damages for, any trespass or other wrong; and he may enforce all covenants and conditions in leases of the property.

Part 4

TRANSFER OF RIGHTS

Sect. 1. Death of Mortgagor

Under section 35 of the Aministration of Estates Act 1925 unless the deceased mortgagor has shown a contrary intention[75] in any document (whether his will or some other document) the mortgaged property devolves upon the person entitled under the will or intestacy subject to the mortgage or charge; but these provisions do not extend

---

[69] *Ante*, pp. 473 *et seq.*
[70] *Ante*, p. 475 *et seq.*
[71] *Post*, p. 524.
[72] L.P.A. 1925, ss. 91, 95, 96.
[73] See, *e.g. Turner* v. *Walsh* [1909] 2 K.B. 484.
[74] L.P.A. 1925, ss. 98, 141, replacing earlier legislation.
[75] See *Re Wakefield* [1943] 2 All E.R. 29; *Re Neeld* [1962] Ch. 643; Parry & Clark, *The Law of Succession* (7th ed.), pp. 267–272.

to a person who takes not as legatee or devisee but, *e.g.* as a purchaser under an option given to him by the will.[76]

These provisions do not affect any rights the mortgagee may have against the estate of the mortgagor; they merely ensure that as between the person taking the mortgaged property and the other beneficiaries, the burden of the mortgage should fall upon the former, in the absence of any contrary intention.

Sect. 2. Death of Mortgagee

A. Death of Sole Mortgagee

Under the Administration of Estates Act 1925[77] the mortagee's right to the money lent and his interest in the mortgaged property both pass to his personal representatives.

B. Death of One of Several Mortgagees

1. At law. Where two or more persons lent money on mortgage of freeholds or leaseholds, the legal estate was usually conveyed to them as joint tenants. On the death of one, his interest passed to the others by virtue of the *jus accrescendi*, and the survivors could reconvey the legal estate to the mortgagor when he redeemed.

2. In equity. In equity, however, there is a presumption of a tenancy in common where two or more together lend money on mortgage.[78] Accordingly, in the absence of any provision to the contrary, when one of the mortgagees died his share passed to his personal representatives, and if the mortgagor redeemed they would have to join in the transaction. If the mortgagees were trustees lending trust money, the disclosure of this fact would be sufficient to rebut the presumption, for trustees are always joint tenants[79]; but this would have the disadvantage of bringing the trusts on to the title.[80]

3. Joint account clause. The practice accordingly grew up of inserting a "joint account clause" in mortgages where two or more persons lent money. This clause rebutted the presumption of a tenancy in common so far as the mortgagor was concerned and made it safe for him to pay his money to the surviving mortgagees. Since 1881 such a clause is unnecessary, for statute[81] has provided that as between the mortgagor and the mortgagees, the mortgagees are

---

[76] *Re Fison's W.T.* [1950] Ch. 394.
[77] A.E.A. 1925, ss. 1 (1), 3 (1).
[78] *Ante*, p. 304.
[79] *Ante*, p. 300.
[80] See, *e.g. Re Blaiberg and Abrahams* [1899] 2 Ch. 340.
[81] C.A. 1881, s. 61, replaced by L.P.A. 1925, s. 111.

deemed to have advanced the money on a joint account unless a contrary intention appears. The result is that the survivor or survivors can give a complete discharge for all moneys due, notwithstanding any notice of severance which the mortgagor may have. This, however, is mere conveyancing machinery; it does not affect the position of the mortgagees *inter se*, and if they are beneficially entitled and not trustees, the survivors must account to the personal representatives of the deceased mortgagee for his share.[82] Although a joint account clause in a mortgage today is thus strictly unnecessary, it is often inserted *ex abundanti cautela*.

Sect. 3. Transfer of Equity of Redemption Inter Vivos

A mortgagor may at any time without the mortgagee's consent make a conveyance of his property subject to the mortgage. However, notwithstanding any such conveyance, the mortgagor remains personally liable on the covenant to pay the money.[83] He therefore usually takes an express covenant for indemnity from the transferee, although such an obligation is implied.[84]

A mortgagor who wishes to sell free from the mortgage may do so—

(i) if he redeems; or
(ii) if the mortgagee consents (as he may well do if the security is adequate or if some other property is substituted for the property in question); or
(iii) if the mortgagor takes advantage of the statutory provision enabling the court to declare property free from an incumbrance upon sufficient money being paid into court.[85]

An assignee of the equity of redemption in general steps into the shoes of the mortgagor; but he does not merely by the assignment become personally liable to the mortgagee to pay the mortgage debt.[86]

Sect. 4. Transfer of Mortgages Inter Vivos

A. In General

A mortgagee may transfer his mortgage at any time without the concurrence of the mortgagor. However, for various reasons it is advisable for the mortgagor's concurrence to be obtained, *e.g.* in order to obtain his admission of the state of accounts showing the amount still due under the mortgage.[87]

---

[82] See *Re Jackson* (1887) 34 Ch.D. 732.
[83] *Kinnaird* v. *Trollope* (1888) 39 Ch.D. 636.
[84] *Bridgman* v. *Daw* (1891) 40 W.R. 253.
[85] L.P.A. 1925, s. 50, replacing C.A. 1881, s. 5 (1).
[86] *Re Errington* [1894] 1 Q.B. 11.
[87] See *Turner* v. *Smith* [1901] 1 Ch. 213.

Once the transfer has been made, the transferee should give notice of it to the mortgagor, unless the mortgagor has notice already, *e.g.* because he was a party to the transfer. If the mortgagor has no actual or constructive notice, the transferee cannot complain if the mortgagor pays to the transferor money due under the mortgage.[88]

B. Sub-Mortgages

A sub-mortgage is a mortgage of a mortgage. A mortgagee may, instead of transferring his mortgage, borrow money upon the security of it. A well-secured debt can itself be good security for a loan to the creditor. Thus if X has lent £20,000 upon a mortgage made by B, and X then wishes to raise a temporary loan of £2,000 himself, it would clearly be inadvisable for X to transfer the mortgage to Y for £20,000 or to call in the whole of his loan. Consequently, X would raise the money by mortgaging his mortgage, *i.e.* by making a sub-mortgage.

Before 1926, a sub-mortgage was effected by a transfer of the mortgage subject to a proviso for redemption. After 1925, this form is still available if the mortgage is equitable or is a legal charge; but where it has been created by the grant of a term of years, a legal sub-mortgage can be made only by the grant of a sub-term or by a legal charge.[89] In general, the sub-mortgagee takes over the mortgagee's rights of enforcing payment under the original mortgage; thus he may sell the property. Alternatively, he may exercise his remedies against the mortgage itself, as by selling it.[90]

Sect. 5. Discharge of Mortgage

A. Before 1926

Upon the redemption of a legal mortgage of a fee simple before 1926, the mortgagee had to execute a reconveyance of the fee simple. In the case of leaseholds, there was a reassignment or, if the mortgage had been made by subdemise, a surrender of the sub-lease. In each case, the document contained a receipt for the money paid. However, in the case of a mortgage to a building society, a mere receipt indorsed on the mortgage deed operated both as a discharge of the mortgage and a reconveyance of the estate[91]; and an equitable mortgage was sufficiently discharged by an indorsed receipt.

B. After 1925

In the case of any mortgage discharged after 1925, a receipt indorsed on or annexed to the mortgage deed, signed[92] by the mortgagee and

---

[88] *Dixon* v. *Winch* [1900] 1 Ch. 736 at p. 742.
[89] L.P.A. 1925, s. 86 (1), (3).
[90] See generally Fisher & Lightwood, *Mortgages* (9th ed., 1977), pp. 260–263.
[91] Building Societies Acts 1836, s. 5; 1874, s. 42.
[92] See *Simpson* v. *Geoghegan* [1934] W.N. 232.

stating the name of the person paying the money, normally operates as a surrender of the mortgage term or a reconveyance, as the case may be, and discharges the mortgage.[93] But if the receipt shows that the person paying the money was not entitled to the immediate equity of redemption and makes no provision to the contrary, it operates as a transfer of the mortgage to him.[94] Building society mortgages may still be discharged by a special form of receipt,[95] which does not state who paid the money and which cannot operate as a transfer of the mortgage.

Apart from these provisions, once a mortgage by subdemise has been redeemed, the sub-term becomes a satisfied term and ceases forthwith.[96] But although when coupled with this provision it might be thought that an ordinary receipt (*i.e.* one not complying with the conditions relating to indorsed receipts) would operate as a sufficient discharge, conveyancers do not in practice rely upon such a receipt, for it is only prima facie proof of payment.

C. Registered Land

A registered charge has to be discharged by deletion from the register. The charge certificate and Form 53 signed by the chargee (or other satisfactory evidence such as an indorsed receipt under the Building Societies Act 1962) must be delivered to the Registry.

Part 5

PRIORITY OF MORTGAGES

Where there is more than one mortgage on the same property, it is sometimes necessary to determine the priority of the mortgages, *e.g.* if the property is sold by one mortgagee and there is not enough money to satisfy all. The general rules for determining priority (which are a particular application of the general rules relating to the enforceability of competing legal and equitable interests) will be discussed first, followed by the rules relating to tacking of further advances, which is a mode of altering the priorities settled by the general rules.

---

[93] L.P.A. 1925, s. 115 (1).
[94] *Ibid.* s. 115 (2).
[95] See now Building Societies Act 1962, s. 37, which has broadly equated the two forms, though the building society form has some advantages: see Wurtzburg and Mills, *Building Society Law* (13th ed., 1970), p. 220.
[96] L.P.A. 1925, ss. 5, 116, *ante*, p. 464.

Sect. 1. Unregistered Land After 1925

A. General Rules

I. MORTGAGES OF A LEGAL ESTATE[97]

1. All mortgages included. It should be noted that this head includes all mortgages of a legal estate, whether the mortgage itself is legal or equitable. The question is "Has a legal estate been mortgaged?" not "Is the mortgage legal or equitable?"

2. Principles. The two main principles are these: (a) *Mortgages protected by deeds*: a mortgage "protected by a deposit of documents relating to the legal estate affected" is expressly excepted from the provisions of the 1925 legislation requiring registration of land charges,[98] since the absence of the title deeds will proclaim the mortgage to anyone seeking to deal with the land.[99] It seems likely that "protected" means "originally protected."[1]

(b) *Mortgages not protected by deeds*: a mortgage made after 1925 and not protected by a deposit of documents relating to the legal estate affected should be registered as a land charge. If the mortgage is legal, it should be registered as a puisne mortgage (Class C (i)); if the mortgage is equitable, it should be registered as a general equitable charge (Class C (iii)).[2]

3. Reasons for registration. The reasons for registering a puisne mortgage or a general equitable charge are as follows:

(a) *Priority*. Section 97 of the Law of Property Act 1925 provides that every such mortgage "shall rank according to its date of registration as a land charge pursuant to the Land Charges Act 1925 or 1972."[3]

(b) *Void for want of registration*. Section 4(5) of the Land Charges Act 1972 provides that a Class C land charge created after 1925 shall "be void as against a purchaser of the land charged therewith, or of any interest in such land, unless the land charge is registered in the appropriate register before the completion of the purchase."[4] In the Act, unless the context otherwise requires, "purchaser" means "any person (including a mortgagee or lessee) who, for valuable considera-

---

[97] See the discussion in (1940) 7 Cam.L.J. 243.
[98] L.C.A. 1972, s. 2 (4), replacing L.C.A. 1925, s. 10. It does not seem that they can be protected as Class C (iv) estate contracts. M & W, p. 971.
[99] Unless a lessee unable to see the freehold title who is not deemed to have constructive notice of those matters he would have discovered had he contracted to see the freehold title: L.P.A. 1925 s. 44 (2), (5).
[1] M. & W., p. 969.
[2] See *ante*, p. 92.
[3] See L.C.A. 1972, s. 18 (6).
[4] Formerly L.C.A. 1925, s. 13 (2).

tion, takes any interest in land or in a charge of land."[5] Thus an unregistered puisne mortgage or an unregistered general equitable charge is void against a purchaser of the fee simple, even if he had actual knowledge of it; for where an interest is void for non-registration as against a purchaser, he is not prejudicially affected by notice of it.[6]

4. Effect. The effect of these provisions upon two successive mortgages must be considered under the four possible heads.

(A) *Each mortgage protected by a deposit of deeds.* There is nothing to require the deposit of all the deeds, so that it may be possible for two or more mortgages of the same property to be exempted from registration and fall under this head.[7] Also a mortgagor might recover his deposited deeds on a pretext (*e.g.* to check his boundaries or show his law student son) and then deposit them with a second mortgagee. In such cases the mortgages will rank in the order of their creation, subject to the old law as to loss of priority.[8]

The conflict between two mortgages protected by deposit may fall under any of four heads:

  (i) Where both mortgages are legal.
  (ii) Where the first is legal and the second equitable.
  (iii) Where the first is equitable and the second legal.
  (iv) Where both are equitable.

These will be considered in turn.

(i) *Both mortgages legal.* The first mortgage will prevail ("*qui prior est tempore, potior est jure*"—he who is first in time is stronger in law) unless the first mortgagee is postponed by virtue of fraud, estoppel or gross negligence as discussed below.

(ii) *Legal mortgage followed by equitable mortgage.* Where a legal mortgage is followed by an equitable mortgage, the legal mortgage has a double claim to priority, both as being prior in point of time and as being a legal mortgage in competition with a mere equitable mortgage.

However, this natural priority may be displaced in a number of ways.

(a) BY FRAUD. If the legal mortgagee is guilty of some fraud whereby the equitable mortgagee was deceived into believing that

---

[5] L.C.A. 1972, s. 17 (1).
[6] L.P.A. 1925, s. 199, *Midland Bank Trust Co. Ltd.* v. *Green* [1981] A.C. 513.
[7] *Cf.* the facts in *Weston* v. *Henshaw* [1950] Ch. 510, *ante*, p. 249.
[8] This assumes that "protected" by deposit of title deeds means "originally protected" and not "continuously protected."

there was no legal mortgage on the property, the legal mortgagee will be postponed to the equitable mortgagee.[9]

(b) BY ESTOPPEL. If the legal mortgagee either expressly or by implication made some misrepresentation by which the equitable mortgagee was deceived, the legal mortgagee will be estopped from asserting his priority.[10] Thus if the legal mortgagee indorsed a receipt for his money on the mortgage and somebody was thereby induced to lend money on an equitable mortgage of the property, the legal mortgagee cannot afterwards claim priority for his loan if in fact it had not been discharged.[11] Again, if the legal mortgagee parted with the deeds to the mortgagor to enable him to raise money, he will be postponed to any subsequent mortgagee who lent money without notice of the first mortgage, even if the mortgagor had agreed to inform the second mortgagee of the first mortgage, or had agreed to borrow only a limited amount which in fact he exceeded.[12] Once the mortgagee had clothed the mortgagor with apparent authority to deal with the property freely, he cannot afterwards claim the protection of any undisclosed limits set to this authority.

(c) BY GROSS NEGLIGENCE IN RELATION TO THE TITLE DEEDS. If the legal mortgagee was grossly negligent in failing to obtain the title deeds, he was postponed to a subsequent equitable mortgagee who had exercised due diligence. Failure to ask for the deeds at all would postpone a legal mortgagee[13]; it was otherwise if he inquired for them and was given a reasonable excuse.[14]

If the legal mortgagee obtained the deeds, it appears from one case[15] that no amount of carelessness in failing to keep them in safe custody will postpone him, *e.g.* where the deeds were kept in a safe to which the mortgagor had a key as manager working for the mortgagee. This has been questioned so that a gross failure to retain the deeds might well postpone priority nowadays.[16]

(iii) *Equitable mortgage followed by legal mortgage.* Where an equitable mortgage was followed by a legal mortgage, the primary rule that the mortgages rank in the order of creation may be displaced by the superiority of a legal estate. For this to occur, the legal mortgagee has to show that he is a bona fide purchaser for value of a legal estate without notice of the prior equitable mortgage.[17] Usually

---

[9] *Peter* v. *Russel* (1716) 1 Eq.Ca.Abr. 321.
[10] *Dixon* v. *Muckleston* (1872) 8 Ch.App. 155 at p. 160.
[11] *Rimmer* v. *Webster* [1902] 2 Ch. 163.
[12] *Perry Herrick* v. *Attwood* (1857) 2 De G. & J. 21.
[13] *Walker* v. *Linom* [1907] 2 Ch. 104; *Colyer* v. *Finch* (1856) 5 H.L.C. 905.
[14] *Manners* v. *Mew* (1885) 29 Ch.D. 725. Since 1926 such mortgage not protected by deposit is registrable as a Class C (i) land charge.
[15] *Northern Counties, etc. Insurance Co.* v. *Whipp* (1884) 26 Ch.D. 482.
[16] M. & W., p. 961.
[17] *Pilcher* v. *Rawlins* (1872) 7 Ch.App. 259; *Att.-Gen.* v. *Biphosphated Guano Co.* (1879) 11 Ch.D. 327.

the inability of the mortgagor to produce the title deeds will amount to notice to the legal mortgagee that some prior mortgage already existed[18]; but if the legal mortgagee's inquiries for the deeds were met by a reasonable excuse (*e.g.* that the deeds had been destroyed in a fire), he will succeed in his claim to be a purchaser without notice and so to have priority over the equitable mortgagee. Unfortunately, in examining the mortgagor's excuses for not producing the title deeds the courts have confused themselves in considering cases where the first mortgage was legal and would lose priority if the first mortgagee had been grossly negligent in relation to the title deeds and have concluded that a subsequent legal mortgagee will only lose priority if guilty of gross negligence.[19] Accepting the excuse that the deeds were in Ireland was not gross negligence[20] but accepting the excuse that the deeds also relate to other property was gross negligence.[21]

(iv) *Both mortgages equitable.* Where both mortgages are equitable, the primary rule is that priority depends upon the order in which the mortgages were created; this, however, is subject to the equities being in other respects equal,[22] so that the prior mortgagee may lose his priority on the ground of fraud, estoppel or gross negligence.[23] Accordingly, a first mortgagee who failed to ask for the title deeds, or who, having obtained them, redelivered them to the mortgagor without pressing for their early return, might be postponed to a second mortgagee who took all proper precautions but who was nevertheless deceived.[24]

(B) *Neither mortgage protected by a deposit of deeds.* (i) CONCORD. If neither mortgage is protected by a deposit of deeds, no difficulty arises if the first mortgage is duly registered before the second is made. Even if the first is equitable and the second legal, the first prevails, for section 97 expressly provides that they shall rank in the order of registration, and the provision that registration amounts to notice prevents the legal mortgagee from claiming to be a purchaser without notice. Nor is there any difficulty if neither mortgage is registered. Even if the first mortgage is legal and the second equitable, under section 4 (5) the first is void against the second for want of registration and so the second has priority. Indeed, if there are several successive registrable mortgages, none of which has been

---

[18] *Oliver* v. *Hinton* [1899] 2 Ch. 264 at 268, *Walker* v. *Linom* [1907] 2 Ch. 104 at p. 114.
[19] *Agra Bank Ltd.* v. *Barry* (1874) L.R. 7 H.L. 135; *Hewitt* v. *Loosemore* (1851) 9 Hare 449; *Oliver* v. *Hinton* [1899] 2 Ch. 264.
[20] *Agra Bank Ltd.* v. *Barry* (*supra*).
[21] *Oliver* v. *Hinton* (*supra*).
[22] *Rice* v. *Rice* (1853) 2 Drew. 73.
[23] See *Taylor* v. *Russell* [1891] 1 Ch. 8; *Rimmer* v. *Webster* [1902] 2 Ch. 163.
[24] *Farrand* v. *Yorkshire Banking Co.* (1888) 40 Ch.D. 182. A mortgage not originally protected by deposit is now registrable as a Class C (iii) land charge.

registered, the priority accorded by date of creation will be reversed for the last will rank first and so on.

(ii) DISCORD. The difficult case is where the first mortgage was registered after the creation of the second mortgage. For example:

January 1	A grants a mortgage to X
February 2	A grants a mortgage to Y
March 3	X registers
March 4	Y registers

In such a case, the order according to section 97 is X, Y; according to section 4 (5) it is Y, X, for X's mortgage is void against Y. It is not clear which section prevails. In favour of section 97, the chief point is that it is expressly dealing with the priority of mortgages, whereas section 4 (5) makes unregistered mortgages void against subsequent mortgages only by virtue of the provision that "purchaser" includes a mortgagee. On the other hand, the provision in section 4 (5) that an unregistered land charge is void against a subsequent purchaser makes it hard to see how the registration of X's mortgage can give priority to something which, as regards Y, has no existence.[25] The problem still awaits solution; probably section 4 (5) will prevail since Y will have been induced to lend his money by the fact that no earlier charge appeared to exist and X could easily have protected himself by speedier registration.[26] Even more complicated problems can be constructed, *e.g.* where X has priority over Y who has priority over Z who has priority over X; but these need not be discussed here.[27]

(iii) PRIORITY NOTICES AND OFFICIAL SEARCHES. At the beginning of 1926, there was the difficulty that it was physically impossible to register a land charge the instant after it had been created; thus there was a dangerous gap between the creation of a mortgage and its registration. Further, even if a search for prior incumbrances was made, the mortgagee could not be sure that no incumbrance had been registered between the time of his search and the completion of the mortgage. These difficulties have been met by the devices of the priority notice and the official search, which have been dealt with earlier.[28]

(C) *First but not second mortgage protected by a deposit of deeds.* In this case, the first mortgage, by taking its priority from the date of its creation, will normally have priority over the second mortgage, subject to the old rules as to loss of priority by fraud, estoppel or gross negligence.[29]

[25] *Cf. Kitney* v. *M.E.P.C.* [1977] 1 W.L.R. 981.
[26] See M. & W., p. 973, Fairest, *Mortgages* (2nd ed.), pp. 146–147.
[27] See M. & W., 971–974; W.A. Lee (1968) 32 Conv. 325.
[28] *Ante*, p. 105.
[29] Discussed *ante*, pp. 506–507.

(D) *Second but not first mortgage protected by a deposit of deeds.* Here, sections 4 (5) and 97 work in harmony. If the first mortgage is registered before the second is made, the first ranks for priority "according to its date of registration" (s. 97), *i.e.* prior to the second mortgage, and section 4 (5) has no application. If the first mortgage is not registered when the second mortgage is made, the first mortgage is void against the second for want of registration, and even if it is subsequently registered, it takes priority from the date of registration.

5. Summary. (a) *Deposit of deeds.* A mortgage protected by a deposit of deeds ranks according to the date on which it was created. The mortgagee may lose priority—

    (i) by fraud, estoppel or gross negligence; or

    (ii) if his mortgage is equitable, by a legal mortgage being made to a mortgagee for value without notice (or, perhaps, to a legal mortgagee who is not grossly negligent through not asking for the deeds or accepting an unreasonable excuse for the absence of the deeds).

(b) *No deposit of deeds.* A mortgage not protected by deposit of deeds should be protected by registration. If the mortgagee fails to do this, he will not, it seems, be protected against a subsequent mortgagee (s. 4 (5)). If he does register he will be protected against all mortgages made thereafter.

II. MORTGAGES OF AN EQUITABLE INTEREST

Where the subject-matter of a mortgage is an equitable interest in any property, whether land or pure personalty, the Rule in *Dearle* v. *Hall*,[30] as amended by the Law of Property Act 1925,[31] now applies.

1. The Rule. The Rule makes priority depend upon the order in which notice of the mortgage is *received*[32] by the owner of the legal estate or interest. However, a mortgagee who, *when he lent his money*, had actual or constructive notice of a prior mortgage could not gain priority over it by giving notice first.[33]

2. It is advisable to give notice to all of the trustees. This may be amplified as follows:

    (i) Notice given to all the existing trustees remains effective even

---

[30] See M. & W., pp. 965–968, 976–978.
[31] ss. 137, 138.
[32] *Calisher* v. *Forbes* (1871) 7 Ch.App. 109; *Ipswich Permanent Money Club Ltd.* v. *Arthy* [1920] 2 Ch. 257.
[33] *Re Holmes* (1885) 29 Ch.D. 786; *Mutual Life Assurance Society* v. *Langley* (1886) 32 Ch.D. 460.

though they all retire or die without communicating the notice to their successors.[34]

(ii) Notice given to one of several trustees is effective against all incumbrances created during his trusteeship, and remain effective despite his death or retirement.[35]

(iii) But, notice given to one of several trustees is not effective against incumbrancers who advance money after the death or retirement of that trustee unless he had communicated the notice to one or more of the continuing trustees.[36]

(iv) If the mortgagor is a trustee, the mere fact that he knows of the transaction will not affect priorities, for such notice affords no protection to subsequent mortgagees.[37] But if the mortgagee is a trustee his knowledge of the transaction does affect priorities; for to protect his mortgage he will readily disclose its existence to any prospective incumbrancers.[38]

3. The amendments made by the Law of Property Act 1925 are as follows: (i) *Notice in writing.* No notice given or received after 1925 can affect priority unless it is in writing.[39] Apart from this, no alteration has been made in the rule relating to notice.

(ii) *Persons to be served.* The persons to be served with notice are[40]:

(a) in the case of settled land, the trustees of the settlement;
(b) in the case of a trust for sale, the trustees for sale;
(c) in the case of any other land, the estate owner of the land affected.

Thus the person to be served is normally the owner of the legal estate, except in the case of settled land, where notice to the tenant for life might well be no protection, *e.g.* if it was his life interest which had been mortgaged. In cases other than the three mentioned above, no special provision has been made, so that notice must be given to the legal owner as before 1926. Nor has any alteration been made to the law relating to notice received by one of several trustees.

(iii) *Indorsement of notice.* If for any reason a valid notice cannot be served (*e.g.* where there are no trustees), or can be served only at unreasonable cost or delay, a purchaser may require that a memorandum be indorsed on or permanently annexed to the instrument creating the trust, and this has the same effect as notice to

---

[34] *Re Wasdale* [1899] 1 Ch. 163.
[35] *Ward* v. *Duncombe* [1893] A.C. 369.
[36] *Re Phillips' Trusts* [1903] 1 Ch. 183.
[37] *Lloyds Bank* v. *Pearson* [1901] 1 Ch. 865.
[38] *Browne* v. *Savage* (1859) 4 Drew. 635.
[39] L.P.A. 1925, s. 137 (3).
[40] *Ibid.* s. 137 (2).

the trustees. In the case of settled land, the trust instrument, and in the case of a trust for sale, the instrument creating the equitable interest, is the document to be used for this purpose.[41]

(iv) *Notice to trust corporation.* The instrument creating the trust, the trustees or the court may nominate a trust corporation to receive notices instead of the trustees. In such cases, only notice to the trust corporation affects priority; notice to the trustees has no effect until they deliver it to the trust corporation, which they are bound to do forthwith. Provision is made for the indorsement of notice of the appointment on the instrument upon which notices may be indorsed, for the keeping of a register of notices, for the inspection of the register, for the answering of inquiries and for payments of fees therefor.[42] In practice, little use is made of these provisions.

(v) *Production of notices.* On the application of any person interested in the equitable interest, the trustees or estate owner must now produce any notices served on them or their predecessors.[43] This emasculates *Low* v. *Bouverie*.[44]

B. Tacking

Tacking is a method by which the rules relating to priorities may be modified, both for realty and for personalty. Before 1926, there were two forms of tacking:

(i) The *tabula in naufragio* ("the plank in the shipwreck").
(ii) The tacking of further advances.

The first form of tacking is not available after 1925 for determining priority as between competing mortgages.[45] However, it can still be relied upon in other cases, *e.g.* where an equitable mortgagee who has acquired the legal estate (under a power of attorney conferred by the mortgage) claims to prevail over a prior equitable incumbrancer having an unregistered estate contract.[46]

I. THE TABULA IN NAUFRAGIO

1. The doctrine. If an equitable mortgagee lent money without notice of a prior equitable mortgage, he could gain priority over it if he subsequently acquired a legal estate in the land with priority over it.[47] This was so because, apart from the order of creation, between the mortgagees the equities were equal and so the holder of a legal

---

[41] *Ibid.* s. 137 (4), (5).
[42] *Ibid.* s. 138.
[43] *Ibid.* s. 137 (8), (9).
[44] See M. & W., pp. 967–968.
[45] L.P.A. 1925, s. 94 (3), (4).
[46] *McCarthy & Stone Ltd.* v. *Hodge Ltd.* [1971] 1 W.L.R. 1547; P.B. Fairest [1972A] Cam. L.J. 34.
[47] *Marsh* v. *Lee* (1671) 2 Ventr. 337.

estate prevailed[48]; the subsequent mortgagee could tack, or attach, his mortgage to the legal estate. Thus if A mortgaged his property to X by a legal mortgage and then to Y and Z by successive equitable mortgages, Z's mortgage would take priority over Y's if Z bought X's mortgage, provided Z had no notice of Y's mortgage when he advanced his money.[49] X's legal mortgage was the plank in the shipwreck, and whichever of Y and Z acquired it had the better chance of being saved if there was not enough money to pay both.

2. Legal estate. Normally the mortgagee seeking to tack actually took a transfer of the legal estate; but this was not essential, for he could tack if he had the best right to call for the legal estate,[50] as where the legal estate was held on trust for him. Further, if the mortgagee acquired a legal estate, it was not necessary that it should be the estate mortgaged; a mere term of years sufficed.[51] And even a legal estate created subsequently to the mortgage against which tacking was to be effected might suffice.[52] But a legal estate could not be used to alter priorities if it was acquired with notice that the conveyance was a breach of trust, for this made the mortgagee a trustee himself.[53]

3. Later mortgage. Although tacking under this head usually took place when a later equitable mortgagee acquired a legal estate, the doctrine applied equally to a legal mortgagee who acquired a later mortgage without notice of an intervening incumbrance.[54]

II. TACKING OF FURTHER ADVANCES

A mortgagee might lend the money and later make a further advance to the mortgagor. Since 1925 there are three[55] cases in which the mortgagee can tack his further advance to his original mortgage and claim priority over an intervening incumbrancer for both loans.

1. Agreement of intervening incumbrancers. The mortgagee can tack if the intervening incumbrancer agrees. Building estates sometimes provided examples of this: the owner requires more money to build on his estate and thus make it a better security. The second mortgagee, not wishing to lend any more money, may agree to the first mortgagee making a further advance to be expended on further building and to rank in priority to the second mortgage.

---

[48] *Wortley* v. *Birkhead* (1754) 2 Ves.Sen. 571 at p. 574.
[49] *Brace* v. *Duchess of Marlborough* (1728) 2 P.Wms.491. Subsequent notice is immaterial: *Taylor* v. *Russell* [1892] A.C. 244 at p. 259.
[50] *Wilkes* v. *Bodington* (1707) 2 Vern. 599 at p. 600.
[51] *Willoughby* v. *Willoughby* (1756) 1 T.R. 763.
[52] *Cooke* v. *Wilton* (1860) 29 Beav. 100.
[53] *Saunders* v. *Dehew* (1692) 2 Vern. 271; *Taylor* v. *Russell* [1892] A.C. 244 at p. 259, *Taylor* v. *London & County Banking Co.* [1901] 2 Ch. 231 at p. 256.
[54] *Morret* v. *Paske* (1740) 2 Atk. 52 at p. 53.
[55] L.P.A. 1925 s. 94 (1).

2. No notice of intervening incumbrancers. Any mortgagee, whether legal or equitable, may tack a further advance if it was made without notice of the intervening mortgage. Where the intervening mortgage is protected by a deposit of deeds and is thus not registrable, the normal rules as to notice operate. If the mortgage is not protected in this way and is accordingly registrable, the rule that registration amounts to notice will apply and so protect it if it is registered. In one case, however, registration is not deemed to be notice; if the prior mortgage was made expressly for securing further advances, such as on a current account (*e.g.* an overdraft at a bank, where the debt is increased and decreased as sums are drawn out or paid in), registration alone is not deemed to be notice, unless the intervening mortgage was registered when the last search was made by the mortgagee.[56] This applies to a spouse's right of occupation which is registered after a mortgage has been made.[57]

An example may make this clearer. Mortgages have been made to A (who took the deeds) and B, in that order, and A has made further advances. If when A made his further advances he had actual, constructive or imputed notice of B's mortgage, he cannot tack under this head even if his mortgage, without obliging him to make further advances, was stated to be security for any further advances he might choose to make. If he had no such notice of B's mortgage when he made his further advances, but B's mortgage was registered at that time, then if A's mortgage is silent as to further advances, the registration amounts to notice and prevents A from tacking. But if A's mortgage was expressed to be security for any further advances that he might make, the registration will not prevent him from tacking, and thus he need not search before making each further advance.

This points a practical moral. Even if a second mortgage has been duly registered, the mortgagee should give express notice of his mortgage to the first mortgagee, for this—

(i) prevents tacking under this head; and
(ii) compels the first mortgagee to hand over the deeds to him when the first mortgage is discharged.[58]

3. Obligation to make further advance. A further advance may be tacked if the prior mortgage imposes an obligation on the mortgagee to make it. In this case, not even express notice will prevent tacking.[59] If in return for a mortgage a bank binds itself to honour a customer's cheques up to an overdraft of £10,000 there is no question of the bank having to search before honouring each cheque, for not

---

[56] *Ibid.* s. 94 (2).
[57] Matrimonial Homes Act 1967, s. 2 (8). For the Act, see *ante*, p. 95.
[58] *Ante*, p. 486.
[59] L.P.A., s. 94 (1) (c).

even express notice will prevent the bank from tacking each further advance.

Sect. 2. Registered Land

1. Registered charges. Under section 29 of the Land Registration Act "Subject to any entry to the contrary in the register, registered charges on the same land shall rank according to the order in which they are entered on the register and not according to the order in which they are created." This is straightforward.

2. Tacking of further advances. Where the proprietor of a registered charge is under an obligation noted on the register to make further advances then any subsequent registered charge takes effect subject to any further advance made pursuant to the obligation.[60] Where no such obligation exists but the charge is expressed to cover such further advances, if any, that may happen to be made, then the Registrar, before making any entry which would prejudicially affect the priority of any further advances, has to notify the registered chargee of the intended entry, *e.g.* of a second registered charge. If, after the date when the notification should have arrived in due course of post, further advances are made they will not have priority over the second registered charge.[61] If this occasions loss to the first chargee he will, exceptionally, be entitled to an indemnity where failure on the part of the Post Office or the Land Registry meant that he had no notification of the second charge.[62] Tacking is only available in respect of registered charges.

3. Minor interest followed by registered charge. If it has been possible to register a charge because the earlier mortgage ranking as a minor interest has not been protected either by entry on the register or by deposit of the land certificate then the registered charge has priority.[63] If the minor interest has been protected then the charge could only have become a registered charge subject to a notice preserving priority for the earlier minor interest[64] or subject to the earlier interest being converted into a prior registered charge.

4. Unprotected minor interest followed by minor interest. As between these two competing equitable interests general equitable principles apply,[65] namely that the first in time prevails unless the first

---

[60] L.R.A. 1925, s. 30 (3).
[61] *Ibid.* s. 30 (1).
[62] *Ibid.* s. 30 (2).
[63] *Ibid.* ss. 19 (2), 22 (2), 20 (1), 23 (1).
[64] A cautioner must upgrade his caution to a notice if his interest is to bind the registered charge: Ruoff & Roper, pp. 734, 736.
[65] *Barclays Bank* v. *Taylor* [1974] Ch. 137.

incumbrancer is prevented from having priority on grounds of fraud, estoppel or gross negligence.[66] It is standard conveyancing practice to protect mortgages, so that failure to protect a mortgage, ranking as a minor interest, by entry on the register or by deposit of the land certificate, holds the property out as unencumbered by any such interest. The first incumbrancer should thus be estopped from claiming priority.[67]

5. Protected minor interest followed by minor interest. Obviously, the first incumbrancer, since protected, has priority over the second incumbrancer who should know about the first mortgage.[68]

6. The dates of entries on the register do not govern priorities except for registered charges. If A's unprotected minor interest mortgage is created on March 1, then B's unprotected minor interest is created on April 2, then A protects his interest on May 3, and B protects his interest on June 4, it seems that priority is not governed by the dates of entries on the register.[69] In the absence of statutory rules one has to fall back on general equitable principles as in paragraph 4 above. Cautions have no effect except to enable the cautioner to take action when informed of proposed dealings.[70] Notices are only effective so far as the interest protected by the notice is valid,[71] and, on general equitable principles, A's interest is not valid against B's interest for the reasons in paragraph 4 above.

7. Liens by deposit of the land certificate. Where a mortgage is actually created by deposit of the land certificate, as opposed to being created by deed to which the deposit of the land certificate is merely ancillary,[72] section 66 seems to create a special rule. It provides that a proprietor may, subject to overriding interests and to interests protected on the register at the date of deposit, create a lien and such lien shall, subject as aforesaid, be equivalent to a mortgage of unregistered land by deposit of title deeds. By implication it can be said that such lien-holder takes free from minor interests created before the deposit but not then protected on the register. This is clearly proper where the earlier minor interest is a mortgage where it is standard conveyancing practice to protect such interest and the position conforms to the unregistered land position. However, where

---

[66] *Abigail* v. *Lapin* [1934] A.C. 491; *Butler* v. *Fairclough* (1917) 23 C.L.R. 78 *ante*, p. 70.
[67] See Hayton: Ch. 8.
[68] *Parkash* v. *Irani Finance Ltd.* [1970] Ch. 101, Hayton pp. 151–153.
[69] See Hayton, pp. 140–153, Ruoff & Roper, p. 124.
[70] L.R.A., s. 56 (2).
[71] *Ibid.* s. 52; *Kitney* v. *M.E.P.C.* [1971] 1 W.L.R. 981.
[72] *Re White Rose Cottage* [1964] Ch. 483 at pp. 490–491.

the earlier interest is an ordinary estate contract it would reverse the unregistered land position.[73]

8. Reform. Even with registered land circular priorities can arise. Suppose O charges his house to A who does not protect his charge. Then O charges his house to B by deed supported by deposit of the land certificate.[74] Then A enters a caution. Then O, with the excuse that he wants to show the land certificate to his law student son (though, in fact, he has no children), persuades B to return the land certificate, O then charges the house to C by deed supported by deposit of the land certificate. C seeks to become registered chargee so A objects. A has priority over C (since protected when C took his charge) but C has priority over B (since B was unprotected when C took his charge) but B has priority over A (since A was unprotected when B took his charge). Priority problems would not arise if mortgages could not be protected by deposit of the land certificate alone but had to be protected by entry on the register, and if priorities were determined by date of entry on the register. Legislation along these lines would be straightforward and worthwhile.

Part 6

PARTICULAR PRIORITY PROBLEMS OF MORTGAGEES

A. Tenancies by Estoppel

1. Unregistered land. If P, a purchaser, is allowed possession of the purchased house by V, the vendor, before completion of the purchase and purports to grant a tenancy to T, then T has a tenancy by estoppel.[75] When P completes the purchase with the assistance of a mortgage from M, P obtains the legal estate a split second before M obtains a legal mortgage. In this *scintilla temporis* P's legal estate feeds T's tenancy by estoppel so that T obtains a legal lease just before M obtains a legal mortgage. T's lease thus binds M.[76] Mortgagees must therefore do their best to ensure that no such tenancies exist, since any provision in the mortgage excluding the mortgagor's powers of leasing is of no avail against leases granted prior to the mortgage.

If T merely had an informal lease or agreement for a lease then this would not bind M if not registered as a Class C (iv) land charge. However, any legal periodic tenancy arising out of going into

---

[73] *McCarthy & Stone Ltd.* v. *Hodge Ltd.* [1971] 1 W.L.R. 1547, Hayton, pp. 143, 160.
[74] L.R.A., s. 66 is thus inapplicable since it only applies where the charge is created by the deposit: note 72 *ante*.
[75] *Ante*, p. 347.
[76] *Church of England B.S.* v. *Piskor* [1954] Ch. 553.

possession and paying rent accepted by the landlord would still bind M.[77]

2. Registered land. A mortgagee of registered land is faced with even worse problems since he will be bound by T's interest as an overriding interest within section 70 (1)(*k*) (legal leases not exceeding 21 years granted at a rent without taking a fine) or section 70 (1)(*g*) (rights of a person in actual occupation save where inquiry is made of such person and such rights are not disclosed).[78]

B. Rights of Equitable Co-Owners

1. Unregistered land. A legal mortgagee dealing with a sole legal owner will be bound by the equitable interests of co-owners of whom he has notice.[79] Occupation amounts to notice and it would seem all adults and, probably, persons over 16 years of age living in emancipated state on the premises must be asked if they claim any interest. A written disclaimer of interest should be obtained or the persons should agree in writing to the postponement of their interests, if any, to the mortgage, or they should join in the mortgage as concurring parties. Even if there were two legal owners, whether originally or by appointment of a co-trustee for sale,[80] a mortgagee would probably need to check that the loan was within the powers of the trustees for sale[81] without the need for the consent of all the beneficiaries.

2. Registered land. Where the mortgagor is buying a new house the position is even worse for a mortgagee of registered land since the mortgagee only obtains legal title as registered chargee when the documents are delivered to the Land Registry and *at that date* takes subject to then-existing overriding interests.[82] He can thus be bound by the section 70 (1)(*g*) rights[83] of actual occupiers who move into the house after the mortgage moneys have been paid over but before he becomes registered chargee.[84] He can question the mortgagor about such possibilities (where co-habitees may be contributing to the purchase-moneys) but can do little if the mortgagor is untruthful, especially if, when matters come to light, the mortgagor has disappeared or is penniless.

---

[77] *Cf. Hollington Bros. Ltd.* v. *Rhodes* [1951] 2 T.L.R. 691.
[78] See Hayton, pp. 125–129.
[79] *Ante*, pp. 66–69, 108.
[80] In the case of two persons holding expressly on trust for sale they may have express powers of absolute beneficial owners conferred on them by the deed.
[81] L.P.A. 1925, s. 28 (1); S.L.A. 1925, s. 71.
[82] *Re Boyle's Claim* [1961] 1 W.L.R. 339; *London & Cheshire Insurance Co.* v. *Laplagrene* [1971] Ch. 499.
[83] On "rights" see Hayton, pp. 127–128, 138–139.
[84] Hayton, p. 104.

C. Settled Land

If *Weston* v. *Henshaw*[85] is good law the ultimate nightmare for a mortgagee is to lend money to an apparent sole beneficial owner when the mortgaged unregistered land, in fact, is the subject of a Settled Land Act vesting instrument, for such mortgage will be void.

---

[85] [1950] Ch. 510; *ante*, pp. 249–252.

CHAPTER 14

LIMITATION

THE fundamental principle of the Limitation Act 1980,[1] which consolidates earlier legislation, is that unless claims are enforced within a limited time, they become barred. It is more important that long and undisturbed possession of land should be protected, even if initially it was wrongful, than that the law should lend its aid to the enforcement of stale claims.

1. Limitation and prescription. Limitation must be distinguished from prescription.[2] Two differences may be mentioned.

(a) *Subject-matter.* Limitation often concerns the ownership of the land itself, whereas prescription is directed to the acquisition of easements and profits over the land of another.

(b) *Limitation negative.* Prescription operates positively so as to presume the grant of an easement or profit by the owner of the land; title is thus derived from him. Limitation, on the other hand, operates negatively so as to bar a claim to the land, thus leaving some other claimant to the land free from the competing claim. Limitation may operate differentially, barring one person but not another. Thus it may bar a tenant under a lease but not his landlord.

2. Possession as the basis of title. In English law, the basis of title to land is possession. Possession of land by itself gives a title to the land good against the whole world except a person with a better right to possession.[3] If X takes possession of A's land, X has a title which will avail against all save A; a title acquired by wrong is still a title. X has a fee simple, and so has A; but all titles are relative, and so although X's fee is good, A's is better.[4] If, however, A fails to take steps to recover the land in due time, his claim will be barred by limitation, and X's fee, freed from the superior claims of A's fee, will be good against all the world.

3. Elements of limitation. In every case of limitation, three points must be considered, namely—

(1) The length of the period;
(2) When time starts to run; and
(3) The effect of the lapse of time.

These will be taken in turn.

---

[1] The Limitation Act 1939 as affecting land was amended by the Limitation Amendment Act 1980 and both were repealed and replaced by the present Act.
[2] *Ante*, p. 415.
[3] *Asher* v. *Whitlock* (1865) L.R. 1 Q.B. 1; *ante*, p. 133.
[4] See *Leach* v. *Jay* (1878) 9 Ch.D. 42 at pp. 44, 45.

Part 1

THE LENGTH OF THE PERIOD

1. The main periods. There are two main periods of limitation:

(a) *Six years*: a period of six years for actions on simple contracts (*e.g.* for money lent without security) or claims for rent, and actions in tort.[5]

(b) *Twelve years*: a period of 12 years for the recovery of land or of money charged on land, as by a mortgage.[6] Under the Real Property Limitation Act 1833 the period was 20 years, but the Real Property Limitation Act 1874 reduced it to 12. Twelve years is also now the period for actions for money due upon a covenant, in place of the former period of 20 years.

2. Special provisions. There are also certain special provisions.

(a) *Crown land.* In the case of Crown lands the period is now 30 years.[7] Formerly it was 60 years, a period which has been retained in the one case of foreshore owned by the Crown.[8]

(b) *Charitable corporation sole.* A spiritual or eleemosynary (*i.e.* charitable) corporation sole, such as a bishop or the master of a hospital, is barred after 30 years.[9]

Part 2

THE RUNNING OF TIME

The running of time falls into three sections: first, when time begins to run; second, what will postpone this date; third, what will start time running afresh. In general,[10] once time has begun to run, it runs continuously.[11]

Sect. 1. When Time Begins to Run

In the case of actions for the recovery of land or capital sums charged on land, time begins to run in accordance with the following rules.

1. Owner in possession. Where the owner of land is entitled in

---

[5] Limitation Act 1980, ss. 2, 5, 19.
[6] *Ibid.* ss. 15, 20.
[7] *Ibid.* Sched. 1 para. 10.
[8] *Ibid.* para 11.
[9] *Ibid.* para 10.
[10] Time is suspended during any period in which a party is an enemy or detained in enemy territory: Limitation (Enemies and War Prisoners) Act 1945.
[11] *Bowring-Hanbury's Trustee* v. *Bowring-Hanbury* [1943] Ch. 104.

possession, time runs against him from the moment "adverse possession" is taken by another.[12] This requires either discontinuance of possession by the paper owner followed by another's possession or dispossession of the paper owner by another.[13] A claimant will have possession if he has continuous and exclusive possession in fact coupled with the necessary *animus possidendi*.[14] If the paper owner has no present use for the land (*e.g.* waste land) but has in mind some specific purpose in the future the courts[15] are very ready to treat a claimant as not having acquired a sufficient degree of exclusive occupation to constitute possession or as not having manifested the appropriate *animus possidendi*.[16] Where the claimant's acts have not been inconsistent with the paper owner's intended purposes some courts,[17] controversially, have even been prepared as a matter of law to impute a licence by the paper owner in favour of the claimant but this is no longer possible.[18]

2. Future interests. A person entitled in reversion or in remainder at the time when adverse possession is taken has alternative periods: he has 12 years from adverse possession being taken or six years from the falling of his interest into possession, whichever is the longer.[19] Thus if land is settled on A for life with remainder to B, and X dispossesses A 10 years before A dies, B has six years from A's death in which to sue; but if X had dispossessed A three years before A's death, B would have 12 years from the dispossession of A. If X had not taken adverse possession until after A's death, B's interest would no longer have been a future interest, and he would have the normal period of 12 years from the taking of adverse possession. Further, if A's interest had been an entail, then if he had been dispossessed by X, B would have been barred 12 years later; the alternative six years' period does not extend to a reversioner or remainderman whose interest was liable to be barred by the barring of a prior interest in tail.[20]

3. Leaseholds. The above provisions do not apply to a reversioner on a lease for a term of years when the tenant has been ousted.

[12] Limitation Act 1980, Sched. 1 paras. 1, 8.
[13] *Treloar* v. *Nute* [1976] 1 W.L.R. 1295.
[14] *Ibid. Red House Farms (Thorndon) Ltd.* v. *Catchpole* (1976) 244 E.G. 295, *Powell* v. *McFarlane* (1979) 38 P. & C.R. 452. The *animus possidendi* is the intent to exclude the world at large so far as reasonably practicable.
[15] *Leigh* v. *Jack* (1879) 5 Ex.D. 264; *Williams Brothers Direct Supply Ltd.* v. *Raftery* [1958] 1 Q.B. 159; *Tecbild Ltd.* v. *Chamberlain* (1969) 20 P. & C.R. 633; *Wallis' Cayton Bay Holiday Camp Ltd.* v. *Shell-Mex* [1975] Q.B. 94.
[16] *Powell* v. *McFarlane* (*supra*).
[17] *Wallis' Cayton Bay Holiday Camp Ltd.* v. *Shell-Mex* (*supra*; *Gray* v. *Wykeham-Martin* [1977] Bar Library Transcript No. 10A (C.A.).
[18] Limitation Act 1980, Sched. 1, para. 8 (4), *post*, p. 523. This still leaves scope for a finding of express or implied licence if the facts actually justify it. See *Hyde* v. *Pearce, The Times*, November 26, 1981.
[19] Limitation Act 1980, s. 15 (2), Sched. 1, para. 4.
[20] *Ibid.* ss. 15 (3), 38 (5).

Irrespective of when the dispossession occurred, time does not run against the reversioner until the lease expires, because, until then, he has no right to possession.[21] Thus if L grants T a lease for 99 years and T is dispossessed by X, the 12 year period runs against T from the dispossession but against L only from the determination of the lease.

A tenant cannot acquire a title to the land demised against his landlord during the currency of the lease, even by prolonged failure to pay rent. There is one exception to this in the case of a lease capable of enlargement into a fee simple. If a rent not exceeding £1 per annum reserved by such a lease has not been paid for a continuous period of 20 years, five of which have elapsed since 1925 the rent ceases to be payable; neither the arrears nor any future payment can be recovered and the lease may be enlarged into a fee simple.[22] Further, where the tenant takes possession of adjoining land of the landlord, there is a presumption, which may be rebutted.[23] that he takes it as an extension of his lease,[24] and it becomes subject to the terms of the tenancy.[25] Similarly a tenant's adverse possession of adjoining land of a third party is prima facie for the benefit of the landlord as well as the tenant.[26]

A landlord may be barred if adverse possession is taken not of the land but of the rent from it; for if for 12 years the tenant under a lease in writing pays a rent of at least £10 per annum to some person who wrongfully claims the reversion, this bars the landlord's right to the reversion.[27]

4. Licensees, tenants at will and at sufferance. A licensee does not have adverse possession since he is in possession with the consent of the owner.[28] Where a person claims to be in adverse possession he is not as a matter of law to be treated as in possession by licence or permission of the owner merely because his possession is not inconsistent with the owner's present or future enjoyment of the land.[29] However, a finding of fact that he is in possession under an implied licence or permission may be made if justified on the actual facts.[30] A tenant at will is now in the same position as a licensee.[31]

In the case of a tenancy at sufferance, time runs against the landlord from the commencement of the tenancy at sufferance.

---

[21] *Ibid.* Sched. 1, para. 4.
[22] L.P.A. 1925, s. 153; *ante*, p. 358.
[23] See *Kingsmill* v. *Millard* (1855) 11 Exch. 313 at pp. 318, 319.
[24] *Smirk* v. *Lyndale Developments Ltd.* [1975] Ch. 317 reversed on appeal but not on this point.
[25] *J.F. Perrott & Co. Ltd.* v. *Cohen* [1951] 1 K.B. 705.
[26] *King* v. *Smith* [1950] 1 All E.R. 554.
[27] Limitation Act 1980 Sched. 1, para. 6.
[28] *Cobb* v. *Lane* [1952] 1 All E.R. 1199; *Heslop* v. *Burns* [1974] 1 W.L.R. 1241; *Hughes* v. *Griffin* [1969] 1 W.L.R. 23.
[29] Limitation Act 1980, Sched. 1, para. 8 (4)
[30] *Ibid.* Also see *Hyde* v. *Pearce, The Times*, November 26, 1981.
[31] Limitation Amendment Act 1980, s. 3 (2) repealing Limitation Act 1939, s. 9 (1).

5. Yearly or periodic tenants. Where a tenant under a yearly or other periodic tenancy does not hold under a written lease time runs from the end of the first year or other period of the tenancy, subject to extension by payment of rent or written acknowledgement.[32] If there is a lease in writing, time runs from the determination of the tenancy.

6. Rentcharges. In the case of a rentcharge in possession, time runs from the last payment of rent to the owner of the rentcharge.[33] Thus the owner's rights are barred—

(i) if no rent is paid for 12 years, in which case the rentcharge is extinguished; or

(ii) if the rent is paid to a stranger for 12 years, in which case the rentcharge remains enforceable against the land but the former owner's claim to it is extinguish in favour of the stranger.

Similar rules apply to other rents not due under a lease.

7. Mortgages. As soon as a mortgagee goes into possession, time begins to run against subsequent mortgagees and the mortgagor so as to bar their rights to redeem.[34] As regards the mortgagee's right to recover the money charged on the land, or to foreclose, time runs against him from the date upon which the money was due[35]; and when he is barred, his mortgage ceases to exist.[36] In each case, any written acknowledgment or any payment on account of principal or interest starts time running afresh.[37]

8. Claims through Crown or corporation sole. It has been seen that the Crown is entitled to a 30 years' period instead of the usual 12.[38] If a person against whom time has started to run conveys his land to the Crown, the only change is that the limitation period becomes 30 years from the dispossession instead of 12. But in the converse case where time has started to run against the Crown and the Crown then conveys the land to X, the rule is that X is barred at the expiration of 30 years from the original dispossession or 12 years from the conveyance to him, whichever is the shorter.[39] Thus X is entitled to 12 years from the date of the conveyance unless at that time there

---

[32] Limitation Act 1980, Sched. 1, paras. 5, 6; see, *e.g. Moses* v. *Lovegrove* [1952] 2 Q.B. 533; *Hayward* v. *Chaloner* [1968] 1 Q.B. 107; *Jessamine Investment Co.* v. *Schwartz* [1978] Q.B. 264.

[33] Limitation Act 1980, s. 38 (8).

[34] *Ibid.* s. 16; see, *e.g. Young* v. *Clarey* [1948] Ch. 191.

[35] Limitation Act 1980, s. 20.

[36] *Cotterell* v. *Price* [1960] 1 W.L.R. 1097.

[37] Limitation Act 1939, s. 29.

[38] *Ante*, p. 521.

[39] Limitation Act 1980, Sched. 1, para 12.

were less than 12 years of the Crown period unexpired, in which case X merely has the residue of that period.

Similar rules apply[40] to the 30 years' period for a spiritual or eleemosynary corporation sole.[41]

9. Trusts. (a) *Adverse possession by stranger.* Equitable interests in land or under trusts for sale of land are in general treated as "land," and so as subject to the 12 years' period.[42] But adverse possession of trust property by a stranger does not bar the trustee's title to the property until all the beneficiaries have been barred.[43] Thus if land is held on trust for A for life with remainder to B, 12 years' adverse possession of the land by X bars A's equitable interest and, but for the provision just mentioned, would bar the trustee's legal estate. But time will not start to run against B's equitable interest until A's death,[44] and the same accordingly applies to the trustee's legal estate. Consequently, after the 12 years have run, the trustee will hold the legal estate on trust for X for the life of A, and subject thereto on trust for B. This is so even if A is the trustee, as will normally be the case with settled land.

(b) *Adverse possession by trustee.* Trustees cannot obtain a title against their beneficiaries by adverse possession of the trust property; for there is no period of limitation for an action by a beneficiary to recover from his trustees the trust property or its proceeds in their possession or converted to their use, or in respect of any fraud by the trustees.[45] Thus if land is conveyed to X and Y as tenants in common, X cannot obtain a title to the land as against Y, no matter how long he excludes Y from the land or its rents and profits; for X and Y hold the legal estate on the statutory trusts for themselves as tenants in common,[46] and X is thus trustee for Y.[47] But subject to this, the period in respect of a breach of trust (*e.g.* for paying income to the wrong person) is six years.[48]

Exceptionally, if a trustee who is also a beneficiary receives or retains trust property or its proceeds as his beneficial share and acted honestly and reasonably, then his liability will be limited to the excess over his proper share if an action is brought to recover that trust property after six years have elapsed since the distribution.[49] Thus if

---

[40] *Ibid.*
[41] *Ante*, p. 521.
[42] Limitation Act 1980, ss. 18, 20.
[43] *Ibid.* s. 18.
[44] *Ante*, p. 522.
[45] Limitation Act 1980, s. 21.
[46] *Ante*, p. 306.
[47] See *Re Landi* [1939] Ch. 828.
[48] Limitation Act 1980, s. 21.
[49] *Ibid.*

T has distributed one-third of the trust property to himself, honestly and reasonably believing that only three beneficiaries exist, he will be liable to a fourth beneficiary after six years only for the one-twelfth difference between the one-third share he took and the one-quarter share which was truly his, instead of for the whole one quarter share.

(c) *Adverse possession by beneficiary.* Time does not begin to run against the trustees or beneficiaries if settled land or land held on trust for sale is in the possession of a beneficiary who is not solely and absolutely entitled.[50]

Sect. 2. Postponement of the Period

The date from which time begins to run may be postponed for disability, fraudulent concealment, or mistake.

A. Disability

If the owner of an interest in land is under disability when the right of action accrues, then even if the normal period of limitation expires, the period is extended to six years from the time when he ceases to be under a disability or dies, whichever happens first, with a maximum period in the case of land of 30 years from the date when the right of action first accrued[51] Thus if X takes possession of A's land at a time when A is insane,[52] A will have 12 years from the dispossession or six years from his recovery in which to bring his action, whichever period is the longer, except that A's claim will be barred in any event after 30 years from the dispossession. The following points should be noted:

(a) *Disability.* A person is under a disability for this purpose if he is a minor or insane.[53]

(b) *Supervening disability.* A disability is immaterial unless it existed at the time when the cause of action accrued. Thus if A becomes insane the day before he is dispossessed, the provisions for disability apply, whereas if he becomes insane the day after he has been dispossessed, they do not.

(c) *Successive disabilities.* In the case of successive disabilities, if a person is under one disability and before that ceases another disability begins, the period is extended until both disabilities cease, subject to the maximum of 30 years. But if one disability comes to an end before another disability starts, or if the person under disability is succeeded by another person under disability, time runs from the ceasing of the first disability. For example, A is a minor when the cause of action accrues. If later, during his minority, he becomes

---

[50] Limitation Act 1980, Sched. 1, para. 9.
[51] *Ibid.* s. 28.
[52] For brevity: "person of unsound mind" is the term in the Act.
[53] Limitation Act 1980 s. 38 (2); Mental Health Act 1959, 7th Sched.

insane, the six years does not start to run until he is both sane and of full age. But if he reaches full age before he becomes insane, or if he dies a minor and B, a mental patient, becomes entitled to the land, the six years run from A's majority in the first case and his death in the second.

B. Fraud, Deliberate Concealment and Mistake

Where—

(i) an action is based on the fraud of the defendant or his agent, or of any person through whom he claims, or his agent, or
(ii) any fact relevant to the plaintiff's right of action has been deliberately concealed from him by any such person, or
(iii) the action is for relief from the consequences of a mistake,

then time does not begin to run against the landowner until he discovers the fraud, concealment or mistake or could with reasonable diligence have discovered it.[54] Deliberate concealment is a more appropriate formula to replace the old statutory formula of fraudulent concealment which envisaged conduct that was unconscionable having regard to the relationship of the parties rather than common law fraud.[55] Deliberate commission of a breach of duty in circumstances in which it is unlikely to be discovered for some time amounts to deliberate concealment of the facts involved in that breach of duty.[56]

The rule as to mistake applies only where mistake is the basis of the action, as where the action is to recover money paid under a mistake of fact. There is no general doctrine that making a mistake (*e.g.* as to the true position of a boundary) stops time running.[57]

Neither fraud nor mistake will postpone the running of time as against a subsequent purchaser for value without knowledge or reason to believe that there was fraud or mistake.[58]

Sect. 3. Starting Time Running Afresh

Time may be started running afresh by—

(i) a signed acknowledgment in writing of the plaintiff's title; or
(ii) part payment of principal or interest.[59]

The acknowledgment or payment must be signed or made by the person in whose favour time is running, or by his agent, and must be

---

[54] Limitation Act 1980, s. 32.
[55] *Applegate* v. *Moss* [1971] 1 Q.B. 406; *Bartlett* v. *Barclays Bank Trust Co. Ltd.* [1980] Ch. 515; and see *Vane* v. *Vane* (1872) 8 Ch.App. 383 (illegitimacy concealed).
[56] Limitation Act 1980, s. 32 (2).
[57] See *Phillips-Higgins* v. *Harper* [1954] 1 Q.B. 411.
[58] Limitation Act 1980, s. 32 (3).
[59] *Ibid.* s. 29.

made to the person whose title is being barred, or to his agent.[60] The acknowledgment must be of existing liability[61] and not merely of facts which might give rise to liability,[62] or merely that there might be a claim.[63] Once, however, the full period has run, no payment or acknowledgment can revive any right to recover land, for the lapse of time will have extinguished not only the owner's remedies for recovering the land but also his right to it.[64] It is otherwise in the case of other actions, where lapse of time bars only the remedy and not the right.

Part 3

THE EFFECT OF THE LAPSE OF TIME

Sect. 1. Title to Land

1. The squatter's title. (a) *No "Parliamentary conveyance."* Although the effect of the Limitation Act 1980[65] is to extinguish the title of the former owner, it is not correct to say that the former owner's title is transferred to the "squatter," *i.e.* the person who has occupied the land and in whose favour time has run. There is no "Parliamentary conveyance" of the former owner's title in the case of unregistered land.[66] The effect of the Act is not positive but negative; it transfers nothing and merely extinguishes the former owner's claim. A squatter may thus see his title improved as lapse of time successively bars different persons with claims to the land, until ultimately his fee simple is free from rival claims.

In the case of a squatter registered as proprietor of a registered estate acquired by adverse possession it may, perhaps, be that the registered estate is vested in the squatter by Parliamentary transfer under the scheme of the Land Registration Act 1925, but the courts have not yet had to decide the point.[67]

(b) *Burdens binding the squatter.* Even if a squatter can show that the fee simple owner has been barred, however, he may not be able to take a clean title; for burdens which bound the land will continue to bind it in the hands of the squatter. For example, a squatter will be bound by a restrictive covenant attached to the land unless he can

---

[60] *Ibid.* s. 30.
[61] As in *Moodie* v. *Bannister* (1859) 4 Drew. 432; *Dungate* v. *Dungate* [1965] 1 W.L.R. 1477.
[62] *Re Flynn (No. 2)* [1969] 2 Ch. 403.
[63] *Good* v. *Parry* [1963] 2 Q.B. 418.
[64] *Ibid.* s. 17; *Nicholson* v. *England* [1926] 2 K.B. 93.
[65] *Ibid.* s. 17.
[66] *Tichborne* v. *Weir* (1892) 67 L.T. 735 at p. 737.
[67] *Spectrum Investment Co.* v. *Holmes* [1981] 1 W.L.R. 221; and see L.R.A. 1925, ss. 75, 9, 10, 11 and *Fairweather* v. *St. Marylebone Property Co. Ltd.* [1963] A.C. 510.

show that it is no longer enforceable, *e.g.* by lapse of time since a breach of it, for until a breach occurs the covenantee has no right of action and time does not run against him; a squatter without notice is not a purchaser without notice.[68] Again, a squatter on unregistered leasehold land who obtains a title against the tenant but not against the landlord is not in the position of an assignee of the lease. An assignee is liable to be sued for a breach of covenant committed while he held the lease, even if at the time of the action the lease has expired[69] but a squatter cannot be sued after the expiration of a lease for breaches of covenant committed while he was in possession of unregistered land.[70] Yet during the term of the lease, he can be forced to pay the rent and perform the covenants by the threat of forfeiture, if the lease contains a forfeiture clause; yet he has no right to apply for relief against forfeiture[71] and he is of course bound by any restrictive covenants. Moreover, if the squatter takes advantage of some clause in the lease, such as a proviso that the rent should be halved if the covenants are observed, he cannot "blow hot and cold"; if he accepts the benefits of the lease, he cannot refuse the burdens. Consequently, he will be estopped from denying that he is bound by the lease.[72] But the mere payment of rent under a lease with no such clause will not operate as an estoppel.[73]

(c) *Barred leaseholds.* If a squatter bars a tenant but not the freeholder, and then the tenant acquires the freehold, time begins to run against the freehold; but until it has run, the tenant, by virtue of owning the freehold, may evict the squatter: for the freehold is not barred, and the former tenancy has merged in the freehold.[74] Further, if instead the tenant surrenders his tenancy to the freeholder, this enables the freeholder to evict the squatter forthwith, for the surrender removes the only interest which prevented the freeholder from claiming possession of the land that he owns.[75] However, the position is different in the case of registered land where the squatter has actually become registered proprietor of the lease. The ousted tenant no longer has a registered estate capable of surrender[76] or, it seems, of merger.

2. Proof of title. It should be noted that a good title cannot be shown merely by proving adverse possession of land, however long the period. If A and his predecessors in the title have been in

---

[68] *Re Nisbet & Pott's Contract* [1906] 1 Ch. 386.
[69] *Ante*, p. 382.
[70] *Tichborne* v. *Weir* (1892) 67 L.T. 735, and see *ante* p. 381.
[71] *Tickner* v. *Buzzacott* [1965] Ch. 426.
[72] *Ashe* v. *Hogan* [1920] 1 I.R. 159; *Tito* v. *Waddell* (*No.* 2) [1977] Ch. 106 at pp. 299–302.
[73] *Tichborne* v. *Weir*, *supra*.
[74] *Taylor* v. *Twinberrow* [1930] 2 K.B. 16.
[75] *Fairweather* v. *St. Marylebone Property Co. Ltd.* [1963] A.C. 510; but see 78 L.Q.R. 33.
[76] *Spectrum Investment Co.* v. *Holmes* [1981] 1 W.L.R. 221.

possession of land for 20, 50, or a 100 years, that alone does not prove A is entitled to it, for the true owner—

(a) might have been under disability at the time of dispossession; or
(b) might have been the Crown; or
(c) might have been the reversioner or remainderman under a settlement; or
(d) might be the reversioner on a long lease.

Consequently, to establish a good title by the operation of the Act it must be shown—

(i) who was the true owner of the interest in land in question; and
(ii) that he has been barred by lapse of time.

A vendor who can do this can establish a title which the courts will force even an unwilling purchaser to accept.[77] However, in practice, it is comparatively unusual for a title to land to be acquired by limitation, except in the case of encroachments upon neighbouring land.

3. Successive squatters. Even before the statutory period has expired, a squatter has a title good against everyone except the true owner.[78] To hold otherwise would mean that a squatter who had not barred the true owner would have no remedy against somebody who dispossessed him; this might lead to breaches of the peace by competing squatters. Consequently, if a squatter who has not barred the true owner sells the land he can give the purchaser a right to the land which is valid against all except the true owner. The same applies to devises, gifts or other dispositions by the squatter; in each case the person taking the squatter's interest can add the squatter's period of possession to his own.[79] Thus if X, who has occupied A's land for eight years, sells the land to Y, A will be barred after Y has held the land for a further four years. Again, if a squatter is himself dispossessed, the second squatter can add the former period of occupation to his own. For example, if land owned by A has been ocuppied by X for eight years, and Y dispossesses X, A will be barred when 12 years have elapsed from X first taking possession. But although at the end of that time A is barred, X will not be barred until 12 years from Y's first taking possession, for Y cannot claim to be absolutely entitled until he can show that everybody with any claim to the land has been barred by the lapse of the full period.

There is no right to add together two periods of adverse possession if a squatter abandons possession before the full period has run and

---

[77] *Re Atkinson & Horsell's Contract* [1912] 2 Ch. 1; contrast *George Wimpey & Co. Ltd.* v. *Sohn* [1967] Ch. 487.
[78] *Perry* v. *Clissold* [1907] A.C. 73; *ante*, p. 520.
[79] *Asher* v. *Whitlock* (1865) L.R. 1 Q.B. 1.

some time elapses before another person takes possession of the land. During the interval, there was no person in adverse possession whom the true owner could sue; thus time started to run afresh when the second squatter took possession of the land.[80]

Sect. 2. Arrears of Income

The question of the recovery of arrears of income is distinct from that of the recovery of the land or capital money which produces it. The arrears of rent which the landlord or the owner of a rentcharge can recover by action or distress are limited to the arrears accrued due during the previous six years.[81] In the case of agricultural holdings, the landlord's right of distress is further restricted to the year preceding the distress[82] and special provisions exist for bankruptcy.[83]

There is also a six years' period for arrears of mortgage interest.[84] But a mortgagee who exercises his power of sale may retain all arrears of interest out of the proceeds of sale, for this is not recovery by action[85]; and a mortgagor who seeks to redeem can do so only on the equitable terms of paying all arrears, however old.[86]

---

[80] *Trustees, Executors and Agency Co. Ltd.* v. *Short* (1888) 13 App.Cas. 793; Limitation Act 1980, Sched. 1, para. 8 (2).
[81] Limitation Act 1980, ss. 19, 38.
[82] Agricultural Holdings Act 1948, s. 18.
[83] Bankruptcy Act 1914, s. 35.
[84] Limitation Act 1980, s. 20.
[85] *Re Marshfield* (1887) 34 Ch.D. 721.
[86] *Dingle* v. *Coppen* [1899] 1 Ch. 726; *Holmes* v. *Cowcher* [1970] 1 W.L.R. 834.

CHAPTER 15

RECTIFICATION AND INDEMNITY IN REGISTERED LAND

Now that the different sorts of interests in land have been fully examined it is possible properly to explore the operation of those provisions in the Land Registration Act that enable the register of title to be rectified and that enable an indemnity to be paid out of state funds to someone who suffers loss by reason of rectification or by reason of non-rectification.

Part 1

RECTIFICATION

Sect. 1 Rectification Jurisdiction

It is clearly provided that rectification may occur "notwithstanding that the rectification may affect any estates, rights, charges or interests acquired or protected by registration, or by entry on the register, or otherwise,"[1] *e.g.* a right protected as an overriding interest.

Thus a rectification claim may be for replacement of the registered proprietor by the claimant, for cancellation of a notice or caution wrongly entered on the register, for entry of a notice burdening the registered title, or for any other matter requiring the register to be altered to reflect the true position.

By section 82 (1) (*a*) and (*b*) the register may be rectified by the court alone where the court:

(a) has decided that any person is or is not entitled to any estate right or interest in or to any registered land or charge and, as a consequence of such decision, it orders rectification;

(b) on the application of any person, who is aggrieved by any entry made in or omitted from the register or by any default being made, or unnecessary delay taking place in the making of an entry in the register, orders rectification.

By section 82 (1) (*c*) to (*h*) the register may be rectified by the court or by the Registrar:

(c) in any case and at any time with the consent of all persons interested;

(d) where either is satisfied that any entry has been obtained by fraud;

---

[1] L.R.A. 1925, s. 82 (2); *Chowood* v. *Lyall* [1930] 2 Ch. 156 at pp. 164–165.

(e) where two or more persons are mistakenly registered as proprietors of the same registered estate or charge;

(f) where a mortgagee has been registered as proprietor of the land instead of as proprietor of the charge and a right of redemption is subsisting;

(g) where a legal estate has been registered in the name of a person who, if the land had not been registered, would not have been the estate owner;

(h) in any other case where, because of error or omission in the register or any mistaken entry, it may be deemed just to rectify the register.

There is also a miscellaneous collection of instances of powers of correction which sometimes verge on full rectification. They are to be found in rule 13 (clerical errors), rule 14 (larger clerical errors), rule 131 (where the powers of disposition have become vested in some person other than the proprietor), and rules 276 to 277 (fixing boundaries).

Sect. 2. Implicit Restrictions on Rectification

1. The Registrar's darling. At first sight there seems to be an awesome—or awful—blanket discretionary jurisdiction to rectify conferred by section 82 (1), paras, (*a*) to (*h*). However, just as Lord Radcliffe[2] made it clear that it is wrong to treat the Income Tax Act 1952 as if it made law but could not itself contain principle so with the Land Registration Act. Just as in unregistered land there is the fundamental "equity's darling" principle, enabling a bona fide purchaser of a legal interest for value without notice to take free of equitable interests, so in registered land there is the fundamental "registrar's darling" principle, enabling a purchaser of a registered interest for value to take free of interests not then protected as overriding interests or by entry as minor interests,[3] though what exactly amounts to a sufficient entry on the register can raise problems.[4]

2. Paragraph (a). In section 82 (1) (*a*) it seems that in deciding whether or not a person is entitled to any interest in registered land the court must decide on registered land principles. Thus, if someone has a minor interest which is unprotected when a purchaser for value becomes the new registered proprietor of the property, the court should not be able to ignore registered land principles and decide on unregistered land principles that such person has an interest in

[2] *Sharkey* v. *Wernher* [1956] A.C. 58 at p. 80.
[3] L.R.A., ss. 5, 9, 20, 23, 59, 74; *Freer* v. *Unwins Ltd.* [1976] Ch. 288; *Williams & Glyn's Bank* v. *Boland* [1981] A.C. 487.
[4] *Post*, p. 538.

registered land, enabling the register to be rectified by entry of a notice or caution. However, even registered land principles are subject to the equitable *in personam* jurisdiction (operating by a court order personally compelling the defendant to do something, *e.g.* execute a transfer in the plaintiff's favour) that prevents statutes being used as instruments of fraud.[5] If, indeed, the dealings between the minor interest holder and the new registered proprietor are such as to invoke the equitable jurisdiction then it seems the court may directly rectify the register under paragraph (*h*). Generally, however, where there is an omission within paragraph (*b*) or (*h*) that is the fault of the claimant (in failing to protect his interest) rectification should not be ordered. Indeed, even if the omission is the fault of Registry officials, the new registered proprietor, the Registrar's darling, should not be liable to rectification, an indemnity instead being given to the aggrieved claimant. "Having searched the register, the purchaser must be able to rely on that search and (apart from overriding interests) must surely be entitled to rely on a title free from all that does not actually appear on that title before completing."[6]

3. Paragraph (d). Paragraph (*d*) raises two questions: what is meant by "fraud" and whose fraud is it that is material? It would seem that fraud should be brought home to the person whose registered title is being impeached or his agents so that an innocent successor in title to a "fraudster" should not be liable to rectification.[7] However, if it be shown that his suspicions were aroused and that he abstained from making inquiries for fear of learning the truth (*i.e.* he has Nelsonian, as opposed to actual knowledge, through having turned a Nelsonian blind eye to problems) then fraud might properly be ascribed to him.[8] "Fraud" would seem to require some want of probity, some personal dishonesty or moral turpitude and be capable of extending to a case of undue influence.[9] Mere notice of an unprotected interest which the new registered proprietor then claims to take free from should certainly not invoke rectification under paragraph (*d*).[10] "It is not fraud to take advantage of legal rights" said Lord Cozens-Hardy M.R. in *Re Monolithic Building Co. Ltd.*[11] where a later mortgagee with express notice of an earlier unregistered mortgage had priority over an earlier mortgagee. An essential feature of registration of title "is to substitute a system of registration of rights for the doctrine of

---

[5] *Frazer* v. *Walker* [1967] A.C. 569 at p. 585; *Lyus* v. *Prowse* (1982) 79 L.S. Gaz. 369.
[6] *Strand Securities Ltd.* v. *Caswell* [1965] Ch. 958 at p. 987 *per* Russell L. J.
[7] *Assets Co.* v. *Mere Roihi* [1905] A.C. 176 at p. 210.
[8] *Ibid.*
[9] *Re Leighton's Conveyance* [1936] 1 All E.R. 667.
[10] *De Lusignan* v. *Johnson* (1973) 230 E.G. 49; *Williams & Glyn's Bank* v. *Boland* [1981] A.C. 487.
[11] [1915] 1 Ch. 643.

notice"[12] so if the right is not registered then *cadit quaestio* (unless it is an overriding interest or was not registered owing to the fraud of the defendant registered proprietor).

4. Paragraph (g). Paragraph (g) at first sight is startlingly broad in apparently allowing rectification wherever the registered proprietor is someone who would not have been the estate owner if the land had been unregistered land. Thus where, say, land has actually been registered for 50 years one can treat the land hypothetically as if it had been unregistered throughout the period, and if unregistered land principles produce as estate owner someone different from the registered proprietor then rectification is possible! Obviously, unregistered land principles cannot be allowed to be perpetually pervasive and so undermine registered land law completely.[13] The position of the Registrar's darling must surely be sacrosanct and full effect must be given to sections 20, 23, 59, 74 and 75 of the Land Registration Act. It may well be that the paragraph should only be available against a first registered proprietor.

It is further submitted that paragraph (g) should be considered in the light of paragraph (f), also introduced for the first time by the Law of Property (Amendment) Act 1924, Sched. 8, para. 16, both of which were probably intended to allow for changes to be made to the register to make it accord with the system of mortgages and the vesting of legal estates introduced by L.P.A. 1925, ss. 85 (2), 86 (2) and First Schedule. Thus, in 1926 it was possible to rectify the register to make the tenant for life of settled land the registered proprietor and to make the mortgagor of mortgaged land the registered proprietor. It seems, though, that rectification was not just to be available to give effect to the transitional provisions of L.P.A., s. 39 and First Schedule. It was also to be available where a post 1925 purported outright transfer was in substance only a mortgage and where a registered disposition was made in favour of a minor and, presumably, where a S.L.A. settlement was not properly effected *inter vivos* by two deeds so that no legal estate in unregistered land would pass by virtue of S.L.A., s. 4, *e.g.* if W transferred her house to S absolutely but only upon S undertaking to allow her a life interest therein. If, however, the first registered proprietor liable to a rectification claim managed to transfer the property to the Registrar's darling then it is submitted that no rectification claim should lie.

5. Paragraph (h). Paragraph (h) also appears to give the court or the Chief Land Registrar an enormous discretion to rectify the register. However, just as if in unregistered land law there were such

---

[12] *Parkash* v. *Irani Finance Ltd.* [1970] Ch. 101 at p. 109; also *Miles* v. *Bull* (*No. 2*) [1969] 3 All E.R. 1585 at p. 1590.
[13] See *Spectrum Investment Co. Ltd.* v. *Holmes* [1981] 1 All E.R. 6.

a vast statutory discretion in the Court on grounds of error, omission or mistake to alter a person's title to land then the court's decision would be subject to certain fundamental principles, so with the position in registered land. Can it ever be just to rectify the register if this would detrimentally affect the Registrar's darling? It would seem sensible to limit paragraph (*h*) just to the transaction immediately affected by the error, omission or mistake.[14] It would be possible to submit that the error or omission or mistake within paragraph (*h*) refers only to some act or neglect or default of the Registry, *e.g.* where a registration is not in conformity with the instrument on which it was based. However, such a submission is more likely to succeed in relation to paragraph (*b*), the court being very happy to retain its sizeable discretion in paragraph (*h*); a self-denying refusal of jurisdiction (and power) tends to go against human—and judicial—nature. Retention of jurisdiction can be justified on the ground that mistakes in paragraph (*h*) must surely extend to a transaction itself based on a mistake, though a person detrimentally affected by such a mistake might have an alternative remedy under the court's equitable *in personam* jurisdiction under which the person benefiting from the mistake could personally be ordered to take certain steps.[15] Jurisdiction under paragraph (*h*) might also be exercised to regularise an *Ives* v. *High*[16] situation where the defendant is bound on the *in personam* principle that he who takes the benefit must also bear the burden.

Sect. 3. Statutory Restrictions on Rectification

Although section 82 (1) provides that the register may be rectified in the cases we have already noted, section 82 (3) as amended goes on to provide that "The register *shall not* be rectified, except for the purpose of giving effect to an overriding interest or an order of the court, so as to affect the title of the proprietor who is in possession" except in two instances.

A. No Rectification Against Proprietor in Possession

The expression "in possession" creates difficulty since it is defined by section 3 (xviii) as including the "receipt of rents and profits or the right to receive the same, if any" "unless the context otherwise requires." There is no doubt that physical occupation by the registered proprietor protects him under section 83 (3). Of course, an Englishman's home should not be taken away from him by rectification, except in very special circumstances, for a financial indemnity is inadequate recompense.

---

[14] *Cf. Franzom* v. *Register of Titles* [1975] A.L.J.R. 4.
[15] *Magee* v. *Pennine Insurance Co.* [1969] 2 Q.B. 507; *Lawrence* v. *Lexcourt Holdings Ltd.* [1978] 1 W.L.R. 1128.
[16] [1967] 2 Q.B. 379.

Without argument, Walton J. in *Freer* v. *Unwins Ltd.*[17] has assumed that "possession" includes the receipt of rents and profits. This is probably correct.[18] It would seem that possession cannot include the right to receive rents and profits for *all* registered proprietors have this right by virtue of their registration and section 82 (3) is clearly intended to apply not to all but just to *some* registered proprietors.

B. The Four Exceptional Instances

1. Rectification to give effect to a court order. Does a proprietor in possession really have much protection if the shield of section 82 (3) can always be taken away to give effect to a court order? This depends on the number of circumstances in which a court may order rectification of the register, *e.g.* under section 82 (1). It has already been submitted that the astonishing width of application of section 82 (1) cannot be taken at face value since there must be some implicit restrictions in order to protect the Registrar's darling and to prevent all registered titles being precarious.

Nevertheless section 82 (1) allows much scope for rectification. Indeed, it is *the* statutory rectification provision giving such scope for rectification that the restriction on rectification against a proprietor in possession is rendered almost nugatory if the restriction is always to be lifted to give effect to court orders under section 82 (1). Can a more sensible interpretation be put upon the court order exception?

This exception was first introduced as part of the Adminstration of Justice Act 1977, s. 24. The section was barely discussed and no one perceived that the court order exception at face value took away most of the protection hitherto afforded to a proprietor in possession.[19] It would seem probable that this was not intended but that the words "order of the Court" were included to deal with orders of the court other than those made under the statutory jurisdiction in section 82 (1). Thus, rectification against a proprietor in possession might be directly ordered by the court where the court held a disposition to be void in bankruptcy proceedings under section 42 of the Bankruptcy Act 1914. It is hoped that a court would strive to place a restrictive interpretation upon the court order exception but it may well be that further legislation is needed.

2. Rectification to give effect to an overriding interest. A registered proprietor's title is always subject to overriding interests by virtue of sections 5, 9, 20, 23 and 70 and so, in law, rectification to give effect to them cannot be prejudicial since it alters the legal position not at

---

[17] [1976] Ch. 288 at p. 294.
[18] Hayton, pp. 171–173.
[19] For similar Parliamentry blindness see L.R.A. 1966, s. 1 (4) criticised by Cretney & Dworkin (1968) 84 L.Q.R. 528 and remedied by Land Registration and Land Charges Act 1971, s. 3 (1).

all. For this very reason, as we shall see, no indemnity is payable in such cases. The number of interests capable of existing as overriding interests[20] makes this a very serious exception. It should be noted that the time for ascertaining whether a proprietor is in possession is the date of the rectification hearing, whilst the time for ascertaining whether a person has an overriding interest is the date of the registration of the proprietor.[21]

3. Rectification because proprietor caused or substantially contributed to error or omission by fraud or negligence. Section 24 of the Administration of Justice Act 1977 most usefully and sensibly substituted a narrower exceptional case than that originally provided in L.R.A., s. 82 (3) (*a*). Originally, there could be rectification against a proprietor in possession if he had "caused or substantially contributed by his *act* neglect or default to the fraud mistake or omission in consequence of which" rectification was sought. Judicial interpretation treated this as covering not just cases where the proprietor intentionally or negligently misled the Registry but also cases where the proprietor innocently lodged documents for first registration of title, which did not in fact convey the exact estate in the particular parcel of land in question, *e.g.* " a conveyance which by itself is inoperative to pass title."[22] (where part of the land had earlier been conveyed to someone else, before registration of title had become compulsory, and this had been overlooked) or "a document which contains a misdescription of the property."[23] This interpretation deprived a first registered proprietor in possession of the apparent protection of section 82 (3) if there were any defect in the conveyance to him which he lodged with the Registry. Subsequent registered proprietors were safe since it was only the first proprietor who was treated as responsible for the mistaken registration of title.[24]

Under the new section 82 (3) (*a*) rectification against a proprietor in possession is only available if he "caused or substantially contributed to the error or omission by fraud or lack of proper care." It remains to be seen how rigorous is the standard of proper care but it would seem that failure to carry out the usual conveyancing inquiries and inspections should amount to lack of proper care, which, probably, should be judged objectively and not subjectively.

Take the case of a registered proprietor, V, who granted O an option to purchase his land, such option expiring on May 1, 1981 but containing a provision that upon payment of £500 O may before May 1, 1981 extend the option to May 1, 1982. Pursuant to rule 190 and Form 59 a notice is entered by the Registrar which, misleadingly, only states that the option is exercisable until May 1, 1981.

[20] *Ante*, pp. 121–124.
[21] *London & Cheshire Insurance Co.* v. *Laplagrene* [1971] Ch. 499.
[22] *Chowood* v. *Lyall (No. 2)* [1930] 1 Ch. 426 at p. 435.
[23] *Re Sea View Gardens* [1967] 1 W.L.R. 134 at p. 141.
[24] *Epps* v. *Esso Petroleum* [1973] 1 W.L.R. 1071 at p. 1079.

In October 1981 P becomes new registered proprietor for value, having been told by V that the option has expired so that the notice no longer protects a valid right under section 52. In fact, O had validly extended the option to May 1982 and in December 1981 he exercises the option, claiming the notice sufficiently protects him or, alternatively, the register should be rectified to refer to the option being exercisable until 1982 if the extension provision were invoked by O.

P claims he should be entitled to rely on the entry in the register so as not to have to make any inquiries about the option and that, anyhow, O should have checked that the Registrar made the proper entry.

O maintains that, having sent in the basic application with a copy of the option, he should be able to rely on the Registrar making a proper entry and that no sensible purchaser should have proceeded without insisting on the vendor having the notice removed, an easy matter if the option had expired as alleged by the vendor.

This last point will probably carry the day for O—and prevent any indemnity being payable to P.

4. Where for any other reason, in any particular case, it is considered that it would be unjust not to rectify the register against the proprietor (s. 82 (3) (c). The words "unjust not to rectify" show that it is necessary to show more than that it would be just to rectify the register. These provisions are indefinite and broad; indeed, broad enough to give a blanket discretion. They have only been considered in five cases. A little guidance can be found in *Re 139 High Street, Deptford*[25] where the following factors were considered relevant in not rectifying the register; the true owner had no genuine need for the land; he would be sufficiently compensated by an indemnity; the proprietor in possession had expended money on the land. In *Epps v. Esso Petroleum*[26] it was considered relevant to review the indemnity position of each party on the footing that the claimant obtained rectification or was refused rectification as the case may be, and to take into account the failure of the claimant to take all proper conveyancing precautions before purchasing the property.

In *Freer v. Unwins*[27] the new registered proprietor had in 1974 taken a transfer from the old registered proprietor when there was no notice or other entry on the register relating to a 1955 restrictive covenant. Walton J. expressed "very great surprise" that the Registrar had rectified the register under section 82 (3) (c) to enter a notice of the covenant and stated[28] "I cannot see that there was any ground whatsoever for rectifying the register against the freehold

---

[25] [1951] Ch. 884 at p. 892.
[26] [1973] 1 W.L.R. 1071.
[27] [1976] Ch. 288.
[28] *Ibid.* at p. 295.

proprietor." After all, "The general scheme of the Act is that one obtains priority according to the date of registration and one is subject or not subject to matters appearing on the register according to whether they were there before one took one's interest or after."[29] It surely cannot be unjust not to rectify the register against the Registrar's darling.

Reliance may now be placed upon section 82 (3) (c) in situations covered by section 82 (3) (b) until repealed by Administration of Justice Act 1977, s. 24. Rectification used to be possible under section 82 (3) (b) where the immediate disposition to the proprietor was void or the disposition to any person through whom he claimed otherwise than for value was void, *e.g.* for forgery or *non est factum*. It seems section 82 (3) (b) was repealed on the basis that if the proprietor was himself guilty of fraud or negligence in relation to the void disposition then section 82 (3) (a) was available whilst, if he were innocent, rectification ought not *prima facie* to follow as a matter of course under section 82 (3) (b) (*e.g.* if he had spent £30,000 on building a house on the land) but should be left to the court's broad discretion under section 82 (3) (c).[30] This overlooks the fact that in all the exceptional section 82 (3) instances there still remains the general discretion under section 82 (1) as will now be seen.

Sect. 4. Discretion to Rectify

1. The Discretion. Since (1) section 82 (1) gives a discretion to rectify in certain cases but (2) section 82 (3) states that the discretion must not be exercised against a proprietor in possession except in certain instances, it has (3) been judicially assumed that in those instances the discretion must be exercised so as to rectify the register against the proprietor.[31] However, this third step does not follow, for if one of the exceptional instances arises, so as to prevent the general rule in section 82 (3) applying, then, only the first step remains, *i.e.* there is a discretion which may be exercised for or against the proprietor in possession. Pennycuick J. seemed to appreciate this[32] but it was left to Templeman J.[33] to make it clear that the discretion remains where any of the exceptional instances are established. However, in the case of the new court order exception, of course, effect must be given to the order, the court having decided to make the order.

---

[29] *Ibid.* at p. 298.
[30] See Law Commission Working Paper No. 45, para. 81. Whilst rectification might be possible against an innocent first registered proprietor it should not be possible against an innocent subsequent registered proprietor who is the "registrar's darling."
[31] *Re 139 High St. Deptford.* [1951] Ch. 884 at p. 889.
[32] *Re Sea View Gardens* [1967] 1 W.L.R. 134 at p. 141.
[33] *Epps* v. *Esso Petroleum* [1973] 1 W.L.R. 1071 at pp. 1078, 1079.

2. The Rule in Saunders v. Vautier. One area which has not yet been judicially explored is the extent to which advantage might be taken of the rule in *Saunders* v. *Vautier*[34] to circumvent the discretion to rectify conferred by the Act. The rule in *Saunders* v. *Vautier* confers upon an absolutely entitled beneficiary the right to call for a transfer of the legal estate vested in his trustee. Thus, if a registered proprietor has the legal estate and the victim, V, of a wrongful or mistaken *first* registration arising from forgery or double conveyancing retains the equitable interest, as he does according to Templeman J. in *Epps* v. *Esso Petroleum,* V can call for the legal estate to be transferred to him by the proprietor and can obtain a court order to this effect. Upon complying with this (on pain of committal for contempt or execution of a transfer by a Chancery Master) the proprietor will find that he has no claim to an indemnity since he did not suffer loss by reason of rectification but by reason of himself transferring the title to V. If he seeks to preserve his indemnity claim the proprietor may force V to take him to court and then persuade the court to take the short cut of directly rectifying the register under section 82 (1) (*a*) as Harman J. seems to have done in *Bridges* v. *Mees,*[35] though there the plaintiff actually sought an order for the defendant to transfer the property to him or a court order for rectification. Section 82 (1) (*a*) seems broadly drafted enough to enable a court of its own motion to rectify thereunder. However, it may be that still no indemnity claim will lie since the proprietor may be treated as having suffered no loss by reason of rectification, having throughout been subject to V's interest,[36] though it may be preferable to restrict this principle to overriding interests alone.

Of course, these problems do not arise if the views of Templeman J. are erroneous and registration confers on the first proprietor the whole legal and equitable estate even in cases of forgery and of double conveyancing as has already been submitted.[37] Registration should confer the full legal and equitable estate upon the proprietor, subject to minor interests then protected on the register and to overriding interests: sections 5, 9. Thus, if the overriding interest is the full equitable estate under section 70 (1) (*f*) or (*g*) (*e.g.* in Mrs. Hodgson's case in *Hodgson* v. *Marks*[38] or where the victim of a forgery is in actual occupation) then it is open to the person with the overriding interest to take advantage of the rule in *Saunders* v. *Vautier,* so circumventing any judicial discretion under section 82. No indemnity claim lies in any event where overriding interests are concerned.[39]

---

[34] (1841) 4 Beav. 115.
[35] [1957] Ch. 475.
[36] *Cf. Re Chowood's Registered Land* [1933] Ch. 574.
[37] *Ante,* pp. 119–120.
[38] [1971] Ch. 892.
[39] *Post,* p. 548.

3. A problematical example. Suppose C Ltd. purchased three acres
of waste land in 1938 and sold and conveyed one acre thereof in 1942
to D. Not realising this had been done, no mention of the 1942
conveyance having been indorsed on the 1938 conveyance (or the
1938 conveyance having been destroyed in a war-time fire) C Ltd.
purportedly sold and conveyed the three acres to E Ltd. in 1977 when
the area had become a compulsory registration area. E Ltd. duly
became registered proprietor of the three acres.

E Ltd. left the land alone until six months ago when it began
building two houses on the acre conveyed to D in 1942. It retains one
house, in which resides its managing director, but it has just
transferred the other to P for £80,000 so that P is now registered
proprietor thereof.

D had made no use of the land since 1942 and had been ill in
hospital and then convalescing with his sister while the houses were
being built. He has just returned to the locality and discovered the
position. No adverse possession of his acre occurred until six months
ago.

P, as second registered proprietor, takes the legal estate subject to
entries in the register and overriding interests, but free from all other
interests whatsoever as if E Ltd., the transferor, had been entitled to
the land in fee simple for its own benefit, *i.e.* as equitable owner.[40]
Thus P takes free of any interest of D and D has no interest entitling
him to claim rectification.[41] D will only be entitled to an indemnity
for his loss if not guilty of lack of proper care.[42] Failure to indorse the
existence of the 1942 conveyance on the 1938 conveyance is strong
evidence of lack of proper care but it might be that C Ltd.'s solicitors
had informed D's solicitors that this had been done, when, in fact, it
had not been done.

E Ltd., as first registered proprietor, holds the legal estate on trust
for D, the victim of the double conveyancing mistake if the views of
Templeman J.[43] are correct, namely that the equitable interest
remains in D. On this basis D can demand the legal estate under the
rule in *Saunders* v. *Vautier*[44] when it may well be the case that no
indemnity can be claimed by E Ltd. The alternative view that E Ltd.
has the legal and equitable interest seems preferable.[45] However, on
first registration the legal estate has been registered in the name of a
person who, if the land had not been registered, would not have been
the estate owner so that D may claim rectification,[46] though it should

[40] L.R.A. 1925, s. 20 (1), *ante*, p. 120.
[41] L.R.A., s. 82 (1) (g) must, it seems, be restricted to first registered proprietors
(except where needed to give effect to the transitional provisions of the 1925
Legislation): *ante*, p. 535.
[42] L.R.A., s. 83 (5).
[43] *Epps* v. *Esso Petroleum* [1973] 1 W.L.R. 1071.
[44] (1841) 4 Beav. 115.
[45] *Ante*, p. 120.
[46] L.R.A., s. 82 (1) (g).

not be ordered unless it would be unjust not to rectify the register against E Ltd.[47] If E had taken all necessary conveyancing precautions and D had not, then it would be unjust to rectify the register against E Ltd.[48] D could claim an indemnity only if not guilty of lack of proper care.[49]

If D, for £50 per annum payable yearly in advance, had granted a yearly tenancy of his acre to T, T wishing to assure himself of full shooting and sporting rights,[50] then E Ltd. and P will hold their estates subject to T's overriding interest under section 70 (1) (*k*) and to D's overriding interest under section 70 (1) (*g*).

If E Ltd. and P had known of T's presence they should have learned of the interests of T and D and so they should be liable to have D replace them as registered proprietor and should be unable to claim an indemnity through their lack of proper care.

If E Ltd. and P had not known of T (*e.g.* if he had been working abroad or ill at the time and so had not been shooting, etc., on the acre) then, it seems, the register should still be rectified to give effect to the overriding interests of T and D, to which the estates of E Ltd. and P are subject,[51] and E Ltd. and P can claim no indemnity, rectification merely formalising the existing position so that no loss is suffered by reason of rectification.[52] It seems likely that the court has no discretion to manufacture a satisfactory solution and ignore the statutory principle that registered estates are subject to overriding interests, so that the court cannot under rule 197 order entry to be made on the register to the effect that T and D have no overriding interest and then order an indemnity to be paid to T and D.

Sect. 5. The Effect of Rectification

1. New edition. When the register is rectified it is the Registrar's practice to issue a new edition of the register, all interests then bearing the date of the new edition, the date being that of the rectification application rather than that of the resolution of the application.[53] Thus, when a successful claimant replaces the registered proprietor the new register will reveal to what registered charges and minor interests the land is then subject, though it must be remembered that interests protected by a notice are only effective to the extent that they are inherently valid[54] and that cautioners will either be "warned off" or their protection upgraded.

---

[47] *Ibid.* s. 82 (3) (*c*).
[48] *Cf. Epps* v. *Esso Petroleum* [1973] 1 W.L.R. 1071.
[49] L.R.A., s. 83 (5).
[50] If an equitable sporting profit had been granted before the sale to E Ltd. it would have been void if not registered as a Class D (iii) land charge.
[51] L.R.A., s. 20 (1).
[52] *Re Chowood's Registered Land* [1933] Ch. 574.
[53] *Freer* v. *Unwins Ltd.* [1976] Ch. 288; L.R.R., r. 83.
[54] L.R.A., s. 52, *Kitney* v. *M.E.P.C.* [1977] 1 W.L.R. 981.

2. Partial rectification. In *Re Leighton's Conveyance*[55] a daughter, fraudulently using undue influence, had her mother transfer the mother's house to the daughter, the mother being too prepared to sign whatever the daughter put before her without examining the documents at all. The daughter as registered proprietor created charges upon the house in favour of chargees who were ignorant of the fraud. The mother obtained rectification by replacing the daughter as registered proprietor but the charges were left on the charges register of the property on the footing, it seems, that the mother was estopped by her conduct, in enabling the daughter to appear as unincumbered proprietor, from having priority over the chargees.

There can be no quarrel with this if the mother did not have an overriding interest, but *prima facie* she did have by virtue of her actual occupation, if her right to set aside the disposition for undue influence is a "right" within section 70 (1) (*g*), as it seems to be.[56]

However, if the mother had an overriding interest then "a person who remains in actual occupation does not do anything to abandon the rights which her actual occupation protects unless on inquiry she does not reveal them: that is what section 70 (1) (*g*) enacts. The [mother] did not arm [the daughter] with the apparent ability or power to deal with the property free from overriding interests."[57]

3. Freer v. Unwins Ltd. Where a successful rectification claim results in entry of a notice on the register it seems that, whilst the registered proprietor will then be bound (as of the date of the rectification application) by the interest protected by the notice, earlier dispositions (*e.g.* leases for 21 years or less, charges, easements, restrictive covenants, liens created by deposit) will not be subject to the notice, the notice having no retrospective effect.

In *Freer* v. *Unwins Ltd.*[58] the plaintiff, a shop owner in a parade, had surprisingly obtained rectification against the freehold registered title of a nearby shop, of which the defendant was tenant, by obtaining entry of a notice relating to a valid restrictive covenant created in 1955. Then the shops were unregistered land so the plaintiff had duly registered his covenant against the name of the nearby shop owner under the Land Charges Act. The nearby shop was later sold when the area had become a compulsory registration area, but somehow the new registered title omitted the burden of the covenant. The proprietor of the nearby shop in 1969 leased it for 21 years to S who, in 1974, assigned the lease to the defendant. Having obtained rectification the plaintiff sued the defendant to

---

[55] [1936] 1 All E.R. 667.
[56] *Blacklocks* v. *J.B. Developments (Godalming) Ltd.* [1981] 3 All E.R. 392 (right to rectify a deed is within s. 70 (1) (*g*)).
[57] *Per* Russell L.J. in *Hodgson* v. *Marks* [1971] Ch. 892 at p. 934.
[58] [1976] Ch. 288.

enforce the covenant, but failed, since Walton J. held that the notice, though binding the proprietor, had no effect against S or the defendant. By section 19 (2) the 1969 lease (though not itself capable of being registered with a separate land certificate and not noted on the freehold title) took effect as if it were a registered disposition. Thus, by sections 20 (1) and 59 (6) the lessee, S, *then* took subject to minor interests protected on the register and to overriding interests, but free from all other interests whatsoever. The entry of the notice to protect the covenant, a minor interest, was dated April 28, 1975, pursuant to the successful rectification claim and took effect by section 50 (2) subject to "incumbrancers or other persons who at the time when the notice is entered may not be bound by the covenant." Since the 1969 lease (with the benefit of section 20 (1) and 59 (6)) was well prior to the 1975 notice the lessee, S, took free from the covenant and the defendant assignee was "in exactly a similar position."[59]

In essence, the lessee was treated as if he had the rights of a bona fide purchaser for value without notice under ordinary land law principles and the defendant assignee as a successor in title[60] to such "equity's darling." In registered conveyancing the "Registrar's darling" seems to be merely a transferee of a registered estate for value without there being any entry then on the register (or any overriding interest). It would thus seem that even if the defendant somehow had notice of the plaintiff's covenant when he took the assignment there is no reason why he should not still have been able to take advantage of the lease's priority according to the state of the register in 1969. Presumably, if the 1969 lease had been for 22 years and so registered with a separate title of which rectification was then sought, in circumstances where the assignee somehow had notice of the covenant when he took the assignment, the assignee should also be able to rely conclusively on the register.[61] Rectification should thus not be ordered against him under section 82 (3) (c).

At least the freeholder in *Freer* v. *Unwins Ltd.* was bound by virtue of section 50 (2): "Where such a notice is entered *the proprietor* of the land and the persons deriving title under him (except incumbrancers or other persons who *at the time when the notice is entered* may not be bound by the covenant) *shall be deemed to be affected with notice* of the covenant as being an incumbrance on the land."

It seems implicit in the fact that the sub-section is concerned with the date when the notice is entered and not an earlier date (such as the date of creation of the covenant) that it is not possible to rectify restrospectively. This is also the case in section 48 (1) (as extended by

[59] *Ibid.* at p. 298.
[60] *Wilkes* v. *Spooner* [1911] 2 K.B. 473.
[61] *De Lusignan* v. *Johnson* (1973) 230 E.G. 499; *Williams & Glyn's Bank* v. *Boland* [1981] A.C. 487; *Midland Bank Trusts Co.* v. *Green* [1981] A.C. 513.

s. 49) concerned with notices of minor interests other than restrictive covenants, and in section 66 concerned with liens by deposit. The possiblity of retrospective rectification would, indeed, breach what Walton J. refers as "the general scheme of the Act that one obtains priority according to the date of registration and one is subject or not subject to matters appearing on the register according to whether they were there before one took one's interest or after one took one's interest."[62]

Part 2

INDEMNITY

Sect. 1. Indemnity Jurisdiction

The provisions for indemnity are supposedly intended to complement the provisions for rectification so that by section 83 a person who suffers loss by reason of: (1) rectification of the register; or (2) non rectification of the register; or (3) destruction of documents in the Registry, inaccurate land certificates, searches, etc., can claim compensation. Unlike the position in some jurisdictions there is, quite sensibly, no need before seeking compensation for the claimant to bring or attempt to bring any proceedings against the person who caused the loss. However, the Registrar as insurer is subrogated to the rights of the claimant by section 83 (10).

Although where the register *is* rectified, the amount payable relates to the value (if there had been no rectification) of the estate, interest or charge immediately before the time of rectification, where the register is *not* rectified the amount payable cannot exceed the value of the estate interest or charge at the time when the error or omission which caused the loss was made.[63] The claimant, where some years have elapsed, will thus recover very much less than the present value of the land and will wonder what are the advantages of the registered system. He will also need to see if too many years have not elapsed for where the land has been registered with absolute title or good leasehold title he will usually only have six years from the date of registration of the title in dispute in which to bring his claim for an indemnity.[64] Thus the plaintiffs in *Epps* v. *Esso Petroleum*[65] could not claim any indemnity though suffering loss from non-rectification. The difference between this six year period and the ordinary 12 year limitation period for the recovery of land seems anomalous. If the indemnity claim does not arise in consequence of a

---

[62] [1976] Ch. 288 at p. 297.
[63] L.R.A., s. 83 (6).
[64] L.R.A., s. 83 (11).
[65] [1973] 1 W.L.R. 1071.

registration with absolute or good leasehold title the six year period does not commence until the claimant knows, or but for his own default might have known, of the existence of his claim.[66]

It should be noted that it is the court that has the power to determine questions as to right or to amount of any indemnity, though nothing is to preclude the Registrar from settling by agreement claims for indemnity. The practice is first to seek agreement with the Registrar and only if the claim is refused, either on merit or quantum, to look to the High Court.[67]

Sect. 2. No Indemnity

1. Bars on indemnity. No indemnity is payable in many instances. In *Freer* v. *Unwins Ltd.*[68] Walton J. opined that there would be no indemnity where a claimant successfully obtains rectification but still suffers loss, the loss not being occasioned by reason of any rectification of the register. However, Ruoff and Roper (4th ed.)[69] coyly states, "Happily events did not turn out in that way" and in correspondence the Chief Land Registrar has refused to disclose his legal reasoning for allowing Mr. Freer's claim for an indemnity. At least a flexible liberal approach to granting compensation is to be welcomed: if a person innocently suffers under a state-imposed registration system then the state should compensate him. It is expressly provided that there is no indemnity on account of any mines or minerals unless a note has been expressly entered on the register showing that mines and minerals are included in the registered title.[70] There is no indemnity if the limitation period is breached.[71] There is no indemnity for costs incurred in taking or defending legal proceedings without the consent of the Registrar, as insurer, except there is nothing to prevent an applicant for an indemnity from applying to the court without any such consent. The costs of any such application or of any legal proceedings arising out of it may be recovered.[72]

2. Lack of proper care. More significantly there is no indemnity where the applicant or a person from whom he derives title (otherwise than under a disposition for value registered or protected on the register) has caused or substantially contributed to the loss by fraud or lack of proper care.[73] It is an open question whether lack of

---

[66] L.R.A., s. 83 (11).
[67] Ruoff & Roper, pp. 802–803.
[68] [1976] Ch. 288.
[69] p. 794, note 93.
[70] L.R.A., s. 83 (5) (*b*).
[71] *Ibid.* s. 83 (11), *ante*, p. 546.
[72] *Ibid.* s. 83 (5) (*c*), (8), Land Registration and Land Charges Act 1971, s. 2.
[73] L.R.A., s. 83 (5) (*a*). Any contributory negligence bars a claim: this can be unjust. *Cf.* Land Registration (Scotland) Act 1979, s. 13 (4).

proper care is to be judged objectively or subjectively and it remains to be seen how rigorous the standard of proper care is to be.

For example, a registered proprietor, M, might transfer her house to her 35 year-old son or nephew, S, living with her on the express arrangement that she is to have a *life* interest, but otherwise the facts are as in *Hodgson* v. *Marks*,[74] S selling to T, who becomes registered proprietor. T then discovers M still residing there and claiming rectification by entry of herself as registered proprietor, being Settled Land Act tenant for life.[75] If, since T is not a proprietor in possession, rectification were ordered by the Registrar under section 82 (1) (*g*) (for if the land were unregistered M and not T would be the estate owner)[76] then T would seek an indemnity.

Is he guilty of lack of proper care if he failed to make any inquiry as to M's rights? Is his age, shyness, poor understanding of English (being a foreigner) relevant? What if his solicitors had asked S's solicitors whether any overriding interests existed and obtained the truthful reply that none existed so far as they knew (M having a minor interest only under section 86 (2)), so his solicitors then relied upon section 20 to obtain the legal estate free from minor interests not then protected on the register. Indeed, since T is the Registrar's darling it seems that M's prima facie claim to rectification under section 82 (1) (*g*) ought not to have been allowed in the first place or, if allowed, it should then have been overcome by a further claim to rectification made by T under section 82 (1) (*a*). The question would then arise whether M's lack of proper care prevented an indemnity being payable to her.

3. Overriding interests. It is most significant that where rectification is ordered to give effect to an overriding interest no indemnity is payable for no loss is suffered by reason of rectification, since the proprietor's title has in any event been subject to the overriding interest all the time under sections 5, 9, 20 or 23. Rectification merely formalises the existing situation.[77] It is thus vital to purchasers to check up on the rights of actual occupiers.[78]

Exceptionally, where rectification is ordered to give effect to an overriding interest (or for any other reason) against "a proprietor of any registered land or charge claiming in good faith under a forged disposition" the proprietor is deemed to have suffered loss by reason of the rectification so as to be entitled to an indemnity—if not guilty of lack of proper care, of course.[79] It would seem that the right of a victim of forgery to claim rectification under section 82 (1)(*g*) amounts to a "right" of an occupier or receiver of rents under section 70 (1) (*g*).[80]

[74] [1971] Ch. 892.
[75] *Bannister* v. *Bannister* [1948] 2 All E.R. 133; L.R.A., ss. 86 (1), 87 (3).
[76] S.L.A. 1925, s. 4 (1).
[77] *Re Chowood's Registered Land* [1933] Ch. 574.
[78] *e.g. Hodgson* v. *Marks* [1971] Ch. 892.
[79] L.R.A., s. 83 (4) circumventing *Att.-Gen.* v. *Odell* [1906] 2 Ch. 47.
[80] See Hayton, pp. 95–96.

4. Haigh's Case. It is impossible to leave the topic without mentioning a practical and unforgettable instance of the payment of an indemnity. John Haigh, the acid-bath murderer, by means of a clever forgery had himself registered as proprietor in place of one of his victims and then sold the property to a purchaser for value, who upon registration thereof obtained a valid title. The victim's personal representative, upon discovering the whole horrible truth, sought and obtained a full indemnity from the insurance fund: he could not obtain rectification since there was an innocent proprietor in possession protected by section 82 (3).[81] By way of comparison, it should be noted that in unregistered conveyancing the personal representative would have no effective remedy against Haigh after he was hanged since Haigh had no assets to speak of, but he would have been able to recover the land from the innocent purchaser who would have had no defence, having taken under a forged and therefore void conveyance. The innocent purchaser would have lost out completely. Registered conveyancing thus has clear advantages though there is still plenty of scope for reform.

[81] Ruoff & Roper (3rd ed.), p. 853.

CHAPTER 16

OWNERSHIP AND ITS LIMITS

AT the beginning of the twentieth century the restrictions placed upon the user and enjoyment and upon the disposition of land by the general law were minimal. The owner of a fee simple estate in 1900 had enormous latitude to do as he pleased with his own, and could often act with impunity to the detriment of the environment and of society. In the course of the ensuing 80 years the position has altered radically: massive statutory innovation has overlaid the traditional freedom to act with a complex network of restrictions. The enactments concerned were necessitated by the pressure of social and economic forces working in the community, whilst the progress of this statutory intervention was much accelerated by the effects of the two world wars. The legislature has had to grapple with problems involving:

(a) the need to protect the environment and its resources from the ravages of unregulated exploitation;

(b) the need to provide for a rational and integrated pattern in the process of land development;

(c) the need to overcome the obstacle to community interests sometimes presented by the hitherto almost inviolable rights of land ownership[1];

(d) the needs of industry, commerce and agriculture for sufficient security of tenure to stimulate investment by allowing for continuity and growth;

(e) the need, in the face of a rising population and a continuing scarcity of residential accommodation, to prevent rent levels from reflecting the full impact of the market, and to provide security of tenure for tenants.

The way in which Parliament has responded to these challenges is described in Parts 3 and 4 of this chapter. The earlier two parts set up the contrast by dealing with what may be described as the traditional freedom of ownership (in Part 1), subject only to the restrictions imposed by the common law (described in Part 2).

Part 1

GENERAL RIGHTS OF OWNERS

The owner of the largest estate known to the law, the fee simple absolute in possession, has traditionally enjoyed wide powers of control, disposition and use of the land in which his estate subsists.

---

[1] Incursion really began with the building of the railways in the first half of the nineteenth century. And see Land Clauses Consolidation Act 1845.

1. Ownership. The maxim is *cujus est solum, ejus est usque and coelum et ad inferos*; he who owns the soil is presumed to own everything "up to the sky and down to the centre of the earth."[2] This prima facie includes all mines and minerals,[3] and any chattel not the property of any known person[4] which is found under or attached to the land, *e.g.* in the bed of a canal[5]; but it probably does not include a chattel merely resting on the surface.[6] Where land is bounded by water gradual imperceptible natural changes are taken into account by treating the title of the owner as extending to the land as added to or detracted from by accretion or diluvion.[7]

2. Disposition. The owner can dispose of his land or part of it as he wishes. Thus he may sever it horizontally, as by disposing separately of an upper floor of a building.

3. Use. The owner may in general use the land in the natural course of user in any way he thinks fit. He may waste or despoil it as he pleases and is not liable merely because he neglects it.[8]

Part 2

COMMON LAW RESTRICTIONS ON OWNERSHIP

1. Liability in tort. A landowner may be liable in tort for injuries caused to third parties by his acts and omissions in respect of things brought or artificially stored on the land, *e.g.* if water in a reservoir escapes, or if a lamp projecting over the highway gets into a dangerous state of repair and injures a passer-by. He may similarly be liable for nuisance, *e.g.* if he makes an unusual and excessive collection of manure which attracts flies and causes a smell.[9]

2. Gold and silver. The Crown is entitled to all gold and silver occurring in any mine,[10] and is also entitled to all "treasure trove." Objects amount to treasure trove only if—

   (i) they consist of gold or silver, whether in bullion, coin or some manufactured object;

---

[2] *Corbett* v. *Hill* (1870) L.R. 9 Eq. 671 at p. 673; and see *Commissioner for Railways* v. *Valuer-General* [1974] A.C. 328 at pp. 351, 352; *Grigsby* v. *Melville* [1974] 1 W.L.R. 81.
[3] *Mitchell* v. *Mosley* [1914] 1 Ch. 438 at p. 450; for exceptions, see *post*, p. 566.
[4] See *Moffatt* v. *Kazana* [1968] 3 All E.R. 271.
[5] *Elwes* v. *Brigg Gas Co.* (1886) 33 Ch.D. 562.
[6] *Hannah* v. *Peel* [1945] K.B. 509; *Parker* v. *B. A. Board* [1982] 2 W.L.R. 503.
[7] *Southern Theosophy Inc.* v. *South Australia* [1982] 1 All E.R. 283.
[8] *Giles* v. *Walker* (1890) 24 Q.B.D. 656.
[9] *Bland* v. *Yates* (1914) 58 S.J. 612.
[10] See *Att.-Gen.* v. *Morgan* [1891] 1 Ch. 432.

(ii) they have been hidden in or on the land deliberately, and not merely lost; and

(iii) the true owner is unknown.[11]

3. Wild animals. Wild animals are not the subject of ownership.[12] But a landowner has what is sometimes called a "qualified property" in them, consisting of the exclusive right to catch, kill and appropriate the animals on his land; and as soon as the animals are killed they fall into the ownership of the landowner, even if killed by a trespasser.[13]

4. Water. A landowner has no property in water which either percolates through his land or flows through it in a defined channel. In the case of percolating water, the landowner may draw off any or all of it without regard to the claims of neighbouring owners.[14] In the case of water flowing through a defined channel, the riparian owner (the owner of the land through which the water flows) cannot always take all the water but has certain valuable rights. The owner of only one bank of a stream prima facie may exercise riparian rights up to the middle of the stream.

(a) *Fishing.* As part of his natural right of ownership he has the sole right to fish in the water. Except in tidal waters, the public has no right of fishing even if there is a public right of navigation.[15]

(b) *Flow.* He is entitled to the flow of water through the land unaltered in volume or quality, subject to ordinary and reasonable use by the upper riparian owners; and he is bound by a corresponding obligation to the lower riparian owners.[16]

(c) *Abstraction.* The ordinary and reasonable use which a riparian owner was formerly entitled to make of the water flowing through his land was[17]—

(i) the right to take and use all water necessary for ordinary purposes connected with his riparian tenement (such as for watering his cattle or for domestic purposes, or, possibly, in some manufacturing districts, for manufacturing purposes), even though this completely exhausted the stream; and

(ii) the right to use the water for extraordinary purposes connected with his riparian tenement, provided the use was reasonable and the water was restored substantially undim-

[11] See *Att.-Gen.* v. *Trustees of the British Museum* [1903] 2 Ch. 598 at pp. 608–611; *Att.-Gen. of Duchy of Lancaster* v. *G. E. Overton Farms Ltd.* [1982] 1 All E.R. 524.
[12] *The Case of Swans* (1592) 7 Co. Rep. 15b at p. 17b.
[13] *Blade* v. *Higgs* (1865) 11 H.L.C. 621.
[14] *Chasemore* v. *Richards* (1859) 7 H.L.C. 349.
[15] See *Blount* v. *Layard* [1891] 2 Ch. 681.
[16] *John Young & Co.* v. *The Bankier Distillery Co.* [1893] A.C. 691.
[17] *McCartney* v. *Londonderry and Lough Swilly Ry.* [1904] A.C. 301 at pp. 306, 307.

inished in volume and unaltered in character. Such purposes include irrigation and, in all districts, manufacturing purposes, such as for cooling apparatus. The amount by which the flow might be diminished was a question of degree in each case.[18]

These rights have now been curtailed by statute. An owner of land cannot take any water without the licence of a river authority. Exceptions are water taken for—

(i) the domestic purposes of the occupier's household, or
(ii) agricultural purposes other than spray irrigation.[19]

Part 3

STATUTORY RESTRICTIONS ON USE AND ENJOYMENT

Sect. 1. Planning Control

A. Growth of Control

1. Control by schemes. At common law, any landowner was free to develop his land as he wished, provided he did not infringe the rights of others. He could erect whatever buildings he wished, however unsuitable they might be, and however injurious to the amenities of the district. Not until the Housing, Town Planning, etc., Act 1909 was enacted was there any general power for local authorities to control the development of land. Successive statutes strengthened and extended this control, culminating in the Town and Country Planning Act 1932, which for the first time conferred planning powers over land in the country, as distinct from towns. The essence of this and the earlier Acts was the preparation of a scheme. Each local authority was empowered to prepare a scheme showing what development would be permitted on each part of the land: and there were powers of enforcement against those who carried out development contravening the scheme.

2. Interim development control. (a) *Defects.* The system suffered from a number of defects. First, it was optional: there was no obligation for any local authority to prepare a scheme, and many did not. Secondly, there was the long period which usually elapsed between the decision of the local authority to prepare a scheme and the final approval of the scheme. During this period, the land was subject to "interim development control." Under this, any landowner could develop his land at his own risk: if when at last the scheme was made the development accorded with the scheme, it was safe,

---

[18] See *Rugby Joint Water Board* v. *Walters* [1967] Ch. 397.
[19] Water Resources Act 1963, ss. 23, 24 (2), 135 (1).

554 *Ownership and its Limits*

whereas if it did not accord with it, the local authority could take enforcement action under the scheme and, for example, secure the removal of any offending buildings.

(b) *Permission.* To guard against this risk, an application for interim development permission could be made before carrying out the work. If this was given, the development was immune from enforcement action even if ultimately it was found to contravene the scheme. But if development was carried out without interim development permission, there was no power to take enforcement action against it during the interim development period; and some speculative developers relied successfully on the probability that no scheme would come into force until they had been able to reap the profits of their development.

3. The Act of 1943. This system continued until the Town and Country Planning (Interim Development) Act 1943 was pased. At that time, a mere 4 per cent. of England and Wales was subject to operative schemes; another 70 per cent. was subject to interim development control; and the remaining 26 per cent. was subject to no control. The Act imposed interim development control on all land in this last category, so that thenceforward the whole of the land in the country was under interim development control save for the 4 per cent. governed by schemes.[20] Secondly, the Act enabled local authorities to take enforcement proceedings against those who subsequently developed their land without obtaining interim development permission: unauthorised buildings could be demolished, and unauthorised uses penalised.[21]

These provisions transformed planning control. Formerly, over a quarter of the country was free from control, and all save some 4 per cent. of the rest was free from any control save the indefinite risk of a scheme ultimately being made which would be inconsistent with the development. After the Act of 1943, the whole of the country was subject to a system under which effective action could forthwith be taken against any future development carried out without permission.

B. Town and Country Planning Acts

1. Acts of 1947 to 1960. The Town and Country Planning Act 1947 was passed on August 6, 1947, and came into operation on the "appointed day," July 1, 1948.[22] It was subsequently amended extensively, notably by the Town and Country Planning Acts 1953, 1954 and 1959, and the Caravan Sites and Control of Development Act 1960. The Act of 1947, which was complex and far-reaching and

[20] s. 1.
[21] s. 5.
[22] S.I. 1948 No. 213.

repealed all the previous law, had two main objects: first, a general revision and strengthening of the existing system of planning control; and secondly, the imposition of a new system of "development charges." The main object of development charges was to prevent landowners profiting from the great increase in value of their land which accrued without effort on their part when, for example, the spread of a town transformed into valuable building land some meadows which had previously had only a low value for agricultural purposes. The system of development charges proved unworkable and was abolished by the Act of 1953, but the planning provisions of the Act of 1947 remained.

2. Acts of 1962 to 1968. In 1962 the previous legislation from the Act of 1947 onwards was repealed and re-enacted in the consolidating Town and Country Planning Act 1962. This was subsequently amended by the Town and Country Planning Acts 1963 and 1968, the Control of Office and Industrial Development Act 1965, and Part 3 of the Industrial Development Act 1966. Furthermore, by the Land Commission Act 1967 a new attempt was made to secure for the State a part of the increased value which accrues to land as a result of surrounding development. The new charge was known as "betterment levy." After a change of government betterment levy was abolished by the Land Commission (Dissolution) Act 1971.

3. Acts of 1971 to 1980. In 1971 the legislation was again repealed and consolidated. The current principal Act, the Town and Country Planning Act 1971, has itself been amended, initially by the Town and Country Planning (Amendment) Act 1972 and the Town and Country Amenities Act 1974. These Acts are together known as the Town and Country Planning Acts 1971 to 1974. Further attempts were then made to secure development value for the State. The Finance Act 1974 introduced a special capital gains tax on gains realised from disposing of or letting land known as "development gains tax." Capital gains tax was then paid on the gain in the current use value whilst development gains tax was paid on the extra gain arising from the realised development value. This system was replaced by "development land tax" under the Development Land Tax Act 1976, which applies not just to land held as a capital investment but also to land held as stock in trade. The amount of realised development value chargeable to D.L.T. is available as a deduction in computing chargeable gains or profits of a trade as the case may be. The new tax is designed to operate in conjunction with the system imposed by the far-reaching Community Land Act 1975.

The Act of 1975 had two objectives: first, to enable the community, acting through local authorities, to control the development of land in accordance with the needs and priorities of the community as a

whole, and, secondly, to ensure that the increase in the value of the
land resulting from development was reaped by the community itself.
Powers were conferred upon local authorities to act directly in the
development of land or in co-operation with the private sector. In
achieving the aims of the Act what, in effect, was contemplated was
the nationalisation, or "municipalisation," of all land ripe for
development. A change in the political climate resulted in the repeal
of Act of 1975 by the Local Government Planning and Land Act
1980,[23] although the Act of 1980 re-enacts some of the provisions of
the earlier Act.[24] The Development Land Tax survives. The Act of
1980 also made various other amendments to planning legislation: the
number of county planning authorities is reduced, powers are
conferred for the charging of fees in respect of planning applications,
and the procedures for the approval or adoption of structure and
local plans have been modified. Local planning authorities are
enabled to repeal and replace structure plans.[25] Other Acts passed
since 1974 are the Town and Country Planning (Amendment) Act
1977 and the Control of Office Development Act 1977.

4. Administration. The central administration of the Acts is under
the Secretary of State for the Environment, but all the routine
administration is carried out by local planning authorities, which for
most purposes are district councils, but for some functions, *e.g.* the
preparation of structure (as opposed to local) plans,[26] county councils
are the local planning authorities.

C. Control of Development

1. Development. The fundamental concept underlying the planning
legislation is "development," which is defined as meaning—

  (i) "the carrying out of building, engineering, mining or other
      operations in, on, over or under land," or
 (ii) "the making of any material change[27] in the use of any
      buildings or other lands."[28]

Many of the expressions in the definition are themselves defined by
the Act, though the only phrase which need be mentioned here is that
"engineering operations" includes "the formation or laying out of
means of access to highways."[29] The Act makes it clear that it is
development to begin using one dwelling-house as two or more

---

[23] Act of 1980, Pt. XI (s. 101, Sched. 17).
[24] Act of 1980, Pt. XIV.
[25] Act of 1980, Pt. 1X, (ss. 86–92, Scheds. 14, 15).
[26] For these, see *post*, p. 000.
[27] See *Guildford R.D.C.* v. *Fortescue* [1959] 2 Q.B. 112 (intensification of use not a
    change); *East Barnet U.D.C.* v. *British Transport Commission* [1962] 2 Q.B. 484;
    Jennings Motors Ltd. v. *Sec. of State* [1982] 1 All E.R. 471.
[28] Act of 1971, s. 22.
[29] *Ibid.* s. 290.

separate dwelling-houses,[30] or to extend dumps of refuse or waste materials. On the other hand, "development" does not include improvements or alterations to a building which do not materially affect its external appearance, the use of any buildings or other land within the curtilage of a dwelling-house for any purpose incidental to the enjoyment of the dwelling-house as such, the use of any land for agricultural purposes, and any change from one use to another use within the same class in the 18 classes of use set out in the Town and Country Planning (Use Classes) Order 1972.[31] The Act further provides in effect that the definition does not include certain cases of reverting to a former use.[32]

2. Planning permission. (a) *Permission.* The general rule is that any person who proproses to develop land must first obtain planning permission from the local planning authority or from the Secretary of State on appeal; and such permission may be granted either unconditionally or subject to such conditions as are thought fit, or it may be refused.[33] The conditions must reasonably relate to the proposed development.[34] Although the refusal of permission may be a very serious matter for the landowner, no compensation is payable except in a very limited class of cases.[35]

An applicant must give prior notice of his application to certain other persons owning interests in the property; and in a few cases of development likely to offend neighbours, he must first advertise his application, so that they may be able to object before permission is given.[36] An applicant for planning permission does not need to have a legal interest in the property concerned: applications are frequently made by prospective purchasers and lessees. Every local planning authority is bound to maintain a register of applications for permission and the results of such applications[37]; this is quite different from the local land charges register.[38]

(b) *Development, structure and local plans.* Each local planning authority was bound to prepare a development plan by July 1, 1951, showing the proposed development of its area.[39] These plans, which had to be reconsidered every five years, form a prophecy of the permissions likely to be granted and those likely to be refused; but unlike planning schemes under the old system, the plan itself

[30] *Ibid.* s. 22 (3) (*a*); and see *Ealing Corporation* v. *Ryan* [1965] 2 Q.B. 486.
[31] Act of 1971, s. 22; S.I. 1972 No. 1385.
[32] Act of 1971, s. 23.
[33] *Ibid.* s. 29.
[34] See *Fawcett Properties Ltd.* v. *Buckinghamshire C.C.* [1961] A.C. 636; *R.* v. *Hillingdon L.B.C., ex p. Royco Homes Ltd.* [1974] Q.B. 720; *Newbury D.C.* v. *Sec. of State* [1980] 1 All E.R. 731.
[35] Act of 1971, Pts. VII and VIII.
[36] *Ibid.* ss. 26, 27.
[37] *Ibid.* s. 34.
[38] See *ante*, p. 106.
[39] Act of 1947, s. 5.

authorises no development, and it is as necessary to obtain planning permission after the plan has come into force as before. All development plans were subject to amendment and approval by the Minister after holding a public inquiry. This proved cumbersome, and consequently the Act of 1968 introduced a more flexible system, involving a gradual replacement of development plans by less detailed "structure plans" which sketch in general lines of development.[40] Despite its name a structure plan does not comprise a map: it is in the form of a written statement containing or accompanied by diagrams, illustrations and descriptive matter. A structure plan must formulate the planning authority's policy and general proposals in respect of the development and other use of land in their area (including measures for the improvement of the physical environment and the management of traffic). Structure plans require the approval of the Secretary of State and may be supplemented by local plans which will not normally be under the Secretary of State's control.[41] A local plan consists of a map and a written statement. A structure plan must indicate any part of the planning authority's area which they have singled out for comprehensive treatment in accordance with a local plan to be prepared later. Such an area is known as an "action area" and the local plan in due course of time prepard for it as an "action area plan." There are many types of local plan which can be prepared under the overriding scheme of a structure plan.

(c) *Permitted development.* By the Town and Country Planning General Development Order 1977 planning permission is given[42] for 23 classes of development, subject to certain conditions, and so in these cases there is no need to apply to the local planning authority for permission.[43] The Order includes such matters as minor alterations to dwellings, tempory uses, and much development by gas, water, electricity and other undertakings.

(d) *Industrial and office development.* For much industrial and office development there is an overriding requirement. In districts prescribed by the Secretary of State an Industrial Development Certificate or Office Development Permit must be obtained from the Secretary of State before applying for planning permission to erect an industrial or office building, or to change the use of a building to industrial or office use.[44] There are exceptions in the case of small developments.

[40] Act of 1968, Pt. 1, now Act of 1971, Pt. II.
[41] Act of 1971, ss. 11–14.
[42] See *Cater* v. *Essex C.C.* [1960] 1 Q.B. 424.
[43] S.I. 1977 No. 289.
[44] Act of 1971, ss. 66–68; Act of 1972, s. 5.

(e) *Caravan sites.* Caravan sites proved very hard to control under the general law of town and country planning, the main difficulty being that the mere development of land without planning permission is not an offence. Sites could be exploited and the vans moved on before enforcement proceedings could be brought to a successful conclusion. To remedy this abuse the Caravan Sites and Control of Development Act 1960 makes it an offence in most cases to use land as a caravan site without a site licence granted by the local authority, which is only issued if the requisite planning permission for the use of the land as a caravan site has been obtained.[45] The licence will usually be subject to conditions relating to the physical use of he land, *e.g.* conditions aimed at preventing overcrowding.[46] The Local Government Planning and Land Act 1980, Part XVII concerns the duty of local authorities to provide caravan sites for gipsies, and deals with exemptions from the requirement for site licences.

3. Enforcement notices. (a) *The notice.* If development is carried out without the requisite permission, or if any conditions to which a permission was subject have not been complied with, the local planning authority may serve an enforcement notice on the owner and occupier of the land, specifying the unauthorised development or breach of condition and the reasons for service. The notice takes effect at the date specified in it, being at least 28 days after service; and it should require any appropriate remedial steps to be taken within a further specified period, *e.g.* the discontinuance of a use, or the removal of offending structures.[47] An enforcement notice which does not fairly comply with the statutory requirements (*e.g.* by not stating correctly what is complained of) is void.[48]

(b) *Time limit.* A notice enforcing the discontinuance of an unauthorised use may be served at any time, unless the use began before 1964 or consists of changing the use of a building to use as a single dwelling-house.[49] Notices to enforce all other breaches of planning control (including a change to use as a single dwelling-house) must be served within four years and 28 days of the breach.[50]

(c) *Stop notice.* A local planning authority may, on or after serving an enforcement notice, serve a stop notice. Its effect is to prohibit the continuance of the operations which are alleged to be a breach of planning control. Its purpose is to stay operations until the validity or

---

[45] ss. 1, 2, 1st Sched.
[46] *Ibid.* ss. 3, 5.
[47] Act of 1971, s. 87; *Burgess* v. *Jarvis* [1952] 2 Q.B. 41.
[48] *East Riding C.C.* v. *Park Estate (Bridlington) Ltd.* [1957] A.C. 223; *Francis* v. *Yiewsley and West Drayton U.D.C.* [1958] 1 Q.B. 478.
[49] Act of 1971, s. 87, amended by Local Government and Planning (Amendment) Act 1981.
[50] *Ibid.*

otherwise of the enforcement notice has been established and so nullify the effects of delaying tactics by developers.[51]

(d) *Appeal.* An appeal to the Minister against an enforcement notice may be made before it has taken effect. The Minister has wide powers to grant permission for the development, or vary or quash the enforcement notice; and a further appeal lies to the High Court, but only on a point of law.[52]

(e) *Penalties.* If an enforcement notice or a stop notice is not obeyed, the penalty is a fine not exceeding £1,000 on summary conviction, or an unrestricted fine on conviction on indictment. In addition, there may be a daily penalty not exceeding £100 for continued disobedience after conviction; and except where a use is required to be discontinued, the local planning authority may enter the land, take the steps required by the notice (*e.g.* the demolition of an offending structure), and sue the owner for the cost of so doing.[53] Further, if these powers prove an insufficent deterrent, the Attorney-General may permit the local planning authority to sue in his name for an injunction.[54]

4. Additional controls. In addition to regulating development the Act provides for certain additional controls. Local planning author-ities can make Tree Preservation Orders, prohibiting in the interests of amenity the cutting of trees.[55] The demolition or alteration of buildings of special architectural or historic interest may be prevented by "listing," that is, inclusion in a list compiled by the Secretary of State.[56] Moreover, any area of special architectural or historic interest may be designated a "conservation area" by the local planning authority, which means that no building in it may be demolished without consent and the trees are protected as if they were subject to a tree preservation order.[57] Further, a local planning authority may serve on the owner and occupier of any garden, vacant sites or other open land which seriously interferes with the local amenities a notice to abate the injury[58]; and there is an elaborate system for the control of advertisements on land.[59]

---

[51] Act of 1971, s. 90 (as amended by the Town and Country Planning (Amendment) Act 1977). s. 92A of the Act of 1971 (inserted by para. 6 of the Sched. to the Local Government and Planning (Amendment) Act 1981) requires every district planning authority and every London Borough Council to maintain a register of enforcement and stop notices which relate to land in their area for notices issued or served after November 26, 1981.

[52] Act of 1971, ss. 88, 246; Town and Country Planning Enforcement (Inquiries Procedure) Rules (1981 S.I. 1743).

[53] *Ibid.* ss. 89–91.

[54] *Att.-Gen.* v. *Smith* [1958] 2 Q.B. 173. Also see *Gouriet* v. *Union of Post Office Workers* [1978] A.C. 435; Local Government Act 1972, s. 222.

[55] Act of 1971, ss. 60–62. See also Act of 1974, s. 10.

[56] Act of 1971, ss. 54–58.

[57] Act of 1974, ss. 1, 8.

[58] Act of 1971, s. 65. See *Britt* v. *Buckinghamshire C.C.* [1964] 1 Q.B. 77.

[59] Act of 1971, ss. 63, 64, 109; S.I. 1969 No. 1532; S.I. 1972 No. 489; S.I. 1974 No. 185; S.I. 1975 No. 898.

D. Effect on the Law of Property

When the Act of 1947 was enacted, some strange suggestions were made as to its fundamental effect on English land law. It was even contended that the fee simple in land no longer existed, but instead each landowner had merely a fee simple in the existing or permitted use of his land. This view appears to have been based on the need to obtain permission for any development, and on the obligation to pay a development charge to re-acquire the development rights which the state was acquiring. The substance of the first of these changes, however, had already been made by the Act of 1943 (which none had regarded as being epoch-making), and the second of the changes more resembled a tax on development than anything else. The subsequent betterment levy, development gains tax, and development land tax are even more purely fiscal measures and involve no element of purchasing rights in land from the State. Further, on this view, no purchaser of land in, say, 1950, received more than a fee simple in an existing use, and so today, despite the abolition of development charges, he still has no fee simple in the land. Yet again, it ignored "existing or permitted buildings" in which the landowner had the same kind of rights as in the "existing or permitted use."

In truth, the theory would not bear examination, and it has gained no foothold in the courts or among practioners. Planning control affects the use and enjoyment of land, but not the estates or interests in it; and the various charges, levies or taxes are a purely fiscal burden. Planning matters must be duly investigated for the protection of purchasers, but they are not technically matters of title. The right to use property in a particular way is not in itself property.[60] The fee simple in land remains the same fee simple as before. All that has happened is that the fruits of ownership have become less sweet; but that is nothing new in land law.

Sect. 2. Miscellaneous Controls

A number of other statutes control the use and enjoyment of land and the buildings on it, of which the following are the most important:

1. The Housing Acts 1957 to 1980. Under these Acts the appropriate local authority, subject in some cases to the consent of the Secretary of State for the Environment, has power to require a landowner to repair certain houses, to demolish insanitary or obstructive houses, or to clear his land of buildings. Compulsory purchase procedures exist to enable a local authority to acquire land for clearance and redevelopment. The Housing (Homeless Persons)

---

[60] *Belfast Corporation* v. *O.D. Cars Ltd.* [1960] A.C. 490.

Act 1977 places local authorities under a duty to provide permanent rehousing for families within its area of responsibility who are either homeless or are threatened with homelessness.[61] Assistance may also be given by the Secretary of State or by a local authority to voluntary organisations which are concerned with homelessness.

2. The Public Health Acts 1936 to 1974. These Acts formerly empowered local authorities to make by-laws regulating such matters as the construction, materials, height, lighting, ventilation, sanitation and size of rooms of new buildings. They now empower the Secretary of State to make building regulations for the same matters.[62] What may be termed the public health code now extends to include the Health Service and Public Health Act 1968, the Public Health (Recurring Nuisances) Act 1969, and the Control of Pollution Act 1974. This 1974 Act is concerned with the disposal of waste, the pollution of the atmosphere and of water and noise.

3. Offices, Shops and Railway Premises Act 1963. The purpose of this Act is to secure the health, safety and welfare of persons employed to work in the various kinds of premises named in the title by ensuring that the premises are sufficiently spacious and airy, and have proper amenities and safety precautions. This Act and the parallel legislation such as the Factories Act 1961 and the Mines and Quarries Act 1954 may be replaced eventually by regulations made under the all-encompassing Health and Safety at Work, etc., Act 1974.

4. Agricultural control. The Agricultural Act 1947 gave the Minister of Agriculture, Fisheries and Food (acting through the County Agricultural Executive Committees) wide powers of controlling farming operations and of securing a proper standard of good estate management, especially in the provision and maintenance of fixed equipment. It was repealed by the Agriculture Act 1958. All that remains is a limited power in the Agricultural Land Tribunal (the successor to some of the functions of the County Agricultural Executive Committees) to direct a landlord to provide fixed equipment required to enable the tenant to comply with statutory provisions (*e.g.* for producing clean milk); but failure to comply is treated merely as a breach of the terms of the tenancy, giving the tenant the right to do the work himself and to recover the cost from the landlord.[63]

---

[61] See *Din* v. *London Borough of Wandsworth* [1981] 3 All E.R. 881; *Islam* v. *London Borough of Hillingdon* [1981] 3 All E.R. 901.
[62] See Act of 1936, ss. 61, 62; Act of 1961, ss. 4–11; Fire Precautions Act 1971, ss. 11–13.
[63] Agriculture Act 1958, s. 4.

5. Air-space. Even at common law, probably no action lay for trespass in respect of passage through the air-space above the land in such circumstances as to involve no interference with the reasonable use of it.[64] This has now been reinforced by the Civil Aviation Act 1949,[65] which provides that no action shall lie in respect of trespass or nuisance merely by reason of the flight of aircraft over property at a height which is reasonable under the circumstances, provided the proper regulations are observed. But an action for nuisance lies for the passage of dangerous projectiles 75 feet over land[66]; and the permanent occupation of the air-space over the land of another without his consent, *e.g.* by telephone wires or a cornice or branches of a tree, is both a nuisance[67] and a trespass.[68]

Part 4

STATUTORY RESTRICTIONS ON OWNERSHIP AND DISPOSITION

Sect. 1. Compulsory Purchase

1. Powers. A landowner is subject to what is sometimes called "eminent domain," namely, the right of Parliament, as part of its legislative omnipotence, to authorise the compulsory acquisition of land by some government department, public authority or public utility company. There are many Acts authorising such acquisition.

(a) *General.* Ever since the building of the railways in the first half of the last century there has been an increasing spate of legislation authorising all kinds of public bodies to acquire land compulsorily for the purpose of carrying out their various functions.[69]

(b) *Planning.* A new departure was made by the Town and Country Planning Act 1947.[70] Under that Act a development plan might designate land as subject to compulsory acquisition not only when it was required for the specific functions of some public body but also when it was necessary to secure its development in

---

[64] *Bernstein* v. *Skyviews & General Ltd.* [1978] Q.B. 479. In *Wollerton and Wilson Ltd.* v. *Richard Costain Ltd.* [1970] 1 W.L.R. 411, a crane jib swinging 50 feet above roof level was admitted to be a trespass.

[65] s. 40, replacing Air Navigation Act 1920, s. 9.

[66] *Clifton* v. *Viscount Bury* (1887) 4 T.L.R. 8.

[67] See McNair, *Law of the Air* (3rd ed., 1964), Chap. 3.

[68] *Kelsen* v. *Imperial Tobacco Co. (of Great Britain and Ireland) Ltd.* [1957] 2 Q.B. 334.

[69] Stewart-Brown *Guide to Compulsory Purchase and Compensation* (5th ed., 1962) has a list of over 70 "main Acts" in its appendices. A.S. Wisdom, *Local Authorities' Powers of Purchase* (5th ed., 1974) summarises the powers under 87 heads.

[70] It had been foreshadowed by the more limited Town and Country Planning Act 1944.

accordance with the plan.[71] Under the present provision[72] the Secretary of State may authorise a local authority to acquire land compulsorily for the following purposes:

  (i) that the land is required to secure the treatment as a whole by development, redevelopment or improvement of it; or
 (ii) that it is expedient in the public interest that the land should be held together with the land so required; or
(iii) that the land is required for development or redevelopment as a whole to provide for the relocation of population or industry; or
 (iv) that it is expedient to acquire the land immediately for a purpose which it is necessary to achieve in the interests of the proper planning of an area in which it is situated.

(c) *Useless land.* A form of compulsory purchase in reverse was introduced by the Town and Country Planning Act 1947.[73] Where planning permission is refused or conditions are imposed, a land-owner may sometimes serve on the local authority a notice requiring the authority to purchase the land compulsorily. He can do this only if "the land has become incapable of reasonably beneficial use in its existing state,"[74] and cannot be rendered capable of reasonably beneficial use by carrying out any development that is permitted.[75] There is a similar right in some circumstances where land is "blighted" by planning proposals in a development or structure plan or other document which shows land as being required for a public authority, a highway or other purposes.[76]

2. Procedure. It is, of course, possible that the Act which confers the power to acquire land compulsorily should also lay down the procedure to be followed. But for the most part the procedure has become standardised, and is to be found in enabling Acts which are incorporated by reference into the Act which confers the power of compulsory acquisition.[77] The main steps are as follows.

(a) *Order.* When an authority wishes to make a specific purchase, it makes a provisional compulsory purchase order. The order is not effective unless and until it is confirmed by the appropriate Minister, who has to hear any objections, usually at a public inquiry conducted by an inspector.

---

[71] Act of 1947, s. 38.
[72] Act of 1971, s. 112.
[73] Act of 1947, s. 19.
[74] See *R.* v. *Minister of Housing and Local Government, ex p. Chichester R.D.C.* [1960] 1 W.L.R. 587.
[75] Act of 1971, ss. 180–191.
[76] *Ibid.* ss. 192–208; Land Compensation Act 1973, Pt. V.
[77] Acquisition of Land (Authorisation Procedure) Act 1946 now replaced by Acquisition of Land Act 1981; Compulsory Purchase Act 1965.

(b) *Notice to treat.* After the order has become operative, the next step is for the acquiring authority to serve a notice on the owner known as a notice to treat.[78] The notice does not by itself create a contract for sale, but it gives either party the right to have the compensation assessed. When the price has been ascertained, by the Lands Tribunal in default of agreement, there is then an enforceable contract of which specific performance will be granted.

(c) *Entry.* After the compensation has been assessed, the acquiring authority naturally can obtain possession by completing the contract. Yet any time after the notice to treat and before completion the acquiring authority can enter on 14 days' notice. In such a case the authority will pay interest running from the date of entry on the compensation money after it has been assessed.[79]

3. Compensation. The Town and Country Planning Act 1947 laid down a new basis for compensation payable on compulsory purchase which gave the owner only the value of the land in its "existing use." No payment was made for its potential development value.[80] This basis was abandoned in 1959 after the abolition of development charges, and compensation is now based on "open market" value. The change was effected by the Town and Country Planning Act 1959 and its provisions on this point have now been consolidated and replaced by corresponding provisions in the Land Compensation Act 1961.

(a) *Open market value.* The most important result of the Act of 1959 was the restoration of the open market value of the land as the measure of compensation to be paid on a compulsory acquisition. This value depends not only on any actual planning permissions that have been granted but also on what planning permissions would have been likely to be granted. It is accordingly provided that for this purpose it is to be assumed that various forms of development would be permitted, including the development for which the compulsory acquisition is being made, any development foreshadowed by the development plan, and any development certified by the local planning authority as being appropriate.[81] Compensation may also be paid for disturbance (*e.g.* loss of goodwill, and removal expenses),[82] and injurious affection, that is, injury to other lands caused by the acquisition.[83]

---

[78] Compulsory Purchase Act 1965, s. 5.
[79] *Ibid.* s. 11 (1).
[80] Act of 1947, ss. 51, 52.
[81] Act of 1959, s. 1 and ss. 2–5, replaced by Act of 1961, ss. 14–17. See *Provincial Properties (London) Ltd.* v. *Caterham and Warlingham U.D.C.* [1972] Q.B. 453.
[82] Land Compensation Act 1973, Pt. III.
[83] *Ibid.* Pt. VI.

(b) *Variations.* If the landowner has become entitled to any compensation for the refusal of planning permission, this must be deducted; and any enhancement in the value of the land due to the acquiring authority's proposals for other land must be excluded.[84] On the other hand, if within five years after the completion of the sale planning permission is given for other development on the land that would make it more valuable, the vendor is entitled to correspondingly additional compensation.[85]

(c) *No market.* If the land is devoted (and but for the acquisition would continue to be devoted) to a purpose for which there is no general demand or market (*e.g.* a church), compensation may be assessed on the basis of equivalent reinstatement, provided that reinstatement in some other place is intended.[86]

Sect. 2. Minerals

As has been seen, the Crown is entitled at common law to all gold and silver occurring in any mine. Statute has deprived landowners of certain other minerals occurring in or under their land.

1. Petroleum and natural gas. Under the Petroleum (Production) Act 1934 there was vested in the Crown petroleum existing in its natural condition in strata, including any mineral oil or relative hydrocarbon and natural gas.[87]

2. Coal. Under the Coal Act 1938, all interests in coal (except interests arising under a coal-mining lease) were vested in the Coal Commission in return for compensation; and these interests (including coal-mining leases) have now vested in the National Coal Board.[88]

Sect. 3. Protection of Tenants

The modern tendency is to enact legislation designed to protect tenants against their landlords. At common law, the matter was in general one of contract: provided a landlord did not contravene the terms of his bargain, he might at will evict his tenant, or under the threat of eviction secure his agreement to pay an increased rent of whatever amount he could exact. Although a number of matters such as fixtures, emblements and the like are of importance, the two crucial matters in any scheme for protecting tenants are protection

[84] Act of 1959, ss. 9, 17, replaced by Act of 1961, ss. 6–9, 12, 1st Sched.
[85] Act of 1959, ss. 18–21, replaced by Act of 1961, ss. 23–26.
[86] Act of 1961, s. 5 (5). See *Birmingham Corporation* v. *West Midland Baptist (Trust) Association* [1970] A.C. 874.
[87] s. 1; *Earl of Lonsdale* v. *Att.-Gen., The Times*, January 19, 1982.
[88] Coal Industry Nationalisation Act 1946.

against eviction, and control of rent: and these subjects will be dealt with here.

Legislation has been piecemeal. Apart from some relatively mild provisions concerning agricultural land, beginning with the Agricultural Holdings (England) Act 1875, no real system of control existed until the first of the Rent Acts was enacted in 1915. There is little common design to be found in the various statutes: as will be seen, protection against eviction is provided by a wide variety of devices, and so is control of rent. The general basis of the various systems will be considered in turn.

A. Business Premises

1. The Act of 1927. Business premises were first protected[89] by Part I of the Landlord and Tenant Act 1927. This gave the tenant the right to a new lease (or compensation in lieu thereof) provided he could establish that by reason of the carrying on by him or his predecessors in title at the premises of a trade or business for not less than five years, goodwill had become attached to the premises by reason whereof they could be let at a higher rent than they otherwise would have realised.[90] The mere building up of goodwill was thus not enough, for often the tenant, on leaving, would carry much of it with him. What had to be shown was goodwill which remained adherent to the premises after the tenant had gone. This was usually difficult to prove and, indeed, normally impossible except in the case of shops; and tenancies of professional premises were outside these provisions. The procedural requirements for making a valid claim under the Act were complicated, too, and many claims failed on purely technical grounds. These relatively ineffectual provisions were replaced by the far-reaching terms of the Landlord and Tenant Act 1954, Part II, to which a number of detailed amendments were made by the Law of Property Act 1969, Part I. The closely restricted right for business tenants to claim compensation for improvements, subject to certain conditions, continues in an amended form.[91]

2. The Act of 1954. (a) *Tenancies within the Act.* Part II of the Landlord and Tenant Act 1954 applies to any tenancy where the property comprised in it is or includes premises occupied by the tenant for the purposes of any trade, profession or employment[92]; there is no requirement of adherent goodwill. The principle exceptions from the Act are the following: agricultural holdings; regulated tenancies under the Rent Act 1977[93]; mining leases; most licensed premises other than bona fide hotels and restaurants; and

---

[89] Apart from nearly a year's protection under the Rent Acts: Act of 1920, s. 13.
[90] Landlord and Tenant Act 1927, ss. 4, 5.
[91] *Post*, p. 570.
[92] Landlord and Tenant Act 1954, s. 23.
[93] Rent Act 1977, s. 24 (3).

certain tenancies granted to a servant during his employment, or granted for not more than six months.[94] Tenancies at will or at sufferance are also outside the Act.[95]

(b) *Security of tenure.* Security of tenure is secured by the simple provision that a tenancy within Part II "shall not come to an end unless terminated in accordance with the provisions of this Part of this Act."[96] Thus a tenancy for a fixed term may continue indefinitely despite the expiration of the fixed term, and an ordinary notice to quit given by the landlord will be inoperative; but the tenancy may still determine by notice to quit given by the tenant or by surrender or forfeiture.[97] In order to determine the tenancy the landlord must give not less than six nor more than 12 months' notice in the statutory form, to expire not earlier than the date when, apart from the Act, the tenancy could have been determined by notice to quit, or would have expired.[98] If within two months of receiving this notice the tenant gives the landlord notice that he is not willing to give up possession of the premises, he may, not less than two or more than four months after the landlord's notice was given, apply to the court for a new tenancy.[99] Alternatively, a tenant holding for a fixed term (and not merely under a periodical tenancy) may serve on the landlord a statutory form of request for a new tenancy in place of the old, to begin not less than six nor more than 12 months later; and not less than two nor more than four months after serving this request he must apply to the court.[1]

(c) *Opposition to new tenancy.* The court is bound to grant the tenant a new tenancy unless the landlord establishes one of the seven statutory grounds of opposition. The landlord can rely only on the grounds stated in his statutory notice or in a notice served on the tenant within two months of receiving a request for a new tenancy. Some of the grounds are based on default by the tenant and others on the landlord's need; and only the first three and the fifth, by using the word "ought," give the court any discretion. The seven grounds are as follows.[2]

(1) REPAIR: that the tenant ought not to be granted a new tenancy in view of the state of the "holding" (*i.e.* the premises let, excluding any part not occupied by the tenant or a service tenant of his) due to the tenant's failure to comply with his repairing obligations.

---

[94] Landlord and Tenant Act 1954, s. 43, as amended.
[95] *Wheeler* v. *Mercer* [1957] A.C. 416; *Hagee (London) Ltd.* v. *A.B. Erikson and Larson* [1975] 3 W.L.R. 272.
[96] Act of 1954, s. 24.
[97] But see L.P.A. 1969, s. 4 (ineffective if during first month of occupation).
[98] Act of 1954, s. 25.
[99] *Ibid.* s. 29; *Dodds* v. *Walker* [1981] 2 All E.R. 609. (The four months expire on the corresponding date in the fourth month but if such month has no corresponding date because it is too short the period expires on the last day of the month.)
[1] *Ibid.* ss. 26, 29.
[2] *Ibid.* ss. 29, 30.

(2) RENT: that the tenant ought not to be granted a new tenancy in view of his persistent delay in paying rent.

(3) OTHER BREACHES: that the tenant ought not to be granted a new tenancy in view of other substantial breaches by him of his obligations under the tenancy, or for any other reason connected with his use or management of the holding.

(4) ALTERNATIVE ACCOMMODATION: that the landlord has offered and is willing to provide or secure the provision of suitable alternative accommodation on reasonable terms.

(5) PART OF WHOLE: that the premises are part of larger premises held by the landlord and the tenant ought not to be granted a new tenancy because the landlord could obtain a substantially greater rent for the property as a whole than for the parts separately.

(6) DEMOLITION OR RECONSTRUCTION: "that on the termination of the current tenancy the landlord intends to demolish or reconstruct the premises comprised in the holding or a substantial part of those premises or to carry out substantial work of construction on the holding or part thereof and that he could not reasonably do so without obtaining possession of the holding." The landlord cannot succeed on this ground if he has a right under the current tenancy to enter and do the work,[3] or if the tenant is willing to give the landlord facilities for the work without unduly interfering with the tenant's business, or the tenant is willing to accept a tenancy of an economically separable part of the holding.[4]

(7) OWN OCCUPATION: "that on the termination of the current tenancy the landlord intends to occupy the holding for the purposes, or partly for the purposes, of a business to be carried on by him therein, or as his residence." But this head is not open to a landlord whose interest was purchased or created less than five years before the termination of the current tenancy.

The landlord cannot have the intention required by the last two heads unless at the date of the hearing he has not a mere hope but a firm, settled intention, not likely to be changed, to do something that he has a reasonable prospect of bringing about.[5] Normally an undertaking to the court given by a responsible person or body conclusively shows an intention to do what is undertaken, *e.g.* to demolish the premises.[6] A landlord who genuinely intends to reconstruct the premises and then occupy them himself is not affected by the five years rule, for the existence of Ground 7 does not prevent him from relying on Ground 6.[7]

---

[3] *Heath* v. *Drown* [1973] A.C. 498.
[4] Landlord and Tenant Act 1954, s. 31A, added by L.P.A. 1969, s. 7.
[5] *Betty's Cafes Ltd.* v. *Phillips Furnishing Stores Ltd.* [1959] A.C. 20.
[6] *Expresso Coffee Machine Co. Ltd.* v. *Guardian Assurance Co. Ltd.* [1959] 1 W.L.R. 250.
[7] *Fisher* v. *Taylors Furnishing Stores Ltd.* [1956] 2 Q.B. 78.

(d) *Terms of new tenancy.* When premises are first let to a business tenant, there is no restriction on the amount of rent he may be charged, and no power, except by contract,[8] to secure its revision while the initial tenancy continues. But if the tenant obtains a new tenancy under the Act, the rent is to be the open market rent, though a rent review clause may be included; and in default of agreement the court will determine the rent and other terms of the tenancy.[9] The rent may thus be raised or lowered, but the tenant is protected against unreasonable demands by the landlord. The duration of any new tenancy is whatever the court considers reasonable, not exceeding 14 years[10]; but there is no limit to the number of renewals. The basic idea of the Act is thus that a business tenant has a prima facie right to continue his business indefinitely in the premises, and although there is no restriction on the terms of the tenancy under which he first occupies the premises, any renewals are controlled by the court.

(e) *Compensation for eviction.* A tenant who does not obtain a new tenancy is entitled to no compensation unless this occurs because the landlord objects to the grant of a new tenancy solely by reason of one or more of the last three grounds set out above, all of which are for the landlord's benefit. In these cases, the landlord must pay the tenant compensation equal to the rateable value of the premises, or twice that sum if the tenant and his predecessors in the business have occupied the premises for business purposes for the previous 14 years.[11]

(f) *Compensation for improvements.* Under the Landlord and Tenant Act 1927,[12] if a tenant of premises used for a trade, business or profession carries out improvements to the premises which added to their letting value, the tenant may recover compensation from the landlord on leaving. But the tenant must satisfy a number of conditions; in addition to making his claim at the right time and in due form, he must give the landlord three months' notice of his intention to make the improvement. The landlord may then exclude the tenant's right to compensation if he successfully objects to the improvement, or carries it out himself in return for a reasonable increase of rent.

B. Agricultural Holdings

1. Introduction. The Agricultural Holdings (England) Act 1875 was the first of a long series of Acts regulating agricultural holdings.

---

[8] As a result of inflation rent review clauses are normally inserted into leases at the date of grant.
[9] Landlord and Tenant Act 1954, ss. 32, 34, 35, as amended by L.P.A. 1969, ss. 1, 2, 8; see *O'May* v. *City of London Real Property Co. Ltd.* [1981] 2 All E.R. 660.
[10] Landlord and Tenant Act 1954, s. 33.
[11] *Ibid.* s. 37, as amended by L.P.A. 1969, s. 11.
[12] ss. 1–3, as amended by the Landlord and Tenant Act 1954, Pt. III.

At first, the Acts were mainly directed towards securing proper compensation for the tenant, initially for improvements and, latterly, also if his tenancy was determined without good cause.[13] The Agriculture Act 1947 first gave security of tenure and protection as to rent, in place of the limited security of tenure provided during the war by Defence Regulations. The principal Act today is the Agricultural Holdings Act 1948, which consolidated the Act of 1947 with the Agricultural Holdings Act 1923, and was itself amended by the Agricultural Act 1958. Further amendments to the law were effected by the Agriculture (Miscellaneous Provisions) Act 1976, and the Agricultural Holdings (Notices to Quit) Act 1977.

2. Jurisdiction. The Acts confer many powers on the Minister of Agriculture, Fisheries and Food, on Agricultural Lands Tribunals, and on arbitrators. In general, the Act of 1958 transferred powers of determining disputes from the Minister and the former County Agricultural Executive Committees to the Tribunals, which previously had mainly appellate functions. Each of the eight areas into which England and Wales are divided has a Tribunal presided over by a lawyer appointed by the Lord Chancellor; and the Council on Tribunals supervises both the Tribunals and any arbitrators (unless appointed by agreement).[14]

3. "Agricultural holding." The Acts apply to any "agricultural holding." This means the aggregate of land used for the trade or business of agriculture which is comprised in a contract of tenancy for years, or from year to year; but, oddly enough, tenancies for more than one but less than two years are not included.[15] The definition also extends to agreements for value for a tenancy or licence for an interest less than a tenancy from year to year in circumstances which would otherwise make the land an agricultural holding. But this does not apply to agreements approved by the Minister, nor to those made in contemplation of the land being used only for grazing or mowing during some specified period of the year, even if the period is 364 days.[16] "Agriculture" is widely defined, and includes horticulture, fruit growing, seed growing and market gardening.[17] On mixed lettings (*e.g.* of pasture, an orchard and an inn), the Acts apply to all or none; the test is whether as a whole the tenancy is in substance a tenancy of agricultural land.[18]

---

[13] A.H.A. 1923, s. 12.
[14] Agriculture Act 1947, s. 73, 9th Sched.; Agriculture Act 1958, ss. 8, 10, 1st and 2nd Scheds.; Tribunals and Inquiries Act 1958, s. 1, 1st Sched; Agricultural (Miscellaneous Provisions) Act 1972, s. 21 (abolishing the C.A.E. Committees); S.I. 1959 Nos. 81, 83, as amended; S.I. 1974 No. 66.
[15] *Gladstone* v. *Bower* [1960] 2 Q.B. 384.
[16] A.H.A. 1948, ss. 1, 2; *Goldsack* v. *Shore* [1950] 1 K.B. 708; *Scene Estate Ltd.* v. *Amos* [1957] 2 Q.B. 205; contrast *Rutherford* v. *Maurer* [1962] 1 Q.B. 16.
[17] A.H.A. 1948, s. 94.
[18] *Dunn* v. *Fidoe* [1950] 2 All E.R. 685; *Howkins* v. *Jardine* [1951] 1 K.B. 614; *Monson* v. *Bound* [1954] 1 W.L.R. 1321.

4. Notices to quit. As under earlier legislation, a notice to quit an agricultural holding (including a notice exercising an option of termination in the tenancy agreement[19]) is invalid if it purports to determine the tenancy in any way save by 12 months' notice to expire at the end of a year of the tenancy[20] and this is so even if the notice was given by the tenant.[21] Further, a tenancy for a fixed term of two years or more granted since 1920 will determine at the end of the fixed period only if written notice to quit has been given by one party to the other not more than two years nor less than one year before the end of the term; if this is not done, the tenancy continues as a tenancy from year to year, notwithstanding any contrary agreement.[22]

5. Security of tenure. The landlord's right to serve a notice to quit, as modified in this way, remains unaffected. However, if within one month of receiving a notice to quit the tenant gives the landlord a counter-notice,[23] then, with eight exceptions, the notice to quit becomes ineffective unless the Agricultural Land Tribunal consents to it taking effect: and only in five cases can the Tribunal give that consent.[24] There are thus three categories.

(a) *No security.* The notice to quit will be effective if either the tenant fails to serve a counter-notice or else the case falls within one of the following eight heads. In the latter case the notice to quit must make it plain on which of the eight heads the landlord will rely.[25]

(1) PRIOR CONSENT: the Tribunal has previously consented to the notice being given.

(2) PLANNING PERMISSION: the land is required for some non-agricultural uses for which planning permission has been given or (in certain cases) is not required.

(3) BAD HUSBANDRY: on an application made within the previous six months the Tribunal has certified that the tenant was not farming in accordance with the rules of good husbandry.

(4) UNREMEDIED BREACH: the tenant has failed to comply fully[26] with a written notice by the landlord in the prescribed form requiring him to remedy a breach of a term of his tenancy within a specified time.

---

[19] See *Edell* v. *Dulieu* [1924] A.C. 38.
[20] Agricultural Holdings (Notices to Quit) Act 1977, s. 1.
[21] *Flather* v. *Hood* (1928) 44 T.L.R. 698. A shorter notice may be given if both parties agree: *Elsden* v. *Pick* [1980] 1 W.L.R. 899.
[22] A.H.A. 1948, s. 3.
[23] See *Mountford* v. *Hodkinson* [1956] 1 W.L.R. 422 (abusive letter), and contrast *Frankland* v. *Capstick* [1959] 1 W.L.R. 204.
[24] Agricultural Holdings (Notices to Quit) Act 1977, ss. 2, 3. For a ninth case (no security for sub-tenant where notice served on tenant), see M. & W., p. 1122.
[25] Agricultural Holdings (Notices to Quit) Act 1977, s. 2, *Cowan* v. *Wrayford* [1953] 1 W.L.R. 1340.
[26] *Price* v. *Romilly* [1960] 1 W.L.R. 1360.

(5) IRREPARABLE BREACH: the landlord's interest in the holding has been materially prejudiced by an irreparable breach of a term of the tenancy.

(6) BANKRUPTCY: the tenant is bankrupt or has compounded with his creditors.

(7) DEATH: the notice is given within three months after the death of the tenant with whom the *original* contract of tenancy was made, or the death of the last survivor of original joint tenants and either no application is made to succeed to the tenancy within three months of the tenant's death or the applicant is not a "suitable person."[27] If the tenancy was not for a fixed term with more than 27 months left to run then an application can be made by an "eligible person." This is the tenant's spouse, sibling or child whose principal source of livelihood was the holding and who, at the tenant's death, was not already the occupier of a commercial unit of agriculture. If the Tribunal considers the eligible person to be a suitable person to become tenant of the holding then the landlord must be given the chance to apply for the Tribunal to consent to the operation of his notice to quit in the same way as if he had served a notice not relying on any of the eight exceptional grounds (see (b) below). If the landlord does not so apply or his application is unsuccessful then the Tribunal will order a new tenancy to be granted to the suitable person. These succession provisions can operate twice only but they are treated as having operated where the tenant in his lifetime agreed to the holding being let to someone who could have claimed to succeed had the tenant kept on farming until his death.

(8) MINISTER'S NOTICE: the notice to quit is given by the appropriate Minister to enable him to effect any amalgamation within the meaning of the Agriculture Act 1967, or the reshaping of any agricultural unit.

(b) *Security dependent on reasonableness.* If the landlord satisfies the Agricultural Land Tribunal that the case falls within any of five heads, the Tribunal must consent to the notice to quit taking effect unless it appears that a fair and reasonable landlord would not insist on possession, in which case the Tribunal must withhold consent.[28] Any consent may be made subject to conditions (which may later be varied or revoked) to ensure that the land is used for the purposes stated by the landlord. The five heads are as follows.

(1) GOOD HUSBANDRY: the landlord proposes to terminate the tenancy in order to carry out a purpose desirable in the interests of good husbandry of the holding.

[27] Agriculture (Miscellaneous Provisions) Act 1976, ss. 18–24.
[28] Agricultural Holdings (Notices to Quit) Act 1977, s. 3.

(2) SOUND MANAGEMENT: that purpose is desirable in the interests of the estate of which the holding constitutes all or part.[29]

(3) RESEARCH: that purpose is desirable for the purposes of agricultural research, education, experiment or demonstration, or for the purposes of statutes relating to smallholdings or allotments.

(4) GREATER HARDSHIP: withholding consent would cause greater hardship than granting it.

(5) NON-AGRICULTURAL USE: the land is required for some non-agricultural use not within paragraph (2) of the foregoing list of eight cases.

(c) *Full security*. In all cases not falling within the foregoing heads, the notice to quit is ineffective and the tenancy continues unaffected.

6. Protection as to rent. When an agricultural tenancy is first granted, the parties are free to agree whatever rent they please. However, not more frequently than once in every three years, either party may require the amount of the rent to be submitted to arbitration. Any increase or decrease awarded by the arbitrator takes effect as from the next day on which the tenancy could have been determined by a notice to quit given when the reference to arbitration was demanded.[30] Accordingly, no revision of rent is possible during a tenancy for a fixed term which is not determinable by notice to quit. In addition, the landlord may increase the rent in respect of certain improvements carried out by him.[31]

7. Compensation for disturbance. If a tenant quits the holding in consequence of a notice to quit given by the landlord (even if the notice is in fact invalid,[32]) he is entitled to compensation for disturbance of not more than two years' rent nor less than one.[33] No agreement can exclude this or any other provision in the Act as to compensation,[34] and a provision which by implication does this (*e.g.* by providing for determination of the tenancy at such short notice as to leave no time to claim compensation) is void.[35]

8. Compensation for improvements. When an agricultural tenant quits his holding at the end of his tenancy, he is entitled to compensation for certain improvements carried out by him, provided he has observed the necessary conditions. Such improvements fall in

---

[29] See *Evans* v. *Roper* [1960] W.L.R. 814.
[30] A.H.A. 1948, s. 8; see *Sclater* v. *Horton* [1954] 2 Q.B. 1; *Edell* v. *Dulieu* [1924] A.C. 38.
[31] A.H.A. 1948, s. 9.
[32] *Kestell* v. *Langmaid* [1950] 1 K.B. 233.
[33] A.H.A. 1948, s. 34, replacing earlier provisions.
[34] *Ibid.* s. 65.
[35] *Coates* v. *Diment* [1951] 1 All E.R. 890.

three main categories. First, there are certain long-term improvements (*e.g.* planting orchards) for which the landlord's consent is
required. Secondly, there are other long-term inmprovements (*e.g.*
the erection of buildings) for which either the landlord's consent or
the Tribunal's approval is necessary. Thirdly, there are some
short-term improvements (*e.g.* the chalking or liming of land) for
which neither consent nor approval is needed. The measure of
compensation is the increase in the value of the holding, or, in the
case of a short-term improvement, the value of the improvement to
an incoming tenant.[36]

C. Dwellings

The statutes. Over 67 years have passed since the first statute
protecting tenants of dwelling-houses appeared.[37] It was later
repealed and replaced by a series of statutes commencing in 1920 and
known as the Rent Acts.[38] These statutes were in turn repealed and
replaced by the consolidating Rent Act 1968. This Act was amended
by the Housing Act 1969, the Housing Finance Act 1972, the
Counter-Inflation Act 1973, and the Rent Act 1974. There then
followed a further consolidation in the Rent Act 1977 which was in
turn amended by the Housing Act 1980. In addition, security of
tenure for agricultural workers housed by their employers was
provided by the Rent (Agriculture) Act 1976, which also deals with
the control of rent in respect of dwellings in such occupation.

Until the enactment of the Housing Act 1980 protection had always
operated in the private sector, but the Act of 1980 introduced
important provisions relating to security of residential tenure in what
may be called the public sector. Included in the scope of this
protection are tenancies granted by local authorities, also by the
Housing Corporation, the Commission for the New Towns, housing
associations, housing trusts and housing co-operatives.

Rights protective of tenure have also been conferred on some
tenants holding long tenancies by the Landlord and Tenant Act 1954,
Part I.

Under the Leasehold Reform Act 1967 qualifying long leaseholders are given the right to purchase the reversion or to obtain a
new long lease.[39] As a matter of some political controversy, the
Housing Act 1980 has conferred on tenants in the public sector rights
somewhat similar to those existing under the Act of 1967.

At the present time protection exists under various statutes and in
various forms in respect of the following species of residential
occupation.

---

[36] A.H.A. 1948, ss. 46–51, 3rd and 4th Scheds., as amended by Agriculture Act 1958.
[37] Increase of Rent and Mortgage Interest (War Restrictions) Act 1915.
[38] Rent and Mortgage Interest Restrictions Acts 1920–1939; Furnished Houses (Rent
Control) Act 1946; Landlord and Tenant (Rent Control) Act 1949; Housing Repairs
and Rents Act 1954; Rent Act 1957; Rent Act 1965.
[39] *Post*, p. 588.

(a) Private sector protection.
   (i)   Regulated tenancies (Rent Act 1977)
   (ii) Restricted contracts (Rent Act 1977)
   (iii) Long tenancies (Landlord and Tenant Act 1954, Part I; Leasehold Reform Act 1967)
   (iv) Protected occupancies (Rent (Agriculture) Act 1976)
   (v)   Assured tenancies (Housing Act 1980)

(b) Public sector protection.
   (vi) Secure tenancies (Housing Act 1980)

It will now be necessary to look at each of these categories in some detail.

A Private Sector Protection

I. TENANCIES PROTECTED BY THE RENT ACT

1. "Controlled" and "regulated" tenancies. When the Rent Act 1977 came into operation two main systems of protection existed under the Act, closely similar except for the method of restricting the rent. First, there were "controlled" tenancies, steadily dimishing in number and subject to an older system whereby the rent was fixed in relation to some objective criterion. In the past this had been the "standard rent," the rent at which the dwelling had been let on a particular date, but after the Rent Act 1957 it was based on the gross value of the dwelling for rating purposes in 1956. Secondly, there were "regulated" tenancies (introduced by the Rent Act 1965), under which the existing rent is replaced by a rent fixed by a rent officer or, on appeal, by a rent assessment committee. These committees are distinct from the rent tribunals which have jurisdiction over restricted contracts. By 1980 it was estimated that there were fewer than 2,000 controlled tenancies still existing in England and Wales. The Housing Finance Act 1972 had instituted a programme of conversion of controlled tenancies into regulated tenancies, commencing with those having the highest annual rateable value.[40] This process was halted after a change of government. The Housing Act 1980 provides for the automatic conversion of all[41] controlled tenancies into regulated tenancies so that this latter category will in the future comprise all protected and statutory tenancies under the Rent Act 1977. The Housing Act 1980 also introduced a new and important category of protected regulated tenancy into the scheme of the Act of 1977: the

[40] Conversion occurred of all controlled tenancies with a rateable value on March 31, 1972 of £70 or more in London and £35 elsewhere. In addition, conversion occurred if a landlord obtained a "qualification certificate" from a local authority for a particular house, certifying that it had standard amenities, was in good repair and was otherwise fit for habitation; Housing Finance Act 1972, s. 27. For standard amenities, see Housing Act 1974, s. 58, 6th Sched.
[41] Except for those involving an element of business user which are brought under the Landlord and Tenant Act 1954, Pt. 11.

"protected shorthold tenancy." This form of tenancy is a term certain of not less than one year nor more than five years in respect of which prescribed conditions are satisfied. The landlord may recover possession of premises let on such a tenancy at the expiry of the term.

2. Application of the Act. The Rent Act 1977 applies to every "dwelling-house" of an appropriate rateable value[42] which satisfies certain conditions. "Dwelling-house" means any house (or part of a house) which is "let as a separate dwelling."[43] Thus the existence of a tenancy is essential; this requirement excludes a mere licence from the Act, but not a tenant at will or at sufferance. Whether the premises are let "as" a dwelling depends on the use provided for or contemplated by the tenancy agreement, or, in default, by the *de facto* user at the time in question.[44] And the letting must be as "a" (*i.e.* one) dwelling and not as two or more dwellings.[45]

The word "separate" formerly excluded lettings where the tenant was required to share living accommodation such as a kitchen.[46] However, statute has modified the rule, so that where the sharing is with the landlord the tenant is given restricted contract protection,[47] and where the sharing is with other tenants, the tenant has normal protection, subject to certain modifications.[48] Often what is structurally a single dwelling-house contains many "dwelling-houses" for the purposes of the Rent Act, even if it has not been physically divided into self-contained flats; for one or two rooms, with a right to share the bathroom and lavatory, may for this purpose constitute a "dwelling-house."

3. Exceptions. Certain tenancies which would otherwise fall within the Act are nevertheless excluded. In some cases, the exception is personal to the landlord. Thus, the Crown is generally not bound by the Act[49] (but tenants are protected where the interest of the Crown is under the management of the Crown Estate Commissioners), nor are local authorities, new town development corporations or certain housing associations or housing trusts.[50] In such cases, the exemption does not operate in favour of other persons concerned with the property, such as sub-tenants or purchasers. Other exceptions depend on the nature of the tenancies. Thus the Act does not apply where the letting is rent free or the rent is less than two-thirds of the rateable value.[51] Again, the Act is excluded where the tenancy was

---

[42] See *post*, p. 578.
[43] Act of 1977, s. 1 (1).
[44] *Wolve* v. *Hogan* [1949] 2 K.B. 194.
[45] *Horford Investments* v. *Lambert* [1976] Ch. 39.
[46] *Neale* v. *Del Soto* [1945] K.B. 144.
[47] Act of 1977, s. 21. See *post*, p. 585.
[48] Act of 1977, s. 22.
[49] Act of 1977, s. 13 (as substituted by the Housing Act 1980, s. 73).
[50] Act of 1977, ss. 14, 15; and see Housing Act 1980, s. 74.
[51] Act of 1977, s. 5 (1).

granted in order to give the tenant the right to occupy the dwelling for a holiday, or if the tenant is pursuing or intends to pursue a course of study provided by a specified institution, and the tenancy was granted by that or some other specified body.[52] The Act is also excluded where the rent includes payments in respect of board or attendance[53]; payments for the use of furniture formerly excluded the Acts but no longer do so.[54]

Most of the exceptions, however, depend on the nature or status of the premises themselves. Thus for diverse reasons, public houses,[55] and parsonage houses of the Church of England[56] (*e.g.* the ordinary rectory or vicarage), are outside the Act. Agricultural holdings occupied by the farmer are also outside the Act (but, of course, within the Agricultural Holdings Act 1948).[57] Although in general any land or premises let together with a dwelling-house are treated as being part of the dwelling-house, if the dwelling-house is let together with more than two acres of agricultural land, both house and land are excluded from the Act.[58]

Particular mention must be made of the important exception where the tenancy is granted by a "resident landlord," that is, a landlord of a dwelling which is part of a building, another part of which is occupied throughout the tenancy by the landlord as his residence. The provision does not apply to a purpose built block of flats except in a case where the dwelling which is let is part of a flat in such a block. Where after August 13, 1974, any such landlord grants such a tenancy, the tenancy is outside the normal protection, so long as the landlord continues to be resident, though it constitutes a restricted contract.[59] But such a tenancy is not excluded from normal protection if it is granted to an existing tenant of the building holding under either a protected or statutory tenancy.[60]

4. Rateable value. To be protected the dwelling must have the appropriate rateable value. This has varied throughout the years. The present position is that to escape protection the dwelling has to have an annual rateable value exceeding specified limits on three prescribed dates of which one, two or all three may be applicable depending on when the "appropriate day" in respect of the dwelling happens to fall.[61] The appropriate day means the date on which a

---

[52] *Ibid.* ss. 8, 9.
[53] *Ibid.* s. 7: restricted contract protection may apply in some cases.
[54] Rent Act 1974, s. 1. Furnished tenancies granted before August 14, 1974, where the landlord is a resident landlord continue to be excluded from normal protection, but retain protection as restricted contracts.
[55] Act of 1977, s. 11.
[56] *Bishop of Gloucester* v. *Cunnington* [1943] K.B. 101.
[57] A.H.A. 1948, 7th Sched.
[58] Act of 1977, s. 26.
[59] *Ibid.* s. 20.
[60] *Ibid.* s. 12. Note the significant amendments made to this section by the Housing Act 1980, s. 65.
[61] Act of 1977, s. 4.

rateable value for the dwelling first appeared in the valuation list, but if that date happens to fall before March 23, 1965, this latter date is declared to be the appropriate day. The relevant dates and figures are as follows (the higher figure is the rateable value applicable in Greater London and the lower figure is the rateable value which applies elsewhere).

    March 23, 1965: £400 and £200
    March 22, 1973: £600 and £300
    April 1, 1973: £1,500 and £750

The increase in the figures represents an increase by the Government under the Counter-Inflation Act 1973 followed by new rating assessments. It will be seen that in order to be outside the scope of statutory protection the great majority of rented property has to exceed the relevant limits on all three dates.

Controlled tenancies had to have come into existence before July 6, 1957, and be in respect of dwellings with a rateable value which on November 7, 1956, did not exceed £40 in Greater London and £30 elsewhere.

5. Statutory tenancy. The Rent Act protects a tenant from eviction by prohibiting the courts from making any order for possession except on specified grounds, and giving him the right to continue in possession of the premises despite the termination of the tenancy by notice to quit or otherwise. The Act thus brings into being what is usually called a "statutory tenancy"; this is the right of the tenant to remain in possession, despite the determination of his contractual tenancy, on all the terms of the contractual tenancy which are not inconsistent with the Act,[62] until the court makes an order for possession against him. A statutory tenancy is not really a "tenancy" at all, in the common law sense of the word; the tenant has no estate or interest in the land, but a mere personal right of occupation. This has been graphically described as a "status of irremovability."[63] He cannot dispose of his statutory tenancy by assignment[64] or by will, and it will not vest in his trustee in bankruptcy.

Further, a statutory tenancy will cease to exist if the tenant ceases to occupy the premises as his home[65] or one of his homes.[66] Mere temporary absences are immaterial; but once an absent tenant has lost either his *animus revertendi* (intention of returning) or his *corpus possessionis* (visible indication of his animus, such as the presence on the premises of some caretaker on his behalf), his statutory tenancy is at an end.[67] If a house is totally destroyed, any statutory tenancy

---

[62] *Ibid.* s. 3.
[63] *Jessamine Investment Co.* v. *Schwartz* [1977] 2 W.L.R. 145.
[64] But see Act of 1977, s. 3 (5), Sched. 1, para. 13.
[65] *Skinner* v. *Geary* [1931] 2 K.B. 546.
[66] *Hallwood Estates Ltd.* v. *Flack* (1950) 66 (2) T.L.R. 368.
[67] *Brown* v. *Brash* [1948] 2 K.B. 247; *Tickner* v. *Hearn* [1960] 1 W.L.R. 1406.

perishes with the house, whereas a contractual tenancy might still continue to exist in the ruins.[68] A statutory tenancy is thus an anomaly which fits into no recognised category of property law. If the tenant dies, his widow, if residing with him at his death, or otherwise any member of his family who has resided with him for at least the previous six months, becomes statutory tenant in his place.[69] Two such transmissions are permitted.

6. Order for possession. If a landlord seeks an order for possession, he must satisfy one of the following two heads.

(a) *Reasonableness and a ground for possession.* The landlord must satisfy the court on the overriding requirement, namely, that in all the circumstances of the case it is reasonable to make an order for possession.[70] In addition, he must further establish one of the "discretionary" grounds for possession. Some of these are based on misconduct by the tenant, others on the landlord's needs, or the existence of alternative accommodation. The grounds fall under the following heads.[71]

(1) BREACH: rent lawfully due has not been paid, or some other obligation of the tenancy that is consistent with the Act has been broken.

(2) NUISANCE: the tenant, his lodger or sub-tenant has been guilty of conduct which is a nuisance or annoyance to adjoining occupiers, or has been convicted of illegal or immoral user of the premises.

(3) WASTE: the tenant, his lodger or sub-tenant has permitted the condition of the premises to deteriorate.

(4) DAMAGE TO FURNITURE: the tenant, his lodger or sub-tenant has, by ill-treatment, caused the condition of furniture provided under the tenancy to deteriorate.

(5) TENANT'S NOTICE TO QUIT: the tenant has given notice to quit and the landlord has acted upon it so as to be seriously prejudiced if he could not obtain possession.

(6) ASSIGNING OR SUB-LETTING WITHOUT CONSENT: the tenant, without the landlord's consent, has assigned or sub-let the whole of the premises, or has sub-let part, the remainder being already sub-let.

(7) NEEDED FOR LANDLORD'S SERVANT: the premises are reasonably required as a residence for a whole-time servant of the landlord, and

[68] *Ellis & Sons Amalgamated Properties Ltd.* v. *Sisman* [1948] 1 K.B. 653; *National Carriers Ltd.* v. *Panalpina Ltd.* [1980] 1 All E.R. 161.
[69] Act of 1977, s. 2, Sched. 1, Pt. 1, as amended by the Housing Act 1980, s. 76. As to 'family' see *Dyson Holdings Ltd.* v. *Fox* [1976] Q.B. 503, *Helby* v. *Rafferty* [1979] 1 W.L.R. 13; *Watson* v. *Lucas* [1980] 1 W.L.R. 1493; *Carega Properties S.A.* v. *Sharratt* [1979] 1 W.L.R. 925.
[70] Act of 1977, s. 98.
[71] Act of 1977, s. 98, Sched. 15, Pt. 1.

they were let to the tenant in consequence of his former employment by the landlord or a previous landlord.

(8) NEEDED FOR LANDLORD OR HIS FAMILY: the landlord reasonably requires the premises for occupation as a residence for himself, a child of his over 18 years old, or one of his parents (or parents-in-law). There are two exceptions. First, this head is not available to a landlord who became landlord by purchasing[72] any interest in the premises after March 23, 1965. This prevents a landlord who buys the premises subject to an existing tenancy from evicting the tenant under this head.[73] Secondly, this does not apply if the tenant satisfies the court that in all the circumstances "greater hardship" would be caused to all persons likely to be affected[74] by making the order for possession than by refusing it.

(9) EXCESSIVE RENT ON SUB-LETTING: the tenant has sub-let part of the premises at an excessive rent.

(10) ALTERNATIVE ACCOMMODATION: suitable alternative accommodation is available for the tenant, or will be availabe when the order for possession takes effect. This accommodation need not be as suitable as the existing accommodation and may even be part of it.[75]

(b) *Unrestricted ground for possession.* There are a number of exceptional cases ("mandatory grounds") where the landlord can obtain an order for possession as of right without proof of reasonableness.[76] They were never available in respect of a controlled tenancy. It is very important to note that all of the mandatory grounds are only available if the appropriate notice has been served on the tenant by not later than the relevant date, which is generally the date of the commencement of the tenancy. The notice alerts the tenant to the fact that the landlord may recover the premises by relying on a ground of this class. The grounds are as follows.

(1) OWNER-OCCUPIER: the landlord was an owner-occupier of the dwelling when he let it and possession is sought on the ground that, of the conditions set out below, one of those in paragraphs (a) and (c) to (f) is satisfied.

(2) RETIREMENT HOME: the landlord let the dwelling prior to his retirement and possession is sought on the ground that, of the same set of prescribed conditions mentioned above, one of those in paragraphs (b) to (e) is satisfied.
The conditions referred to are:

---

[72] See *Thomas* v. *Fryer* [1970] 1 W.L.R. 845.
[73] See, *e.g. Wright* v. *Walford* [1955] 1 K.B. 363.
[74] See *Harte* v. *Frampton* [1948] 1 K.B. 73.
[75] *Parmee* v. *Mitchell* [1950] 2 K.B. 199; *Mykolyshyn* v. *Noah* [1970] 1 W.L.R. 1271.
[76] Act of 1977, s. 98, Sched. 15, Pts. 2 and 5. The Housing Act 1980, s. 66 made important amendments to some of the mandatory cases and inserted Pt. 5 into Sched. 15 of the Act of 1977.

(a) the dwelling is required as a residence for the owner or any member of his family who resided with him when he last occupied the dwelling;

(b) the owner has retired from regular employment and requires the dwelling as his residence;

(c) the owner has died and the dwelling is required for a member of his family residing with him at the time of his death;

(d) the owner has died and the dwelling is required by a successor in title as his residence or for the purpose of disposing of it with vacant possession;

(e) the dwelling is subject to a mortgage which pre-dates the tenancy and the mortgagee requires the dwelling for the purpose of disposing of it with vacant possession pursuant to his mortgagee's power of sale;

(f) the dwelling is not suitably proximate to the owner's place of work and he needs the proceeds of a sale with vacant possession in order to acquire a dwelling more suitable to his needs.

(3) HOLIDAY HOME: the tenancy was granted for a fixed term of not more than eight months, and sometime during the previous 12 months the dwelling was occupied under a right to occupy it for a holiday.

(4) STUDENT RESIDENCE: the tenancy was granted for a fixed term of not more than 12 months and sometime during the previous 12 months the dwelling was subject to a tenancy granted by a specified institution to a student at a specified educational institution.

(5) MINISTER OF RELIGION: the house is held in order to be available for occupation by a minister of religion as a residence from which to perform his duties, and is required for this purpose.

(6) AGRICULTURAL WORKER: the house is required for an agricultural worker.

(7) REDUNDANT FARMHOUSE: a farmhouse made redundant by an amalgamation of farms or other circumstances is required for an agricultural worker.

(8) PROTECTED SHORTHOLD TENANCY[77]: this special new species of protected tenancy has already been referred to above. Such a tenancy is a protected tenancy granted after the commencement of the Housing Act 1980 for a term certain of not less than one year nor more than five years. It must satisfy specified conditions, which include the service of a notice on the tenant before the grant of the

---

[77] Housing Act 1980, ss. 51–55, Protected Shorthold Tenancies (Rent Registration) Order (1981 S.I. 1578). Case 19 under which possession may be recovered is inserted by s. 55 into Sched. 15, Pt. 2 of the Act of 1977.

tenancy stating that it is to be a protected shorthold tenancy, and the requirement for London, but not elsewhere, that either a rent for the dwelling is registered at the time the tenancy is granted, or, before the grant, a certificate of fair rent has been issued and an application for the registration of a rent is made not later than 28 days after the beginning of the term. If at the expiry of the term the tenant does not give up possession the landlord may commence proceedings for possession not later than three months after the expiry of a notice to the tenant of the landlord's intention to do so. The protected shorthold tenancy is a radical innovation intended to stimulate the supply of residential lettings by offering landlords a guaranteed right to recover possesion.

(9) SERVICEMEN: possession may be recovered where the letting is by a person who both at the time when he acquired the dwelling and at the time of the grant of the tenancy was a member of the regular armed forces. The court must be of the opinion that the dwelling is required as a residence for the owner, or, that of the conditions set out under (2) above, one of those in paragraphs (c) to (f) is satisfied.[78]

Apart from the mandatory grounds of possession already listed, recovery of possession is mandatory where the dwelling is overcrowded[79] within the meaning of the Housing Act 1957,[80] in circumstances which render the occupier guilty of an offence. The provision applies to "premises used as a separate dwelling by members of the working classes or of a type suitable for such use."[81] In such a case there is no requirement that any notice should have been served on the tenant at the commencement of the tenancy.

7. Rent limit. (a) *Contractual rent.* There is now no restriction on the amount of rent that can be charged on the grant of a protected regulated tenancy to an entirely new tenant. Under an existing protected tenancy, *i.e.* during its contractual period, an increase in rent is not restricted in amount, but in terms of form there has to be compliance with the requirements laid down in respect of a rent agreement.[82] Non-compliance makes the amount of the increase irrecoverable.[83] One of the requirements is that the tenant has to be informed of his right to apply for the registration of a fair rent.

(b) *Registered rent.* The landlord, the tenant or the local authority may apply to the rent officer for the area for the registration of a rent.

---

[78] Inserted into Sched. 15, Pt. 2 of the Act of 1977 by the Housing Act 1980, s. 67.
[79] Act of 1977, s. 101.
[80] s. 77 (1).
[81] See *Guinness Trust* v. *Green* [1955] 1 W.L.R. 872.
[82] Act of 1977, s. 51.
[83] *Ibid.* s. 54.

The rent officer, after giving the parties an opportunity to make representations, registers the rent if he thinks it fair, or, if not, determines and registers what he thinks would be a fair rent. There is a right of appeal to a rent assessment committee. For a period of two years after registration neither party can apply for the registration of a different rent without the concurrence of the other.[84]

(c) *Fair rent.* In determining what is a fair rent, regard must be had "to all the circumstances (other than personal circumstances) and in particular to the age, character, and locality and state of repair of the dwelling-house," and any furniture provided. There must, however, be disregarded the effect of local shortages of accommodation, and disrepair or default attributable to a failure by the tenant to comply with his obligations, and any voluntary improvement carried out by the tenant.[85] The disregard of scarcity is especially significant: it has the result that registered rents are commonly much below the level of market rents.

8. Premiums. There are wide provisions prohibiting any person[86] from requiring a premium as a condition of the grant, renewal, continuance or assignment of any tenancy within the Act,[87] and preventing a statutory tenant (who has no assignable interest) from asking or receiving any consideration from any person except the landlord as a condition of giving up possession.[88]

9. Mortgages. Where the Act restricts a landlord's rights (*e.g.* as to rent) against his tenant, it was thought that the landlord should be correspondingly protected against any mortgagee of the property; and the Act so provides,[89] except in the case of a mortgage created after December 7, 1965,[90] or a mere equitable charge or mortgage.[91] There were two systems of protection, one where the property was on that date subject to a controlled tenancy, and the other where the tenancy was regulated. Only the latter system now survives. There is no automatic protection of a mortgagor under a regulated mortgage, but he may apply to the court for relief if he will be caused "severe financial hardship" by an increase in mortgage interest, the enforcement of the mortgage, or the registration of a reduced rent.[92] The court has wide powers to vary the terms of the mortgage or restrain the exercise of any remedies under it.

---

[84] *Ibid.* s. 67, as amended by the Housing Act 1980, s. 60: the period used to be three years.
[85] Act of 1977, s. 70.
[86] "any person" includes landlords, tenants, agents or middlemen: *Farrell* v. *Alexander* [1977] A.C. 59 at p. 71.
[87] See *Elmdene Estates Ltd.* v. *White* [1960] A.C. 528.
[88] Act of 1977, s. 8 (5), Sched. 1, Pt. 2.
[89] *Ibid.* ss. 129, 131.
[90] *Ibid.* s. 93.
[91] *London County and Westminster Bank Ltd.* v. *Tompkins* [1918] 1 K.B. 515.
[92] Act of 1977, s. 132.

II. RESTRICTED CONTRACTS

1. The legislation. Until the Furnished Houses (Rent Control) Act 1946 was passed, there was no effective provision to protect residential tenants of premises let with furniture or services. The Act established a system of control by setting up a number of rent tribunals, which are now under the control of the Council on Tribunals.[93] The Act was amended by the Landlord and Tenant (Rent Control) Act 1949, and the statutory provisions regulating furnished lettings were consolidated and replaced by Part VI of the Rent Act 1968. The protection is now contained in the Rent Act 1977. Under the Act of 1946 protection applied however great the rateable value of the premises, but since July 6, 1957,[94] only those premises within the general limits of rateable value for the purposes of the Rent Act currently in force are protected.[95]

2. Application. The protection afforded by the Rent Act 1977 applies to any contract whereby a person has been granted the right to occupy as a residence[96] a house or part of a house at a rent which includes payment for the use of furniture or for services, or on terms that he shares living accommodation with his landlord. It also applies to tenancies which are excluded from normal Rent Act protection because they were granted by a "resident landlord." But the provisions are excluded if a substantial part of the rent is for board, or if the contract creates a regulated tenancy conferring normal protection, as many furnished tenancies granted by non-resident landlords now do.[97] It is important to appreciate that restricted contracts do not merely embrace "non-qualifying tenancies," the protection extends to licences provided that the occupier is entitled to exclusive occupation of at least some accommodation within a dwelling. It follows that if occupation is not exclusive there will be no protection of any kind under the Act. This has led to the evasion of the Act by the use of non-exclusive sharing arrangements. Such an arrangement will be upheld by the court as valid provided it is not a mere sham.[98]

3. Rent. Either party or the local authority may refer the contract to the rent tribunal, which, after hearing the parties, may approve the rent or reduce or increase it to an amount which the tribunal

---

[93] Tribunals and Inquiries Act 1958, s. 1, 1st Sched.
[94] See Rent Act 1957, s. 12, now repealed. The date is that on which the Act came into force.
[95] See the Act of 1977, s. 19.
[96] See *Luganda* v. *Service Hotels Ltd.* [1969] 2 Ch. 209. (long-term occupation of hotel room suffices).
[97] Act of 1977, ss. 19, 85, 107: see *ante*, p. 577.
[98] See *Somma* v. *Hazlehurst* [1978] 1 W.L.R. 1014. Contrast *Walsh* v. *Griffiths-Jones* [1978] 2 All E.R. 1002.

considers reasonable.[99] The rent determined by the tribunal is then registered with the local authority, and thereafter it becomes an offence to require or receive more than the registered rent, or to charge any premium, in respect of the premises.[1] A registered rent may be reconsidered, but the tribunal cannot be required to reconsider it within three years (two years in the case of registrations effected after the commencement of the Housing Act 1980)[2] unless the application is made by the landlord and tenant jointly, or there has been a change of circumstances so that the registered rent is no longer reasonable.[3] The rent tribunal is still bound to consider the reference even if the tenant quits before the hearing.[4]

4. Security of tenure. If these provisions stood alone, a landlord could usually deter tenants from referring cases to the tribunal by the threat of serving a notice to quit. Accordingly, security is provided by one of two alternative systems, depending on whether the restricted contract was granted before or after the Housing Act 1980.

(a) *Restricted contracts granted prior to the Housing Act 1980.* There are two methods of providing security in the case of restricted contracts which were granted before the commencement of the Act of 1980.

(1) *Automatic.* Where a tenant has referred a contract to the tribunal, no notice to quit subsequently served on him is to take effect before the expiration of a period of six months after the decision of the tribunal; the tribunal may, however, substitute a shorter period for the statutory six months.[5] Further, any period of security under this and the next head may be reduced by the tribunal if the tenant or those residing with him have been guilty of misconduct or have broken the terms of the tenancy, *e.g.* by maltreating the house or the furniture.[6]

(2) *On application.* Except where a reduction has been made for misconduct, applications may be made for successive extensions of security of tenure. Where any contract has been referred to a tribunal and a notice to quit has been served (whether before or after making the reference) then at any time before the expiration of the period of the end of which the notice to quit will take effect, the tenant may apply to the tribunal for the extension of that period; and the tribunal may extend that period for not more than six months.[7] Thus, if a

---

[99] Act of 1977, ss. 77, 78.
[1] Act of 1977, ss. 79, 81, 122.
[2] Act of 1980, s. 70 (1).
[3] Act of 1977, s. 80 (2).
[4] *R.* v. *West London Rent Tribunal, ex p. Napper* [1967] 1 Q.B. 169.
[5] Act of 1977, s. 103.
[6] *Ibid.* s. 106.
[7] *Ibid.* s. 104.

weekly tenant refers a contract to the tribunal, and the landlord promptly serves a notice to quit, the tenant should apply for further security of tenure within six months of the decision of the tribunal; and provided he makes successive (and successful) applications every six months, the operation of the notice to quit will be repeatedly postponed. If the landlord had served no notice to quit until, say, a year after the first reference to the tribunal, the tenant can apply for security of tenure at any time before the notice to quit expires.[8]

(3) *Exceptions.* (1) NO NOTICE. If the tenancy, being for a fixed period, requires no notice to quit to determine it, the provisions as to security of tenure do not apply at all.[9]

(2) OWNER-OCCUPIER. The provisions for security of tenure do not apply where an owner-occupier lets the house with written notice that he is owner-occupier, and the house is later required for occupation by him or a resident member of his family.[10]

(b) *Restricted contracts granted after the commencement of the Housing Act 1980.* In the case of restricted contracts granted after the commencement of section 69 of the Act of 1980, the provisions just described have no application, and so tenants are in a weak position. However, the county court is given jurisdiction where it makes an order for possession to stay or suspend the execution of the order, or postpone the date for possession for a maximum of three months.[11] If a stay or postponement is granted the court must, unless it considers that it would cause exceptional hardship, impose conditions with regard to payment by the tenant of any arrears of rent. A post-1980 Act occupier cannot be evicted except by court order even if he is merely a licensee.[12]

III. LONG TENANCIES

A long tenancy is one granted for a term exceeding 21 years.[13] From 1957[14] to 1967[15] all long tenancies were outside the Rent Acts, but then they were brought within the scope of the Rent Act 1968 regardless of the length of the term. However, many long tenancies are outside the scope of Rent Act protection because the rent is less than two-thirds of the rateable value.[16] This particularly applies where the original lease was a building lease so that the rent is a

[8] See *Preston and Area Rent Tribunal* v. *Pickavance* [1953] A.C. 562.
[9] Nevertheless, despite "notice to quit," the protective jurisdiction has been held to apply in the case of the termination of a licence where no notice to quit in the technical sense is required: *Luganda* v. *Service Hotels Ltd.* [1969] 2 Ch. 209.
[10] Act of 1977, s. 105.
[11] Housing Act 1980, s. 69 introducing s. 106A into the Rent Act 1977.
[12] Amendment to the Protection from Eviction Act 1977, s. 3, introduced by the Housing Act 1980, s. 60 (1).
[13] Landlord and Tenant Act 1954, s. 2 (5); Leasehold Reform Act 1967, s. 3 (1).
[14] Rent Act 1957, s. 21 (1).
[15] Leasehold Reform Act 1967, s. 39.
[16] See *ante*, p. 577.

ground rent only. Long tenancies at low rents have two forms of protection: Part I of the Landlord and Tenant Act 1954 and Part I of the Leasehold Reform Act 1967.

A. Landlord and Tenant Act 1954

1. Tenancies protected. A tenant under a long tenancy will be protected by Part I of the Act of 1954 at the end of the term if he would then have been entitled to the protection of the Rent Act 1977 but for the lowness of the rent.[17] Thus Part I protects only residential tenants in occupation of premises of a type within the Rent Act 1977.

2. The protection. When Part I applies, the tenancy is automatically continued, if the tenant so desires.[18] The landlord may terminate the tenancy in two ways. First, he may serve a "notice to resume possession" and apply to the court for possession on grounds similar to those under the Rent Act.[19] Secondly, he may instead serve a notice proposing a statutory tenancy. In this case the parties (or in default of agreement the county court) determine the rent and other terms of the tenancy. The statutory tenancy is a regulated tenancy and so subject to the provisions for assessment and registration applicable to the rents of such tenancies.[20]

B. Leasehold Reform Act 1967

1. General. The Leasehold Reform Act 1967 gives further protection to some tenants holding long leases at low rents. It is based on the "principle" that under a building lease "the land belongs in equity to the landowner and the house belongs in equity to the occupying leaseholder,"[21] thus abrogating the normal rule" *quicquid plantatur solo, solo cedit.*"[22] The Act allows the tenants to whom it applies to exercise one of two rights, either to demand the conveyance of the freehold, or to demand the grant of a new lease of 50 years.

2. Tenancies protected. The tenancy must be a long tenancy at a low rent of premises having a rateable value of not more than £400 in Greater London or £200 elsewhere on March 23, 1965[23]; and two further conditions must be satisfied.[24]

---

[17] Landlord and Tenant Act 1954, ss. 1, 2.
[18] *Ibid.* ss. 5, 17.
[19] *Ibid.* s. 12, 3rd Sched.
[20] Leasehold Reform Act 1967, s. 39 (1), 1st Sched., paras. 3, 4; Rent Act 1977, s. 18 (1). See *ante*, pp. 579, 583.
[21] White Paper on Leasehold Reform (1966, Cmnd. 2916), para. 4.
[22] See *ante*, p. 19.
[23] Or the first subsequent day if the valuation list showed no rateable value for the premises on that day. In such a case the figures are increased to keep in step with rating revaluations; for details, see Housing Act 1974, s. 118.
[24] Leasehold Reform Act 1967, ss. 1, 2.

(a) *Residence*. At the time of his claim the tenant must have occupied the house or part of it as his only or main residence for the last three years,[25] or for periods totalling three years during the last 10 years.

(b) *House*. The premises must be a house. This includes a semi-detached or terraced house, but not a flat. Long leases of flats at low rents are thus protected only by the Act of 1954.

3. Mode of claiming. A qualified tenant who wishes to acquire the freehold or a new lease has to serve a notice in a prescribed form upon his landlord. The service of the notice constitutes a contract to convey the freehold or grant a new lease, as the case may be; it is registrable as an estate contract and may be the subject of a notice or caution if the title to the land is registered.[26] The tenant may serve his notice at any time during the continuance of his long tenancy, including any period during which it is being continued by Part I of the Act of 1954, but if the landlord has served a notice under that Act,[27] the tenant must serve his notice within two months or he will lose his rights.[28]

4. Enfranchisement. If the tenant has elected to purchase the freehold he is entitled to have the estate in fee simple conveyed to him subject to the tenancy and incumbrances on it, but free from other incumbrances such as mortgages and rentcharges charged on the freehold interest.[29] The price is based on the market value of the land, but disregarding the value of the buildings on it,[30] so that it is very favourable to the tenant. In addition the tenant has to pay the landlord's reasonable costs and expenses.

5. New lease. If the tenant is claiming a new lease, he is entitled to a lease in substitution for his existing lease to run for a period to end 50 years after the expiry date of the existing lease. The rent is to be the current letting value of the site only. It may be revised after 25 of the 50 years has run.[31] The tenant has to pay the landlord's reasonable costs and expenses.

6. Exemptions. The landlord may defeat or modify one or both of the claims in five cases, subject to paying compensation in the first two.

---

[25] The Housing Act 1980, s. 141, Sched. 21, reduced the qualifying period from five to three years.
[26] Leasehold Reform Act 1967, s. 5. See *ante* pp. 93, 125, 127.
[27] See *ante*, p. 588.
[28] Leasehold Reform Act 1967, 3rd Sched., para. 2.
[29] *Ibid*. s. 8.
[30] See, *ibid.* s. 9, as amended by Housing Act 1969, s. 82.
[31] Leasehold Reform Act 1967, ss. 14, 15.

(a) *Residence.* A landlord may defeat a claim either to the freehold or an extended lease if he reasonably requires the house as a residence for himself or a member of his family.[32]

(b) *Redevelopment.* A landlord may resist a claim to an extended lease (or determine it, if it has already been granted) if he proposes to demolish or reconstruct the house.[33] This does not entitle him to resist a claim for enfranchisement.

(c) *Public authorities.* Local authorities and similar public bodies may retain land if they have a certificate from a minister that it will be required for development for the purposes of the authority within the next 10 years.[34]

(d) *Crown land.* A direct tenant of the Crown cannot make a claim.[35]

(e) *Management powers.* Before 1970, the landlord of an estate containing many long leaseholds or an approved tenants' association could apply to the appropriate Minister for a certificate that it was in the general interest to retain management powers and control over the development and use of the houses in the area of the estate. The scheme of management then became effective if the court approved it[36]; but it did not prevent enfranchisement or extension.

IV. AGRICULTURAL WORKERS

The Rent (Agriculture) Act 1976 provides security of tenure for agricultural workers housed by their employers, and the successors of such workers within the meaning of the Act. The Act also imposes rent control, and places housing authorities under a duty, in certain circumstances, to provide accommodation.

1. Protected occupancies and statutory tenancies. A protected occupancy exists when a qualifying worker occupies a dwelling-house in qualifying ownership under a relevant licence or tenancy.[37] Protection also extends, in certain circumstances, to a person who is no longer such a worker and to a dwelling-house that is no longer in qualifying ownership. A qualifying worker means a whole-time agricultural worker or a person who has worked in agriculture for not less than 91 out of the last 104 weeks.[38] A dwelling is in qualifying ownership at any time when the occupier is employed in agriculture and his employer either owns the dwelling or has arranged with the

---

[32] *Ibid.* s. 18.
[33] *Ibid.* s. 17.
[34] *Ibid.* s. 28, and see s. 29.
[35] *Ibid.* s. 33.
[36] *Ibid.* s. 19.
[37] Rent (Agriculture) Act 1976, s. 2.
[38] *Ibid.* Sched. 3, Pt. 1, para. 1.

owner for it to be used to house his employees.[39] Relevant licence connotes exclusive occupation of a separate dwelling such that if it were a tenancy, and not otherwise excluded, Rent Act protection would apply. Relevant tenancy means a tenancy which would similarly be protected.[40] Where a notice to quit terminates a protected occupancy or a protected occupier is served with a notice of rent increase the protected occupancy is transformed into a statutory tenancy. The Act provides for rights of succession on death in respect of both protected occupancies and statutory tenancies[41] Under the security of tenure provisions there are specified grounds on which possession of the dwelling may be recovered by the landlord and which resemble the grounds of possession contained in the Rent Act 1977.[42]

2. Restriction of rents. The Rent (Agriculture) Act 1976 imposes a mechanism of control in respect of statutory tenancies. A rent may be registered, and the provisions of the Rent Act 1977 apply.[43]

V. ASSURED TENANCIES

Assured tenancies are the creation of the Housing Act 1980.[44] A dwelling, the construction of which was begun after the passing of the Act, and in respect of which prescribed conditions are satisfied, including that the interest of the landlord belongs to an approved body specified by the Secretary of State, may be let under a tenancy which is an assured tenancy and not a housing association tenancy or a protected tenancy. Protection for tenants is provided by the application, in suitably modified form, of Part II of the Landlord and Tenant Act 1954.[45]

B. Public Sector Protection

VI. SECURE TENANCIES

The category of tenancies now to be considered comprises public sector lettings by local authorities, and lettings in the "quasi-public sector" by the Housing Corporation, the Commission for the New Towns, housing associations, housing co-operatives and housing trusts, etc. The protection accorded is due to the innovation of the Housing Act 1980.[46]

1. The operative conditions. A tenancy under which a dwelling-house is let as a separate dwelling is a secure tenancy at any time

---

[39] *Ibid.* Sched. 3, Pt. 1, para. 3.
[40] *Ibid.* Sched. 2, paras. 1, 2.
[41] *Ibid.* ss. 3, 4.
[42] *Ibid.* s. 6, Sched. 4.
[43] *Ibid.* s. 13.
[44] Housing Act 1980, ss. 56–58.
[45] *Ibid.* s. 58, Sched. 5.
[46] *Ibid.* s. 28.

when two conditions, known as the landlord condition and the tenant condition, are satisfied. The first condition is fulfilled when the interest of the landlord belongs to such a body as is named above, and the second condition is fulfilled when the tenant is an individual and occupies the dwelling-house as his only or principal home. In the event of a disposition of a landlord's interest the tenancy might pass into or out of protection depending on whether or not the new landlord is a qualifying body under the Act. Where a secure tenancy is a tenancy for a fixed term and it comes to an end by effluxion of time, protection is not lost so long as the two conditions remain satisfied, because a periodic tenancy at once arises.[47] There is provision for a single statutory succession on the death of the secure tenant.[48]

2. Security of tenure. Security of tenure is effected by restricting the landlord's ability to recover possession except on specified grounds under a system resembling that contained in the Rent Act 1977.[49]

3. Restriction of rent. No formal control exists in relation to local authority rent levels. Local authorities have power to make such reasonable charges as they may determine.[50] In relation to quasi-public sector lettings, a fair rent scheme operates in a similar way to the fair rent scheme applicable to protected tenancies under the Rent Act 1977.

4. Tenant's right to purchase. Where a secure tenant has been such for not less than three years the tenant is given the right to purchase the reversion at a price which the property would achieve on the open market, less a discount ranging from 33 to 50 per cent. depending on the previous duration of the secure tenancy. The relevant provisions are contained in Part I of the Housing Act 1980.

C. Other Protection for Residential Occupiers

The Protection from Eviction Act 1977 makes it a criminal offence unlawfully to deprive a residential occupier of any premises of his occupation of those premises or any part of them.[51] A residential occupier is a person occupying premises as a residence under a contract or by any right given by law.[52] Trespassers and lodgers residing informally on the premises are therefore not included. Harassment of a residential occupier or members of his household with the intention of causing the residential occupier to give up

---

[47] *Ibid.* s. 29.
[48] *Ibid.* s. 30.
[49] *Ibid.* ss. 32–24, Sched. 4.
[50] Housing Act 1957, s. 111.
[51] Protection from Eviction Act 1977, s. 1 (2).
[52] *Ibid.* s. 1 (1).

occupation or to refrain from exercising any right or pursuing any remedy in respect of the premises is also a punishable offence. The persistent withdrawal or withholding of services reasonably required for the residential occupation of the premises may be harassment if done with the requisite intent.[53]

Where premises are let as a dwelling, any right of re-entry or forfeiture can only be enforced by proceedings in court so long as any person is lawfully residing in the dwelling.[54] Eviction without due process of law is prohibited where any tenancy (which is not a statutorily protected tenancy) and certain restricted contracts within the meaning of the Rent Act 1977 come to an end but the occupiers continue to reside in the dwelling.[55] Where a landlord (or a tenant) serves notice to quit a dwelling, such notice is not valid unless it is given not less than four weeks before the date on which it is to take effect and it is in writing and contains information prescribed by regulations made by the Secretary of State.[56] The prescribed information spells out the requirement for court proceedings by the landlord, even after the notice to quit has expired, in order to obtain the tenant's lawful eviction. The possibilities of some form of statutory protection for the tenant and free legal advice in connection therewith are also included in the information.[57] No notice to quit, however, is required in the case of a tenancy for a fixed term or a licence.

D. Status

1. Protection. Today, most tenants in this country are protected by some statutory provision or other. Leasehold tenants, who in early law were regarded as holding mere contracts, and not until the sixteenth century became recognised as the owners of estates,[58] have some claim now to have travelled from contract via estate to status; for their more important rights depend in large part not on the contracts which they have made but on the positive protection conferred on them by statute, overriding any contractual arrangements. Yet the variations between the statutory provisions are so great that it is difficult to discern much common ground between the systems.

2. Rent. Thus as regards rent, even though the premises have been let before, there may or may not be initial control as to rent; contrast business and agricultural lettings with the Rent Act. Again, control as to rent may attach only on a renewal of the tenancy (business), or at

---

[53] *Ibid.* s. 1 (3).
[54] *Ibid.* s. 2.
[55] *Ibid.* s. 3.
[56] Protection from Eviction Act 1977, s. 5.
[57] Notices to Quit (Prescribed Information) Regulations 1980, S.I. 1980 No. 1624.
[58] *Ante*, pp. 17, 18, 33.

stated intervals (agriculture), or on application to a tribunal (restricted contracts). Yet again, the rent may be fixed by the court (business, and statutory tenancies under the Act of 1954), a leasehold valuation tribunal (50 year leases under the Act of 1967), an arbitrator (agriculture), or a rent officer or rent assessment committee (regulated tenancies under the Act of 1977).

3. Security of tenure. Security of tenure is equally varied. There are six main methods by which it may be provided. First, there is the drastic method of giving the tenant the right to purchase the landlord's interest (long lease and secure tenancy). Secondly, there may be a restriction on determining the existing tenancy until the tenant has been able to apply to the court for a new tenancy (business and assured tenancy). Thirdly, there may be a power for the tenant to paralyse a notice to quit by serving a counter-notice unless the landlord obtains permission from a tribunal for his notice to operate (agriculture). Fourthly, there is the automatic suspension of a notice to quit for a limited period, with power for the tenant to apply to a tribunal for an extension (pre-1980 restricted contracts). Fifthly, there is power in the court to postpone the operation of a notice to quit for a limited period (restricted contracts granted after the commencement of the new provisions introduced by the Housing Act 1980). Sixthly, there is the mere passive right for the tenant to remain, despite the termination of the contractual tenancy, until ordered to go by the court (Rent Act tenancies, secure tenancies, and licences and tenancies under the Rent (Agriculture) Act 1976).

4. Status. The variations are thus great. Yet both on major issues and on many minor matters a tenant today will look more often to the rights conferred on him by the Statute-Book than to the terms of his tenancy. In that sense it is perhaps true to say that there is an ill-defined but nevertheless real status of protected tenant.

INDEX